DIE STAATSGALERIE STUTTGART
THE STAATSGALERIE STUTTGART

PETER BEYE

DIE STAATSGALERIE STUTTGART

THE STAATSGALERIE STUTTGART

GUNTHER THIEM

GRAPHISCHE SAMMLUNG

DEPARTMENT OF PRINTS AND DRAWINGS

HATJE

© 1991 Verlag Gerd Hatje
und Autoren
© 1991 der abgebildeten Werke soweit nicht aufgeführt bei den
Künstlern und ihren Rechtsnachfolgern;
Hans Arp, Max Beckmann, Joseph Beuys, Georges Braque,
Giorgio de Chirico, Marcel Duchamp, Max Ernst, Alberto Giacometti,
George Grosz, Paul Klee, Oskar Kokoschka, Käthe Kollwitz,
Fernand Léger, René Magritte, Henri Matisse, Piet Mondrian,
Claude Monet, Francis Picabia, Pablo Picasso, Jackson Pollock,
Mark Rothko, Karl Schmidt-Rottluff, Max Slevogt, Wols
bei VG Bildkunst, Bonn;
Willi Baumeister bei Baumeister Archiv, Stuttgart;
Erich Heckel bei Nachlaß Erich Heckel, Hemmenhofen;
Ernst Ludwig Kirchner bei Dr. Wolfgang und Ingeborg Henze,
Campione d'Italia;
Emil Nolde bei Stiftung Seebüll Ada und Emil Nolde;
Oskar Schlemmer bei Familie Schlemmer, Badenweiler

Übersetzungen ins Englische
Jill Lloyd (Texte Beye)
Stephen Reader (Texte Thiem)

Lektorat englisch
Ina Conzen-Meairs, Elsbeth Wiemann (Texte Beye)
Karla Schlaepfer (Texte Thiem)

Fotos
Anthony d'Offay, London
Seite 25
Städtisches Museum Ludwigsburg
Seite 48
Hauptstaatsarchiv Stuttgart
Seite 49
Adalbert Helwig, Sindelfingen
Seiten 58, 60, 61
Alle andern
Franziska Adriani, Heinz Vogelmann
Staatsgalerie Stuttgart

Frontispitz
Piet Mondrian
Composition dans le carré
Komposition im Quadrat
Öl auf Leinwand, 1922

Gesamtherstellung
Dr. Cantz'sche Druckerei, Ostfildern bei Stuttgart

Druckfarben von Kast + Ehinger

© 1991 Verlag Gerd Hatje
and authors
© 1991 the reproduced works in this volume, unless otherwise
stated are reserved by artists and their legal successors;
Hans Arp, Max Beckmann, Joseph Beuys, Georges Braque,
Giorgio de Chirico, Marcel Duchamp, Max Ernst, Alberto Giacometti,
George Grosz, Paul Klee, Oskar Kokoschka, Käthe Kollwitz,
Fernand Léger, René Magritte, Henri Matisse, Piet Mondrian,
Claude Monet, Francis Picabia, Pablo Picasso, Jackson Pollock,
Mark Rothko, Karl Schmidt-Rottluff, Max Slevogt, Wols
by VG Bildkunst, Bonn;
Willi Baumeister by Baumeister Archiv, Stuttgart;
Erich Heckel by Nachlaß Erich Heckel, Hemmenhofen;
Ernst Ludwig Kirchner by Dr. Wolfgang and Ingeborg Henze,
Campione d'Italia;
Emil Nolde by Stiftung Seebüll Ada and Emil Nolde;
Oskar Schlemmer by Familie Schlemmer, Badenweiler

Translation in English
Jill Lloyd (texts Beye)
Stephen Reader (texts Thiem)

House Editor english
Ina Conzen-Meairs, Elsbeth Wiemann (texts Beye)
Karla Schlaepfer (texts Thiem)

Photographic credits
Anthony d'Offay, London
Page 25
Städtisches Museum Ludwigsburg
Page 48
Hauptstaatsarchiv Stuttgart
Page 49
Adalbert Helwig, Sindelfingen
Pages 58, 60, 61
All others
Franziska Adriani, Heinz Vogelmann
Staatsgalerie Stuttgart

Frontispiece
Piet Mondrian
Composition dans le carré
Composition in Squares
Oil on canvas, 1922

Printed by
Dr. Cantz'sche Druckerei, Ostfildern by Stuttgart

Colour Ink by Kast + Ehinger

ISBN 3-7757-0346-2

INHALT

CONTENTS

PETER BEYE

———

STAATSGALERIE
STUTTGART
AUFTRAG UND GESCHICHTE

———

THE STAATSGALERIE
STUTTGART
MANDATE AND HISTORY

Stellenwert und Funktion des Museums haben sich während der vergangenen Jahrzehnte entscheidend verändert. Vor allem hat das wachsende Interesse für die künstlerischen Probleme der eigenen Zeit dem Museum neue, bis dahin noch weitgehend ungenutzte Wirkungsmöglichkeiten erschlossen. Nach dem relativ kurzen, doch für das kulturelle Leben in Deutschland verhängnisvollen Naziregime vollzog sich dieser Prozeß mit auffallender Vehemenz und dazu in einem durch ideologische Vorstellungen nahezu unbelasteten Freiraum. Kunst — während der 30er und zu Beginn der 40er Jahre politisch mißbraucht — wurde wiederum erlebbar als Schöpfung, das heißt als ein denkbar komplexes, unser Wahrnehmungs- und Urteilsvermögen vielfältig schärfendes Phänomen. Was die Gegenwart an künstlerischer Leistung hervorbrachte, wurde für viele nicht nur zum Maßstab der eigenen Standortbestimmung, sondern auch Grundlage einer sich wandelnden Einstellung zur Geschichte. Nichts verdeutlicht dies mehr als die folgenden, bereits 1943 formulierten Sätze von Willi Baumeister: »Die Entdeckung der Kunst ist (zugleich) die Erhebung von vordem unbeachteten Objekten zu Kunstwerken ... sie geht parallel zur jeweiligen Kunstproduktion ... ein neu entstandenes Werk dokumentiert unter anderem dadurch seine Macht, daß es mit seiner Erstmaligkeit bereits Vorhandenes (wiederum) aktuell macht.« Es steht außer Frage, daß sich in diesen Worten ein evolutionsbedingtes, doch gerade deshalb dynamisches Geschichtsverständnis manifestiert. Was aber beinhaltet diese Aussage, bezogen auf die Funktion des Museums? Setzt man voraus, daß das Museum aus klar erkennbarem Engagement und nicht nur beiläufig der Kunst der eigenen Zeit folgt, wird sich ihm auch Geschichte nicht aus neutraler Distanz und auf der Basis prästabilisierter Urteilskriterien erschließen, sondern als Leistung, die vom jeweiligen Standpunkt der Gegenwart her neu überprüft und reflektiert werden muß. Kunst ist — das wissen wir alle — evolutionär, Ausdruck sich ständig erneuernder Selbstfindung. Selbst da, wo sie auf der äußersten Höhe ihrer Entfaltung am Ziel ist, bleibt sie verfügbar, ist sie wirkungsfähig in verschiedener Richtung, weil — um mit Jacob Burckhardt zu sprechen — »jede Zeit neue Gesichtspunkte, neue Spiegelungsweisen für die alten Kulturen hervorbringt«. Dieses der Kunst immanente Prinzip der Evolution auch als Institution zu verwirklichen, ist Aufgabe, ja zentrales Anliegen mehr oder weniger jedes modernen Museums.

Die Stuttgarter Staatsgalerie ist ein solches Museum. Sie ist dies mit Priorität, doch nicht ausschließlich. Auch wenn sie ihre entscheidende Formung erst während der letzten Jahrzehnte erhielt, ist sie — wie die Mehrzahl aller deutschen Museen — aus einer landesfürstlichen Sammlung hervorgegangen. Folgt man der Spur ihrer wechselvollen Geschichte, so reicht diese bis ins 17. Jahrhundert, in ihren Anfängen sogar noch weiter zurück. Von den Bildern, die in den herzoglichen Schloßinventaren jener Zeit aufgeführt sind, läßt sich allerdings

The significance and function of the museum have changed decisively during the past decades. Growing interest in the artistic issues of our own times has opened up new and previously unexplored fields of activity for the museum. After the relatively short, but for cultural life nevertheless disastrous interlude of the Nazi era, this process of change proceeded with exceptional intensity and was, moreover, virtually undisturbed by ideological presuppositions. Art, which had been politically misused in the 1930s and early 1940s, was once again experienced as a creative process of particular complexity, as a phenomenon able to increase our capacities for perception and critical understanding. The artistic achievements of our own times became for many not just a measure for defining their personal attitude, but also the basis for a changing interpretation of history. The following lines by Willi Baumeister, already formulated in 1943, show that most clearly: "Artistic discovery involves (at the same time) the elevation of previously unnoticed objects into works of art ... this process runs parallel to the current art ... among other things a work of art manifests its value by rising again to actuality what has always been existent." These words reflect an evolutionary and dynamic conception of history. But what does that statement imply in relation to the function of a museum? If we presuppose that the museum deals with the art of its time with real engagement rather than just casual interest, then history too will not be interpretated from a neutral distance and in terms of previously established criteria of judgement, but rather as an achievement which must be reexamined and reinterpreted in the context of the present. Art, as we know, is evolutionary. It expresses a constantly regenerating self-determination. Even when art reaches its highest level of achievement it remains relevant and effective because, as Jacob Burckhardt remarked, "each age brings forth new perspectives, new ways of mirroring past cultures." The task and central concern of virtually every modern museum as an institution is to incorporate this evolutionary principle immanent to art.

This is indeed the central purpose of the Staatsgalerie, but not its only one. Although the gallery has achieved its definitive form only in recent decades, it originated, like most German museums, from a sovereign collection. Its changing history reaches back to the 17th century, and even beyond that. However, none of the items mentioned in the ducal inventories can be traced with certainty back to the present collection. Apparently their artistic value was not very high. They were mostly portraits of ancestors, of members and friends of the ducal house of Württemberg, presentations of biblical and allegorical subjects, of hunting scenes and curiosities from natural history[1]. Only after the construction of the Baroque residence in Ludwigsburg (after 1704) did collecting activities increase considerably and lead in 1736 to the purchase of the qualitatively not insignificant collection from the Prussian envoy in Vienna, Count Gustav von Gotter[2]. The insight of this cultivated and enthusiastic man of the world was responsible for the acquisition of the gallery's first significant works in-

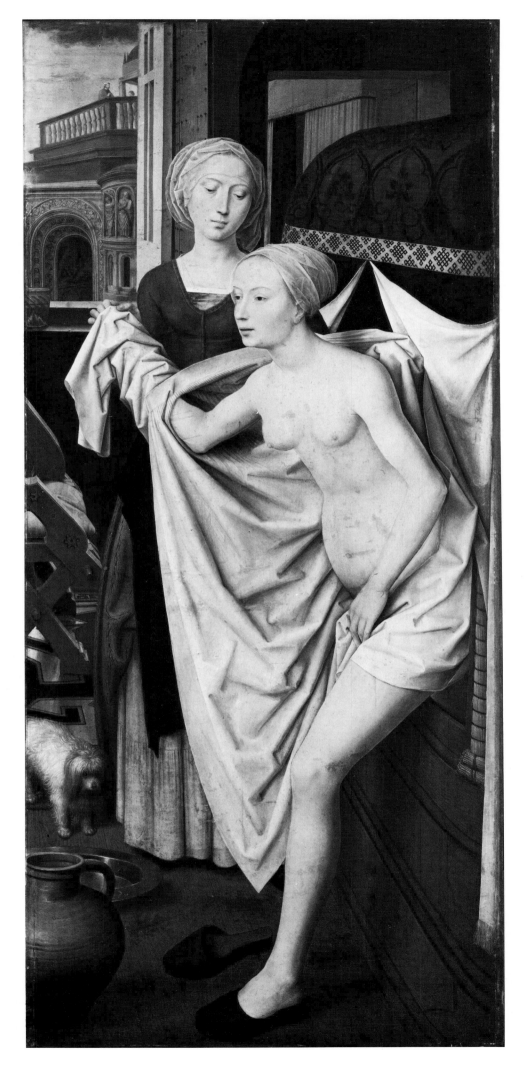

1
Hans Memling
Bathseba im Bade
um 1485

1
Hans Memling
Bathsheba at her Bath,
circa 1485

keines mit Sicherheit bis in den heutigen Bestand verfolgen. Ihr künstlerischer Wert scheint nicht hoch gewesen zu sein. Es waren meist Bilder von Ahnen, von Mitgliedern und Freunden des württembergischen Herzoghauses, daneben biblische und allegorische Szenen sowie Darstellungen von Jagden und naturwissenschaftlichen Kuriositäten.[1] Erst durch den Bau des barocken Residenzschlosses in Ludwigsburg (ab 1704) wurden sammlerische Initiativen gefördert, die 1736 zum Ankauf der auch qualitativ nicht unbedeutenden Sammlung des preußischen Gesandten in Wien, Graf Gustav Adolf von Gotter, führten.[2] Dem Spürsinn dieses ebenso kultivierten wie begeisterungsfähigen Weltmannes verdankt die Galerie erste Akzente, vor allem einen außergewöhnlichen Memling (Abb. 1, S. 9; Tafel 7, S. 82) sowie zahlreiche Bilder der holländischen Schule und des deutschen Barock. Zu Gotters Sammlung dürften auch jene Bilder gehört haben, die — in den Inventaren als »Wiener Malereien« klassifiziert — aus dem Besitz des Burggrafen Reinhard von Roeder 1748 nach Stuttgart gelangten.[3] Von den wichtigeren Werken dieses Ensembles sei hier nur Jan van Amstels »Christi Einzug in Jerusalem« genannt (Tafel 9, S. 86). Seit 1760 stand der Ludwigsburger Sammlung ein »directeur« vor — der erste war der Hofmaler Nicolas Guibal —, während die eigentliche Aufsicht über die Bestände einem »garçon de galerie« — ebenfalls einem Maler — übertragen war. Beider Funktion beschränkte sich auf Pflege und Registrierung, nicht aber auf einen systematischen Ausbau der Sammlung. Das 19. Jahrhundert stand ganz im Zeichen der malenden Galeriedirektoren. In den Jahren, da allenthalben das Interesse für die altdeutsche Kunst sich zu regen begann, bestimmten in Stuttgart die Klassizisten — oder besser gesagt deren epigonale Nachfahren — Werturteil und Geschmack, was sich im Bereich der Museumspolitik verheerend auswirken sollte. Das durch die Säkularisierung freigewordene Kunstgut der schwäbischen Klöster und Stifte wanderte einspruchslos in einzelne Privatsammlungen ab und mit diesen bisweilen gar außer Landes. Die weltberühmte Sammlung der Brüder Boisserée, ein einzigartiger Bestand altdeutscher und altniederländischer Bilder, der acht Jahre, von 1819 bis 1827, auf Staatskosten in Stuttgart ausgestellt war, fiel schließlich — angeblich wegen des zu hohen Kaufpreises — an Ludwig I. in München. Sparsamkeit am falschen Platz, dazu Engstirnigkeit im politischen Raum, fanden in der zurückhaltenden, ja kühlen Beurteilung der Sammlung durch die einheimische Professorenschaft eine willkommene Stütze. Zwar attestierte selbst Eberhard Wächter — Leitfigur der damaligen Stuttgarter Kunstszene — den Bildern »kunsthistorisches Interesse«, nicht aber stilbildende Wirkung im Sinne der von ihm verfochtenen Ideale des Klassizismus. Bildung und Lehre als integrierende Bestandteile der klassizistischen Kunsttheorie haben das Wachstum einer in ihrem Spektrum reicher gefächerten Sammlung in Stuttgart zunächst erheblich behindert. Fördernd wirkten sie freilich auf didaktischem

cluding the unusual painting by Memling (ill. 1, p. 9; plate 7, p. 82), numerous works by the Dutch school and the German Baroque. Gotter's collection probably also included the paintings (classified as "Viennese paintings" in the inventories), which came to the museum in 1748 via the collection of Count Reinhard von Roeder[5]. Among the more important works of this ensemble was Jan von Amstel's "The Entry of Christ in Jerusalem" (plate 9, p. 86). After 1760 a "directeur" headed the Ludwigsburg collection. The first was the court painter Nicolas Guibal. The actual responsibility for the care of the works was in the hands of a "garçon de galerie", who was also a painter. Both functions were limited to care and registration of the works and excluded any systematic extension of the collection.

During the 19th century collection politics were determined by directors, whose main vocation was painting. While interest in early German art everywhere else increased, the Classicists in Stuttgart — or rather their later imitators — dominated judgement and taste with disasterous effects in the realm of museum politics. Artistic treasures from Swabian monasteries, which had been liberated by secularization, drifted without opposition into private collections sometimes even outside the state. The world-famous collection of the Boisserée brothers, a unique selection of early German and early Netherlandish paintings, which was exhibited in the Stuttgart gallery for eight years from 1819 to 1827, eventually passed to Ludwig I of Munich — supposedly because of its excessive price. Economy at the wrong moment and political short-sightedness were reinforced by the reserved and cool attitude of the local professors towards the gallery collection. For instance, Eberhard Wächter, the leading figure in Stuttgart art life at the time, attested "art historical interest" to the paintings but denied to them any stylistic influence in the sense of the classical ideals he stood for.

Education and instruction, mutually supportive ingredients of neoclassical art theory, seriously impeded the development of a collection in Stuttgart rich in scope and variety. But of course they were supportive in the didactic field: for example in the organisation of the "art school", which was newly founded in 1829 and combined idealistic aims with practical expediency in the tradition of the "académie des arts". Art education at this institution was basically conceived as human education; consequently it was not solely related to the free development of fine arts, but also included the education of art lovers of all classes and the support of decorative arts. These pluralistic aims, although certainly attesting to a democratic disposition, were nevertheless limited from the outset, due to the general orientation of the teaching program towards the canon of Classicism. Both Dannecker's "room of antique casts", which owes its name to a collection of casts of classical masterpieces brought together by the artist, and the royal print room with its numerous, often high-quality graphic reproductions, substituted mostly second hand visual material for originals[4]. Even the museum holdings — which were admittedly limited at this time — were misused as a simple "collection

2
Johann Heinrich Dannecker
Schillerbüste
1794

2
Johann Heinrich Dannecker
Bust of Schiller,
1794

11

Feld: so bei der Einrichtung der 1829 neu gegründeten »Kunstschule«, die in der Nachfolge der »académie des arts« idealistische Ziele mit praktischem Nützlichkeitsdenken verband. Kunstbildung wurde an dieser Institution durchaus programmatisch als Menschenbildung verstanden, war also nicht allein auf die freie Entfaltung der hohen Künste bezogen, sondern schloß auch die Erziehung von Kunstliebhabern aller Stände und die Förderung des Kunsthandwerks ein. Dieser pluralistischen Zielsetzung, der man einen demokratischen Ansatz kaum absprechen kann, waren aber a priori Grenzen gesetzt, da sich das Lehrprogramm weitgehend am Kanon klassizistischer Formvorstellungen orientierte. Danneckers »Antikensaal«, der seinen Namen einer vom Künstler zusammengetragenen Abgußsammlung klassischer Meisterwerke verdankt, und das königliche Kupferstichkabinett mit seinen zahlreichen, zum Teil hochwertigen Stichreproduktionen, ersetzten das Original durch überwiegend aus zweiter Hand stammendes Anschauungsmaterial.[4] Selbst der bis dahin nicht eben reiche museale Bestand wurde als reine »Vorbildersammlung« mißbraucht, nicht aber um seiner selbst willen geachtet und planvoll erweitert. Ankaufsmittel wurden, wenn überhaupt, so mit Vorrang für den Erwerb klassizistischer Werke verwendet (Abb. 2, S. 10).[5]

Erst nach dem Bau eines eigenen Museums (1838−1843), welches freilich auch die erwähnte Kunstschule aufnehmen mußte, regten sich Kräfte, die auf eine stärkere Profilierung der Stuttgarter Sammlung hinwirken sollten. Begünstigt wurde diese Entwicklung durch das persönliche Engagement König Wilhelms I. von Württemberg, der 1852 die »Pinacotheca Barbini-Breganze« − eine nach Umfang und Rang nicht unbedeutende Sammlung italienischer Bilder − für Stuttgart sicherte. Glanzstücke des in Venedig erworbenen Gemäldeensembles waren zwei Gemälde Vittore Carpaccios (Tafel 13, S. 96) und Giovanni Battista Tiepolos furios gemalter Entwurf für das 1752 vollendete Deckenbild im Kaisersaal der Würzburger Residenz (Tafel 18, S. 106). Aber auch die spärlichen Bestände an altdeutscher, vor allem an altschwäbischer Kunst, wurden in jenen Jahren beträchtlich erweitert. Zumal aus der Sammlung des Stuttgarter Obertribunalprokurators Karl Gustav Abel kamen wichtige Werke vom Meister der Sterzinger Altarflügel und zwei Altäre von Bartholomäus Zeitblom hinzu (Tafel 3, 4, S. 72). Zusammen mit dem »Hl. Benedikt« des Meisters von Meßkirch (Tafel 5, S. 74), der 1866 mit einigen anderen Bildern aus der Sammlung des Tübinger Theologieprofessors und späteren Domdekans Hirscher angekauft wurde, setzten diese Gemälde in der dominierenden Nachbarschaft der Klassizisten einen zwar ebenfalls nur regionalen, doch spürbaren Akzent. Standen allerdings Sammlungen von Weltrang zur Diskussion, verhielten sich Stuttgarts Bildereinkäufer eher bescheiden. Auf der berühmten Auktion des Gräflich Schönbornschen Kunstbesitzes in Schloß Pommersfelden (1867) wurden lediglich vier Bilder erworben, darunter frei-

of models" rather than being appreciated for their own qualities and systematically expanded. Purchase funds, when available, were preferably used for the acquisition of works from Classicism (ill. 2, p. 10)[5].

Only after the construction of a separate museum from 1838 to 1843, which naturally also had to include the above mentioned art school, were forces set free which had a stronger impact on shaping the Stuttgart collection. This development was encouraged by the personal efforts of King Wilhelm I of Württemberg, who in 1852 secured for Stuttgart the "Barbini-Breganze Pinacotheca", a not unimportant collection of Italian paintings. High-lights of this collection, which was purchased in Venice, included two paintings by Vittore Carpaccio (plate 13, p. 96) and Giovanni Battista Tiepolo's spirited sketch for the ceiling painting in the "Kaisersaal" at the Würzburg Residence, completed in 1752 (plate 18, p. 106). But above all, the sparse holdings of early German art, primarily early Swabian art, were significantly increased in these years − especially when such important works as those by the "Master of the Sterzing Altarpiece" and the two altars by Bartholomäus Zeitblom from the collection of the Chief Tribunal Procurator in Stuttgart, Karl Gustav Abel (plates 3, 4, p. 72) could be added. Together with the "Sanct Benedict" by the "Master of Meßkirch" (plate 5, p. 74), which was bought together with some other pictures from the collection of the Tübingen theology professor and later dean of the cathedral, Hirscher, these paintings provided − next to the still dominating presence of neoclassical art − a regional but nevertheless noticeable emphasis. However, when internationally renowned collections were presented for acquisition, the Stuttgart purchasers behaved rather modestly. At the famous auction of the art collection of the Schönborn Countship in Pommersfelden Castle in 1867, only four paintings were purchased, including Rembrandt's indisputable masterpiece "St Paul in Prison" (plate 10, p. 88). In 1872, Feuerbach's "Iphegenia" was acquired and immediately became a landmark of the collection. It retained this position, not unjustifiably, for many years to come.

At the turn of the century the "painter gallery directors" were replaced by art historians. This change proved to be very beneficial for the gallery. Especially Konrad von Lange, who was director only for six years from 1901 to 1907, accomplished a decisive transformation of the museum. The early German collection was systematically augmented with works such as "The Virgin as Throne of Solomon" from Bebenhausen and "The Prague Altarpiece" (plates 1, 2, p. 68). The foundations of a modern collection were laid with works by Slevogt (plate 22, p. 114), Liebermann, Pissarro, Vuillard and Uhde. The Stuttgart "Galerieverein", founded in 1906 at Lange's instigation, signaled the beginning of a new era with its first spectacular purchase, "Spring Meadows" by Claude Monet (plate 21, p. 112). Indeed, Lange was the first gallery director in Stuttgart, whose purchase activities were focused and systematical − an atypical procedure for this state, which aroused enthusiasm as well as scepticism. Unfor-

3
Anselm Feuerbach
Iphigenie
1871

3
Anselm Feuerbach
Iphegenia,
1871

4
Hendrick Terbrugghen
Lautespielender Sänger
1629

4
Hendrick Terbrugghen
Singer playing a Lute,
1629

5
Rembrandt
Selbstbildnis mit roter Mütze
um 1660

5
Rembrandt
Self-portrait with a red beret,
circa 1660

6
Edward Burne-Jones
Das Schreckenshaupt
1887

6
Edward Burne-Jones
The baleful Head,
1887

16

lich ein Hauptwerk: der »Paulus im Gefängnis« von Rembrandt (Tafel 10, S. 88). 1872 folgte Feuerbachs »Iphigenie«, die sogleich zum Wahrzeichen der Stuttgarter Sammlung avancierte und sich dieser Gunst noch lange und nicht zu Unrecht erfreute (Abb. 3, S. 13).

Um die Jahrhundertwende wurden die malenden Galeriedirektoren erstmals durch Kunstwissenschaftler ersetzt, sehr zum Vorteil der Galerie, wie sich bald herausstellen sollte. Vor allem unter Konrad von Lange, der nur sechs Jahre, von 1901 bis 1907, im Amt war, vollzog sich innerhalb des Museums eine entscheidende Wandlung. Der altdeutsche Bestand wurde systematisch ergänzt (Bebenhauser »Maria als Thron Salomonis«, Prager Altar [Tafel 1, 2, S. 66 und 68]), der Grundstock für eine moderne Abteilung mit Werken von Slevogt (Tafel 22, S. 114), Liebermann, Pissarro, Vuillard und Uhde gelegt. Der auf Langes Betreiben 1906 gegründete Stuttgarter Galerieverein signalisierte schon mit seiner ersten spektakulären Erwerbung, den »Feldern im Frühling« von Claude Monet (Tafel 21, S. 112), den Beginn einer neuen Ära. Tatsächlich war Lange der erste Museumsdirektor in Stuttgart, dessen Ankaufstätigkeit auf Schwerpunktbildungen abzielte — ein in diesem Lande ungewöhnlicher Vorgang, der Begeisterung, aber auch Skepsis auslöste. Leider besaßen die Nachfolger Langes weder Mut genug noch den Elan, um die Aufbauarbeit ihres Vorgängers mit der notwendigen Entschiedenheit fortzuführen. Max Dietz, der von 1907 bis 1915 als Direktor amtierte, galt als verlängerter Arm der konservativen Kräfte innerhalb der Akademie, aus deren Produktion er mit Vorliebe aufkaufte. Dem Werk Adolf Hölzels und seiner Schüler Baumeister und Schlemmer schenkte er so gut wie keine Beachtung. Heinrich Weizsäcker, der Ordinarius für Kunstgeschichte an der Stuttgarter Technischen Hochschule, nahm die Galeriedirektion im Ersten Weltkrieg nebenamtlich wahr. Der spätere Reichskunstwart Edwin Redslob und der Direktor des Schloßmuseums Hans Buchheit machten nur kurze Visiten, die ohne Auswirkung blieben. Erst unter Otto Fischer (Direktor von 1921—1927), der sich mit seiner konsequenten Sammelpolitik gegen vielfältige Widerstände, vor allem aus dem Bereich der lokalen Presse und Künstlerschaft, durchsetzen mußte, gelangten wieder bedeutende Werke in das Museum: allen voran Jerg Ratgebs von visionärer Gestaltungskraft durchdrungener »Herrenberger Altar« (Tafel 6, S. 76) und Caspar David Friedrichs »Böhmische Landschaft« (Tafel 20, S. 110) sowie ein zahlenmäßig kleines, doch ausgewählt gutes Ensemble deutscher Expressionisten. 1930 — bereits unter Fischers Nachfolger Heinz Braune — erhielt das Museum zu seiner räumlichen Entlastung mit dem Kronprinzenpalais ein zweites Ausstellungsgebäude, das die Graphische Sammlung und Werke württembergischer Künstler von der Nachbiedermeierzeit bis zur Gegenwart aufnahm.

Im übrigen standen die 30er Jahre ganz im Schatten der unheilvollen Kulturpolitik des Naziregimes. 1937 wurde fast der gesamte

tunately, Lange's successors had neither the courage nor the spirit to decisively continue the constructive work of their predecessor. Max Diez, who was director from 1907 to 1915, furthered the conservative forces within the academy and also preferably purchased their own productions. He paid little or no attention to the work of Adolf Hölzel and his pupils, Willi Baumeister and Oskar Schlemmer. Heinrich Weizsäcker, professor of art history at the Stuttgart Technical College, was also concurrently the gallery director during the First World War. The later "Reichskunstwart" Edwin Redslob and Hans Buchheit, the director of the "Württembergisches Landesmuseum", made only short and uninfluential appearances. It was under the directorship of Otto Fischer (1921—1927), who carried through his consistent collecting policies in spite of multiple opposition from the press and local artists, that important works again entered the museum. These included Jerg Ratgeb's visionary "Herrenberg Altarpiece" (plate 6, p. 76) and Caspar David Friedrich's "Bohemian Landscape" (plate 20, p. 110), as well as a numerically small but well-chosen collection of German Expressionism. In 1930, during the directorship of Fischer's successor Heinz Braune, the museum gained a second much-needed building with the "Kronprinzenpalais", which took over the collection of prints and drawings, as well as works by Württemberg artists from the post-Biedermeier period onwards.

The 1930s were completely overshadowed by the destructive cultural policies of the Nazi regime. In 1937, virtually the whole collection of modern art was confiscated as "entartet" ("degenerated"), including works by Kirchner, Klee, Baumeister, Schlemmer, Nolde, Beckmann, Lehmbruck and Barlach[6]. In 1944, both museum buildings were bombed and burnt down to the exterior walls. Fortunately the paintings had been removed from the museum and were deposited at twenty different locations. With the bombardement of Waldenburg Castle, the war losses, primarily of more recent Swabian paintings, were limited in comparison to those suffered by other German museums. After 1945, the reconstruction of the Staatsgalerie proceeded in small steps. A former army barrack served as its first quarters. In 1958, the gallery building in the former upper Neckarstraße — today named Konrad-Adenauer-Straße — was officially reopened by the President of the Federal Republic, Theodor Heuss. The "Kronprinzenpalais", whose original location is now occupied by the monstrous concrete buildings of the "Kleiner Schloßplatz", was substituted by James Stirling's extension to the Staatsgalerie in 1984.

The central task of the post-war period was the expansion of the still very heterogeneous collection. Despite an initial reduction in the budget, which was sometimes supplemented by special funds, works by Rembrandt (plate 11, p. 90) and Frans Hals could be acquired. Thanks to the bequest of the industrialist Dr. h. c. Heinrich Scheufelen from Oberlenningen, who died in 1948, a rich selection of Baroque paintings could be added to the collection (ill. 4, p. 14)[7]. Pictures by

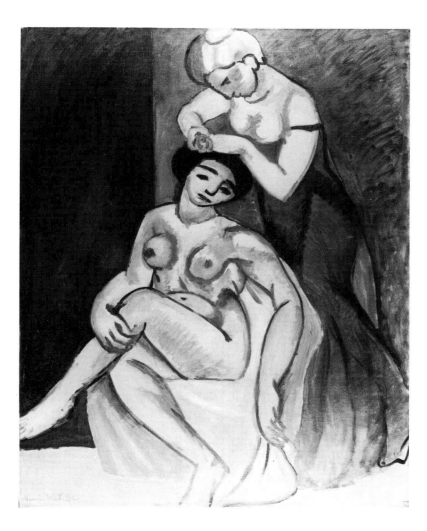

7
Henri Matisse
La Coiffure
1907

7
Henri Matisse
La Coiffure,
1907

Besitz an moderner Kunst als »entartet« beschlagnahmt, darunter Werke von Kirchner und Klee, von Baumeister und Schlemmer, von Nolde und Beckmann, von Lehmbruck und Barlach.[6] 1944 fielen beide Museumsgebäude den Bomben zum Opfer und brannten bis auf die Umfassungsmauern aus. Glücklicherweise waren die Gemäldebestände vorher an zwanzig Bergungsorte verlagert worden. Die bei der Beschießung von Schloß Waldenburg entstandenen Kriegsverluste vor allem neuerer schwäbischer Bilder hielten sich im Vergleich zu den Verlusten anderer deutscher Museen in Grenzen.

Nach 1945 vollzog sich der Wiederaufbau der Staatsgalerie zunächst in kleineren Etappen. Eine alte Wehrmachtsbaracke diente als erstes Quartier. 1958 wurde das Gebäude in der oberen Neckarstraße — der heutigen Konrad-Adenauer-Straße — in Anwesenheit des damaligen Bundespräsidenten Theodor Heuss mit einem feierlichen Staatsakt wieder eröffnet. Für das Kronprinzenpalais, an dessen Stelle inzwischen die monströsen Betonbauten des Kleinen Stuttgarter Schloßplatzes stehen, konnte erst der 1984 vollendete Erweiterungsbau von James Stirling angemessenen Ersatz bieten.

Im Zentrum aller Aktivitäten der Nachkriegszeit stand der Ausbau der noch immer sehr heterogenen Sammlungsbestände.

Munch, Kirchner, Nolde, Kokoschka, Beckmann and Grosz constituted the beginning of a modern collection (plates 35, p. 142; 36, p. 144; 42, p. 156, ill. 10, p. 20). The real turning point came with the introduction of the "National Lottery Laws", which passed the parliament in 1958[8]. The substantial financial support provided by the lottery enabled the Staatsgalerie for the first time in its history to escape provincial limitations and to develop a collection of more than regional importance. The achievements of Heinrich Theodor Musper, the first director after the war, and especially those of his successor Erwin Petermann, must be considered as epoch-making. The purchase of the Moltzau collection in 1959, praised in Germany and even abroad as the "Stuttgart museum miracle", secured masterpieces for the museum which earlier directors could only have dreamed of: among others paintings by Renoir, Gauguin, Cézanne, Matisse, Picasso, Léger and Braque (plates 23, p. 116; 25, p. 120; 28, p. 126; 29, p. 128; 31, p. 134; ill. 7, p. 18; 8, p. 19)[9]. The modern department of the Staatsgalerie as well as the no less remarkable department of prints and drawings immediately ranked as one of the foremost collections in Germany. The acquisition of the collection of the former president of the "Galerieverein", Hugo Borst, which will be discussed later in detail, added significant

18

8
Pablo Picasso
Violine – Jolie Eva
1912

8
Pablo Picasso
Violin – Jolie Eva,
1912

9
Fernand Léger
Eléments
géométriques
1913

9
Fernand Léger
Eléments
géométriques,
1913

19

10
Max Beckmann
Selbstbildnis mit rotem Schal
1917

10
Max Beckmann
Self-portrait with a red scarf,
1917

Trotz zunächst geringer Etatmittel, die aber bisweilen durch Sonderzuschüsse aufgestockt wurden, konnten der alten Abteilung Werke von Rembrandt (Tafel 11, S. 90) und Frans Hals zugeführt werden. Dem Vermächtnis des 1948 verstorbenen Industriellen Dr. h. c. Heinrich Scheufelen aus Oberlenningen verdankt das Museum einen auch zahlenmäßig eindrucksvollen Bestand vor allem barocker Gemälde (Abb. 4, S. 14).[7] Bilder von Munch, Kirchner und Nolde, von Kokoschka, Beckmann und Grosz bildeten den Auftakt der neu zu begründenden modernen Abteilung (Tafel 35, S. 142; 36, S. 144; 42, S. 156; Abb. 10, S. 20). Die entscheidende Weichenstellung ermöglichte aber erst das denkwürdige Lottogesetz, welches 1958 im Landtag verabschiedet wurde.[8] Dank der Bereitstellung erheblicher Mittel erhielt die Staatsgalerie erstmals in ihrer Geschichte die Chance, aus provinzieller Enge herauszutreten und sich zu einer Sammlung von überregionalem Rang zu entwickeln. Was seitdem unter Heinrich Theodor Musper, dem ersten Direktor nach Kriegsende, und mehr noch unter seinem Nachfolger Erwin Petermann erreicht worden ist, stellt sich selbst aus der kurzen zeitlichen Distanz unserer Tage als bahnbrechende Leistung, wenn auch nicht als etwas Abgeschlossenes dar. Bereits mit dem Ankauf der Sammlung Moltzau im Jahre 1959, der allenthalben in Deutschland, ja sogar im Ausland als »Stuttgarter Museumswunder« apostrophiert wurde, gelangten Werke ins Haus, von denen frühere Museumsdirektoren nur zu träumen gewagt hätten, darunter Spitzenbilder von Renoir, Gauguin, Cézanne, Matisse, Picasso, Léger und Braque (Tafel 23, S. 116; 25, S. 120; 28, S. 126; 29, S. 128; 31, S. 134; Abb. 7, S. 18; 8, S. 19).[9] Schlagartig rückten die moderne Abteilung der Staatsgalerie und zugleich ihre nicht minder bedeutende Graphische Sammlung auf einen der vorderen Plätze in Deutschland. Mit dem Ankauf der Sammlung des früheren Galerievereinsvorsitzenden Hugo Borst, über den noch gesondert zu sprechen sein wird, kamen wichtige Expressionisten hinzu. Selbst die zahlenmäßig zwar großen, doch qualitativ noch wenig akzentuierten Bestände älterer Kunst konnten durch Werke von Rembrandt (Abb. 5, S. 15) und Rubens, von Jacob van Ruisdael und Albert Bouts (Tafel 8a, b, S. 84), durch gezielte Erwerbungen vor allem im Bereich des Barock, aber auch der altdeutschen Malerei und der Frühitaliener deutlich verstärkt werden.[10] Der Perseus-Zyklus von Edward Burne-Jones setzte in der Abteilung des 19. Jahrhunderts einen für deutsche Verhältnisse singulären Akzent (Abb. 6, S. 16).[11]

Nach dem Ausscheiden Erwin Petermanns aus dem Amt im Jahre 1969 vollzog sich der Ausbau der Galerie konsequent in der von ihm eingeschlagenen Richtung: dem reichhaltigen Picasso- und Kubistenensemble folgten exemplarische Werke der maßgeblichen Repräsentanten der DADA-Bewegung, der Pittura Metafisica und des Surrealismus (Abb. 11, S. 22; Tafel 43, S. 158; 46, S. 166; 47, S. 168; 48, S. 170). Ebenso erhielt der bis dahin im wesentlichen von Lehmbruck, Barlach, Lipchitz und Moore bestimmte

Expressionist paintings. Even the numerically large but qualitatively less impressive old masters collection could be considerably strengthened with works by Rembrandt (ill. 5, p. 15), Rubens, Jacob von Ruisdael and Albert Bouts (plate 8a, b, p. 84) and also by intelligent purchases of early German, Italian and Baroque art[10]. The "Perseus Series" by Edward Burne-Jones set, for German standards, a unique accent in the nineteenth century collection (ill. 6, p. 16).

After Erwin Petermann's retirement in 1969, the gallery continued to develop steadily in the direction he had initiated. The rich collection of works by Picasso and of Cubism was augmented by exemplary works by the major artists of Pittura Metafisica, Dadaism and Surrealism (ill. 11, p. 22; plates 43, p. 158; 46, p. 166; 47, p. 168; 48, p. 170). Similarly the sculpture collection, characterized up to this point mainly by Lehmbruck, Barlach, Lipchitz and Moore, was considerably enlarged with works by Gonzales and Giacometti (ill. 13, p. 24). The American section that Petermann initiated — he had already purchased an important painting by Pollock in 1964! (plate 53, p. 182) — was extended with Pop Art and Hard Edge, with Conceptual Art and Environments (ill. 14, p. 25).

At the same time, a collection of recent European art was assembled, which like the section of Constructivist art, still has its gaps. The Oskar Schlemmer archive, Will Grohmann's archival estate, and the Sohm archive (Fluxus and Happening) became the basis of a documentary center that has much potential for development[12]. Private donations backed up the financial engagement of the state and were sometimes even granted as an award for state support. Baron Preuschen donated his collection of early Italian art, Mrs. Elly Koehler contributed paintings by Gauguin (plate 24, p. 18) and Kokoschka, and Mrs. Marguerite Arp donated a sculpture collection by Hans Arp (ill. 12, p. 23). Mrs. Hilla Lörcher gave the complete estate of the Stuttgart sculptor Alfred Lörcher to the museum[13]. Donations of works by Morris Louis, George Segal, Yves Klein and Tinguely are owed to the LTG ("Lufttechnische Gesellschaft Stuttgart-Zuffenhausen").

With the help of substantial donations, the Stuttgart "Galerieverein" was also able to purchase a number of excellent paintings (see below). As a conclusion it can be stated that modern art is better represented in Stuttgart than in most other German museums; comparable collections are only to be found in the Rhineland (namely in Düsseldorf and Cologne) where the broad panorama of contemporary art is displayed in a similarly impressive way.

After this historical survey let us return to our initial theme: the "functions" of the museum as they can be defined from present perspective. In the complex network of these functions collecting is only one — although the most important — of our tasks. Without a doubt character and individuality of every museum are primarily defined by the structure of its collection. Therefore acquisition policy should have special, accentuating focal points in order to avoid any uniformity of our museums. This applies equally to historical

11
Marcel Duchamp
La Bagarre d'Austerlitz
1921

11
Marcel Duchamp
La Bagarre d'Austerlitz,
1921

12
Hans Arp
Torse des Pyrénées
1959

12
Hans Arp
Torse des Pyrénées,
1959

Plastikbestand entscheidenden Zuwachs durch Werke von Gonzales und Giacometti (Abb. 13, S. 24). Was Petermann mit der amerikanischen Abteilung begründet hatte — er erwarb unter anderem schon 1964 (!) ein bedeutendes Gemälde von Pollock (Tafel 53, S. 182) —, wurde gezielt und konzentriert mit Pop Art und Hard-Edge, mit Concept Art und Beispielen des Environments (Abb. 14, S. 25) erweitert. Parallel dazu entstand eine Sammlung neuester europäischer Kunst, in der es freilich — wie auch im Konstruktivismus — noch Lücken gibt. Das Oskar-Schlemmer-Archiv, der archivalische Nachlaß Will Grohmanns und das Archiv Sohm (Fluxus und Happening) legten den Grundstein für ein noch ausbaufähiges Dokumentationszentrum.[12] Private Stiftungen in Millionenhöhe bestätigten das staatliche Engagement und wurden nicht selten ausdrücklich als Prämie dafür

and to contemporary art; and in the future all efforts in this area should be in accordance with the character of the collection. It should be expanded or supplemented in instances which make sense in relation to what is already there.

Works of high and comprehensive validity define the range and quality of a collection. Corresponding to the changing tide of history they must be able to convey multiple resonances and to reveal changing aspects. In the context of the museum they have to undergo new and changing interpretations as well. These demands necessitate not only a suitable architectural framework, but also a readiness to question inflexible principles, for example, dogmatic chronological ordering — particularly when artistic relationships are stronger than chronological ties. It is inadequate to decide on the basis of inherited concepts which art works belong in the museum

13
Alberto Giacometti
Femme debout
1948

13
Alberto Giacometti
Femme debout,
1948

14
Joseph Beuys
Dernier espace avec introspecteur
1964—1982

14
Joseph Beuys
Dernier espace avec introspecteur,
1964—1982

gegeben. Baron Preuschen schenkte seine Sammlung frühitalienischer Bilder, Frau Elly Koehler Gemälde von Gauguin (Tafel 24, S. 118) und Kokoschka, Frau Marguerite Arp ein Skulpturenensemble von Hans Arp (Abb. 12, S. 23), Frau Hilla Lörcher den kompletten Nachlaß des Stuttgarter Bildhauers Alfred Lörcher.[15] Der LTG (Lufttechnische Gesellschaft Stuttgart-Zuffenhausen) sind unter anderem Stiftungen von Morris Louis, George Segal, Yves Klein und Tinguely zu danken. Auch der Stuttgarter Galerieverein erwarb mit Hilfe beträchtlicher Spenden eine Reihe hervorragender Bilder, auf die wir noch später zurückkommen werden. Alles in allem ist die Moderne in Stuttgart heute so gut repräsentiert wie nur selten in Deutschland; vergleichbare Sammlungen gibt es eigentlich nur im Rheinland, so in Düsseldorf und in Köln, wo sich das weitgespannte Panorama der neueren Kunst auf ähnlich eindrucksvolle Weise erschließt.

Kehren wir nach diesem historischen Rückblick nochmals zum Beginn unserer Überlegungen und damit zu den »Funktionen« des Museums zurück, so wie sich diese aus aktueller Sicht darstellen. Im komplexen Bezugsfeld dieser Funktionen ist das Sammeln nur eine, allerdings die wohl wichtigste Aufgabe. Ihr verdankt mehr oder weniger jedes Museum seine Struktur oder sagen wir richtiger noch: seine Individualität. Demzufolge muß die Ankaufspolitik von Museen zu Schwerpunktbildungen mit dem Ziel qualitativer Akzentuierung tendieren, um so der allenthalben drohenden Gefahr der Uniformierung unserer Museumslandschaft entgegenzuwirken. Dies trifft gleichermaßen auf die Gebiete der älteren wie der neueren Kunst zu, die es auch künftig dort zu stärken gilt, wo die Struktur der Sammlung Erweiterungen fordert oder solche aufgrund bereits vorhandener Ansätze nahelegt.

Werke von hoher Aussagekraft, gleich welcher Art und Zielsetzung, sind bestimmend für den Rang einer Sammlung. Im Laufe der Geschichte vielfältiger Wirkungen fähig und sich immer wieder unter veränderten Aspekten erschließend, müssen sie im Bezugssystem des Museums ständig aufs neue erhellt und interpretiert werden. Dies setzt nicht nur einen angemessenen architektonischen Rahmen, sondern auch die Bereitschaft voraus, allzu starre Prinzipien wie zum Beispiel das der schulmäßig chronologischen Ordnung in Frage zu stellen, im besonderen dann, wenn die künstlerischen Bindungen stärker als die zeitlichen sind. Auch geht es nicht an, von überlieferten Bildvorstellungen aus die Grenzen noch »museumsfähiger« Kunst zu fixieren, da Kunst die Form ihrer Verwirklichung immer selber bestimmt und sich damit auch die Voraussetzungen ihrer Beurteilung ändern. Um die Spannweite künstlerischer Auseinandersetzungen sichtbar zu machen, wird selbst der sogenannten »Kunst der Kunstlosigkeit« (DADA), die sich vielfach nur im musealen Kontext erschließt, stärkere Beachtung geschenkt werden müssen, will man die Rezeptionsmöglichkeiten des Betrachters nicht einengen.

and which do not. Art determines its value steadily anew and in doing so also changes the preconditions of its judgement. In order to make the scope of artistic positions evident and to enrich the ways of receiving the visitor, even the so-called "anti-art" (Dada), which often becomes comprehensible only in the context of the museum, deserves more attention.

The tasks of the museum are not, however, exhausted in the choice and presentation of its contents; simultaneously these activities are conditioned by initiatives in the field of art historical research. Only where this exists are a progressive handling of the collection, a reasonable policy for future purchases, and effective educational activities possible. In this sense museums with a contemporary collection — and Stuttgart is one of these — have the particular task of developing an educational program on the basis of contemporary consciousness. In other words, they must activate the memory of historical heritage exactly where this heritage becomes meaningful in the consciousness of today. This should operate not only via supplementary activities like lectures and guided tours; rather it should be made convincingly evident in the development and changing presentation of the collections. Only with the interaction of all these functions does the museum gain a profile, becoming at one and the same time a unity and an organism with clear ambitions.

It is absolutely necessary that adequate scope is maintained for contemporary information. The museum cannot limit itself by responding to increasing knowledge with historical examples; rather it should have confidence in the growing maturity of its visitors and stimulate discussion about the trends and directions whose meaning only become evident gradually, via critical engagement. The direct link between permanent exhibition rooms and the temporal exhibition space, which is now realized in the new museum extension, offers a convenient solution to this problem. It makes the museum more flexible and allows it at the same time to become a place within the city where art is not simply preserved, but rather presented in its primary form. Precisely in exhibitions and particularly in those devoted to contemporary art, we should remain most conscious of the fact that effectiveness and "survival" of art are dependent on its "living-conditions". In the coming years we have therefore to reflect upon these questions, and also upon the fact that today not only art defies the museum, but also that sometimes the museum defies the art.

Die Aufgabe des Museums erschöpft sich aber nicht nur in Auswahl und Darbietung seiner Bestände, sondern wird gleichwohl bestimmt von den Initiativen, die es auf dem Gebiet der kunstgeschichtlichen Forschung entwickelt. Nur wo diese die Grundlage bildet, sind eine progressive Bearbeitung des vorhandenen Besitzes, eine sinnvolle Planung des weiteren Ausbaus sowie eine von Verantwortungsbewußtsein getragene und wirksame Bildungsarbeit möglich. Dabei fällt den der Moderne zugewandten Museen — und zu ihnen zählt die Stuttgarter Staatsgalerie — die besondere Aufgabe zu, ihr Bildungsprogramm auf der Grundlage der Vorstellungswelt der Gegenwart zu entwickeln oder mit anderen Worten: die Erinnerung an das historische Erbe gerade dort zu aktivieren, wo dieses Erbe im Bewußtsein unserer Tage virulent wird. Dies sollte aber nicht nur durch flankierende Maßnahmen wie Vorträge, Führungen oder dergleichen geschehen, sondern schon in der Erweiterung und in der wechselnden Präsentation der Sammlungsbestände überzeugend sichtbar gemacht werden. Erst im Ineinandergreifen aller dieser Funktionen gewinnt das Museum Profil, wird es gleichsam als »Einheit«, als ein von klaren Zielvorstellungen geprägter Organismus erlebbar.

Unabdingbar ist es, daß der aktuellen Information ein angemessener Spielraum gewährt wird. Das Museum kann sich nicht nur darauf beschränken, Wissen am Beispiel historisch gesicherter Werte zu mehren, sondern es sollte im Vertrauen auf die wachsende Mündigkeit seiner Besucher auch Tendenzen und Strömungen zur Diskussion stellen, deren Bedeutung sich erst allmählich, in der kritischen Auseinandersetzung erschließt. Die für den Erweiterungsbau der Staatsgalerie geforderte und inzwischen realisierte Verbindung von Schausammlung und Ausstellungsbereich erscheint unter diesem Aspekt als besonders geeignete Lösung, steigert sie doch die »Elastizität« des Museums und läßt es zu jenem Ort im Gefüge einer Stadt werden, an dem Kunst nicht ausschließlich bewahrt, sondern auch in ihren primären Erscheinungen vorgestellt wird. Gerade Ausstellungen, und im besonderen solche zeitgenössischer Kunst, können der Erkenntnis förderlich sein, daß sowohl Wirkung wie das »Überleben« der Kunst nicht zuletzt auf den ihr zuerkannten »Lebensbedingungen« gründen. Über diese Fragen wird man in den kommenden Jahren nachdenken müssen und ebenso darüber, daß sich heute keineswegs nur die Kunst dem Museum verweigert, sondern bisweilen auch das Museum der Kunst.

DER STUTTGARTER
GALERIEVEREIN

THE STUTTGART
GALERIEVEREIN

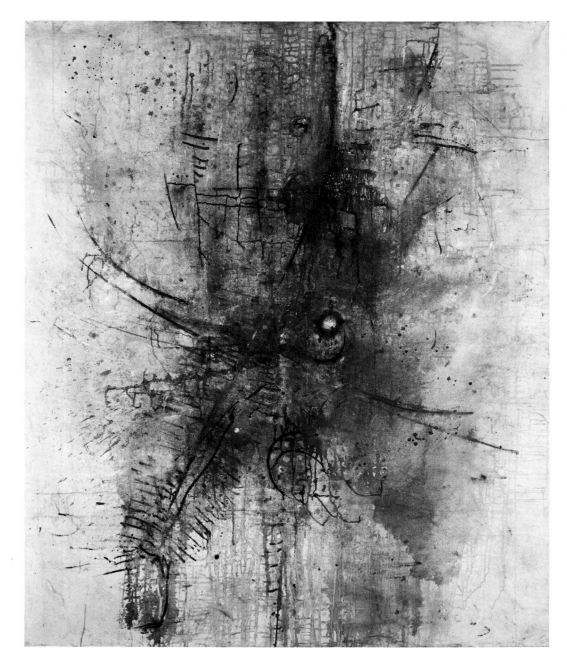

Auf- und Ausbau kultureller Institutionen setzen nicht nur staatliches Engagement, sondern auch weitreichende private Initiativen voraus. Beide können, ja sollten einander ergänzen, die Schwerpunkte ihrer Aktivitäten also gemeinsam bestimmen, um der Gefahr divergierender Interessenbildung entgegenzuwirken. In diesem Zusammenhang spielen Theater-, Bibliotheks- und Museumsvereine eine entscheidende, in politisch oder ökonomisch schwierigen Zeiten sogar unverzichtbare Rolle. So auch in Stuttgart, wo sich die private Initiative freilich nur zögernd, dann aber mit um so größerer Entschiedenheit regte. Denn anders als in Berlin, wo unter Wilhelm von Bodes souveräner Regie der Kaiser-Friedrich-Museums-Verein schon vor der Jahrhundertwende seinen glanzvollen Part zu spielen begann, mußten im sparsamen Schwaben erst Interessen und Kräfte geweckt werden, bevor es 1906 zur Gründung eines in seiner Zielsetzung vergleichbaren Forums, dem Stuttgarter Galerieverein, kam.[14]

The development of cultural institutions requires not only state involvement but also extensive private initiatives. Both can and should be mutually supportive, deciding cooperatively the emphasis of their activities. In this context theater, library, and museum support groups play a decisive, and in times of political or economic difficulties, even an essential role. This is also the case in Stuttgart where private initiatives were reluctantly awoken but then developed with great enthusiasm. In contrast to Berlin, where the friends of the Kaiser-Friedrich-Museum under the superior direction of Wilhelm von Bode already played a brilliant role before the turn of the century, interest and energy had to be stimulated in frugal Swabia, before the foundation of an organization with comparable aims, the Stuttgart "Galerieverein", was realizable in 1906. The summons to constitute this group, for which Konrad von Lange, the then director of the Staatsgalerie cautiously prepared ground, met with considerable response.

Der Aufruf zur Konstituierung dieses Vereins, den Konrad von Lange, der damalige Direktor der Staatsgalerie, behutsam vorbereitet hatte, fand ein beachtliches Echo. 140 Mitglieder wurden bereits im ersten Jahr nach der Gründung gewonnen, das entspricht einem Fünftel der heutigen Mitgliederzahl. Die Schirmherrschaft übernahm König Wilhelm II. von Württemberg, den Vorstandsvorsitz der Intendant des Königlichen Hoftheaters Baron Joachim zu Putlitz. Außerdem gehörten dem Vorstand maßgebliche Repräsentanten aus Politik, Verwaltung und Künstlerschaft an. Die Mitglieder kamen aus Kreisen des Hofes, des Adels, ferner aus Wirtschaft und Wissenschaft des ganzen Landes. Nach der Satzung vom 20. Januar 1906 sollte die Aufgabe des Vereins vornehmlich darin bestehen, »für die weitere Entwicklung der königlichen Gemäldegalerie durch Heranziehung privater Mittel zu wirken«. Diese Mittel sollten zwar nicht ausschließlich, doch mit Priorität zum Ausbau der Sammlungen eingesetzt werden. So erwarb der Verein schon im ersten Jahr seines Bestehens eine Reihe bedeutender Werke, darunter auch eines von unbestreitbarem Weltrang: Claude Monets »Felder im Frühling« (Abb. 16, S. 32; Tafel 21, S. 112). Zieht man überdies in Betracht, daß Lange bereits 1904 aus staatlichen Mitteln Max Slevogts »d'Andrade« (Tafel 22, S. 114) für Stuttgart gesichert hatte, so läßt sich ermessen, wie überlegt dieser Museumsmann staatliche und private Initiativen zu koordinieren und im Interesse einer zielstrebigen Ankaufsstrategie zu nutzen verstand.

Als Lange 1907 sein Mandat im Vereinsvorstand aufgab, verlor der Galerieverein nicht nur seinen Gründer und Spiritus rector, sondern er büßte auch bald an Attraktivität und Effizienz ein. Die Zahl der Mitglieder sank, bereits unter Lange initiierte Ausstellungs- und Vortragsaktivitäten gingen zurück. Immerhin konnten aber unter dem neuen Galeriedirektor Max Diez bis 1915 so namhafte Kunsthistoriker wie Heinrich Wölfflin und Julius Meier-Graefe für Vorträge gewonnen und einige, vornehmlich einheimischen Künstlern gewidmete Ausstellungen veranstaltet werden. Von einer sinnvollen Abstimmung dieser Aktivitäten auf den weiteren Ausbau der Sammlung war indes wenig zu spüren. Pluralismus sollte ersetzen, was Lange noch als ein auf Koordination basierendes Programm verstanden hatte. Unter den Erwerbungen jener Jahre ragen ein »Schmerzensmann« von Hans Baldung Grien und Ferdinand Hodlers »Genfer See« (Abb. 18, S. 34) hervor. Dazu kamen — wohl unter wachsendem Druck regionaler Interessen — Bilder schwäbischer Impressionisten, deren Qualität freilich nur selten dem hohen Anspruch früherer Erwerbungen genügte. Einige dieser Gemälde wurden später an die Staatsgalerie weiterverkauft; damit ergab sich ein Präzedenzfall, auf den man sich auch in der Zukunft bisweilen bezog, um die Ankaufspolitik des Museums im ganzen beweglicher zu gestalten.

Weltkrieg und Inflation brachten dem Verein starke Einbußen. Das Vermögen, soweit es in Kriegsanleihen angelegt war, wurde

140 members joined already in the first year after the foundation (today the Galerieverein has 3000 members). Nominal patronage was assumed by King Wilhelm II of Württemberg. The director of the Royal Court Theater, Baron Joachim zu Putlitz, became the first president. Other influential representatives from politics, administration, and the arts were members of the board of directors. The members came from court circles, from the aristocracy, and from business and education throughout the whole state. According to the statute of 20 January 1906, the main task of the association consisted in the further development of the royal art gallery via the support of private funds. These funds were meant to be used primarily but not exclusively to build up the collection. Thus the association already purchased a number of important works during the first year of its existence; among others one of unquestionable world class, Claude Monet's "Spring Meadows" (ill. 16, p. 32; plate 21, p. 112). When we take into account that Lange had already purchased Max Slevogt's "d'Andrade" (plate 22, p. 114) in 1904 with state funds, we can see how intelligently this museum director understood how state and private initiatives could be coordinated in the interests of a consistent acquisition policy.

In 1907, when Lange gave up his mandate on the board of directors, the "Galerieverein" lost not only its founder and guiding spirit, it also suffered by losing attraction and efficiency. The number of members decreased, the exhibiting and lecturing activities introduced by Lange were reduced. Nevertheless, under the new gallery director Max Diez until 1915, famous art historians like Heinrich Wölfflin and Julius Meier-Graefe gave lectures and a few exhibitions were arranged, mostly of local artists. But there was little trace of intelligent decision-making directed towards the further development of the collection. Pluralism replaced Lange's concept of a program based on coordination. Among the purchases of these years Hans Baldung Grien's "Man of Sorrows" and Ferdinand Hodler's "Lake of Geneva" (Ill. 18, p. 34) stand out. Probably because of growing pressure of regional influences, paintings by Swabian impressionists whose quality only seldom corresponded to the high quality of earlier purchases were added to the collection. Some of these paintings were later sold to the Staatsgalerie. This created a precedent which shaped future acquisition policy of the museum in a flexible way.

World War I and inflation produced heavy losses for the "Galerieverein". Capital given over to war loans lost its value from one day to the next. In order to take these new conditions into account the association altered its statutes in 1923 after Otto Fischer took over the gallery directorship. The Privy Counsellor Dr. Ernst Sieglin succeeded Baron zu Putlitz and became the new president. Because the funds for spectacular new purchases could no longer be raised, the focus shifted to more intensive exhibiting activities. In 1924 the "Galerieverein" contributed to the exhibition "Neue Deutsche Kunst", the first representative exhibi-

16
Claude Monet
Felder im Frühling
1887
(Ausschnitt)

16
Claude Monet
Spring Meadows,
1887
(Detail)

17
Camille Pissarro
Der Gärtner
1899

17
Camille Pissarro
The Gardener,
1889

18
Ferdinand Hodler
Der Genfer See mit den Savoyer Alpen
1906

18
Ferdinand Hodler
The Lake of Geneva with the Alps of Savoy,
1906

von einem auf den anderen Tag wertlos. Um den neuen Verhältnissen Rechnung zu tragen, änderte der Verein 1923, nachdem Otto Fischer die Galeriedirektion übernommen hatte, seine Satzungen. Der Geheime Hofrat Dr. Ernst Sieglin löste Baron zu Putlitz ab und wurde neuer Vorsitzender. Da die notwendigen Mittel für spektakuläre Erwerbungen nicht mehr aufgebracht werden konnten, verlagerte sich das Interesse auf eine Intensivierung der Ausstellungstätigkeit. So beteiligte sich der Verein 1924 an der Ausstellung »Neue deutsche Kunst«, der ersten repräsentativen Darstellung des Expressionismus in Stuttgart, und ein Jahr später, also 1925, an der bis heute umfassendsten Präsentation schwäbischer Malerei im 19. Jahrhundert. Die Mischung regionaler und überregionaler Ausstellungsthemen wirkte gleichsam »neutralisierend« auf Gegner der Staatsgalerie; sie war eine notwendige Korrektur des von Diez eingeschlagenen Kurses und stärkte im besonderen die Position des Museums.

Seit 1927 hatte Hugo Borst, geschäftsführender Direktor bei der Robert Bosch GmbH, den Vorstandsvorsitz inne. Sein mutiges Engagement für die neuere Kunst kann kaum hoch genug eingeschätzt werden. Als die deutschen Museen während der 30er Jahre fast ihren gesamten modernen Kunstbesitz verloren, baute er — unbeirrt von den politischen Gefahren und Wirren — eine für damalige Verhältnisse einzigartige Sammlung neuerer Kunst auf, deren Schwerpunkte im Expressionismus, der südwestdeutschen und der Schweizer Kunst lagen. Werke von Beckmann (Tafel 45, S. 164) und Klee, Baumeister und

tion of Expressionism in Stuttgart. One year later, in 1925, it contributed to the most comprehensive presentation of Swabian 19th century painting organized up to now. The combination of regional and supra-regional exhibition themes had a neutralizing effect on the opponents of the Staatsgalerie; it provided a necessary corrective to the course pursued by Diez and particularly strengthened the position of the museum.

After 1927, Hugo Borst, the business director of Robert Bosch GmbH, took over the presidency. His courageous commitment to contemporary art can hardly be overestimated. While the German museums came close to losing their total holdings of modern art in the 1930s, he built up a collection of recent art which was unique for its time and whose strong points were Expressionism, southwestern German art, and Swiss art. Works by Beckmann (plate 45, p. 164), Klee, Baumeister, Schlemmer, Hodler and Marc, were thus saved from assault and purchased by the Staatsgalerie from Borst's heirs in 1968[15]. In 1936, the "Galerieverein" changed its name to "Freunde der Württembergischen Staatsgalerie" and constituted new statutes, consistent with language rules of that time, to establish a "broader basis" of efficiency.

Under Heinrich Theodor Musper, the first director after the war, a meeting of members reconvened in 1948. The statutes of 1936 were repealed and the original name was reassumed. Gerhard Freiherr von Preuschen was elected new president. Like Borst, he had an industrial background and was highly respected as a collector, especially of early Italian art. Preuschen not only

19
Gottlieb Schick
Wilhelmine von Cotta
1802 (Ausschnitt)

19
Gottlieb Schick
Wilhelmine von Cotta,
1802 (Detail)

20
Giovanni di Paolo
Hl. Christopherus

20
Giovanni di Paolo
Saint Christopher

Schlemmer, von Hodler und Marc konnten so dem Zugriff der Nationalsozialisten entzogen und 1968 von der Staatsgalerie über die Erben des Sammlers erworben werden.[15] 1936 änderte der Galerieverein seinen Namen in »Freunde der Württembergischen Staatsgalerie« und gab sich neue Satzungen, um sein Wirken — damaliger Sprachregelung folgend — auf »eine breitere Basis« zu stellen.

Unter Heinrich Theodor Musper, dem ersten Direktor nach Kriegsende, fand 1948 wieder eine Mitgliederversammlung statt. Sie revidierte die Satzungen von 1936 und führte den ursprünglichen Namen wieder ein. Zum neuen Vorstandsvorsitzenden wurde Gerhard Freiherr von Preuschen gewählt, der wie Borst aus der Industrie kam und als Sammler, allerdings frühitalienischer Kunst, in hohem Ansehen stand. Preuschen reaktivierte nicht nur das Ausstellungswesen, er setzte auch in der Ankaufspolitik neue Akzente: außer Gottlieb Schicks »Frau von Cotta« (Abb. 19, S. 35; Tafel 19, S. 108), einem Hauptwerk des schwäbischen Klassizismus, gelangten damals Gemälde von Hölzel sowie Zeichnungen von Dürer, Renoir und Käthe Kollwitz in den Besitz des Vereins. Der Werbefunk des Süddeutschen Rundfunks war an diesen Erwerbungen durch Spenden entscheidend beteiligt. Die Ära Preuschen stand überdies im Zeichen bedeutender Stiftungen: Schon 1948 erhielt die Staatsgalerie als Vermächtnis die Sammlung Scheufelen (vgl. S. 17), und 1952 schenkte die Max-Kade-Foundation New York dem Verein 120 vornehmlich von Hans Burgkmair d. Ä. geschaffene Holzschnittillustrationen.[16] Auch Baron von Preuschen vermachte — wie eingangs erwähnt — der Staatsgalerie 1972 seine beachtliche Sammlung frühitalienischer Bilder (Abb. 20, S. 36).[17]

Im Mai 1957 übernahm Josef Eberle, Mitinhaber und Herausgeber der Stuttgarter Zeitung, den Vorstandsvorsitz. Das damals schon überfällige 50jährige Jubiläum des Vereins wurde mit der feierlichen Wiedereröffnung der Staatsgalerie im Jahre 1958 verbunden. Anläßlich dieses Jubiläums erhielt der Verein aus Kreisen der Industrie und des Handels zahlreiche Geschenke, darunter ein bedeutendes Selbstbildnis von Lovis Corinth. Nur ein Jahr später — die Lottoregelung hatte gerade den Ankauf des doppelseitigen Picassos (Tafel 26, S. 122; 27, S. 124) ermöglicht — mobilisierte Eberle alle politisch relevanten Kräfte des Landes, um die Sammlung Moltzau für Stuttgart zu sichern. Nachdrücklich unterstützte er so das Engagement des damaligen Kultusministers Gerhard Storz, seines Kunstreferenten Wolf Donndorf und des späteren Direktors der Staatsgalerie Erwin Petermann, der die zentrale Bedeutung gerade dieser Erwerbung als erster erkannt und im internen Kreis seiner südwestdeutschen Museumskollegen durchgesetzt hatte. Daß Eberle — ein Zeitungsverleger von profunder humanistischer Bildung — nicht nur der neueren, sondern ebenso der älteren Kunst zugewandt war, belegen auch die unter ihm erfolgten Ankäufe des Vereins, deren hervorragendste der »Gärtner« von Camille Pissarro, eine Tafel vom Meister der Darmstädter

reactivated the exhibition program, he also gave new impulses to the acquisition policy; besides Gottlieb Schick's "Frau von Cotta (ill. 19, plate 19), a masterpiece of Swabian Classicism, paintings by Hölzel and drawings by Dürer, Renoir, and Käthe Kollwitz were acquired. The advertising section of the "Süddeutscher Rundfunk" made important contributions towards these purchases. Preuschen's era also witnessed some important donations; in 1948 the Staatsgalerie had already received the Scheufelen collection as a bequest (see p. 17), and in 1952 the Max-Kade-Foundation in New York gave 120 woodcuts, mostly by Hans Burgkmair the elder, to the "Galerieverein"[16]. As already mentioned, Baron von Preuschen also bequeathed his remarkable collection of early Italian paintings in 1972[17].

In May 1957, Josef Eberle, editor and joint owner of the "Stuttgarter Zeitung", took over the precidency. The postponed 50th anniversary of the "Galerieverein" was combined with the celebrated reopening of the Staatsgalerie in 1958. On this occasion, the organisation received numerous gifts from industry and business, including an important self-portrait by Lovis Corinth. Just one year later, the "National Lottery Laws" rendered possible the purchase of the double-sided Picasso (plates 26, p. 122; 27, p. 124), and Eberle mobilized all politically relevant forces of the state to secure the Moltzau collection for Stuttgart. He thus strongly supported the Minister of Culture, Gerhard Storz, and his referee for visual arts, Wolf Donndorf, as well as the efforts of Erwin Petermann, who was to become the next director of the Staatsgalerie. Petermann was actually the first to recognize the central importance of this purchase and it was he who convinced the inner circle of his southwestern German museum colleagues of this. Eberle's commitment not only to recent art, but also to the historical collection, is demonstrated by the successful acquisitions of the "Galerieverein" during his directorship. Most significant were "The Gardener" by Camille Pissarro, a panel by the Master of the Darmstadt Passion and Vanvitelli's "The Tiber Island in Rome" (ill. 17, p. 33; 21, p. 39, plate 16, p. 102). Above all, however, in these years of general and noticeable prosperity, the "Galerieverein" received the most valuable and comprehensive donation in its history: the main part of Max Kade's collection of European prints with masterpieces by Mantegna, Schongauer, Dürer and Rembrandt[18].

Josef Eberle gave up his presidency in 1972. Hans Bausch, director of the "Süddeutscher Rundfunk", became his successor. His election was understood by insiders as a political decision, because it was Bausch who, encouraged by Wolf Donndorf, had proposed the introduction of the "National Lottery Laws" in 1958 when he was parliamentary delegate. And it was Bausch, who had carried it through against vehement parliamentary opposition. Thus it could be expected that the new president would successfully continue the purchasing activities so promisingly introduced by his predecessors, and that he would even be able to im-

Passion und Vanvittellis »Rom-Vedute« sind (Abb. 17, S. 33; 21, S. 39; Tafel 16, S. 102). Vor allem aber wurde dem Galerieverein in jenen Jahren einer allenthalben spürbaren Prosperität die wohl umfassendste und wertvollste Stiftung in seiner Geschichte zuteil: der Hauptbestand der von Max Kade aufgebauten Sammlung europäischer Druckgraphik mit Meisterwerken von Mantegna, Schongauer, Dürer und Rembrandt.[18] Josef Eberle schied 1972 aus dem Vereinsvorstand aus. Zu seinem Nachfolger wurde Hans Bausch, der Intendant des Süddeutschen Rundfunks, gewählt. Seine Wahl kam für Insider einem »Politikum« gleich, war es doch Bausch, der — stimuliert von Wolf Donndorf — 1958 als Landtagsabgeordneter den Antrag zur Einführung der Lottoregelung gestellt und gegen zum Teil vehementen Widerstand seiner Kollegen im Parlament durchgesetzt hatte. Man durfte von dem neuen Vorstandsvorsitzenden also erwarten, daß er die unter seinen Vorgängern so verheißungsvoll eingeleitete Sammeltätigkeit erfolgreich fortsetzen würde und die Verbindungen zu Politik und Wirtschaft sogar werde festigen können. Wie berechtigt diese Erwartung war, zeigte sich schon bei der ersten von Bausch initiierten Spendenaktion zum Ankauf eines in seiner existentiellen Hellsichtigkeit erschütternden Bildes von Wols (Abb. 15, S. 30; Tafel 54, S. 184), dem nur wenig später ein Gemälde von Morris Louis, die Gilgamesch-Zeichnungen von Willi Baumeister und als spektakuläre Stiftung der Landesgirokasse die Originalfigurinen des Triadischen Balletts von Oskar Schlemmer (Tafel 51, S. 176) folgten. Der außergewöhnliche Rang dieser Werke, aber auch ihr Stellenwert im Kontext der neueren Kunst, signalisierten einen sammelpolitischen Anspruch, der in überzeugendem Einklang mit der Ankaufstätigkeit der Staatsgalerie selbst stand. Unter diesem Aspekt kommt auch der Erwerbung des Bildes »Der Prophet« von Egon Schiele (Tafel 40, S. 152) zur Eröffnung des Stirlingschen Neubaus erhöhte Bedeutung zu. Konsequenz, anhaltendes Engagement und politischer Einfluß haben das Handeln des Stuttgarter Galerievereins in neuerer Zeit in zunehmendem Maße bestimmt. Niemand, der die aktuelle Kunstszene mit all ihren Unwägbarkeiten und Gefährdungen kennt, wird an der Notwendigkeit dieses Einflusses zweifeln. Auch die politische Führung des Landes ist sich dessen bewußt und durchaus bestrebt, private Impulse nach Kräften zu fördern, soweit sich diese gewinnbringend auf die Substanz und Entwicklung unserer Kunstsammlungen auswirken. Daß die von Ministerpräsident Lothar Späth 1981 gegründete »Museumsstiftung Baden-Württemberg« in Absprache mit dem Vorsitzenden des Galerievereins konzipiert worden ist, läßt deutlich erkennen, in welch erheblichem Umfang selbst staatliche Entscheidungen vom zielstrebigen Einsatz privater Initiative mitbestimmt sind.[19] Mehr Verständnis und Einsicht in das komplexe Bezugsfeld musealer Probleme kann man von einem Verein, der sich als Mittler zwischen der Kunst, ihren Institutionen und der Öffentlichkeit versteht, schwerlich erwarten.

prove the "Galerieverein's" relation to politically and economically influential circles. That these expectations were fully justified, was already confirmed by the first donations Bausch secured for the purchase of Wol's painting of moving existential vision (ill. 15, p. 30; plate 54, p. 184). Shortly afterwards followed a painting by Morris Louis, Willi Baumeister's "Gilgamesch"-drawings and the original figurines from Oskar Schlemmer's "Triadic Ballet" (plate 51, p. 176) a spectacular donation of the "Landesgirokasse". The outstanding quality of these works, as well as their importance in the context of recent art, indicated high demands on acquisition politics which complemented with the purchasing activities of the Staatsgalerie. In this context we must also mention the acquisition of Egon Schiele's "The Prophet" (plate 40, p. 152) to celebrate the opening of Stirling's extension. Consistency, continuous commitment and political influence have increasingly characterized the activities of the "Galerieverein" in recent years. None who is familiar with the unpredictability and riskiness of the contemporary art scene would doubt the necessity of this support. The political leaders are also aware of this, and they attempt to encourage private initiatives, in as far as these are profitable for the substance and development of our art collections. The fact that the "Museumsstiftung Baden-Württemberg", founded by the Minister President Lothar Späth in 1981, was conceived in consultation with the president of the "Galerieverein", shows the considerable extent to which the firm intentions of private initiative contribute even to state decisions[19]. It would be hard to conceive of better understanding and insight into the complex field of museum problems than that shown by this association, organized as a mediator between art, its institutions, and the public forum.

21
Meister der Darmstädter Passion
Christus heilt einen Blinden

21
Master of the Darmstadt Passion
Christ healing a Blindman

DAS MUSEUM
DER BILDENDEN KÜNSTE
VON GOTTLOB GEORG
VON BARTH

———

THE MUSEUM
OF FINE ARTS
BY GOTTLOB GEORG
VON BARTH

Kunstgebäude.

22
Friedrich Keller
Kunstgebäude in Stuttgart
Stahlstich

22
Friedrich Keller
Kunstgebäude (Art Building) in Stuttgart,
steel engraving

Mit der Planungs- und Baugeschichte des alten Museums der bildenden Künste haben sich vor allem Volker Plagemann und Irene Antoni befaßt.[20] Beider Recherchen ergaben, daß der Realisierung dieses Bauprojeks vielfältige Kontroversen vorausgingen, die einen bisweilen erschreckenden Mangel an Einsicht in die Probleme eines Museums offenbaren. Deutlich erkennbare Mängel lagen schon im Konzept. Das Gebäude sollte nämlich nicht nur die königlichen Sammlungen aufnehmen, sondern auch die 1829 neu gegründete Kunstschule, eine nur bescheidene Nachfahrin ihrer berühmten Vorgängerin, der »Hohen Carlsschule«. Die Idee einer solchen Symbiose von Akademie, die in Stuttgart zunächst unter der Sparformel »Schule« firmierte, und einer ihr zugeordneten Sammlung, war freilich nicht neu. Sie hatte sich bereits im Zeitalter der Aufklärung in Frankreich gebildet und war an der Wende des 18. zum 19. Jahrhundert aktualisiert, doch selten in die Praxis umgesetzt worden.[21] Die Gefahr einer einseitigen Ausrichtung musealer Interessen auf gerade aktuelle ästhetische Normen lag nahe; sie wurde auch allenthalben, nur nicht in Stuttgart erkannt. Anstatt einer institutionellen Entflechtung und damit der »freien« Entfaltung sammlerischer Ambitionen den Vorrang zu geben, legte man sich hier schon im Stadium der Planung auf eine Kunstschule mit angeschlossener »Lehrsammlung« fest. Sammlung und Lehre sollten einander ergänzen, die Kunst primär als »Material« eines am klassizistischen Kanon gereiften Lehrprogramms dienen.

Auch über den Standort dieser in Deutschland zwar singulären, in ihrer Doppelfunk-

The history of the design and construction of the old Museum of Fine Arts has been presented in the works of Volker Plagemann and Irene Antoni[20]. Both studies demonstrate that the realization of this building project was preceded by multiple controversies that reveal a sometimes quite shocking lack of insight into the problems of a museum. A lack of understanding was already evident in the conception. The building was to house not only the royal collection but also the newly founded art school (1829), which was a modest alternative to its famous predecessor, the "Hohe Carlsschule". The idea of combining an academy (known depreciatingly in Stuttgart as a "school"), and a supporting collection was certainly not new. It was already current in the period of the Enlightenment in France and it was brought up to date at the turn of the 19th century, but seldom put into practice[21]. There was a strong danger of a one-sided museum concept orientated solely towards contemporary aesthetic norms; this was acknowledged everywhere, but not in Stuttgart. Rather than supporting the independent development of both institutions which would have given priority to the "free" expansion of the collection, the authorities insisted in the planning phase on an art school with a linked "study collection". The collection and the teaching activities were conceived as mutually interdependent, the art serving primarily as "material" for an educational program committed to the neoclassical canon.

There were also divergent opinions about the location of this institution which was certainly unique in Germany, however ques-

23
Modell für die Erweiterung der Staatsgalerie
1907

23
Model for the extension of the Staatsgalerie,
1907

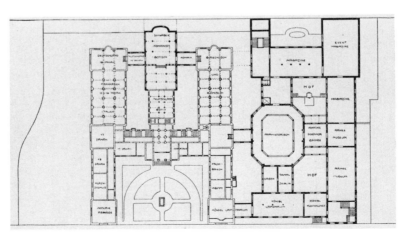

24
Entwurf für die Erweiterung der Staatsgalerie
(Grundriß des Erdgeschosses)
1907

24
Sketch for the extension of the Staatsgalerie
(Plan for the ground floor),
1907

tion gleichwohl fragwürdigen Institution gingen die Meinungen weit auseinander. So wurden zunächst diverse Plätze im Innern der Stadt und ihrer Anlagen ins Auge gefaßt, bevor sich der König — wohl angeregt durch ein städtebauliches Gutachten des Architekten Nicolaus von Thouret — für den damals noch außerhalb des eigentlichen Stadtgebiets gelegenen oberen Teil der Neckarstraße als endgültigen Standort entschied. Von Thouret stammen auch verschiedene Pläne für das Museum, unter denen vor allem ein 1837/38 entstandener Entwurf bereits wesentliche Elemente der späteren Anlage enthielt (Abb. 26, S. 47). Dies trifft im besonderen auf den U-förmigen Grundriß des Gebäudes und die Anordnung der Galerieräume zu. Den Bauauftrag erhielt aber nicht er, sondern der königliche Oberbaurat im Finanzministerium Gottlob Georg von Barth, der sich in abschließender Konkurrenz sowohl gegen Thouret wie gegen den Wilhelma-Erbauer Zanth (Abb. 27, S. 48; 28, S. 48) durchgesetzt hatte. Die Bauarbeiten selbst nahmen insgesamt vier Jahre in Anspruch. Am 1. Mai 1843 wurde das Museum eröffnet, nachdem die Skulpturensammlung und das Kupferstichkabinett schon im Winter 1842/43 eingezogen waren.

Ein zeitgenössischer Stich von Friedrich Keller zeigt den Bau kurz nach seiner Vollendung (Abb. 22, S. 42). Als Dreiflügelanlage mit offenem Ehrenhof verbindet er die repräsentative Grundform eines Barockschlosses mit der zurückhaltenden Gliederung des späten Klassizismus. Eingangsbereich und Eckrisalite sind als stärker akzentuierte Gebäudeblöcke hervorgehoben. Der zweigeschossige Bau ruht auf einem Sandsteinsockel, seine Wände sind glatt verputzt. Die gerahmten Sprossenfenster verbindet ein durchlaufendes Sandsteinsims. Die anspruchsvoller gestalteten Fenster der Eckrisalite sind durch Pilaster unterteilt, die im Obergeschoß einen plastischen Sturz tragen. Auf dem südlichen Sturz hat der Bildhauer Theodor von Wagner eine Allegorie der Malerei, auf dem nördlichen eine solche zum Thema der Plastik — jeweils mit deutlichem Hinweis auf die Funktion des Kunstunterrichts — geschaffen.[22] Im Ehrenhof stand — auf dem Stich noch erkennbar — eine Vase des Bildhauers Friedrich Distelbarth, deren Platz seit 1884 ein von Johann Ludwig Hofer geschaffenes Reiterstandbild des Galeriegründers Wilhelm I. von Württemberg einnimmt.[23]

Die ursprüngliche Disposition des Innern ist, da Barths Pläne verlorengingen, nur auf der Grundlage späterer Berichte und Erweiterungspläne, die Irene Antoni eingehend analysierte, rekonstruierbar (Abb. 29, S. 50; 30, S. 51).[24] Demnach lag hinter der Eingangshalle ein Vestibül. Das Treppenhaus, für das Thouret noch einen apsidenartigen Anbau vorgesehen hatte, bezog Barth in den Mitteltrakt ein. Im übrigen folgte er weitgehend der Raumaufteilung Thourets. Der Mitteltrakt war der Kunstschule vorbehalten, während sich die Skulpturensammlung auf das Erdgeschoß der Flügel erstreckte. Ein rückwärtiger Anbau beherbergte u. a. das Lapidarium, dessen Bestän-

tionnable it was in its double function. First of all, different sites in the city center were proposed, before the King (certainly persuaded by an appraisal made by the architect Nicolaus von Thouret), decided on the final site on the upper section of the Neckarstraße, which was still at that time outside the city limits. Thouret proposed various plans for the museum, including his sketch from 1837/38 which already contained important elements of the later construction (ill. 26, p. 47). This applies particularly to the U-shaped ground plan of the building and the distribution of the galleries. However, he did not get the commission; rather it was the royal Head of the Building Control Office in the Ministry of Finance, Gottlob Georg von Barth, who succeeded in the final competition against Thouret and Zanth (architect of the zoological gardens "Wilhelma"). The construction work took four years. After the sculpture collection and the department of prints and drawings were installed in winter 1842/43, the museum was opened on May 1, 1843.

A contemporary engraving by Friedrich Keller shows the building shortly after its completion (ill. 22, p. 42). The 3-winged construction combined the ground plan of a Baroque palace with the unobtrusive design of late classicism. The entrance and wing pavilions are accentuated as strong protruding building blocks. The two-storied building rests on a sandstone plinth and has plastered walls. The framed, stepped windows are connected by a continuous sandstone moulding. The more ambitiously designed windows of the wing pavilions are subdivided by pilasters, which in the upper floor support a carved lintel. On the south roof the sculptor Theodor von Wagner placed a relief showing the allegory of painting, on the north roof a relief representing the allegory of sculpture, both making a clear reference to the function of art education[22]. In the court yard a vase by the sculptor Friedrich Distelbarth was placed — a situation still recognizable in the engraving —, which was substituted in 1884 by an equestrian portrait of the founder of the museum, Wilhelm I of Württemberg, by Johann Ludwig Hofer[23].

Because Barth's plans were lost, the original interior design can only be reconstructed from later reports and extension plans which have been analysed by Irene Antoni (ill. 29, p. 50; 30, p. 51)[24]. According to these sources a vestibule was located behind the entrance hall. The stairway, for which Thouret had planned an apse-like extension, was integrated by Barth into the central section. Otherwise he mainly followed the room divisions proposed by Thouret. The central section was reserved for the art school, while the sculpture collection was extended across the ground floor of the two wings. A back extension also housed the lapidarium, which today belongs to the "Württembergisches Landesmuseum". The picture gallery and department of prints and drawings occupied the upper floor, which also had to accomodate rooms for the temporary art and industrial exhibitions. From 1881 to 1888 the gallery was extended by two posterior wings following

de heute dem Württembergischen Landesmuseum gehören. Gemäldegalerie und Kupferstichkabinett belegten das Obergeschoß, das zusätzlich Räume für wechselnde Kunst- und Industrieausstellungen aufnehmen mußte. 1881–1888 wurde die Galerie nach Plänen Albert von Boks um die beiden rückwärtigen Flügel erweitert und die Kunstschule bis auf nur wenige Räume in ein eigens für sie errichtetes Gebäude in die Urbanstraße verlegt. 1902 stattete Konrad Lange die Galerie mit Oberlicht aus.[25] 1909 wollte Julius Baum das Museum gar um einen zweiten Gebäudekomplex erweitern, um — nach dem Vorbild des Bayerischen Nationalmuseums in München und des Schweizerischen Landesmuseums in Zürich — die räumlichen Voraussetzungen zur Errichtung einer zentralen Landeskunstsammlung zu schaffen.[26] Seinem Vorschlag waren Pläne und ein Modell des Stuttgarter Architekten Osswald beigefügt, die weder formal noch in der gewaltsamen Anbindung an das alte Museum überzeugen (Abb. 23, S. 43; 24, S. 43). Im übrigen hätte die von Baum erstrebte Vereinigung aller auf Stuttgart verteilten Kunstbestände über kurz oder lang zu katastrophaler Raumnot geführt; denn schon 1930 mußten das Kupferstichkabinett und die Abteilung neuerer württembergischer Kunst in das Kronprinzenpalais am Schloßplatz (Abb. 25) verlegt werden.[27] 1944 zerstörten dann Bomben beide Sammlungsgebäude bis auf die Umfassungsmauern. Während das Kronprinzenpalais — ein durchaus nobler, museumstechnisch aber problematischer Bau aus der Mitte des 19. Jahrhun-

plans by Albert von Bok. The main sections of the art school were moved to a building especially erected for this purpose in the Urbanstraße. In 1902, Konrad Lange installed overhead lighting in the gallery[25]. In 1909, Julius Baum even thought of extending the building by a second complex on the model of the Bavarian National Museum in Munich and the Swiss State Museum in Zürich in order to create a central state art collection[26]. Plans and a model by the Stuttgart architect Osswald were made to illustrate his concept, but they are unconvincing both formally and in terms of the inharmonious connection with the old museum (ill. 23, p. 43; 24, p. 43). Moreover, Baum's attempts to unite all the holdings of art distributed throughout Stuttgart would have finally led to a catastrophic lack of space, since already in 1930 the department of prints and drawings and the collection of recent Württemberg art had to be moved to the "Kronprinzenpalais" at the Schloßplatz (ill. 25)[27]. In 1944, both buildings were destroyed by bombs down to the exterior walls. While the "Kronprinzenpalais" — a building from the mid-19th century — fell victim to later traffic circulation projects, the old museum was restored and reopened in 1958. The administrative offices and the print department occupied the ground floor, the picture gallery took up the upper story of the building, whose interior was renovated and modernized under the direction of Maximilian Debus. During the following years all activities were focused on the extension of the collection. As a consequence, the old museum soon proved to be

25
Friedrich Keller
Kronprinzenpalais
Bleistiftzeichnung

25
Friedrich Keller
Kronprinzenpalais,
pencil drawing

derts — der späteren Verkehrsplanung zum Opfer fiel, wurde das alte Museum wieder aufgebaut und 1958 neu eröffnet. Direktion und Graphische Sammlung bezogen das Erdgeschoß, die Gemäldegalerie das Obergeschoß des in seinem Innern unter Beratung von Maximilian Debus renovierten und modernisierten Gebäudes. Auf- und Ausbau der Sammlungsbestände standen im Mittelpunkt aller Aktivitäten der folgenden Jahre. Das alte Museum erwies sich schon bald als zu eng. Auch bot es keinerlei Möglichkeit, Ausstellungen von überregionalem Rang zu veranstalten. Pläne für einen Erweiterungsbau wurden bereits 1961–1967 und nach einer durch Sparmaßnahmen bedingten Zäsur im Rahmen eines städtebaulichen Ideenwettbewerbs im Jahre 1974 entwickelt.[28] Doch erst 1977 fand auf Initiative des damaligen Ministerpräsidenten Hans Filbinger ein allein auf die Erweiterung der Staatsgalerie und den Neubau des Kammertheaters beschränkter Wettbewerb statt, aus dem als Sieger der Engländer James Stirling hervorging.[29] Mit der Realisierung seines Entwurfs, über den noch zu sprechen sein wird, lösten sich nahezu alle die Galeriearbeit bis dahin belastenden Probleme. Funktionen und Sammlungsbestände konnten erstmals auf zwei annähernd gleich große Häuser verteilt und damit im alten Museum Platz für eine angemessene Präsentation der älteren Gemälde sowie notwendige Erweiterungen der Graphischen Sammlung geschaffen werden. Überlegungen der gegenwärtigen Landesregierung, Teile der alten Galerie in das Ludwigsburger Schloß — den historischen Stammsitz der Staatsgalerie — zu verlegen, kämen nicht nur dem Wachstum der Sammlung, sondern vor allem einer repräsentativen Ausgestaltung des Schlosses entgegen, das sich idealerweise in anschaulich erlebbarer Verbindung barocker Architektur und gleichzeitig entstandener Kunstbestände darstellen sollte.

too small. It also offered no possibilities for showing large exhibitions of more than regional importance. Plans for an extension were already proposed during the years from 1961 to 1967 and again in 1974 in a competition for town-planning, which took place after an interval of inactivity necessitated by a savings campaign[28]. Only in 1977 followed a more focused competition limited to the extension of the Staatsgalerie and the new wing of the theater. This competition, initiated by the Minister President Hans Filbinger, was won by the British architect James Stirling[29]. The realization of his plans, to which we shall return later, provided a solution to most of the gallery's problems. The collection and the administrative offices could be divided between two houses of similar size, thus freeing the old museum for the presentation of old master paintings and a much needed extension for the print department. The plans of the present state government to move part of the old collection to Ludwigsburg Palace — the original site of the Staatsgalerie — would answer both the growth of the collection and, above all, would provide the palace with a representative decoration, thus constituting a harmonious union of the Baroque architecture with an art collection developed during the same period.

Nicolaus Friedrich von Thouret

Geboren 1767 in Ludwigsburg, gestorben 1845 in Stuttgart.

Thouret hat seit 1833 insgesamt vier Entwürfe für das Stuttgarter Kunstgebäude entwickelt, das erst 1843 den Namen »Museum der bildenden Künste« erhielt. Sein letzter, 1837/38 entstandener Entwurf gilt in der überarbeiteten Endfassung als der reifste und beste. An der Neckarstraße gelegen, deren oberen Teil Thouret bereits 1818 (!) als »künftiges Kulturzentrum« ausgewiesen hatte, ist der Bau in Form einer Dreiflügelanlage konzipiert. Die rustikale, in einer Planvariante noch stärker aufgelöste Fassadengestaltung mit ihren Rundbogenfenstern ist von Münchner Bauten Leo von Klenzes beeinflußt. Waren im Innern Ausstellungsräume und Ateliers den Flügeln zugeordnet, sollte der Mitteltrakt die Kunstschule aufnehmen. Die Eckrisalite sind mit Oberlicht ausgestattet. Durch die Verlegung des Treppenhauses erhielt das Foyer besondere Bedeutung. Thourets Entwurf diente Barth im Grundriß als Vorbild.

Nicolaus Friedrich von Thouret

Born 1967 in Ludwigsburg, died 1845 in Stuttgart.

Since 1833, Thouret made four proposals for the Stuttgart art museum, which was only later, in 1843, named "Museum of Fine Arts". His last sketch from 1837/38, a revised final version, is considered the best. The building was located at the Neckarstraße, whose upper section Thouret had already coined a "future culture·center" in 1818! It was conceived as a 3-winged arrangement. The rusticated façade with its round arched windows, which is even more broken up in one of the design variations, is influenced by the buildings by Leo von Klenze in Munich. Exhibition halls and ateliers were relegated to the wings, while the middle section was intended to house the art school. The wing pavilions were provided with overhead lighting. The setting-back of the stairway endowed the foyer with extra importance. Concerning the ground plan, Thouret's sketch served Barth as a model.

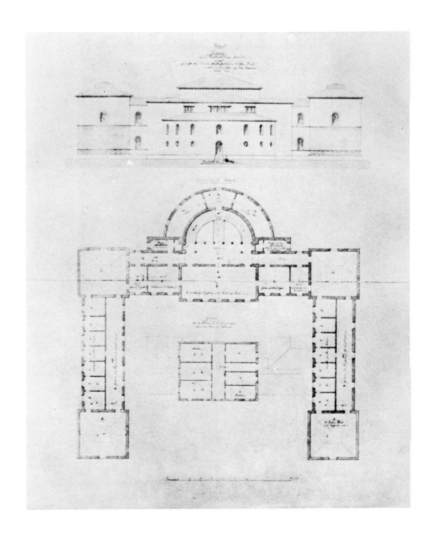

26
Nicolaus Friedrich von Thouret
Entwurf für das
Stuttgarter Kunstgebäude
(Fassadenaufriß und Grundriß)
1837/38

26
Nicolaus Friedrich von Thouret
Sketch for the Stuttgart Kunstgebäude
(Art Building)
(section of the façade and groundplan),
1837/38

Karl Ludwig Wilhelm von Zanth

Geboren 1796 in Breslau, gestorben 1857 in Stuttgart.

Zanths Entwurf eines »Kunstgebäudes« vom 6. Februar 1838 ist im Unterschied zu den Entwürfen von Thouret und Barth als Vierflügelanlage mit geräumigem Innenhof konzipiert. Die Schließung zur Straßenseite erfolgte mit Rücksicht auf die durchgehende Häuserfront. Vorder- und Rückseite weisen jeweils zwei Eckrisalite und einen zum Hof hin erweiterten Mittelrisalit auf. Der Haupteingang liegt im Innern des zur Nekkarstraße gelegenen Flügels. Ein zweiter Zugang — für Lehrer und Schüler der Kunstschule — war am Südflügel geplant. Besondere Aufmerksamkeit hatte Zanth der skulpturalen Gestaltung der Fassade gewidmet, die Macht und musischen Anspruch des Königs, aber auch Größe, Vielfalt und Wirkung der Künste seit der Antike verherrlichen sollte. Der König favorisierte diesen Entwurf und entschied sich erst nach eingehender Beratung mit seinem Finanzministerium für den billigeren von Barth, der im ganzen freilich auch klarer und in der Anordnung der Funktionsbereiche überzeugender war.

Karl Ludwig Wilhelm von Zanth

Born 1796 in Breslau, died in 1857 in Stuttgart.

Zanth's sketch for a "building for art", dating from 6 February 1838, is, in contrast to the sketches by Thouret and Barth, conceived as a 4-winged arrangement with a spacious inner courtyard. The closed front aligning to the street harmonized with the façades of the neighbouring houses. The front and back wings were accentuated with two wing pavillions and a central projection extending towards the courtyard. The main entrance is situated inside the wing aligning to the Neckarstraße. A second entrance — for teachers and pupils of the art school — was planned for the south wing. Zanth paid particular attention to the sculptural decoration of the façade, which aimed at glorifying the power and inspiration claims of the King as well as the greatness, multiplicity and influence of the arts since ancient times. The King preferred this design. Only after consultation with his finance ministry he decided in favour of Barth's less expensive plan. This latter plan was certainly more clearly arranged and its disposition of the various museum functions was more convincing.

28
Karl Ludwig Wilhelm von Zanth
Entwurf eines
Kunstgebäudes für Stuttgart
(Grundriß des Erdgeschosses)
1838

28
Karl Ludwig Wilhelm von Zanth
Sketch for an
Art Building in Stuttgart
(Plan of the ground floor),
1838

27
Karl Ludwig Wilhelm von Zanth
Entwurf eines Kunstgebäudes
für Stuttgart
(Fassadenaufriß)
1838

27
Karl Ludwig Wilhelm von Zanth
Sketch for an Art Building
in Stuttgart
(section of the façade),
1838

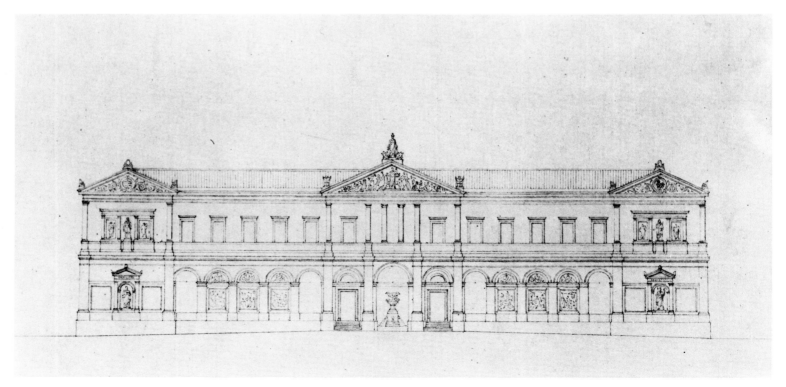

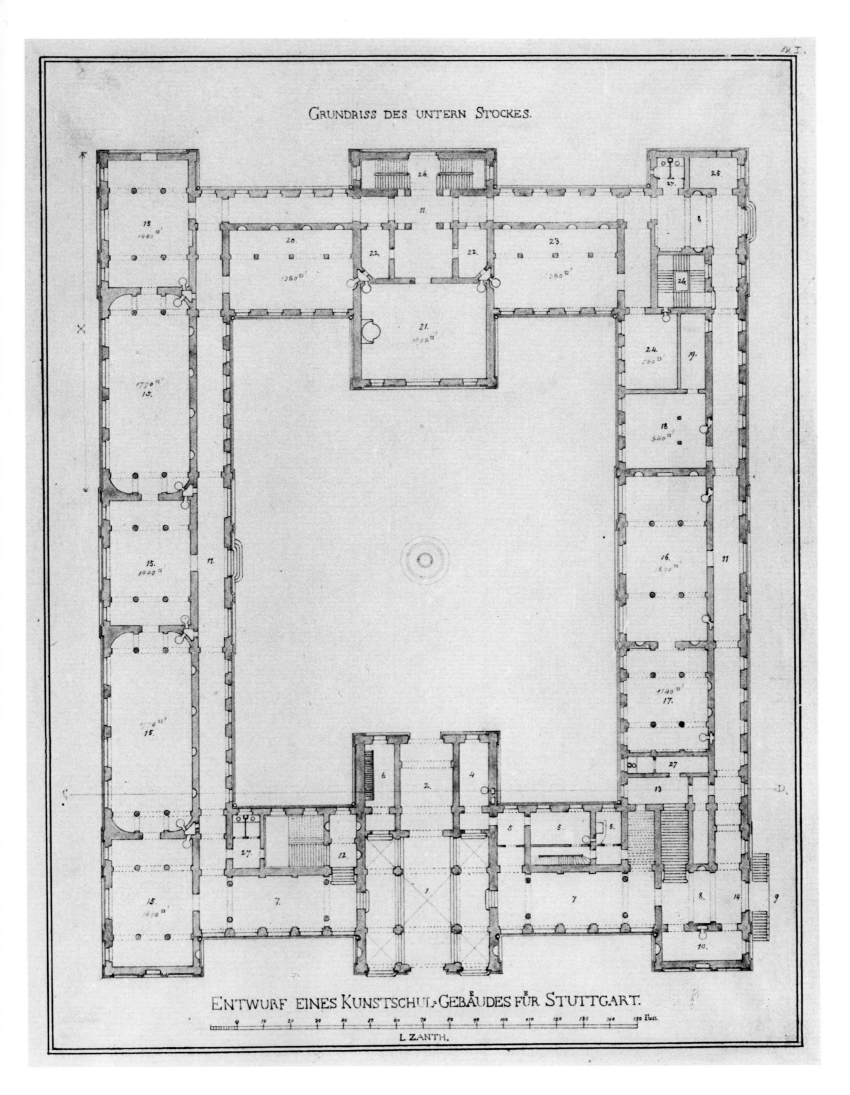

GRUNDRISS DES UNTERN STOCKES.

ENTWURF EINES KUNSTSCHUL-GEBÄUDES FÜR STUTTGART.

L. ZANTH.

Albert von Bok

Geboren 1825 in Eltershofen bei Schwäbisch Hall, gestorben 1814 in Stuttgart.

Die abgebildeten, von Irene Antoni erstmals veröffentlichten Pläne von Boks aus den Jahren 1880—1884 geben wahrscheinlich die ursprüngliche Anlage wieder. Demnach waren die Räume der Flügelbauten durch zum Süden gelegene Korridore erreichbar, während Mitteltrakt und Eckrisalite — von geringfügigen Abweichungen abgesehen — dem heutigen Grundriß entsprachen. Im Vestibül befanden sich vier im Quadrat aufgestellte Säulen. Boks Erweite-

Albert von Bok

Born 1825 in Eltershofen near Schwäbisch Hall, died 1914 in Stuttgart.

The illustrated plans by Bok from 1880 to 1884, first published by Irene Antoni, probably show the original arrangement. The rooms of the side wings were reached by south corridors, while the center tract and the wing pavilions — apart from minor alternations — correspond to the present ground plan. The vestibule was accentuated by four columns laid out in a square design. Bok's extension showed large rooms on the ground floor with paired columns. These

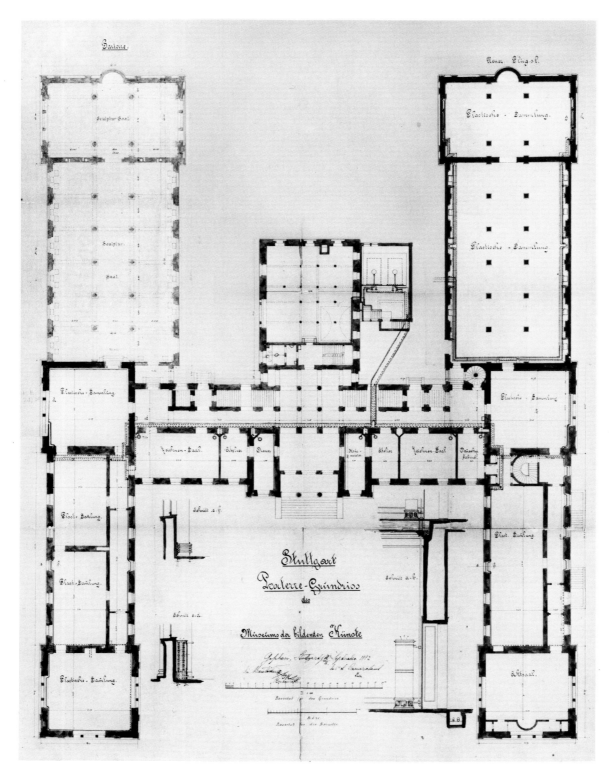

29
Albert von Bok
Erweiterungsplan für das
Museum der bildenden Künste
(Grundriß des Erdgeschosses)
1880—1884

29
Albert von Bok
Extension plan for the
Museum of Fine Arts
(Plan of the ground floor),
1880—1884

rung sah im Erdgeschoß große Säle mit paarweise eingestellten Säulen vor, die sich im heutigen Saal südwestdeutscher Kunst, dessen Boden erst 1960 auf das Niveau der unteren Galerieräume angehoben wurde, noch erhalten haben. Im Obergeschoß waren im Südflügel fünf große Gemäldesäle, im Nordflügel vier über einen seitlichen Korridor erreichbare Kabinette und der »Festsaal« untergebracht.[50] Die kabinettartige Aufteilung des Nordflügels wurde nach dem Zweiten Weltkrieg zunächst beibehalten; sie wich erst Anfang der 60er Jahre der heutigen Disposition.

have been retained in the present room for southwestern German art, whose floor was first raised to the level of the lower galleries in 1960. In the upper floor of the south wing were five large rooms for paintings. The north wing included four cabinets, which could be reached via a side corridor, as well as the "ball-room".[50] The division of the north wing into small cabinets was retained after the second World War; the present disposition of the other rooms was introduced only at the beginning of the 1960s.

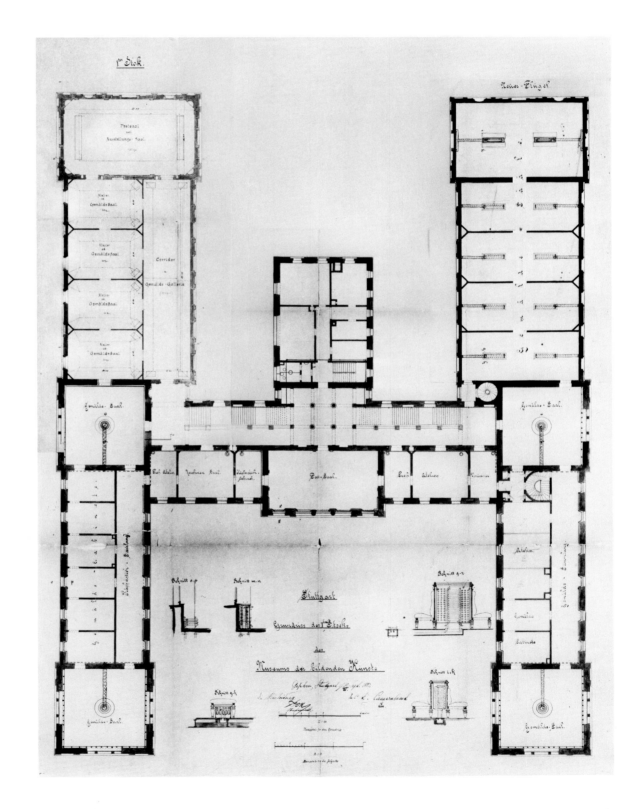

30
Albert von Bok
Erweiterungsplan für das
Museum der bildenden Künste
(Grundriß des Obergeschosses)
1880–1884

30
Albert von Bok
Extension plan for the
Museum of Fine Arts
(Plan for the upper floor),
1880–1884

DIE NEUE STAATSGALERIE
VON
JAMES STIRLING

———

THE NEW
STAATSGALERIE
BY JAMES STIRLING

Die Frage, ob sich die Architektur unserer Zeit auch im Museumsbau artikuliert, ist in der Tat eine eher akademische, wenn nicht gar müßige Frage. Allein am Beispiel des Guggenheim-Museums in New York, des dortigen Whitney-Museums, des Centre Pompidou in Paris oder des Museums in Mönchengladbach läßt sich unschwer ermessen, daß das Museum als architektonische Aufgabe bedeutende Architekten zu inspirieren vermochte, wenngleich die Gestalt der von ihnen geschaffenen Bauten keinerlei Rückschlüsse auf einen allgemein verbindlichen Museumstyp zuläßt, wie ihn noch das 19. Jahrhundert hervorgebracht hat. Die Gründe dafür liegen weniger in der nur »scheinbaren« Geschichtslosigkeit unserer Architektur, als in der divergierenden Entwicklung der Künste in unserem Jahrhundert. Emanzipation ist ein in diesem Zusammenhang nicht ungern verwendetes Schlagwort. Emanzipation heißt Befreiung, und das meint Entbindung von der Verpflichtung, einer Sache zu dienen, die nicht zugleich die eigene ist. Die Architektur war von dieser Entwicklung kaum minder betroffen als Malerei und Skulptur. Bezogen auf die Eigendynamik künstlerischer Gestaltungsfaktoren kam diesem Prozeß fundamentale Bedeutung zu, bezogen auf den interdisziplinären Kontakt der einzelnen Künste hat er freilich auch zur Entfremdung geführt. Nichts verdeutlicht dies mehr als das bisweilen totale Debakel der »Kunst am Bau« oder die mangelnde Integrationsfähigkeit selbst qualifizierter moderner Architektur. Im Museumsbau stellt sich dieses Problem noch zugespitzt dar, weil nämlich hier die Symbiose — oder sagen wir richtiger: »die korrespondierende Beziehung von Kunst und Architektur« zwar nicht unabdingbar gefordert, doch nahegelegt werden kann. Daß dabei der Spielraum des Architekten nicht eingeschränkt, sondern im Gegenteil freigesetzt werden sollte, ist sicherlich richtig und allein möglich, wenn die Funktion des Museums schon im Stadium der Ausschreibung klar definiert, im übrigen aber die Architektur in der Freiheit ihrer Entfaltung nicht beeinträchtigt wird.

Es kommt hinzu, daß der Kontext, in dem ein Museum entsteht, aber auch seine topographische Lage, einen nicht unerheblichen Einfluß auf Planung und Ausformung seiner Gestalt haben können. In Stuttgart spielten diese Faktoren eine entscheidende Rolle. Der durch Kriegseinwirkung zwar stark reduzierte, doch noch immer fühlbare spätklassizistische Umraum, die unmittelbare Nachbarschaft des 1843 vollendeten Museums der bildenden Künste, die Reihung nahezu aller landeseigenen Kulturbauten entlang einer nicht nur optisch brutalen, zu Beginn der 60er Jahre auf einem ehemaligen Boulevard angelegten »Stadtautobahn«, das alles waren und sind heute noch Vorgaben, die keineswegs nur stimulieren, sondern auch Resignation auslösen können. Immerhin stellte schon der Ausschreibungstext die Beseitigung, und das kann nur heißen die »Versenkung« der Konrad-Adenauer-Straße vage in Aussicht. Sollte dies tatsächlich geschehen, dann wird im Herzen der Stadt ein kulturelles Zentrum entstehen, das auf überschaubarem Raum

The issue of whether or not the architecture of our times manifests itself in museum buildings is in fact an academic if not a wholly redundant question. Alone the examples of the Guggenheim and Whitney Museums in New York, of the Pompidou Center in Paris, or the museum in Mönchengladbach clearly prove that the museum as an architectural project has inspired important architects — even though the structure of their buildings do not reflect the constitution of an obligatory museum "type", such as the 19th century produced. The reason for this have less to do with the apparent "ahistoricity" of our architecture than with the divergent development of the various arts in our century. Emancipation is a catchword not seldom used in this context. Emancipation means liberation, and that signifies liberation from the duty of serving a goal which is not one's own. Architecture has been scarcely less effected by this development than painting and sculpture. In relation to the internal dynamics of artistic creation, this process was fundamentally significant; in relation to interdisciplinary contact between the individual arts it certainly also led to distance and alienation. The total debacle of the "art for buildings" program as well as the inability of even qualified modern architecture to achieve integration, both exemplify this problem. In museum buildings, this problem gets intensified because here the synthesis — or better expressed — "the corresponding relation of art and architecture" is not absolutely necessary but certainly more relevant. In order not to limit but rather to liberate the architect's creative scope, it is necessary to define clearly the function of the museum at the outset, and not to impair the free development of architecture.

Moreover, the context in which a museum comes into being, and also its topographical location, should not be unimportant for its planning and construction. In Stuttgart these factors played a decisive role. The late neoclassical surroundings, which were reduced by war but are nevertheless still palpable, the direct proximity of the adjacent Museum of Fine Arts, completed in 1843, as well as the disposition of nearly all public cultural buildings along a modern city motorway which replaced a boulevard at the beginning of the 1960s — all these are preconditions which were and are bound to provoke not only a stimulated response but also resignation. Nevertheless, the terms of the competitions already vaguely proposed the removal — and this can only mean the "covering" — of the Konrad-Adenauer-Straße. If this should really take place, then there would exist a cultural center at the heart of the city, combining in a single panorama the Staatsgalerie and the theater, the music school and the opera, archives and libraries, and in its extension also the "Kunstverein" and the "Städtische Galerie". It would represent a closed ensemble and thus a unity within the urban structure. Even if this unity would be seriously compromised by the monstrous neighbouring concrete buildings opposite the Staatsgalerie, it can hardly be denied that the interlacing of all the important cultural institutions

Staatsgalerie und Theater, Musikhochschule und Oper, Archive und Bibliotheken, in der Erweiterung auch Kunstverein und Städtische Sammlung so miteinander verknüpft, daß sich diese als ein geschlossenes Ensemble und damit als Einheit im Gefüge der Stadt darstellen können. Auch wenn diese Einheit durch den monströsen Betonbau des Kulissengebäudes gegenüber der Staatsgalerie empfindlich gestört bleiben dürfte, ist doch kaum zu bestreiten, daß die Verflechtung aller wichtigen Kulturinstitutionen auf einem Terrain vielfältige Möglichkeiten der Kooperation und vor allem der interdisziplinären Nutzung erschließen wird, von dem Gewinn an Urbanität ganz zu schweigen.

Doch kehren wir nach diesem Exkurs zum Ausgangspunkt unserer Überlegungen und damit zum Thema »Museum« zurück. Was war in Stuttgart verlangt, was — bezogen auf die Funktion des Museums — gefordert? Auf jeden Fall nicht die offene Struktur einer Containerarchitektur, die das Prinzip totaler Flexibilität unreflektiert auf den gesamten Musterkomplex überträgt. Daß in sich variable Großräume improvisierender Gestaltung dienlich sein können, wollen wir gar nicht bestreiten. Jeder Ausstellungsleiter ist sich dessen bewußt. Andererseits kommt ein Kunstwerk zu ungleich stärkerer Geltung, wenn seine Präsenz bei der Konzeption eines Raumes »mitgedacht« und es nicht nachträglich als Requisit oder gar als Versatzstück in beliebig manipulierbare Ausstellungshallen eingebracht wird. Kunst — und ich beziehe mich damit keineswegs nur auf bestimmte Phänomene derselben, sondern auf Kunst allgemein — bedarf eines Umraums, der sich durch ein hohes Maß an Zurückhaltung auszeichnet, der optische Störelemente wie Installationsschächte oder dergleichen verdrängt und — gleichsam »dienend« — die Wirkungsfähigkeit des einzelnen Kunstwerkes fördert, also ein kontemplatives Erleben desselben ermöglicht. In diesem Zusammenhang stellt sich auch die zunehmende Bedeutung der Museumsdidaktik als ein Problem besonderer Art dar, und zwar namentlich dort, wo sie innerhalb der Schausammlungen unserer Museen so stark dominiert, daß das einzelne Kunstwerk dabei nicht selten zum Illustrationsobjekt degradiert wird.

Das Museum also nicht als multimedialer »Gemischtwarenladen«, wohl aber als Haus, das unterschiedliche Nutzungen zuläßt, das Lektion und Anschauung sorgfältig trennt und auch zwischen wechselnder und dauernder Ausstellung scheidet, das war — auf eine knappe Formel gebracht — unser Programm, ein Programm, das freilich in enger Verknüpfung mit der künftigen Nutzung des Altbaus entwickelt und formuliert werden mußte. Da dieser im Untergeschoß die Graphische Sammlung, im Obergeschoß die alte Malerei bis zum Impressionismus aufnehmen sollte, ergaben sich für den Neubau folgende Forderungen:

1. in gangartiger Verbindung zum Obergeschoß des Altbaus die Schausammlungsräume für die neuere Sammlung, welche die hauseigenen Bestände des 20. Jahrhunderts umfaßt. Eine dem Wettbewerb vorausgegangene Analyse dieser Bestän-

in one area would open up multiple possibilities for cooperation and above all for interdisciplinary functions — not to mention the urban advantages of such a plan.

But let us return to the starting point of our deliberations after this deviation and thus back to the subject of the "museum". What was required in Stuttgart — what was demanded in relation to the function of the museum? Certainly not the open structure of "container architecture" that would impose the principle of total flexibility directly onto the whole complex of the museum. The potential of large changeable rooms for improvisation and variation cannot be denied. Every exhibition organizer is aware of their advantage. On the other hand, a work of art is much more powerful if its presence is taken into account at the very moment of the conception of the corresponding room. It looses this power when it is added subsequently like a requisite or a displaced object in any given exhibition hall. Art — and I am not referring to its individual manifestations but rather to art in general — requires a setting that is characterized by a high degree of reserve. It has to supress visual irritations like installation shafts and the like and thus — while "serving" — it will increase the impact of every individual art work and facilitate a contemplative experience. In this context the didactic functions of the museum become especially problematic; for in the exhibition spaces they can become so dominating a factor that the individual art works are sometimes degraded to the level of illustrations.

In shortened form our concept was the following: instead of a "multi-media" general store the museum as a house that allows for different uses, which separates the "lesson" from "looking" and also distinguishes between temporary and permanent exhibition. This program had of course to be developed and formulated in close relation to the future use of the old museum. Because this was to contain the print collection on the lower floor and, on the upper floor, old master paintings up to Impressionism, the criteria of the new museum were as follows:

1. The visitor should be able to walk from the upper floor of the old building to the exhibition space for new art, which had to include the museum collection of 20th century art. A study of the collection that preceded the competition specified two room sizes: 200 sq metres × 6 metres high for larger sculptures, objects and paintings; 100 sq metres × 4 metres high for works with smaller dimensions. These rooms should be devided by temporary walls and be furnished with overhead lighting.

2. The entrance floor should include a foyer and café, seminar rooms, a lecture hall and a dividable exhibition hall. For the latter a system of variable lighting should be devised to render possible interdisciplinary events and, above all, exhibitions of light sensitive graphics.

3. The placing of the depots should take into account not only the delivery point but also the possibility of uncomplicated and quick access to all exhibition spaces.

de hatte zwei Raumgrößen nahegelegt: für größere Skulpturen, Objekte und Bilder 200 qm bei 6 m Höhe, für Arbeiten kleineren Maßstabs 100 qm bei 4 m Höhe. Diese Räume sollten durch Wandelemente beschränkt unterteilbar und mit Oberlicht ausgestattet sein.

2. Auf einer unteren Geschoßebene Foyer und Café, Seminarräume und Vortragssaal sowie eine beliebig unterteilbare Ausstellungshalle, für die ein System variabler Beleuchtung gefordert wurde, um auch interdisziplinäre Veranstaltungen und vor allem Ausstellungen lichtempfindlicher Graphik zu ermöglichen.

3. Über die Anordnung der Depots sollten nicht nur der Standort der Anlieferung, sondern auch die Möglichkeit einer unkomplizierten und raschen Versorgung aller Ausstellungsbereiche entscheiden.

4. Bibliothek und Direktion wurden in einer Einheit zusammengefaßt. Sie sollten mit dem Museumsbau zwar verbunden, ihm aber nicht unbedingt integriert sein.

5. Ein größerer Plastikhof sollte möglichst geschützt sein und in überschaubarer Verbindung zur Schausammlung stehen.

6. Außerdem sollte der Neubau einen eigenen Eingang erhalten, weil eine zentrale Erschließung sowohl des alten wie des neuen Museums zwischen den beiden Gebäuden aus mancherlei Gründen, vor allem wegen einer unverlegbaren Feuergasse, nicht möglich war.

Daß darüber hinaus auch Erwägungen der Denkmalpflege, Probleme der sehr fragwürdigen, doch hoffentlich korrigierbaren städtebaulichen Situation zu berücksichtigen waren, darf als bekannt vorausgesetzt werden. Zumal der Wunsch nach Erhaltung einiger historischer Gebäude in der Urbanstraße und die Forderung einer diagonalen Fußgängerverbindung zwischen Urban- und Konrad-Adenauer-Straße hat die Entwicklung brauchbarer Lösungsvorschläge — wie sich nach dem Wettbewerb herausstellen sollte — eher belastet.

Mit einer Ausnahme freilich — dem Entwurf von James Stirling (Abb. 32, S. 58; 35, S. 62; 36, S. 62).[31] Im Unterschied nämlich zur Mehrzahl seiner Kollegen (Abb. 33, S. 60; 34, S. 61) entschied er sich nicht zur Trennung zwischen Museum und einer Fußgängerzone, die sich seitlich durch mehr oder weniger amputierte Grünräume windet, sondern für eine rein architekturbezogene Lösung. Die Rotunde — vom Passanten über eine Rampe erreichbar — ist nicht nur optischer Mittelpunkt des Museums, sondern auch Schnittpunkt und damit Ort der Begegnung zwischen Museum und Öffentlichkeit. In freier Abwandlung einer Idee von Karl Friedrich Schinkel (Abb. 31, S. 57) alle Ebenen des Museums durchdringend, sich aber nach oben hin öffnend, nimmt sie weniger applikatorisch als collagierende Stilzitate auch früherer Zeit auf, so Sinn und Funktion des Gebäudes erschließend, das sich in seinem Innern ja ebenfalls als eine großangelegte Collage künstlerischer Erscheinungsformen aus verschiedener Zeit darstellt.[32] »A museum is a museum« — so könnte man argumentieren und seine Form aus seiner inhaltlichen Funktion heraus bestimmen. Das Prinzip

4. The library and administration were to be conceived as a unity. They should be connected to the museum building but not necessarily be integrated with it.

5. A large sculpture courtyard should be as protected as possible and clearly connected with the exhibition rooms.

6. In addition the new building should have an extra entrance, because a central entrance for the old and the new museum, situated between the two buildings, was impossible for several reasons, above all because of an unalterable access route for fire engines.

Moreover there were considerations of conservation and the problems of an awkward but hopefully correctible urban situation that had to be observed. After the competition it turned out that the desire to preserve some of the historical buildings in the Urbanstraße and the demand for a diagonal public footpath connecting Urbanstraße and Konrad-Adenauer-Straße, hindered the formulation of satisfactory solutions.

There was one exception, however: the plan by James Stirling (ill. 32, p. 58; 35, p. 62; 36, p. 62)[31]. In contrast to the majority of his colleagues (ill. 33, p. 60; 34, p. 61), he decided against separating the museum and the public footpath, that wound its way laterally through more or less marked off green spaces. Stirling went for a purely architectural solution instead. The rotunda, reached by a ramp for pedestrians, is not only the optical center of the museum, but also the point of intersection and the meeting point between the museum and its public. The rotunda is a free variation on an idea by Karl Friedrich Schinkel (ill. 31, p. 57), pervading all levels of the museum, but open to the sky. It represents less an appliqué than a collage of stylistic quotations from earlier times, revealing both the meaning and function of the building which, in its interior, presents a large-scale collage of artistic visions from various periods[32]. "A museum is a museum" — this is a possible argument which would lead us to derive its form from its function. In this sense, the principle of collage is not at all an old one, but rather actual, and it makes itself clearly felt even when Stirling is less obviously concerned with history. This is particularly noticeable in the form of the facade, in the ramps and the walls, in the circular elements and curves, but also in the lively variation of natural stone facing, translucent building materials and colour, forming an architectural ensemble with sculptural effects that culminates impressively in the cascade-like construction of the glass-fronted foyer. The character of the building is sculptural in all its aspects; even in the terrace-like construction, which is an excellent adaptation to the sloping terrain. Above the base level, — where the carpark and maintenance services are housed — a terrace extends which, while conceived as a pedestrian walkway, can also be used for open air sculpture. The sideways orientation of the entrance is in counterpoint to the axiality of the building, leading into a foyer that can be viewed from outside and which also affords space for the presentation of art works. The cloakroom, information counter and mu-

der Collage ist indes keineswegs alt, sondern im Gegenteil neu und läßt sich selbst dort, wo Stirling Geschichte weniger fühlbar bemüht, sehr deutlich nachweisen. Besonders auffallend in der Fassadengestaltung, bei der Rampen und Wände, Kreissegmente und Kurven, aber auch der lebhafte Wechsel von Natursteinverkleidung, transluziden Baumaterialien und Farbe ein architektonisches Ensemble von geradezu plastischer Wirksamkeit bilden, das in dem kaskadenartigen Aufbau der Foyerverglasung eindrucksvoll kulminiert. Plastisch ist dieser Bau allenthalben, auch in seiner terrassierenden Anlage, die sich dem steigenden Gelände hervorragend anpaßt. Über dem Sockelgeschoß, in dem Parkraum und technische Anlagen untergebracht sind, bildet sich eine Terrasse, die — als Fußgängerzone gedacht — zur Aufstellung von Freiplastiken genutzt werden kann (Abb. 35, S. 62). Der seitlich gelegene Eingang wirkt der Axialität des Gebäudes entgegen. Er mündet im Foyer, das von außen einsehbar ist und ebenfalls Platz für die Präsentation von Kunstwerken bietet. Garderobe, Informations und Verkaufsstand sind dort untergebracht, seitlich noch ein Café, das Stirling gleichsam als Klammer zwischen Museum und Kammertheater plaziert, also für beide Institutionen nutzbar gemacht hat. Vom Foyer aus erschließen sich auf einem Niveau Ausstellungshalle und Vortragssaal, also jene Bereiche, die transitorischer Wirksamkeit dienen. Die Schausammlung — über Rampe, Treppen oder Aufzüge erreichbar — ist U-förmig angelegt und nimmt damit den originalen Grundriß des Altbaus in die Gestaltung mit auf (Abb. 36, S. 62). Die Größe der Schausammlungsräume folgt — wenngleich nicht pedantisch — den in der Ausschreibung fixierten Richtwerten. Die Verbindung zwischen Alt- und Neubau soll dem Besucher die Möglichkeit bieten, sich den gesamten Museumskomplex entweder von der Gegenwart oder der Vergangenheit her zu erschließen. Der obere Plastikhof ist piazzaartig angelegt und von der Galerie aus ohne Umweg, also direkt zu betreten. Über eine Treppe mit dem öffentlich einseum shop are housed here, as well as to the side a café, that Stirling placed as a "clip" between the museum and the theater so that it can be used by both institutions. Adjoining to the foyer and on the same level are the exhibition and the lecture hall — that means those areas are reserved for events of a transitory nature. The lay-out of the exhibitions rooms for the permanent collection follows unpedantically the specifications prescribed in the original recommendation. The link between the old and the new building makes the whole museum complex accessible from the point of view of the present or of the past. The upper sculpture courtyard is designed like a piazza and is directly accessible from the galleries. Connected to the rotunda by a stairway, its rectangular ground plan presents an exciting contrast to the roundness of the latter. To summarize: the differentiated forms of the well-proportioned exhibition rooms correspond to the equally differentiated sites for the display of sculpture, which can be distributed in no less than three locations: in the rotunda, in the upper sculpture courtyard and on the public terrace that fronts the museum. The communicative advantages of these multiple sites for the presentation of sculpture is obvious. This was not achieved by any of the other competitors. Stirling was also unsurpassed in the convincing integration of his building with its city setting. He pays respect to the historical conditions of the surroundings, taking these up here and there in the forms of his own creation, which nevertheless insists on its own architectural individuality and character. The sculptural content of Stirling's building and his idiosyncratic use of collage methods have little in common with the modest late neoclassical disposition of the old museum. Does this mean that Stirling's architecture is monumental, as some critics have suggested? Monumentality, as Stirling has made clear on one occasion, has less to do with the dimensions of a building than with its "presence". Stirling's architecture fulfills this ambition on two counts: for it both makes demands on

31
Karl Friedrich Schinkel
Altes Museum Berlin
(Grundriß des Erdgeschosses)
1823—1830

31
Karl Friedrich Schinkel
Altes Museum, Berlin
(Plan of the ground floor),
1823—1830

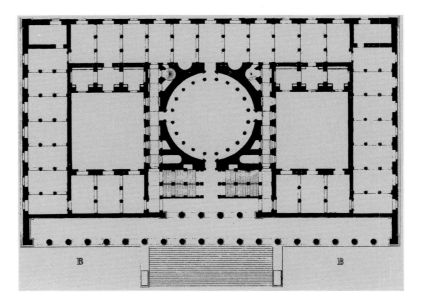

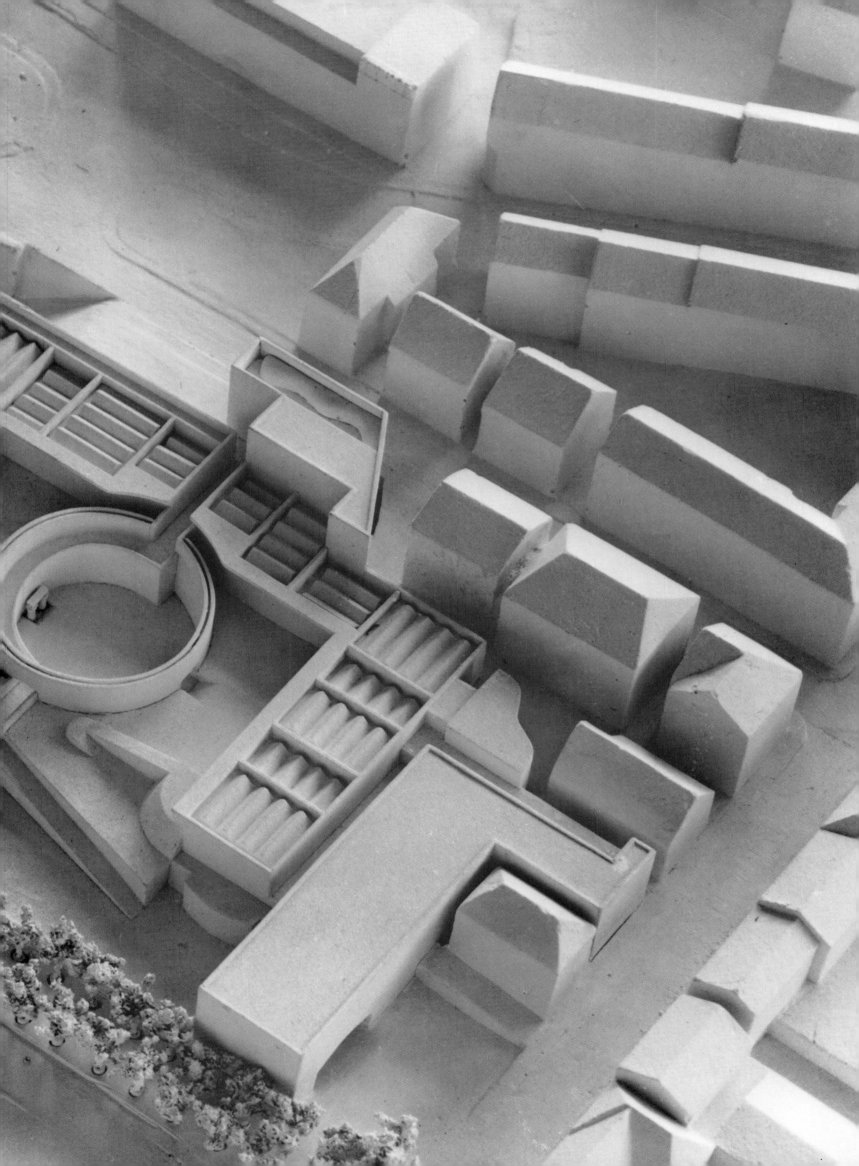

33
Jørgen Bo und Vilhelm Wohlert
Wettbewerbsmodell
Neue Staatsgalerie
1977

33
Jørgen Bo and Vilhelm Wohlert
Competition Model for the
New Staatsgalerie,
1977

32
James Stirling
Wettbewerbsmodell Neue Staatsgalerie
1977
Seiten 58 und 59

32
James Stirling
Competition model for the New Staatsgalerie,
1977
(pages 58, 59)

34
Arbeitsgemeinschaft
Günther Behnisch & Partner / Hans Kammerer,
Walter Belz & Partner
Wettbewerbsmodell
Neue Staatsgalerie
1977

34
Joint Project
Günther Behnisch and Partner/
Hans Kammerer, Walter Belz and Partner
Competition model for the
New Staatsgalerie,
1977

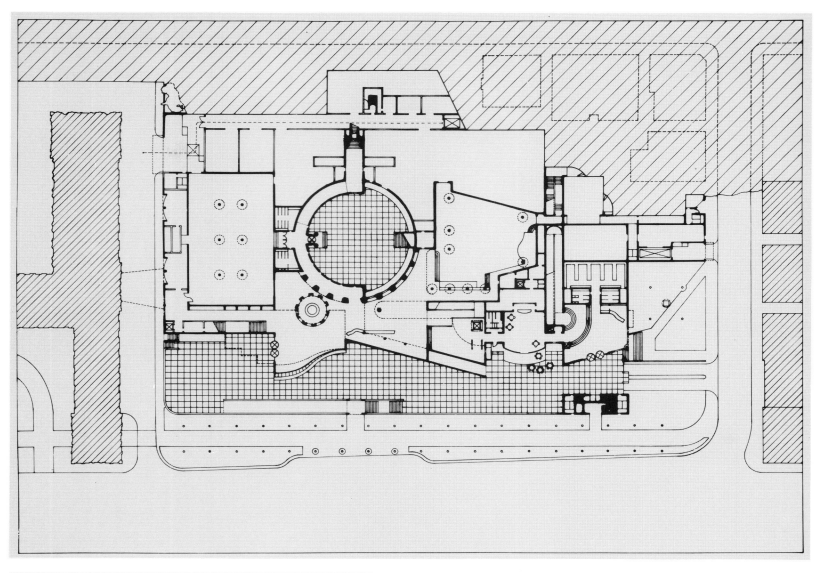

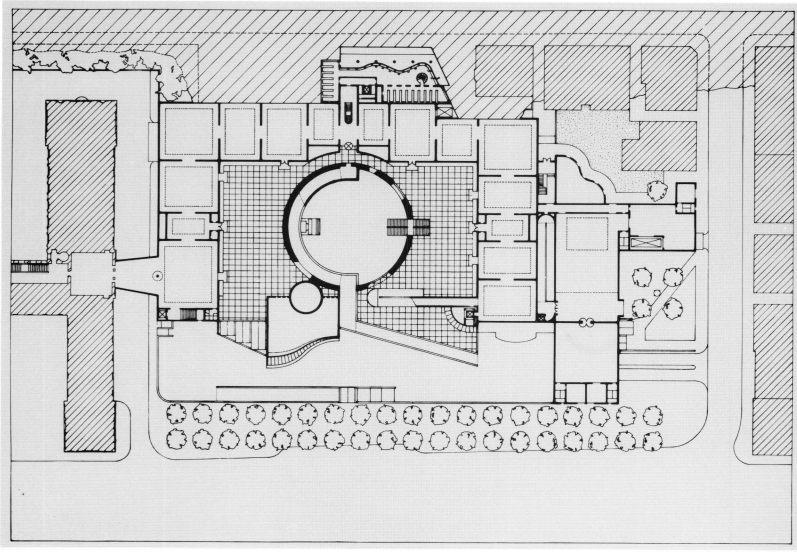

35
James Stirling
Grundriß der Neuen Staatsgalerie
(Eingangsgeschoß)

35
James Stirling
Groundplan for the New Staatsgalerie
(entrance level)

sehbaren Plastikbezirk der Rotunde verbunden, bildet sein rechteckiger Grundriß einen spannungsvollen Kontrast zu deren Rundform. Fazit: der differenzierenden Gestaltung in sich wohl proportionierter Schausammlungsräume entspricht ein nicht minder differenziertes Angebot für die Aufstellung von Plastik, die auf nicht weniger als drei Bereiche verteilt werden kann: auf Rotunde und oberen Plastikhof, aber auch auf die dem Bauwerk vorgelagerte, öffentlich zugängliche Terrasse. Der Kommunikationswert so vielfältiger Präsentationsmöglichkeiten für Plastik ist offenkundig und wurde von keinem der anderen Wettbewerbsteilnehmer erreicht. Unübertroffen blieb Stirling auch in der überzeugenden städtebaulichen Einbindung seines Gebäudes, das den historischen Bedingungen des Umraums Rechnung trägt, sie da und dort auch in die eigene Gestaltung mit aufnimmt, sich im übrigen aber als Architektur von unverwechselbarer Eigenart und Prägung erweist. Der plastische Gehalt des Stirlingschen Baus und der eigenwillige Einsatz collagierender Mittel haben mit der eher zurückhaltenden spätklassizistischen Gliederung des Altbaus nur wenig gemein. Ist Stirlings vitale Architektur deshalb gleich »monumental« — wie einige Kritiker meinen? Monumentalität — das hat Stirling einmal deutlich zum Ausdruck gebracht — bezieht sich weniger auf den äußeren Maßstab eines Gebäudes als auf seine »Präsenz«. Stirlings Architektur wird diesem Anspruch in doppelter Weise gerecht, indem sie fordernd und zugleich dienend in eine korrespondierende Partnerschaft zu den Kunstwerken tritt. Nicht zuletzt deshalb erschließt sich sein Bau sowohl als ein Stück wiedergewonnener urbaner Architektur, als auch vor allem als das, was wir eigentlich wollten: ein in der Durchdringung von Funktion und Gestalt perfektes Museum.

the works of art and serves them simultaneously in a corresponding partnership. Accordingly, his building works both as a piece of reconquered urban architecture and also — and above all — as that what we really hoped for: a perfect museum in its interaction of function and form.

36
James Stirling
Grundriß der Neuen Staatsgalerie
(Galeriegeschoß)

36
James Stirling
Groundplan for the New Staatsgalerie
(Gallery level)

DIE WERKE

THE WORKS OF ART

Bodenseeschule,

um 1335

1

Maria als Thron Salomonis

Tempera auf Leinwand über Holz (Eiche und Fichte), 107 × 195 cm, Goldgrund. Zisterzienserabtei Bebenhausen bei Tübingen. – Erworben 1904.

School of Lake Constance,

circa 1335.

1

The Virgin as the Throne of Solomon

Distemper on canvas over wood (oak and spruce), 107 × 195 cm, gold ground. Cistercian Abbey Bebenhausen near Tübingen.
Purchased 1904.

Das Tympanonbild — es ist das älteste erhaltene schwäbische Tafelgemälde überhaupt — stammt vom Kreuzgangsportal des Sommerrefektoriums im Zisterzienserkloster Bebenhausen bei Tübingen. Sein tradierter Anbringungsort verweist auf den engen Zusammenhang von Malerei und Architektur, die im Mittelalter eine unauflösbare, anschaulich erlebbare Einheit bildeten. Dargestellt ist in Anlehnung an das themengleiche Relief der Straßburger Münsterfassade »Maria als Thron Salomonis«, oder richtiger noch: »Maria als Thron des neuen Salomo.« Der in der unteren Bogennische inmitten des Stufenaufbaus thronende Salomo ist »Sinnbild für die sich in Christus offenbarende Weisheit«, gilt also nach der typologischen Deutung des Mittelalters als die alttestamentliche Entsprechung bzw. als Vorläufer Christi. Aber auch Maria, die mit dem Kind (als dem neuen Salomo) auf der obersten Stufe des Thrones sitzt, diesen also — selbst thronend — im Wortsinn besetzt, wird im hohen Mittelalter als »Sedes Sapientiae« (Sitz der Weisheit) gedeutet. Die zwölf Löwen zu beiden Seiten auf den Stufen des Thrones werden sowohl mit den zwölf Stämmen Israels (den Urvätern der Maria), als auch neutestamentlich — mit den zwölf Aposteln gleichgesetzt. Acht Frauenfiguren in den Tabernakelnischen verkörpern die »Tugenden«, durch die Maria zur Mutter Gottes wurde. Apostel und Propheten, jeweils im Brustbild, vervollständigen das Programm; ihre Schriftbänder verweisen auf Menschwerdung und Wiederkehr des Erlösers. Die Tafel ist — ihrer ursprünglichen Funktion gemäß — symmetrisch gegliedert. Der Goldgrund stellt Tiefe nicht dar, wohl aber »symbolisiert« er sie. Auch die Figuren sind auffallend flach, also ohne körperhaftes Volumen. In Gebärde und Haltung wahrnehmbar unterschieden, heben sie sich kaum mehr vom Hintergrund ab als die sie rahmenden Architekturen. Die Grazie ihrer Bewegungen und der Linienfluß ihrer Gewänder stehen im Einklang mit der kalligraphischen Klarheit der Umrisse, die sich — damaligem Zeitstil entsprechend — mehr oder weniger der geschwungenen Form der S-Kurve annähern. Die Tiefenlinien von Sockel und Boden verkürzen sich nicht, sondern erweitern sich in »umgekehrer Perspektive« nach hinten. Das Kolorit zeichnet sich durch ein hohes Maß an Zurückhaltung aus; gleichwohl sind die wenigen, den Bildaufbau dominierenden Farben durch die »Vielfalt ihrer Kombinationen« reich nuanciert.

The tympanum painting (the oldest surviving example of Swabian panel painting) comes from the cloister door of the summer refectory in the Cistercian monastery of Bebenhausen near Tübingen. Its original setting demonstrates the close relationship between painting and architecture, which formed an inseparable unity in the medieval age. The image represents "The Virgin as the Throne of Solomon", or, more exactly, "The Virgin as the Throne of the New Solomon", imitating the relief with a similar subject on the facade of Straßburg Cathedral. Solomon, throned in the lower arch within the stairway, is "the symbol of Christ's manifest wisdom", the Old Testament equivalent for or forerunner of Christ, according to the typological interpretation of the Middle Ages. But the Virgin too, seated with her child (the new Solomon) on the highest step of the throne, literally "crowning the throne", was understood as "sedes Sapientiae" (the seat of wisdom) during the High Middle Ages. The twelve lions on both sides of the steps of the throne were identified with the twelve tribes of Israel, (the ancestors of Mary), and, as regards the New Testament, with the twelve Apostles. The eight female figures in small tabernacles embody the "virtues" that enabled Mary to become the mother of God. Apostles and prophets, both represented in half-length portraits, complete the scheme; their inscribed ribbons refer to the incarnation and second coming of the Saviour. The panel is symmetrically composed in accordance with its original function. The gold ground does not represent but rather "symbolizes" depth. The figures too are conspicuously flat, that is without bodily volume. With marked variations of gesture and pose, the figures are hardly more raised from the gold background than the architecture that frames them. The grace of their movements and the flowing lines of their robes correspond to the calligraphic clarity of the contours which, in line with contemporary period style, more or less conform to the swinging serpentine curve. The lines conveying depth in the socle and floor are not foreshortened, rather they broaden out in a form of "inverted perspective". The colour is distinguished by a high degree of reserve; but the limited number of hues which dominate the composition are nevertheless richly nuanced by the "multiplicity of their combinations".

Literatur: Kat. Lange, Nr. 95 a. – Kat. 1931, S. 156 ff. – Kat. 1957, S. 43 ff. mit Abb. – Kat. 1962, Alte Meister, S. 40 ff. mit Abb. – Christiane Michna, Maria als Thron Salomonis, Dissertation (Maschinenschrift), Wien 1950, Nr. 26 (ausführliche Darstellung der Ikonographie). – Heinrich Theodor Musper, Gotische Malerei nördlich der Alpen, Köln 1961, S. 47 mit Abb. – Kurt Löcher, Staatsgalerie Stuttgart – Altdeutsche Meister, 1972/73 (Maschinenschrift). – Edeltraud Rettich, Staatsgalerie Stuttgart – Altdeutsche Abteilung, Stuttgart 1978, mit Abb.

Bibliography: Cat. Lange, no. 95 a – Cat. 1931, p. 156 f. – Cat. 1957, p. 43 f. with ill. – Cat. 1962, Alte Meister, p. 40 f. with ill. – Christiane Michna, Maria als Thron Salomonis, thesis (typescript), Vienna 1950, no. 26 (detailed description of iconography). – Heinrich Theodor Musper, Gotische Malerei nördlich der Alpen, Cologne 1961, p. 47 with ill. – Kurt Löcher, Staatsgalerie Stuttgart – Altdeutsche Meister, 1972/73 (typescript). – Edeltraud Rettich, Staatsgalerie Stuttgart – Altdeutsche Abteilung, Stuttgart 1978, with ill.

Prager Schule,
1385

2

Flügelaltar aus Mühlhausen

Tempera auf Leinwand über Fichtenholz
mit Eichenholzeinlagen, 233,5 ×233,5 cm
(mit Rahmen)
St. Veitskapelle in Mühlhausen bei
Stuttgart. — Erworben 1902.

School of Prague,
1385.

2

Triptych from Mühlhausen

Distemper on canvas over spruce with
inlaid oak, 233.5 × 233.5 cm (with frame).
St. Vitus' Chapel in Mühlhausen near
Stuttgart. — Purchased 1902.

Der sogenannte Prager Altar, ein Werk der böhmischen Kunst, gehörte ursprünglich als Hauptaltar zur künstlerischen Ausstattung der St.-Veits-Kapelle in Mühlhausen bei Stuttgart. Er wurde von Reinhart von Mühlhausen zum Gedächtnis seines 1380 in Prag verstorbenen Bruders Eberhart gestiftet und laut rückseitiger Inschrift »am sant wensceszlaustag«, dem 28. September 1385, vollendet. Geöffnet zeigt der Altar die vor Goldgrund stehenden böhmischen Nationalheiligen Veit, Wenzel und Sigismund; geschlossen vor rotem, teils goldgemusterten Grund zur Linken Christus als Schmerzensmann, dem sich der kniende Stifter empfiehlt, zur Rechten den Gekreuzigten, flankiert von Maria und Johannes, in der Mitte die Verkündigung und darüber das seltene Motiv der gekrönten Maria als Sponsa (Himmelsbraut) Christi. Die Rückseite trägt die Stiftungsinschrift, außerdem Bildnisse der Brüder Reinhart und Eberhart sowie eine weitere Darstellung des Gekreuzigten, den wiederum Maria und Johannes umgeben.

Stilistisch gehört der Altar in den Ausstrahlungsbereich der Kunst des Theoderich von Prag, der als Hauptmeister der böhmischen Malerschule des 14. Jahrhunderts Anregungen sowohl der Parler als auch der oberitalienischen Kunst (Tomaso da Modena) aufnahm, diese aber in den Dienst einer eher rustikal anmutenden Formanschauung stellte. Die Figuren zeichnen sich durch Standfestigkeit aus, ihre Bewegungen sind organisch entwickelt. Ein klar ausgeprägtes Empfinden für Plastizität macht sich im Aufbau der Körper und in der Modellierung der Köpfe bemerkbar. Die schweren Gewänder fallen weich und gleichen sich den Bewegungen an. Architekturen fehlen. Sokkel und Throne sind aber annähernd folgerichtig verkürzt, nehmen also deutlich Bezug auf die körperhafte Präsenz der Figuren. Der Maler des Altars ist — wie vor allem Edeltraud Rettich herausstellte — sicher kein Schwabe, sondern wohl böhmischer Herkunft. Geprägt von der Prager Kunst seiner Zeit, hat er deren höfische Aspekte aber weitgehend getilgt und einen durchaus eigenen, in seinem Ausdrucksgehalt eher spröden und herben, als »bürgerlich« apostrophierbaren Stil entwickelt.

The so-called Prague Altar, a bohemian work of art, was originally the main altarpiece in the artistic adornment of St. Vitus' chapel in Mühlhausen near Stuttgart. It was donated by Reinhart von Mühlhausen in memory of his brother Eberhart who died in Prague in 1380 and, according to the inscription on the rear, it was completed "am sant Wenceszlaustag" (on Stw. Wenceslav's day), the 28th September 1385. The open altar shows the bohemian national saints Vitus, Wenceslav and Sigismund standing before a gold ground. The closed altar depicts, on the left, the Man of Sorrows, to whom the kneeling donor commends himself; to the right we find the crucified Christ flanked by Mary and John, in the centre the annunciation and above the rare motif of Mary crowned as Christ's heavenly bride. On the rear there is the commemorative inscription and in addition portraits of the brothers Reinhart and Eberhart, as well as a second depiction of the crucified Christ with Mary and John.

Stylistically the altar relates to the circle of influence radiating from Theoderic of Prague, who, as the major artist of the bohemian school of painting in the fourteenth century, adopted stimuli from the Parler and the North Italian art (Tomaso da Modena), but employed this knowledge in the service of a formal language with a more rustic appearance. The figures are distinguished by their stability, their movements are organically conceived. A marked sensitivity for sculptural form is noticeable in the construction of the bodies and the modelling of the heads. The heavy robes fall in soft folds, complementing the figures' movements. Architecture is absent, but the socles and thrones are more or less logically foreshortened, refering clearly to the sculptural presence of the figures. The painter of the altar — as Edeltraud Rettich above all points out — was certainly not Swabian, but rather of bohemian origins. Bearing the imprint of contemporary art in Prague, he nevertheless largely expunged its courtly aspects to develop an individual style which we might apostrophise as rough and austere rather than "bourgeois" in tone.

Literatur: Kat. Lange, Nr. 94. — Kat. 1931, S. 123 ff. — Kat. 1957, S. 204 mit Abb. — Kat. 1962, Alte Meister, S. 153 ff. — Kurt Löcher, Staatsgalerie Stuttgart — Altdeutsche Meister, 1972/73 (Maschinenschrift). — Edeltraud Rettich, Staatsgalerie Stuttgart — Altdeutsche Abteilung, Stuttgart 1978, mit Abb. — Edeltraud Rettich, Der Flügelaltar aus Mühlhausen von 1385, in: Die Parler und der Schöne Stil 1350—1400, Bd. I, Köln 1978, S. 338 ff.

Bibliography: Cat. Lange no. 94. — Cat. 1931, p. 123 f. — Cat. 1957, p. 204 with ill. — Cat. 1962, Alte Meister, p. 153 f. — Kurt Löcher, Staatsgalerie Stuttgart — Altdeutsche Meister, 1972/73 (typescript). — Edeltraud Rettich, Staatsgalerie Stuttgart — Altdeutsche Abteilung, Stuttgart 1978, with ill. — Edeltraud Rettich, "Der Flügelaltar aus Mühlhausen von 1385", in: Die Parler und der Schöne Stil 1350—1400, vol. 1, Cologne 1978, p. 338 f.

Meister der Sterzinger Altarflügel

Jüngerer Mitarbeiter Hans Multschers (tätig in Ulm zwischen 1427 und 1467). Benannt nach den im Rathaus zu Sterzing aufbewahrten Flügelbildern des 1456 bis 1458 von Multscher gelieferten ehemaligen Hochaltars der Pfarrkirche zu Sterzing (Südtirol).

3

Das Gefolge der Heiligen Drei Könige

Öl und Tempera auf Fichtenholz, 165 × 142,5 cm, damaszierter Goldgrund. Ehemaliges Zisterziensernonnenkloster Heiligkreuztal bei Riedlingen. — Sammlung Abel, Stuttgart. — Erworben 1859.

Master of the Sterzing Altarpaneles

Junior colleague of Hans Multscher (active in Ulm from 1427 to 1467). Named after the altar wings of the former highaltar of the parish church at Sterzing (South Tyrol), supplied by Multscher in 1456–1458, preserved in Sterzing town hall.

3

The Retinue of the Magi

Oil and distemper on spruce, 165 × 142.5 cm, gold damask ground. Former Cistercian convent "Heiligkreuztal" near Riedlingen. — Collection Karl Gustav Abel, Stuttgart. — Purchased 1859.

In der altdeutschen Abteilung der Staatsgalerie stellt die um 1450 von einem jüngeren Werkstattgenossen Hans Multschers geschaffene Tafel in mancher Hinsicht ein Unikum dar. Schon das Sujet — das Gefolge der Heiligen Drei Könige — ist ungewöhnlich, da es auf uns sonst bekannten Altartafeln so gut wie nie isoliert, dafür um so häufiger in Verbindung mit dem Zug oder mit der Anbetung der Heiligen Drei Könige dargestellt wurde.

Aber nicht nur thematisch, auch formal erweist sich die Tafel als eine Arbeit von außergewöhnlichem Rang. Das Gespräch der beiden vorderen Reiter, das in dem fragenden Blick des einen und in dem nachdenklichen des anderen seinen bildhaften Ausdruck findet, ist sowohl »inhaltliches« Zentrum der Darstellung wie Ausgangspunkt der Komposition. Diese entwickelt sich — der Marschrichtung des Zuges entsprechend — von recht nach links, wo auf einer benachbarten Tafel oder im geschnitzten Mittelschrein die Anbetung der Könige zu sehen war. Farblich schließt sich die Gruppe der Reiter zu einer reichen, in sich lebensvollen Einheit zusammen, während der in einem warmen Ocker gehaltene Weg auf das mattschimmernde Gold des Hintergrunds abgestimmt ist. Diese mildleuchtende Farbenharmonie, die technisch vollendete Malerei und der reliefhafte — mittelbar auf niederländischem Einfluß basierende — Aufbau der Komposition verleihen der Tafel um so mehr Bedeutung, als der hier entwikkelte stille und großflächige Stil die Ulmer Malerei noch ein halbes Jahrhundert geprägt hat.

Die Tafel gehörte als Flügelinnenseite zu einem Altar im ehemaligen Zisterziensernonnenkloster Heiligkreuztal bei Riedlingen. Die abgetrennte Flügelaußenseite, eine Grablegung Christi darstellend, befindet sich ebenfalls in der Staatsgalerie. Zwei weitere Tafeln mit Marientod und Kreuzigung besitzt die Kunsthalle Karlsruhe. Die fast quadratische Form sämtlicher Tafeln legt nahe, daß sie ursprünglich zu »einem zweigeschossigen Wandelaltar gehörten, wie er in der Multscher-Werkstatt üblich war« (Edeltraud Rettich). Die Marienszenen waren innen, die Passionsszenen außen dargestellt. Der Reiterzug wurde 1940 vom damaligen »Reichsstatthalter« Murr als Geschenk für Hermann Göring annektiert und nach Karinhall gebracht, 1945 nach Österreich verschleppt und 1946 — zum Glück unversehrt — zurückerstattet.

The panel painted by a younger member of Hans Multscher's workshop circa 1450 has been described as a unique piece in the old master painting collection of the Stuttgart Staatsgalerie. Even the subject — the retinue of the Magi — is unusual, as in other known altarpieces it virtually never occurs in isolation but more often in combination with depictions of the procession of the Magi or the adoration scene.

In formal as well as thematic terms the panel emerges as a work of extraordinary rank. The conversation taking place between the two horsemen in the foreground, which finds plastic expression in the questioning look of the one and the thoughtful gaze of the other, is both the thematic focus of the image and the compositional point of departure. This develops — corresponding to the movement of the procession — from right to left, where the adoration of the Magi was to be seen on an adjacent panel or in a carved central shrine. Colouristically, the group of riders forms a rich unity full of inner life, while the warm ochre pathway harmonizes with the dim shimmer of the gold background. This gently glowing colour orchestration, the technical perfection of the painting and the illusion of relief in the construction of the composition — indirectly based on Netherlandish example — endow the panel with increased significance, in that the tranquility and the broadly conceived style we find developed here were to characterize Ulm painting for a further half century.

The panel is the inner lateral wing from an altar in the former Cistercian convent of "Heiligkreuztal" near Riedlingen. The detached exterior wing, depicting the Burial of Christ, is also located in the Staatsgalerie. Two other panels with the Death of the Virgin and the Crucifixion are in the collection of the Karlsruhe Kunsthalle. The virtual square formed by the assembled panels suggests that they originally belonged to a "two-storeyed convertible altar as was customary in the Multscher workshop" (Edeltraud Rettich). Depicted on the interior were scenes from the life of the Virgin, on the exterior, the Passion. The "Retinue of the Magi" was annexed by the former Reichsstatthalter ("governer of the Reich") Murr as a gift for Hermann Göring; it was taken to Karinhall and in 1945 removed to Austria. In 1946 — with unexpected good fortune — it was restored to Stuttgart.

Literatur: Kat. Lange, Nr. 13. — Kat. 1931, S. 180. — Kat. 1957, S. 273 ff. mit Abb. — Kat. 1962, Alte Meister, S. 202 ff. mit Abb. — Zur Kompositionsform vgl. Hans Fegers, Zur Frage der Bildkomposition bei einem Werk der altdeutschen Malerei, Festschrift Julius Baum, Stuttgart 1952, S. 83 ff. — Kurt Löcher, Staatsgalerie Stuttgart — Altdeutsche Meister, 1972/73 (Maschinenschrift). — Edeltraud Rettich, Staatsgalerie Stuttgart — Altdeutsche Abteilung, Stuttgart 1978, mit Abb.

Bibliography: Cat. Lange, no. 13. — Cat. 1931, p. 180. — Cat. 1957, p. 273 f. with ill. — Cat. 1962, Alte Meister, p. 202 f. with ill. — For discussion of the composition see Hans Fegers "Zur Frage der Bildkomposition bei einem Werk der altdeutschen Malerei" in: *Festschrift Julius Baum*, Stuttgart 1952, p. 83 f. — Kurt Löcher, Staatsgalerie Stuttgart — Altdeutsche Meister, 1972/73 (typescript). — Edeltraud Rettich, Staatsgalerie Stuttgart — Altdeutsche Abteilung, Stuttgart 1978, with ill.

Bartholomäus Zeitblom

Geboren um 1455–1460 in Nördlingen, gestorben zwischen 1518–1522 in Ulm. Seit 1482 in Ulm nachweisbar. Schwiegersohn des Friedrich Herlin und in zweiter Ehe des Hans Schüchlin. Tätig in Ulm.

4

Heimsuchung Mariae, 1496

aus dem Eschacher Altar

*Öl und Tempera auf Fichtenholz,
214 × 107,3 cm
Pfarrkirche Eschach bei Gaildorf. – 1818
dem Bildhauer Johann Heinrich Dannecker
angeboten. – Sammlung von Hirscher,
Tübingen und später Freiburg i. Br. –
Sammlung Abel, Stuttgart. – Erworben
1859.*

Bartholomäus Zeitblom

Born circa 1455–1460 in Nördlingen, died between 1518 and 1522 in Ulm. Presence documented in Ulm after 1482. Son in law of Friedrich Herlin and then (in his second marriage) of Hans Schüchlin. Active in Ulm.

4

Visitation of the Virgin, 1496

from the Eschach Altar

*Oil and distemper on spruce, 214 × 107.3 cm
Parish church in Eschach near Gaildorf. –
1818 offered to the sculptor Johann
Heinrich Dannecker. – Collection von
Hirscher, Tübingen and later Freiburg i. Br.
– Collection of Karl Gustav Abel,
Stuttgart. – Purchased 1859.*

Der 1496 entstandene Marienaltar aus der Johanneskirche in Eschach war ein dreiteiliger Flügelaltar, von dem nur der Schrein mit den lebensgroßen Figuren der von Engeln gekrönten Maria in Eschach verblieben ist. Die gemalten Tafeln wurden 1818 von der Gemeinde aus Geldnot verkauft und gelangten 1859 mit Ausnahme der Predellenrückseite (heute Gemäldegalerie Berlin) in den Besitz der Staatsgalerie. Dargestellt sind auf den Flügeln innen die Verkündigung und die Heimsuchung Mariae, außen die beiden Johannes, auf der Predella die vier Kirchenväter und rückseitig das von Engeln gehaltene Schweißtuch der heiligen Veronika.

Auf der hier abgebildeten Tafel der Heimsuchung stehen Maria und Elisabeth aufrecht nebeneinander. Sie vereinigen ihre ausgestreckten rechten Hände, ohne daß sich ihre Blicke begegnen. Nach außen wird die Gruppe durch die steil ansteigenden Umrißlinien der Gewänder begrenzt. In folgerichtiger Entsprechung zum hohen Bildformat sind die Figuren auffallend schlank und gestreckt. Die Architektur mit gleichem Belag auf Boden und Wand rechnet mit der Schrägstellung der Figuren. Dennoch meidet Zeitblom die Tiefe. Knapp hinter den statuengleichen Gestalten sind die Mauern emporgeführt, die Figuren zugleich rahmend und so fest an sich bindend, daß sich kaum eine freie Bewegung entwickeln kann. Jeder Versuch, eine Handlung zu veranschaulichen, hat sich einem strengen Formwillen untergeordnet. – Im Unterschied zum kraftvollen Realismus der fränkischen Schule, dem der junge Dürer erste Impulse verdankt, ist Zeitbloms stille, sich in reiner »Zuständlichkeit« erfüllende Kunst Zeugnis eines in den Eschacher Tafeln kulminierenden Spätstils, der zugleich das Ende der spätgotischen Ulmer Tafelmalerei ankündigt.

The altar to Mary dating from 1496 in the church of St John in Eschach was a three-part winged altar, of which only the shrine with life-size figures of the Virgin crowned by angels remains in Eschach. The painted panels were sold by the parish in 1818 to raise necessary funds and they entered the possession of the Staatsgalerie in 1859, excepting the reverse side of the predella (now in the Gemäldegalerie Berlin). On the inner wings is a depiction of the annunciation and visitation of Mary, on the outer, the two Johns, on the predella, the four church fathers, and, on the reverse, St Veronica's shroud borne by angels.

In the panel representing the visitation which is illustrated here, Mary and Elizabeth are standing erectly next to each other. They join their extended right hands, without meeting each others' eye. Outwardly the group is contained by the steeply sloping contours of their robes. Logically corresponding to the high format of the painting, the figures are noticeably thin and elongated. The architecture, with the same facing on the floor and walls, answers the inclination of the figures. But Zeitblom avoids depth. The walls are placed directly behind the statue-like figures, simultaneously framing and binding them, so that there is little possibility of free movement. Attempts to visualize the action of the story have been subordinated to a strict formal discipline. – In contrast to the realism of the Franconian school, to which the young Dürer owed his first stimuli, Zeitblom's quiet and static art bears witness to the culmination of a late style in the Eschach panels, which also announces the end of late gothic panel painting in Ulm.

Literatur: Kat. Lange, Nr. 62. – Kat. 1931, S. 221 ff. – Kat. 1957, S. 326 ff. – Kat. 1962, Alte Meister, S. 253 ff. – Kurt Löcher, Staatsgalerie Stuttgart – Altdeutsche Meister, 1972/73 (Maschinenschrift). – Edeltraud Rettich, Staatsgalerie Stuttgart – Altdeutsche Abteilung, Stuttgart 1978, mit Abb.

Bibliography: Cat. Lange, no. 62. – Cat. 1931, p. 221 f. – Cat. 1957, p. 326 f. – Cat. 1962, Alte Meister, p. 253 f. – Kurt Löcher, Staatsgalerie Stuttgart – Altdeutsche Meister, 1972/73 (typescript). – Edeltraud Rettich, Staatsgalerie Stuttgart – Altdeutsche Abteilung, Stuttgart 1978, with ill.

Meister von Meßkirch

Oberschwäbischer Maler, der nach seinem Hauptwerk, dem Hochaltar und acht Nebenaltären für die Stiftskirche in Meßkirch (Kreis Konstanz) benannt wird. Geboren um 1500 im Fränkischen. Ausbildung im Dürerkreis. Seit etwa 1530, vielleicht auch schon früher, in Meßkirch tätig, wo er um 1543 (?) verstorben sein soll.

5

Der heilige Benedikt im Gebet

Entstanden um 1540
Öl und Tempera auf Tannenholz,
106 × 75 cm
1726 laut Inschrift auf der Innenseite einer Schubleiste (»S. Peter den. 31. Jenner anno. 1726.«) im Besitz des Klosters Petershausen bei Konstanz oder St. Peter bei Freiburg i. Br. — Sammlung von Hirscher, Tübingen und später Freiburg i. Br. — Erworben 1866.

Master of Meßkirch

Upper Swabian painter, named after his major work, the highaltar and eight ancillary altars for the collegiate church in Meßkirch (district of Konstanz). Born circa 1500 in Franconia. Trained in Dürer's circle. Active by 1530, (possibly earlier) in Meßkirch, where he is thought to have died in 1543 (?).

5

St Benedict in Prayer

Circa 1540
Oil and distemper on fir-wood,
106 × 75 cm. 1726 in possession of the Petershausen monastry near Konstanz or the church St Peter near Freiburg i. Br., according to an inscription on the reverse. — Collection Hirscher, Tübingen and later Freiburg i. Br. — Purchased 1866.

Nach der Legenda Aurea zog sich der heilige Benedikt für drei Jahre zum Gebet in eine Felsenhöhle zurück, wo ihn der Mönch Romanus versorgte, obwohl der Teufel die Glocke, mit der Romanus die Speisung anzukündigen pflegte, zerschlagen hatte. Auffallenderweise widmet der Maler der Darstellung des Heiligen, der vor dem Kreuz kniet, kaum mehr Interesse als der ihn umgebenden Landschaft, deren üppig wuchernde Vegetation sie nach damaliger Vorstellung als »Ort der Abgeschiedenheit« ausweist. Der Landschaftsausschnitt öffnet sich auf ein Kloster, auf eine Burg und eine Stadt, die sich sinnbildlich auf die drei Stände, Mönchstum, Fürstentum und Bürgertum, beziehen. Vielfalt und Reichtum des Motivischen sind in einen stimmungsvollen Kontext eingebunden, der seine Formung einem den Bildaufbau harmonisierenden Kolorit und dem zarten Filigran einer gleichwohl prägnanten, am Vorbild des Dürerkreises geschulten Zeichnung verdankt. Auch Erinnerungen an die Landschaftsmalerei der Donauschule spielen herein, ordnen sich aber einer eher »volkstümlichen« Art der Legendendarstellung zu. Ob das Gemälde — wie bisweilen vermutet — ursprünglich zum Hausaltar eines Benediktinerabtes gehörte, ist — obschon vom Thema und von der Provenienz her naheliegend — mit Sicherheit nicht zu beweisen.

According to the Legenda Aurea, St Benedict withdrew for three years to a cave to pray where he was cared for by the monk Romanus, although the devil had smashed to pieces the bell Romanus used to announce his meals. Remarkably, the painter pays little more attention to the depiction of the saint kneeling in front of the cross than he does to the surrounding landscape, whose lush and luxuriantly growing vegetation signifies a "place of seclusion" as this was conceived at the time. The landscape opens onto a view of a monastery, a castle and a town, which are symbols of the three estates: priesthood, princedom and citizenship. The complexity and richness of the motif are unified by the poetic whole resulting from the harmonious colour composition and the delicate yet precise filagree of drawing, which is indebted to the example of Dürer's circle. Echoes of the landscape painting of the Danube school also play a rôle, but this is combined with a more "popular" style of depicting legends. Whether or not the painting was originally part of a private altar belonging to a Benedictine abbot — as has sometimes been suggested — cannot be firmly established, although the subject and provenance point to this.

Literatur: Kat. Lange, Nr. 82. — Kat. 1931, S. 99. — Kat. 1957, S. 171 mit Abb. — Kat. 1962, Alte Meister, S. 127ff. mit Abb. — Kurt Löcher, Staatsgalerie Stuttgart — Altdeutsche Meister, 1972/73 (Maschinenschrift). — Edeltraud Rettich, Staatsgalerie Stuttgart — Altdeutsche Abteilung, Stuttgart 1978, mit Abb.

Bibliography: Cat. Lange, no. 82. — Cat. 1931, p. 99. — Cat. 1957, p. 171 with ill. — Cat. 1962, Alte Meister, p. 127f. with ill. — Kurt Löcher, Staatsgalerie Stuttgart — Altdeutsche Meister, 1972/73 (typescript). — Edeltraud Rettich, Staatsgalerie Stuttgart — Altdeutsche Abteilung, Stuttgart 1978, with ill.

Jerg Ratgeb

Geboren um 1480 in Schwäbisch Gmünd oder Herrenberg, 1526 in die Bauernkriege verwickelt und aus politischen Gründen in Pforzheim geviertelt. Wohnhaft in Stuttgart, wo er 1508 erstmals erwähnt wird. Tätig in Heilbronn (1509–1512), Schwaigern (1510), Frankfurt a. M. (1514–1517) und Herrenberg (1518–1519).

6

Herrenberger Altar

Entstanden 1518–1519
Öl und Tempera auf Fichtenholz, die einzelnen Tafeln mit leicht abweichenden Maßen: Abendmahl und Auferstehung 274 × 147 cm, Geißelung und Kreuzigung 262 × 142,5 cm.
Bezeichnet auf Vorder- und Rückseite, jeweils zwischen Verkündigungsengel und Maria: R. 1519.

Jerg Ratgeb

Born in Schwäbisch Gmünd or Herrenberg in Swabia circa 1480. Involved in the Peasants War in 1526 and for political reasons quartered in Pforzheim. Resident in Stuttgart where he is first mentioned in 1508. Active in Heilbronn (1509–1512), Schwaigern (1510), Frankfurt a. M. (1514–1517) and Herrenberg (1518–1519)

6

Herrenberg Altar

1518–1519
Oil and distemper on spruce, individual panels with slightly differing dimensions:
Last Supper and Resurrection 274 × 147 cm, Flagellation and Crucifixion 262 × 142.5 cm
Signed front and back, both times in between the angel of the annunciation and the Virgin: R 1519

Der ehemalige Hochaltar der Stiftskirche zur heiligen Maria in Herrenberg gelangte 1924 aus der Württembergischen Altertumssammlung in die Staatsgalerie. Der geschnitzte Mittelschrein und die geschnitzte Predella sind verloren. In geschlossenem Zustand zeigt der Altar den Abschied der Apostel, einmal geöffnet die Passion Christi, zweimal geöffnet Szenen aus dem Marienleben. Von der Rückseite der Predella hat sich die gemalte Darstellung des Schweißtuchs der heiligen Veronika erhalten. Eine Verkündigung an Maria schließt das Programm in den geschweiften Ecküberhöhungen der Innenflügel ab. Auf den bemalten Originalrahmen finden sich Zitate aus dem Alten und aus dem Neuen Testament in lateinischer Sprache.

Die Passion Christi zeigt die folgenden, hier abgebildeten Szenen: zur Linken das Abendmahl und Christus am Ölberg; daran anschließend die Geißelung Christi, die Dornenkrönung und Christus vor Pilatus; halbrechts die Kreuzigung, außerdem Kreuztragung und Grablegung; rechts die Auferstehung sowie Noli me tangere und die Frauen am Grabe.

Die Verbindung verschiedener, zeitlich auseinander liegender Ereignisse auf einem Bild (Simultan-Darstellung) folgt mittelalterlicher Tradition, ebenso der Wechsel im Maßstab der Figuren, die ihrer Bedeutung entsprechend einmal größer (Christus), einmal kleiner (Jünger) erscheinen. Die Realistik der Darstellung (man beachte – um beim Abendmahl zu bleiben – den sich schneuzenden Apostel zur Linken) ist mit den Passionsspielen in Verbindung gebracht worden. Das nur scheinbar triviale Motiv symbolisiert nach mittelalterlicher Vorstellung die Reinigung des Körpers von der Sünde. Die beiden Vögel auf der Brüstung beziehen sich auf Christus und den nahenden Verrat; die Fliege, die Judas mit dem Brot des Abendmahls empfängt, galt als Teufelssymbol. Ungeachtet dieser themenbedingten Bezüge ist die Darstellung von spannungsgeladener, ja explosiver Dramatik. Der gelbgekleidete Verräter springt unter Christi Wort »Einer von euch wird mich verraten« auf und wirft den Wein des Abendmahls um, »verwirft das Sakrament« (Bushart). Zwischen seinem sich in der Erregung rötenden Gesicht und Christus liegt das geschlachtete Passahlamm, Hinweis auf den Opfertod Christi. Auf der zweiten Tafel folgt die Aufzählung der Vergehen, für die Christus leidet; auf der dritten die Kreuzigung und die Zeichnung der Auserwählten durch Christi Blut; auf dem Schlußbild der Triumph des verklärten Christus und – das Hauptmotiv gleichsam begleitend – Hinweise auf die Auferstehung der auf Christus Hoffenden. Der gesamte Zyklus nimmt deutlich Bezug »auf das sacramentum, auf das Mysterium von Einsetzung, Besiegelung und Fortwirken des Opferwerks Christi und deren unblutige Erneuerung im Meßopfer auf dem Altar« (Bushart).

Formal stellt der Altar innerhalb der schwäbischen Malerei einen absoluten Höhepunkt dar. Die Figuren sind überdehnt und verzerrt, oft bis zur völligen Mißachtung der Anatomie. In der Skala des Ausdrucks stehen Extreme einander hart gegenüber:

The former high altar from the collegiate church of Holy Mary in Herrenberg was transferred in 1924 from the Württemberg collection of antiquities to the Staatsgalerie. The carved central shrine and the carved predella are lost. Closed, the altar shows the leave taking of the apostles, opened once, Christ's passion, and, opened twice, scenes from the life of Mary. On the reverse of the predella, the painted depiction of St Veronica's shroud has survived. The Annunciation to the Virgin completes the programme in the curved corner elevations of the inner wings. On the original painted frame there are quotations from the Old and New Testaments in Latin.

Christ's passion consists of the following scenes illustrated here: on the left, the Last Supper and Christ on the Mount of Olives; in addition the Flagellation of Christ, Christ Crowned with Thorns and Christ before Pilate; to the right, the Crucifixion, Christ Carrying the Cross and the Burial of Christ; extreme right, the Resurrection as well as Noli me Tangere and the Women at the Graveside.

The combination of different temporally separate events in a single work (simultaneous representation) conforms to medieval tradition, as does the changing scale of the figures who, according to their importance appear larger (Christ) or smaller (disciples). The realism of depiction (see the left hand apostle blowing his nose in the Last Supper) relates to Passion plays. This apparently trivial motif symbolized in the medieval mind the purification of the body from its sins. The two birds on the parapet refer to the approaching betrayal; the fly, which Judas is catching with the bread of the Last Supper, was intended as a symbol of the devil. Regardless of these thematic references the image is full of suspense-filled, even explosive drama. The traitor in yellow jumps up at Christ's words, "One of you shall betray me" and upsets the wine of the Last Supper, "repudiating the sacrament" (Bushart). Between his face, red with excitement, and Christ lies the slaughtered lamb of the passover, referring to the sacrifice of Christ. On the second panel the torments follow which caused Christ's suffering; on the third panel the Crucifixion and the marking out of the chosen ones through Christ's bloody; in the final painting the triumph of Christ's transfiguration and – accompanying the central motif – references to the resurrection of those who put their hope in Christ. The entire cycle clearly refers to "the sacrament, the mystery of Christ's intervention, his vanquishment and the continuing effects of his sacrifice and its reiteration without bloodshed in the sacrificial mass at the highaltar" (Bushart).

In formal terms the altar represents an absolute peak of Swabian painting. The figures are stretched and distorted, often in total disregard of anatomy. In the gamut of expression extremes are set in direct confrontation: the visionary presence of the resurrected Christ – reminiscent of Grünewald – and the oppressive proximity of his persecutors and despisers. A strongly marked polarity permeates the paintings, surfacing in the lively construction of the sce-

Literatur: Kat. 1931, S. 129 ff. – Kat. 1957,
S. 211 ff. mit Abb. – Kat. 1962, Alte Meister,
S. 158 ff. mit Abb. – Bruno Bushart und
H. R. Fuhrmann, Jörg Ratgeb – der Maler des
Herrenberger Altars, Sonderdruck von »Aus
Schönbuch und Gäu«, 1959. – Kurt Löcher,
Staatsgalerie Stuttgart – Altdeutsche Meister,
1972/73 (Maschinenschrift). – Edeltraud
Rettich, Staatsgalerie Stuttgart – Altdeutsche
Abteilung, Stuttgart 1978, mit Abb. – Edeltraud
Rettich, in: Große Gemäldegalerien,
herausgegeben von Erich Steingräber, München
1980, S. 447 mit Abb.

Bibliography: Cat. 1931, p. 129 f. – Cat. 1957,
p. 211 f. with ill. – Cat. 1962, Alte Meister,
p. 158 f. with ill. – Bruno Bushart and
H. R. Fuhrmann, "Jörg Ratgeb – der Maler des
Herrenberger Altars", off-print from: Aus
Schönbuch und Gäu, 1959. – Kurt Löcher,
Staatsgalerie Stuttgart – Altdeutsche Meister,
1972/73 (typescript). – Edeltraud Rettich,
Staatsgalerie Stuttgart – Altdeutsche Abteilung,
Stuttgart 1978, with ill. – Edeltraud Rettich, in:
Große Gemäldegalerien, ed. by Erich
Steingräber, Munich 1980, p. 447 with ill.

die erscheinungshafte Präsenz des Auferstandenen, bei dem man an Grünewald denkt, und die beklemmende Nähe seiner Verfolger und Ächter. Eine stark ausgeprägte Polarität durchdringt die Gemälde, tritt sowohl im bewegten Aufbau der szenischen Darstellung als auch in Architektur und Landschaft zutage. Formen der Renaissance – sie sind weitgehend Augsburger Prägung – werden ebenso kühn wie frei kombiniert und versatzstückartig so arrangiert, daß sich ihre Funktion primär vom Geschehen her ableitet. Souverän nutzt Ratgeb die perspektivischen Mittel, die rahmend und damit die Komposition übergreifend (kassettierte Decke), aber auch aktionsstützend (man beachte die Schräge, die im Abendmahl von Christus auf Judas hinführt) eingesetzt werden. Selbst die Landschaft ist frei von nur abbildhaften Bezügen, erweist sich im Wechsel von Expression, Realität und Vision durchaus als Variable, ist »Grund und Begründung des Inhaltlichen« in einem.

nes as well as in the architecture and landscape. Renaissance forms – mostly bearing the stamp of Augsburg painting – are set in free and daring combinations, employed theatrically so that their function derives from the playing out of events. Ratgeb brilliantly employs perspectival means to frame and to encroach on the composition (in the coffered ceiling), but also to underline the action (witness the diagonals leading from Christ to Judas in the Last Supper). Even the landscape is free from illustrative trappings; non-uniform in its changing balance of expression, realism and visionary intensity it both reinforces and exemplifies the content of the paintings.

Hans Memling

Geboren um 1433 in Seligenstadt/Main, gestorben 1494 in Brügge. Beeinflußt von Rogier van der Weyden und Hugo van der Goes. Seit 1465 in Brügge tätig.

7

Bathseba im Bade

Entstanden um 1485
Öl und Tempera auf Eichenholz,
191,5 × 84,6 cm
Sammlung Graf Gustav Adolf von Gotter. —
Erworben 1736.

Hans Memling

Born circa 1433 in Seligenstadt/Main, died 1494 in Bruges. Influenced by Rogier van der Weyden and Hugo van der Goes. Active after 1465 in Bruges.

7

Bathsheba at her Bath

Circa 1485
Oil and distemper on oak, 191.5 × 84.6 cm
Collection Count Gustav Adolf von Gotter. — Purchased 1736.

Biblischer Überlieferung zufolge erblickte König David vom Dach seines Palastes aus Bathseba, des Urias Frau, beim Bade. Von ihrer Schönheit geblendet, verführte er sie und schickte Uria bei der Belagerung von Rabba in den Tod. Bald darauf nahm David Bathseba zum Weib. Obwohl er auf Vorhaltungen des Propheten Nathan hin in tiefe Reue verfiel, starb zur Sühne seines Vergehens der aus dem Ehebruch hervorgegangene Sohn. Sein zweiter Sohn Salomo folgte ihm später als König (geraffte Inhaltsbeschreibung nach Klapproth, a. a. O.). Memling schildert in seinem Gemälde den ersten Teil dieses Berichts. Schauplatz des Geschehens ist ein Innenraum, in dem man zur Rechten ein Badegehäuse aus Bottich mit baldachinartigem Abschluß erkennt. Abweichend zur spätmittelalterlichen Bildüberlieferung ist Bathseba aber nicht in höfischer Kleidung und beim Fußbad, sondern als lebensgroßer Akt (!) und in betont »bürgerlichem« Milieu dargestellt. Sie hat ihr Bad gerade beendet und läßt sich von der Magd in einen umhangartigen Mantel helfen. Wassertropfen schimmern auf der zarten Haut ihres Körpers, der drei Viertel der Höhe des schmalen Bildfeldes einnimmt und dem Betrachter am nächsten gerückt ist. Auch Boden und Klappstuhl entwickeln sich kaum in die Tiefe, sondern nehmen — steil ansteigend — die gotische Vertikalität des Bildaufbaus auf. Die Rückwand des Raumes ist zweimal durchbrochen, einmal durch eine Tür, die in das Schlafzimmer führt, dann durch ein geöffnetes Fenster, das den Blick auf einen Palast freigibt, auf dessen Balkon man König David mit dem Boten erkennt. An der Portalarchitektur des Palastes sind Abraham und Moses (als Gesetzesvertreter), im Relief des Torbogens Urias Tod im Kampf dargestellt. Leider ist der durch das Fenster begrenzte obere Bildausschnitt zur Hälfte eine aus dem 17. Jahrhundert stammende Zutat; das originale Eckstück, das David mit dem Boten in Halbfigur zeigt, befindet sich im Eigentum des Art Institute in Chicago.
Formal steht das Gemälde noch ganz im Banne spätgotischer Bildtradition, die sich bei Memling aber nicht in dramatischer, sondern in auffallend »maßvoller« Gestaltung manifestiert. Die Leidenschaftlichkeit und den »unbeugsamen Stilwillen« (M. J. Friedländer) seines Lehrmeisters Rogier wandelt Memling ins Empfindsame ab, die gesteigerte, spannungsgeladene Intensität eines Hugo van der Goes mildert er zu ernster, verhaltener Schönheit. Das Lineare ist betont, verbindet sich aber einem erlesenen Kolorit, das ganz in den Dienst einer das stoffliche Erscheinungsbild der Dinge einfühlsam charakterisierenden Formanschauung gestellt ist. Der gestreckte Figurentyp mit den abfallenden Schultern entspricht noch dem gotischen Schönheitsideal, doch sind die Bewegungen — obschon in erkennbarer Korrespondenz zum eckigen Faltenwurf stehend — frei entwickelt. Auch im beseelten Ausdruck der Köpfe, die den großen Bildnismaler verraten, beweist diese Kunst ihre Tiefe und Kraft.

In accordance with the biblical story, King David is watching Bathsheba, Uria's wife, at her bath from the roof of his palace. Dazzled by her beauty he seduced her and sent Uria to his death at the siege of Rabba. Shortly afterwards David married Bathsheba. Although he became deeply repentant in response to the remonstrances of the prophet Nathan, his son resulting from this act of adultery died to atone for David's sin. His second son Salomon later succeeded him as King.
Memling portrays in his painting the first part of this story. The scene of events is an interior, to the right of which we find a tub, recognized by its baldachinno-like cover. Departing from late medieval pictorial tradition, Bathsheba is not shown in courtly dress in a foot bath but rather as a lifesize nude (!), depicted in a markedly "bourgeois" milieu. She has just finished her bath and is being wrapped by her maid in a loose coat. Drops of water glisten on the delicate skin of her body, which takes up three-quarters of the narrow field of the image and is pused close up to the spectator. Similarly the floor and folding stool are hardly extended into depth, rather they assume the gothic verticality of the composition, inclining steeply. The back wall of the room is interrupted twice: once by a door which leads into the bedroom; also by an open window, giving a view onto the palace on whose balcony King David and a courtier are to be seen. Abraham and Moses (as representatives of the law) are represented on the portal and in sculptural relief on the gateway arch we find a depiction of Uria's death. Half of the upper part of the painting bordered by the window is a seventeenth century addition; the original corner section showing David and the courtier — formerly in the Art Institute of Chicago — could be purchased by the Staatsgalerie Stuttgart in 1986. — In formal terms the painting remains under the spell of late gothic pictorial tradition which manifests itself in Memling's work in a temperate rather than a dramatic form. Memling transforms the passion and the "unbending stylistic will" (M. J. Friedländer) of his master Rogier into a new sensitivity; he tones down the heightened suspense-filled intensity of Hugo van der Goes to achieve a serious, controlled beauty. Line is emphasized, linked however, to a selective colour range, which is put at the service of a formal vision characterized by an empathetic response to the material appearance of objects. The elongated figure-type with sloping shoulders still corresponds to the gothic ideal of beauty, but the movements, although patently related to the angular drapery, are freely conceived. Similarly the lively expression of the heads, which betrays the touch of the great portrait painter, demonstrates the profundity and power of this art.

Memlings Gemälde ist nicht als autonomes,
also für sich stehendes Einzelwerk anzusehen, sondern gehörte vermutlich zu einem
dreiteiligen »Gerechtigkeitsbild«, dessen
zweiter, bis heute verschollener Flügel eine
Susannendarstellung gezeigt haben könnte.
Die Thematik beider Gemälde legt nahe,
daß sie ursprünglich zum Schmuck eines
Rathaus- oder Gerichtssaales bestimmt waren, wo sie Richtern und Parteien am Beispiel der alttestamentlichen Frauengestal-
ten das Walten göttlicher Gerechtigkeit vor
Augen führen sollten.

Memling's painting is not to be seen as an
autonomous, that is to say, as an independent single work; it probably belongs to a
three-part "painting of justice", whose second wing — to date untraced — could have
shown a depiction of Susanna and the El-
ders. The subject of both paintings suggests
that they were originally intended as deco-
rations for a town hall or law court, where
judges and officials would have been inspired by the example of the Old Testament
women to demonstrate the rules of heavenly justice.

Literatur: Kat. Lange, Nr. 111. — Kat. 1931,
S. 98. — Kat. 1957, S. 168 mit Abb. — Kat. 1962,
Alte Meister, S. 125 ff. mit Abb. — Rüdiger
Klapproth, in: Große Gemäldegalerien,
herausgegeben von Erich Steingräber, München
1980, S. 447 ff. mit Abb.

Bibliography: Cat. Lange, no. 111. — Cat. 1931,
p. 98. — Cat. 1957, p. 168 with ill. — Cat. 1962,
Alte Meister, p. 125 f. with ill. — Rüdiger
Klapproth, in: Große Gemäldegalerien, ed.
by Erich Steingräber, Munich 1980, p. 447 f.
with ill.

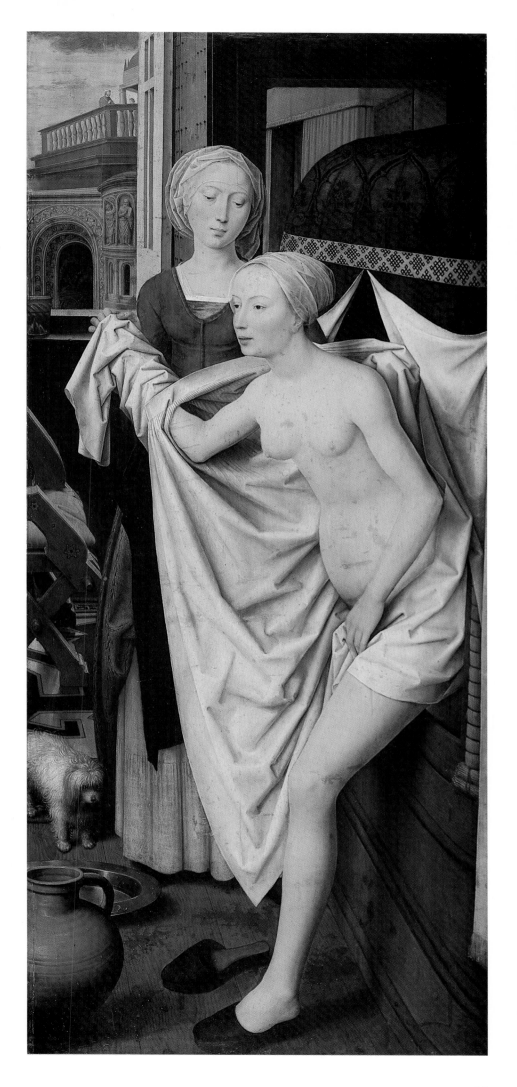

Albert Bouts

Zweiter Sohn des Dieric Bouts d. Ä. Geboren 1455–1460 in Löwen, gestorben ebenda 1549. Beeinflußt von seinem Vater und Hugo van der Goes. Tätig vor allem in Löwen.

8 a

Schmerzensmann

Öl und Tempera auf Eichenholz,
34,3 × 26 cm

8 b

Mater dolorosa

Öl und Tempera auf Eichenholz,
34,3 × 25,7 cm
Beide erworben aus Privatbesitz 1972.

Albert Bouts

Second son of Dieric Bouts the elder. Born 1455–1460 in Louvain, died there in 1549. Influenced by his father and by Hugo van der Goes. Active primarily in Louvain.

8 a

Man of Sorrows

Oil and distemper on oak, 34.3 × 26 cm

8 b

Virgo doloris

Oil and distemper on oak, 34.3 × 25.7 cm
Both purchased from a private collection in 1972.

Überzeugender als in der monumentalen Historie hat sich die Kunst des Albert Bouts im kleinen Format religiöser Andachtsbilder verwirklicht. Das Stuttgarter Diptychon variiert einen in der altniederländischen Malerei weit verbreiteten Bildtyp. Während Maria die Hände betend erhoben und den Blick unter fast geschlossenen Lidern gesenkt hat, ist Christus, der seine Wundmale zeigt, von qualvollem Leiden gezeichnet. Die Spitzen der Dornenkrone wölben sich unter der gespannten Haut seiner Stirn; Blut rinnt über Wangen und Hals und strömt aus den offenen Wunden der Hände. Aus den müden, schmerzvoll geröteten Augen tropfen Tränen herab. Auf dem Brustkorb zeichnen sich noch die Spuren der Geißelung ab.

Luftumflossen und vom Bildgrund gelöst, sind die Figuren nicht in starrer Frontalität dargestellt, sondern in leicht zugewandter Haltung aufeinander bezogen. Die vom Licht unterstützte Modellierung der Köpfe und Hände, der Nuancenreichtum der Farbe und die subtil-differenzierende Zeichnung bedingen und steigern einander, sind also frei von aller »trockenen Handwerklichkeit«, die Albert Bouts bisweilen mit Recht attestiert wird. Die auch thematisch begründbare Realistik der Darstellung durchdringt und eint alle Teile des Bildes; sie äußerst sich aber nicht in bewegter Dramatik, da alle Bewegung in das Innere der Figuren verlegt ist, sich gleichsam in »stiller Zuständlichkeit« mitteilt.

The art of Albert Bouts was more convincingly realized in small religious devotional paintings than in monumental historical subjects. The Stuttgart diptych is a variation on a widespread pictorial type in early Netherlandish painting. While the Virgin is shown with her hands raised in prayer and her lowered glance is veiled by virtually closed eyelids, Christ, who is showing his stigmata, is represented in agony. The sharp points of his crown of thorns curve and pierce the tense skin of his forehead; blood runs down his cheeks and neck and streams from the open wounds in his hands. Tears are falling from his tired, painfully reddened eyes. Traces of the flagellation are still to be seen on his chest.

The figures, who are detatched from the ground and placed in a pocket of space, are not presented with rigid frontality, rather they lean gently towards each other. The observation of light in the modelling of hands and heads, the richly nuanced colouration and the subtle differentiations of the drawing are mutually dependant and reinforcing; they are free from every trace of the "dry craftmanship", of which Albert Bouts has sometimes been rightly accused. The realism of the image, which is also justified in thematic terms, permeates and unifies each part of the painting; but this is not expressed in active drama, as all movement is transfered to the inner reality of the figures, manifesting itself as "quiet state of being".

Literatur: Jahrbuch der Staatlichen Kunstsammlungen in Baden-Württemberg, X, 1973, S. 229 mit Abb.

Bibliography: Jahrbuch der Staatlichen Kunstsammlungen in Baden-Württemberg, X, 1973, p. 229 with ill.

Jan Aertson van Amstel

Geboren um 1500 in Amsterdam, gestorben 1540–1542 (Winkler: nach 1543) in Antwerpen. Nach Hoogewerff Bruder des Pieter Aertsen. 1528 Meister der Lucasgilde, 1535 Bürger in Antwerpen. Schwager des Lehrers von Pieter Brueghel d. Ä., Pieter Coecke.

9

Einzug Christi in Jerusalem

Entstanden um 1540
Öl und Tempera auf Eichenholz,
83,3 × 102,5 cm.
Laut rückseitiger Inschrift bereits 1613 im
Besitz des Kurfürsten Maximilian von
Bayern. — Wahrscheinlich im Spanischen
Erbfolgekrieg um 1706 nach Wien
verschleppt. — Sammlung Reinhard von
Roeder, Wien/Stuttgart. — Erworben 1748.

Jan Aertson van Amstel

Born circa 1500 in Amsterdam, died 1540/1542 (Winkler: after 1543) in Antwerp. According to Hoogewerff, a brother of Pieter Aertsen. 1528 master in the Guild of St Luke, 1535 citizen in Antwerp. Brother-in-law of Pieter Coecke, the teacher of Pieter Brueghel the elder.

9

The Entry of Christ in Jerusalem

Circa 1540
Oil and distemper on oak, 83.3 × 102.5 cm
According to an inscription on the reverse
already in 1613 in the collection of
Maximilian, the Elector of Bavaria. —
Probably brought to Vienna circa 1706 in
the war of Spanish succession. Collection
Reinhard von Roeder, Wien/Stuttgart. —
Purchased 1748.

Entwicklungsgeschichtlich zwischen Patinir und Pieter Brueghel d. Ä. stehend, gehört Jan van Amstel zu den Mitbegründern einer zunehmend »realistischen« Auffassung in der niederländischen Landschaftsmalerei des 16. Jahrhunderts. Zwar stellt er die Landschaft noch nicht um ihrer selbst willen, sondern vorzugsweise in Verbindung mit einer Massenszenerie dar. So auch auf dem Stuttgarter Bild, das Christus auf dem Weg nach Jerusalem zeigt. Bar aller Reminiszenzen an den kulissenhaften Aufbau, der noch Patinirs ideale »Weltlandschaften« kennzeichnet, ist die Landschaft, in die van Amstel den biblischen Vorgang verlegt, von erkennbarem Streben nach naturnaher Gestaltung erfüllt. Sie hat Weite und Tiefe, die auf genauer Beobachtung des Atmosphärischen und einer kontinuierlichen Aufhellung der Farbe beruhen (Weiterführung der von van Eyck begründeten Farb- und Luftperspektive). Der Vordergrund ist in einem satten Rotbraun gehalten, von dem sich das kräftige Grün der Vegetation wirkungsvoll abhebt. Im Mittel- und Hintergrund spielen Grün, Blau, Grau und Weiß ineinander; Felsen und Bäume sind hier in nahezu gleichem Ton, also weitgehend ohne Differenzierung gegeben. Die Figuren sind von miniaturhafter Kleinheit, doch prägnant in ihrer plastischen Durchbildung. Der Zug entwickelt sich von einer Bergkuppe aus und staffelt sich vorne in lockerer Reihung wie auf einer Bühne. Christus, der auf dem Esel reitend den Blick auf das entfernte Jerusalem richtet, ist weder durch Größe noch durch Nimbus hervorgehoben. Seine Gestalt geht vollkommen auf in der bunten Vielfalt einer eher »volkstümlich« anmutenden Szenerie, die auch das Treiben der Landleute anschaulich schildert. Gerade in der Einbindung des Biblischen in die Sphäre des Alltäglichen liegt die spezifisch niederländische Auffassung der Darstellung begründet.

Standing between Patinir and Pieter Brueghel the elder in terms of historical development, Jan van Amstel is one of the founders of an increasingly realistic conception of Netherlandish landscape painting in the 16th century. Admittedly he does not yet represent landscape for its own sake, but mostly in combination with a crowd scene. This is also the case in the Stuttgart painting, which shows Christ on his way to Jerusalem. No longer recalling the constructed effects of theatrical scenery still characteristic of Patinir's ideal "universal landscapes", the landscape in which van Amstel locates the religious events reflects his discernable efforts to achieve naturalistic configuration. The landscape has scope and depth, due to an exact observation of atmosphere and a continuous lightening of colour (extending the chromatic and atmospheric perspective first practiced by van Eyck). The foreground is rendered in a deep red-brown, against which the intense green of the vegetation contrasts effectively. In the middle-ground and background green, blue, grey and white sparkle and blend; rocks and trees are rendered here in virtually the same tone, that is to say largely undifferentiated. The figures conform to a miniature scale, yet they are exact in their plastic design. The train of figures leads from a mountain top an groups into loose and staggered rows in the foreground, as if on a stage. Christ, riding on a donkey and looking in the direction of distant Jerusalem, is neither emphasized by means of scale nor by a halo. His figure is wholly incorporated in the colourful diversity of the "popular" scenery, which also vividly depicts the activity of the countryside folk. It is precisely the integration of the biblical story in the sphere of everyday life that establishes the specifically Netherlandish interpretation of the scene.

Literatur: Kat. Lange, Nr. 114. – Kat. 1931, S. 3 ff. – Kat. 1957, S. 23 ff. mit Abb. – Kat. 1962, Alte Meister, S. 26 mit Abb.

Bibliography: Cat. Lange, no. 114. – Cat. 1931, p. 3 f. – Cat. 1957, p. 23 f. with ill. – Cat. 1962, Alte Meister, p. 26 with ill.

Rembrandt Harmensz van Rijn

Geboren 1606 in Leiden, gestorben 1669 in Amsterdam. Schüler des Jacob van Swanenburgh in Leiden und des Pieter Lastman in Amsterdam. 1624 für einige Monate im Atelier des Jacob Pynas. Seit 1625 wieder in Leiden. 1631 Übersiedlung nach Amsterdam.

10

Paulus im Gefängnis

Öl auf Eichenholz, 72,8 × 60,3 cm
Zweifach bezeichnet; an der Lagerstatt:
R.f. 1627, auf dem Manuskript: Rembrand
fecit.
Sammlung Graf Schönborn,
Pommersfelden (dort seit 1719)
nachweisbar. — Erworben 1867.

Rembrandt Harmensz van Rijn

Born 1606 in Leyden; died 1669 in Amsterdam. Apprenticed to Jacob van Swanenburgh in Leyden and Pieter Lastman in Amsterdam. In 1624 he spent several months in Jacob Pynas' studio. From 1625 resident in Leyden. 1631 settled in Amsterdam.

10

St Paul in Prison

Oil on oak, 72.8 × 60.3 cm
Signed twice: once on the bed, R.f. 1627,
once on the manuscript, "Rembrand fecit".
Collection Count Schönborn,
Pommersfelden (documented after 1719).
Purchased in 1867.

In seiner Leidener Zeit hat Rembrandt wiederholt Apostel, Propheten oder Gelehrte in kontrastreich beleuchteten Innenräumen gemalt. Stets sind sie nicht nur das Abbild einer bestimmten religiösen oder profanen Figur, sondern Verkörperungen ihrer eigenen »Historie«. Als Modelle dienten Rembrandt Menschen seiner Umgebung — zumeist Greise, deren vom Leben geprägte Physiognomien ihn faszinierten. Auch der Stuttgarter Paulus gewinnt seine Intensität aus der menschlichen Durchdringung der Darstellung. Hinter der hohen Stirn und den drängenden Schläfen arbeitet es in seinem mächtigen Schädel. Die weit geöffneten Augen sind meditierend in die Ferne gerichtet. Die Rechte liegt wie vergessen am Mund, den schütteres Barthaar umgibt, die Linke hält das zerlesene Buch. Das Schwert, durch das der Apostel sein Martyrium erlitt, lehnt an dem steinernen Lager, auf dem sich Folianten und Habseligkeiten türmen. Sonnenlicht fällt durch das vergitterte Fenster; es erhellt die Rückwand der Zelle, während die Gestalt des Apostels ihr eigenes, sie modellierendes Licht von vorne empfängt. Der Raum ist — wie fast immer bei Rembrandt — »physiognomisch« gesehen: der abgetretene Boden, die vom Putz partiell schon freie, »gealterte« Wand beziehen sich korrespondierend auf das Erscheinungsbild der Figur, deren schicksalhafte Präsenz bestimmend für den gesamten Bildaufbau ist.

During his Leyden years, Rembrandt frequently painted apostles, prophets and scholars in interiors with strong contrasts of light and shade. These figures do not simply illustrate a particular religious or profane character, rather they always embody their own "historia". Rembrandt drew his models from his surroundings: mostly old men whose physiognomies, so deeply imprinted by life, fascinated him. The Stuttgart St Paul also gains intensity from the depth of humanity that permeates the image. Behind his high forehead and pulsing temples, St Paul's spirit is powerfully alive in his great skull. His wide open eyes look meditatively into the distance; his right hand is held, as if unaware, next to his mouth which is framed by a ragged beard. In his left hand he holds a well-thumbed book. The sword which was to be the agent of his martyrdom is propped against the wall, flanked by folios and other effects. Sunlight streams through the barred window, lighting up the back wall, while the figure is lit and modelled frontally. The space — as is so often the case in Rembrandt's painting — is a physiognomic space. The worn floor, the ageing crumbling wall both correspond to the phenotype of the figure, whose fateful presence is the fulcrum around which the entire composition is built.

Literatur: Kat. Lange, Nr. 265. — Kat. 1931, S. 131 ff. — Kat. 1957, S. 217 mit Abb. — Kat. 1962, Alte Meister, S. 161 mit Abb. — Rüdiger Klapproth, in: Große Gemäldegalerien, herausgegeben von Erich Steingräber, München 1980, S. 450 mit Abb.

Bibliography: Cat. Lange, no. 265. — Cat. 1931, p. 131 f. — Cat. 1957, p. 217 with ill. — Cat. 1962, Alte Meister, p. 161 with ill. — Rüdiger Klapproth, in: Große Gemäldegalerien, ed. by Erich Steingräber, Munich 1980, p. 450 with ill.

Rembrandt Harmensz van Rijn

11

Tobias heilt seinen Vater

Öl auf Eichenholz, 47,2 × 38,8 cm
Bezeichnet links auf der Stuhllehne:
Rembrandt f. 1636. Sammlung
Herzog von Arenberg, Brüssel. —
Erworben aus dem Londoner Kunsthandel
1958.

Rembrandt Harmensz van Rijn

11

Tobias Healing his Father

Oil on oak, 47.2 × 38.8 cm
Signed left on the arm of the chair:
Rembrandt f. 1636. Collection Duke von
Arenberg, Brussels. —
Purchased from the London art market in
1958.

Abweichend vom Text der Apokryphen, nach dem Tobias seinen Vater auf Geheiß des Erzengels Raphael mit der Galle des Fisches von der Blindheit erlöst, stellt Rembrandt den Vorgang der Heilung als zeitgenössische Staroperation dar, die er in die alltägliche Sphäre einer Bauernkate verlegt. Der junge Tobias, dessen Haupt ein orientalischer Turban bedeckt, beugt sich über den Vater, der in einem Lehnstuhl sitzt. Während er mit seiner Linken das rechte Augenlid des Vaters emporzieht, führt er mit der anderen Hand die Starnadel ein. Raphael und die Frau des alten Tobias folgen gebannt dem Geschehen. Licht ergießt sich durch ein offenes Fenster und erhellt die Szenerie. Eine zweite Lichtquelle — ein wärmendes Feuer — schafft sowohl Distanz als auch Einblick in das ärmliche Ambiente des Raumes, das sich nur schemenhaft aus dem Dunkel herauslöst. Licht und Schatten sind aber nicht hart voneinander getrennt (wie z. B. bei Caravaggio), sondern wachsen einander gleichsam entgegen, um in einem raumbildenden Hell-Dunkel zu verschmelzen, das entscheidend zur atmosphärischen Verdichtung und damit zur »Verinnerlichung« der Darstellung beiträgt. Das intime, noch der Leidener Zeit entlehnte Bildformat verstärkt diese Wirkung. Wahrnehmbar unterscheidet Rembrandt zwischen dem Reallicht des Feuers und der gesteigerten, »immateriellen« Erscheinungsweise des Lichtes, darin die handlungstragenden Figuren getaucht sind. Solcherart gewinnt die Lichtregie eine über die unmittelbare Beobachtung hinausweisende, den Vorgang transzendierende Bedeutung. Eine zeitgenössische Kopie des Stuttgarter Bildes im Herzog-Anton-Ulrich-Museum in Braunschweig ist rechts um mehr als ein Drittel breiter; das Original wurde demnach beschnitten, die Komposition dadurch stärker »zentriert«.

Departing from the text of the apocrypha, according to which, on the command of the archangel Raphael, Tobias delivered his father from blindness using the gall of a fish, Rembrandt represents the process of healing as a contemporary operation to remove a cataract, which he sets in the everyday ambience of a farmer's cottage. The young Tobias, whose head is wrapped in an oriental turban, leans over his father who is sitting in an armchair. While he pulls back his father's eyelid with his left hand, his right hand inserts the needle used to remove cataracts. Raphael and Tobias senior's wife follow the events spellbound. Light pours in through an open window and illuminates the scene. A second light source, namely a warming fire, creates distance and allows us a glimpse of the meagre interior, which only schematically emerges from the surrounding darkness. Light and shadow are not, however, clearly divided (as they are for example in Caravaggio); rather they move simultaneously in each other's direction, to fuse in a spatial chiaroscuro, which is essential for the atmospheric concentration and thereby the "spiritualization" of the image. The intimate format carried over from his Leyden period, strengthens this effect. Rembrandt distinguishes perceptibly between the real light of the fire and the intensified "immaterial" visionary light in which the figures acting out the events are bathed. In this way the orchestration of light gains a significance that points beyond direct observation and transcends the proceedings. A contemporary copy of the Stuttgart painting in the Herzog Anton Ulrich-Museum in Braunschweig is wider by more than a third on the right hand side; the original was consequently cropped, resulting in a more strongly centred composition.

Literatur: Kat. 1962, Alte Meister, S. 162 mit Abb.

Bibliography: Cat. 1962, Alte Meister, p. 162 with ill.

Neapolitanischer Meister

um 1330–1340

12

Szenen aus der Apokalypse

Tempera auf Pappelholz, je 34,9 × 86,3 cm
Erworben aus Privatbesitz 1970

Neapolitan Master

circa 1330–1340

12

Scenes from the Apocalypse

Distemper on poplar, each panel
34.9 × 86.3 cm
Purchased from a private collection in
1970.

Literatur: Annegrit Schmitt, Die Apokalypse
des Robert von Anjou, in: Pantheon, XXVIII,
1970, S. 475 ff. – Jahrbuch der Staatlichen
Kunstsammlungen in Baden-Württemberg, VIII,
1971, S. 283 ff. mit Abb. (Gerhard Ewald).

Bibliography: Annegrit Schmitt, "Die
Apokalypse des Robert von Anjou", in:
Pantheon, XXVIII, 1970, p. 475 f. – Jahrbuch
der Staatlichen Kunstsammlungen in Baden-
Württemberg, VIII, 1971, p. 283 f. with ill.
(Gerhard Ewald).

Die beiden aus der Sammlung des Grafen zu Erbach-Fürstenau erworbenen Tafelbilder mit den Visionen aus der Apokalypse des heiligen Johannes gehören zu den bedeutendsten Werken frühitalienischer Malerei in deutschem Museumsbesitz. Sie befanden sich bis 1905 im Nachlaß des Frankfurter Malers Edward Jakob von Steinle. Mündlicher Überlieferung zufolge soll Goethes Schwager Johann Georg Schlosser sie aus Italien mitgebracht und im Stift Neuberg bei Heidelberg aufbewahrt haben, bevor sie in den Besitz Jakob von Steinles gelangten.

Insgesamt 44 Szenen aus der Apokalypse sind auf den beiden Tafeln wiedergegeben, lesbar jeweils von links oben nach rechts unten, beginnend mit der Darstellung des Johannes auf Patmos und endend in der Vision der heiligen Stadt, des neuen Jerusalem. Die ursprüngliche Verwendung der Tafeln ist ungeklärt. Spuren einer alten Montage schließen nicht aus, daß sie möglicherweise nicht als Tafelbilder, sondern als bildhafte Verkleidung, vielleicht eines Reliquienschreins (Johannesreliquie?) dienten. Die einzelnen Szenen sind – dem Text folgend – nebeneinander, doch in inselhafter Isolation dargestellt. Sie »schwimmen« gleichsam auf tiefblauem Grund. Obschon sie keinerlei stabilisierende Rahmung, also keine »Verankerung« haben, eignet ihnen ein hohes Maß anschaulich erlebbarer Plastizität. Die Formgebung im einzelnen ist von minutiöser Prägnanz. Architekturen und Landschaft sind zwar noch nicht perspektivisch folgerichtig, doch immerhin räumlich erfaßt. Daß der Raum in der Regel auf den Aktionsraum der Figuren beschränkt bleibt, diesen also nicht oder kaum überschreitet, folgt im Prinzip der von Giotto begründeten Form räumlicher Darstellung. Für die Entstehungszeit kennzeichnend – und möglicherweise auf sienesischen Anregungen gründend – ist die lebhafte Schilderung der szenischen Handlung, die zudem auf genauer Kenntnis des apokalyptischen Textes beruht. Dieser Eindruck wird noch verstärkt durch die Strahlkraft der Farbe, die den visionären Charakter der miniaturhaften Darstellungen eindringlich steigert.

Der »in sich reich facettierte«, auf Einflüssen verschiedenster Art basierende Stil der Stuttgarter Tafeln, aber auch ihre singuläre Stellung innerhalb der Malerei des Trecento, haben ihre Datierung und Lokalisierung erschwert. Von einigen Forschern dem Giusto de'Menabuoi, einem Paduaner Meister oder dessen Werkstatt zugeschrieben, werden sie von anderen in die Nähe Cavallinis geteilt, der als Freskant sowohl in Rom wie in Neapel nachweisbar ist. Vor allem Annegrit Schmitt stützt unter erweiterter Bezugnahme auf Neapolitaner Wandmalereien und illuminierte Handschriften die ursprüngliche These der Lokalisierung nach Neapel und gelangt aufgrund einer Gruppe datierbarer Miniaturen, welche die Existenz der Stuttgarter Tafeln voraussetzen, zu deren zeitlicher Ansetzung zwischen 1330 und 1340.

The two panel paintings depicting visions from the Apocalypse of St John, purchased from the collection of the Count of Erbach-Fürstenau, are among the most important works of early Italian art in German museums. Until 1905 they were in the estate of the Frankfurt painter Edward Jakob von Steinle. According to oral tradition, Goethe's brother-in-law Johann Georg Schlosser brought them with him from Italy and deposited them in the monastery at Neuburg near Heidelberg before they passed into the possession of Jakob von Steinle.

In total 44 scenes from the apocalypse are reproduced on the two panels, to be read respectively from top left to bottom right, beginning with the depiction of St John on Patmos and ending with the vision of the holy city, the new Jerusalem. The original function of the panels is unclear. Traces of an old mounting do not exclude the possibility that they served as a pictorial facing rather than as panel paintings, perhaps for a reliquary (a reliquary to St John?).

The individual scenes — following the text — are consecutive, but represented as isolated islands. They "swim", so to speak, on a deep blue ground. Although they do not have a stabilizing frame, that is to say an "anchor", they are characterized by a high degree of inherent plasticity. Detailed forms are rendered with a miniature-like exactitude. Architectural structures and landscape are not yet logically perspectival but they are nevertheless spatially conceived. The limitation of space to the immediate field of figurative action, which it exceeds hardly or not at all, follows in principle the form of spatial representation instituted by Giotto. The lively depiction of scenic action is characteristic of the period of origin — and is possibly based on the inspiration of Sienese painting; it refers, moreover, to an exact knowledge of the apocalyptic text. This impression is further strengthened by the radiating intensity of the colours, which emphatically heightens the visionary nature of the miniature-like representations. The "rich and multifaceted" style of the Stuttgart panels, which refer to influences of the most various kinds, combined with their highly singular position in the context of Trecento painting, have made it difficult to specify date and location. Attributed by some researchers to Giusto de'Menabuoi, to a Paduan master or his workshop, they have been associated by others with Cavallini, who can be traced as a fresco painter both in Rome and in Naples. Annegrit Schmitt above all supports the thesis of Neapolitan origin with further reference to Neapolitan murals and illuminated manuscripts, and succeeds in fixing their date between 1330 and 1340 on the grounds of a group of dateable miniatures which presuppose the existence of the Stuttgart panels.

93

Neapolitanische Meister um 1330–1340. Szenen aus der Apokalypse (Ausschnitt)

Neapolitan Master circa 1330–1340. Scenes from the Apocalypse (Detail).

Neapolitanische Meister um 1330–1340. Szenen aus der Apokalypse (Ausschnitt)

Neapolitan Master circa 1330–1340. Scenes from the Apocalypse (Detail).

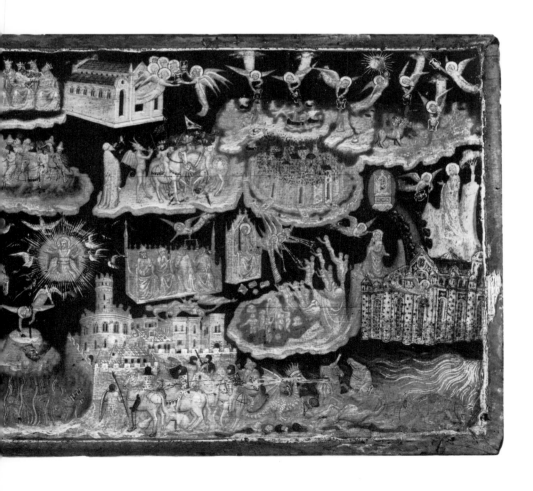

Vittore Carpaccio

Geboren 1460–1465 in Venedig (?), gestorben 1526 ebenda. Beeinflußt von Antonello da Messina und vor allem von Giovanni Bellini, mit dem er 1507 gemeinsam im Dogenpalast arbeitete. Tätig in Venedig.

13

Der heilige Thomas von Aquin thronend zwischen den Heiligen Markus und Ludwig von Toulouse, verehrt von einem jugendlichen Stifter; oben Maria mit Kind und Engeln

Tempera mit starker Ölphase auf Pappelholz, 264 × 171 cm
Bezeichnet unten Mitte auf einem gemalten Zettel: OP(US) VICTOR CARPATHIUS M. D. VII (1507). Sammlung Barbini-Breganze. – Erworben 1852.

Vittore Carpaccio

Born 1460–1465 in Venice (?), died 1526 in Venice. Influenced by Antonello da Messina and above all by Giovanni Bellini, with whom he worked in the Doges Palace in 1507. Active in Venice.

13

St Thomas Aquinas throned between St Mark and St Louis of Toulouse, worshipped by a young donor; above the Virgin with child and angels

Distemper with strong traces of oil on poplar, 264 × 171 cm
Signed lower centre on a painted note: OP(US) VICTOR CARPATHIUS M.D.VII (1507)
Collection Barbini-Breganze. – Purchased 1852.

Der heilige Thomas von Aquin thront in der Mitte des Bildes. Ihn flankierten zur Linken der Apostel Markus, zur Rechten in bischöflichem Ornat der heilige Ludwig von Toulouse. Zu Füßen des heiligen Ludwig kniet Alvise Licinio, der Sohn des Stifters. Aus einer Engelsglorie blicken Maria und der Jesusknabe herab. Vier geflügelte Engel halten ein weinrotes Band, das vor sinnlicher Anfechtung schützende Cingulum. Doch nicht allein das Cingulum, auch der in der mariologischen Überlieferung auf die »Reinheit« der Gottesmutter bezogene Text im Buch des heiligen Ludwig (Offenbarung Johannes, 22, 1 ff.) lassen den Schluß zu, daß hier ein Disput über die Immaculata Conceptio (die unbefleckte Empfängnis) der Maria dargestellt ist.

Die Komposition, die vom geläufigen Bildtyp der Sacra Conversazione (Heiligen Unterhaltung) mit der thronenden Madonna nur geringfügig abweicht, ist symmetrisch gegliedert. Der Wechsel vom Profil der Heiligen Markus und Ludwig zur Frontalität des heiligen Thomas fördert die Klarheit der räumlichen Disposition. Auch der Thron ist perspektivisch folgerichtig verkürzt. Die Figuren zeichnen sich durch statuarische Geschlossenheit aus; sie sind annähernd lebensgroß in einer vorderen Bildzone angeordnet, während die Landschaft nur als eine den Bildraum öffnende Zutat erscheint. Anders als in den klassischen Werken der Hochrenaissance, wo Figur und Raum einander durchdringen, sind die einzelnen Bildgründe bei Carpaccio streng voneinander geschieden. Das Kolorit wirkt metallisch und hart und ist ganz in den Dienst einer das skulpturale Erscheinungsbild der Figuren steigernden Formanschauung gestellt. Die dem Künstler oft attestierte Naturnähe der Darstellung drückt sich nicht nur im Detailreichtum des Thrones und der Gewänder, sondern besonders in der individuellen Prägung der Gesichter wahrnehmbar aus.

Die Altartafel wurde von dem Glasfabrikanten Tommaso Licinio für die Kirche San Pietro Martire in seiner Heimatstadt Murano gestiftet. Der heilige Ludwig war der Namenspatron seines auf dem Bild dargestellten Sohnes Alvise Licinio. – 1507 datiert, fällt die Entstehung der Tafel bereits in die Zeit der Hochrenaissance, doch ist ihr formaler Aufbau noch deutlich von den Bildvorstellungen des Quattrocento bestimmt.

St Thomas Aquinas is throned in the centre of the painting. He is flanked on the left by the apostle Mark, and on the right by St Louis of Toulouse in bishop's vestments. At St Louis' feet kneels Alvise Licinio, the donor's son. The Virgin and her child look down from a host of angels. Four winged angels are bearing a wine-red ribbon, the Cingulum that guards against sensual temptation. Not only the Cingulum but also the text in the book of St Louis (Revelation of St John, 22, 1 f.), refering to the "purity" of the Mother of God in the mariological tradition, allows us to conclude that a dispute about Mary's immaculate conception is represented here.

The composition, which departs only negligibly from the familiar pictorial paradigm of the sacra conversazione with Mary throned, is symmetrically articulated. The transition from the profile views of St Mark and St Louis to the frontality of St Thomas reinforces the clarity of spatial disposition. The foreshortening of the throne too is perspectively consistent. The figures are distinguished by their statuesque self-containment; they are grouped almost life-size in the foreground zone, while the landscape appears merely as an addition to open up pictorial space. In contrast to classical works of the High Renaissance, where figure and space are mutually interdependent, the separate pictorial planes in Carpaccio's painting are radically separated. The colouration has a hard metallic effect and it is put wholly in service of a formal conception that enhances the sculptural phenotype of the figures. The life-like representation with which the artist is often credited is not only expressed in the rich details of the throne and robes, but is particularly noticeable in the individual character of the faces. The altar panel was commissioned by the glass factory owner Tommaso Licinio for the church of San Pietro Martire in his home town of Murano. St Louis was the name saint of Alvise Licinio who is represented in the painting. – Dated 1507, the genesis of the painting already falls into the period of the High Renaissance, but its formal construction is still clearly conditioned by the pictorial ideas of the Quatrocento.

Literatur: Kat. Lange, Nr. 451. – Kat. 1931, S. 30. – Kat. 1957, S. 60 mit Abb. – Kat. 1962, Alte Meister, S. 51 mit Abb.

Bibliography: Cat. Lange, no. 451. – Cat. 1931, p. 30. – Cat. 1957, p. 60 with ill. – Cat. 1962, Alte Meister, p. 51 with ill.

Giorgio Vasari

Maler, Architekt und Literat. Geboren 1511 in Arezzo, gestorben 1574 in Florenz. Ausgebildet unter Andrea del Sarto und dem Bildhauer Baccio Bandinelli, beeinflußt von Michelangelo und Raffael. 1550 erste Ausgabe seiner berühmten Sammlung italienischer Künstlerbiographien. 1561 Gründung der Accademia del Disegno in Florenz. Tätig in Florenz und Rom. Universeller Hofkünstler der Medici.

14

Toilette der Venus

Entstanden 1558
Öl auf Pappelholz, 154 × 124,5 cm
Erworben aus römischem Privatbesitz 1967.

Giorgio Vasari

Painter, architect and man of letters. Born 1511 in Arezzo, died 1574 in Florence. Trained by Andrea del Sarto and the sculptor Baccio Bandinelli, influenced by Michelangelo and Raphael. 1550 first edition of his famous anthology of Italian artists' biographies. 1561 foundation of the Accademia del Disegno in Florence. Active in Florence and Rome. Allround court artist for the Medici.

14

Toilet of Venus

1558.
Oil on poplar, 154 × 124.5 cm
Purchased from a private collection in Rome in 1967.

Venus, die Göttin der Liebe, thront auf einem niedrigen Sitz, bedient von drei Grazien, die Wirkung des Perlengeschmeides in ihren goldgelben Haarflechten prüfend. Amor fliegt mit Blumen herbei. Eine der Grazien gießt Wasser in ein Metallbecken, aus dem zwei Tauben — die Attribute der Venus — »wohl in Anlehnung an das antike Vogel-Vasen-Motiv« (Monika Kopplin) zu trinken suchen. Die Darstellung gilt der »Verherrlichung der weiblichen Schönheit«, spielt aber auch auf deren Vergänglichkeit (Vanitas) an; denn im konvexen Spiegel erscheint das Gesicht der Venus leicht verzerrt, seltsam streng und gealtert.

Die Szenerie entwickelt sich kaum in die Tiefe, sondern füllt in ihrem kompakten, reliefhaften Aufbau fast die gesamte Bildfläche aus. Beherrschend nimmt die junge Göttin die Mittelachse der Komposition ein, die übrigen Gestalten sind im Halbrund um sie gruppiert. Der kraftvolle Frauentypus verbindet Anregungen aus dem Werk Raffaels mit der gesteigerten Plastizität Michelangelos, auf den sich der Künstler auch in der gedrängten, doch stärker »reglementierten« Anordnung der Figuren bezieht. Fast lehrbuchhaft werden Profil, Halbprofil, Vorder- und Rückenansicht im Wechsel der Kopf-, Arm- und Handhaltungen vor Augen geführt. Auch die distanzierende Kühle der koloristischen Instrumentierung und die virtuose Behandlung der ornamentalen Details entsprechen der manieristischen Kunstauffassung Vasaris und ihrer betont akademischen Prägung.

Vasari hat das Thema der »Toilette der Venus« mehrfach gemalt. Die Stuttgarter Fassung ist vermutlich identisch mit dem Werk, das er selbst in seinen »Ricordanze« unter den 1558 für den Florentiner Sammler Luca Torrigani gemalten Bildern aufgeführt hat. Ein Gegenstück, den Triumph des Bacchus darstellend, ist leider verschollen, doch zusammen mit dem Stuttgarter Gemälde in einem 1786 in Florenz erschienenen Stickwerk »Raccolta di ottanta stampe rappresentanti i quadri più scelti de' Sig. ri March. si Gerini di Firenze« überliefert.

Venus, the goddess of love, throned on a low stool and attended by three graces, is observing the effect of a string of pearls in her yellow-gold tresses. Cupid bearing flowers flies above. One of the graces pours water into a metal bowl, from which two doves — the attributes of Venus — "certainly derived from the antique bird-vase motif" (Monika Kopplin), are attempting to drink. The representation is a "glorification of female beauty", but it also alludes to its transience (vanitas); for in the convex mirror Venus' face appears slightly distorted, unusually strict and aged.

The scene hardly extends into spatial depth, rather its compact relief-like construction fills up virtually the whole of the picture plane. The young goddess dominates, occupying the central axis of the composition; the remaining figures are grouped around her in a semi-circle. The powerful female type combines inspiration from Raphael's work with the exaggerated plasticity of Michelangelo, to whose example the artist also refers in the crowded but more strictly "regimented" organization of the figures. Almost as if in a pattern book, profile, half-profile, frontal and back-views are presented to us in the changing positions of heads, arms and hands. The distanced coolness of the colour and the virtuosity of handling in the ornamental details also accord with Vasari's mannerist conception of art and the markedly academic character of such.

Vasari painted the subject of "The Toilet of Venus" several times. The Stuttgart version is probably the work that Vasari himself in his "Ricordanze" listed as one of the paintings executed in 1558 for the Florentine collector Luca Torrigani. A companion piece, representing the triumph of Bacchus, is unfortunately lost, but together with the Stuttgart painting this has passed down to us in an embroidery executed in Florence in 1786: "Raccolta di ottanta stampe rappresentanti i quadri più scelti de' Sig. ri March. si Gerini di Firenze."

Literatur: Jahrbuch der Staatlichen Kunstsammlungen in Baden-Württemberg, V, 1968, S. 202 mit Abb. (Gerhard Ewald). – Ausst.-Kat. Vom Manierismus zum Barock, Staatsgalerie Stuttgart, 1982/83, S. 128 ff. mit Abb. (Gerhard Ewald und Monika Kopplin).

Bibliography: Jahrbuch der Staatlichen Kunstsammlungen in Baden-Württemberg, V, 1968, p. 202 with ill. (Gerhard Ewald). – Cat. Vom Manierismus zum Barock, Staatsgalerie Stuttgart, 1982/83, p. 128 f. with ill. (Gerhard Ewald and Monika Kopplin).

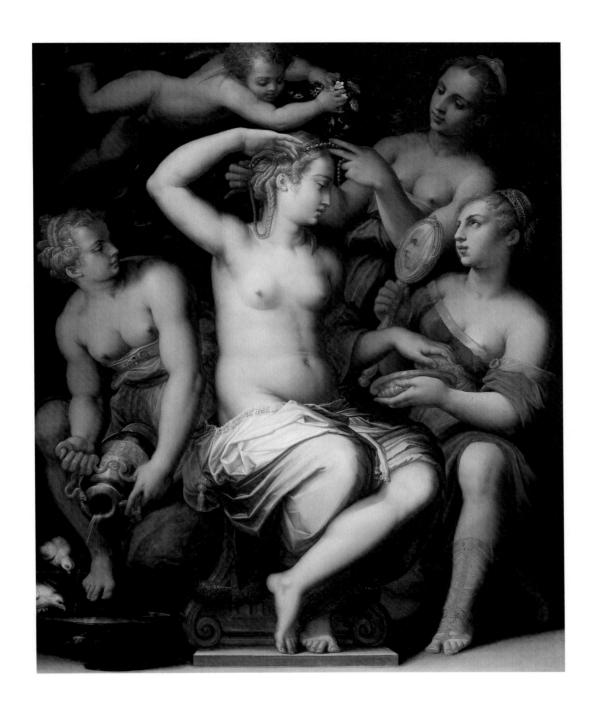

Annibale Carracci

Geboren 1560 in Bologna, gestorben 1609 in Rom. Schüler seines Vetters Lodovico Carracci, Bruder des Agostino Carracci, mit denen er später die »Accademia degli Incamminati« gründet, in der »nach der Natur« gezeichnet wurde. Seit 1595 in Rom, dort zunehmend unter dem Einfluß Michelangelos und vor allem Raffaels.

15

Der Leichnam Christi mit den Leidenswerkzeugen

Entstanden um 1582
Öl auf Leinwand, 70,7 × 88,8 cm
Erworben aus italienischem Privatbesitz 1967.

Annibale Carracci

Born 1560 in Bologna, died 1609 in Rome. Pupil of his cousin Lodovico Carracci, brother of Agostino Carracci, with both he later founded the "Accademia degli Incamminati", where drawing "from nature" was practiced. After 1595 in Rome and increasingly under the influence of Michelangelo and above all Raphael.

15

Dead Christ with the Tools of Sorrow

Circa 1582
Oil on canvas, 70.7 × 88.8 cm
Purchased from an Italian private collection in 1967.

Angeregt durch Andrea Mantegnas berühmten »Toten Christus« in der Mailänder Brera hat Annibale Carracci den Leichnam Christi — genauer gesagt ist es der aufgebahrte Leichnam mit den Leidenswerkzeugen — in extremer Verkürzung dargestellt. Die offenkundig nach einem Modell gemalte Gestalt des Toten ist von einer solchen Monumentalität, daß sie den Rahmen des nur mittelgroßen Gemäldes fast zu sprengen scheint. Im Unterschied zu Mantegna verzichtet Carracci auf die trauernden Assistenzfiguren der Maria und des Johannes, die zuweilen auch durch Engel ersetzt werden. Durch die — in der ikonographischen Überlieferung bereits früher belegbare — Isolation des zentralen Motivs gewinnt die Darstellung an Intensität und Dramatik. Dieser Eindruck wird durch die bedrängende Enge des Bildraums und die kontrastreiche Modellierung des Körpers noch entscheidend verstärkt. An die Stelle einer idealisierenden Überhöhung des Themas, die im Frühbarock vorherrscht, ist eine in der Realistik der Darstellung beklemmende Sicht des Todes getreten, die in so außergewöhnlicher Zuspitzung selten — in anderer Themenbindung allenfalls bei Caravaggio — zu finden ist.

Die von Robert Longhi vorgeschlagene Zuschreibung des Bildes an Annibale Carracci wurde inzwischen allgemein anerkannt, ebenso seine Datierung in die Zeit »um 1582«, die auf Forschungen Donald Posners zurückgeht. Bar aller manieristischen Reminiszenzen belegt das Gemälde beispielhaft die von Carracci auch programmatisch erhobene Forderung nach naturnaher Gestaltung, die vor allem sein Frühwerk vom »klassischen« (unter dem zunehmenden Einfluß Raffaels stehenden) Stil seiner römischen Jahre unterscheidet.

Inspired by Andrea Mantegna's famous "Dead Christ" in the Brera in Milan, Annibale Carracci represents Christ's dead body — more exactly Christ's entombed body with the tools of sorrow — extremely foreshortened. The dead figure — quite obviously painted from the model — is so monumental that it appears almost to burst the frame of the middle sized painting. In contrast to Mantegna, Carracci leaves out the mourning assistant figures of Mary and John, who are sometimes replaced by an angel. Through the isolation of the central motif — already previously verifiable in iconographical tradition — the image gains in intensity and drama. This effect is decidedly strengthened by the pressing narrowness of the pictorial space and by forceful contrasts in the modelling of the body. In place of an idealizing superelevation of the subject, such as held sway in the early Baroque period, he presents a view of the dead Christ that is oppressive in the realism of its representation, seldom found pushed to this pitch (at best by Caravaggio in the context of other subjects).

Roberto Longhi's attribution of the painting to Annibale Carracci is now generally accepted, as is his dating in the period "around 1582", which was first suggested by Donald Posner's research. Excluding all traces of mannerism, the painting verifies in an exemplary way Carracci's programmatically elevated demand for realistic configuration, which separates his early work above all from the classical style of his Roman years under the increasing influence of Raphael.

Literatur: Jahrbuch der Staatlichen Kunstsammlungen in Baden-Württemberg, V, 1968, S. 203 ff. mit Abb. — Donald Posner, Annibale Carracci — A Study in the reform of Italian painting around 1590, London 1971, Bd. II, Kat. Nr. 3. — Ausst.-Kat. Vom Manierismus zum Barock, Staatsgalerie Stuttgart 1982/83, S. 29 mit Abb. (Gerhard Ewald und Monika Kopplin).

Bibliography: Jahrbuch der Staatlichen Kunstsammlungen in Baden-Württemberg, V, 1968, p. 203 f. with ill. — Donald Posner, Annibale Carracci — A Study in the reform of Italian painting around 1590, London 1971, vol. 11, Cat. no. 3. — Cat. Vom Manierismus zum Barock, Staatsgalerie Stuttgart 1982/83, p. 29 with ill. (Gerhard Ewald and Monika Kopplin).

Gaspar van Wittel, genannt Vanvitelli

Geboren 1653 in Amersfoort bei Utrecht, gestorben 1736 in Rom. Ausbildung bei dem Landschafts- und Stillebenmaler Mathias Withoos, Schüler des Architekten van Campen. Seit 1673 in Rom, zunächst als topographischer Zeichner; Weiterbildung bei dem flämischen Maler Abraham Genoels. Seit 1680 ausschließlich als Vedutenmaler tätig. Zahlreiche Reisen, u.a. in die Lombardei, nach Venedig, Bologna, Florenz, Neapel und Messina.

16

Die Tiberinsel in Rom

Öl auf Leinwand, 64,5 × 102 cm
Erworben aus Pariser Privatbesitz 1966.
Leihgabe des Stuttgarter Galerievereins.

Gaspar van Wittel, known as Vanvitelli

Born 1653 in Amersfoort near Utrecht, died 1736 in Rome. Training under the landscape and still life painter Mathias Withoos, pupil of the architect van Campen. After 1673 in Rome, first as a topographical draftsman; further education with the Flemish painter Abraham Genoels. After 1680 active exclusively as a "Vedute painter". Numerous journeys, including Lombardy, Venice, Bologna, Florence, Naples and Messina.

16

The Tiber Island in Rome

Oil on canvas, 64.5 × 102 cm
Purchased from a Parisian private collection in 1966.
On loan from the Stuttgart Galerieverein.

Dargestellt ist die Tiberinsel in Rom mit ihren mittelalterlichen Bauten, aus denen der romanische Campanile von San Bartolomeo und der barocke Turm von San Giovanni Calibita herausragen. Die Cestiusbrücke zur Linken und der Ponte Quattro Capi zur Rechten verbinden die Insel mit den benachbarten Ufern der Stadt. Die ruinöse Brücke im Vordergrund, ihres zerstörten Zustandes wegen der »Ponte Rotto« genannt, stützt in repoussoirhafter Funktion die Tiefenwirkung der Darstellung. Die Barke rechts vorne trägt auf ihrem Bug das Wappen der Familie Pignatelli, bekrönt von den päpstlichen Insignien — ein für den Kundigen unübersehbarer Hinweis auf die Datierung des Bildes, das während des Pontifikats von Innozenz XII. Pignatelli (1691 bis 1700) entstanden sein dürfte. Formal besticht das Gemälde durch die Prägnanz der topographischen Darstellung, die Vanvitelli selbst bei extrem weitem Blickwinkel »mit den Erfordernissen bildmäßiger Wirkung und perspektivischer Gesetzmäßigkeit« (Voss) zu verbinden weiß. Hinzu kommt ein stark ausgeprägtes Empfinden des Holländers für das Atmosphärische, ohne daß die Klarheit der Zeichnung und die Bestimmtheit der Lokaltöne darunter leiden. Auch an der einfühlsam-differenzierenden Gestaltung der Figurenstaffage erkennt man die niederländische Schulung des Malers. Die Spiegelung im Wasser fördert die Stimmung des Bildes; sie faßt die Farben der Häuser und Boote, der Wolken und des sich nach oben lichtenden Himmels nochmals gerafft, in vibrierender Bewegung zusammen. — Auf der Tradition seiner holländischen Vorläufer Berckheyde und Jan van der Heyden aufbauend, jene aber mit einem intuitiven Gespür für Klarheit und Weite seiner südländischen Wahlheimat verbindend, darf Vanvitelli als der Begründer der italienischen Vedutenmalerei angesehen werden.

The Tiber Island in Rome is represented with its medieval buildings, among which the Roman bell tower of San Bartolomeo and the Baroque tower of San Giovanni Calibita stand out. The Cestius Bridge on the left and the Ponte Quattro Capi on the right link the island with the neighbouring shores of the city. The bridge in ruins in the foreground, known as the "Ponte Rotto" on account of its decrepid condition, acts as a repoussoir device to convey recession in the image. The right-hand boat bears the coat of arms of the Pignatelli family on its bow, crowned by the papal insignia; for experts this is an unmistakeable clue to the date of the painting, which must have been painted during the pontificate of Innocent XII. Pignatelli (1691–1700). Formally the painting is convincing through the exactitude of topographical representation, that Vanvitelli knows how to unify in line with "the demands of pictorial effect and perspectival order" (Voss) even when he employs an extremely wide angle of vision. In addition we find a highly developed sensitivity for atmospheric effect in this Dutchman's art, which does not interfere with the clarity of drawing nor the precision of local tones. We also recognize the Dutch training of the painter in the emphatically differentiated arrangement of the decorative figure groups. The reflection in the water augments the mood of the painting; it combines in shimmering movement the colours of the houses and boats, the clouds and the upwardly directed light in the sky which it picks up again. Building on the tradition of his Dutch precursors, Berckheyde and Jan van der Heyden, but combined with an intuitive feeling for the clarity and expanse of his chosen southern homeland, Vanvitelli may be seen as the founder of Italian "Vedute" painting.

Literatur: Jahrbuch der Staatlichen Kunstsammlungen in Baden-Württemberg, IV, 1967, S. 179 mit Abb. — Ausst.-Kat. Das Jahrhundert Tiepolos, Italienische Gemälde des 18. Jahrhunderts aus dem Besitz der Staatsgalerie Stuttgart, 1977/78, S. 123 ff. mit Abb. (Gerhard Ewald).

Bibliography: Jahrbuch der Staatlichen Kunstsammlungen in Baden-Württemberg, IV, 1967, p. 179 with ill. — Cat. Das Jahrhundert Tiepolos, Italienische Gemälde des 18. Jahrhunderts aus dem Besitz der Staatsgalerie Stuttgart, 1977/78, p. 123 f. with ill. (Gerhard Ewald).

Giovanni Paolo Panini

Maler und Architekt. Geboren 1691/92 in Piacenza, gestorben 1765 in Rom. Geschult an der emilianischen Perspektiv- und Architekturmalerei des Ferdinando Galli Bibiena. Seit 1711 in Rom, wo er sich in der Privatakademie Benedetto Lutis weiterbildet. Beeinflußt von Ghisolfi, Salvatore Rosa, Andrea Locattelli und P. L. Ghezzi. Tätig vor allem in Rom.

17

»Roma Antica«

Imaginäre Galerie mit Ansichten der berühmtesten antiken Bauten und Skulpturen Roms
Öl auf Leinwand, 186 × 227 cm
Sammlung Earl of Ellesmere. — Erworben aus dem Londoner Kunsthandel 1978.

Giovanni Paolo Panini

Painter and architect. Born 1691/92 in Piacenza, died 1765 in Rome. Schooled in the Emilian perspectival and architectural painting of Ferdinando Galli Bibiena. After 1711 in Rome, where he continued his education in the private academy of Benedetto Luti. Influenced by Ghisolfi, Salvatore Rosa, Andrea Locattelli and P. L. Ghezzi. Active mostly in Rome.

17

"Roma Antica"

Imaginary gallery with views of the most famous Roman antique buildings and sculptures.
Oil on canvas, 186 × 227 cm
Collection Earl of Ellesmere. — Purchased from the London art market in 1978.

Das Gemälde erschließt sich in der anspruchsvollen Pracht einer barocken Bühne: ein monumentaler, Elemente sakraler und weltlicher Architektur phantasievoll vereinender Raum ist dicht mit Gemälden behängt, auf denen berühmte Bauten des antiken Rom dargestellt sind. Unschwer erkennt man das Kolosseum, das Pantheon, die Maxentiusbasilika, die Diokletiansthermen, das Reiterstandbild des Marc Aurel auf dem Kapitol u. a. m. Nicht minder berühmte Skulpturen wie die »Laokoongruppe«, der »Herkules Farnese«, der »Apoll von Belvedere« und »der sterbende Gallier« vervollständigen in exemplarischer Auswahl den Bestand des hier dargestellten »Musée imaginaire«. Einige Kavaliere sind in das Studium einer Kopie der »Aldobrandinischen Hochzeit« vertieft, unter ihnen steht Panini mit Palette und Pinsel. Die Figuren sind in zwangloser Gruppierung verteilt, sie verlieren sich fast in der Weite des Raumes, dem aber insoweit erhöhte Bedeutung zukommt, als sein Inventar auf die Sphäre ihrer geistigen Herkunft und Bildung verweist. Auch die »freie«, in gebauter Realität so nicht belegbare Verknüpfung von »Innen« (Raum) und »Außen« (Park) ist inhaltlich auf den unteilbaren Anspruch barocker Weltanschauung zurückzuführen. Der Tiefensog der Bild-Wände nimmt der Architektur alle Schwere und steigert den imaginären Charakter der Darstellung. Selbst der Unterschied zwischen dem »Freilicht« des Parks und dem lichtdurchdrungenen Himmel der Bilder hebt sich im Illusionismus reiner Malerei auf.

Das Gemälde — zweifellos ein Hauptwerk Paninis und auch als Zeit-Bild von hohem dokumentarischen Wert — gehört zu einer Gruppe von vier Bildern, die Etienne-François Comte de Stainville, späterer Duc de Choiseul, als französischer Gesandter am Päpstlichen Stuhl 1756 bei Panini in Auftrag gab. Das Gegenstück »Roma Moderna«, eine imaginäre Galerie mit den bedeutendsten Bauten des barocken Rom, befindet sich heute im Museum of Fine Arts in Boston, eine Variante des Stuttgarter Bildes im Metropolitan Museum in New York.

The painting opens on the pretentious splendour of a Baroque stage: a monumental room imaginatively uniting elements of sacred and profane architecture is densely hung with paintings depicting the famous buildings of ancient Rome. We recognize with ease the Colosseum, the Pantheon, the Basilica of Maxentius, the Baths of Diocletian, the equestrian statue of Marcus Aurelius on the Capitol Hill and much more. Equally famous sculptures like the "Laocoon group", the "Farnese Hercules", the "Apollo Belvedere" and the "Dying gaul" complete the holdings of this "musée imaginaire", rendered there in a representative selection. Several cavaliers are sunk in the study of a copy of the "Nozze Aldobrandine" (Aldobrandini's Wedding); among them stands Panini with a palette and brush. The figures are distributed in casual groups almost in the wide room, which they nevertheless endow with added significance in as much as its inventory refers to their intellectual origins and education. The freely conceived association of interior (the room) and exterior (the park) space, not verifiable in real architectural terms, also refers to the inseparable ideal of the Baroque worldview. The funnel effect of the walls covered with paintings dematerializes the architecture and intensifies the imaginary character of the image. Even the contrast between the "plein air" of the park and the light saturated skies in the paintings is dissolved in the illusionism of pure painting.

The painting — undoubtedly a major work of Panini and also of great documentary value as a record of the time — belongs to a group of four paintings commissioned in 1756 by the French envoy to the papal seat, Etienne-François Comte de Stainville, the later Duc de Choiseul. The companion piece "Roma Moderna", an imaginary gallery with the most important buildings in Baroque Rome, is found today in the Museum of Fine Arts in Boston; a variation on the Stuttgart painting is in the Metropolitan Museum in New York.

Literatur: Jahrbuch der Staatlichen Kunstsammlungen in Baden-Württemberg, XVI, 1979, S. 230 mit Abb. — Gerhard Ewald, in: Große Gemäldegalerien, herausgegeben von Erich Steingräber, München 1980, S. 452 mit Abb.

Bibliography: Jahrbuch der Staatlichen Kunstsammlungen in Baden-Württemberg, XVI, 1979, p. 230 with ill. — Gerhard Ewald, in: Große Gemäldegalerien, ed. by Erich Steingräber, Munich 1980, p. 452 with ill.

Giovanni Battista Tiepolo

Geboren 1696 in Venedig, gestorben 1770 in Madrid. Studium bei Gregorio Lazzarini in Venedig, beeinflußt von Giovanni Battista Piazetta und Sebastiano Ricci. Tätig in Venedig und Oberitalien, 1750–1753 in Würzburg und seit 1762 für den spanischen Hof in Madrid.

18

Apollo führt Beatrix von Burgund dem Kaiser Friedrich I. Barbarossa als Braut zu

Öl auf Leinwand, 65,3 × 106,5 cm
Sammlung Barbini-Breganze. –
Erworben 1852.

Giovanni Battista Tiepolo

Born 1696 in Venice, died 1770 in Madrid. Studied under Gregorio Lazzarini in Venice, influenced by Giovanni Battista Piazetta and Sebastiano Ricci. Active in Venice and North Italy, 1750–1753 in Würzburg and after 1762 serving the Spanish court in Madrid.

18

Apollo carries Beatrice of Burgundy as a Bride to Frederick Barbarossa

Oil on canvas, 65.3 × 106.5 cm
Collection Barbini-Breganze. –
Purchased 1852.

Apollo führt Beatrix, die »Braut Burgund«, auf seinem Sonnengespann dem »Genius Imperii« Friedrich von Hohenstaufen zu. Hymenos, der Hochzeitsgott mit Fackel, fliegt voraus. Auf den Wolken lagern zur Rechten Venus, die Göttin der Liebe, umgeben von Ceres und Bacchus, Gottheiten der Fruchtbarkeit. Links erkennt man den Flußgott Main mit einer Quellnymphe. Zu Füßen des Thrones drängen sich allegorische Gestalten und Bannerträger mit der kaiserlichen Fahne und der rotweiß quadrierten des Herzogtums Franken. Ein vor dem Sockel des Thrones schwebener Putto hält das Herzogsschwert.

Das Bild ist der Entwurf für das von Tiepolo im Auftrag des Fürstbischofs Carl Philipp von Greiffenklau 1751/52 gemalte Deckenfresko im Kaisersaal der Würzburger Residenz, dessen Programm sich auf bereits damals weit zurückliegende historische Ereignisse bezieht: auf die Aufenthalte Friedrich Barbarossas anläßlich seiner Eheschließung (1156) und auf die Belehnung des Bistums mit dem Herzogtum Franken (1168). Auf Wunsch des Auftraggebers hat Tiepolo in seinem Deckenfresko beide Begebenheiten in einer mythologischen Allegorie überhöht.

Der formale Aufbau des Bildes ist vom Oval des Deckenspiegels bestimmt. Schon in der dem Deckenbild vorausgehenden Skizze sind Figuren und Gruppen souverän arrangiert und in großzügiger, raum-greifender Disposition auf das zentrale Motiv der heransprengenden, in kühner Verkürzung dargestellten Sonnenrosse bezogen. Licht und Farbe durchdringen und steigern einander; sie heben die körperhafte Schwere der Figuren und Tierleiber nahezu vollkommen auf und tragen — unterstützt von der Linear- und Luftperspektive — entscheidend zur illusionistischen Raumwirkung bei.

Tiepolos Werk markiert Höhepunkt und Vollendung, aber auch Ende der großen europäischen Barockmalerei. Sein szenischer Illusionismus ist noch kaum überschattet vom erwachenden Zeitgeist der Aufklärung, der die alte Einheit von Glaube, staatlicher Machtentfaltung und Bildung auflösen sollte. Es folgte ein kurzer Übergangsstil, in dem der Mythos barocker Phantasie zunehmend verblaßte. Anschauung und ordnendes Bilden reiften schon bald zur Maxime; sie wirkten sich vielfältig aus: in emanzipierender Betrachtung vor allem der Landschaft und des Porträts, aber auch in der strengen Gesetzmäßigkeit klassizistischer Bildform.

Apollo carries Beatrice, the bride of Burgundy, on his sun chariot towards Frederick of Hohenstaufen, the "Genius Imperii". Hymen, the marital god with a torch, leads the way. Reclining on a cloud we find, to the right, Venus the goddess of love flanked by Ceres and Bacchus, gods of fertility. To the left we recognize the river god Main with a water nymph. At the foot of the throne crowd allegorical figures and banner carriers with the Imperial flag and the checked red and white flag of the Dukedom of Franconia. A putto floating at the base of the throne holds the ducal sword.

The painting is a sketch for the ceiling fresco in the "Kaisersaal" (Imperial hall) of the Würzburg residence, which Tiepolo painted in 1751/52, commissioned by the prince-bishop Carl Philipp von Greiffenklau. The decorative scheme refers to events already far back in history: to the visit of Frederick Barbarossa on the occasion of his marriage (1156) and to the enfeoffment of the bishopric with the Dukedom of Franconia (1168). In line with the wishes of the commissioner, Tiepolo elevated both events to the level of a mythological allegory.

The formal construction of the painting is dependent on the oval ceiling mirror. Already in the preparatory sketch for the ceiling painting the figures and groupings are regally arranged and oriented in a generous spatial disposition around the central motif of the forward moving, daringly foreshortened sun chariot. Light and colour fuse and mutually intensify each other, almost dissolving the bodily weight of the figures and animals and, underpinned by linear and aerial perspective, helping to convey a sense of illusionistic space. Tiepolo's work marks the high point and perfection but also the end of great European Baroque painting. His theatrical illusionism is, as yet, hardly shadowed by the awakening spirit of the Enlightenment, which was to dissolve the old unity of belief, power and education. There followed a short transitional style, when the mythology of the Baroque imagination grew increasingly pale. Observation and disciplined form soon reached full maturity, becoming evident in various ways: in the emancipatory observation from life in landscape and portraiture above all, but also in the disciplined order of neoclassical pictorial form.

Literatur: Kat. Lange, Nr. 587. – Kat. 1931, S. 195. – Kat. 1957, S. 290. – Kat. 1962, S. 218 mit Abb. – Ausst.-Kat. Das Jahrhundert Tiepolos, Italienische Gemälde des 18. Jahrhunderts in der Staatsgalerie, 1977/78, S. 113 ff. mit Abb. (Gerhard Ewald). – Ders. in: Große Gemäldegalerien, herausgegeben von Erich Steingräber, München 1980, S. 450 ff. mit Abb. – Die hier in Anlehnung an Ewald, a.a.O., geraffte Inhaltsbeschreibung bezieht sich auf eine ausführliche Darstellung aus der deutschen Version des Tiepolo übersandten Programms für die Ausmalung des Kaisersaales, abgedruckt im Katalog »Die Zeit der Staufer«, Württembergisches Landesmuseum, Stuttgart 1977, Bd. 1, Nr. 1039.

Bibliography: Cat. Lange, no. 587. – Cat. 1931, p. 195. – Cat. 1957, p. 290. – Cat. 1962, *Alte Meister*, p. 218 with ill. – Cat. Das Jahrhundert Tiepolos, Italienische Gemälde des 18. Jahrhunderts in der Staatsgalerie, 1977/78, p. 113 f. with ill. (Gerhard Ewald). – Also in: Große Gemäldegalerien, ed. by Erich Steingräber, Munich 1980, p. 450 f. with ill. – The outline of the content of the painting, taken from Ewald (see above), relates to a full description in the German version of the programme for the decoration of the "Kaisersaal" sent to Tiepolo and reprinted in the catalogue Die Zeit der Staufer, Württembergisches Landesmuseum, Stuttgart 1977, vol. 1, no. 1039.

Christian Gottlieb Schick

Geboren 1776 in Stuttgart, gestorben 1812 ebenda. 1787–1794 an der Hohen Carlsschule in Stuttgart bei Philipp Friedrich Hetsch, anschließend starke Bindung an Johann Heinrich Dannecker. 1798–1802 in Paris im Atelier von Jacques Louis David. 1802 vorübergehend in Stuttgart, danach bis 1811 in Rom.

19

Wilhelmine von Cotta

Öl auf Leinwand, 133 × 140 cm
Bezeichnet rechts an der Brüstung: Schick
faciebat 1802
Freiherr Cotta von Cottendorf, Tübingen. –
Erworben 1951.
Leihgabe des Stuttgarter Galerievereins.

Christian Gottlieb Schick

Born 1776 in Stuttgart, died 1812 in Stuttgart. 1787–1794 studied at the "Hohen Carlsschule" in Stuttgart under Philipp Friedrich Hetsch, subsequently a strong connection to Johann Heinrich Dannecker. 1798 till 1802 in Paris in Jaques Louis David's studio. 1802 temporarily in Stuttgart, then until 1811 in Rome.

19

Wilhelmine von Cotta

Oil on canvas, 133 × 140 cm
Signed to the right on the balustrade:
Schick faciebat 1802
Freiherr Cotta von Cottendorf, Tübingen. –
Purchased 1951.
On loan from the Stuttgart Galerieverein.

Gottlieb Schick gilt als der bedeutendste Maler des Klassizismus in Schwaben. Bereits in jungen Jahren war er durch seine Lehrer, den Bildhauer Johann Heinrich Dannecker und den Maler Jacques Louis David, mit der Gedanken- und Formenwelt der Antike in Berührung gekommen. Wiederholte Aufenthalte in seiner späteren Wahlheimat Rom führten zu einer Vertiefung dieser Eindrücke. Zahlreiche, zu Lebzeiten des Künstlers besonders geschätzte Historienbilder und eine Reihe nicht minder bekannter Porträts zeugen von seinem Bemühen, die aus Anschauung und Studium gewonnenen Anregungen mit den eigenen malerischen Intentionen in Einklang zu bringen. Das 1802 datierte Porträt der ersten Frau des berühmten Stuttgarter Verlegers Johann Friedrich von Cotta bezeichnet einen Höhepunkt dieser Entwicklung. In der Haltung der Dargestellten noch dem Vorbild der Madame Récamier von David verpflichtet, beeindruckt es durch seinen ruhigen, wohlausgewogenen Aufbau, durch die Unmittelbarkeit und Frische des Ausdrucks sowie den Wohlklang der auf Weiß-Rot-Grün gestimmten, sich herrlich steigernden Farben. Auch in der freien Verbindung der figürlichen Darstellung mit einer kaum historisch-idealisierten, sondern auffallend naturnahen, unverkennbar schwäbischen Landschaft erweist sich das Bild als eine der eigenständigsten Schöpfungen, die der Klassizismus in Deutschland hervorgebracht hat.

Gottlieb Schick is considered to be the most important neoclassical painter in Swabia. Already in his youth he came into contact with the intellectual and formal world of antiquity via his teachers, the sculptor Johann Heinrich Dannecker and the painter Jacques Louis David. Repeated periods of residence in Rome, his later chosen homeland, helped to deepen these impressions. Numerous history paintings (highly appreciated during his lifetime) and his no less famous portraits bear witness to his attempts to combine the stimuli won from observation and study with his own painterly intentions. His 1802 portrait of the first wife of the famous Stuttgart publisher, Johann Friedrich von Cotta, marks a high point in this development. While the pose is still indebted to David's portrait of Madame Récamier, the painting impresses us with its calm, well balanced composition, with its direct and fresh expression, and with its harmonious colour gradation, pitched around white, red and green. The combination of the figurative representation and a landscape which bares little trace of heroic idealism and is rather markedly naturalistic and insistently Swabian, also makes the painting one of the most independent creations produced by the neoclassical movement in Germany.

Literatur: Kat. 1962, S. 182 mit Abb. – Kat. 1982, 19. Jahrhundert, S. 128 ff. mit Abb. – Ausst.-Kat. Gottlieb Schick – ein Maler des Klassizismus, Staatsgalerie Stuttgart 1976, Nr. 39, Farbtafel S. 83.

Bibliography: Cat. 1962, Alte Meister, p. 182 with ill. – Cat. 1982, 19. Jahrhundert, p. 128 f. with ill. – Cat. Gottlieb Schick – ein Maler des Klassizismus, Staatsgalerie Stuttgart 1976, no. 39, colour plate p. 83.

Caspar David Friedrich

Geboren 1774 in Greifswald, gestorben 1840 in Dresden. Erster Unterricht bei dem Universitätszeichenlehrer Quistorp in Greifswald. 1794—1798 an der Kopenhagener Akademie. Seit 1798 in Dresden. Zahlreiche Reisen nach Pommern, Rügen, Böhmen und in den Harz.

20

Böhmische Landschaft

Entstanden um 1808
Öl auf Leinwand, 70 × 104,5 cm
Graf F. v. Thun und Hohenstein, Tetschen
a. d. Elbe (mit dem Dresdener Pendant). —
Erworben 1921.

Caspar David Friedrich

Born 1774 in Greifswald, died 1840 in Dresden. Earliest training with the university drawing master Quistorp in Greifswald. 1794—1798 at the Copenhagen Academy. After 1798 in Dresden. Numerous journeys to Pomerania, Rügen, Bohemia and the Harz region.

20

Bohemian Landscape

Circa 1808
Oil on canvas, 70 × 104.5 cm
Count F.v. Thun und Hohenstein,
Tetschen a.d. Elbe (with the Dresden
pendant). — Purchased 1921.

Wie sein Gegenstück — eine morgendliche »Böhmische Landschaft« der Dresdener Galerie — stellt auch das Stuttgarter Bild den Milleschauer bei Teplitz, diesmal in abendlicher Dämmerung dar. Menschenleer und doch auf den Menschen bezogen, breitet sich die Landschaft in ruhiger Lagerung und Schichtung der Bildgründe aus, um in der fast »körperlosen« Lichtsilhouette des sanft ansteigenden Gebirges zu kulminieren. Die romantisch empfundene Spannung zwischen Nähe und Ferne wird durch den »Riegel« eines Waldsaums entscheidend intensiviert und klingt auch in der Aufhellung der Farben an. Das »Portalmotiv« der Bäume steht in enger Beziehung zu dem überragenden, dem Betrachter gleichwohl entrückten Berg und betont — wie Börsch-Supan hervorhebt — »als sakrales Motiv die Bedeutung des Berges als Sinnbild Gottes«. Skizzen unterschiedlicher topographischer Provenienz und Datierung liegen dem Gemälde zugrunde: die beiden Buchen, welche das »Tor« suggerieren, sind in verschiedenen Jahren und an verschiedenen Orten entstanden, im Mai 1797 in Sachsen und im Juli 1799 in Neubrandenburg. Auch Waldsaum, kahler Ast und Distel (im Bildvordergrund) lassen sich auf Studien früherer Jahre belegen. Trotz so weitergeholter Einzelmotive erschließt sich das Erscheinungsbild dieser Landschaft als Einheit, da Anschauung und Vorstellung, gestaltende Phantasie und Empfindung zu völliger Deckung gebracht sind. Wie immer bei Friedrich stellen die Motive sowohl sich selbst dar, als sie auch einen »die Wahrnehmungsfakten überschreitenden Sinnzusammenhang« (Werner Hofmann) bilden. Weder als »Landschaftsporträt« noch als »Stimmungslandschaft« bestimmbar, ist das Gemälde Abbild und Sinnbild, Erinnerungsbild und Vision in einem.

Like its companion piece — a Bohemian morning landscape in the Dresden Gallery — the Stuttgart painting also represents the Milleschauer near Teplitz, this time in the evening twilight. Devoid of figures and yet oriented towards a human presence, the landscape spreads out across the pictorial plane in calm stratifications, culminating in the almost immaterial silhouette of the gently rising mountain. The romantically sensed tension between near and far is intensified decisively by the "cross-beam" of a fringe of woodland, and this is also evoked by the paling of the colours. The "gateway motif" of the trees relates closely to the overtowering mountain which is nevertheless removed from the spectator, thus emphasizing — as Börsch-Supan points out — "the significance of the mountain as a sacred motif, as a symbol of God". Sketches with various topographic and temporal origins lie behind the painting. The two beech trees which suggest the gateway were sketched in different locations in May 1797 in Saxony and July 1799 in Neubrandenburg. Similarly the fringe of woodland, the bare bough and the thistle in the foreground can be traced back to studies made in earlier years. Despite the disparate origins of individual motifs, the landscape unfolds as a unity because observation and idea, pictorial imagination and sensitivity throw a fine and complete net over the whole. As always in Friedrich's work, the motifs are both realistic and representative of a "totality of meaning that exceeds perceptual fact" (Werner Hofmann). Classifiable neither as a "portrait of a landscape" nor as a "landscape of mood", the painting is both representative and symbolic, a memory painting and a vision in one.

Literatur: Kat. 1931, S. 54. — Kat. 1957, S. 98 mit Abb. — Kat. 1968, S. 65 mit Abb. — Kat. 1982, 19. Jahrhundert, S. 84 mit Abb. — Helmut Börsch-Supan/Karl Wilhelm Jähnig, Caspar David Friedrich, München 1973, S. 314 f., Nr. 189 mit Abb. — Zur Datierung: Eva Reitharová/Werner Sumowski, Beiträge zu Caspar David Friedrich, in: Pantheon, XXXV, 1977, S. 47 mit Abb. — Christian von Holst, in: Große Gemäldegalerien, herausgegeben von Erich Steingräber, München 1980, S. 452 ff. mit Abb. — Karl-Ludwig Hoch, Caspar David Friedrichs Frömmigkeit und seine Ehrfurcht vor der Natur — dargestellt im Hinblick auf die Bildsymbolik der wiedererkannten böhmischen Bilder, Dissertation (Maschinenschrift), Karl-Marx-Universität Leipzig 1981, Bd. II, S. 203 ff.

Bibliography: Cat. 1931, p. 54. — Cat. 1957, p. 98 with ill. — Cat. 1968, p. 65 with ill. — Cat. 1982, 19. Jahrhundert, p. 84 with ill. Helmut Börsch-Supan/Karl Wilhelm Jähnig, Caspar David Friedrich, Munich 1973, p. 314 f., no. 189 with ill. — With regard to dating: Eva Reitharová/Werner Sumowski, "Beiträge zu Caspar David Friedrich", in: Pantheon, XXXV, 1977, p. 47 with ill. — Christian von Holst, in: Große Gemäldegalerien, ed. by Erich Steingräber, Munich 1980, p. 452 f. with ill. — Karl-Ludwig Hoch, Caspar David Friedrichs Frömmigkeit und seine Ehrfurcht vor der Natur — dargestellt im Hinblick auf die Bildsymbolik der wiedererkannten böhmischen Bilder, thesis (typescript), Karl-Marx-University Leipzig 1981, vol. 11, p. 203 f.

Claude Monet

Geboren 1840 in Paris, gestorben 1926 in Giverny/Seine. Erster Malunterricht bei Boudin. 1859/60 in Paris, Bekanntschaft mit Pissarro. 1860–1862 Militärdienst in Algerien. 1862/63 im Atelier von Gleyre in Paris, zusammen mit Renoir und Sisley. Seit 1866 überwiegend in Argenteuil. Seit 1883 in Giverny. Zahlreiche Reisen, u.a. nach London, Holland, Italien, Spanien und Norwegen.

21

Felder im Frühling

Öl auf Leinwand, 74,3 × 93 cm
Bezeichnet rechts unten: Claude Monet 87
Opernsänger Jean Baptiste Faure, Paris. –
Erworben 1906.
Leihgabe des Stuttgarter Galerievereins.

Claude Monet

Born 1840 in Paris, died 1926 in Giverny/Seine. First painting lessons with Boudin. 1859/60 in Paris, aquaintance with Pissarro. 1860–1862 military service in algeria. 1862/63 attended Gleyre's studio in Paris together with Renoir and Sisley. After 1866 mostly in Argenteuil. After 1883 in Giverny. Numerous travels, including London, Holland, Italy, Spain and Norway.

21

Spring Meadows

Oil on canvas, 74.3 × 93 cm
Signed lower right: Claude Monet 87
Opera singer Jean Baptiste Faure, Paris. –
Purchased 1906.
On loan from the Stuttgart Galerieverein.

»Impression, soleil levant« hatte Monet eines seiner Bilder benannt, das 1874 zusammen mit Werken von Renoir, Pissarro, Sisley u.a. im Atelier des Pariser Fotografen Nadar ausgestellt war. Der Kunstkritiker Leroy griff diese Bezeichnung auf und disqualifizierte die Maler höhnisch als »Impressionisten« – ein »Spottname«, der schon bald zum »Stilbegriff« werden sollte. – Bar aller Reminiszenzen an die tradierte Ateliermalerei gibt das impressionistische Landschaftsgemälde den unmittelbaren Natureindruck wieder, da es von der ersten Anlage bis zur Vollendung en plein air, d.h. im Freien, gemalt wurde. Monet war nicht der erste, der diese Forderung der Freilichtmalerei erfüllte, aber er zog die äußersten Konsequenzen daraus. Ausgehend von der Beobachtung, daß Licht und Atmosphäre die Erscheinungsform der Dinge ständig verändern, hat er bereits in den 70er und zu Beginn der 80er Jahre Werke geschaffen, in denen sein Impressionismus zu voller Entfaltung gelangt ist. So auch im Stuttgarter Bild, das – obschon »komponiert« – vor allem durch seinen freien malerischen Aufbau besticht. Ein stürmischer Wirbel von Farbflocken löst Formen, Volumina und Umrisse auf. Die Lokalfarben weichen leuchtenden Farbflecken verschiedener Struktur, die in mehreren Lagen über- und nebeneinander, bald locker angedeutet, bald fester hingestrichen sind. Grün spaltet sich zu Gelb und Blau, Orange zu Rot und Gelb. Erst das Auge des Betrachters schließt diese Farben wieder zum Eindruck eines windbewegten Frühlingsfeldes zusammen. – Indem Monet das Transitorische thematisiert, verletzt er nicht nur den (akademischen) Glauben an bildhafte Statik; er relativiert ebenso die (bleibende) Gültigkeit des Motivs, das sich in der »Zeitlichkeit« seiner Bilder einer über den »Moment« der Rezeption hinausweisenden Fixierung versagt. In diesem Tatbestand liegt die das reine »Augenerlebnis« erst sinnfällig machende »Modernität« des Impressionisten Monet. Seine sich im Reflex des jeweiligen »Jetzt« erfüllende Kunst schließt freilich nicht allein Relativierung, sondern in deren Konsequenz auch das zunehmende Entgleiten des Motivischen und damit den Primat reiner Malerei ein.

"Impression, soleil levant" was the title given by Monet to one of his paintings exhibited in 1874 alongside works by Renoir, Pissarro and Sisley in the studio of the Parisian photographer Nadar. The art critic Leroy picked up this name and dismissed the painters scornfully as "impressionists" – a "nickname" which quickly became a stylistic concept. Departing completely from traditional studio painting, impressionist landscape reproduced the direct impact of nature, being painted from beginning to end "en plein air", that is to say, outside. Monet was not the first to fulfil the demands of open air painting, but he drew the most extreme consequences from this development. Building on the observation that light and atmosphere continually change the appearance of things, he already achieved works in the 1870s and early 1880s in which his impressionism was in ful flower. For example, the Stuttgart painting – although it is "composed" – impresses us above all with its free painterly structure. A stormy vortex of coloured strokes dissolves forms, volumes and contours. Local colours give way to variously structured luminous coloured strokes in several layers, adjacent to and on top of each other, now sketchily suggested, now more decisively laid in. Green breaks up into yellow and blue, orange into red and yellow. The eye of the spectator alone recombines these colours into the impression of a windy spring meadow. By thematizing the transitory, Monet did not only attack the (academic) belief in pictorial stasis; he also relativised the (eternal) validity of his motif which, in the temporality of his paintings, is denied a fixity that transcends the "moment" of reception. In this we can locate the "modernity" of Monet's impressionism, manifested as a pure optical experience. His art which materialized the reflex of a changing "moment" does not only involve relativism but also, as a consequence of this, a "loosening" of the subject in favour of the primacy of pure painting.

Literatur: Kat. Lange, Nr. 663a. – Kat. 1931, S. 103. – Kat. 1957, S. 178 mit Abb. – Kat. 1968, S. 127 mit Abb. – Kat. 1982, 19. Jahrhundert, S. 110 mit Abb. – Werner Deusch, Neuere Malerei in der Staatsgalerie Stuttgart, S. 14 ff. mit Abb. – Christian von Holst, in: Große Gemäldegalerien, herausgegeben von Erich Steingräber, München 1980, S. 454 mit Abb.

Bibliography: Cat. Lange, no. 663a. – Cat. 1931, p. 103. Cat. 1957, p. 178 with ill. – Cat. 1968, p. 127 with ill. – Cat. 1982, 19. Jahrhundert, p. 110 with ill. – Werner Deusch, Neuere Malerei in der Staatsgalerie Stuttgart, p. 14f. with ill. – Christian von Holst, in: Große Gemäldegalerien, ed. by Erich Steingräber, Munich 1980, p. 454 with ill.

Max Slevogt

Geboren 1868 in Landshut, gestorben 1932 in Neukastel/Pfalz. 1885—1889 an der Münchner Akademie, u. a. bei Herterich und v. Diez. 1889 an der Académie Julian in Paris. 1890 in Italien, danach in München. 1898 in Holland. Seit 1901 in Berlin. 1914 Ägyptenreise. Häufige Aufenthalte in seinem Landhaus in Neukastel.

22

Das Champagnerlied

Auch »Der weiße d'Andrade« genannt

Öl auf Leinwand, 215 × 160 cm
Bezeichnet rechts unten: Slevogt 1902.
Erworben vom Künstler 1904.

Max Slevogt

Born 1868 in Landshut, died 1932 in Neukastel/Pfalz. 1885—1889 studied at the Munich Academy under Herterich and v. Diez. 1889 attended the Académie Julian in Paris. 1890 in Italy, afterwards in Munich. 1898 in Holland. After 1901 in Berlin. 1914 journey to Egypt. Frequent periods in his country house in Neukastel.

22

The Champagne Song

Also known as "The White d'Andrade"

Oil on canvas, 215 × 160 cm
Signed lower right: Slevogt 1902
Purchased from the artist in 1904.

Dargestellt ist der portugiesische Sänger Francisco d'Andrade (Lissabon 1859—1921 Berlin) in der berühmten Champagnerarie des Don Juan. Das Thema des Bildes kam Slevogt, der mit d'Andrade befreundet und ein begeisterter Liebhaber und Kenner Mozartscher Musik war, besonders entgegen. Zahlreiche Studien und Skizzen belegen sein Bemühen um eine die Gestalt des Sängers zunehmend isolierende Bildform. Selbst Haltung, Gestik und Mimik des Dargestellten beruhen, so spontan sie auch anmuten, auf »einer bis ins einzelne überdachten Komposition der Figur in dem sie umgebenden Raum« (Deusch). Gerade der Vergleich mit Manets Studie des Schauspielers Faure als Hamlet in der Hamburger Kunsthalle verdeutlicht sowohl Nähe als auch Distanz Slevogts zum französischen Impressionismus. Im Unterschied zur formauflösenden, alle Bildteile gleichermaßen durchdringenden Malerei des Franzosen ist der koloristische Aufbau des Slevogtschen Gemäldes einer noch stärkeren Themenbindung verpflichtet. Zumal das Gesicht des d'Andrade ist porträthaft erfaßt und hebt sich in kraftvoller Modellierung vom furiosen Impasto des Gewandes und dem nur skizzenhaft angedeuteten Hintergrund wahrnehmbar ab. Allein die Strahlkraft der Farbe und die im Ganzen doch improvisierende Handschrift lassen erkennen, daß auch Slevogt vom Impressionismus geprägt wurde, dessen Mittel er aber — und das ist entscheidend — in differenzierender, die inhaltlichen Bezüge des Bildes stärker akzentuierender Weise eingesetzt hat.

The Portugese singer Francisco d'Andrade (Lisbon 1859—1921 Berlin) is depicted here in the famous "Champagne Song" of Don Giovanni. The subject of the painting was particularly attractive for Slevogt, who was friendly with d'Andrade and an enthusiastic lover and scholar of Mozart's music. Numerous studies and sketches illustrate his attempts to achieve a pictorial solution which increasingly isolated the singer's form. Even the bearing, gesticulation and mimicry of d'Andrade, however spontaneous they might appear, refer to "a composition worked out in detail relating the figure to his surroundings" (Deusch). A comparison with Manet's study of the actor Faure as Hamlet in the Kunsthalle Hamburg precisely clarifies Slevogt's proximity to and distance from French Impressionism. In contrast to the form dissolving painterliness of the French artist which is equally applied in all pictorial zones, the colouristic construction of Slevogt's painting is more closely bound to his subject. D'Andrade's face in particular is rendered as a portrait and its powerful modelling stands out noticeably from the wild impasto of the costume and the sketchily suggested background. The luminosity of the colour and the improvisational brushwork of the painting as a whole make clear that Slevogt was also influenced by impressionism whose means — and this is the decisive point — he employed in a more finely differentiated way, accentuating more strongly the thematic structure of the painting.

Literatur: Kat. Lange, Nr. 891 a. — Kat. 1931, S. 175. — Kat. 1957, S. 267 mit Abb. — Kat. 1961, S. 112 mit Abb. — Kat. 1968, S. 172 mit Abb. — Kat. 1982, 19. Jahrhundert, S. 148 ff. mit Abb. — Bruno Bushart, Der Sänger d'Andrade als Don Giovanni, Reclams Werkmonographien 47, Stuttgart 1959. — Werner Deusch, Neue Malerei in der Staatsgalerie Stuttgart, S. 40 ff. mit Abb.

Bibliography: Cat. Lange, no. 891 a. — Cat. 1931, p. 175. — Cat. 1957, p. 267 with ill. — Cat. 1961, p. 112 with ill. — Cat. 1968, p. 172 with ill. — Cat. 1982, 19. Jahrhundert, p. 148 f. with ill. — Bruno Bushart, Der Sänger d'Andrade als Don Giovanni, Reclams Werkmonographien 47, Stuttgart 1959. — Werner Deusch, Neue Malerei in der Staatsgalerie Stuttgart, p. 40 f. with ill.

Paul Cézanne

Geboren in Aix-en-Provence 1839, gestorben 1906 ebenda. Seit 1861 in Paris. Besuch der Académie Suisse, Begegnung mit Pissarro, Sisley, Monet, Renoir und Manet. 1862–1874 mit Pissarro in Auvers-sur-Oise. Danach meist in Aix, unterbrochen durch häufige Aufenthalte in Paris, der Île-de-France und der Provence.

23

Badende vor einem Zelt

Entstanden 1883–1885
Öl auf Leinwand, 63 × 81 cm
Sammlung Klas Fåhreus, Lidingön. –
Sammlung Walter Halvorsen, Oslo. –
Sammlung Ragnar Moltzau, Oslo. –
Erworben 1959.

Paul Cézanne

Born in Aix-en-Provence 1839, died 1906 in Aix-en-Provence. After 1861 in Paris. Attended the Académie Suisse, contact with Pissarro, Sisley, Monet, Renoir and Manet. 1862–1874 with Pissarro in Auvers-sur-Oise. Thereafter mainly in Aix, punctuated by frequent periods in Paris, the Île-de-France and Provence.

Die Beschäftigung mit dem Thema der Badenden reicht bis in die impressionistischen Anfänge Cézannes zurück und nimmt in den 80er Jahren des vergangenen Jahrhunderts konstruktive Formen an. Zahlreiche Studien sind zu den einzelnen, in den verschiedenen Bildversionen immer wiederkehrenden Figuren vorhanden. Sie zu einer sinnvoll-tektonischen Ordnung zu vereinen und zur großen Bildform umzuschmelzen, ist das Anliegen des Künstlers. Auch die Badenden des Stuttgarter Bildes sind nicht als impressionistische »Momentaufnahme« gesehen, sondern zu wohldurchdachter Gruppierung gegliedert. Ihre noch »raumbildende« Disposition kulminiert im pyramidalen Aufbau der Gruppe zur Linken, die durch ein zeltartig drapiertes Tuch hinterlegt ist, das allein der Stabilisierung der Komposition dient. Die Malweise ist von aquarellhafter Zartheit, die Palette auf nur wenige Töne beschränkt: auf ein ruhiges tintiges Blau, auf Ocker und verschiedene Abwandlungen von Grün. Die Linie hat ihr Recht als Umgrenzung der Gestalt wieder erhalten, aber ihr Verlauf wird oftmals gebrochen, verdickt, mitunter sogar verwischt. Der Gegenstand, der sich bei den Impressionisten auflöst, beginnt sich erneut zu verfestigen, wird wieder kompakt und zugleich vereinfacht. Hinter dieser scheinbar asketischen Sehweise verbirgt sich ein neues Verhalten gegenüber der sichtbaren Welt: Natur und Mensch sind für Cézanne nur Ausgangspunkt einer Gestaltung, die ihre Erfüllung im selbständigen, eigenen Gesetzen unterworfenen Kunstwerk findet.

Cézanne's engagement with the subject of bathers dates back to his impressionist beginnings and in the 1880s it assumed constructive forms. Numerous studies exist for the individual figures which reoccur again and again in different pictorial versions. The artist's concern is to arrange the figures in a logical tectonic order and to recast them in a monumental pictorial form. Correspondingly, the bathers in the Stuttgart painting are not seen as impressionist "snapshots", but rather they are articulated in a well considered group. Their disposition, which is still "spatially diagramatic", culminates in the pyramid structure of the left-hand group, backed by a tent-like draped cloth which serves only to stabilize the composition. The painterly technique has the delicacy of watercolour, the palette is limited to only a few tones: restful blue, ochre and various modifications of green. Line has rediscovered its rôle as a border to form; but its continuity is often broken, compressed, at times even erased. The integrity of the object which was dissolved by the impressionists begins to resolidify; it is made compact and at the same time simplified. Behind this apparently ascetic "way of seeing" there lies concealed a new attitude to the visual world. For Cézanne nature and man are only a point of departure for form, which reaches fulfillment in an independent artwork, subject to its own laws.

23

Bathers in front of a Tent

1883–1885
Oil on canvas, 63.5 × 81 cm
Collection Klas Fåreus, Lidingön. –
Collection Walter Halvorsen, Oslo –
Collection Ragnar Moltzau, Oslo. –
Purchased 1959.

Literatur: Kat. 1961, S. 31 mit Abb., – Kat. 1968, S. 40ff. mit Abb. – Kat. 1982, 19. Jahrhundert, S. 49 mit Abb. – Werner Deusch, Neuere Malerei in der Staatsgalerie Stuttgart, S. 26ff. mit Abb.

Bibliography: Cat. 1961, p. 31 with ill. – Cat. 1968, p. 40f. with ill. – Cat. 1982, 19. Jahrhundert, p. 49 with ill. – Werner Deusch, Neuere Malerei in der Staatsgalerie Stuttgart, p. 26f. with ill.

Paul Gauguin

Geboren 1848 in Paris, gestorben 1903 in Atuana auf den Marquesas. Kindheit in Peru. Zunächst Matrose und Kaufmann, 1871 Bankangestellter. Seit 1874 als Maler tätig, anfänglich unter dem Einfluß Pissarros. 1884 in Dänemark, 1885 in Paris, 1886 erster Aufenthalt in Pont-Aven. 1887 Reise nach Martinique. 1888 wieder in Pont-Aven, im Herbst desselben Jahres mit van Gogh in Arles. 1889/90 in Pont-Aven und Le Pouldu. Seit 1891, abgesehen von einem Frankreich-Aufenthalt, auf Tahiti. 1901 Übersiedlung auf die Marquesas.

24

E HAERE OE I HIA

Wohin gehst Du?

Öl auf Leinwand, 96 × 69 cm
Bezeichnet rechts unten: 92 P. Gauguin;
links unten betitelt.
Sammlung Bernhard Koehler, Berlin. –
Stiftung Elly Koehler, München, 1969.

Paul Gauguin

Born 1848 in Paris, died 1903 in Atuana in the Marquesan Isles. Childhood in Peru. First a sailor and salesman, 1871 employed in a bank. After 1874 active as a painter, first under the influence of Pissarro. 1884 in Denmark, 1885 in Paris, 1886 first visit to Pont-Aven. 1887 journey to Martinique. 1888 again in Pont-Aven, in the autumn with van Gogh in Arles. 1889/90 in Pont-Aven and Le Pouldu. After 1891, apart from one visit to France, in Tahiti. 1901 moved to the Marquesan Isles.

24

E HAERE OE I HIA

Where are you going?

Oil on canvas, 96 × 69 cm
Signed lower right:
92 P. Gauguin; titled lower left.
Collection Bernard Koehler, Berlin. –
Donated by Elly Koehler, Munich, 1969.

Das Thema des Bildes »Wohin gehst Du?« wird bisweilen mit der Maori-Mythologie in Verbindung gebracht. Demnach wäre die halbnackte Eingeborene, die ein Wolfsjunges trägt, als Oviri, die Todesgöttin der Maori, zu deuten. An sie richtet sich – folgt man einem Interpretationsvorschlag Seilers – die Frage der beiden kauernden Frauen, in welche Hütte der Tod wohl eintreten werde. Das jugendliche Erscheinungsbild der blumengeschmückten Oviri hat aber auch Anlaß gegeben, ihre mythologische Nähe zu Natur- und Fruchtbarkeitsgottheiten, im besonderen zu Hina, der Göttin des Mondes und der Liebe, hervorzuheben. – So ambivalent das Bild in seiner Aussage bleibt, sich thematischer Fixierung sogar verschließt, sicher ist eines: Gauguin geht es nicht um die Illustration eines Mythos, wohl aber bezieht er Elemente eines fremden Schöpfungsmythos in seine Gestaltungen ein, um den schöpferischen Anspruch der Kunst zu legitimieren. Die Neuartigkeit seiner sich vom klassischen Impressionismus klar distanzierenden Bildform, ihr ruhiger, Stille suggerierender, flächiger Aufbau, die Betonung wiederum der Kontur und der ungebrochenen Farbe – dies alles ist den formauflösenden Tendenzen der Impressionisten diametral entgegengesetzt und weist in ganz anderer Richtung auf eine Verselbständigung der künstlerischen Ausdrucksmittel hin. Die Fragwürdigkeit einer nur mythologischen, den formalen Gehalt weitgehend negierenden Deutung des Bildes läßt sich auch daran ermessen, daß auf einer zweiten Fassung des Themas in der Leningrader Eremitage das Wolfsjunge (als Attribut der Oviri) durch ein Gefäß ersetzt ist.

The subject of the painting "Where are you going?" has sometimes been associated with Maori mythology. According to this theory, the half-nude native, who is holding a wolf cub, is meant as Oviri, the Maori goddess of death. The two crouching women – if we follow Seiler's proposed interpretation – in whose hut death is about to enter, address their question to her. The youthful appearance of the flower-clad Oviri has given cause, however, to acknowledge her mythological proximity to nature and fertility deities, in particular to Hina, the goddess of the moon and of love. However, ambivalent the message of the painting remains, even resisting thematic determination, one thing is sure: Gauguin is not interested in illustrating a myth, rather he incorporates elements of a foreign myth of creation in his own work in order to legitimize art's creative demands. The novelty of his pictorial form is clearly far from impressionism. The calm planar construction suggestive of silence, the new emphasis on contour and unbroken colour – all this is diametrically opposed to the form dissolving tendencies of impressionism, and points in a quite different direction, towards a new independent use of artistic means. The questionable relevance of an exclusively mythological interpretation of the painting that largely negates its formal substance becomes obvious when compared to a second version of the subject in the Hermitage in Leningrad, where the wolf cub (an attribute of Oviri) is replaced by a pot.

Literatur: Kat. 1968, S. 67 ff. mit Abb. –
Kat. 1982, 19. Jahrhundert, S. 86 mit Abb.

Bibliography: Cat. 1968, p. 67 f. with ill. –
Cat. 1982, 19. Jahrhundert, p. 86 with ill.

E Haere oe i hia

Henri Matisse

Geboren 1869 in Le Cateau/Nordfrankreich, gestorben 1954 in Cimiez. Seit 1892 an der Académie Julian und an der École des Beaux-Arts in Paris. 1895–1897 im Atelier Moreau, 1898/99 Aufenthalt auf Korsika und in Toulouse. 1905 erste gemeinsame Ausstellung der »Fauves« (Wilden) im Salon d'Automne. 1908 Reise nach Deutschland. 1908–1910 eigene Kunstschule in Paris. 1910–1913 Reisen nach Spanien, Moskau, Marokko. Seit 1917 im Winter in Nizza. 1930 Reise nach Tahiti und den USA. Seit 1938 in Cimiez bei Nizza. 1943–1948 in Vence, danach wieder in Cimiez.

25

La Coiffure

Bei der Toilette

Entstanden 1907
Öl auf Leinwand, 116 × 89 cm
Bezeichnet links unten: Henri Matisse
Sammlung Michel und Sarah Stein, Paris.
— Sammlung Trygve Sagen, Oslo. —
Sammlung P. Krag, Oslo. — Sammlung
Ragnar Moltzau, Oslo. — Erworben 1959.

Henri Matisse

Born 1869 in Le Cateau/Northern France, died 1954 in Cimiez. After 1892 at the Académie Julian and the École des Beaux-Arts in Paris. 1895–1897 attended Moreau's studio, 1898/99 stay in Corsica and Toulouse. 1905 first group exhibition of the "Fauves" (Wild Beasts) at the Salon d'Automne. 1908 journey to Germany. 1908–1910 directed own art school in Paris. 1910–1913 travelled in Spain, Moscow, Morocco. After 1917 wintered in Nice. 1930 journey to Tahiti and the USA. After 1938 lived in Cimiez near Nice. 1943–1948 in Vence, afterwards back in Cimiez.

25

La Coiffure

The Toilet

1907
Oil on canvas, 116 × 89 cm
Signed lower left: Henri Matisse
Collection Michel and Sarah Stein, Paris. —
Collection Trygve Sagen, Oslo. —
Collection P. Krag, Oslo. —
Collection Ragnar Moltzau, Oslo. —
Purchased 1959.

In der Flächenbindung der Darstellung und im tektonischen Aufbau der Komposition noch auf den Errungenschaften von Gauguin und Cézanne fußend, diese aber frei variierend und eigener Bildgestalt zuführend, ist »La Coiffure« ein für den »Fauvisten« Matisse auffallend streng gegliedertes Werk. Zwei Frauen — eine stehend, die andere sitzend — sind so angeordnet, daß sie in ihrer Gruppierung ein gleichschenkliges Dreieck ergeben, dessen Spitzen außerhalb der Bildfläche liegen. Der Zweizahl der Figuren entspricht die Teilung der Wand in zwei schmucklose Flächen, deren linke etwa ein Drittel des Bildgrundes einnimmt. Auch im Farbigen waltet Ökonomie: hellere und dunklere Töne korrespondieren in freier Symmetrie miteinander. Das »schattenlose Licht« legt Kontur, Farbe und Form in ihrem »Eigenwert« bloß, um die innerhalb des Bildorganismus wirksamen Spannungen zu intensivieren. Der Wechsel zwischen dem kraftvollen Duktus der Zeichnung und schraffierender Modulation in der Art von Cézanne verstärkt diese Wirkung. Bernd Rau hat erkannt, daß »La Coiffure« motivisch auf Renoirs themengleiches Gemälde von 1883 zurückgeht: Matisse wiederholt spiegelbildlich die stehende Gestalt im grünen Kleid, verwandelt das bei Renoir noch bekleidete sitzende Modell jedoch in einen Akt von fast »kubisch« facettierter Plastizität und fügt anstelle des Mobiliars einen betont planen, die ornamentale Verspannung der Figuren stützenden Hintergrund ein. La Coiffure ist 1907, also gleichzeitig mit dem Kubismus, entstanden: während es den Kubisten aber um eine Analyse der Form geht, steigert Matisse vor allem die Eigendynamik der Farbe, die er im »dekorativen« Kontext seiner nur wenig späteren Bilder »reiner Flächigkeit« zuführen sollte.

"La Coiffure" is an exceptionally severely articulated work for the "Fauve" painter Matisse; still based on the achievements of Gauguin and Cézanne in the planar synthesis of the representation and architectural construction, but freely adapting these sources and introducing a personal pictorial form. Two women — one standing, the other seated — are so arranged that their grouping builds an isosceles triangle whose corners lie beyond the picture plane. The two figures correspond to the division of the wall into two undecorated planes, the left of which occupies about one-third of the ground. Colouristically too, economy is the order of the day: lighter and darker tones correspond in a loose symmetry. A "shadowless light" lays bare the intrinsic value of contour, colour and form in order to intensify the effective tensions within the pictorial organism. The interchange between the powerful drawn line and modulated crosshatching in the style of Cézanne strengthens this effect. Bernd Rau has recognized that the motif of "La Coiffure" refers to Renoir's painting of the same subject in 1883. Matisse repeats in inverted form the standing figure in green but transforms the seated model, who is still dressed in Renoir's work, into a nude whose faceted plasticity is "almost cubist". Instead of furniture Matisse introduces an emphatically planar background, which emphasizes the ornamental scaffolding of the figures. "La Coiffure" was painted in 1907, contemporary to the birth of cubism. But while the cubists were concerned with an analysis of form, Matisse intensifies above all the inherent dynamism of colour, which he was to introduce as "pure colour planes" in the "decorative" context of his slightly later paintings.

Literatur: Kat. 1961, S. 77ff. mit Abb. — Kat. 1968, S. 120 mit Abb. — Kat. 1982, 20. Jahrhundert, S. 220ff. mit Abb. — Werner Deusch, Neuere Malerei in der Staatsgalerie Stuttgart, S. 60ff. mit Abb. — Gotthard Jedlicka, Henri Matisse — La Coiffure, Reclams Werkmonographien 107, Stuttgart 1965. — Bernd Rau, Henri Matisse und Auguste Renoir — eine schöpferische Begegnung, in: Studien zur Kunst, Gunther Thiem zum 60. Geburtstag, Stuttgart 1977, S. 45ff. mit Abb.

Bibliography: Cat. 1961, p. 77f. with ill. — Cat. 1968, p. 120 with ill. — Cat. 1982, 20. Jahrhundert, p. 220f. with ill. — Werner Deusch, Neuere Malerei in der Staatsgalerie Stuttgart, p. 60f. with ill. — Gotthard Jedlicka, Henri Matisse — La Coiffure, Reclams Werkmonographien 107, Stuttgart 1965. — Bernd Rau, "Henri Matisse und Auguste Renoir — eine schöpferische Begegnung", in: Studien zur Kunst, Gunther Thiem zum 60. Geburtstag, Stuttgart 1977, p. 45f. with ill.

Pablo Picasso

Pablo Ruiz y Picasso, geboren 1881 in Malaga, gestorben 1973 in Mougins. Ausbildung an den Kunstschulen in La Coruña, Barcelona und Madrid, anschließend in Barcelona tätig. 1900 erster Besuch, 1901 und 1902 weitere Aufenthalte in Paris. »Blaue Periode« ca. 1901–1904. 1904 Übersiedlung nach Paris. »Rosa Periode« ca. 1905/06. 1906 Bekanntschaft mit Braque und Matisse, »Iberische Periode«. 1907 Vollendung der »Demoiselles d'Avignon«, Beginn des Kubismus. 1911–1914 Sommeraufenthalte in Spanien und Südfrankreich mit Derain, Braque und Juan Gris. 1917 Reise nach Italien. Nach 1920 »Neoklassische Periode«. 1937 »Guernica« für den spanischen Pavillon der Pariser Weltausstellung. Seit Kriegsende vor allem in Südfrankreich.

26

Kauernde

Auch »Femme assise au capuchon«, »Femme accroupée«, und »Kauernde Frau an der Mauer« genannt. Entstanden 1902

Auf der Rückseite die »Artisten« von 1905
Öl auf Leinwand, 90 × 71 cm
Bezeichnet rechts oben: Picasso
Sammlung Gertrude Stein, Paris. –
Sammlung Dr. Muthmann, Nassau. –
Dr. Fritz Nathan, Zürich. – Erworben 1959.

Das Bild stammt aus der »Blauen Periode«, die von wachsender Selbständigkeit im Schaffen des jungen Picasso geprägt ist. Erinnerungen an Toulouse, Degas und Steinlen werden allmählich verdrängt oder – soweit ihnen stilbildende Wirkung zukam – auf ihre »Ausdrucksfunktion« hin befragt und gesteigert. Die Farbe, die um die Jahrhundertwende noch reich nuanciert ist, zieht sich auf einen tiefblauen, ins Grünliche spielenden »Generalton« (Haftmann) zurück, der sich – fern aller dinglichen Charakterisierung – als Medium einer die »Grundstimmung« des Bildes fördernden Gestaltung erweist. Das Motiv wird von allem illustrativen Beiwerk befreit, der Bildaufbau selbst stark vereinfacht und auf die Gesetzmäßigkeiten der Fläche bezogen. Steil türmen sich Mauer, Landschaft und Himmel übereinander; Raum weniger darstellend als suggerierend. Die Kauernde selbst ist in strengem, von der Schulter halb verdecktem Profil, doch großflächiger Modulation ihres Gesichts und der sie schützenden Kleidung gegeben. Reglos, in sich zusammengesunken, von Armut und Elend gezeichnet, ist sie auf erschütternde Weise präsent in ihrer ausweglosen Isolation.

The painting dates from the "Blue Period", which is characterized by a growing independence in the art of the young Picasso. Memories of Toulouse Lautrec, of Degas and Steinlen are gradually superceded or – in as far as they constituted a shaping stylistic influence – investigated for their expressive potential and intensified. Colour, which at the turn of the century was still richly nuanced, withdraws into a deep blue "general tone" (Haftmann) touching on green which – removed from all material characterization – serves as a medium to promote the underlying mood of the painting. The motif is freed of all illustrative accessories, the pictorial construction itself is radically simplified and subjected to the inherent laws of the picture plane. Wall, landscape and sky are piled up steeply on top of each other; less representing than suggesting space. The crouching figure herself is rendered in a rigorous profile which is half hidden by her shoulder; but her face and protective clothing are broadly modelled. Motionless, sunk within herself and scarred by poverty and wretchedness, she is movingly affective in her hopeless isolation.

Pablo Picasso

Pablo Ruiz y Picasso, born 1881 in Malaga, died 1973 in Mougins. Training at the art schools in La Coruña, Barcelona and Madrid, subsequently active in Barcelona. 1900 first visit, 1901 and 1902 further stays in Paris. "Blue Period" circa 1901–1904. 1904 moved to Paris. "Rose Period" circa 1905/06. 1906 aquaintance with Braque and Matisse, "Iberian Period". 1907 completed the "Demoiselles d'Avignon", beginning of Cubism. 1911–1914 summered in Spain and the South of France with Derain, Braque and Juan Gris. 1917 journey to Italy. After 1920 "Neoclassical Period". 1937 "Guernica" for the Spanish pavillion at the Paris World Fair. After the war mainly in the South of France.

26

Crouching Woman

Also known as "Femme assise au capuchon", "Femme accroupée" and "Crouching woman by a wall". 1902

Reverse: "Acrobats", 1905
Oil on canvas, 90 × 71 cm
Signed upper right: Picasso
Collection Gertrude Stein, Paris. –
Collection Dr. Muthmann, Nassau. –
Dr. Fritz Nathan, Zürich. – Purchased 1959.

Literatur: Kat. 1961, S. 85 ff. mit Abb. – Kat. 1968, S. 136 ff. mit Abb. – Kat. 1982, 20. Jahrhundert, S. 254 ff. mit Abb. – Werner Deusch, Neuere Malerei in der Staatsgalerie Stuttgart, S. 48 ff. mit Abb. – Gudrun Inboden, in: Große Gemäldegalerien, herausgegeben von Erich Steingräber, München 1980, S. 454 mit Abb.

Bibliography: Cat. 1961, p. 85 f. with ill. – Cat. 1968, p. 136 f. with ill. – Cat. 1982, 20. Jahrhundert, p. 254 f. with ill. – Werner Deusch, Neuere Malerei in der Staatsgalerie Stuttgart, p. 48 f. with ill. – Gudrun Inboden, in: Große Gemäldegalerien, ed. by Erich Steingräber, Munich 1980, p. 454 with ill.

Pablo Picasso

27

Artisten

Auch »Les Baladins«, »Die Gaukler«
oder »Mutter und Kind« genannt

Entstanden 1905
Gouache auf Leinwand, 90 × 71 cm
Sammlung Gertrude Stein, Paris. −
Sammlung Dr. Muthmann, Nassau. −
Dr. Fritz Nathan, Zürich. − Erworben 1959.

Pablo Picasso

27

Acrobats

Also known as "Les Baladins", "The
Clowns" or "Mother and Child"

1905
Gouache on canvas, 90 × 71 cm
Collection Gertrude Stein, Paris −
Collection Dr. Muthmann, Nassau. −
Dr. Fritz Nathan, Zürich. −
Purchased 1959.

Das Bild − Rückseite des Gemäldes die »Kauernde«, von 1902 − ist ein Hauptwerk der »Rosa Periode«, in der Picasso fast ausschließlich Themen aus dem Artisten- und Zirkusmilieu gestaltet hat. Seine Bedeutung liegt weniger im rein malerischen Aufbau der Komposition (vgl. die Kauernde), als in der feiner differenzierenden Zeichnung und dem anschaulich erlebbaren Zusammenwirken von Form, Farbe und Material. Überall tritt der bloße Grund zutage, ein ärmliches braunes Rupfengewebe, dessen rauhe Struktur durch die stumpfen Farben hindurchdringt. Morbides, zum Grau tendierendes Kalkweiß verleiht den Gesichtern krankhafte Blässe. Ein strenger Umriß trennt die Gestalt des Knaben von seiner Mutter, die ihren Kopf in die rechte Hand neigt. Kein warmer Lichtschimmer verklärt die Figuren oder den schäbigen Flitterkram ihrer Kleider. Müde Einsamkeit umgibt die Fahrenden, deren Leben von Entbehrung geprägt ist. Im Unterschied zu den »verhärteten« Zügen der Zigeuner- und Bettlerbildnisse der vorangegangenen Jahre drückt sich in den zarten Physiognomien von Mutter und Sohn ein höheres Maß individueller Beseelung und Empfindsamkeit aus. Die rötliche Tönung des Grundes geht auf das rosafarbene Zelt des Pariser Zirkus Medrano zurück, der den Künstler zu seiner Artistenserie anregte (vgl. Karin v. Maur im Kat. 1982).

The painting − on the reverse of "Crouching Woman", 1902 − is a masterwork of Picasso's "Rose Period", in which he almost exclusively depicted subjects from the milieu of the circus and the variety. Its importance lies less in the purely painterly disposition of the composition (compare "Crouching Woman") than in the finely differentiated drawing an the interplay of form, colour and material. The bare primed canvas appears all over, a simple brown sackcloth weave, whose raw structure penetrates through the muted colours. A morbid chalk-white, tending towards grey, lends the faces a sickly palour. A strong contour separates the boy from his mother, whose head is inclined in her right hand. No warm shimmer of light illuminates the figures or the tawdry finery of their clothes. Weary loneliness surrounds the travelling players, whose life is deeply marked by privation. In contrast to the "hardened" features of the gypsy and beggar portraits of preceding years, a high degree of individual inspiration and sensitivity is expressed in the delicate physiognomies of the mother and son. The red tone of the background refers to the pink coloured marquee of the Parisian Circus Medrano, which inspired the artist's series of acrobats (see Karin v. Maur in Cat. 1982).

Literatur: Kat. 1961, S. 86 mit Abb. − Kat. 1968, S. 137 ff. mit Abb. − Kat. 1982, 20. Jahrhundert, S. 255 mit Abb. − Werner Deusch, Neuere Malerei in der Staatsgalerie Stuttgart, S. 50 ff. mit Abb. − Gudrun Inboden, in: Große Gemäldegalerien, herausgegeben von Erich Steingräber, München 1980, S. 458 mit Abb.

Bibliography: Cat. 1961, p. 86 with ill. − Cat. 1968, p. 137 f. with ill. − Cat. 1982. 20. Jahrhundert, p. 255 with ill. − Werner Deusch, Neuere Malerei in der Staatsgalerie Stuttgart, p. 50 f. with ill. − Gudrun Inboden, in: Große Gemäldegalerien, ed. by Erich Steingräber, Munich 1980, p. 458 with ill.

Pablo Picasso

28

Violine – Jolie Eva

Entstanden 1912
Öl auf Leinwand, 60 × 81 cm
Bezeichnet auf der Rückseite: Picasso.
Sammlung Alphonse Kann,
Saint-Germain-en-Laye. –
Sammlung RagnarMoltzau, Oslo. –
Erworben 1959.

Pablo Picasso

28

Violin – Jolie Eva

1912
Oil on canvas, 60 × 81 cm
Signed on the reverse: Picasso.
Collection Alphonse Kann,
Saint-Germain-en-Laye. –
Collection Ragnar Moltzau, Oslo. –
Purchased 1959.

Innerhalb der Kunst des 20. Jahrhunderts setzte der Kubismus die wohl folgenreichste Zäsur. Begründet wurde er von dem Spanier Picasso und dem Franzosen Georges Braque. Beider Streben galt dem gleichen Ziel: das Bild vom Vorbild zu lösen, es frei und selbständig zu machen, also letzte Konsequenzen aus den Bemühungen Cézannes zu ziehen. Von der Transformation zur Deformation, von vereinfachender Stereometrie zu totaler Zerlegung des Bildmotivs fortschreitend, stand der Kubismus um 1912 auf dem Höhepunkt seiner zweiten, der analytischen Phase. In diesem Jahr ist auch die Stuttgarter Violine entstanden. In kompakter, reliefhafter Schichtung sind die einzelnen Formelemente ineinander verschränkt und kontrapunktisch aufeinander bezogen: Rundung und Fläche, Struktur und Farbe, Bewegung und Gegenbewegung bedingen und steigern einander. Das Kolorit – auf Grau und Braun, die von den Kubisten bevorzugten Farben beschränkt – tendiert jedoch weniger zu monochromer Verschmelzung, als es – unterstützt vom kraftvollen Duktus der Zeichnung – die im Bildorganismus wirksamen Spannungen aufnimmt. Ein autonomes Gemälde ist hier entstanden, das von einer veränderten Einstellung zur Realität, aber auch von einem revolutionären Befreiungsakt künstlerischer Gestaltungskraft zeugt, indem es die Identität zwischen Darstellung und Dargestelltem zugunsten eigenständiger Formbildung aufhebt. Die Inschrift »Jolie Eva« bezieht sich auf die damalige Gefährtin Picassos Eva Gouel, deren Kosename »Ma Jolie« auf den Titel eines zeitgenössischen Chansons zurückgeht.

Cubism certainly effected the break in 20th century art that had the most far reaching consequences. It was founded by the Spaniard Picasso and the Frenchman Georges Braque. Both strove for the same goal: to liberate painting from the model, to render it free and independent, to draw the logical consequences, that is, from Cézanne's endeavours. Progressing from transformation to deformation, from a simplifying stereometry to total disassembly of the pictorial motif, Cubism in 1912 stood at the climax of its second "analytical" phase. In this year the Stuttgart Violin was also painted. In compact relief-like layers the individual formal elements are folded into each other and set in a relation of counterpoint: curve and plane, structure and colour, movement and counter-movement mutually condition and intensify each other. The colour scale, reduced to the preferred cubist colours of grey and brown, tends not so much towards a monochrome fusion but rather, reinforced by the powerful line of the drawing, it takes on the active tensions of the pictorial whole. An autonomous painting is produced that bears witness to a new attitude to reality; but also to a revolutionary liberation of artistic creative force, as the identification of depiction and depicted is set aside in favour of a self-sufficient formal construction. The inscription "Jolie Eva" refers to Picasso's current companion Eva Gonel whose pet name "Ma Jolie" derived from the title of a contemporary popular song.

Literatur: Kat. 1961, S. 87 mit Abb. – Kat. 1968, S. 137 ff. mit Abb. – Kat. 1982, 20. Jahrhundert, S. 256 mit Abb. – Werner Deusch, Neuere Malerei in der Staatsgalerie Stuttgart, S. 64 ff. mit Abb.

Bibliography: Cat. 1961, p. 87 with ill. – Cat. 1968, p. 137 f. with ill. – Cat. 1982, 20. Jahrhundert, p. 256 with ill. – Werner Deusch, Neuere Malerei in der Staatsgalerie Stuttgart, p. 64 f. with ill.

Pablo Picasso

29

Sitzende

Auch »Buste de Femme«
oder »Frau im Hemd« genannt

Öl auf Leinwand, 116 × 73 cm
Bezeichnet rechts unten: Picasso 21.
Sammlung J. Eichmann, Zürich. –
Sammlung Bührle, Zürich. –
Sammlung Ragnar Moltzau, Oslo. –
Erworben 1959.

Pablo Picasso

29

Seated Woman

Also known as "Buste de Femme"
or "Woman in a chemise"

Oil on canvas, 116 × 73 cm
Signed lower right: Picasso 21.
Collection J. Eichmann, Zurich. –
Collection Bührle, Zurich. –
Collection Ragnar Moltzau, Oslo –
Purchased 1959.

Um 1920 entwickelte Pablo Picasso – angeregt durch einen Italienaufenthalt im Jahre 1917 – einen neuen, großen Figuralstil, den seiner »neoklassischen Periode«. Für das Klassische war der Künstler – sowohl motivisch als auch stilistisch – Zeit seines Lebens ohnedies disponiert. Schon 1905/06 – in seiner »iberischen«, dem Kubismus unmittelbar vorausgehenden Periode – hatte er einige Akte gemalt, deren voluminöse Plastizität er im gereiften Stil der frühen 20er Jahre wieder aufnehmen, doch in stärker harmonisierender Gestaltung abwandeln sollte. Die »Sitzende« verkörpert diesen Stil in exemplarischer Ausprägung. Alles in diesem Gemälde ist groß, im Wortsinn »monumental« gesehen: der schwere, massige Körper, der gedrungene, auffallend breite Hals, der mächtige Kopf mit der keilartig vorspringenden Nase, das großzügig gewellte Haar, die klobig erscheinenden Arme und Hände. Jede Einzelform ist in kraftvoll sich steigernder Rundung entwickelt, in fast kolossal anmutender Maßstäblichkeit, die auch den Aufbau der Figur im ganzen bestimmt. Eine urtümliche, gleichsam archaische Wirkung geht von der körperhaften, ja »raumsprengenden« Präsenz dieser Sitzenden aus; selbst das zarte, pastellhafte Kolorit vermag diesen Eindruck nur wenig zu mildern.

Around 1920 – inspired by his stay in Italy in 1917 – Pablo Picasso developed a new great figure style, that of his "neoclassical period". All his life the artist had anyway a disposition towards the classical – both thematically and stylistically. Already in 1905/06 – in his "Iberian" period that immediately preceded Cubism – he had painted several nudes whose voluminous plasticity he was to take up again in the mature style of the early 1920s; yet transformed into a more powerfully harmonic form. The "Seated Woman" embodies this style in an exemplary way. Everything in this painting is large in the sense of "monumental": the heavy solid body, the thickset conspicuously broad neck, the powerful head with its wedge-like protruding nose, the generously wavy hair, the bulky appearance of the arms and hands. Each individual form is developed in a powerful rising roundedness, as if on a seemingly colossal scale which also determines the construction of the figure as a whole. An original, one might say an archaic force emanates from the corporeal, even "spatially transgressive" presence of this seated woman. The delicate pastel toned colouration serves to soften this effect only a little.

Literatur: Kat. 1961, S. 87 ff. mit Abb. –
Kat. 1968, S. 138 mit Abb. – Kat. 1982,
20. Jahrhundert, S. 259 mit Abb.

Bibliography: Cat. 1961, p. 87 f. with ill. –
Cat. 1968, p. 138 with ill. – Cat. 1982,
20. Jahrhundert, p. 259 with ill.

Pablo Picasso

30

Die Badenden

Entstanden 1956
Holz, teils bemalt, teils mit Einritzungen
und Einbrennungen versehen. Ehemals
Sammlung Marina Picasso. — Erworben
aus Mitteln der »Museumsstiftung Baden-
Württemberg« 1981/82.

Die Taucherin
Höhe 264 cm

Mann mit gefalteten Händen
Höhe 214 cm

Der Brunnenmann
Höhe 227 cm

Das Kind
Höhe 136 cm

Frau mit ausgestreckten Armen
Höhe 198 cm

Der junge Mann
Höhe 176 cm

Pablo Picasso

30

The Bathers

1956
Wood, partially painted, partially
furnished with scratches and burns.
Formerly Collection Marina Picasso. —
Purchased with funds from the "Museums-
stiftung Baden-Württemberg" 1981/82.

Woman Diver
Height 264 cm

Man with folded arms
Height 214 cm

Fountain Man
Height 227 cm

Child
Height 136 cm

Woman with outstretched arms
Height 198 cm

Young Man
Height 176 cm

Wohl angeregt durch die monumentale Flächenskulptur eines Kentauren, die er 1955 während der Dreharbeiten für den Film »Le mystère Picasso« von Clouzot geschaffen hatte, faßte Picasso im Sommer 1956 den Entschluß, auch das Bademotiv — eines der Leitthemen seiner Kunst überhaupt — als selbständige plastische Gruppe zu gestalten. Die sechs zum Teil überlebensgroßen Figuren sind aus einfachen, gerade verfügbaren Fundstücken montiert, durch die ihr Erscheinungsbild weitgehend determiniert wird. Nur partiell bemalt oder durch präzisierende Einritzungen und Einbrennungen belebt, bilden sie in ihrer statuarischen Vereinzelung und Frontalität ein Ensemble von suggestiver Eindringlichkeit. In Ausdruck und Haltung an mythische Kultfiguren erinnernd, stehen sie da, pfahlartig aufragend oder weitausgreifend, so daß sich der Eindruck eines Rituals aufdrängt. Diese über das Thema hinausweisende »Mehrschichtigkeit«, die sich auch in einem von Picasso nachträglich in Zeichnungen fixierten badeszenenartigen Arrangement nicht verliert, findet in der Assemblage-Konstruktion ihr formales Äquivalent. Der betont silhouettenhafte Aufbau der Form und ihre durch das »Rohmaterial« noch verstärkte Ausdrucksgewalt verleihen den Einzelgestalten »den Charakter monumentaler Schattenfiguren, die sich in magischer Choreographie gruppieren« (Karin v. Maur). Eine nur wenig spätere Bronzeversion und ein nachträglich noch stark modifizierter Wandbildentwurf (1957) für das Pariser Unesco-Gebäude wiederholen die Komposition in nur geringer Abwandlung der Einzelmotive.

Im Bestand der Staatsgalerie, die über die wohl reichste Picasso-Sammlung in Deutschland verfügt, setzt das aus Mitteln der »Museumsstiftung Baden-Württembergs« erworbene Figurenensemble einen spektakulären Akzent. Als das plastische Hauptwerk aus der Spätzeit des Künstlers wird es durch eine bedeutende frühe Plastik, die Violine von 1912 (Leihgabe), sinnvoll ergänzt. Vor allem aber bildet die Gruppe einen höchst eindrucksvollen Kontrast zu den Figurinen des Triadischen Balletts von Oskar Schlemmer.

Certainly inspired by the monumental sculptural relief of a centaur which he made during the filming of "Le mystère Picasso" by Clouzot in 1955, Picasso decided in 1956 to render the bathers motif too — one of the main themes of his art in general — as an independent sculptural group. The six, partly over life-size figures are assembled from simple readily available found objects, which determine to a large extent their appearance. Only partially painted or animated by descriptive scratches and burns, they form a suggestively forceful ensemble with their statuesque isolation and frontality. Reminiscent of cult figures in their expression and attitude, they stand there, projecting upwards like an arrow or reaching out sideways so that a ritualistic impression obtrudes. This "multilayerdness" which reaches beyond the subject itself and which also persists in the bather-like arrangement Picasso subsequently formulated in drawings, finds its formal equivalent in the assemblage-construction. The emphatically silhouette-like formal construction and the expressive impact which the "raw materials" further augment, lend the individual figures "the character of monumental shadow puppets who come together in a magic choreography" (Karin v. Maur). A slightly later bronze version and a subsequent much modified mural design (1957) for the Paris Unesco building repeat the composition with only minor changes in the individual motifs.

In the Staatsgalerie collection, which certainly is equipped with the richest Picasso collection in Germany, the figure ensemble which was purchased with funds from the "Museumsstiftung Baden-Württemberg", provides a spectacular accent. As the sculptural masterpiece of the artist's late years it is well complemented by an important early sculpture, the Violin from 1912. Above all however, the group forms a most impressive contrast to the figurines in Oskar Schlemmer's Triadic Ballet.

Literatur: Kat. 1982, 20. Jahrhundert, S. 260 ff. mit Abb. — Ausst.-Kat. Picasso — Das plastische Werk, Nationalgalerie Berlin und Kunsthalle Düsseldorf, 1983/84, S. 296 ff. mit Abb. (Werner Spies).

Bibliography: Cat. 1982, 20. Jahrhundert, p. 260 f. with ill. — Cat. Picasso — Das plastische Werk, Nationalgalerie Berlin und Kunsthalle Düsseldorf, 1983/84, p. 296 f. with ill. (Werner Spies).

Georges Braque

Geboren 1882 in Argenteuil-sur-Seine, gestorben 1963 in Paris. 1897–1899 an der Kunstschule in Le Havre und Lehre bei einem Dekorationsmaler. Seit 1900 in Paris. 1902–1904 an der Académie Humbert. 1905–1910 Aufenthalte in L'Estaque. 1911 mit Picasso in Céret. 1914–1916 Soldat. Seit 1917 in Paris, 1928 in Dieppe. Seit 1931 in Varengeville, unterbrochen durch Aufenthalte in Paris.

31

Violine

Entstanden 1912
Öl auf Leinwand, 82 × 61 cm
Bezeichnet auf der Rückseite: Braque.
Daniel-Henry Kahnweiler, Paris. –
Sammlung L. Kochnitzky, Brüssel. –
Sammlung David Thompson, Pittsburgh. –
Sammlung Ragnar Moltzau, Oslo. –
Erworben 1959.

Innerhalb des analytischen Kubismus, der um 1910 einsetzt und seinen Kulminationspunkt um 1912 erreicht, gilt Georges Braque als der neben Picasso führende Künstler. Wie dieser (vgl. Tafel 28, S. 126) entwickelt er seine Kunst vorzugsweise am gleichsam »neutralen« Thema des Stillebens. Auch auf dem Stuttgarter Bild — einer Violine wie auf dem Gemälde Picassos — ist der Gegenstand so weit zerlegt, daß man ihn nur in fragmentarischer Andeutung wahrnimmt. Das in sich reich facettierte Gefüge des Bildes ist von auffallender Transparenz und Klarheit. Die einzelnen Formelemente entbehren aller Plastizität; ihr Erscheinungsbild teilt sich verhalten, fast nur umrißhaft, mit. Das Kolorit wirkt im Vergleich zu Picasso gedämpfter, ordnet sich der das Bild gliedernden Zeichnung wahrnehmbar unter. Die Farben — auf Braun und Grau reduziert — tendieren weit mehr zu monochromer Verschmelzung und entsprechen so noch stärker den Gesetzmäßigkeiten der Fläche. Trotz unterschiedlicher Interpretation des Motivs — die Version Picassos ist vitaler, die Braques rationaler — zielt beider Gestaltung in dieselbe Richtung: der äußeren Realität eine solche der Kunst gegenüberzustellen; denn auch für Braque gilt ein Bild erst dann als vollendet (er selbst verwendet den Terminus »fertig«), »wenn die Idee, die anfänglich darin enthalten war, völlig ausgelöscht ist«.

In the history of analytical Cubism, which began around 1910 and reached its culmination around 1912, Georges Braque is known, with Picasso, as the leading artist. Like Picasso (compare plate 28, p. 126) he preferred to develop his art in the same "neutral" genre of still life. In the Stuttgart work — as in Picasso's painting, a violin — the object is so dismembered that we only recognize it as a fragmentary trace. The richly faceted structure of the work is strikingly transparent and lucid. The individual formal elements lack all plasticity; their appearance is understated, conveyed almost solely by outlines. In comparison with Picasso the colouration seems more subdued, noticeably subordinated to the drawing that articulates the picture. The colours — reduced to brown and grey — tend far more towards a monochrome fusion and correspond accordingly more strongly to the inherent laws of the picture plane. Despite their different readings of the motif — Picasso's version is more vital, Braque's more rational — both paintings have the same objective: to confront exterior reality with the reality of art. For Braque too a picture was only considered complete (he actually employed the terminus "ready"), "when the idea which it originally contained is totally effaced".

Georges Braque

Born 1882 in Argenteuil-sur-Seine, died 1963 in Paris. 1897–1899 at the art school in Le Havre and apprenticeship with a decorator. After 1900 in Paris. 1902–1904 at the Académie Humbert. 1905–1910 visits to L'Estaque. 1911 with Picasso in Céret. 1914–1916 soldier. After 1917 in Paris, 1928 in Dieppe. After 1931 in Varengeville interrupted by periods of residence in Paris.

31

Violin

1912
Oil on canvas, 82 × 61 cm
Signed on reverse: Braque.
Daniel-Henry Kahnweiler, Paris. –
Collection L. Kochnitzky, Brussels. –
Collection David Thompson, Pittsburgh. –
Collection Ragnar Moltzau, Oslo. –
Purchased 1959.

Literatur: Kat. 1961, S. 23. – Kat. 1968, S. 31 ff. mit Abb. – Kat. 1982, 20. Jahrhundert, S. 96 mit Abb. – Werner Deusch, Neuere Malerei in der Staatsgalerie Stuttgart, S. 66 mit Abb.

Bibliography: Cat. 1961, p. 23. – Cat. 1968, p. 31 f. with ill. – Cat. 1982, 20. Jahrhundert, p. 96 with ill. – Werner Deusch, Neuere Malerei in der Staatsgalerie Stuttgart, p. 66 with ill.

Fernand Léger

Geboren 1881 in Argentan/Normandie, gestorben 1955 in Gif-sur-Yvette. 1897–1899 Lehre in einem Architektenbüro in Caen. Seit 1900 in Paris. 1903/04 an der École des Arts Décoratifs. 1910 Verbindung zum Kubismus. 1914–1916 Militärdienst. 1920 Begegnung mit Le Corbusier. 1924 Film »Ballet mécanique«; Italienreise. Verbindung zum holländischen DeStijl. Seit 1928 ausgedehnte Reisen in Europa und nach Amerika. 1940–1945 in den USA. 1945 Rückkehr nach Paris. 1952 Übersiedlung nach Gif-sur-Yvette bei Paris.

32

Étude pour la partie de cartes

Studie zu »Das Kartenspiel«

Entstanden 1918
Öl auf Leinwand, 92,4 × 73,2 cm
Rechts unten bezeichnet und (fälschlich)
1919 datiert.
Sammlung Louis Carré, Paris. –
Sammlung de Montaigu, Paris. – Erworben
aus dem Schweizer Kunsthandel 1963.

Légers Malerei ist weit mehr als die seiner Weggefährten innerhalb des Kubismus vom Erlebnis der Technik bestimmt. Der kraftvolle Bau seiner Bilder beruht auf dem Kontrast plastisch gerundeter und flacher Bestandteile, die lebhaft voneinander abgesetzt und durch starke, die Partikel leuchtend akzentuierende Farben gekennzeichnet sind. Deutlich wird dies am Beispiel des hier reproduzierten Bildes, in dem der Künstler auf ein Motiv aus dem großen, ein Jahr früher entstandenen Gemälde »La partie des cartes« zurückgreift, nun alle anthropomorphen Körper restlos abstrahierend zur technisch-mechanischen Formenwelt hin. Der große optische Reiz besteht in dem Changieren zwischen den exakt modellierten perspektivischen Röhrenformen und den eingesprengten rein geometrischen Farbflächen. Im dynamischen Kräftespiel dieser Formen und Farben treten bildgestaltende Qualitäten zutage, die sich nur themenfixierter Betrachtung entziehen. Die technoiden Elemente werden ihrer funktionellen Bestimmung enthoben und gleichsam zu »Bausteinen« einer – im Unterschied zu vergleichbaren Werken von Picasso und Braque – stark verräumlichten Bildkonstruktion, die sich jedoch einem betont flächig gegliederten Hintergrund zuordnet.

Leger's painting is far more strongly conditioned than his contempories in the cubist movement by the experience of technology. The powerful construction of his pictures depends on the contrast between sculpturally rounded and flat elements which are set off vibrantly from each other and characterized by strong colours that illuminate the separate features. This is clear in the example of the painting reproduced here, where the artist returns to a motif from the large painting "La partie des cartes" finished one year earlier, now completely abstracting all the anthropomorphic bodies into a technico-mechanical formal language. A considerable optical stimulus results from the oscillation between exactly modelled perspectival tubular forms and interspersed pure geometrical colour planes. In a dynamic play of forces between these forms and colours, suggestions of forms emerge which resist specific thematic interpretation. The technological elements are freed from their functional determination and simultaneously used as "building blocks" in a strongly spatial pictorial construction (in contrast to comparable works by Picasso and Braque), which is nevertheless adjoined to a insistently articulated planar background.

Fernand Léger

Born 1881 in Argentan/Normandy, died 1955 in Gif-sur-Yvette. 1897–1899 in an architectural office in Caen. After 1900 in Paris. 1903/04 at the École des Arts Décoratifs. 1910 association with Cubism. 1914 till 1916 military service. 1920 meeting with Le Corbusier. 1924 film "Ballet mécanique"; journey to Italy. Association with the Dutch group De Stijl. After 1928 lengthy journies in Europe and America. 1940–1945 in the USA. 1945 return to Paris. 1952 moved to Gif-sur-Yvette.

32

Étude pour la partie de cartes

Study for "La partie de cartes", 1918

Oil on canvas, 92.4 × 73.2 cm
Signed lower right and (wrongly)
dated 1919.
Collection Louis Carré, Paris. –
Collection de Montaigu, Paris. –
Purchased from the Swiss art market
in 1963.

Literatur: Kat. 1968, S. 106 mit Abb. –
Kat. 1982, 20. Jahrhundert, S. 195 ff. mit Abb.

Bibliography: Cat. 1968, p. 106 with ill. –
Cat. 1982, 20. Jahrhundert, p. 195 f. with ill.

Edvard Munch

Geboren 1863 in Löiten/Norwegen, gestorben 1944 auf Gut Ekely bei Oslo. 1882/83 an der Kunst- und Gewerbeschule Oslo, beeinflußt von H. Heyerdahl und Chr. Krohg. 1885 erster Aufenthalt in Paris. Seit 1889 wiederholte Reisen, u. a. nach Frankreich, Deutschland, Dänemark. Seit 1909 ständig in Norwegen.

33

Mädchenakt auf rotem Tuch

Entstanden 1902
Öl auf Leinwand, 81 × 65 cm
Bezeichnet links unten: E. Munch.
Sammlung Dr. Gustav Schiefler,
Hamburg. – Gedächtnisstiftung des
Stuttgarter Industriellen Dr. A. Klein,
ausgeführt von dessen Erben 1960.

Edvard Munch

Born 1863 in Löiten/Norway, died 1944 on Ekely a country-seat near Oslo. 1882/83 at the school of fine and decorative arts in Oslo, influenced by H. Heyerdahl and Chr. Krohg. 1885 first visit to Paris. After 1889 numerous journies to France, Germany and Denmark. After 1909 permanently in Norway.

33

Nude Girl on a red Cover

1902
Oil on canvas 81 × 65 cm
Signed lower left: E. Munch.
Collection Dr. Gustav Schiefler,
Hamburg. –
Donated in memory of the Stuttgart
industrialist Dr. A. Klein by his heirs
in 1960.

Von seinem Dichterfreund Strindberg als der »esoterische Maler der Liebe, der Eifersucht und des Todes« apostrophiert, steht Edvard Munch um 1900 bereits an der Schwelle zum Expressionismus, der ihm entscheidende Impulse verdankt. Menschen und Landschaft dienen ihm nicht als Objekt abbildhafter Gestaltung, sondern als Gefäß seelischer Empfindungen. Um die Gewalt dieser Empfindungen sichtbar zu machen, mußten Zeichnung und Farbe aus ihrer rein »beschreibenden« Funktion gelöst, in ihrem Ausdrucksgehalt intensiviert und damit instandgesetzt werden, psychische Betroffenheit zu reflektieren. Auch der »Mädchenakt auf rotem Tuch« ist keine »Étude de Nu« im üblichen Sinn, sondern ein symbolträchtiges, zutiefst erregendes Bild. Alles Räumliche ist hier verunklärt, löst sich im Strudel der Farbe und im Atmosphärischen auf. Dergestalt wird der Raum gleichsam zum »Echo« des von der Flut rotbrauner Haare umspielten Gesichts, das von erwachender Liebe, Wollust und angstvoller Spannung gezeichnet ist. Die Farbigkeit – im besonderen das »Blut« assoziierende Rot – verstärkt diese Wirkung. Wie eigentlich immer erweist sich die Bildgestalt Munchs in der existenzbedingten Verflechtung ihres formalen Aufbaus als Einheit, oder mit anderen Worten als das, was Stanislaw Przybyszewski einmal so treffend das »absolute Korrelat des nackten Empfindens« genannt hat.

Invoked as "the esoteric painter of love, of jealousy and of death" by his poet friend Strindberg, Edvard Munch already stood in 1900 on the threshold of Expressionism which owes important stimuli to him. Human beings and landscape do not serve him as objects of representational configuration but rather as recepticles of emotional sensation. To make visible the power of these sensations, drawing and colour are released from their purely "descriptive" function, intensified as vehicles of expression and so put in a position to reflect psychic shock. The "Nude girl on a red cover" is not an "Étude de Nu" in the conventional sense, but rather a symbolically pregnant and deeply provocative picture. Space is obscured here, dissolved in the vortex of colour and atmosphere. In this way space becomes simultaneously an "echo" of the face (surrounded by a flood of red-brown hair), which is characterized by awakening love, lust and anxious tension. The colouration – in particular the red we associate with blood – intensifies this effect. As always Munch's visual creation proves unified in the existential interweaving of its pictorial form or, in other words, as Stanislaw Przybyszewski once so appropriately remarked, it is an "absolute analogue of bare sensation".

Literatur: Kat. 1961, S. 81 mit Abb. – Kat. 1968, S. 129 mit Abb. – Kat. 1982, 20. Jahrhundert, S. 240 ff. mit Abb. – Werner Deusch, Neuere Malerei in der Staatsgalerie Stuttgart, S. 34 mit Abb.

Bibliography: Cat. 1961, p. 81 with ill. – Cat. 1968, p. 129 with ill. – Cat. 1982, 20. Jahrhundert, p. 240 f. with ill. – Werner Deusch, Neuere Malerei in der Staatsgalerie Stuttgart, p. 34 with ill.

Karl Schmidt-Rottluff

Geboren 1884 in Rottluff bei Chemnitz, gestorben 1976 in Berlin. 1903 Bekanntschaft mit Erich Heckel. 1904 Beginn der Malerei. 1905 Architekturstudium an der Technischen Hochschule Dresden. Mitbegründer der Künstlergruppe »Die Brücke«. 1906 bei Emil Nolde auf Alsen. 1907–1912 Sommeraufenthalte in Dangast, zeitweilig mit Heckel. 1911 in Norwegen. Dann Übersiedlung nach Berlin. 1915–1918 Soldat. 1923–1925 Reisen nach Paris, Italien und Dalmatien. 1943 Übersiedlung nach Rottluff. 1947 Berufung an die Hochschule für Bildende Künste Berlin.

34

Oppedal

Hardanger Fjord

Öl auf Leinwand, 76 × 84,5 cm
Bezeichnet rechts unten: S. Rottluff 1911.
Sammlung Dr. Schottelius, Hamburg. –
Sammlung Dr. Max Lütze, Hamburg. –
Erworben 1977.

Ursprünglich zum Architekten bestimmt, hat Karl Schmidt-Rottluff auch in späterer Zeit ein stark ausgeprägtes Empfinden für das Gebaute, für eine tektonische Durchdringung des Bildes bewahrt. Von seinen impressionistischen Anfängen über eine allmähliche Formraffung zu immer stärkerer Vereinfachung fortschreitend, gelangte er um 1910 – und beispielhaft in der hier abgebildeten Landschaft – zu einer großflächigen Bildform, in der das Motivische wenn auch nicht gerade verdrängt, so doch einem strengen Formwillen untergeordnet ist. Unter bewußtem Verzicht auf Detailschilderung und vor allem auf Tiefe werden die Formen zu großen, »mauerhaft« wirksamen Komplexen zusammengefaßt und die Farben auf nur wenige komplementäre Werte beschränkt, die – fern aller Lokalfarbigkeit – ein dynamisches Eigenleben entwickeln. Das lineare Gerüst, das bisweilen zur Verankerung der Farbflächen dient, ist weitgehend getilgt: »das Bild wird zur Einheit miteinander verzahnter Teile, die ... für sich genommen schwer lesbare Umschreibungen für Formen der Natur sind« (Buchheim), obwohl sie – als Ganzes – doch auf ein Naturvorbild hinweisen. In der unaufhebbaren Ambivalenz von Anschaulichkeit und der sich verselbständigenden Ausdrucksgewalt der Farben liegt der außergewöhnliche Rang dieses Bildes.

Originally intended for architecture, Karl Schmidt-Rottluff always retained a strong feeling for construction, for a tectonic presence in the picture. Progressing from his impressionist beginnings by way of a gradual paring down of form to ever greater simplification, he achieved around 1910 a planar pictorial style – exemplified in the landscape illustrated here – in which the motif is not exactly suppressed, but certainly subordinated to a rigorous formal discipline. With a conscious renunciation of detail and above all of depth, the forms are combined in large "wall-like" complexes; and the colours are restricted to a few complimentary values which – without reference to local colour – develop an intense life of their own. The linear scaffolding which occasionally serves to anchor the colour planes is largely dispensed with: "the painting becomes a unity of dovetailed parts which are paraphrases – in themselves difficult to read – for forms in nature" (Buchheim). As a whole, the form nevertheless refer to a model in nature. The exceptional quality of this painting lies in the irreduceable ambivalence of clarity on the one hand and, on the other, the independent expressive power of the colours.

Karl Schmidt-Rottluff

Born 1884 in Rottluff near Chemnitz, died 1976 in Berlin. 1903 acquaintance with Erich Heckel. 1904 first paintings. 1905 student of architecture at the polytechnic in Dresden. Founder member of the artists' group "Die Brücke". 1906 visited Emil Nolde on Alsen. 1907–1912 summer residence in Dangast, intermittently with Heckel. 1911 in Norway. Subsequently moved to Berlin. 1915–1918 military service. 1923–1925 trips to Paris, Italy and Dalmatia. 1943 returned to Rottluff. 1947 appointment at the "Hochschule für Bildende Künste" in Berlin.

34

Oppedal

Hardanger Fjord

Oil on canvas, 76,5 × 84.5 cm
Signed lower right: S. Rottluff 1911.
Collection Dr. Schottelius, Hamburg. –
Collection Dr. Max Lütze, Hamburg. –
Purchased 1977.

Literatur: Kat. 1982, 20. Jahrhundert, S. 304 mit Abb.

Bibliography: Cat. 1982, 20. Jahrhundert, p. 304 with ill.

Ernst Ludwig Kirchner

Geboren 1880 in Aschaffenburg, gestorben 1938 durch Freitod in Davos. 1901–1905 Architekturstudium in Dresden und Malstudien in München. 1905 Mitbegründer der Künstlergemeinschaft »Die Brücke« in Dresden. 1911 Übersiedlung nach Berlin. 1912–1914 Sommeraufenthalte auf Fehmarn. 1914 Meldung zum Militärdienst, 1915 Zusammenbruch und Aufenthalt in einem Sanatorium im Taunus. 1917 Übersiedlung in die Schweiz.

35

Straßenszene

»Friedrichstraße«, Berlin

Entstanden 1914
Öl auf Leinwand, 125 × 91 cm
Bezeichnet links unten: E. L. Kirchner.
Sammlung Dr. Frédéric Bauer, Davos. –
Erworben 1953.

Seit 1912 – ein Jahr vor Auflösung der Künstlergemeinschaft »Die Brücke« – macht sich im Schaffen Kirchners eine entscheidende Wandlung zu stärkerer Dynamisierung der Bildform und einer fühlbaren Aktivierung vor allem der zeichnerischen Mittel bemerkbar. Größen- und Tiefenverhältnisse werden verzerrt, um die innerhalb der Fäche wirksamen Spannungen zu steigern. Wie im Stuttgarter Bild weicht die Kurve der eckig gebrochenen Kontur, und auch die Farbe gleicht sich dem Staccato schraffierender Zeichnung an. Das pulsierende Leben der Großstadt ist hier im zuckenden Duktus des Pinsels präsent. Die maskenhaft typisierten Figuren sind extrem überlängt und in diagonaler Staffelung so angeordnet, daß der Eindruck einer fortlaufenden Bewegung entsteht. Das lineare Kraftfeld des Bodens nimmt diese Bewegung auf und trägt so entscheidend zur Intensivierung der von Hektik und herausfordernder Erotik erfüllten Darstellung bei.

From 1912 – one year before the dissolution of the artists' association "Die Brücke" – a decisive transformation in Kirchner's work is noticeable in the direction of a more intensely dynamic pictorial form and a sensible activation above all of his graphic means. Relations in space and depth are distorted in order to intensify the tensions active in the picture plane. As we see in the Stuttgart painting, curves give way to angular broken contours and colour too becomes one with the drawn staccato cross-hatching. The pulsing life of the big city is already present here in the jerky brushwork. The figures, typified by their mask-like faces, are extremely elongated and so disposed in echelon formation that an impression of continuous movement arises. The lines of force on the ground take up this movement and hence contribute decisively to the intensification of the image, embued with frenzy and challenging eroticism.

Ernst Ludwig Kirchner

Born 1880 in Aschaffenburg, commited suicide in 1938 in Davos. 1901–1905 studied architecture in Dresden and art in Munich. 1905 founder member of "Die Brücke" in Dresden. 1911 moved to Berlin. 1912–1914 summer stays in Fehmarn. 1914 military service, 1915 breakdown and period in a sanatorium in the Taunus hills. 1917 moved to Switzerland.

35

Street Scene

"Friedrichstraße", Berlin

1914
Oil on canvas, 125 × 91 cm
Signed lower left: E. L. Kirchner.
Collection Dr. Frédéric Bauer, Davos. –
Purchased 1953.

Literatur: Kat. 1957, S. 135 ff. – Kat. 1961, S. 61 mit Abb. – Kat. 1968, S. 94 mit Abb. – Kat. 1982, 20. Jahrhundert, S. 172 ff. mit Abb. – Werner Deusch, Neuere Malerei in der Staatsgalerie Stuttgart, S. 76 mit Abb.

Bibliography: Cat. 1957, p. 135 f. – Cat. 1961, p. 61 with ill. Cat. 1968, p. 94 with ill. Cat. 1982, 20. Jahrhundert, p. 172 f. with ill. – Werner Deusch, Neuere Malerei in der Staatsgalerie Stuttgart, p. 76 with ill.

Emil Nolde

Eigentlich Emil Hansen. Geboren 1867 in Nolde/Nordschleswig, gestorben 1956 in Seebüll. 1884–1888 an der Sauermannschen Schnitzschule in Flensburg. 1889 an der Kunstgewerbeschule Karlsruhe. 1892 bis 1898 Lehrtätigkeit an der Gewerbeschule in St. Gallen. Danach in München bei Friedrich Fehr und in Dachau bei Adolf Hölzel. 1900 an der Académie Julian in Paris. 1902 in Berlin. 1906 Mitglied der Künstlergemeinschaft »Die Brücke« in Dresden. Zahlreiche Reisen, u. a. 1913/14 nach Neuguinea. 1917 Umzug nach Unterwarf/Nordschleswig, 1927 nach Seebüll. Winteraufenthalte in Berlin.

36

Tänzerinnen

Entstanden 1920
Öl auf Leinwand, 106 × 88 cm
Bezeichnet links unten: Emil Nolde.
Erworben 1952.

Emil Nolde hatte ein enges Verhältnis zum Ausdruckstanz. Er war mit Mary Wigman und deren Schülerin Palucca befreundet und hatte auch die Tänzerinnen Saharet und Loie Fuller auf der Bühne gesehen. Dazu kam sein Interesse für exotische Kulttänze, das er auf einer Südseereise vertiefte. Es kann also so kaum überraschen, daß der Tanz in Noldes Schaffen einen vergleichsweise breiten Raum einnimmt: Erste Darstellungen zu diesem Thema sind bereits um 1910, weitere zwischen 1912 und 1918 entstanden. Das Stuttgarter Bild steht am Ende dieser ausdrucksstarken Gemälde. Sein betont flächiger Aufbau manifestiert sich schon im Verzicht auf einen räumlich-illusionistischen Bildgrund und in der einfachen Reihung der gnomenhaften Zuschauerköpfe. Die Tanzenden breiten sich in »dekorativer Eurythmie« (Haftmann) in die Fläche. Durch das Zusammenwirken von Bewegung und Gegenbewegung, von wie in Trance vollzogener Ausdrucksgebärde und sich steigernder Leuchtkraft der Farben entsteht eine vibrierende Spannung, die sich selbst im bewegten Dekor der Kleider noch eindringlich mitteilt. Alle am Aufbau des Bildes beteiligten Gestaltungsfaktoren dienen dazu, die in der rauschhaften Motorik des Tanzes freiwerdenden Empfindungen und Kräfte ungehemmt zum Ausdruck zu bringen.

Emil Nolde had close contacts with the free dance movement. He was friends with Mary Wigman and her pupil Palucca; he had also seen the dancers Saharet and Loie Fuller on the stage. On top of this there was his interest in exotic ritual dances which deepened during his South Seas journey. It is thus hardly surprising that dance in Nolde's work plays a comparatively central rôle: the first representations of this subject originated around 1910, later examples date from 1912 to 1918. The Stuttgart picture is one of the last of these powerfully expressive paintings. Its emphatically planar construction is already manifested in the renunciation of a spatially illusionistic pictorial surface and in the simple row of gnome-like spectators' heads. The dancers stretch out in "decorative eurythmics" (Haftmann) across the picture plane. Via the interplay of movement and counter-movement, of expressive gestures performed as if in a trance and the mutually enhancing luminosity of the colours, a vibrating tension arises which even comes across insistently in the lively patterns of the costumes. All the shaping factors that contribute to the construction of the picture serve to give uninhibited expression to the feelings and energies liberated by the intoxicating mechanism of the dance.

Emil Nolde

Real name Emil Hansen. Born 1867 in Nolde/North Schleswig, died 1956 in Seebüll. 1884–1888 at Sauermann's school for wood carving in Flensburg. 1889 at the school for Decorative arts in Karlsruhe. 1892–1898 teaching at the craft school in St Gallen. Afterwards studied under Friedrich Fehr in Munich and Adolf Hölzel in Dachau. 1900 attended the Académie Julian in Paris. 1902 in Berlin. 1906 member of the artists' association "Die Brücke" in Dresden. Numerous travels, among others to New Guinea in 1913/14. 1917 moved to Unterwarf/North Schleswig, 1927 to Seebüll, Winter residences in Berlin.

36

Dancing Women

1920
Oil on canvas, 106 × 88 cm
Signed lower left: Emil Nolde.
Purchased 1952.

Literatur: Kat. 1957, S. 188. – Kat. 1961, S. 83 mit Abb. – Kat. 1968, S. 133 mit Abb. – Kat. 1982, 20. Jahrhundert, S. 244 ff. mit Abb. – Werner Deusch, Neuere Malerei in der Staatsgalerie Stuttgart, S. 86 mit Abb.

Bibliography: Cat. 1957, p. 188. – Cat. 1961, p. 83 with ill. – Cat. 1968, p. 133 with ill. – Cat. 1982, 20. Jahrhundert, p. 244 f. with ill. – Werner Deusch, Neuere Malerei in der Staatsgalerie Stuttgart, p. 86 with ill.

Wassily Kandinsky

Geboren 1866 in Moskau, gestorben 1944 in Neuilly-sur-Seine. 1886 Studium der Rechte und der Volkswirtschaft in Moskau, 1897–1900 an der Azbé-Schule in München und an der Münchner Akademie unter Stuck. Seit 1903 auf Reisen in Holland, Tunesien, Italien und Frankreich. 1908 wieder in München. 1909 Gründung der Neuen Künstler-Vereinigung München. 1911 Austritt mit Marc, Münter, Kubin und Gründung des »Blauen Reiter«. 1914 Rückkehr nach Moskau. 1922–1933 Lehrer am Bauhaus in Weimar, Dessau und Berlin. Seit 1928 deutscher Staatsbürger. 1933 Übersiedlung nach Neuilly-sur-Seine. 1939 französischer Staatsbürger.

37

Improvisation 9

Öl auf Leinwand, 110 × 110 cm
Bezeichnet rechts unten: Kandinsky 1910.
Sammlung Prof. Franz Stadler, München
und später Zürich. — Erworben 1965.

Das 1910 entstandene Gemälde belegt den Übergang zur »abstrakten« Malerei, die — von Kandinsky begründet — im Zeichen einer zunehmenden Verselbständigung der künstlerischen Ausdrucksmittel stand. Noch spielen Erinnerungen an Gegenständliches, möglicherweise an ein russisches Märchen, herein: eine Berglandschaft, eine hochgelegene Kapelle, die Abbreviatur eines Reiters, die rudimentäre Gestalt eines Riesen, eine dichtgedrängte Zuschauergruppe. Aber all dies wird überlagert durch die elementare Strahlkraft der Farben und die expressive Gestik der Linien. Das Motivische dient — wenn überhaupt — so nur als Folie dramatischer Farbklänge, die Anspruch auf eine isolierende Betrachtung erheben. Die im Spannungsfeld der koloristischen Instrumentierung sich steigernde Eigendynamik der Farbe läßt erkennen, daß die abstrakte Kunst weniger einem puristischen Formbedürfnis als einem neuen Ausdrucksverlangen erwuchs, in dieser Stunde ihrer Geburt also zum Expressionismus gehört. Auch entwicklungsgeschichtlich kommt dem Gemälde erhöhte Bedeutsamkeit zu: kurz darauf sollte Kandinsky zur totalen Freisetzung der künstlerischen Ausdrucksmittel und damit zu reiner Abstraktion vorstoßen.

The 1910 picture exemplifies the transition to "abstract" painting (initiated by Kandinsky), which shows increasingly independent means of artistic expression. Memories of figurative forms, possibly from a Russian fairy tale, still play a rôle: a mountain landscape, a chapel on a hill, the abbreviated sign for a rider, the rudimentary form of a giant, a closely packed group of spectators. But all this is overlayed by the elementary luminosity of the colours and the gesturally expressive lines. The motif serves — if at all — only as a foil to the dramatic colour orchestration which asserts its own independent presence. The interior dynamic of the colours — heightened in the electric field of colour instrumentation — makes clear that abstract art grew less out of a demand for pure form than out of a new expressive urge; at the hour of its birth it was synonymous with Expressionism. The picture is particularly important in terms of Kandinsky's historical development: shortly afterwards he pushed forward to a total liberation of artistic expression and so to pure abstraction.

Wassily Kandinsky

Born 1866 in Moscow, died 1944 in Neuilly-sur-Seine. 1886 studied law and political economics in Moscow, 1897–1900 attended the Azbé school in Munich and studied at the Munich Academy under von Stuck. From 1903 travelled in Holland, Tunisia, Italy and France. 1908 back in Munich. 1909 foundation of the "Neue Künstler-Vereinigung München". 1911 left this body with Marc, Münter and Kubin and founded the "Blauer Reiter". 1914 returned to Moscow. 1922–1933 teacher at the Bauhaus in Weimar, Dessau and Berlin. After 1928 German citizenship. 1933 emigrated to Neuilly-sur-Seine. 1939 French citizenship.

37

Improvisation 9

Oil on canvas, 110 × 110 cm
Signed lower right: Kandinsky 1910.
Collection Prof. Franz Stadler, Munich
and later Zürich. — Purchased 1965.

Literatur: Kat. 1968, S. 89 mit Abb. — Kat. 1982, 20. Jahrhundert, S. 164 mit Abb.

Bibliography: Cat. 1968, p. 89 with ill. — Cat. 1982, 20. Jahrhundert, p. 164 with ill.

Franz Marc

Geboren 1880 in München, gefallen 1916 bei Verdun. 1900–1903 an der Münchner Akademie bei Hackl und v. Diez. 1903 und 1907 Reisen nach Paris. Seit 1910 in Sindelsdorf/Obb., Freundschaft mit Macke. 1911 mit Kandinsky Gründung des »Blauen Reiter«. 1912 in Paris, Besuch bei Delaunay. 1914 Übersiedlung nach Ried bei Benediktbeuren, dann Kriegsdienst.

38

Die kleinen gelben Pferde

Entstanden 1912
Öl auf Leinwand, 66 × 104 cm
Bezeichnet links unten: Marc.
Sammlung Bernhard Koehler, Berlin. –
Erworben 1957.

Franz Marc

Born 1880 in Munich, killed in action, 1916 at Verdun. 1900–1903 attended the Munich Academy, studying under Hackl and v. Diez. Visited Paris in 1903 and 1907. From 1910 resident in Sindelsdorf/Bavaria. Friendship with August Macke. 1911 founded the "Blauer Reiter" with Kandinsky. 1912 visited Robert Delaunay in Paris. 1914 moved to Ried near Benediktbeuren. Then war service.

38

Small Yellow Horses

1912
Oil on canvas, 66 × 104 cm
Signed bottom left: Marc.
Collection Bernhard Koehler, Berlin. –
Purchased 1957.

Ausgehend von einer Bleistiftstudie aus dem Jahre 1908 hat Franz Marc 1908–1914 eine Reihe von Pferdedarstellungen geschaffen, die als »Lenggrieser Pferdebilder« bekannt sind. Die Reihe dieser Bilder macht in zunehmender Vereinfachung und farbiger Abstraktion die von ihm erstrebte Symbiose von Landschaft und Tierwelt evident. Die Staatsgalerie besitzt zwei Fassungen des Themas: »Die kleinen blauen Pferde« und die hier abgebildeten »kleinen gelben Pferde«. Die schweren Tierleiber sind dicht an den Betrachter herangerückt und bilden im Ineinandergreifen ihrer sich rundenden Formen eine unauflösbare Einheit. Trotz des »unwirklichen« Gelb werden die Tiere aber erst durch die Landschaft in eine »mythische Sphäre« (Lankheit) gehoben. Das Blau des Bodens schließt die Assoziation an einen Weidegrund aus; es wird vom Blau über den Köpfen wiederaufgenommmen, dessen Rund eher der Erdkugel als einem Berg gleicht. Wolkenbänke schieben sich zwischen Tiere und Grund, Sennhütten tauchen schemenhaft auf. Was Marc hier gestaltet, stellt sich nicht mehr als ein Ausschnitt der Realität, sondern in imaginärer Verdichtung als »Weltlandschaft« dar. Auch das Tier wird so »zum Symbol unteilbaren Seins, das er im großen kosmischen Zusammenhang zu erfühlen versucht« (Deusch).

Beginning with a pencil sketch in 1908, Franz Marc developed a series of horse images, known as the "Lenggrieser horse paintings". In this series we see Marc's desire to affect a synthesis of landscape and animal world, by means of increasing simplification and coloured abstraction. The Staatsgalerie has two versions of the theme: "Small Blue Horses", and, as illustrated here, "Small Yellow Horses". The heavy animal torsos are pulled up close to the observer, and their rounded forms interpenetrate to create an inseparable unity. Despite the "unreal" yellow colouring, it is the landscape that first elevates the animals into a "mythic sphere" (Lankheit). The blue ground excludes associations with a meadow; above the horses' heads blue recurres, suggesting the curve of the earth's horizon rather than the contours of a mountain. Banks of clouds glide between the animals and the ground; alpine huts appear in schematic form. Marc's depiction can no longer be described as a "slice of life"; rather, he presents a universal landscape, distilled by the imagination. The animal is transformed into a symbol of universal being, which Marc endeavours to sense within the great cosmic plan.

Literatur: Kat. 1961, S. 75 ff. mit Abb. – Kat. 1968, S. 117 mit Abb. – Kat. 1982, 20. Jahrhundert, S. 217 mit Abb. – Werner Deusch, Neuere Malerei in der Staatsgalerie Stuttgart, S. 74 mit Abb.

Bibliography: Cat. 1961, p. 75 f. with ill. – Cat. 1968, p. 117 with ill. – Cat. 1982, 20. Jahrhundert, p. 217 with ill. – Werner Deusch, Neue Malerei in der Staatsgalerie Stuttgart, p. 74 with ill.

Paul Klee

Geboren 1879 in Münchenbuchsee bei Bern, gestorben 1940 in Muralto-Locarno. 1898—1901 Studium in München bei Knirr und Stuck. 1902—1906 in Bern. 1906 Übersiedlung nach München. 1911 Bekanntschaft mit Macke und Kandinsky. 1912 Mitglied des »Blauen Reiter« und Bekanntschaft mit Marc; Reise nach Paris, Begegnung mit Delaunay. 1914 Reise nach Tunis mit Macke und Moilliet. 1916—1918 Soldat. 1920 bis 1931 Lehrer am Bauhaus in Weimar und Dessau. 1928/29 Reise nach Ägypten. 1931 Professor an der Akademie in Düsseldorf. 1933 Rückkehr nach Bern.

39

Vierteiliger Palast

*Wasserfarben, gewachst, auf gipsgrundierter
Leinwand, 90,5 × 68 cm
Bezeichnet rechts unten: Klee.
Rückseitig betitelt und datiert: 1933.
Sammlung Davids Thompson, Pittsburgh. —
Erworben aus dem
Schweizer Kunsthandel 1970.*

Paul Klee

Born 1879 in Münchenbuchsee near Bern, died 1940 in Muralto-Locarno. 1898—1901 studied in Munich under Knirr and von Stuck. 1902—1906 in Bern. 1906 moved to Munich. 1911 acquaintance with Macke and Kandinsky. 1912 member of the "Blauer Reiter", an acquaintance with Marc; travelled to Paris, meeting with Delaunay. 1914 travelled to Tunis with Macke and Moilliet. 1916—1918 soldier. 1920—1931 taught at the Bauhaus in Weimar and Dessau. 1928/29 travelled to Egypt. 1931 Professor at the Düsseldorf Academy. 1933 returned to Bern.

39

Palace in Four Parts

*Waxed water soluble colour on a gesso
ground on canvas, 90.5 × 68 cm
Signed lower right: Klee.
Title and date on reverse: 1933.
Collection David Thompson, Pittsburgh. —
Purchased from the Swiss art market 1970.*

Die Lehrtätigkeit am Bauhaus erbrachte für Klee eine Festigung und Klärung der formalen und geistigen Grundlagen, durch die seine Bildideen und deren künstlerische Umsetzung schon früher bestimmt waren. Die Intensivierung der Reflexion führte zur Vereinfachung und konstruktiven Verspannung der Form, in welcher wiederum eine Steigerung der Aussage beschlossen lag. Für die Wahl der Motive und ihre künstlerische Anverwandlung wurde eine Reise nach Ägypten im Winter 1928/29 von größter Bedeutung. Zunächst wird die Bildwelt, soweit sie auf Anregungen jener Reise beruht, noch vom Eindruck des topographisch Ablesbaren und perspektivisch Gebundenen bestimmt. Im »Vierteiligen Palast« — einem erst 1933 entstandenen Gemälde — ist die höchst sensible Oberfläche der Bildgrundierung freilich mehr als nur Reflex auf die Struktur und die in Entfernungen erfahrbare Weite der Landschaft; sie abstrahiert sich zu transparenter, in ihrer Tiefenausdehnung nicht abzumessender Farb-Dichte eines scheinbar unendlichen »Lichtraumes«. Die Gegenstände in ihm sind nicht mehr umgrenzt und eingefügt in eine räumlich ablesbare Beziehung: Die vier Mauerzüge des Palastes können trotz der maßstäblichen Relativierung, die zwischen ihnen angezeigt ist, weder in ihrer gesamten Ausdehnung eindeutig erkannt, noch in ihrem Abstand zueinander genauer bestimmt werden. Die Erscheinung des Gläsernen und Transluziden der einzelnen Farbkompartimente, die von der Struktur des überall durchdringenden »Mal«- und »Bild«-Grundes bewirkt wird, hält Licht, Atmosphäre und Raum in nicht fixierbarer, vibrierender Bewegung und Spannung.

Klee's teaching activities at the Bauhaus involved a consolidation and clarification of the formal and spiritual foundations which had long since conditioned his pictorial ideas and his artistic transposition of such. This heightened reflex led to formal simplification and constructive tension which implied in its turn a more intense message. His choice of motif and its artistic transformation was greatly influenced by a journey to Egypt in the winter of 1928/29. Above all his pictorial vision (in as far as it alluded to the stimuli of each journey) is still conditioned by topographical logic and perspectival associations. In "Palace in four parts" — a late painting from 1933 — the highly sensitive surface of the pictorial ground is far more than a simple reflection of the structure of the landscape and its verifiable scope in the distance. It is abstracted in the direction of a transparent colour seal whose expanse into depth is immeasurable, an apparently infinite "spatial light". The objects it contains are no longer defined and integrated into spatially logical relations: the four continuums of the palace wall, despite their given relative proportions, cannot be clearly read in their totality nor exactly apprehended in their distance from each other. The spectral glassiness and translucence of the individual colour areas, conditioned by the extensive permeation of the "painterly and pictorial ground", contains light, atmosphere and space in indefinite, vibrating movement and tension.

Literatur: Kat. 1982, 20. Jahrhundert, S. 178 ff. mit Abb.

Bibliography: Cat. 1982, 20. Jahrhundert, p. 178 f. with ill.

Egon Schiele

Geboren 1890 in Tulln an der Donau, gestorben 1918 in Wien. 1906–1909 an der Wiener Akademie. 1907 Begegnung mit Gustav Klimt. 1912 Teilnahme an der Kölner Sonderbund-Ausstellung. 1915–1917 Kriegsdienst. Tätig vor allem in Wien.

40

Der Prophet

Doppelselbstbildnis

Öl auf Leinwand, 110,5 × 50,5 cm
Bezeichnet links oben: S. 11.
Sammlung Dr. Oskar Reichel, Wien. –
Sammlung Arthur Stemmer, Wien. –
Dr. M. Dale, New York. –
Schweizer Privatbesitz. –
Erworben mit Hilfe von Spenden 1982/83.
Leihgabe des Stuttgarter Galerievereins.

Egon Schiele

Born 1890 in Tulln on the Danube, died 1918 in Vienna. 1906–1909 at the Academy in Vienna. 1907 met Gustav Klimt. 1912 contributed to the "Sonderbund" exhibition in Cologne. 1915–1917 war service. Active above all in Vienna.

40

The Prophet

Double self-portrait

Oil on canvas, 110.5 × 50.5 cm
Signed above left: S. 11.
Collection Dr. Oskar Reichel, Vienna. –
Collection Arthur Stemmer, Vienna. –
Dr. M. Dale, New York. –
Swiss private collection. –
Purchased with the aid of donations 1982/83.
On loan from the Stuttgart Galerieverein.

Ausgehend vom Wiener Symbolismus um Gustav Klimt, den er selbst als seinen geistigen Mentor bezeichnete, dringt Egon Schiele um 1910 zu einer expressiven, die Grenzbereiche des Psychischen tief auslotenden Bildsprache vor. Zumal auf dem Gebiet des Porträts hat er Werke geschaffen, die ein von Angst und Zwängen bedrohtes Menschenbild spiegeln. Unter den zahlreichen Selbstdarstellungen des Künstlers kommt dem Stuttgarter Gemälde insofern erhöhte Bedeutsamkeit zu, als sich in der »zwitterhaften Verschränkung« gerade dieses Doppelporträts die Ambivalenz zwischen Leben und Tod in extremer Zuspitzung mitteilt. Wie schon Werner Hofmann bemerkt, »ist es Schiele in diesem Bilde gelungen, eine halluzinierte Innenschau, die sich im Doppelbödigen bewegt, auf eine Form zu bringen, deren Syntax so undurchschaubar ist wie ihr Bedeutungsgeflecht«. Der entblößte Körper zur Linken – eine beklemmende Symbiose von Torso und Akt – versinkt zur Hälfte in der dunklen Umhüllung einer zweiten Gestalt, deren blickloser Schädel Schieles Gesichtszüge trägt. Realität und Vision wachsen einander entgegen und verschmelzen in der »stelenhaften« Präsenz der Figuren zu einem Bild von erschütternder Eindringlichkeit. Der Gegensatz von pastoser und rein flächiger Malweise sowie der Hell-Dunkelkontrast stehen in erkennbarer Wechselbeziehung zur existenzbedingten Thematik des Gemäldes, die Schieles Wort »Alles ist lebend tot« in umfassender Deutung erhellt.

Taking as a point of departure Viennese Symbolism in the circles around Gustav Klimt, whom he described as his spiritual mentor, Egon Schiele advanced around 1910 towards an expressive pictorial language, deeply sounding the depths of man's psychic frontiers. Especially in the realm of portraiture he created works which mirror a picture of man threatened by fear and compulsions. The Stuttgart picture is a particularly important example among the numerous self-representations by the artist in that the ambivalent relation between life and death is communicated with extreme poignancy in the "condensed hybrid" of this double portrait. As Werner Hofmann remarked, "Schiele achieved in this painting a hallucinatory glimpse of the interior that hovers as a double image, assuming a form whose syntax is as opaque as the texture of its meanings". The stripped body on the left – an oppressive symbiosis of torso and nude – is half submerged in the dark wrapping of a second figure whose sightless skull bears Schiele's facial features. Reality and vision approach and fuse in the "stele-like" presence of the figures, resulting in a startlingly insistent painting. The opposition of impasto painting and pure colour planes, like the light-dark contrasts, are a visual equivalent for the existential theme of the painting, which provides an illuminating and comprehensive interpretation of Schiele's words "all is living dead".

Literatur: Otto Kallir, Egon Schiele, Wien 1966, S. 260, Nr. 130 mit Abb. – Ausst.-Kat. Experiment Weltuntergang – Wien um 1900, Kunsthalle Hamburg 1974, S. 149 (Werner Hofmann).

Bibliography: Otto Kallir, Egon Schiele, Vienna 1966, p. 260f, no. 130 with ill. – Cat. Experiment Weltuntergang – Wien um 1900, Kunsthalle Hamburg 1974, p. 149 (Werner Hofmann).

Oskar Kokoschka

Geboren 1886 in Pöchlarn/Österreich, gestorben 1980 in Villeneuve/Schweiz. 1905–1909 an der Kunstgewerbeschule in Wien, 1909–1914 in Berlin, Mitarbeit an der Zeitschrift »Der Sturm«, 1914/15 Soldat. 1917–1924 in Dresden, 1924–1931 Reisen in Europa, Nordafrika und Vorderasien. 1931–1934 wechselnd in Wien und Paris. 1934–1938 in Prag. 1938–1953 in London, danach in Villeneuve am Genfer See.

41

Bildnis Herwarth Walden

Entstanden 1910
Öl auf Leinwand, 100 × 69,3 cm
Bezeichnet rechts unten: OK
Sammlung Herwarth Walden, Berlin. –
Sammlung Nell Walden, Schinznach. –
Sammlung Samuel H. Maslon, Wayzata/
Minnesota. –
Sammlung Charles Clore, London. –
Erworben aus
dem Londoner Kunsthandel 1966.

Oskar Kokoschka

Born 1886 in Pöchlarn/Austria, died 1980 in Villeneuve/Switzerland. 1905–1909 at the School of Decorative Art in Vienna, 1909–1914 in Berlin, contributing to the magazine "Der Sturm", 1914/15 soldier. 1917–1924 in Dresden, 1924–1931 travelled in Europe, to North Africa and the Near East. 1931–1934 alternately in Vienna and Paris. 1934–1938 in Prague. 1938–1953 in London, then in Villeneuve on Lake Geneva.

41

Portrait of Herwarth Walden

1910
Oil on canvas, 100 × 69.3 cm
Signed lower right: OK
Collection Herwarth Walden, Berlin. –
Collection Nell Walden, Schinznach. –
Collection Samuel H. Maslon,
Wayzata/Minnesota. –
Collection Charles Clore, London. –
Purchased from the London art market
1966.

Kunstgeschichtlich gehört das Walden-Porträt zu den hervorragendsten Zeugnissen nicht nur im Frühwerk Kokoschkas, sondern – im weiteren Sinne – auch des deutschen Expressionismus. Der Dargestellte, Herwarth Walden, war eine der profiliertesten Erscheinungen seiner Zeit; seine Kennerschaft und sein Spürsinn haben sich auf nahezu allen Gebieten der Kunst entscheidend ausgewirkt. 1910 berief er den erst 24-jährigen Kokoschka von Wien nach Berlin an die Redaktion seiner neugegründeten Zeitschrift »Der Sturm«, dem wichtigsten Organ aller kunstrevolutionären Ideen der damaligen Avantgarde. Neben Dichtern wie Rilke, Lasker-Schüler, Wedekind und den Brüdern Mann zog Waldens Persönlichkeit auch die fortschrittlichen Künstler des Expressionismus und namhafte ausländische Maler wie Boccioni, Delaunay und Léger in ihren Bann. Für Kokoschka war die für Walden im Jahre 1910 bei Paul Cassirer organisierte Ausstellung der erste große Erfolg, nicht zuletzt wegen der aufsehenerregenden Wirkung des erst kurz vor der Ausstellung vollendeten Walden-Porträts. Das Bild offenbart, daß sich der junge Maler ganz der Bedeutung dieser schicksalhaften Begegnung bewußt war; denn kaum eines seiner früheren Werke zeigt diese großartig-schwungvolle Kontur, diese Freiheit und Sicherheit in Handschrift und Kolorit. Wie ein Skalpell ist der Pinsel geführt, ganz darauf gerichtet, das Innere des »streitbaren Stürmers« mit unerbittlicher Schärfe nach außen zu kehren. Die hohe Stirn, der bohrende Blick, das vogelhafte Profil, aber auch die eckige Haltung, kennzeichnen die vorausschauende Kühnheit dieses bedeutenden Geistes. Heftig und grell-leuchtende Farben vor einem in atmosphärischem Dunkel gehaltenen Grund verstärken noch diesen Eindruck.

In art historical terms, the Walden portrait is one of the best products not only of Kokoschka's early work, but also – in a wider sense – of German Expressionism. The sitter, Herwarth Walden, was one of the most prominent personalities of his times; his expertise and his flair decisively influenced almost all artistic manifestations. In 1910 he summoned the young 24 year old Kokoschka from Vienna to Berlin for the editorial board of his newly founded journal "Der Sturm", the most important organ for all the revolutionary artistic ideas of the avantgarde at the time. Alongside poets like Rilke, Lasker-Schüler, Wedekind and the brothers Mann, Walden's personality also captivated the progressive Expressionist artists and renowned foreign painters like Boccioni, Delaunay and Léger. For Kokoschka the exhibition of his work organized by Walden for Paul Cassirer's gallery in 1910 was his first big success, not least due to the sensational effect of his Walden portrait, finished just before the exhibition. The painting makes clear that the young artist was fully aware of the significance of this fateful meeting; for few of his other early works display this splendidly bold contour, this freedom and confidence of brushwork and colour. The brush is used like a scalpel, fully aimed at exposing the inner life of the "combative storm trooper" with pitiless rigour. The high forehead, the piercing glance, the birdlike profile, but also the angular pose, signify the far-sighted daring of this important spirit. Intensive and shrilly shining colours in front of a restrained dark atmospheric ground further strengthen this impression.

Literatur: Kat. 1968, S. 100 ff. mit Abb. –
Kat. 1982, 20. Jahrhundert, S. 182 ff. mit Abb.

Bibliography: Cat. 1968, p. 100 f. with ill. –
Cat. 1982, 20. Jahrhundert, p. 182 f. with ill.

155

George Grosz

Geboren 1893 in Berlin, gestorben 1959 ebenda. 1909/10 Studium in Dresden, 1913 in Berlin und Paris. Zunächst Karikaturist für Zeitschriften. Tätig in Berlin, 1917 bis 1920 Mitglied der dortigen DADA-Gruppe. 1932 Reise, 1933 Übersiedlung nach New York. Seit 1951 mehrere Reisen nach Deutschland. 1959 Rückkehr nach Berlin.

42

Leichenbegängnis –
Widmung an Oskar Panizza

Öl auf Leinwand, 140 × 110 cm
Rückseitig Rohentwurf einer ähnlichen Komposition und mehrfach bezeichnet, u. a.: begonnen 26. Oktober 1917 bis 4. Juni 1918.
Sammlung Heinrich Kirchhoff, Wiesbaden. Erworben 1949.

George Grosz

Born 1893 in Berlin, died 1959 in Berlin. 1909/10 studied in Dresden, 1913 in Berlin and Paris. First cartoonist for magazines. Active in Berlin, 1917–1920 member of Berlin DADA. 1932 travelled to New York, 1933 emigrated there. After 1951 several journies to Germany. 1959 returned to Berlin.

42

Burial –
Dedicated to Oskar Panizza

Oil on canvas, 140 × 110 cm
On reverse rough sketch for a similar composition and multiple inscriptions, among others: begonnen 26 Oktober 1917 bis 4 Juni 1918.
Collection Heinrich Kirchhoff, Wiesbaden. – Purchased 1949.

Einer »apokalyptischen Vision« (Gudrun Inboden) gleicht dieses Gemälde, das George Grosz dem Wiener Irrenarzt und satirischen Schriftsteller Oskar Panizza (1853 bis 1921) gewidmet, nicht aber – wie bisweilen behauptet – als »Begräbnis des Oskar Panizza« gekennzeichnet hat. 1917/18 entstanden, ist es ein flammender Protest gegen den sozialen Verfall der damaligen Gesellschaft, deren Mißstände Grosz schonungslos geißelt. Daß gerade die Arbeit an diesem Gemälde den Künstler besonders bewegte, geht aus den folgenden am 15. Dezember 1917 notierten Zeilen hervor: »Ich male zur Zeit an einem großen Höllenbild – Schnapsgasse grotesker Tode und Verrückter, da spielt sich viel ab –, der Leibhaftige reitet auf dem queren Sarg von links ab durch das Bild, rechts übergibt sich ein Jüngling, speit all die schönen Jugendillusionen in die Leinwand ... darin, daß diese Epoche destruktiv nach unten segelt – bin ich in der Anschauung unverrückbar ...« Treffender läßt sich die zeitträchtige und zersetzende Stimmung des Bildes schwerlich beschreiben. Seine makabre, von Zynismus und Spott durchsetzte Thematik gewinnt durch die gespenstische Wirkung der nächtlichen Szenerie noch an Dramatik. Bedingt durch den eigenwilligen Einsatz perspektivischer Mittel geraten die gläsernen Bauten ins Wanken, haben Menschen und Dinge Basis und Standort verloren. Zur blinden Masse degeneriert und von animalischen Impulsen getrieben, werden die Figuren von drei fratzenhaft entstellten Kreaturen (Allegorien für Trunksucht, Syphillis und religiösen Fanatismus) angeführt, während der Tod triumphierend auf einem Sarg thront und sich betrinkt. Eine glühende, alles durchdringende Farbigkeit faßt das bewegte Geschehen kaleidoskopartig, in vielfältig wirksamer Brechung zusammen. In der dynamischen Durchdringung der Komposition geht das Gemälde auf Anregungen des italienischen Futurismus zurück, von dem es sich aber in der kompromißlosen zeitkritischen Weltsicht eindeutig absetzt.

This painting resembles an "apocalyptic vision" (Gudrun Inboden), dedicated by George Grosz to the Viennese mental doctor and satirical author Oskar Panizza (1853–1921), but not – as is sometimes suggested – entitled "Burial of Oskar Panizza". Painted in 1917/18, it is a burning protest against the social decay of society in his times, whose defects Grosz ruthlessly castigates. The artist's particular engagement while working on this picture is recorded in the following notes dated 15 December 1917: "I'm painting at present a large picture of hell – an alleyway of grotesque corpses and madmen, lots is happening there – the personification of the devil is riding on the diagonal coffin from the left through the painting, on the right a young man is throwing up, vomiting all the beautiful illusions of youth into the canvas ... in as much as this epoch is destructively going under – my conception has not changed...". It would be difficult to describe more accurately the topicality and decaying mood of the painting. Its macabre theme, carried through with cynicism and mockery, gains drama through the ghostly effect of the night-time scenery. Conditioned by the idiosyncratic use of perspectival devices, the glass buildings seem to sway, people and objects have lost their foundations and stability. Degenerating into a blind crowd and driven by animal impulses, the figures are led by three grotesquely distorted creatures (allegories for Drunkenness, Syphillis and Religious Fanaticism), while Death is throned triumphantly on a coffin getting drunk. A glowing, all-permeating colouration combines the restless events in a kaleidoscopic, apparently multiple refraction. The pervasive dynamism of the painting refers to stimuli from Italian Futurism, although the uncompromising topical critique of its world view is a new departure.

Literatur: Kat. 1961, S. 49 ff. mit Abb. – Kat. 1968, S. 73 mit Abb. – Kat. 1982, 20. Jahrhundert, S. 143 ff. mit Abb. – Werner Deusch, Neuere Malerei in der Staatsgalerie Stuttgart, S. 82 mit Abb. – Gudrun Inboden, in: Große Gemäldegalerien, herausgegeben von Erich Steingräber, München 1980, S. 458 mit Abb.

Bibliography: Cat. 1961, p. 49 f. with ill. – Cat. 1968, p. 73 with ill. – Cat. 1982, 20. Jahrhundert, p. 143 f. with ill. – Werner Deusch, Neuere Malerei in der Staatsgalerie Stuttgart, p. 82 with ill. – Gudrun Inboden, in: Große Gemäldegalerien, ed. by Erich Steingräber, Munich 1980, p. 458 with ill.

Kurt Schwitters

Geboren 1887 in Hannover, gestorben 1948 in Kirkby-Kendal/England. 1909–1914 Studium an der Dresdner Akademie. Seit 1915 wieder in Hannover. 1919 erste Merz-Bilder, parallel dazu Merz-Dichtung, Merz-Bau und Merz-Bühne. Kontakte zu den Dadaisten in Zürich, Paris und Berlin. Seit 1923 Herausgabe der Zeitschrift »Merz«. 1937 Emigration nach Lysaker bei Oslo. 1940 Flucht nach England.

43

Das Undbild

Collage aus verschiedenen Materialien und Gouache auf Pappe, 35,8 × 28 cm (mit originalem Rahmen: 40,2 × 32,3 cm)
Bezeichnet links unten: K. Schwitters 1919; rückseitig signiert, datiert, betitelt.
Erworben aus dem Londoner Kunsthandel 1969.

Kurt Schwitters

Born 1887 in Hannover, died 1948 in Kirkby-Kendal/England. 1909–1914 studied at the Dresden Academy. After 1915 back in Hannover. 1919 first Merz-paintings, parallel to which Merz-poetry, Merz-building and Merz-stage. Contacts with the DADA artists in Zurich, Paris and Berlin. After 1923 editor of the journal "Merz". 1937 emigrated to Lysaker near Oslo. 1940 fled to England.

43

Das Undbild
The And-Painting

Collage with various materials and gouache on cardboard, 35.8 × 28 cm (with original frame: 40.2 × 32.3 cm)
Signed lower left: K. Schwitters 1919; Signed, dated, titled on reverse.
Purchased from the London art market in 1969.

Vom konventionellen Akademiestudium herkommend, hat Schwitters erst 1917 »Abstraktionen« gemalt, in denen sich die Freisetzung einzelner Bildformen ankündigt. In den beiden folgenden Jahren entstanden — wohl angeregt durch ähnliche Bestrebungen innerhalb des Kubismus und Futurismus — die ersten »Collagen«, die freilich mehr als nur dies, nämlich »Materialbilder« waren. Das Undbild steht am Beginn dieser Entwicklung. Es gehört in die Reihe der Merz-Bilder, der wichtigsten Werkgruppe im Schaffen des Künstlers. »Das Wort Merz (aus einer Anzeige der Commerzbank entnommen und bildhaft verwendet) bedeutet wesentlich die Zusammenfassung aller erdenklichen Materialien für künstlerische Zwecke und technisch die prinzipiell gleiche Wertung der einzelnen Materialien« (Schwitters). Solcherart für den »Wert des Wertlosen« eintretend, bezieht Schwitters als erster Produkte — genauer gesagt sind es Abfallprodukte — konsequent und nicht nur partiell in seine Gestaltungen ein. Den festen Pappgrund nahezu völlig verdeckend und eine höchst sensible Reliefschichtung bildend, sind Fahrkarten, Geld, Papierfetzen, Leder- und Filzstreifen neben- oder übereinander montiert und durch eine teilweise Übermalung so miteinander verbunden, daß eine (auch Elemente der späteren »Combine Painting« antizipierende) Bildform entsteht, die nicht zuletzt durch die gattungsübergreifende Verwendung des Titels von ungewöhnlichem Reiz ist. Das Prinzip der Collage steht somit bei Schwitters für etwas Entscheidendes ein, nämlich für die Idee einer zusammenfassenden Durchdringung der Künste, zu der er sich auch in seinen programmatischen Schriften bekannte. — 1969 erworben, gehört das »Undbild« zu einer zahlenmäßig kleinen, doch für deutsche Verhältnisse wohl singulären Gruppe dadaistischer Werke in der Staatsgalerie, die außerdem exemplarische Arbeiten von Marcel Duchamp, Man Ray und Picabia umfaßt.

Coming from a conventional background of academic training, Schwitters first painted "abstractions" in 1917, which announced the liberation of individual pictorial forms. In the next two years — certainly influenced by similar endeavours in Cubism and Futurism — the first "collages" were created, which were certainly more than this, being in fact "material pictures". The And-Painting stands at the beginning of this development. It belongs to the series of Merz-paintings, the most important group of work in the artists œuvre. "The word Merz (taken from an advertisement for the Commerzbank [Commercial Bank] and used pictorially) means essentially the bringing together of all conceivable materials for artistic purposes, and technically the principally equal evaluation of individual materials" (Schwitters). Standing up for the "worth of the worthless" along these lines, Schwitters was the first to incorporate products — more exactly waste products — in a thoroughgoing rather than partial way into his configurations. Tram tickets, money, scraps of paper, strips of leather and felt, which almost totally cover the firm cardboard ground and form a highly differentiated layered relief, are assembled next to or over each other and combined by partial overpainting. In this way a pictorial form arises (also anticipating the later "combine painting"), whose unusual fascination relates not least to the use of the title to transverse genres. The principle of collage thus vouches for something quite decisive in Schwitter's work, namely the idea of an all-embracing pervasion of the arts, which he also acknowledges in his programmatic writings. Purchased in 1969, the And-Painting belongs to the numerically small, and yet, for Germany, certainly unique group of DADA works in the Staatsgalerie, which also includes exemplary works by Marcel Duchamp, Man Ray and Picabia.

Literatur: Jahrbuch der Staatlichen Kunstsammlungen in Baden-Württemberg, VII, 1970, S. 152 mit Abb. — Kat. 1982, 20. Jahrhundert, S. 307 ff. mit Abb.

Bibliography: Jahrbuch der Staatlichen Kunstsammlungen in Baden-Württemberg, VII 1970, p. 152 with ill. — Cat. 1982, 20. Jahrhundert, p. 307 f. with ill.

Max Beckmann

Geboren 1884 in Leipzig, gestorben 1950 in New York. 1900–1903 an der Großherzoglichen Kunstschule in Weimar. 1903/04 in Paris. 1904 Übersiedlung nach Berlin. 1914/15 Sanitätssoldat. 1915 Übersiedlung nach Frankfurt/M., 1925–1933 Professur an der Städelschen Kunstschule. 1929 bis 1932 überwiegend in Paris. 1947–1949 in St. Louis/USA. 1949/50 in New York, Professur für Malerei am Brooklyn Museum.

44

Die Auferstehung

Entstanden 1916–1918
Öl und Kohle auf Leinwand, 345 × 497 cm
Erworben vom Sohn des Künstlers,
Dr. Peter Beckmann, 1964.

Max Beckmann

Born 1884 in Leipzig, died 1950 in New York. 1900–1903 at the "Großherzogliche Kunstschule" (Grand Ducal Art School) in Weimar. 1903/04 in Paris. 1904 moved to Berlin. 1914/15 medical orderly. 1915 moved to Frankfurt/M., 1925–1933 Professor at the "Städelschen Kunstschule" (...) (Städel Art School). 1929–1932 mostly in Paris. 1947–1949 in St Louis/USA. 1949/50 in New York, Professor of painting at Brooklyn Museum.

44

The Resurrection

1916–1918
Oil and charcoal on canvas, 345 × 497 cm
Purchased from the artist's son,
Dr. Peter Beckmann, 1964.

Literatur: Kat. 1968, S. 21 mit Abb. – Kat. 1982, 20. Jahrhundert, S. 85 ff. mit Abb. – Wolf Dieter Dube, Auferstehung im Werke Max Beckmanns, in: Kunst und Kirche, Heft 2, 1982, S. 67 ff. mit Abb.

Bibliography: Cat. 1968, p. 21 with ill. – Cat. 1982, 20. Jahrhundert, p. 85 f. with ill. – Wolf Dieter Dube, "Auferstehung im Werke Max Beckmanns" in: Kunst und Kirche, vol. 2, 1982 p. 67 f. with ill.

Mit der Arbeit an der »Großen Auferstehung« hat Max Beckmann nach der Entlassung aus dem Kriegsdienst 1916 begonnen. Das Bild ist unvollendet, weil es sich in seiner spannungsbeladenen, von apokalyptischen Vorstellungen genährten Thematik einer Ausführung im klassischen Sinne verweigert (und dies, obwohl Beckmann gesagt hat: »Wenn mir jemand den Auftrag gibt, es fertigzumachen, soll es sein.«) Im Unterschied zu einer früheren, 1909 entstandenen Auferstehung, in welcher der Künstler noch an das tradierte Hochformat themengleicher Darstellungen anschließt, ist die große Auferstehung ein monumentales Querformat, das keinerlei Ausblick in einen lichtdurchdrungenen, erlösenden Himmel gewährt. Es ist ein Bild des Untergangs, geprägt vom Inferno des Krieges. Die Figuren – zum Teil noch in Bandagen (= Leichentücher) gehüllt – sind bis zur Unkenntlichkeit deformiert oder expressiv überzeichnet. Lemurenhaft kriechen sie aus klaffenden Spalten, wälzen sich über den Boden, um dann in aufgerichteter oder gewaltsam sich spreizender Haltung das Bild zu besetzen. Das Problem des Erwachens – ein Leitmotiv der Auferstehung – ist auf beklemmende Weise gegenwärtig. Auch Zerstörung und Chaos drängen sich auf: Häuser und Mauern stürzen zusammen oder fallen ins Nichts, Menschen rotten sich in verzweifelter Panik zusammen. »Der Maler stellt dar, was übrigbleibt, wenn die bewährten Projektionen versagen und die tröstliche Überblendung einer katastrophalen Realität nicht mehr möglich ist« (F. W. Fischer). Der Ausblick weckt keinerlei Hoffnung, mündet gleichsam ins Leere, wo sich das Bild der erloschenen Sonne (Off. 6,12) und ein apokalyptisches Feuerrad abzeichnen. Ein Bildzitat zur Linken verdient besondere Erwähnung: es ist die begonnene Komposition eines Gesellschaftsbildes, wie es Beckmann vor 1914 mehrfach gemalt hat. Unfertig oder verworfen, wie es hier – als Bild im Bilde – erscheint, schließt es den Gedanken des Scheiterns und das heißt zugleich die Unmöglichkeit ein, früher gültige Bild- und Wertvorstellungen im Angesicht einer durch den Krieg total veränderten Welt zu erneuern. Innerhalb des Bildzitats findet sich die erschreckende Aufschrift: zur Sache. Seitlich entdeckt man Beckmann mit seinen Vertrauten, die sich hinter einer aufgebrochenen Erdspalte – »wie in einem Schützengraben« – verbergen. Außer ihm, seiner Frau und Sohn Peter, der mit halbem Gesicht über die Erdspalte blickt, sind noch der Malerfreund Battenberg und dessen Frau zu identifizieren. – Für das in Verbindung mit dem Auferstehungsthema ungewöhnliche Breitformat hat unlängst Wolf Dieter Dube eine neue Deutung versucht: demnach wären – in freier Anlehnung an ältere Weltgerichtsbilder – jeweils im oberen Bildausschnitt zur Linken die Verdammten, zur Rechten die Erlösten dargestellt. Sollte sich diese Deutung als schlüssig erweisen, wäre die Dreiteilung der Komposition, die durch die kreisende Anordnung der Gruppen um die Mittelfigur nur wenig modifiziert wird, als Keimzelle der späteren Triptychen Beckmanns anzusehen.

Beckmann began work on the "Large Resurrection" in 1916 soon after his release from the army, where he served as a medical orderly. The painting is uncompleted, because its tension filled subject, nourished by apocalyptic thoughts, evaded realization in the classical sense; (despite Beckmann's statement: "if someone gives me the commission to finish it, then so be it.") In contrast to an earlier "Resurrection" (1909), where the artist followed the traditional vertical format of thematically comparable representations, the "Large Resurrection" has a monumental horizontal format, which offers no prospect of a light-drenched, redemptive heaven. It is a painting of destruction marked by the inferno of the war. The figures – partly still wrapped in bandages (= shrouds) are unrecognizably deformed or expressively overdrawn. Lemur-like, they creep out from gaping cracks, roll across the ground, then take possession of the painting in erect or forced sprawling poses. The question of awakening – a leitmotiv of the resurrection – is present in an oppressive way. Destruction too and chaos obtrude: houses and walls collapse or fall apart, humans flock together in despairing panic. "The artist represents that which remains, when conventional expectations fail and a comforting soft focus on a catastrophic reality is no longer possible" (F. W. Fischer). The prospect awakens no hope at all ending, as it were, in emptiness where the image of a dying sun (Off. 6,12) and an apocalyptic catherine-wheel are sketched. A pictorial quote on the left-hand side deserves particular mention: the early compositional stages of a society painting, which Beckmann painted several times before 1914. Unfinished or discarded as it appears here – a painting within a painting – it comprises thoughts of failure, and that also means the impossibility, in the face of a world totally altered by war, to renew formerly valid notions of picture-making and values. Within the pictorial quote there is a frightening inscription: to the point. To the side we discover Beckmann with his intimates, concealed behind an open chasm, "as if in a trench". Besides Beckmann, his wife and son Peter, whose half-hidden face peeps over the chasm, his painter friend Battenberg and his wife are also identifiable. – Wolf Dieter Dube has recently proposed a new interpretation of the unusual horizontal format in relation to the resurrection theme: a free imitation of traditional Last Judgement pictures – representing respectively, in the upper section of the painting, the damned on the left and, on the right, the saved. Should this interpretation prove conclusive, the tripartite division of the composition, which is only slightly modified by the circular organization of the groups around the central figure, could justifiably be seen as the germ of Beckmann's later triptychs.

Max Beckmann
Die Auferstehung
1916—1918
(Ausschnitt)

Max Beckmann
The Resurrection,
1916—1918
(Detail)

Max Beckmann

45

Die Loge

Öl auf Leinwand, 121 × 85 cm
Bezeichnet rechts unten: Beckmann F 28.
Sammlung Hugo Borst, Stuttgart. –
Erworben 1968.

Max Beckmann

45

The Theatre Box

Oil on canvas, 121 × 85 cm
Signed lower right: Beckmann F 28.
Collection Hugo Borst, Stuttgart. –
Purchased 1968.

Für »Die Loge« – das Hauptbild der ehemaligen Sammlung Borst in Stuttgart – hat Beckmann 1929 den Carnegie-Preis erhalten. Es war stets ein besonders beliebtes, weil in Motiv und Farbe sehr suggestiv wirksames Gemälde des Künstlers. Renoirs themengleiche Darstellung in London (Courtauld Institute) hat bei der Genese des Bildes Pate gestanden, doch ist aus der »spielerisch-heiteren«, impressionistisch locker gemalten Version des Franzosen etwas vollkommen anderes, ein typischer Beckmann geworden. Einem »asiatischen Götzenbild« (G. Busch) gleich thront die Dame starr und unbewegt hinter der Brüstung. Alles in ihr ist Sammlung und Konzentration. Selbst ihr Dekolleté – durch den Fächer zur Hälfte verdeckt – entzieht sich voyeurhafter Zudringlichkeit. Ihr Begleiter – ein Weltmann im Smoking – hat sich abgewendet, sucht oder besser gesagt »zielt« mit dem Glas in eine andere Richtung. Das Theater – skandalumwitterter Schauplatz der Szene – ist durch nur wenige, symbolträchtige »Versatzstücke« angedeutet: durch Säulen und Bogen, die schräg kippend oder sich rundend, teils stürzend, teils fliehend ein dynamisch wirksames Kräftefeld bilden, in dem sich Gestik und Haltung des Mannes verfangen. Er und mehr noch den Raum erscheinen hier als das Bewegte, als polarer Gegenpart zur »statuarischen Isolation« der Frau, deren stille Präsenz sich nachdrücklich einprägt. Die inhaltliche Spannung des Bildes klingt auch in der stark kontrastierenden Farbgebung an: ein tiefes samtenes Schwarz dominiert; dieses Schwarz – die wohl schwierigste, doch Beckmann immer wieder faszinierende Farbe – ist »nicht ein Abstraktum der Form, sondern Ausgangspunkt einer rein malerischen Gestaltung, Grundton eines Akkordes, der mit wenigen Griffen von Rot oder Gelb oder Grün bis in das reine Weiß hineinwächst« (Glaser). Das Raffinement der koloristischen Instrumentierung mag – wie bisweilen angenommen – französisch beeinflußt sein; der kraftvolle Einsatz der Farbe und deren themenbedingte gesteigerte Intensität suchen jedoch innerhalb der französischen Kunst ihresgleichen.

In 1929 Beckmann received the Carnegie Prize for "The Theatre Box", the most important painting in the former Borst collection in Stuttgart. It was always a particularly well-loved painting, due to the affective suggestiveness of its motif and colour. Renoir's painting with a similar theme in London (Courtauld Institute) influenced the genesis of the painting, but something quite different has been made out of the "playful gaiety" of the loosely painted impressionist version by the Frenchman; it has become a typical Beckmann. Like an "Asian idol" (G. Busch) the lady is throned, stiff and rigid, behind the balustrade. She is all composure and concentration. Even her decolletage – half-hidden by the fan – evades voyeuristic approaches. Her companion – a dandy in a tuxedo – has turned away, searching or rather "aiming" in another direction with his opera glasses. The theatre – the scandalous scene of action – is suggested by a few symbolic "props": by pillars and archways which topple obliquely or swell, plunge and spring – creating a dynamic field of force in which the gesture and pose of the man are caught. He – like the spatial context – appears animated, in polar opposition to the "statuesque isolation" of the woman, whose immobile presence makes an emphatic impression. The thematic tension of the painting is also echoed in the strongly contrasting colouration: a deep velvety black dominates. This black – certainly the most difficult but for Beckmann always the most fascinating colour – is "not an abstraction of form, but rather the springboard for a pure painterly design, the key tone of a chord which, with a few strokes of red or yellow or green, crescendos into a pure white" (Glaser). The refined instrumentation of colour may – as is sometimes assumed – bespeak a French influence; but we would have to search far in French art for a comparably strong employment of colour whose intensity is heightened in response to the theme.

Literatur: Jahrbuch der Staatlichen Kunstsammlungen in Baden-Württemberg, VI, 1969, S. 322 mit Abb. – Kat. 1982, 20. Jahrhundert, S. 89 mit Abb.

Bibliography: Jahrbuch der Staatlichen Kunstsammlungen in Baden-Württemberg, VI, 1969, p. 322 with ill. – Cat. 1982, 20. Jahrhundert, p. 89 with ill.

Giorgio de Chirico

Geboren 1888 in Volos/Thessalien, gestorben 1978 in Rom. 1906–1909 in München, Studium an der Akademie, beeinflußt von Böcklin und Klinger. Anschließend in Mailand, Florenz und Turin. 1911–1915 in Paris. Bekanntschaft mit Apollinaire. 1917 Freundschaft mit Carrá und Gründung der »Metaphysischen Schule«. Seit 1919 in Rom. 1925–1931 wieder in Paris, Kontakt zu den Surrealisten. Seit 1931 überwiegend in Italien, 1935/36 in den USA, 1945 Niederlassung in Rom.

46

Interno metafisico con grande officina

Metaphysisches Interieur mit großer Fabrik

Öl auf Leinwand, 96,3 × 73,8 cm
Bezeichnet links Mitte: G. de Chirico 1916.
Sammlung Carlo Frua de Angeli, Mailand.
Erworben aus dem Schweizer Kunsthandel 1970.

1916 entstanden, gehört das Gemälde zu den Inkunabeln der Pittura Metafisica, deren Begründer und wichtigster Repräsentant Giorgio de Chirico war. Dargestellt ist ein Bild im Bild: eine Fabriklandschaft von abweisender Anonymität innerhalb eines Interieurs, das sich seitlich auf eine in gleißendes Mondlicht getauchte Palastwand hin öffnet. Den Raum verstellen Winkel, Schablonen, stereometrische Körper und Stäbe, die teils gruppiert, teils in gewagter Balance isoliert sind. Die Schärfe in der Fixierung der Gegenstände, bei freibleibender Deutung ihres Zusammenhangs, und die auf Veränderung drängende Unruhe im Stabilen lösen einen Irrationseffekt aus, der durch den eigenwilligen Einsatz perspektivischer Mittel noch intensiviert wird. Ein Podest – zunächst als Basis für das Fabrikbild gedacht – schiebt sich nach vorn, von unten gesehen verwandelt es sich in eine »fliehende« Decke, so daß das Fabrikbild in einen seltsamen, unser Raumgefühl dislozierenden »Schwebezustand« gerät. Oben und Unten sind austauschbar, also variabel erlebbar wie mehr oder weniger alle Erscheinungsformen der Realität, sobald sie im Aufbau des »metaphysischen« Bildes ihrer Kausalität enthoben und dadurch vieldeutiger, die Magie des Realen steigernder Wirkung zugeführt werden.

Painted in 1916, the picture belongs to the incunabula of Pittura Metafisica, whose founder and most important representative was Giorgio de Chirico. A picture within a picture is represented: a landscape with an unfriendly, anonymous factory – in an interior that opens at the side onto a palace wall bathed in gleaming moonlight. The room is obstructed by angle measures, stencils, stereometric forms and poles, partially grouped and partially isolated in a precarious balance. The exact rendition of the objects together with the unspecified significance of their combination, and the transformative disquiet in the midst of stability, release an irrational effect which is further intensified by the idiosyncratic employment of perspectival means. A pedestal – intended in the first instance as a base for the factory picture – pushes forwards; seen from beneath it changes into a "flying carpet", so that the factory painting assumes a peculiar "suspended state", disorienting our own sense of space. Above and below are interchangeable; that is, contingently apprehendable, like all manifestations of reality are to a lesser or greater extent, as soon as their causality is suspended in the structure of the "metaphysical" painting. In this way they are imbued with a more ambiguous effect that intensifies the magic of reality.

Giorgio de Chirico

Born 1888 in Volos/Thessaly, died 1978 in Rome. 1906–1909 in Munich, studied at the Academy, influenced by Böcklin and Klinger. Subsequently in Milan, Florence and Turin. 1911–1915 in Paris. Acquaintance with Apollinaire. 1917 acquaintance with Carrà and foundation of the "Scuola Metafisica" (School of Metaphysical Painting). After 1919 in Rome. 1925–1931 back in Paris, contact with the Surrealists. After 1931 mainly in Italy, 1935/36 in the USA, 1945 settled in Rome.

46

Interno metafisico con grande officina

Metaphysical Interior with Large Factory

Oil on canvas, 96.3 × 73.8 cm
Signed middle left: G. de Chirico 1916.
Collection Carlo Frua de Angeli, Milan. –
Purchased from the Swiss art market in 1970.

Literatur: Jahrbuch der Staatlichen Kunstsammlungen in Baden-Württemberg, VIII, 1971, S. 289 ff. mit Abb. – Kat. 1982, 20. Jahrhundert, S. 107 ff. mit Abb. – Karin von Maur, in: Große Gemäldegalerien, herausgegeben von Erich Steingräber, München 1980, S. 459 mit Abb.

Bibliography: Jahrbuch der Staatlichen Kunstsammlungen in Baden-Württemberg, VIII, 1971, p. 289 f. with ill. – Cat. 1982, 20. Jahrhundert, p. 107 f. with ill. – Karin von Maur, in: Große Gemäldegalerien, ed. by Erich Steingräber, Munich 1980, p. 459 with ill.

Max Ernst

Geboren 1891 in Brühl bei Köln, gestorben 1976 in Paris. 1909–1914 Studium der Philosophie in Bonn. 1913 in Paris. 1914 Begegnung mit Arp in Köln. Danach Kriegsdienst. 1919 Gründung der Kölner DADA-Gruppe mit Arp. Seit 1922 in Paris. 1924 Mitbegründer der surrealistischen Bewegung ebenda. 1941–1953 mit Unterbrechungen in den USA. 1954 wieder in Paris. 1968 Niederlassung in Seillans. Seit 1958 französischer Staatsbürger.

47

Sainte Cécile –
Le piano invisible

Heilige Cäcilie – Das unsichtbare Klavier

Öl auf Leinwand, 101 × 82 cm
Bezeichnet rechts unten: max ernst/23;
links unten: sainte cécile.
Sammlung Johanna Ey, Düsseldorf. –
Süddeutscher Privatbesitz. –
Erworben 1973.

Max Ernst

Born 1891 in Brühl near Cologne, died 1976 in Paris. 1909–1914 studied philosophy in Bonn. 1913 in Paris. 1914 met Arp in Cologne. Then war service. 1919 founded the Cologne DADA-group with Arp. After 1922 in Paris. 1924 founding member of the Paris, Surrealist group. 1941–1953 interruptedly in the USA. 1954 back in Paris. 1968 settled in Seillans. After 1958 French citizenship.

47

Sainte Cécile –
Le piano invisible

St Cecilia – The Invisible Piano

Oil on canvas, 101 × 82 cm
Signed lower right: max ernst/23;
Lower left: sainte cécile.
Collection Johanna Ey, Düsseldorf. –
South German private collection. –
Purchased 1973.

Die Darstellung geht auf die Legende der heiligen Cäcilie zurück, die im 3. Jahrhundert ein grausames Martyrium erleiden mußte, weil sie sich weigerte, den heidnischen Göttern zu huldigen. Da während ihres Leidens die himmlische Orgel gespielt haben soll, wurde Cäcilie seit dem späten Mittelalter auch als Schutzpatronin der Kirchenmusik verehrt. Die Ummauerung, in der sie auf dem Stuttgarter Gemälde erscheint, stellt das Caldarium dar, in dem sie ersticken oder verbrennen sollte. Kraft ihres Glaubens konnte sie jedoch zunächst überleben (geraffte Inhaltsbeschreibung nach Karin v. Maur im Kat. 1982). – Max Ernst verarbeitet in seinem Gemälde verschiedene Quellen dieses in der Hagiographie eher umstrittenen, weil auf unterschiedlicher Überlieferung basierenden Berichts. Auch in der freien Verwendung älterer Bildmotive macht sich sein Hang zu »surrealistischer Kombinatorik« bemerkbar. Haltung und im besonderen Gestik der Heiligen erinnern an das Gemälde »Die heilige Cäcilie an der Orgel« von Carlo Dolci in Dresden, das Max Ernsts Vater kopiert hatte. Die Ummauerung geht — wie Stefanie Poley nachweisen konnte — auf einen Stich von Pierre Jean Mariette aus dem 18. Jahrhundert zurück, der den Aufbau der gipsernen Ummantelung für den Bronzeguß eines Reiterstandbildes von Ludwig XV. zeigt. Es entspricht durchaus dem Arbeitsprinzip der Collage, daß Max Ernst auch als Maler eine fremde Bildidee nahezu wörtlich zitiert, aber insoweit verfremdet, als er sie veränderter Sinngebung zuführt. Das Gemäuer hat ausgesprochenen Zerfallscharakter; die in den unregelmäßigen Vertiefungen befindlichen Ösen blicken wie Augen aus dem Gestein, die sich sinnbildlich auf die »Kraft geistigen Sehens« beziehen. Die Heilige ist nur physisch blind und deshalb außerstande, ihre Umwelt auf »natürlichem« Weg zu erfahren, schon ihr Name »Cécile« spielt auf »cécité«, Blindheit, an. Dieser Eindruck wird noch dadurch verstärkt, daß ihre Hände die aufbrechende Verschalung durchdringen und nach den imaginären Tasten eines sich aus Steinen (!) formenden Klaviers greifen. In der ambivalenten Verknüpfung von Hülle und Kern, von Bewegung und Starre, von Metamorphose und Zeit ist das Gemälde ein Leitbild des Surrealismus geworden, und dies um so mehr, als auch der visionäre Charakter der Darstellung den programmatischen Vorstellungen der Surrealisten entsprach.

The depiction refers to the legend of St Cecilia who suffered a grisly martyrdom in the 3rd century because she refused to worship the heathen gods. Because heavenly organs are said to have played while she suffered, Cecilia has been honoured since the late Middle Ages as the patron saint of church music. The encasing wall in which she appears in the Stuttgart painting represents the caldarium in which she was to suffocate or burn. By virtue of her faith however, she was able to survive for the present (outline of the content as described by Karin v. Maur in the 1982 catalogue). — Max Ernst integrates into his painting various sources of this legend, disputed in hagiography because it is based on different traditions. Also his free use of older pictorial motifs makes evident his bent for "the surrealist art of combination". The pose and above all the gestures of the saint recall the painting "St Cecilia at the Organ" by Carlo Dolci in Dresden, which Max Ernst's father had copied. The encasement refers — as Stefanie Poley has proved — to an 18th century engraving by Pierre Jean Mariette, which shows the construction of the plaster casing for the bronze cast of an equestrian portrait of Ludwig XV. This corresponds throughout to the working principle of collage, which Max Ernst almost literally quotes even when he is painting a foreign pictorial concept; but he "alienates" by introducing a different interpretation. The crumbling wall is clearly a ruin; the loops in the irregular hollows look out like eyes from the rock, referring symbolically to the "strength of spiritual sight". The saint is only physically blind, and therefore not in a position to experience her surroundings in a "natural" way; even her name "Cécile" alludes to "cécité" (blindness). This impression is further strengthened by the way her hands pierce through the cracking encasement and reach for the imaginary keyboard of a piano which metamorphoses out of the stone (!). In its ambivalent combination of case and kernel, of movement and rigidity, of metamorphosis and time, the painting has come to exemplify Surrealism, all the more because the visionary character of the representation corresponded to the programmatic ideas of the Surrealists.

Literatur: Stefanie Poley, Die Bildquellen zu »Sainte Cécile« und »Ubu Imperator« von Max Ernst, in: Jahrbuch der Staatlichen Kunstsammlungen in Baden-Württemberg, X, 1973, S. 89 ff. mit Abb. – Kat. 1982, 20. Jahrhundert, S. 123 mit Abb. – Karin von Maur, in: Große Gemäldegalerien, herausgegeben von Erich Steingräber, München 1980, S. 459 mit Abb.

Bibliography: Stefanie Poley, "Die Bildquellen zu 'Sainte Cécile' und 'Ubu Imperator' von Max Ernst" in: Jahrbuch der Staatlichen Kunstsammlungen in Baden-Württemberg, X, 1973, p. 89 f. with ill. – Cat. 1982, 20. Jahrhundert, p. 123 with ill. – Karin von Maur, in: Große Gemäldegalerien, ed. by Erich Steingräber, Munich 1980, p. 459 with ill.

René Magritte

Geboren 1898 in Lessines/Belgien, gestorben 1967 in Brüssel. 1916–1918 Studium an der Akademie in Brüssel. Beeinflußt von de Chirico. 1927–1930 in Paris; enge Kontakte zu Breton, Eluard, Miró und Arp. 1929 Sommeraufenthalt bei Dali in Cadaquès. Seit 1930 wieder in Brüssel.

48

L'Apparition

Die Erscheinung

Entstanden 1928
Öl auf Leinwand, 82,5 × 116 cm
Rückseitig betitelt.
Sammlung E. L. T. Mesens, Brüssel. –
Sammlung Betty Barman, Brüssel. –
Erworben aus Brüsseler Privatbesitz 1972.

René Magritte

Born 1898 in Lessines/Belgium, died 1967 in Brussels. 1916–1918 studied at the Academy in Brussels. Influenced by de Chirico. 1927–1930 in Paris; close contact with Breton, Eluard, Miró and Arp. 1929 spent the summer with Dali in Cadaquès. After 1930 back in Brussels.

48

L'Apparition

The Apparition

Oil on canvas, 82.5 × 116 cm
Title on reverse.
Collection E. L. T. Mesens, Brussels. –
Collection Betty Barman, Brussels. –
Purchased from a Brussels private
collection in 1972.

Sprache und Darstellung in einander erhellender Funktion kombinierend, erschließt das Gemälde ein von Magritte auch in seinen theoretischen Schriften eingehend erläutertes »Abbildungsproblem«. Ein Mann mit Bowler, der gegen den nächtlichen Horizont schreitet, ist umgeben von nahezu gleichartigen abstrakten Formelementen, die genaue Bezeichnungen tragen: fusil (Gewehr), fauteuil (Sessel), cheval (Pferd), horizon (Horizont) und nuage (Wolke). Fast wörtlich weist Magritte einmal darauf hin, daß die Aussage Wolke (nuage) im Bereich der üblichen mündlichen Mitteilung eine Aneinanderreihung von Lauten ist, die sich ebenso wie ihre schriftliche Fixierung an die Stelle eines Gegenstandes setzen. »Genau diesen Vorgang, dessen wir uns im einzelnen gar nicht so bewußt sind, reproduziert das Gemälde ›l'apparition‹, indem es das bildliche Zeichen durch das sprachliche ersetzt« (Schneede). Durch die Konfrontation der Figur mit der Leere des Horizonts, aber auch durch die rätselhafte Verknüpfung der verbalen Motive entsteht eine ungewohnte, die Phantasie des Betrachters aktivierende Konstellation, die wohl auf einen »Geschehnis«-Zusammenhang der einzelnen Bildgegenstände hindeuten könnte, ohne daß sie diesen Zusammenhang aber tatsächlich preisgibt. Das geheimnisvolle Dunkel, aus dem sich Figur und Dingbezeichnungen wie Schattenformen herauslösen, verstärkt diesen Eindruck. – Ungeachtet der stimulierenden Wirkung, die von de Chiricos »Dingverfremdung« auf Magritte ausging, bezeichnen die verschlüsselten »Wort-Bild-Malereien« des belgischen Surrealisten eine eigene Leistung, die sich auch von der provokativen (zu alogischer Fragmentierung tendierenden) Wort-Collage der Dadaisten eindeutig absetzt.

Combining language and representation in a mutually illuminating relation, the painting addresses a "problem of illustration" that Magritte also expounds in detail in his theoretical writings. A man in a bowler hat, who is walking towards the nocturnal horizon, is surrounded by almost similar abstract formal elements, which carry exact designations; fusil (gun), fauteuil (chair), cheval (horse), horizon (horizon) and nuage (cloud). Magritte refers almost literally to the fact that the expression cloud (nuage) is a stringing together of sounds in the realm of conventional oral communication which, just like its written form, stands in for an object. "The painting 'l'apparition' exactly reproduces this process (which we are not so aware of in its particularity) by substituting the spoken for the pictorial sign" (Schneede). By means of the confrontation between the figure and the empty horizon, but also by means of the ambiguous conjunction of verbal motifs, an unfamiliar constellation arises that activates the viewer's imagination. Certainly the correlation of the separate pictorial elements might suggest an "event", but this correlation is not actually revealed. The mysterious darkness out of which the figure and the "object-signs" emerge like shadows strengthens this impression. Leaving aside the stimulus for Magritte of de Chirico's "alienated objects", the encoded "word-image-painting" of the Belgian surrealist represents an independent achievement that also clearly contrasts with the Dadaists' provocative word-collage (tending to allogical fragmentation).

Literatur: Jahrbuch der Staatlichen Kunstsammlungen in Baden-Württemberg, X, 1973, S. 238 mit Abb. – Uwe M. Schneede, René Magritte, Leben und Werk, Köln 1973, S. 42 mit Abb. – Kat. 1982, 20. Jahrhundert, S. 211 ff. mit Abb.

Bibliography: Jahrbuch der Staatlichen Kunstsammlungen in Baden-Württemberg, X, 1973, p. 238 with ill. – Uwe M. Schneede, René Magritte, Leben und Werk, Cologne 1973, p. 42 with ill. – Cat. 1982, 20. Jahrhundert, p. 211 f. with ill.

Piet Mondrian

Geboren 1872 in Amersfoort bei Utrecht, gestorben 1944 in New York. 1892–1894 Studium der Malerei an der Rijksakademie in Amsterdam. 1908–1910 wiederholt in Domburg; Begegnung mit Jan Toorop. 1911–1914 in Paris. 1915 Bekanntschaft mit Van Doesburg. 1917 Mitbegründer von De Stijl. 1919–1938 in Paris. Seit 1930 Teilnahme an den Ausstellungen von Abstraction – Création. 1938–1940 in London, danach in New York.

49

Komposition in Weiß, Rot und Blau

Öl auf Leinwand, 98,5 × 80,3 cm
Bezeichnet halbblinks unten: P. M. 36.
Sammlung Felix Witzinger, Basel. –
Erworben 1966.

Piet Mondrian

Born 1872 in Amersfoort near Utrecht, died 1944 in New York. 1892–1894 studied painting at the "Rijksakademie" in Amsterdam. 1908–1910 repeated visits to Domburg; meeting with Jan Toorop. 1911–1914 in Paris. 1915 acquaintance with van Doesburg. 1917 founder member of De Stijl. 1919–1938 in Paris. After 1930 took part in the Abstraction-Création exhibitions. 1938–1940 in London, then in New York.

49

Composition in White, Red and Blue

Oil on canvas, 98.5 × 80.3 cm
Signed lower middle left: P. M. 36.
Collection Felix Witzinger, Basel. –
Purchased 1966.

»Die Kunstkultur, die zur reinsten und wirklichsten Darstellung des Eigentlichen in der Kunst hinleitet, mußte zwangsläufig zur Kunst ohne Objekte führen. Die Gestaltungselemente, die diese Kunst benützt, können wir neutral nennen, da sie keinen einschränkenden Charakter haben.« In diesen Sätzen Mondrians ist unmißverständlich zum Ausdruck gebracht, daß seine Kunst sich auf der Höhe ihrer Entfaltung in autonomer, vom Naturvorbild abgelöster Gestaltung verwirklichen mußte. Vom Kubismus ausgehend, war Mondrian schon vor dem Ersten Weltkrieg bestrebt, Struktur und Farbe aus ihrer gegenständlichen Bindung zu lösen und zunehmend zu verselbständigen. Es bedurfte freilich noch einiger Jahre, bevor das lineare Gefüge seiner Bilder aller räumlich-illusionistischen Wirkungen entbunden und auf wenige sich rechtwinklig kreuzende Teilungslinien zurückgeführt war, durch welche die Farbkompartimente sowohl getrennt wie in ihrer Beziehung zueinander aktiviert wurden. Das war ebenso neu wie bedeutsam; denn auf der Grundlage der von Mondrian verwendeten Bauelemente und ihrer Kontraste ließen sich – frei von deskriptiver Befrachtung – ausgleichende Beziehungen herstellen, ein »elementares Gleichgewicht«, in dem »ästhetische Harmonie« als formelhaftes Gleichnis »universaler Harmonie« darstellbar wurde. Das Stuttgarter Bild gehört bereits in die Spätzeit dieser Entwicklung. 1936 entstanden, vereint es alle für Mondrian charakteristischen Gestaltungsfaktoren: die strenge Flächenbindung der Darstellung, aber auch die lineare Verspannung der Komposition, in der die Farbe als reine Primärfarbe (Rot und Blau) in ein konstituierendes Spannungsverhältnis zu den nichtfarbigen Bildzonen gesetzt ist. Anders als auf einem 1922 entstandenen, das Bildfeld weitgehend freistellenden Gemälde des Künstlers in der Staatsgalerie (siehe Frontispiz) ist das lineare Gerüst hier dem Achsenkreuz angenähert, das Bild so vierfach teilend, wobei jeder Teil – obschon in einem übergreifenden Zusammenhang stehend – nochmals unterschiedliche Möglichkeiten der Bildteilung aufzeigt.

"The artistic culture that steers towards the purest and most real representation of what is unique to art must necessarily lead to a non-objective art. We could call the elements of design that this art employs neutral, because they do not have a restrictive character." With these words Mondrian voiced unequivocally his belief that his art at the height of its development must realize an autonomous form divorced from the natural model. Taking Cubism as a point of departure, Mondrian had already attempted, before the First World War, to free structure and colour from their representational function and to render them increasingly self-sufficient. To be sure, it took several more years before the linear structure of his paintings was liberated from all spatial illusionistic effects and reduced to a few dividing lines crossing at rightangles, which both separated the coloured areas and activated their interrelation. This was just as innovative as it was significant: because, on the basis of the constructive elements Mondrian used and their contrasts, it was possible to achieve balanced relationships – free from all descriptive burden; an "elemental balance" which rendered possible the depiction of an "universal harmony" in prescriptive terms. The Stuttgart painting already belongs to a late stage in this development. Painted in 1936, it combines all Mondrian's characteristic principles of design: the uncompromising planarity of representation, but also the linear bracing of the composition, in which colour as pure primary hue (red and blue) is set in a relationship of constructive tension with the uncoloured pictorial zones. In contrast to a 1922 painting by the artist in the Staatsgalerie (see frontispiece), where the picture plane is largely left open, the linear scaffolding here is near to the central axis, thus dividing the picture into four parts, in which each part – although placed in overlapping association – presents different possibilities of pictorial division.

Literatur: Kat. 1968, S. 126 mit Abb. – Kat. 1982, 20. Jahrhundert, S. 234 mit Abb. – Karin von Maur, in: Große Gemäldegalerien, herausgegeben von Erich Steingräber, München 1980, S. 468 mit Abb.

Bibliography: Cat. 1968, p. 126 with ill. – Cat. 1982, 20. Jahrhundert, p. 234 with ill. – Karin von Maur, in: Große Gemäldegalerien, ed. by Erich Steingräber, Munich 1980, p. 468 with ill.

Oskar Schlemmer

Geboren 1888 in Stuttgart, gestorben 1943 in Baden-Baden. 1906–1914 Studium an der Stuttgarter Akademie unter Friedrich von Keller, Landenberger und Hölzel. Freundschaft mit Meyer-Amden und Baumeister. 1911/12 in Berlin. 1914 in Paris. 1914–1918 Kriegsdienst. 1921–1928 am Bauhaus in Weimar und Dessau; Leiter der Bildhauerei, Wandmalerei und Bauhausbühne. 1929–1932 Professor an der Breslauer Akademie, 1932/33 an den Vereinigten Staatsschulen Berlin-Charlottenburg. 1934 in der Schweiz. Seit 1935 in Südbaden. 1939–1943 Tätigkeit in Stuttgart für ein Malergeschäft und in Wuppertal bei der Lackfabrik Dr. Herberts.

50

Plan mit Figuren

Entstanden 1919
Öl und Collage (Metallfolie) auf Leinwand,
93 × 130 cm
Bezeichnet rückseitig: Oskar/Schlemmer/
Plan mit Figuren.
Erworben 1965 aus dem Nachlaß.

Zu betont figurativen Resultaten gelangte die konstruktive Malerei im wesentlichen auf deutschem Boden. Vor allem bei Schlemmer erwies sich die menschliche Gestalt als zentrales, sein ganzes Schaffen bestimmendes Thema. Schlemmer stellt den Menschen nicht in seiner zeitbedingten individuellen Erscheinung, sondern als autonome »Kunstfigur« dar, die in enger Verknüpfung zum Bezugsfeld ihrer Präsenz – zu Fläche und Raum – steht. So auch im »Plan mit Figuren«, der 1919, noch vor der Berufung des Künstlers an das Staatliche Bauhaus in Weimar, entstand. Zehn Figuren – teils stehend, teils liegend – sind so angeordnet, daß sie in ihrer Gruppierung mehrfach die Kreuzung von Senkrecht und Waagrecht wiederholen. Alle Gestalten sind geometrisierend vereinfacht; Profil-, Vorder- und Rückenansicht werden gleichsam modellhaft vor Augen geführt. Die Darstellung ist an die Fläche gebunden. Allein die Wandlungen im Maßstab und der Wechsel zwischen flächiger und modellierender Malweise lassen den Eindruck entstehen, als ob sich die Figuren in verschiedenen Raum-Ebenen halten. Das Bild steht also an der Schwelle zu den späteren Gemälden des Künstlers, in denen der Raum die Fläche vollends verdrängt und die Figur »rundplastischer« Gestaltung zugeführt wird.

Constructivist painting gave rise first and foremost to figurative results in Germany. Above all in Schlemmer's work the human form proved to be the central theme, determining his entire creative production. Schlemmer does not represent humans in their temporal and individual form, but rather as autonomous "art figures", which stand in close association with their relational field – the pictorial plane and space that answer their presence. This also holds true for "Plan with Figures", painted in 1919 before the artist was appointed to the Bauhaus in Weimar. Ten figures – some standing, some reclining – are so disposed that their grouping frequently repeats the intersection of perpendicular and horizontal lines. All the figures are geometrically simplified: profile, frontal and back views are presented, all similarly mannequin-like. The representation is bound to the picture plane. Only the changing proportions and the alternation between a planar painterly style and modelling give rise to the impression that the figures remain in separate spatial pockets. Thus the picture stands on the threshold of Schlemmer's later paintings, in which space is totally subordinated to flatness and the figure is endowed with a "spherical plasticity".

Oskar Schlemmer

Born 1888 in Stuttgart, died 1943 in Baden-Baden. 1906–1914 studied at the Stuttgart Academy under Friedrich von Keller, Landenberger and Hölzel. Friendship with Meyer-Amden and Baumeister. 1911/12 in Berlin. 1914 in Paris. 1914–1918 war service. 1921–1928 at the Bauhaus in Weimar and Dessau; head of sculpture, mural painting and the Bauhaus theatre. 1929–1932 Professor at the Breslau Academy, 1932/33 at the "Vereinigten Staatsschulen" Berlin-Charlottenburg. 1934 in Switzerland. After 1935 in South Baden. 1939–1943 worked in Stuttgart for an artists' supplies shop and in Wuppertal in Dr. Herberts' lacquer factory.

50

Plan with Figures

1919
Oil and collage (silver foil)
on canvas, 93 × 130 cm
Signed on reverse: Oskar/Schlemmer/Plan
mit Figuren.
Purchased 1965 from the estate.

Literatur: Kat. 1968, S. 160. – Kat. 1982, 20. Jahrhundert, S. 287 mit Abb.

Bibliography: Cat. 1968, p. 160. – Cat. 1982, 20. Jahrhundert, p. 287, with ill.

Oskar Schlemmer

51

Figurinen zum
Triadischen Ballett

*Ausgeführt 1920–1922 in Stuttgart,
1926 teilweise erneuert von der Firma
Theaterkunst in Berlin. Seit 1975 restauriert
in der Staatsgalerie Stuttgart unter Leitung
von Siegfried Cremer. Verschiedene
Materialien, auf neue Trägerfiguren
montiert, Höhe 185 cm bis 205 cm
Erworben 1979 aus dem Nachlaß. Stiftung
der Landesgirokasse an den Stuttgarter
Galerieverein.*

Oskar Schlemmer

51

Figurines for the
Triadic Ballet

*Executed 1920–1922 in Stuttgart,
1926 partially renewed by the firm
"Theaterkunst" in Berlin.
After 1975 restored in the
Staatsgalerie Stuttgart under the direction
of Siegfried Cremer
Various materials, mounted onto new
models, height 185 cm–205 cm.
Purchased 1979 from the estate.
Donated by the Landesgirokasse to the
Stuttgart Galerieverein.*

Zu Beginn seiner Lehrtätigkeit am Staatlichen Bauhaus in Weimar hat sich Schlemmer zunehmend mit Problemen der Plastik befaßt, auch hier das Räumliche in der Durchdringung stereometrischer Grundformen suchend. Aber diese materielle Einführung der dritten Dimension befriedigte ihn nur bedingt, da die Fixierung aller Bewegung in der End-Gestalt des einzelnen plastischen Werks die von ihm erstrebte »korrespondierende« Beziehung zwischen Figur und Raum weitgehend einschränkte. Möglichkeiten zur Lösung dieses Problems boten sich allenfalls dort, wo die bildhafte Statik (die Schlemmer selbst bisweilen als »tragisch« empfand) in Bewegung aufgelöst werden konnte, nämlich auf der Bühne und hier im besonderen beim Tanz. Schlemmer war ein begeisterter Theatermensch. Schon in seiner Jugend hatte ihn die Bühne als reiner »Kunstraum« gefesselt. Er war selbst Tänzer und arbeitete gerade in diesen Jahren an der Vollendung seines »Triadischen Balletts«, das 1922 seine Uraufführung erlebte. Konstruktive Überlegungen spielten darin eine nicht minder bestimmende Rolle wie sein Verhältnis zur Zahlensymbolik. Der Dreiteilung des Spielplans in Gelb (heiter-burlesk), Rosa (festlich-getragen) und Schwarz (heroisch-mystisch) entsprach die Dreizahl der Tänzer, die er einzeln, paarweise oder zu dritt auftreten ließ, den Raum so immer neu ausdeutend oder — um in der Sprache Schlemmers zu bleiben — »modulierend«. Kostüme und Masken der »Triaden« stellten sich Schlemmer als »raumplastische« Schöpfungen dar, die freilich erst durch das Medium des menschlichen Körpers zu »mobilen« Plastiken wurden. Von den vielen Möglichkeiten, die Schwerkraft des Physischen im Tanz aufzuheben, wählte er bezeichnenderweise die der expressiven Suggestion entgegengesetzte: die strenge Disziplin mechanisch wirksamer Gesten. Schlemmers Figurinen sind dem Raum nicht neutral, sondern in einer ihn interpretierenden Funktion zugeordnet. Der Raum entsteht erst im Dialog mit den Figuren, die ihn durchdringen und gliedern, und so Ausgangspunkt und Mittler sich ständig wandelnder Raumdeutung werden, in der sich die Intention des Plastikers und des Choreographen Schlemmer vollendet.

When he took up his teaching position at the Weimar Bauhaus, Schlemmer was increasingly concerned with the problems of sculpture, still searching for spatiality by penetrating stereometric elementary forms. But this material introduction of the third dimension was only partially satisfying, because the fixation of all movement in the final form of individual sculptures largely restricted the "corresponding" relationship between figure and space that he strove to realize. Possibilities of solving this problem arose where pictorial statics (which Schlemmer himself in the meantime experienced as "tragic"), could be broken down — namely on the stage, and particularly in dance. Schlemmer was an enthusiastic theatre-goer. In his youth the stage had already captivated him as a pure "artistic space". He was a dancer himself and was currently working on the completion of his "Triadic Ballet", first performed in 1922. Constructive principles and numerical symbolism both played a rôle here. The tripartite division of the programme into yellow (gay burlesque), pink (sober-solemn) and black (heroic-mystical) corresponded to the triad of dancers, which he made appear individually, in pairs or as a threesome, always interpreting or — to use Schlemmer's words — "modelling" the space anew. Schlemmer designed "spatial-sculptural" costumes and masks for the "triad", which certainly only became "mobile" sculptures through the medium of the human body. Significantly, he chose from the many possibilities of dissolving physical gravity by dance that which is diametrically opposed to expressive suggestion: the uncompromising discipline of mechanistic gestures. Schlemmer's figurines do not neutrally confront space, rather they are coordinated with it by means of their interpretative rôle. Space only materializes in a dialogue with the figures, which penetrate and articulate the void, becoming the springboard and mediator of a constantly transforming spatial construction, in which Schlemmer's intentions as a sculptor and as a choreographer are fully realized.

Literatur: Kat. 1982, 20. Jahrhundert, S. 292 ff. mit Abb.

Bibliography: Cat. 1982, 20. Jahrhundert, p. 292 f. with ill.

Oskar Schlemmer
Figurinen zum Triadischen Ballett
1920—1922

Oskar Schlemmer
Figurines for the Triadic Ballet,
1920—1922

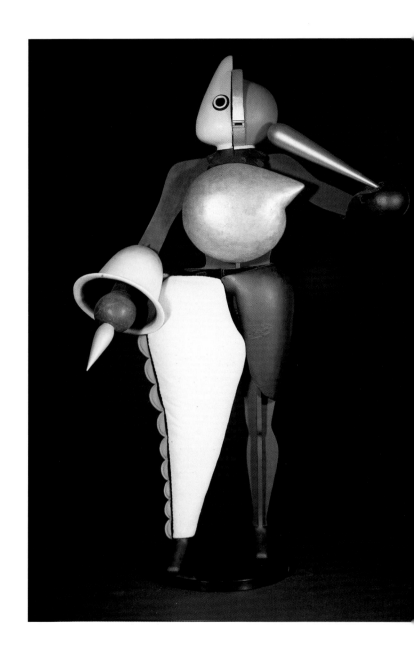

Oskar Schlemmer
Der Abstrakte
Figurine aus dem
Triadischen Ballett

Oskar Schlemmer
The Abstract
Figurine from the
Triadic Ballet

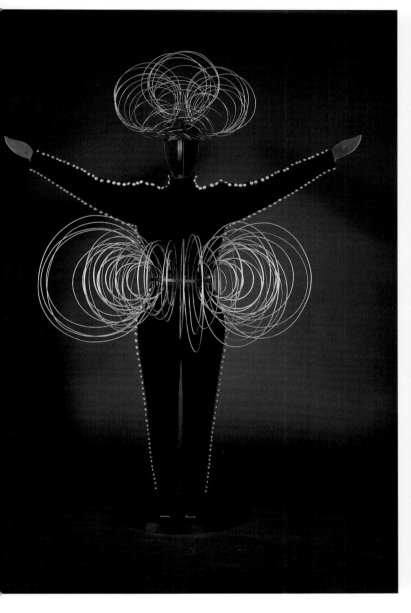

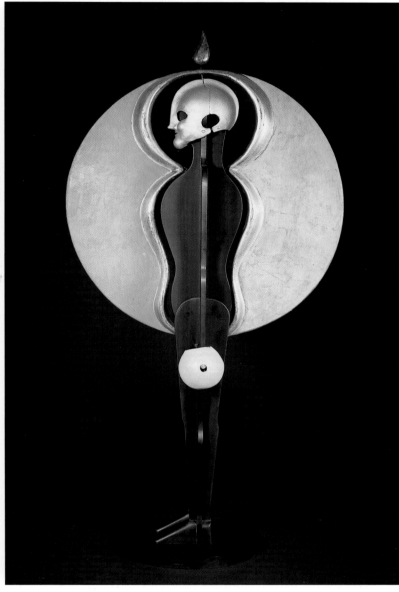

Oskar Schlemmer
Drahtfigur
Figurine aus dem
Triadischen Ballett

Oskar Schlemmer
Wire Figure
Figurine from
the Triadic Ballet

Oskar Schlemmer
Scheibentänzer
Figurine aus dem
Triadischen Ballett

Oskar Schlemmer
Disc-Dancer
Figurine from the
Triadic Ballet

Willi Baumeister

Geboren 1889 in Stuttgart, gestorben 1955 ebenda. 1905–1907 Lehre als Dekorationsmaler und Besuch der Zeichenklasse an der Stuttgarter Akademie. Freundschaft mit Schlemmer und Meyer-Amden. 1910 in der Komponierklasse von Adolf Hölzel. 1911 in Paris, 1913 in Amden/Schweiz. 1914 erneut in Paris. 1914–1918 Kriegsdienst. Seit 1919 wieder in Stuttgart. 1924 in Paris, Bekanntschaft mit Léger, Ozenfant und Le Corbusier. 1928–1933 Professor an der Städelschen Kunstschule in Frankfurt/M. Danach in Stuttgart. 1943–1945 in Urach. 1946–1955 Professor an der Stuttgarter Akademie.

52

Variante zu Eidos I

Auch »Amöbe« oder »Östliche Legende« genannt

Öl auf Leinwand, 58 × 38 cm
Bezeichnet rechts unten: Baumeister 38.
Erworben aus Stuttgarter Privatbesitz 1950.

Das Bild gehört in die Reihe der Eidos-Bilder, die Baumeister auf dem Höhepunkt seines Durchbruchs zur »absoluten« Malerei zeigen. Eidos heißt »Idee«, bisweilen auch »Bild«, »Amöbe« suggeriert Teilung und Wachstum, »Östliche Legende« weist auf Mythisches hin. So ambivalent wie der Titel ist auch die Darstellung selbst, Baumeister arbeitet nicht nach, sondern wie die Natur. Die Formenwelt erscheint fragmentarisch, unfertig. Rein aus der Farbe oder aus »fließender« Zeichnung entwickelte Formen überlagern und durchdringen einander in schwebender Konstellation. Ein kopfähnliches Gebilde, eine Hand, tauchen umrißhaft auf, aber der Umriß legt die Gestalt nicht endgültig fest. Alles ist im Stadium der Wandlung begriffen, deutet auf genetische Vorgänge hin, wird als reine Vergegenwärtigung des Schöpferischen erlebbar. Für Baumeister ist der Kern des Künstlerischen weder »Ableitung« noch »Abstraktion«, sondern die »autonome Urkraft des Bildens«. Damit steht Eidos für etwas Entscheidendes ein, nämlich für die »Idee«, daß die gestaltbildenden Kräfte der Kunst »ein unmittelbarer Teil der Naturkraft selbst« (Baumeister) sind.

The picture belongs to the series of Eidos-pictures that show Baumeister at the climax of his breakthrough to "absolute" painting. Eidos means "idea", occasionally "picture" too, "Amoeba" suggests division and growing. "Eastern Tale" suggests a mythic dimension. The representation is just as ambivalent as the title. Baumeister does not imitate but rather works in harmony with nature. The formal vocabulary seems fragmentary, unfinished. Forms developed straight from the colour or from "flowing" drawings, overlap or penetrate each other in a floating constellation. A head-like shape, a hand, emerge in outline – but the outline does not finally determine the form. Everything is conceived in a stage of transformation, intimating genetic processes, becoming apprehensible as a pure realization of creativity. For Baumeister, the core of artistic activity is neither "derivation" nor "abstraction", but rather the "autonomous primal force of creating". Thereby Eidos vouches for something quite crucial, namely the "idea" that the creative force of art is "a direct aspect of Nature's own forces" (Baumeister).

Willi Baumeister

Born 1889 in Stuttgart, died 1955 in Stuttgart. 1905–1907 apprenticed as a decorator and attended the drawing class at the Stuttgart Academy. Friendship with Schlemmer and Meyer-Amden. 1910 in Adolf Hölzel's composition class. 1911 in Paris, 1913 in Amden/Switzerland. 1914 back in Paris. 1914–1918 war service. After 1919 back in Stuttgart. 1924 in Paris, acquaintance with Léger, Ozenfant and Le Corbusier. 1928 till 1933 Professor at the "Städelsche Kunstschule" (Städel Art School) in Frankfurt/M. Thereafter in Stuttgart. 1943–1945 in Urach. 1946–1955 Professor at the Stuttgart Academy.

52

Variation on Eidos I

Also known as "Amoeba" or "Eastern Tale"

Oil on canvas, 58 × 38 cm
Signed lower right: Baumeister 38.
Purchased from a Stuttgart private collection in 1950.

Literatur: Kat. 1957, S. 54. – Kat. 1961, S. 16. – Kat. 1968, S. 21 ff. mit Abb. – Werner Deusch, Neuere Malerei in der Staatsgalerie Stuttgart, S. 112 mit Abb.

Bibliography: Cat. 1957, p. 34. – Cat. 1961, p. 16. – Cat. 1968, p. 21 f. with ill. – Werner Deusch, Neuere Malerei in der Staatsgalerie Stuttgart, p. 112 with ill.

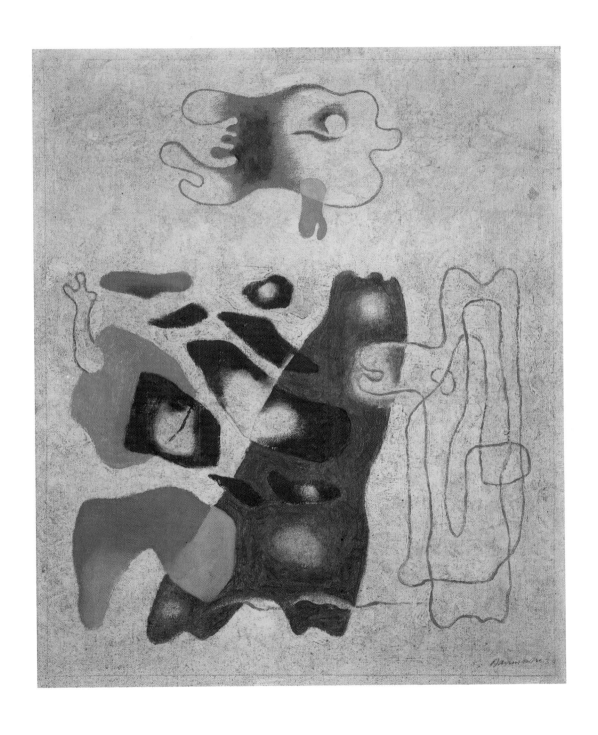

Jackson Pollock

Geboren 1912 in Cody/Wyoming, gestorben 1956 in East Hampton/Long Island. 1930–1932 Studium an der Art Students League in New York, 1931 in der Klasse für Wandmalerei. 1930–1935 verschiedene Aufenthalte in den Weststaaten und Besuche bei den Navaho-Indianern in New Mexico (Sandbilder). 1936 Zusammenarbeit mit Siqueiros. 1942 Begegnung mit Motherwell und Hans Hofmann, 1943 mit Peggy Guggenheim.

53

Out of the Web: Number 7

Aus dem Gewebe heraus: Nummer 7

Öl und Lackfarbe auf Masonit,
121,5 × 244 cm
Bezeichnet rechts unten:
Jackson Pollock 49; rückseitig betitelt.
Erworben 1964.

Jackson Pollock

Born 1912 in Cody/Wyoming, died 1956 in East Hampton/Long Island. 1930–32 studied at the Art Students League in New York, 1931 in the class for mural painting. 1930–1935 various visits to the western states and to the Navaho Indians in New Mexico (sand paintings). 1936 worked with Siqueiros. 1942 met Motherwell and Hans Hofmann, 1943 Peggy Guggenheim.

53

Out of the Web: Number 7

Oil and lacquer on masonite,
121.5 × 244 cm
Signed lower right:
Jackson Pollock 49; titled on reverse.
Purchased 1964.

Das Werk Jackson Pollocks erschließt ein malerisches Prinzip, das als »Action Painting« bezeichnet, rigoros mit allen bis dahin gültigen Bildvorstellungen bricht. Das Gemälde »Out of the Web« ist hierfür nur ein allerdings sehr frühes, doch charakteristisches Beispiel. Es ist keine bildhaft geschlossene Komposition im Sinne des konventionellen Staffeleibildes. Der Malgrund dient Pollock vielmehr als »Aktionsfeld«, auf dem er in weit ausholender spontaner Bewegung flüssige Farbe verträufelt (dripping) oder verspritzt, die Spuren seiner Gestik so in ein dichtes, sich allseits (all-over) ausbreitendes Filigran einwebend. Die formalen Energien entladen sich ohne Rücksicht auf die Begrenzung durch das Format, das wie ein »Ausschnitt grenzenloser Bewegung« (W. Schmalenbach) erscheint. Der Malakt selbst ist von größter Direktheit, weil er die Eigendynamik der Körperbewegungen voll in sich aufnimmt. Die Anwendung des »dripping« zielt darauf ab, »die Integrität der Mittel zu zerstören, die ihnen innewohnenden Kräfte zu befreien und ihre Bindungen an Maße, Gewicht und Körperlichkeit aufzuheben« (Sam Hunter). Selbst die innerhalb der all-over-Struktur ausgeschnittenen biomorphen Schattenformen wirken weniger stabilisierend als »fließend«, ordnen sich dem bewegten Rhythmus des Bildes also vollkommen ein.

Jackson Pollock's work developed a painterly principle, known as "action painting", which broke rigorously with all pictorial ideas valid until that time. The painting "Out of the Web" is just one, albeit a very early but characteristic example of this. It is not a pictorially closed composition in the sense of a conventional easel painting. The painterly ground serves Pollock far more as a "field of action" on which he drips or splatters liquid colour with a broad swinging, spontaneous movement, thus interweaving traces of his gestures in a dense "all over" expansive filigree. The formal energies are discharged without reference to the limitations of format, which seems like a "segment of unbounded movement" (W. Schmalenbach). The painterly act itself is extremely direct, because it fully assumes the interior dynamic of the body movements. The use of the "dripping" technique is intended "to destroy the integrity of the means, to liberate their integral forces and free them from their dependency on size, weight and corporality" (Sam Hunter). Even the biomorpic shadow forms, cut out from within the allover structure, seem less stabilizing than "flowing", thus fully integrated with the lively rhythm of the painting.

Literatur: Kat. 1968, S. 143 mit Abb. – Kat. 1982, 20. Jahrhundert, S. 265 ff. mit Abb.

Bibliography: Cat. 1968, p. 143 with ill. – Cat. 1982, 20. Jahrhundert, p. 265 f. with ill.

Wols

Eigentlich Alfred Otto Wolfgang Schulze. Geboren 1913 in Berlin, gestorben 1951 in Paris. 1931 Fotograf in Dresden. 1932 in Berlin, Begegnung mit Moholy-Nagy; im selben Jahr in Paris. Bekanntschaft mit Léger und Arp. Seit 1933 Kontakte zum Kreis der Surrealisten; in den frühen Aquarellen von Klee beeinflußt. 1939/40 in Internierungslagern in Südfrankreich. Flucht vor der Gestapo und ständig wechselnde Wohnsitze. 1945 Freundschaft mit Jean Paul Sartre, Mathieu und Giacometti.

54

Komposition

Entstanden 1946
Öl auf Leinwand, 162 × 130,5 cm
Bezeichnet rechts unten: Wols.
Sammlung Carlo Frua de Angeli, Mailand.
Erworben mit Hilfe von Spenden aus dem
Schweizer Kunsthandel 1973.
Leihgabe des Stuttgarter Galerievereins.

Das Bild — eines der beiden größten Ölgemälde des Künstlers — gehört zu den frühesten Beispielen einer rein gestischen Malerei, die als europäische »art informel« annähernd zeitgleich mit der amerikanischen »Action Painting« entstand. Anders als Pollock verbindet Wols auch »Handschriftlichkeit« mit intuitivem Gespür für die Bedingungen einer bildhaft geschlossenen Komposition. Seine Malerei erschließt sich »als direktes Handeln aus der Existenz« (Haftmann), ist unmittelbarer Reflex innerer Regungen, die sich im »Psychogramm« des Stuttgarter Bildes zu dramatischen Formvorgängen verdichten. Die Leinwand gleicht einer brüchigen Haut, ihr Zentrum einer offenen Wunde, und selbst im Geäder gerinnender Farben und zerfaserter Linien klingen die Spannungen des Psychischen auf. Das fragile, von Farbnebeln durchdrungene Gespinst nervöser Graphismen evoziert wohl assoziationsträchtige Formbildungen, die sich aber motivischer Fixierung entziehen, da sie aus freier, allein vom Impuls bestimmter Gestaltung hervorgingen.

This picture — one of the two largest oil paintings by Wols — is one of the earliest examples of pure gestural painting, known in Europe as "art informel", which evolved roughly contemporary to American "action painting". In contrast to Pollock, Wols combines gestural "handwriting" with an intuitive sense for the conditions of a pictorially closed composition. His painting can be understood as "a direct transaction in response to existence" (Haftmann); it is an unmediated reflection of inner impulses which, in the "psychograph" of the Stuttgart painting, condense into dramatic configurations. The canvas is like a brittle skin, at its centre an open wound. The tensions of the psyche even sound in the veins of coursing colours and fraying lines. This fragile web of nervous graphic activity, permeated by mists of colour, certainly evokes figurative associations which, however, resist specific definition. This is because the image results from a free roving and instinctive creative impulse.

Wols

Real name Alfred Otto Wolfgang Schulze. Born 1913 in Berlin, died 1951 in Paris. 1931 worked as a photographer in Dresden. 1932 in Berlin, meeting with Moholy-Nagy; also in Paris that year. Acquaintance with Léger and Arp. After 1933 in contact with the Surrealist circle; influenced by Klee in his early watercolours. 1939/40 interned in the South of France. Fled from the Gestapo and no fixed abode. 1945 friendship with Jean Paul Sartre, Mathieu and Giacometti.

54

Composition

1946
Oil on canvas, 162 × 130.5 cm
Signed lower right: Wols.
Collection Carlo Frua de Angeli, Milan. —
Purchased with the aid of donations from
the Swiss art market in 1973.
On loan from the Stuttgart Galerieverein.

Literatur: Jahrbuch der Staatlichen Kunstsammlungen in Baden-Württemberg, XI, 1974, S. 226ff. mit Abb. — Kat. 1982, 20. Jahrhundert, S. 332ff. mit Abb.

Bibliography: Jahrbuch der Staatlichen Kunstsammlungen in Baden-Württemberg, XI, 1974, p. 226f. with ill. — Cat. 1982, 20. Jahrhundert, p. 332f. with ill.

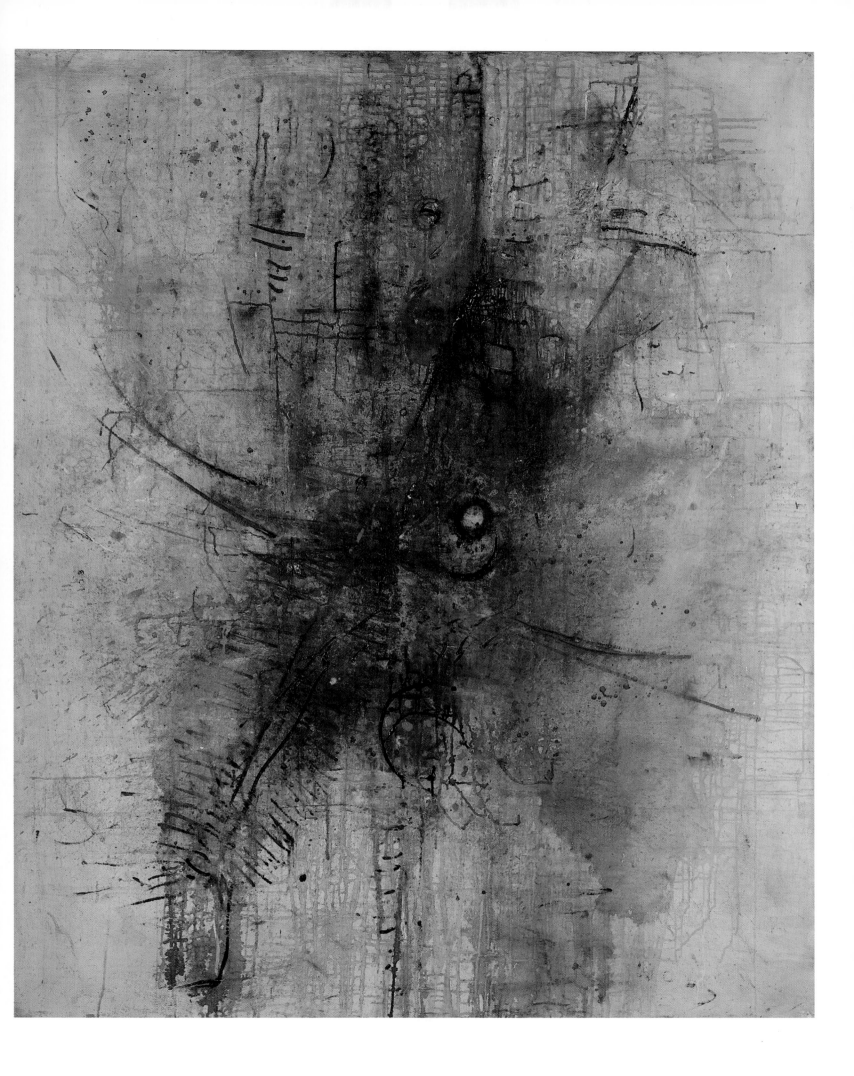

Mark Rothko

Geboren 1903 in Dwinsk/Rußland, gestorben 1970 in New York. 1913 Einwanderung in die USA. 1921–1923 Kunststudium an der Yale University, New Haven. 1925 Studium an der Art Students League in New York. 1929–1952 Kunsterzieher in Brooklyn. 1948 Zusammenarbeit mit Robert Motherwell und Barnett Newman. 1950 und 1959 Reisen nach Europa.

55

Ohne Titel

Kunstharzfarbe auf Leinwand,
206,5 × 193 cm
Bezeichnet auf der Rückseite: Mark Rothko
1962.
Erworben aus dem
Schweizer Kunsthandel 1969.

Mark Rothko

Born 1903 in Dwinsk/Russia, died 1970 in New York. 1913 emigrated to the USA. 1921–1923 studied art at Yale University, New Haven. 1925 studied at the Art Students League in New York. 1929–1952 art teacher in Brooklyn. 1948 worked with Robert Motherwell and Barnett Newman. 1950 and 1959 trips to Europe.

55

Untitled

Artificial resin on canvas 206.5 × 193 cm
Signed on reverse: Mark Rothko 1962.
Purchased from the Swiss art market in
1969.

Seit dem Ende der 40er Jahre verselbständigt sich die Farbe bei Rothko zum ausschließlichen Medium seiner Malerei. Innerhalb der Leinwand setzt er verschiedene, oft auf einen Grundton bezogene Farbfelder mit unbestimmten, sich auflösenden Randverläufen in ein entschiedenes Spannungsverhältnis. Die in sich schwingenden und schwebend-vibrierenden Farbflächen suggerieren Bewegungsmomente, die sich durch die Kombination nur leicht divergierender Ton-Werte ergeben. Die Leinwand verliert in diesen atmosphärischen Strömungen, die gleichsam nach hinten zurückweichen oder sich nach vorne hin ausdehnen, ihre ursprüngliche Funktion als fest zu bestimmende Bildträger-Ebene. Durch den Verzicht auf eine »begrenzende« Rahmung und die lumineszierenden Farben wird der Eindruck einer beinahe atmenden, »allseits ausstrahlenden Räumlichkeit« (Gudrun Inboden) noch entschieden verstärkt. Daß der Betrachter sich in diese »kontemplativen Bildräume« versenken möge, hat Rothko mehrfach betont. Seine Bilder sind — streng genommen — keine »Galeriebilder« mehr, sondern monumentale Ikonen, unauslotbar in ihrer geheimnisvollen Verknüpfung von Transzendenz und Materialität, von Mystik und Rationalität. Im Unterschied zur Kunst Jackson Pollocks, die den äußersten Pol des abstrakten Expressionismus markiert, bezeichnet das Werk Rothkos innerhalb der amerikanischen Malerei den äußersten Pol bildnerischer Meditation.

Since the late 1940s, Rothko's colour achieved independence as the exclusive medium of his painting. He places various colour fields on the canvas, often corresponding to a basic hue and with unspecified, dissolving borders, in a resolute pictorial tension. The oscillating, floating and vibrating colour planes suggest movement, resulting from the combination of very close tonal values. In this atmospheric flux, which simultaneously recedes backwards and extends forwards, the canvas loses its original function as a definite, even determining plane that supports the picture. The renunciation of a "circumscribing" frame and the luminous colours decisively strengthen the impression of an almost breathing "irradiating spatiality in all directions" (Gudrun Inboden). Rothko repeatedly stressed that the spectator might like to submerge himself in this "contemplatative pictorial space". His paintings are — rigorously understood — no longer "gallery pictures", but rather monumental icons, immeasurable in their mysterious association of transcendence and materialism, of mysticism and rationality. In contrast to the art of Jackson Pollock, which demarcates the most extreme position of abstract expressionism, Mark Rothko's work stands for the ultimate in pictorial meditation in American painting.

Literatur: Jahrbuch der Staatlichen Kunstsammlungen in Baden-Württemberg, VII, 1970, S. 154. – Kat. 1982, 20. Jahrhundert, S. 279 mit Abb.

Bibliography: Jahrbuch der Staatlichen Kunstsammlungen in Baden-Württemberg, VII, 1970, p. 154. – Cat. 1982, 20. Jahrhundert, p. 279 with ill.

ANMERKUNGEN

NOTES

1 Vgl. hierzu: Bruno Bushart, Meisterwerke der Stuttgarter Staatsgalerie, Honnef 1956, S. 11 ff. — Werner Fleischhauer, Zur Vorgeschichte der Staatsgalerie Stuttgart, in: Beiträge zur Landeskunde — Beilage zum Staatsanzeiger für Baden-Württemberg, Nr. 6, 1973, S. 5 ff.

2 Bushart, op. cit., S. 15. Gotters Sammlung umfaßte zum Zeitpunkt ihrer Erwerbung 411 Bilder und kostete 24 000 Taler. Außer dem bereits erwähnten Gemälde von Memling und einer umfänglichen Barock-Kollektion umfaßte die Sammlung u. a. auch Bilder von Lucas Cranach d. J., Hans Baldung Grien und Pencz.

3 Reinhard von Roeder, württembergischer Burggraf und Erboberstallmeister, ist als Sammler sonst unbekannt. Wie schon Bushart hervorhebt, bestanden jedoch enge geschäftliche Beziehungen zum Grafen Gotter, von dem Roeder die insgesamt 110 — in den Inventaren als »Wiener Malereien« klassifizierten — Bilder 1736 in Wien erworben haben dürfte.

4 Die Abgußsammlung, deren durch Kriegseinwirkung stark beschädigte Restbestände 1951 beseitigt wurden, geht auf eine Stiftung es Kronprinzen Wilhelm von Württemberg zurück, der 1806–1808 in Paris eine Kollektion antiker Gipsabgüsse erworben hatte. Für die Auswahl war der Bildhauer Johann Heinrich Dannecker verantwortlich, dem auch die Erweiterung und Pflege der Sammlung anvertraut wurde. Vgl. hierzu im einzelnen Bushart, op. cit., S. 17 ff. — Der oft auch in Verbindung mit der Sammlung Boisserée zitierte Ausspruch eines württembergischen Abgeordneten »Mir braucha koi Kunscht, Grumbiera (Kartoffeln) braucha mir« fiel in Wahrheit bei der Diskussion um die Bereitstellung von Mitteln zur Einrichtung des »Antikensaals«.

5 Die Schillerbüste des Bildhauers Johann Heinrich Dannecker wurde vom Künstler »seinem Vaterland als Vermächtnis« hinterlassen und dann von König Wilhelm I. von Württemberg dem Museum übergeben. Sie gehörte also nicht einmal zu den durch Kauf erworbenen Werken aus dem Bereich des Klassizismus. Diese sind weitgehend erfaßt in dem von Christian von Holst bearbeiteten Katalog des 19. Jahrhunderts, Staatsgalerie Stuttgart, 1982.

6 Es kann leider nicht unerwähnt bleiben, daß ein ehemaliger Konservator der Staatsgalerie, Dr. Klaus Graf von Baudissin, der dem Naziregime zunächst durchaus distanziert gegenüberstand, später an der »Erfassung« des zu beschlagnahmenden Kunstgutes deutscher Museen beteiligt war.

7 Der Sammlungsbestand, der außer einer großen Zahl barocker Gemälde auch einige altdeutsche und altniederländische Tafelbilder enthielt, ist vollständig erfaßt im Ausstellungskatalog »Sammlung Dr. Ing. e. h. Heinrich Scheufelen«, Württembergische Staatsgalerie, 1948.

8 Vgl. hierzu auch S. 33 ff. Nach dem Lottogesetz standen den Staatlichen Museen Baden-Württembergs (außer der Stuttgarter Staatsgalerie der Staatlichen Kunsthalle in Karlsruhe, dem Badischen Landesmuseum in Karlsruhe, dem Württembergischen Landesmuseum in Stuttgart und neuerdings auch dem Stuttgarter Linden-Museum für Völkerkunde) jährlich aus den Lotto-Einnahmen zwischen 10 bis 15 Millionen DM

1 See: Bruno Bushart, Meisterwerke der Stuttgarter Staatsgalerie, Honnef 1956, p. 11 f. — Werner Fleischhauer, "Zur Vorgeschichte der Staatsgalerie Stuttgart", in: Beiträge zur Landeskunde — Beilage zum Staatsanzeiger für Baden-Württemberg, no. 6, 1973, p. 5 f.

2 Bushart, op. cit. p. 15. At the time of purchase Gotters' collection included 411 paintings and cost 24 000 Taler. Apart from the aforementioned painting by Memling and an extensive group of Baroque pictures the collection included paintings by Lucas Cranach the younger, Hans Baldung Grien and Pencz, among others.

3 Reinhard von Roeder, Württembergian Count and Head Equerry, is otherwise unknown as a collector. As Bushart points out, he had close business ties to Count Gotter, from whom he must have purchased altogether 110 paintings in Vienna in 1736 — classified in the inventories as "Viennese paintings".

4 The collection of casts, the remainder of which are heavily damaged in the war and removed in 1951, was originally donated by Crown Prince Wilhelm von Württemberg, who had purchased a collection of antique plaster casts in Paris in 1806–1808. The sculptor Johann Heinrich Dannecker was responsible for the selection, and also for the growth and upkeep of the collection. For details see Bushart, op. cit., p. 17 f. — The remark of a Württembergian deputy, often cited in relation to the Boisserée collection, "We don't need art, potatoes are what we need" really was made during the discussion concerning the release of funds for the installation of the "antique" room".

5 The Schiller bust by the sculptor Johann Heinrich Dannecker was left by the artist as a "bequest to his fatherland", and then handed over to the museum by King Wilhelm I of Württemberg. It never belonged therefore to the purchased neoclassical works. These are largely documented in the 19th century catalogue by Christian von Holst, Staatsgalerie Stuttgart, 1982.

6 Unfortunately, it cannot remain unmentioned that a former curator of the Staatsgalerie, D. Klaus Graf von Baudissin, who initially kept his distance from the Nazi régime, was later involved in the "registration" of art treasures confiscated from German museums.

7 The contents of the collection, which, apart from a large number of Baroque paintings, also comprised several early German and Dutch panel paintings, is comprehensively recorded in the exhibition catalogue "Sammlung Dr.-Ing. e. h. Heinrich Scheufelen", Württembergische Staatsgalerie, 1948.

8 See here also p. 33 f. According to the National Lottery Laws (Lottogesetz), the state museums in Baden-Württemberg (apart from the Stuttgart Staatsgalerie, the Badische Landesmuseum in Karlsruhe, the Württembergische Landesmuseum in Stuttgart, and recently also the Stuttgart Linden-Museum for Ethnology) have a yearly sum from the pools of the National Lottery revenue of between 10 and 15 million DM at their disposal for the purchase of artistic masterpieces. The amount of these funds changes according to the amount of the lottery revenue. The percentage allocation to the museums is repeatedly altered, above all in favour of the preservation of monuments. Luckily this did not involve serious losses for the museums because the lottery income mostly increased. At the present time, however, income

zum Ankauf von Spitzenwerken der Kunst zur Verfügung. Die Höhe der Mittel wechselte entsprechend der Höhe des Lotto-Aufkommens. Die prozentuale Zuteilung an die Museen wurde wiederholt vor allem zugunsten der Denkmalpflege verändert, glücklicherweise ohne entscheidende Einbußen für die Museen, weil sich die Lottoeinnahmen gleichzeitig meistens erhöhten. Da die Lottoeinnahmen inzwischen stagnieren, kann vor einer weiteren Kürzung zu Lasten der Museen nur eindringlich gewarnt werden.

9   Der Gesamtbetrag der für ca. 10 Millionen DM erworbenen Sammlung ist aufgeführt im Ausstellungskatalog »Neuere französische Malerei aus der Staatsgalerie Stuttgart«, Staatliche Kunsthalle Karlsruhe 1962; außerdem in den Sammlungskatalogen der Staatsgalerie von 1961 und 1968, jeweils mit Angabe der Provenienz.

10   Auf- und Ausbau der Italienersammlung in der Staatsgalerie sind im wesentlichen das Verdienst des früheren Vizedirektors der Staatsgalerie und heutigen Direktors des deutschen Kunsthistorischen Institutes in Florenz, Gerhard Ewald.

11   Zu dem Zyklus von Edward Burne-Jones vgl. Kurt Löcher. Der Perseus-Zyklus von Edward Burne-Jones, Staatsgalerie Stuttgart, 1973. Kurt Löcher, heute Direktor am Germanischen Nationalmuseum in Nürnberg, gab auch die entscheidende Anregung zur Erwerbung des Zyklus.

12   Das Oskar-Schlemmer-Archiv wurde der Staatsgalerie 1969 von der Witwe des Künstlers, Frau Tut Schlemmer, gestiftet. Der archivalische Nachlaß Grohmanns wurde 1970 erworben; das Archiv Sohm 1981.

13   Das Vermächtnis Preuschen erfolgte 1972; die Stiftungen Frau Elly Koehlers 1969 (Gauguin) und 1971 (Kokoschka); die Stiftung Arp 1975; die Stiftung Lörcher 1981. Zur Arp-Stiftung vgl. die Sonderpublikation der Staatsgalerie, Stiftung Marguerite Arp, Staatsgalerie Stuttgart 1975, bearbeitet von Stephan v. Wiese, Stuttgart 1975.

14   Zur Geschichte des Stuttgarter Galerievereins vgl. auch: Bruno Bushart, Der Stuttgarter Galerieverein, Stuttgart 1964. — Meisterwerke des Stuttgarter Galerievereins, Ausstellungskatalog des Stuttgarter Galerievereins e.V., Staatsgalerie Stuttgart 1974.

15   Zur Sammlung Borst vgl.: Die Sammlung Hugo Borst in Stuttgart, Dokumentation und Chronik, herausgegeben von den Erben des Sammlers, Stuttgart 1970.

16   Veröffentlicht in: Kaiser Maximilian I. Weißkunig — in Lichtdruck-Faksimiles nach Frühdrucken. Mit Hilfe der Max-Kade-Foundation Inc. New York für den Stuttgarter Galerieverein herausgegeben von H.Th. Musper u. a., 2 Bände, Stuttgart 1956.

17   Eine Sonderpublikation über die Sammlung Preuschen durch August Bernhard Rave ist in Vorbereitung.

18   Die Sammlung Kade veröffentlicht in: Ausstellungskatalog »Sammlung Kade«, Graphische Sammlung der Staatsgalerie Stuttgart, 1963/64. — Meisterwerke alter Druckgraphik aus der Staatsgalerie Stuttgart — Zum 100. Geburtstag des Stifters Max Kade, Stuttgarter Galerieverein e.V. und Graphische Sammlung der Staatsgalerie Stuttgart, 1982/83.

from the lotteries has stagnated. Further reductions in funding could therefore have serious consequences for the museums.

9   The total holdings of the collection, purchased for 10 million DM (Deutschmark) are detailed in the exhibition catalogue "Neuere französische Malerei aus der Staatsgalerie Stuttgart", Staatliche Kunsthalle Karlsruhe 1962; also in the catalogues of the Staatsgalerie collection 1961 and 1968, with details of provenance in each case.

10   The development and expansion of the Italian collection for the Staatsgalerie are mainly the achievements of the former vice-director of the Staatsgalerie and present director of the Deutsches Kunsthistorisches Institut in Florence, Gerhard Ewald.

11   On the Burne-Jones' series see Kurt Löcher, "Der Perseus-Zyklus von Edward Burne-Jones,, Staatsgalerie Stuttgart 1973. Kurt Löcher, formerly curator at the Staatsgalerie Stuttgart, in the meantime, director at the Germanisches Nationalmuseum in Nürnberg, also proposed to acquire the Burne-Jones paintings.

12   The Oskar-Schlemmer-Archive was donated to the Staatsgalerie in 1969 by the artist's widow, Mrs Tut Schlemmer. Grohmann's archival estate was purchased in 1970; the Sohm archive in 1981.

13   The Preuschen bequest was acquired in 1972; Mrs Elly Koehler's donation in 1969 (Gauguin) and 1971 (Kokoschka): the Arp donation in 1975; the Lörcher donation in 1981. On the Arp donation see the special publication of the Staatsgalerie, "Stiftung of Marguerite Arp", Staatsgalerie Stuttgart 1975, by Stephan von Wiese, Stuttgart 1975.

14   On the history of the Stuttgart Galerieverein see also Bruno Bushart, "Der Stuttgarter Galerieverein", Stuttgart 1964. — "Meisterwerke des Stuttgarter Galerievereins", exhibition catalogue of the Stuttgart Galerieverein/the Staatsgalerie Stuttgart 1974.

15   On the Borst collection see "Die Sammlung Hugo Borst in Stuttgart, Dokumentation und Chronik", edited by the heirs of the collector, Stuttgart 1970.

16   Published in "Kaiser Maximilian Weißkunig — in Lichtdruck-Faksimiles nach Frühdrucken". With the help of the Max-Kade-Foundation Inc., New York, edited for the Stuttgart Galerieverein by H.Th. Musper and others, 2 vols, Stuttgart 1956.

17   A special publication about the Preuschen collection by August Bernhard Rave is in preparation.

18   The Kade collection is published in the exhibition catalogue "Sammlung Kade", Graphische Sammlung der Staatsgalerie Stuttgart, 1963/64. "Meisterwerke alter Druckgraphik aus der Staatsgalerie Stuttgart — Zum 100. Geburtstag des Stifters Max Kade", Stuttgart Galerieverein e.V. und Graphische Sammlung der Staatsgalerie Stuttgart, 1982/83.

19   The financial supplies of the "Museumsstiftung" (Museum's endowment funds) are made up from contributions by the casinos in Baden-Baden and Constance. Contd. The funds — in total some 4 million DM per annum — are supplemented when necessary by the museums' share of the income from the

19 Die finanzielle Ausstattung der Museumsstiftung erfolgt aus Zuwendungen der Spielbanken in Baden-Baden und Konstanz. Der Fonds — insgesamt etwa 4 Millionen DM jährlich — soll nach Bedarf aus dem Anteil der Museen an den Toto- und Lottoeinnahmen aufgestockt werden. Der Fonds ist für die Erwerbung von Meisterwerken der Weltkunst gedacht, die aus den Einzelanteilen der Museen am Zahlenlotto nicht mehr finanzierbar sind. Am Zustandekommen der Stiftung haben außer dem Ministerpräsidenten, dem Präsidenten des Stuttgarter Galerievereins, vor allem der frühere Ministerialdirektor im Finanzministerium Baden-Württemberg Dr. Eberhard Benz, sowie Ministerialdirigent Dr. Dr. Hannes Rettich und Ministerialrat Dr. Helmut Gerber, beide Ministerium für Wissenschaft und Kunst, entscheidenden Anteil.

20 Volker Plagemann, Das deutsche Kunstmuseum 1790–1870, München 1967, S. 102 ff. — Irene Antoni, Das Museum der bildenden Künste zu Stuttgart — Die Architekturgeschichte von der Planung eines Antikensaals zur Errichtung eines autonomen Gebäudes für Kunstschule und Kunstsammlungen, Magisterarbeit (Maschinenschrift), Universität Stuttgart 1981. Johannes Zahlten, »Die Kunstanstalten zur Staats- und Nationalsache gemacht. . .«, Beiträge zur Geschichte der Staatlichen Akademie der Bildenden Künste Stuttgart (2), Stuttgart 1980.

21 Nur bedingt vergleichbar, weil aus einer privaten Stiftung hervorgegangen, ist das Städelsche Kunstinstitut in Frankfurt/M., dem ebenfalls eine Kunstschule angeschlossen ist; vgl. hierzu: Der Städelsche Museums-Verein e.V. und das Städel — Geschichte und Auftrag, Frankfurt/M. 1982.

22 Dem Relief mit der Allegorie der Malerei liegt eine Zeichnung von Eberhard von Wächter zugrunde, vgl. Irene Antoni, op. cit., S. 62.

23 Die Vase — ein Geschenk der Stadt Stuttgart zur Eröffnung des Museums im Jahre 1843 — ist heute im Hofbereich des ebenfalls von Stirling errichteten Kammertheaters aufgestellt.

24 Irene Antoni, op. cit., S. 57 ff. Die Pläne Albert von Boks im Baurechtsamt Stuttgart.

25 Die Ausstattung der Galerie mit Oberlicht führte gleichzeitig zur Vermauerung der Fenster im Obergeschoß beider Flügel im Altbau. Dadurch wurde auch zusätzlich Hängefläche gewonnen.

26 Julius Baum, Die Stuttgarter Kunstsammlungen, in: Museumskunde, V, Heft 4, 1909, S. 193 mit Abb.

27 Das Kronprinzenpalais ist 1846–1849 nach Plänen von Ludwig Friedrich von Gaab als Stadtpalais für den Kronprinzen Karl erbaut worden.

28 Der städtebauliche Ideenwettbewerb von 1974 bezog sich auf die Erweiterung der Staatsgalerie, das Kammertheater, Erweiterungen der Musikhochschule und Erweiterungen des Landtags.

29 An der Vorbereitung der Entscheidung von Ministerpräsident Dr. Hans Filbinger waren der heutige Regierungspräsident und frühere Ministerialdirigent im Staatsministerium Dr. Manfred Bulling und sein damaliger Mitarbeiter Ministerialrat Dr. Helmut Gerber,

"National Lottery". The fund is intended for the purchase of masterpieces of world art which are too expensive to be financed by the individual museums' portions of the lottery income. Those decisively responsible for the origination of the endowment are — apart from the Minister President — the president of the Stuttgart Galerieverein, above all the former Head of Ministry of Finance for Baden-Württemberg, Dr. Eberhard Benz, alongside the Head of Governmental Department Dr. Dr. Hannes Rettich, and the Assistant Head of Governmental Department Dr. Helmut Gerber, both from the Ministry of Science and Art.

20 Volker Plagemann, "Das deutsche Kunstmuseum 1790–1870", Munich 1967 p. 102 f. — Irene Antoni, "Das Museum der bildenden Künste zu Stuttgart — Die Architekturgeschichte von der Planung eines Antikensaals zur Errichtung eines autonomen Gebäudes für Kunstschule und Kunstsammlungen", M. A. report (typescript), University of Stuttgart 1981. — Johannes Zahlten, "Die Kunstanstalt zur Staats- und Nationalsache gemacht. . .", Beiträge zur Geschichte der Staatlichen Akademie der Bildenden Künste Stuttgart (2), Stuttgart 1980.

21 The only comparable institution because it also developed out of a private endowment is the Städelsche Kunstinstitut in Frankfurt/Main, which is also attached to an art school; see "Der Städelsche Museums-Verein e.V. und das Städel — Geschichte und Auftrag", Frankfurt/M. 1982.

22 The relief with the allegory of painting is based on a drawing by Eberhard von Wächter, see Irene Antoni, op. cit. p. 62.

23 The urn — a gift from the city of Stuttgart to celebrate the opening of the museum in 1843 — is exhibited today in the courtyard of the Chambertheatre, also designed by James Stirling.

24 Irene Antoni, op. cit. p. 57 f. The plans by Albert von Bok are in the Office for Planning and Building Laws and Regulations, Stuttgart.

25 The installation of overhead lighting in the gallery also led to the walling up of the windows on the top floors of both wings of the old building. Thus new wall space was won.

26 Julius Baum, "Die Stuttgarter Kunstsammlungen", in: Museumskunde V, no. 4, 1909, p. 193 with ill.

27 The "Kronprinzenpalais" was built in 1846–1849 as a city palace for the Crown Prince Karl, after plans by Ludwig Friedrich von Gaab.

28 The city architecture competition in 1974 related to the extension of the Staatsgalerie, the Chambertheatre, the extension of the Music School and the extension of the state parliament building.

29 The present District Council Chiarman and former Head of Governmental Department in the state ministry Dr. Manfred Bulling and his colleague at that time, Assistant Head of Governmental Department Dr. Helmut Gerber (now representative for museums in the Ministry for Science and Art), were highly involved in the preparations which led to the Minister President Dr. Hans Filbinger's decision.

30 This refers to the present "ball room" in the old building, not the original "ball room", located in the centre of the middle block and

inzwischen Referent für die Museen im Ministerium für Wissenschaft und Kunst, maßgeblich beteiligt.

30 Gemeint ist der heutige »Festsaal« im Altbau, nicht der ursprüngliche, von Alexander Bruckmann ausgemalte, im Zentrum des Mitteltrakts gelegene »Festsaal«. Vgl. dazu im einzelnen Irene Antoni, op. cit., S. 59 und S. 65 ff.

31 Zu James Stirling: John Jacobus, James Stirling — Bauten und Projekte 1950—1974, Verlag Gerd Hatje, Stuttgart 1975. — Zum Stuttgarter Projekt: Peter Beye, Das Projekt für den Erweiterungsbau der Staatsgalerie von James Stirling, in: Katalog Internationaler Kunstmarkt Köln, 1979, S. 19 ff. — Peter Cook, Museum Stuttgart, in: The Architectural Review, März 1983, S. 31 ff. mit zahlreichen, auch farbigen Abbildungen. — Eine Festschrift der Landesregierung über die Neue Staatsgalerie wird zur Eröffnung des Museums im März 1984 erscheinen; eine ausführliche kunstwissenschaftliche Baumonographie von Thorsten Rodiek im Sommer 1984.

32 Die Pläne von Schinkel abgebildet und erläutert bei Volker Plagemann, Das deutsche Kunstmuseum 1790—1870, München 1967, S. 66 ff., Abb. 56 und 57.

decorated by Alexander Bruckmann. See for details Irene Antoni, op. cit. p. 59 and 65 f.

31 On James Stirling: James Jacobus, "James Stirling — Bauten und Projekte 1950—1974", Verlag Gerd Hatje, Stuttgart 1975. On the Stuttgart project: Peter Beye, "Das Projekt für den Erweiterungsbau der Staatsgalerie von James Stirling", in: Katalog Internationaler Kunstmarkt Köln, 1979, p. 19 f. — Peter Cook, "Museum Stuttgart", in The Architectural Review, March 1983, p. 31 f. with numerous, also colour illustrations. — A publication by the state government about the New Staatsgalerie appeared to celebrate the opening of the museum in March 1984; as well as, in summer 1984, a detailed art historical monograph about the building by Thorsten Rodiek.

32 Schinkel's plans are illustrated and commented on by Volker Plagemann in "Das deutsche Kunstmuseum 1790—1870", Munich 1967, p. 66 f. ill. 56 and 57.

LITERATUR

BIBLIOGRAPHY

Die hier aufgeführte Literatur umfaßt nur die wichtigsten Publikationen; weitere Literaturhinweise sind den erwähnten Katalogen der Staatsgalerie zu entnehmen.

Bruno Bushart,
Meisterwerke der Stuttgarter Staatsgalerie,
Dr. Peters Verlag, Honnef/Rhein 1956.

Werner R. Deusch,
Neuere Malerei in der Staatsgalerie Stuttgart, W. Kohlhammer Verlag, Stuttgart 1961.

Bruno Bushart,
Der Stuttgarter Galerieverein, Stuttgart 1964.

Konrad Lange,
Verzeichnis der Gemäldesammlung im Kgl. Museum der bildenden Künste zu Stuttgart, Stuttgart 1903 (abgekürzt: Kat. Lange).

Klaus Graf von Baudissin,
Katalog der Staatsgalerie zu Stuttgart, Stuttgart 1931 (abgekürzt: Kat. 1931).

Bruno Bushart,
Katalog der Staatsgalerie Stuttgart, Stuttgart 1957 (abgekürzt: Kat. 1957).

Peter Beye,
Katalog der Staatsgalerie Stuttgart — Neue Meister, 1961 (abgekürzt: Kat. 1961).

Bruno Bushart und Marlinde Reinold-Kohrs,
Katalog der Staatsgalerie Stuttgart — Alte Meister, 1962 (abgekürzt: Kat. 1962, Alte Meister).

Peter Beye und Kurt Löcher,
Katalog der Staatsgalerie Stuttgart — Neue Meister, 1968 (abgekürzt: Kat. 1968).

Christian v. Holst,
Malerei und Plastik des 19. Jahrhunderts, Staatsgalerie Stuttgart, 1982 (abgekürzt: Kat. 1982, 19. Jahrhundert).

Karin v. Maur und Gudrun Inboden,
Malerei und Plastik des 20. Jahrhunderts, Staatsgalerie Stuttgart, 1982 (abgekürzt: Kat. 1982, 20. Jahrhundert).

The bibliography listed here includes only the most important publications; further bibliographic references are found in the previously mentioned catalogues of the Staatsgalerie.

Bruno Bushart,
Meisterwerke der Stuttgarter Staatsgalerie (Honnef on the Rhine: Dr. Peters Publishers, 1956).

Werner R. Deusch,
Neuere Malerei in der Staatsgalerie Stuttgart (Stuttgart: W. Kohlhammer Publishers, 1961).

Bruno Bushart,
Der Stuttgarter Galerieverein (Stuttgart: 1964).

Konrad Lange,
Verzeichnis der Gemäldesammlung im Kgl. Museum der bildenden Künste zu Stuttgart (Stuttgart: 1903). Abbreviated: Cat. Lange.

Klaus Graf von Baudissin,
Katalog der Staatsgalerie zu Stuttgart (Stuttgart: 1931). Abbreviated: Cat. 1931.

Bruno Bushart,
Katalog der Staatsgalerie Stuttgart (Stuttgart: 1957). Abbreviated: Cat. 1957.

Peter Beye,
Katalog der Staatsgalerie Stuttgart — Neue Meister (1961). Abbreviated: Cat. 1961.

Bruno Bushart and Marlinde Reinold-Kohrs,
Katalog der Staatsgalerie — Alte Meister (1962). Abbreviated: Cat. 1962, Alte Meister.

Peter Beye and Kurt Löcher,
Katalog der Staatsgalerie Stuttgart — Neue Meister (1968). Abbreviated: Cat. 1968.

Christian v. Holst,
Malerie und Plastik des 19. Jahrhunderts, Staatsgalerie Stuttgart (1982). Abbreviated: Cat. 1982, 19. Jahrhundert.

Karin v. Maur and Gudrun Inboden,
Malerei und Plastik des 20. Jahrhunderts, Staatsgalerie Stuttgart (1982). Abbreviated: Cat. 1982, 20. Jahrhundert.

GUNTHER THIEM

———

GRAPHISCHE
SAMMLUNG

———

DEPARTMENT
OF PRINTS
AND DRAWINGS

ZUR GESCHICHTE DER
GRAPHISCHEN SAMMLUNG
DES FRÜHEREN
KÖNIGLICHEN KUPFERSTICHKABINETTS
STUTTGART

———

THE HISTORY
OF THE GRAPHIC ART COLLECTION
OF THE FORMER
ROYAL COLLECTION OF PRINTS
STUTTGART

Die Inventare und Archivalien der Graphischen Sammlung verbrannten 1944 in dem von Bomben getroffenen Kronprinzenpalais am Schloßplatz; sie waren nicht mit den graphischen Blättern ausgelagert worden. Darum kann die frühere Sammlungsgeschichte nicht mehr vollständig geschrieben, sondern nur rekonstruiert werden. Vieles davon wird den Nachforschungen meiner Mitarbeiter verdankt: Dr. Heinrich Geissler im Bereich der alten Graphik, Dr. Ulrike Gauß im Gesamtkatalog der »Zeichnungen und Aquarelle des 19. Jahrhunderts« (1976) und Dr. Christel Thiem im Ausstellungskatalog unserer 166 Tiepolo-Zeichnungen (1970) sowie im Bestandskatalog »Italienische Zeichnungen 1500 bis 1800« (1977); sie entdeckte Zusammenhänge zwischen prominenten Privatsammlern, wie dem Genueser Marchese Jacopo Durazzo (1717–1794), wie dem Franz Freiherrn Koenig-Fachsenfeld (1866–1918) und Ernst Ziegler in Gönningen (1874–1958) — mit dem Ergebnis, »daß sich die von engagierten Sammlern gesteigerten Zeichnungen heute wieder unter dem Dach der Staatsgalerie befinden«.

In summarischer Form hat 1928 der weitblickende Galeriedirektor Otto Fischer über »Die Gemälde- und Kupferstichabteilung der Staatlichen Landeskunstsammlungen« geschrieben (»Kunstpflege in Württemberg«, Stuttgart 1928), und unser früherer Kollege Dr. Bruno Bushart ist in der Einführung seines Buches »Meisterwerke der Stuttgarter Staatsgalerie« (1956) auch auf die Geschichte der Kupferstichsammlung eingegangen, die Herzog Carl Eugen (1728–1793) aus dem Wunsch begründete, »einem Lande ohne eigene bildnerische Tradition« künstlerische Vorbilder zu verschaffen (Abb. 1, S. 201).

Eine graphische Sammlung oder, wie die alte Bezeichnung heißt: ein Kupferstichkabinett, ist nach Funktion und Material etwas anderes als eine Gemäldegalerie — auch heute noch, wo durch neue Medien eine Verwischung der Grenze zwischen Gemaltem einerseits und Gezeichnetem, Gedrucktem, Geklebtem andererseits stattfindet (diese Verwischung der Kunstgattungen beginnt mit der Erfindung der Collage im Jahre 1912 durch Braque und Picasso). In dem Wort »Galerie« liegt schon immer der Anspruch des Repräsentativen, in dem Wort »Kabinett« hingegen die Sphäre des Intimen; ein wesensmäßiger Unterschied, der — wie jede längere berufliche Tätigkeit — auch die damit befaßten Menschen prägt, früher stärker als heute. Die deutschen, englischen und französischen Kabinette brachten einen speziellen Typus des Gelehrten hervor (z. B. Campbell Dodgson in London, Adhémar in Paris, v. Regteren-Altena in Amsterdam, Meder in Wien, Lehrs in Dresden, Winkler in Berlin, Halm in München, Musper in Stuttgart). Letzterer schrieb 1953, als er Direktor der Staatsgalerie und damit ihrer Gemäldegalerie geworden war: »Wer Zeichnungen versteht, versteht erst eigentlich Gemälde, die ja meist und besonders in früherer Zeit auf Zeichnungen beruhen. Erst da, wo den Zeichnungen grundsätzlich die gleiche Achtung entgegengebracht wird wie Gemälden, darf

In 1944, bombs hit the Kronprinzenpalais in Schloßplatz. It went up in flames. The Collection of Prints and Drawings had been evacuated; but not the adjoining inventories and archives. Today, the only access we have to the Collection's earlier history is through reconstructions. Much of this work we owe the research of my colleagues, Dr. Heinrich Geissler for older prints and drawings. Dr. Ulrike Gauss for the comprehensive catalogue of "Zeichnungen und Aquarelle des 19. Jahrhunderts" (1976) and Dr. Christel Thiem for the exhibition catalogue of our 166 Tiepolo drawings (1970) and the stock catalogue of "Italienische Zeichnungen 1500–1800" (1977). Dr. Thiem discovered similarities between prominent private collectors such as the Genoese Marchese Jacopo Durazzo (1717 till 1794), Franz Freiherr Koenig-Fachsenfeld (1866–1918) and Ernst Ziegler of Gönningen (1874–1958), with the result "that the drawings bought at auctions by serious collectors are once again under the roof of the Staatsgalerie".

In 1928 Otto Fischer, the far-sighted director of the Gallery, wrote succinctly in "Kunstpflege in Württemberg" (Stuttgart, 1928) on "Die Gemälde- und Kupferstichabteilung der Staatlichen Landeskunstsammlungen/The Department of Paintings and Engravings of the Province's State Collection" and, in 1958, our former colleague Dr. Bruno Bushart also focussed on the history of the Collection of Prints and Drawing in the introduction to his book "Meisterwerke der Stuttgarter Staatsgalerie" (1956). He began with the collection's foundation by Duke Carl Eugen (1728–1793). Eugen wanted to provide artistic models for "a country without an artistic tradition of its own" (ill. 1, p. 201).

A collection of prints and drawings or, in older terminology, a print room (the German describes the scale more tellingly, as a "copper engraving cabinet"), differs in both function and material from a picture gallery. This is true even today as new media obscure the distinctions between painting and drawing on the one hand, and on the other, between print and collage (this indistinction of artistic genre began in 1912 with Braque and Picasso's invention of the collage). The word "gallery" always connotes pretense and show; the word "Kabinett" conveys an intimate atmosphere. It is a fundamental difference that shapes — like any longer professional activity — those working there, in the past even more so than today. The print collections in Germany, France and Britain educated a certain kind of scholar. Campbell Dodgson in London, Adhémar in Paris, v. Regteren-Altena in Amsterdam, Meder in Vienna, Lehrs in Dresden, Winkler in Berlin, Halm in Munich or Musper in Stuttgart are typical examples. Musper wrote in 1953, after he became director of the Staatsgalerie and thus head of its department of paintings, "Only those who understand drawings will really understand paintings; paintings being based, especially in former times, on drawings. Only where drawings are given the same regard as paintings can a genuine understanding of art be assumed. This is certainly a rarer

1
Herzog Carl Eugen von Württemberg (1744–1793). Kupferstich von J. F. Leybold, 1782, nach einem Gemälde des Zöglings der Carlsschule, C. J. Schlotterbeck (1757–1811).

1
Duke Carl Eugen of Württemberg (1744–93). Copper engraving by J. F. Leybold, 1782, after a painting by C. J. Schlotterbeck (1757–1811), a pupil of the Carlsschule.

2
Selbstbildnis der gefeierten Porträtistin Elisabeth Vigée-Lebrun, gestochen von Johann Gotthard Müller nach dem Gemälde von 1782 in der National Gallery, London.

2
Self-portrait by the celebrated portraitist, Elisabeth Vigée-Lebrun, engraved by Johann Gotthard Müller after the painting of 1782 in the National Gallery, London.

CAROLUS D.G. WIRTEMBERGIÆ
AC TECCIÆ. DUX,
ALMÆ CAROLINÆ STUTTGARDIANÆ
STATOR. AC PATER.

man wirkliches Verständnis für Kunst voraussetzen, das freilich seltener sein mag, als
man im allgemeinen denkt«.[1]Jene Gelehrten betrachteten sich immer als eine Elite,
das ist bis heute spürbar, ihre Nachfahren
halten wie eine Großfamilie zusammen;
seit 1970 treffen sie sich alle zwei Jahre in
einem anderen Kabinett und nennen sich:
»International Advisory Committee of Keepers of Public Collections of Graphic Art«.
Die Darlegungen von Professor Peter Beye
zur Geschichte der Stuttgarter Gemäldegalerie (Seite 8—27) und diese hier zur
Geschichte der Graphischen Sammlung
zeigen, wie verschiedenartig die beiden
entstanden und gewachsen sind. In den
großen deutschen Museumskomplexen
Dresden, Berlin und München sind die
Graphischen Sammlungen seit alters auto-
nom: Dresden schon seit 1720 unter August
dem Starken[2], Berlin erst 1831 auf Betreiben Wilhelm v. Humboldts und Karl
Friedrich Schinkels[3], München bereits 1758
bzw. 1777, denn erst in diesem Jahr gelangte das vom pfälzischen Kurfürsten Karl
Theodor in Mannheim begründete Kupfer-
stich- und Zeichnungskabinett durch seine
Übernahme der Regierung in Bayern nach
München.[4]
Liest man über die Geschichte dieser
Sammlungen nach, das heißt über die Mo-

quality than is generally thought".[1] These
scholars always regarded themselves as an
elite; the effects are noticeable even up to
the present day: their descendants stay together like a large family. Every other year
since 1970 they meet at a different collection. They call themselves the "International Advisory Committee of Keepers of the
Public Collections of Graphic Art".
Professor Peter Beye's elucidations page
8—26 of this catalogue on the history of the
Department of Paintings in Stuttgart and
mine on the history of the Department of
Graphic Arts demonstrate how different the
two areas are in both origin and development. In the large museum complexes of
Germany — Dresden, Berlin and Munich —
the print collections have always been autonomous. Dresden from as early as 1720
under August the Strong[2], Berlin only since
1831 at the instigation of Wilhelm von
Humboldt and Karl Friedrich Schinkel[3].
Munich already in 1758 or, actually, 1777
when the "Prints and Drawings Cabinet"
established in Mannheim by the Elector Pa-
latine Karl Theodor moved with him to Munich when he took over the government in
Bavaria.[4]
Surveying the histories of these collections,
especially the motives for their foundation,
we find that the desire for the "stately self-

3
Joseph Anton Koch, Spottbild auf das Regime
der Hohen Carlsschule in Stuttgart, um 1791,
aquarellierte Federzeichnung über Bleiskizze.
Der Intendant der Akademie, Oberst v. Seeger,
vollzieht mit erhobenem Stock ein Strafgericht
über die wegen der unbeliebten Dekorations-
malerei aufsässigen Zöglinge. Der kleine Mann
links mit Pfeil und Bogen soll der verhaßte
Akademiedirektor A. F. Harper (1725—1806)
sein, hinter ihm sieht aus dem Fenster ein Narr
mit Schelle und Krone, ein Paar Eselsohren
hochhaltend. Vorne liegt Lessings angefeindete
Schrift »Laokoon oder Über die Grenzen der
Poesie und Malerei« (1766).

3
Joseph Anton Koch, caricature on the regime
at the Hohe Carlsschule, Stuttgart, c. 1791; pen
drawing over lead pencil sketch, water-colour
glazes. The Intendant of the Academy, Major von
Seeger, metes out punishment with raised cane
on pupils recalcitrant at lessons in the hated art
of Interior Painting. The small man on the left
with bow and arrow is intended to lampoon the
despised director of the Academy, A. F. Harper
(1725—1806); behind him a jester thrusts his
head through the window, wearing a bell and
crown and holding a pair of asses' ears above
Harper's head. In the foreground lies Lessing's
essay, Laocoön, or on the Limits of Poetry and
Painting (1766), which had met with much
hostility.

tive ihrer Gründung, so verquicken sich dabei »neben der repräsentativen Selbstdarstellung eines barocken Absolutismus rational-erzieherische Züge der Aufklärung« (Halm); außerdem — und damit kommen wir auf Stuttgart zu sprechen — waren merkantile Absichten im Spiel, wenn mit der Kupferstichsammlung eine Kupferstecherschule verbunden wurde, deren Erzeugnisse — wie die französischen und englischen Farbstiche des 18. Jahrhunderts — exportfähig waren. Die von Herzog Carl Eugen 1782 begründete »Hohe Carlsschule« und ihre durch den Stecher Johann Gotthard Müller (1747—1830) zu hohem Ansehen gelangte Kupferstecherschule (Abb. 2, S. 201) ist die Keimzelle des königlichen württembergischen Kupferstichkabinetts; ihre Kupferstichsammlung bildet deren Grundstock! Im Jahre 1810 erhielt sie erstmals einen eigenen Kustos in der Person des Malers Eberhard v. Wächter (1762—1852); er dürfte den in der älteren Literatur, z. B. bei unserer Cranach-Zeichnung (Tafel 2, S. 232) erwähnten, 1943 vernichteten »Catalogue des dessins de S. M. le Roi« von 1810 verfaßt haben. Damit darf das Jahr 1810 als offizielles Geburtsdatum unserer Graphischen Sammlung angesehen werden.

Im Stuttgarter Ausstellungskatalog »Die Hohe Carlsschule« (1960) ist eine der seltenen

representation of baroque absolutism" fuses with those "rationalistic, didactic traits of the Enlightenment" (Halm). In addition, mercantile gains played an important role — Stuttgart is a case in point — where a etching collection was connected to a school of engraving. The school's products, like the 18th century coloured engravings of France and England, were highly exportable. The "Hohe Carlsschule" founded in 1782 by Duke Carl Eugen and the associated engraving school headed by the master engraver Johann Gotthard Müller (1747—1830) (see ill. 2, p. 201) won much recognition. They provided the germ of the Royal Württemberg Print Room and furnished the basis of its collection. In 1819 the collection's first curator, the painter Eberhard v. Wächter (1762—1852), was appointed. He is very probably the complier of the "Catalogue des dessins de S. M. Roi" of 1810, mentioned in older references (see our Cranach drawing, pl. 2, p. 232) but destroyed in 1943. The appointment and the catalogue set 1810 as the official inauguration date of our Collection of Prints and Drawings.

Concealed in the catalogue for the exhibition "Die Hohe Carlsschule" (Stuttgart, 1960) is one of the rare published text by Erwin Petermann, who reestablished our Graphic Arts Collection from 1945 to 1963, "Joh. Gotth. Müller und die Kupferstecher-

4
»Le Baiser a la Wirtembourg«, Karikatur des Engländers James Gillray von 1797 auf die kinderlose Ehe Friedrichs von Württemberg (seit 1806 König) mit seiner Gemahlin Mathilde, einer englischen Prinzessin.

4
Le Baiser de Wirtembourg, James Gillray's caricature of 1797, of the childless marriage between Frederick of Würtemberg (King from 1806) and his Queen, Mathilda, an English princess.

Le Baiser a la Wirtembourg.
Heav'n grant their Happiness complete .
And may they make both Ends to meet in their hard times.

Publikationen Erwin Petermanns, des Neu-
begründers unserer Graphischen Sammlung von 1945 bis 1963, versteckt: »Joh.
Gotth. Müller und die Kupferstecherschule
der Hohen Carlsschule« (S. 71—82); das ist
nicht eine der üblichen trockenen Abhand-
lungen, sondern entwirft ein wie gestochen
scharfes Bild jener Durchbruchzeit der bildenden Kunst Württembergs im Zeichen
des Klassizismus. Als Beispiel sei eine Passage Petermanns herausgegriffen, die sich
mit der durch den Tod Carl Eugens, 1793,
bedingten Auflösung der Carlsschule befaßt. »Das späteste Kind der Carlsschule,
die Kupferstecher-Anstalt, überlebt am zä-
hesten, als endlich nach dem Willen einer
stumpfen, gehässigen Bürokratie von den
unbedarften Nachfolgern Carl Eugens dessen Schöpfung liquidiert wird. Es ist ein
erbärmliches Stück Württemberg wie es
war und ist, was hier mit Hinhalten, Wort-
brüchen und Insolenzen den Künstlern gespielt wird.«
Über Schicksal und Aufbewahrung der Kupferstichsammlung bis zum Jahr 1843, als sie
erstmals in das von Ludwig Friedrich Barth
entworfene Gebäude des »Museums der
Bildenden Künste« einzog, wissen wir
nichts Genaues, nach Busharts Darlegung
befand sie sich im Neuen Schloß. Wegen ihrer didaktischen Qualität als einer Sammlung von Reproduktionen klassischer Werke wurde sie — ähnlich wie die 1806 in Paris erworbene Kollektion von Gipsabgüssen
antiker Skulpturen — geschätzt und in den
vom Bildhauer Dannecker betriebenen
Plan einer umfassenden Kunstschule einbe-
zogen; sie sollte die 1761 von Herzog Carl
Eugen gegründete »Academie des Arts« ersetzen, die seit 1782 in der Hohen Carlsschule auf- und 1793 mit ihr untergegangen
war (siehe dazu: Werner Fleischhauer: Die
Kunst der Hohen Carlsschule, im Ausstellungskatalog »Die Hohe Carlsschule«, Stuttgart 1960). Von Danneckers großzügigem
Plan blieb nach Querelen mit der Finanz-
kommission eine »Elementarschule für
Kunst und Gewerbe« übrig, die 1829 im
umgebauten »Offizierspavillon« in der unteren Königstraße — zusammen mit der Anti-
ken- und Kupferstichsammlung — installiert
wurde. Aus der Bibliothek dieser Kunstschule, die 1843 mit in das neue Museum
der Bildenden Künste zog, 1888 aber in die
Urbanstraße verlegt wurde, stammen das
Bodensee-Reisetagebuch von Joseph Anton
Koch aus dem Jahre seiner Flucht von der
Carlsschule 1791 (Abb. 3, S. 202) und die
19 Klebebände mit Schweizer und italienischen Ansichten von Karl Urban Keller
(1772—1844).
Aus dem »Offizierspavillon« wurde die Kupferstichsammlung dank der Initiative König
Wilhelms I. 1843 befreit, sie zog mit in das
»Museum der Bildenden Künste« ein und
nannte sich seitdem bis 1918 »Königliches
Kupferstichkabinett Stuttgart«.
Nach Mitteilung Dr. Rudolf Hennings von
der Württembergischen Landesbibliothek
wäre das Kupferstichkabinett erst in jenem
Jahre 1843 von der »Kgl. öffentlichen Bibliothek« abgetrennt worden. Das muß
kein Widerspruch zu Busharts Darlegung
sein. Wahrscheinlich wurde damals die
Stichsammlung der ehemaligen Kupferste-

schule der Hohen Carlsschule" (p. 71—82).
This is not one of the familiar dry treatises;
it sets forth an utterly lucid picture of an era
of artistic breakthrough in Württemberg in
the name of Classicism. An example of his
approach is conveyed in a passage where
Petermann deals with the dissolution of the
Carlsschule after Carl Eugen's death in
1793: "The youngest child of the Carlsschule, the Engraving School, is the toughest
survivor, when, at last, the will of a stolid,
malicious bureaucracy asserts itself and
Carl Eugen's witless successors liquidate
his creation. It is a pitiful taste of Württemberg as it was and is, this game of delaying
tactics, breaches of promise and insolences
played out at the artists' expense."
We have no clear facts on the fate of the
Print Collection or its conservation until
1843, when it was first installed in the "Museum der Bildenden Künste" (Museum of
Fine Arts) designed by Ludwig Friedrich
Barth. According to Bushart the collection
was housed in the Neues Schloß. This collection of classical reproductions was highly
valued as an educational tool, much like the
collection of Antique sculpture plaster casts
acquired in Paris in 1806. The sculptor Dannecker included the collection in his plans
for a comprehensive school of art. This was
intended to replace the "Academie des Arts"
which Carl Eugen founded in 1761. In 1782
the Academie was annexed by the Hohe
Carlsschule and dissolved with it in 1793
(see Werner Fleischhauer: "Die Kunst der
Hohen Carlsschule", in the exhibition catalogue "Die Hohe Carlsschule" Stuttgart,
1960). What remained of Dannecker's
grand scheme after the Finance Commission had haggled over it, was the Elementarschule für Kunst und Gewerbe (Elementary School for Art and Crafts) installed in
1829 in the converted "Offizierspavillon"
together with the collection of antiquities
and prints in the lower Königstraße. Joseph
Anton Koch's travel journal of Lake Constance derives from the library of this art
school (the library also moved to the Museum of Fine Arts in 1843 but 1888 was
transfered to the Urbanstraße). Koch compiled the journal in 1791, the year of his
flight from the Carlsschule (ill. 3, p. 202).
Also from this source are the 19 albums
into which Karl Urban Keller (1772—1844)
affixed his views of Switzerland and Italy.
Thanks to the initiative of the King William I, the Print Collection was freed from
the confines of the "Offizierspavillon" and
moved to the Museum of Fine Arts in 1843.
From that date until 1918 it was known as
the "Königliches Kupferstichkabinett Stuttgart" — the Royal Collection of Prints at
Stuttgart.
According to Dr. Rudolf Henning of the
Württemberg State Library, the Print Collection was separated from the "Royal Public Library" in that crucial year of 1843. This
is not necessarily a contradiction of Bushart's inferences. It is probable that the former Engraving School's print collection
was merged at that time with that of the
"Royal Public Library" to form the Royal
Collection of Prints at Stuttgart. By this
time at the latest, a collected volume, mentioned by C. von Fabriczy and O. Fischer,

5
Friedrich, König von Württemberg (seit 1806,
gestorben 1816), Kupferstich von G. Rist nach
einem Porträt von J.B. Seele (1774–1814),
Hofmaler und Galeriedirektor in Stuttgart.

5
Frederick, King of Württemberg (crowned 1806,
d. 1816). Copper engraving by G. Rist after
a portrait by J.B. Seele (1774–1814), Painter
to the Court and Director of the Gallery at
Stuttgart.

cherschule mit derjenigen der »Kgl. öffentlichen Bibliothek« im »Kgl. Kupferstichkabinett« vereint. Spätestens damals gelangte
ein von C. v. Fabriczy und O. Fischer ge-
nannter Sammelband mit 463 Blättern von
der Königlichen Bibliothek ins Kupferstichkabinett (siehe Anm. 8 und 10). — Henning
und Geissler haben festgestellt, daß Sam-
melbände in der Landesbibliothek und Ein-
zelblätter unserer Sammlung — und zwar
vor allem Porträtstiche des frühen 17. Jahrhunderts — das gleiche, in brauner Feder ge-
schriebene Monogramm »I. C.W.« tragen.
Dieses weist nach glaubwürdiger Tradition
auf den 1594 geborenen Heilbronner kaiserlichen Notar Johann Christoph Wolfskeel.[5] Für die historische Fundierung unserer Sammlung, das heißt die Frage, woher
denn die alten Bestände stammen, ist die
Entdeckung jener Zusammenhänge ein
Lichtblick. Desgleichen der Fund eines Do-
kumentes im Stuttgarter Hauptstaatsarchiv,
den Werner Fleischhauer in seinem Buch
über »Die Geschichte der Kunstkammer der
Herzöge von Württemberg in Stuttgart«
1976 veröffentlichte (S. 74): Herzog Eberhard II. erwarb 1671 von dem aus Schorndorf gebürtigen Sixt Hirschmann (um
1614–1671), einem Juristen, der in fremden Diensten tätig gewesen und in Stuttgart ansässig geworden war, 1161 Kupfersti-
che für 1000 Reichstaler, nachdem er schon

containing 463 prints, had found its way
from the Royal Library into the Print Collection (cf. notes 8 & 10). Henning and
Geissler have discovered that such volumes
in the State Library and individual prints in
our collection, especially early 17th century
portrait engravings, bear the identical monogram "I. C.W." written in brown ink. This
would support the attribution to the Imperial Notary, Johann Christoph Wolfskeel,
born in Heilbronn in 1594[5]. For the historical substantiation of our cellection, that is,
the question of older stiock's provenance, is
the discovery of every link in the chain like
a ray of light. Another link is a document
that was found in Stuttgart's State Archive
and published in Werner Fleischhauer's
book "Die Geschichte der Kunstkammer
der Herzöge von Württemberg in Stuttgart"
(1976, p. 74). In 1671, Duke Eberhard II obtained from Sixt Hirschmann (1614–1671),
a lawyer born in Schorndorf who had been
active in the foreign service and later became a resident of Stuttgart, 1161 engravings for 1000 Reichstaler. This was after
Hirschmann had received 45 Gulden for a
"piece in engraving".
It is conspicuous but no coincidence that all
older collections of graphic art have titles
such as "Kupferstichkabinett", "Cabinet des
Estampes", "Print Room", or "Gabinetto
della Stampe" even though they also con-

1664/65 »für Kupferstück« 45 Gulden erhalten hatte.

Es ist auffällig, aber nicht zufällig, daß alle älteren graphischen Sammlungen sich »Kupferstichkabinett«, »Cabinet des Estampes«, »Print Room«, »Gabinetto delle Stampe« nennen, obwohl sie auch Zeichnungen bewahren, — und daß hier bei den unmittelbaren Vorläufern unserer Sammlung noch nicht die Rede von Zeichnungen war; es hat sie bis 1900 wohl vorwiegend nur in Künstlernachlässen gegeben. Aus solchen dürften die 22 Zeichnungen des aus Biberach an der Riß gebürtigen Malers Johann Heinrich Schönfeld (1609—1682) stammen[6], die zusammen mit denen seines Schülers, des Malers und Stechers Gabriel Ehinger (1652—1736), seit der Mitte des 19. Jahrhunderts bei uns nachweisbar sind (siehe auch Text Tafel 4, S. 238). Und in dem zeichnerischen Nachlaß des aus Paris gekommenen Stuttgarter Hofmalers Nicolas Guibal (1725—1784) könnten sich die beachtlichen Zeichnungsgruppen der Franzosen Dandré Bardon (1700—1783) und Jean Restout (1692—1768) befunden haben.[7]

Entscheidend für die langlebige Tradition des Namens »Kupferstichkabinett« ist der Wandel in der Bewertung der Handzeichnung damals und heute. Die Kabinette als Bildungsinstitute sammelten damals, vor der Erfindung der Fotografie, Stiche, weil sie die Werke der bildenden Kunst und Bildnisse großer Persönlichkeiten jedermann vor Augen führten; daß es dabei Stecher gab, die über die bloße Reproduktion hinaus ihr Vorbild übertrafen — wie jener Joh. Gotth. Müller, und außerdem seit Dürer und Rembrandt die autonomen »Peintre graveurs« — konnte den Ruhm der »Köni-

tain drawings. The immediate precursors of our own collection did not yet mention drawings. It seems that until 1900 drawings were limited mainly to the estates of deceased artists. This is the likely source of the 22 drawings by Johann Heinrich Schönfeld (1609—1682)[6], a painter born in Biberach on the Riss. Along with those of his pupil, the painter and engraver Gabriel Ehinger (1652—1736), whose drawings have been documented as part of our collection since the middle of the last century (see also caption for plate 4, p. 239). Likewise, the estate of Nicolas Guibal (1725 till 1784), a Parisian artist who served as a court painter in Stuttgart, may have originally held the notable series of drawings by his compatriots Drandré Bardon (1700 till 1783) and Jean Restout (1692—1768)[7].

A crucial explanation for the persistent tradition of the "print room" terminology lies in the different evaluation of freehand drawings at that time as compared to today. Before the invention of photography, the "cabinets" were considered institutions that collected engravings and presented great works of art and portraiture to a larger public. Some engravers did not merely reproduce works but also surpassed their models. Johann Gotthard Müller, for example, and the autonomous "peintre graveurs" since Dürer and Rembrandt could only enhance the glory of the "queen" of graphic arts. It follows that in the 19th century the "Director of the Royal Print Room" should be an engraver himself (see K. A. Kräutle's visiting card, p. 203 above). Today it may seem regrettable that the art of engraving was preferred over drawing, but due to this preference we have in Stuttgart a collection of German, Dutch, French, Italian and English

6
Friedrich Keller, Das
Kronprinzenpalais in Stuttgart,
Bleistiftzeichnung um 1850;
errichtet 1846—50 von dem
Architekten Gaab, 1930—43 Sitz
des Königlichen Kupferstich-
kabinetts, zerstört 1944.

6
Friedrich Keller, The Kronpri-
zenpalais in Stuttgart, pencil
drawing, c. 1850. The Palais was
built by the architect, Gaab, in
1846—50. From 1930 to 1943 it
housed the Royal Collection of
Prints; destroyed, 1944.

gin« unter den graphischen Künsten nur er-
höhen. Darum war ja auch im 19. Jahrhundert der »Vorstand des königlichen Kupferstichkabinetts« selbst ein Stecher (siehe die
abgebildete Visitenkarte von K. A. Kräutle
S. 203). Man mag aus heutiger Sicht die damalige Bevorzugung der Stecherkunst gegenüber der Handzeichnung bedauern, so
wird ihr doch in Stuttgart ein Ensemble
deutscher, niederländischer, französischer,
italienischer und englischer Druckgraphik
des 15. bis 18. Jahrhunderts verdankt, das
wir nur deswegen nicht genügend hoch-
schätzen, weil es seit eh und je unser wie
selbstverständlicher Besitz ist, weil die Be-
fassung mit alter Druckgraphik (die in der
Generation unserer Großväter als die allein
würdige galt und unübertreffliche Stan-
dardwerke hervorbrachte) sehr nachgelas-
sen hat und — weil der internationale Stellenwert eines Kabinetts heute vorwiegend
nach seinen Zeichnungen bemessen wird.
Dadurch ist auch unser italienischer Bestand, obwohl erst nach der Hochrenaissance einsetzend, interessant geworden. Die
Druckgraphik als vervielfältigende Kunst
kann sich heute nur durch aus der Masse
hervorragende Abzüge (»avant la lettre«
oder wirkliche, nicht nur vom Handel so genannte »épreuves d'artiste«) behaupten.
Zeichnungen hingegen sind Unikate, selbst
eine Nachzeichnung kann für die Forschung bedeutend werden, wie z. B. jene
brillante Kopie nach dem 1867 verbrannten
Tizian-Gemälde »Tod des hl. Petrus Martyr«
von 1530, über die es in Johann Maiers »Beschreibung von Venedig« 1795 heißt: »In
der vortrefflichen Sammlung des Herrn
Consistorialdirektors Ruoff zu Stuttgart findet sich die Originalzeichnung von diesem
Meisterwerke« (siehe Katalog: Italienische
Zeitungen, 1977, Nr. und Abb. 280).
Wenn dem so ist, wenn der Kupferstich früher den Vorrang gegenüber der Zeichnung
hatte, was konnte dann Herzog Carl Eugens
Nachfolger, König Friedrich I. von Württemberg (Abb. 4, 5, S. 203/205) bewegen,
eben diese Sammlung von Zeichnungen
des Herrn Ruoff und dazu die des in Ruß-
land gefallenen Hauptmanns Jakob Notter
(1777—1812) zu erwerben? — Mit einem
Wort: Weil das Sammeln von Zeichnungen
immer ein königliches Vergnügen war; ihm
verdanken die Sammlungen in Dresden
(August der Starke), Paris (Ludwig XIV.),
Stockholm (Königin Christine von Schwe-
den) oder die seit Georg III. immer im Besitz der englischen Krone verbliebene von
Windsor Castle ihre Entstehung — »zu einer
Zeit, als das Sammeln von Zeichnungen zu
den bevorzugten Neigungen von Personen
gehobenen Standes gehörte« (Halm) und,
wie Goethe 1792 an Heinrich Mayer
schrieb: »Wo noch etwas zu haben war.«
Vielleicht fühlte sich auch der württembergische Herzog, als er 1806 König von
Napoleons Gnaden geworden war, zu diesem elitären Vergnügen legitimiert. — Verzeichnisse der Sammlungen Ruoff und
Notter haben sich nicht erhalten. Nur die
kalligraphische Schreibweise der laufenden
Nummern, wie sie sich auf der obengenannten Tizian-Zeichnung findet (No.
116), läßt Rückschlüsse auf die Herkunft
weiterer, in gleicher Weise numerierter

prints from the 15th to the 18th centuries;
and if we fail to appreciate their true value,
then it is because they have been in our possession for so long and have come to be
taken for granted; and because the interest
in old prints (that our grandparents' generation regarded as the only worthy kind and,
about which, they published superlative
standard reference works) has decreased
markedly; and because today the international ranking of a graphic art collection is
measured predominantly by its drawings. It
is also the reason why our stock of Italian
work has become so interesting even
though it begins after the High Renaissance.
Today, the reproductive art of printing can
only assert its value with prints of outstanding quality — "trial proofs" — or genuine (not
simply coined so by the trade) "artist's
proofs". In contrast, drawings are one-of-a-
kind works and even a drawn copy can become important research material. That
brillant copy of Titian's "Death of St. Peter
the Martyr" of 1530, which burned in 1867,
is a prime example. Johann Maier's "Beschreibung von Venedig" (Description of
Venice) of 1795 refers to it: "In the excellent
collection of Director of the Consistory,
Mr. Ruoff, in Stuttgart, is to be found the
original drawing of this masterpiece." (See
catalogue, Christel Thiem, "Italienische
Zeichnungen" (Stuttgart 1977), No. and
ill. 280).
If it is true that engraving used to rank
above drawing, then what could have motivated Duke Carl Eugen's successor, King
Frederick I of Württemberg (ill. 4, 5,
p. 203/205) to acquire the same Herr
Ruoff's collection of drawings and that of a
Captain Jakob Notter (1777—1812) who had
been killed in service in Russia? In a word
— collecting drawings had always been a
royal pastime. It is the "raison d'être" for
the collections at Dresden (August the
Strong), Paris (Louis XVI), Stockholm
(Queen Christina of Sweden) and the collection that has been in the possession of
the English crown at Windsor Castle since
George III: "at a time when the collecting
of drawings was one of the favourite pre-
dilections of persons of high standing"
(Halm), and, as Goethe wrote to Heinrich
Mayer in 1792, "when there was still something to be had". Perhaps the Duke of Württemberg, king since 1806 by appointment of
Napoleon, felt entitled to this privileged
pastime. No index of the Ruoff and Notter
Collections remains. Only from the calligraphic notation of the successive acquisition numbers as found on the Titian drawing mentioned above (No. 116) can we
infer the source of other, similarly number-
ed works. "The sequence of our inventory
numbers allows for only partial conclusions.
The lowest number of the Italian Masters is
1098 (Albani). The Titian drawing is num-
bered 1390. Thus the numbers between are
presumably part of the oldest stock" (Ibid,
p. 9).
Thanks to an essay by the private Scholar,
Cornelius von Fabriczy of Stuttgart, on the
sketchbook of a Dutch artist who drew
French and Italien cities and buildings in
the last third of the 16th century (ill. 9,
p. 211), we know of the large bound collec-

Blätter zu: »Aus der Abfolge unserer Inventarnummern lassen sich nur bedingt Schlüsse ziehen. Die früheste Nummer bei den italienischen Meistern ist 1098 (Albani). Die Tizian-Zeichnung hat die Nr. 1390. Somit gehören die dazwischen liegenden Nummern vermutlich zum ältesten Bestand« (Christel Thiem im Katalog der Italienischen Zeichnungen, 1977, S. 9).

Einem Aufsatz des Stuttgarter Privatgelehrten Cornelius v. Fabriczy über das Skizzenbuch eines Niederländers, der im letzten Drittel des 16. Jahrhunderts französische und italienische Städte und Bauten zeichnete (Abb. 9, S. 211), verdanken wir die Nachricht des obengenannten großen Sammelbandes[8]; er enthielt außer jenen frühen Veduten, die unter dem Namen »Anonymus Fabriczy« in die Literatur Eingang gefunden haben, ohne vollends erforscht zu sein[9]; nicht nur Zeichnungen von Hans Baldung und von Roelant Savery, sondern auch acht rosa eingefärbte Blätter, jeweils auf beiden Seiten mit reizvollen weltlichen und religiösen Szenen (Abb. 8, S. 210), die dreimal 1483 datiert sind und trotz Otto Fischers Publikation von 1923 durch die merkwürdige Perfektheit der Komposition und des Striches Rätsel aufgeben.[10]

Trotz jenes verheißungsvollen Anfangs unter König Friedrich I. hat sich im 19. Jahrhundert nicht mehr viel an gezielten Erwerbungen abgespielt — und auch nicht bis 1945, obwohl, wie Otto Fischer 1928 zutreffend bemerkte, in Stuttgart dazu beste Gelegenheit durch das renommierte Auktionshaus H. G. Gutekunst in der Olgastraße gewesen wäre; aber wie sollte das auch anders sein, wenn Kupferstecher die »Vorstände« des Kabinetts waren — und nicht Kenner der Zeichenkunst, die damals bei Gutekunst Zeichnungen in Lots, in Bündeln steigerten! — Was hat aber den »Vorstand« Karl August Kräutle bewogen, doch zweimal bei Gutekunst zuzugreifen? Zuerst 1872, als die letzte Sammlung des Marchese Jacopo Durazzo im Schiller-Saal der Liederhalle versteigert wurde. Vielleicht war es der Ruf des Marchese, dem die Wiener »Albertina« ihren Grundstock verdankt[11], der Kräutle veranlaßte, ca. 200 italienische, davon 130 genuesische Zeichnungen zu erwerben, darunter von Hauptmeistern Genuas wie Cambiaso, Castiglione (Tafel 12, S. 270) und der Künstlerfamilie Piola. Zum zweiten Male trat Kräutle erst ein Jahrzehnt später, 1882, bei Gutekunst mit einem Geniestreich auf den Plan: für 416 Goldmark erwarb er in 9 Lots 168 Zeichnungen von Giambattista und Domenico Tiepolo (Tafel 13, 14, S. 272/276), darunter viele, die mit dem Hauptwerk Tiepolos, den Fresken im Treppenhaus und Kaisersaal der Würzburger Residenz, zusammenhängen[12] (dadurch gehört Stuttgart mit Leningrad, Triest, London und New York zu den fünf größten Tiepolo-Sammlungen der Welt). Woher nahm Kräutle das Geld dazu? Er dürfte kaum, wie wir heute, einen Erwerbungsetat gehabt haben, aber er hatte Dubletten, mit denen er den Ankauf gegen nur sechs Gegenbieter (wie wir aus den originalen Unterlagen der seit 1914 in Bern niedergelassenen Firma wissen) finanzieren konnte. Dies zu vermuten legt das Titelblatt jenes Auktionskatalo-

tion mentioned above[8]. Apart form the early vedutes (known in the subject literature as "Anonymous Fabriczy" and not yet fully researched[9]) the book also contained drawings by Hans Baldung and Roelant Savery as well as eight pink dyed sheets adorned on both sides with charming secular and religious scenes (ill. 8, p. 210); three are dated 1483. Despite Otto Fischer's publication of 1923, their remarkable perfection of composition and line still presents a riddle[10].

In spite of a promising beginning under King Frederick I, the rest of the 19th century saw little in the way of judicious, specific purchases. This would not change until 1945, although, as Otto Fischer aptly remarked in 1928, the presence of the famed auctioneers, H. G. Gutekunst, in Stuttgart's Olgastraße, provided ample opportunity. How could events have been otherwise, when the "directors" of the Print Room were copperplate engravers not the connoisseurs of draughtsmanship who would buy drawings in lots and bundles at Gutekunst's auctions! This being so, why then did Director Karl August Kräutle bid twice at Gutekunst's? The first time was in 1872, when Marchese Jacopo Durazzo's last collection was auctioned off in the Schiller-Saal of the Liederhalle. Perhaps it was the marquis' reputation as the one responsible for the original stock of the Albertina in Vienna[11] that motivated Kräutle's purchase of some 200 Italian drawings, of which 130 were Genoese, including work by major artists such as Cambiaso, Castiglione (plate 12, p. 270) and the artist family Piola. The second time Kräutle attended Gutekunst's auction was not until a decade later, but then it amounted to a stroke of genius. In 1882 he spent 416 goldmarks on nine lots. They consisted of 168 drawings by Giambattista and Domencio Tiepolo (plates 13, 14, p. 273/276). Many of the drawings are connected with Tiepolo's mainœuvre: the frescoes in the stairwell and the Kaisersaal of the Residence at Würzburg[12]. Stuttgart, along with Leningrad, Triest, London and New York, has one of the largest Tiepolo collections in the world. Where did Kräutle obtain the money for his purchase? He could hardly have had a specific purchase fund as we do today. But he did have duplicate prints that enabled him to finance his bid against only six contenders (the original documents of the firm founded in Bern in 1914 tell us this). That these prints played a role is suggested by the title page of the auction catalogue of 1882. The announcement of the sale of the Bossi-Beyerlen Collection, which included our Tiepolo drawings, is followed by "and the doubles from the Royal Württemb. Print Room here". After 1882 however, all remained quiet at the Collection — as far as we can tell today. The acquisitions that did follow appear to have come by way of donations.

Our catalogue of 19th century drawings and watercolours "Zeichnungen und Aquarelle des 19. Jahrhunderts" of 1976, presents in all detail the drawings acquired from the estates of 19th century artists. Let it suffice to list them here: Johann Heinrich Dannecker (1758—1841), 210 sheets; Philipp Friedrich

7
Hans Burgkmaier, Kaiser Maximilian und Maria
von Burgund im »Liebesgarten«: »Wie der jung
weyß kunig und die jung kunigin yedes des
andern sein sprach lernet«, Holzschnitt (Unikat)
für die unvollendete Biographie des am
1. Januar 1519 in Wels verstorbenen Kaisers,
1514/16 entstanden; aus der Sammlung des
Fürsten Liechtenstein, Vaduz.

7
Hans Burgkmair, The Emperor Maximilian and
Mary of Burgundy in the "Garden of Love" —
"How the young wise king and the young queen
each the other his language learneth", woodcut
(single print) for the unfinished biography of
the Emperor, who died 1st January 1519 in
Wels. C. 1514/16; from the Collection of the
Prince of Liechtenstein, Vaduz.

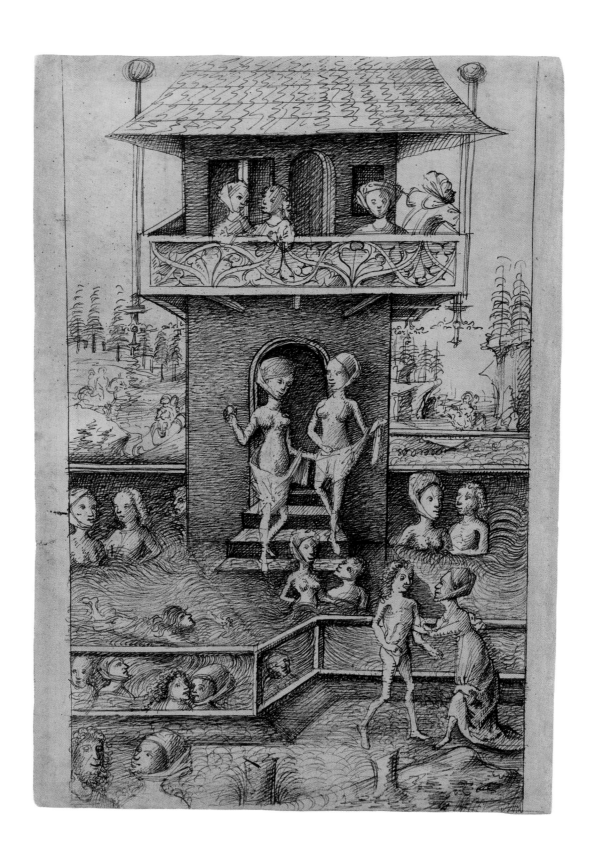

8
Süddeutscher Meister von 1483
Frauenbad
Federzeichnung auf rosa eingefärbtem Papier.

8
South German Master of 1483
Women's Baths
Pen drawing on pink-stained paper.

9
Niederländischer Meister des späten 16. Jahrhunderts, der sogenannte »Anonymus Fabriczy«, Ansicht von Lyon, Federzeichnung.

9
Netherlandish Master of the late 16th century, called "Anonymus Fabriczy", View of Lyons, pen drawing.

ges von 1882 nahe, wo es nach der Ankündigung der Sammlung Bossi-Beyerlen — aus ihr kommen unsere Tiepolo-Zeichnungen — heißt, »sowie der Doubletten des Kgl. Württemb. Kupferstich-Cabinets hier«. — Danach aber, nach 1882, blieb es still im Kupferstichkabinett, soweit wir heute feststellen können. Erwerbungen scheinen sich damals nur mehr in Form von Stiftungen vollzogen zu haben.

Unser Katalog der »Zeichnungen und Aquarelle des 19. Jahrhunderts« von 1976 informiert detailliert über die zeichnerischen Nachlässe von Künstlern des 19. Jahrhunderts. Daher genügt es, diese hier nur zahlenmäßig zu erwähnen: Johann Heinrich Dannecker (1758—1841) 210 Blatt — Philipp Friedrich von Hetsch (1758—1839) 125 Blatt — Eberhard v. Wächter (1762—1852), seit 1810 Custos des Kupferstichkabinetts, ca. 35 Blatt — Georg Konrad Weitbrecht (1796—1838) 943 Blatt — Joseph Anton v. Gegenbaur (1800—1876) 661 Blatt — Bernhard v. Neher (1806—1886) 73 Blatt — Gottlob Friedrich Steinkopf (1779—1860) und sein Sohn Julius Steinkopf (1815 bis 1892) ca. 1500 Zeichnungen und Pausen, dazu 39 Skizzenbücher — Ludwig Knaus (1829—1910) 44 Zeichnungen und 17 Ölskizzen (durch Vermächtnis seines Sohnes Otto 1947) — Karl Friedrich Johann v. Müller (1813—1881) ca. 400 Blatt (nach seinem Tod 1881 und durch Vermächtnis seiner

von Hetsch (1758—1839), 125; Eberhard von Wächter (1762—1852), curator of the Print Collection from 1810, circa 35; Georg Konrad Weitbrecht (1796—1838), 943; Joseph Anton von Gegenbaur (1800—1876), 661; Bernhard von Neher (1806—1886), 73; Gottlob Friedrich Steinkopf (1779—1860) and his son Julius Steinkopf (1815—1892), circa 1500 drawings and tracings, also 39 sketchbooks; Ludwig Knaus (1829—1910), 44 drawings and 17 oil sketches (by the bequest of his son, Otto, 1947); Karl Friedrich Johann von Müller (1813—1881), circa 400 sheets (on his death in 1881 and by bequest of his daughter in 1937); Wilhelm Friedrich Herter (1865—1888) and his brother Robert Johnston Herter (1873—1898), 300 (in 1969 on their descendants' bequest). The closure in 1824 of the porcelain workshops in Ludwigsburg (founded in 1758) brought to our Collection some 450 original designs by the most significant porcelain painters, among them Gottlob Friedrich Riedels (1724 till 1784), who worked at Meissen, Höchst and Frankenthal before his post in Ludwigsburg. This source also brought some 1000 prints.

The manner in which the Collection of Prints and Drawings was accommodated in the newly completed "Museum der Bildenden Künste" in 1843 (the name is still written above the portico of today's Staatsgalerie) was not very advantageous. Placed in

10
Annibale Carracci (1560—1609), Meeresbucht bei Sonnenuntergang, Federzeichnung aus den letzten Jahren des Künstlers, 1972 aus der Ellesmere-Collection erworben.

10
Annibale Carracci (1560—1609), Bay at Sunset pen drawing from the last years of the artist's life, acquired in 1972 from the Ellesmere Collection.

Tochter 1937) — Wilhelm Friedrich Herter (1865–1888) und sein Bruder Robert Johnston Herter (1873–1898) 300 Blatt (1969 durch Vermächtnis ihrer Nachfahren). — Durch die Schließung der 1758 gegründeten Ludwigsburger Porzellanmanufaktur im Jahr 1824 kamen an 450 Entwurfszeichnungen der wichtigsten Porzellanmaler, darunter Gottlob Friedrich Riedels (1724–1784), der zuvor in Meißen, Höchst und Frankenthal tätig war, sowie an 1000 Stiche zu uns. Die Unterbringung der Graphischen Sammlung in dem 1843 vollendeten »Museum der Bildenden Künste« — wie noch heute über dem Portikus der Staatsgalerie zu lesen steht — war nicht glücklich: im Mitteltrakt des Obergeschosses liegend, trennte sie die Galerie und den gewünschten Rundgang in zwei Hälften. In den 20er Jahren entschloß man sich, das am Schloßplatz gelegene Kronprinzenpalais (Abb. 6, S. 206) für Museumszwecke umzubauen: 1930 zog das Kupferstichkabinett dorthin um, zusammen mit der Verwaltung und der »Schwäbischen Malerei« seit 1860.[15] Das dauerte keine 14 Jahre, dann lag Stuttgart in Trümmern. An die Stelle des Kronprinzenpalais setzte man einen Betonklotz — und die Graphische Sammlung wurde wieder in das jetzt »Staatsgalerie« genannte Museum verlegt; sie erhielt vom Erdgeschoß den rechten Flügel mit dem Ausstel-

the central section of the upper storey; the Collection separated the gallery and gallery tour in two halves. In the 1920's it was decided to convert the Kronprinzenpalais at Schloßplatz (ill. 6, p. 206) into a museum. In 1930, the Print Collection moved there along with the museum offices and the Collection of Swabian Paintings since 1860[15]. This constellation lasted not quite 14 years before Stuttgart was reduced to rubble. Where the Kronprinzenpalais had once stood, a concrete block was built. The Collection of Graphic Art was moved back into the museum now restyled "Staatsgalerie". It was allocated the right-hand wing of the ground floor, with an exhibition section and a spacious storeroom.

The history of the Collection of Prints and Drawings in the first half of the 20th century, or more precisely up to 1945, is, in retrospect, a history of the most grievous losses. The lack of inventory lists prevent us from determining what had been acquired up to this time; but thanks to a file headed "Losses", we can reconstruct what was destroyed. The first blow was struck on 28th of August 1937 in the name of "purging the temple of art" under the National Socialist art policy. The artwork sent to Berlin as "accelerated express goods" comprised: 27 drawings, 293 prints and 9 portfolios by contemporary artists. All confiscated and

11
Caspar David Friedrich, Die Ruine der Abtei Eldena bei Greifswald, datiert »den 5 t Mei. 1801«, Federzeichnung über Bleistift, graubraun laviert.

11
Caspar David Friedrich, The Ruins of Eldena Abbey near Greifswald; dated "den 5t Mei. 1801"; pen drawing over pencil, with grey-brown wash.

lungstrakt und einem großzügig konzipierten Magazin.

Die Geschichte der Graphischen Sammlung in der ersten Hälfte des 20. Jahrhunderts, genau gesagt bis 1945, erscheint im Rückblick nur als eine Geschichte schwerster Verluste. Wir können mangels Inventaren nicht mehr feststellen, was bis dahin erworben wurde, aber dank eines Ordners mit dem Titel »Verluste« rekonstruieren, was zugrunde ging. Der erste Schlag erfolgte als »Reinigung des Kunsttempels« durch die nationalsozialistische Kulturpolitik am 28. August 1937; damals wurden als »beschleunigtes Eilgut« nach Berlin abgesandt: 27 Zeichnungen und 293 druckgraphische Blätter sowie neun Mappenwerke moderner Künstler, die als »Entartete Kunst« konfisziert worden waren. Eine Liste nennt 40 prominente Künstler, die Titel ihrer Blätter, die Erwerbungsjahre, die gezahlten Preise und den »Verantwortlichen Direktor«, zumeist Prof. Otto Fischer, der, von 1921 bis 1927 amtierend, erstmals avantgardistisch sammelte, und Prof. Heinz Braune-Krickau. Das früheste Erwerbungsjahr ist 1918 mit sechs Blättern von Adolf Hölzel, dem hervorragenden Stuttgarter Lehrer, der damals verdrossen von der Bureaukratie seinen Dienst an der Akademie quittierte; das letzte Erwerbungsjahr ist 1932 mit zwei Lithographien von Otto Müller für RM 45,—, »verantwortlich Dr. Braune«, der drei weitere Lithographien Otto Müllers hinzugeschenkt hatte, die nichtsdestoweniger auch beschlagnahmt wurden. Sonst hat 1932 kein Ankauf stattgefunden, so groß war damals die wirtschaftliche Not. Auch die 20er Jahre waren keineswegs »golden« gewesen. Was an beschlagnahmten Werken später wieder im Handel auftauchte — wie z. B. laut einer Aktennotiz vom 12. 10. 1949 unser Exemplar der Radierfolge »Krieg« von Otto Dix — konnte nur zurückgekauft werden.[14] Jedoch blieb durch die Zivilcourage eines Beamten eine Mappe wertvollster moderner Blätter sowohl von der Beschlagnahme, wie den Bomben verschont; er hat sie erst mit nach Hause genommen, dann zum Schutz ausgelagert und 1947 vom »Tribunal Militäre du Quartier Général« zurückerhalten: Dieser mutige Beamte wurde 1945 Direktor unseres zerstörten Hauses: Theodor Musper. Er hatte das Beste vom Besten gerettet: 22 Aquarelle und Zeichnungen von Nolde, Pechstein, Heckel, Barlach, Kokoschka, Hofer, Grosz, Dix, Baumeister und Schlemmer. — Zwei frühe Radierungen Picassos, darunter das berühmte »Repas frugal«, bereits 1913 erworben, hatten die Häscher wohl aus Unkenntnis übersehen; es dauerte 33 Jahre, bis wieder ein Blatt Picassos dank einer Stiftung von Kommerzienrat Reusch, 1946, zu uns kam. Dann aber konnte durch rechtzeitigen Zugriff nicht allein bei der Druckgraphik, sondern auch bei den Zeichnungen (Abb. 15, 16, S. 220/221 und Tafel 38, S. 342) sowie bei den illustrierten Büchern erreicht werden, daß Stuttgart wohl nicht nur die älteste, sondern heute auch die größte öffentliche Picasso-Sammlung Deutschlands besitzt (siehe unseren Gesamtkatalog, 1981).

Der zweite und dritte Vernichtungsschlag traf die alte Kunst durch »Kriegseinwir-

classified as "degenerate art". A list names 40 prominent artists, the titles of their works, year of acquisition, price paid and the "director responsible". This was, in most cases, Professor Otto Fischer, who during his period in office from 1921 to 1927, was the first to collect avant-garde pieces; and Professor Heinz Braune-Krickau. The earliest acquisition was made in 1918. Six works by Adolf Hölzel, the brilliant Stuttgart teacher, who resigned from his post in disgust at the governing bureaucracy, were purchased; in 1932 the last purchase were two lithographs by Otto Müller for 45 Reichsmark — "responsible: Dr. Braune". Braune had donated three other Müller lithographs that were confiscated along with the rest. The two prints were the only purchases in 1932 because the economic situation at the time was so dire. The 1920's were not, by any means, "golden" or flourishing.

Those confiscated works that later reappeared at sales and dealers, for example, our set of Otto Dix's cycle of etchings "Krieg" (War), as documented by a memorandum of 12/10/1949, could only be bought back[14]. It was the personal courage of a member of the museum staff that helped preserve a folder of invaluable modern artwork from both confiscation and the bombs. First he took the folder home; then he put it in safe storage. The "Tribunal Militaire de Quartier Général" returned the file to him in 1947. In 1945 this courageous museum official became the director of our destroyed museum. His name: Theodor Musper. He had saved the best of the very best: 22 water-coulours and drawings from Nolde, Pechstein, Heckel, Barlach, Kokoschka, Hofer, Grosz, Dix, Baumeister and Schlemmer. Two early Picasso etchings, including the renowned "Repas Frugal", were acquired as early as 1913, had been overlooked — probably out of ignorance — by the regime's henchmen. It would be another 33 years before another work of Picasso's became part of the Collection and this, thanks to the donation of Kommerzienrat Reusch in 1946. But then, well-timed purchases secured not only prints but also drawings (ills. 15, 16, p. 220/221 and pl. 38, p. 342) and illustrated books, so that Stuttgart became the site of both the oldest and the largest public collection of Picassos in Germany (see our complete catalogue, 1981).

The second and third destructive blows that befell the old masters were through the "effects of war" and, to a greater extent, from the plundering of storage sites at Waldenburg and Taxis. Bombs do not discriminate; but thieves do. The opportunity to recover a stolen item arose only once and that we owe the loyality of a Stuttgart antiquarian book-seller, Kocher-Benzing. In 1971 in the USA he chanced upon an incunabulum bearing our stamp. It was a complete copy of the "Schatzbehalter" (Treasury) printed by Koberger in Nuremberg in 1491 and containing woodcuts by Wolgemut and Pleydenwurff. Apart from this, there were no "windfalls".

Dürer's graphic œuvre suffered in particular; our complete copy of his "Ehrenpforte Kaiser Maximilians I" (Triumphal Gate for

12

Wilhelm Leibl (1844—1900): »Skizze nach
einem bayrischen / Bauernburschen als Haber- /
feldtreiber. / W. Leibl 1889« (eigenhändig),
Federzeichnung braun laviert über Bleistift; von
den Nachfahren Leibls 1871 erworben. — Das
Haberfeldtreiben hat nichts mit der Jagd zu
tun, sondern ist ein bayerischer Rügebrauch
gewesen, besonders in Leibls Wohnort Aibling.

12

Wilhelm Leibl (1844—1900): "Sketch of a Bavarian / country lad as a 'Haberfeldtreiber' ('oatfield beater'). / W. Leibl 1889" (in his hand);
pen drawing with brown wash over pencil.
Acquired from Leibl's descendants in 1971.
"Oatfield driving" (or beating) was not a hunting practice, but a Bavarian ritual reproof,
especially at Aibling, where Leibl lived.

kung« und härter noch durch Plünderungen
an den Auslagerungsorten Waldenburg und
Taxis. Geschosse wüten blind, aber Diebe
nicht. Die Chance, von den letzteren etwas
auf Umwegen zurückzuerhalten, ereignete
sich einmal dank der Loyalität des Stuttgarter Antiquars Kocher-Benzing; er entdeckte
1971 in den USA eine Inkunabel mit unserem Stempel: ein vollständiges Exemplar
des 1491 in Nürnberg von Koberger ge-
druckten »Schatzbehalters« mit Holzschnit-
ten von Wolgemut und Pleydenwurff. —
Sonst aber wurde uns nichts »geschenkt«,
besonders litt das graphische Werk Dürers:
Unser in Meders Œuvrekatalog auf S. 212
genanntes, vollständiges Exemplar der
»Ehrenpforte Kaiser Maximilians I.« in der
1. Ausgabe von 1517/1518 wurde vernichtet
(192 Holzschnitte in 24 Kartons), desgleichen die Kleine und die Große Holzschnitt-
passion und die »Apokalypse«; 22 Kupfer-
stiche wurden gestohlen. Von Altdorfer
wurden 37 Blätter vernichtet, von Rem-

the Emperor Maximilian I) in the first edition of 1517/1518, mentioned on page 212
of Meder's œuvre catalogue, was destroyed
(192 woodcuts in 24 archive boxes) as were
the Little and Great Passion woodcut series,
and the "Apocalypse"; 22 copper engravings were stolen. Also destroyed were 37
works of Altdorfer and 5 large Rembrandt
etchings; 21 Rembrandts were stolen.
Goya's "Caprichos" and "Desastres de la
Guerra" were consumed by the horror of
war he depicted, along with so much else.
Yet, seen as a whole, the "Kupferstichkabinett" got off lightly in that reign of terror.
"Nomen est omen"; the new beginning
for our institute following WWII was hailed
by a new name: the "Graphische Sammlung der Staatsgalerie Stuttgart" or Stuttgart
State Gallery Collection of Graphic Art.
This meant that not only the collecting and
tending of printed graphic works but also
freehand drawings, illustrated books and
posters of equal status[15]. To have fulfilled

brandt fünf große Radierungen – und 21 gestohlen. Goyas »Capricchos« und »Desastres de la Guerra« verschlangen die von ihm geschilderten Kriegsgreuel – außer so vielem anderen. Dennoch ist das »Kupferstichkabinett« aufs Ganze gesehen in jener Schreckenszeit glimpflich davongekommen.

»Nomen est omen« – am Neubeginn nach dem Zweiten Weltkrieg steht ein neuer Name für unser Institut: »Graphische Sammlung der Staatsgalerie Stuttgart«. Das bedeutet: nicht allein gedruckte Graphik soll gepflegt werden, sondern gleichrangig Handzeichnungen, illustrierte Bücher und Plakate.[15] Erfüllt zu haben, was der neue Name versprach: ein virulentes Wachstum mit Schwerpunkten, die uns international bekannt gemacht haben, ist primär das Verdienst von Erwin Petermann, der auch noch nach der Übernahme der Direktion des Gesamthauses im Jahre 1963 seine Hand über die Graphische Sammlung hielt, aber sei-

the expectations of what the new name promised: namely a vigorously expanding collection with an international reputation – this is primarily the achievement of Erwin Petermann. Petermann watched over the Collection of Graphic Art even after he became director of the museum in 1963. Yet, he nonetheless allowed his successor free reign. Perhaps an example will illustrate what I mean. It had not escaped him that I had considerably overdrawn my purchase fund budget. Rather than ask me for an explanation, he said in passing, "Herr Thiem, I think you are going to have to rob a bank before long." Anyone else faced with the task of re-establishing a collection depleted from evacuation, would look first of all to evaluating what had been saved. But Petermann began without delay to collect what he knew and loved; those works which only yesterday had been classified as "degenerate" – Expressionist graphics. By the time their artistic value was acknowledged once

nem Nachfolger nichtsdestoweniger freie Hand ließ. Eine Episode mag das verdeutlichen: Es war ihm nicht verborgen geblieben, daß ich erhebliche Ankaufsschulden gemacht hatte; statt mich zur Rede zu stellen, sagte er im Vorbeigehen: »Herr Thiem, i glaub, Se müsset bald an Bankeinbruch begehe.« Ein anderer hätte beim Wiederaufbau einer mit Verlusten ausgelagerten Sammlung vorerst sein Hauptaugenmerk auf die Sichtung des Erhaltenen gerichtet, er aber fing sofort an zu sammeln, was er liebte und kannte — wie kaum ein anderer: das, was gestern noch als »entartet« gegolten hatte: die Graphik des Expressionismus. Als ihr künstlerischer Rang allgemein wieder erkannt wurde und die Preise heftig anzogen, hatte Petermann mit geringsten Mitteln die größte Sammlung moderner Graphik in öffentlichem Besitz begründet. Von ihren führenden Meistern könnten wir jeweils ganze Ausstellungen aus eigenem Besitz bestreiten. Was für eine eminente sammlerische Leistung steckt dahinter! Ein wichtiger Künstler ist mit drei guten Gemälden meist ausreichend in einem Museum präsentiert, aber nicht mit drei graphischen Blättern.

Die großartigste Stiftung ist uns auf dem Gebiet der alten Meister durch einen Amerikaner zuteil geworden, durch den am Schwäbisch Hall gebürtigen, 1904 nach New York ausgewanderten Industriellen Max Kade (1882–1967); nachdem er in Stuttgart das Studentenwohnheim, die Mensa und den Bibliotheks-Bau der Universität finanziert hatte[16], stiftete er uns aufgrund des jahrelangen Kontaktes zu Erwin Petermann Zug um Zug seine umfassende Sammlung alter Graphik. Als er diese (1953) auf hervorragende Exemplare der großen Meister zu konzentrieren begann, überließ er uns alles übrige — und das war nicht unerheblich; im Jahre 1955 schenkte er uns etwas Singuläres: 120 Frühdrucke der Holzschnitte Burgkmairs (Abb. 7, S. 209), Becks und Schäufeleins zum »Weißkunig«, der Autobiographie Kaiser Maximilians I., aus dem Besitz des Fürsten Liechtenstein[17]; 1964 übergab er uns seinen größten Schatz, die Meister-Graphik, fast vollständig, nachdem sie hier ausgestellt und katalogisiert worden war, vor allem Schongauer, Dürer, Lucas van Leyden, Rembrandt (Tafel 8, S. 256), Mantegna.[18]

Ein unschätzbarer Zuwachs an alten Handzeichnungen ist die seit dem 10. März 1976 »in Verwahrung der Staatsgalerie Stuttgart« befindliche »Sammlung Schloß Fachsenfeld« des Freiherrn v. Koenig. Daß es in Deutschland noch möglich war, im Jahre 1966 eine unberührte, das heißt seit ihrer Begründung unangetastete, aber auch unerforschte Sammlung zu entdecken (Tafel 9, 11, S. 260 und 266), grenzt ans Wunderbare: ca. 2700 Blätter, davon fast 1000 aus der großen Zeit Bolognas im Barock, ca. 900 aus anderen italienischen Schulen sowie aus Frankreich, den Niederlanden und Deutschland, ferner ca. 750 aus dem 19. Jahrhundert, besonders aus Schwaben (B. v. Neher, E. v. Hayn, Reiniger, Pleuer, aber auch C. D. Friedrich und J. G. v. Dillis). Das Team der Graphischen Sammlung hat sich bemüht, in drei Ausstellungen und

again, and prices were rising sharply, Petermann had, with very modest means, begun the largest collection of modern graphic art found in a public institution. We could furnish entire exhibitions of any of the foremost artists in the field solely from own our stock. What an accomplished feat of collecting! An important artist is adequately represented in a museum with three of his/ her good paintings — but never with three prints or drawings.

The most magnificent donation to come our way was a collection of Old Masters. It was owned by an American industrialist, Max Knade (1882–1967), who was born in Schwäbisch Hall and emigrated to New York in 1904. He financed the dormitories, the cafeteria and the library building for the University of Stuttgart[16] and later acknowledged his long-standing close rapport with Erwin Petermann by donating his entire collection of old graphic art. In 1953 when he began concentrating on prime examples of Old Masters, he left us everything else, which was not unconsiderable. In 1955 he gave us something quite unique — 120 early woodcut prints by Burgkmair (ill. 7, p. 209), Beck, Schäufelein for the "Weißkunig", the autobiography of Emperor Maximilian I. The prints were formerly in the possession of the Prince of Liechtenstein[17]. In 1964 we exhibited and catalogued his greatest treasure: the collection of Old Master prints and drawings. Knade presented us with nearly all of the collection, including works by Schongauer, Dürer, Lucas van Leyden, Rembrandt (pl. 8, p. 257) and Mantegna[18]. Drawings of inestimable value from Baron von Koenig's "Schloß Fachsenfeld Collection", were handed over for safe-keeping to the Staatsgalerie Stuttgart on the 10th of March 1976. That it was possible to discover such an untouched collection in Germany in 1976, i. e., one both intact and unresearched since its inception, verges on the miraculous (pl. 9, 11, p. 261 and 267). It comprises some 2700 works, almost 1000 date from the great Bolognese Baroque era, about 900 from other Italian schools and France, the Low Countries and Germany. Furthermore, about 750 19th century pieces, notably from Swabia (B. von Neher, E. von Hayn, Reiniger, Pleuer; also C. D. Friedrich and J. G. von Dillis). The staff at the Collection has been at pains to show themselves worthy of this treasure and has organized three exhibitions and published catalogues[19].

As we all know, France led the field in the art of the 19th century, but Germany's Romantics found the purest expression, in the visual arts as well as in Literature and music, for the longing of the time (ill. 11, p. 213, pl. 20, 21, p. 292/294). Apart from the pieces by Moritz von Schwind and Anselm Feuerbach (pl. 22, 23, p. 296/298), Stuttgart's graphic arts collection contained not one of these Romantic works before 1945. A deficit not to be glossed over even though the Collection did have a significant stock of Classicist drawings by Johann Christian Reinhart, Josef Anton Koch (pl. 19, p. 290), Heinrich Dannecker, Christian Gottlieb Schick[19a] and their pupils. The catalogues of 1960, 1969 and 1976[20] show

Katalogen diesen Schatz zu heben und sich damit seines Besitzes würdig zu zeigen.[19]

Im 19. Jahrhundert war bekanntlich Frankreich in der Kunst führend, aber Deutschlands Romantiker fanden nicht nur in Wort und Musik, sondern ebenso in der bildenden Kunst den reinsten Ausdruck für die Sehnsucht ihrer Zeit (Abb. 11, S. 213 und Tafel 20, 21, S. 292/294). Davon war bis 1945 — abgesehen von Blättern Moritz v. Schwinds und Anselm Feuerbachs (Tafel 22, 23, S. 296/298) — in Stuttgarts graphischer Sammlung nichts vorhanden. Darüber konnte auch nicht der bedeutende Fundus klassizistischer Zeichnungen von Joh. Christian Reinhart, Josef Anton Koch (Tafel 19, S. 290), Heinrich Dannecker, Chr. Gottlieb Schick[19a] und ihrer Schüler hinwegtäuschen. Was auf beiden Gebieten aufgeholt werden konnte, besagen Kataloge von 1960, 1969 und 1976.[20]

Mit zwei Erwerbungsblöcken erhielt die neuere französische Druckgraphik eine Basis: Von Maurice Loncle, Paris, erwarben wir 1961 eine exquisite Kollektion illustrierter französischer Bücher des 19. und 20. Jahrhunderts, das heißt von Delacroix' Faust-Illustrationen bis hin zu den großen »Malerbüchern« von Toulouse-Lautrec, Matisse, Picasso, Braque, Léger, Chagall, Rouault, zumeist in Vorzugsexemplaren, kostbar gebunden.[21] — Von demselben Sammler erwarben wir 1250 der berühmten Lithographien Honoré Daumiers, zumeist in »épreuves sur blanc«, d. h. vor der Auflage in Zeitungen wie »La Caricature« und »Charivari«; dazu 12 Zeichnungen und eine Gouache (Tafel 15, S. 278). — Im französischen 19. Jahrhundert bleibt noch viel zu tun, wenn auch Hauptmeister wie Ingres mit einer, Delacroix und Degas (Abb. 14, S. 219) mit je drei Zeichnungen (darunter von Degas ein monumentales Pastell), Cézanne (Tafel 17, S. 282) mit zwei Aquarellen und van Gogh (Tafel 18, S. 284) mit fünf Arbeiten vorgestellt werden können; zuletzt wurde mit Odilon Redons »Naissance de la Pensée« der Symbolismus in einer inhaltlich wie künstlerisch faszinierenden Darstellung vergegenwärtigt (Tafel 16, S. 280).

Zwischen Erwerbungen und Stiftungen besteht ein sinnvoller Zusammenhang, eines zieht das andere an; in Stuttgart gibt es dafür glänzende Beweise. An erster Stelle ist Tut Schlemmer zu danken, bei ihr kaufte Erwin Petermann längst bevor sich die Erkenntnis von dem Range Oskar Schlemmers (1888—1943) international durchsetzte (Tafel 36, S. 336). So wurden unter vielem anderen, das unseren einzigartigen Schlemmer-Besitz ausmacht, neun der lebensgroßen Pastell-Entwürfe für die zerstörten Folkwang-Wandbilder von 1930 erworben — und 1968 zwölf weitere von Frau Schlemmer geschenkt, als sie diese auf der Bühne ihres Sehringer Hauses entdeckte.[22] Frau Siddi Heckel honorierte 1972 unsere Erwerbungen und eine Ausstellung zum 80. Geburtstag Erich Heckels (1883—1970) mit einer erstklassigen Stiftung von acht Aquarellen und Zeichnungen sowie 14 Blatt Druckgraphik (Tafel 26, S. 306) aus der frühen und späteren Zeit des Künstlers.[23] Frau Luise Seitz stiftete uns 1974 zwanzig ausgewählte Zeichnungen und ein

what we were able to make good in both areas.

Two group acquisitions provided the basis for our collection of more recent French printed graphics. In 1961 we acquired from Maurice Loncle of Paris an exquisite collection of French illustrated books of the 19th and 20th centuries. These ranged from Delacroix's illustrations for "Faust" to the splendid "painters books" of Toulouse-Lautrec, Matisse, Picasso, Braque, Léger, Chagall, Rouault — most of these in special editions with luxury bindings[21]. The same collector endowed us with 1250 of Honoré Daumier's famous lithographs. They are, for the most part, "epreuves sur blanc", i. e. prints pulled before they appeared in journals such as "La Caricature" and "Charivari". These were accompanied by 12 drawings and a gouache (pl. 15, p. 278). There is still much to be done for the French 19th department, although we are able to present definitive masters such as Ingres with one drawing, Delacroix and Degas (ill. 14, p. 219) with three drawings each (including a monumental pastel by Degas), Cézanne (pl. 17, p. 282) with two water colours and van Gogh (pl. 18, p. 285) with 5 works. The latest acquisition in this area, Odilon Redon's "Naissance de la Pensée", exemplies Symbolism in imagery fascinating both in execution and content (pl. 16, p. 280).

There is a meaningful connection between acquisitions and donations — one attracts the other. In Stuttgart this has been the case many times. First and foremost we have to thank Tut Schlemmer; Erwin Petermann purchased pieces from her long before Oskar Schlemmer's (1888—1943) works achieved international acclaim (pl. 36, p. 337). Among the host of works that make up our unique Schlemmer collection, were many, for example nine of the life-size pastel designs for the destroyed Folkwang murals of 1930, acquired this way. In 1968 Frau Schlemmer gave us twelve more pastels after discovering them in the attic of her house in Sehringen[22]. Frau Siddi Heckel acknowledged (1972) our purchases and an exhibition for Erich Heckel's 80th birthday (1883—1970) with a donation of eight first-class water colours and drawings and 14 prints (pl. 26, p. 306) from the artist's early and late periods[23]. In 1974, Frau Luise Seitz donated 20 selected drawings and a sketchbook of her husband's, the sculptor Gustav Seitz (1906—1969). In memory of the painter Adolf Fleischmann, who was born 1892 in Esslingen and returned to Stuttgart in 1964 following years of travel in France and North America (he died in 1968), his wife Elly presented us with mostly coloured works from all his various phases from 1921 on[24]. One gift came quite unexpectedly from the wife of an art historian; in her 1970 bequest, Annemarie Grohmann thanked the land of Baden-Württemberg for the purchase of the entire "Will Grohmann Archive", including the most important print editions on the 1920's — all Bauhaus portfolios and "Die Schaffenden" (The Workers). She did so by donating works by Klee, Kandinsky (pl. 18, p. 285), Miró and Kirchner; works whose importance far outweigh the purchase price of the

14
Edgar Degas (1834—1917),
Frauenakt auf dem Rand einer Wanne,
Kohlezeichnung, 1900/05.

14
Edgar Degas (1834—1917),
Female nude at the edge of a bathtub,
charcoal drawing, 1900/05.

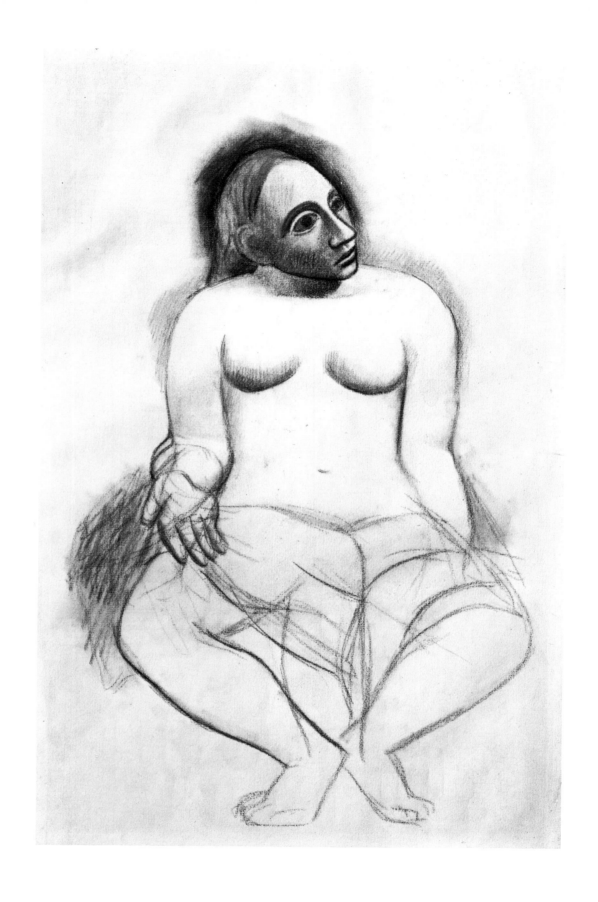

15
Pablo Picasso (1881—1973), Sitzender weiblicher
Akt, Kohlezeichnung von 1906, aus der Samm-
lung H. Lange, Krefeld 1955, mit Mitteln des
Süddeutschen Rundfunks erworben.

15
Pablo Picasso (1881—1973), Seated female nude,
charcoal drawing of 1906; acquired from the
Collection of H. Lange, Krefeld, with financial
assistance from the Süddeutscher Rundfunk, 1955.

16
Pablo Picasso (1881—1973), Kubistischer Akt
(»Nu«), Federzeichnung von 1910, ehemals
Sammlung Frigério, Paris.

16
Pablo Picasso (1881—1973), Cubist Nude (Nu),
pen drawing, 1910, formerly Collection Frigério,
Paris.

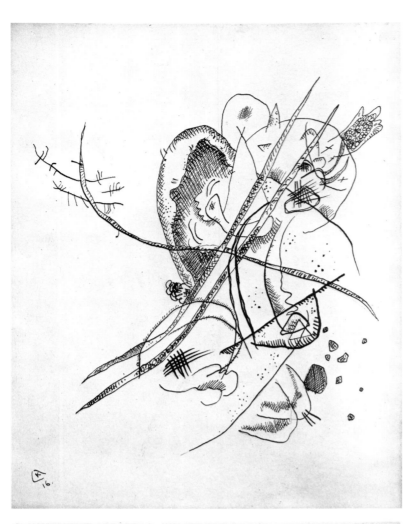

18
Wassily Kandinsky (1866—1944),
Komposition, Tuschfederzeich-
nung, entstanden 1916 während
seines Aufenthaltes in Stockholm.

18
Wassily Kandinsky (1866—1944)
Composition, pen-and-ink
drawing completed while in
Stockholm, 1916.

19
Kasimir Malewitsch
(1878—1935), Suprematistische
Zeichnung aus einem Skizzenbuch von 1915/16, Bleistift.

19
Kasimir Malevich (1878—1935)
Suprematist drawing from a
sketchbook of 1915/16, pencil.

17
Marcel Duchamp (1887—1968),
Tamis (Siebe), Zeichnung in
Blei-, Rot- und Blaustift, datiert
1914, Vorarbeit für sein Hauptwerk »Das große Glas«
(1915 ff.), auch »Junggesellenmaschine« genannt (siehe Text
bei Tafel 31 und 34).

17
Marcel Duchamp (1887—1968),
Tamis (Sieves), drawing in lead,
red and blue pencil, dated 1914.
Draft for his major work, The
Great Glass (begun 1915), also
called The Bachelor Machine
(see text at plates 31 and 34).

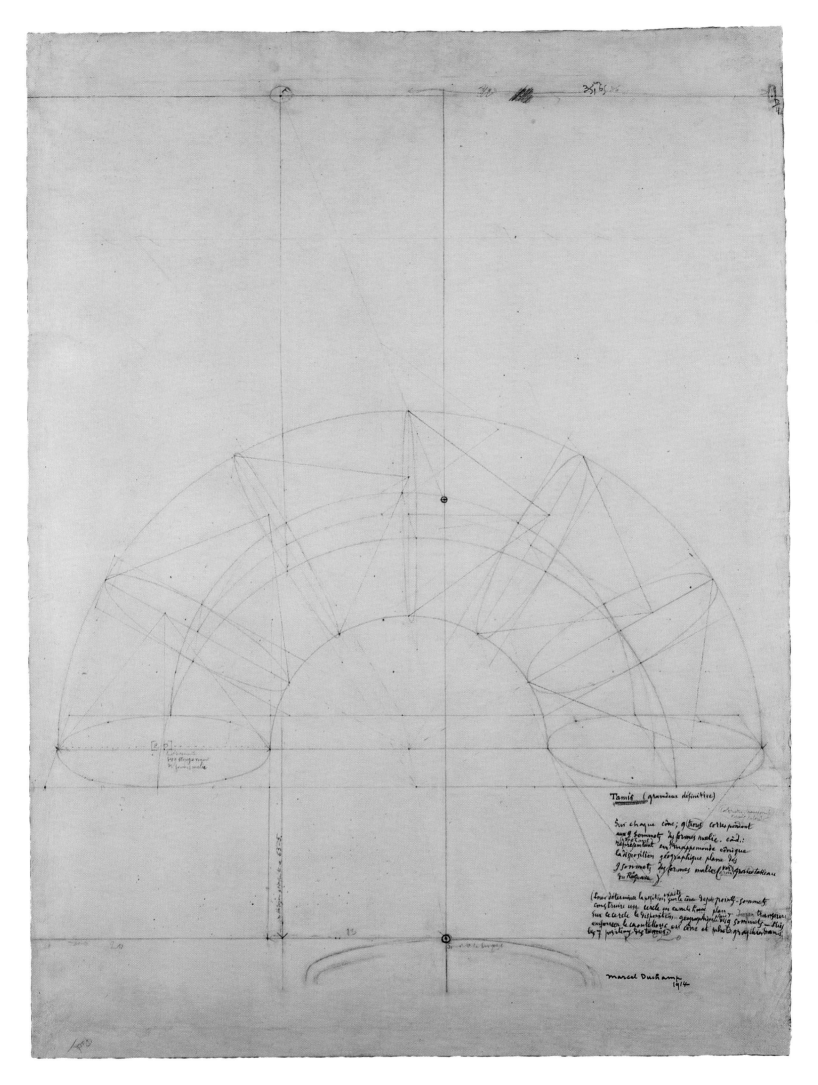

Tamis (grandeur définitive)

Marcel Duchamp
1914

Skizzenbuch ihres Mannes, des Bildhauers Gustav Seitz (1906–1969). – Im Andenken des 1892 in Esslingen geborenen und nach Wanderjahren in Frankreich und Nordamerika 1964 nach Stuttgart heimgekehrten Malers Adolf Fleischmann († 1968) schenkte uns seine Frau Elly eine Gruppe von meist farbigen Blättern aus allen Schaffensphasen seit 1921.[24] Ganz unerwartet wurden wir von der Frau eines Kunsthistorikers beschenkt, von Annemarie Grohmann; sie dankte es uns in ihrem Vermächtnis 1970, daß das Land Baden-Württemberg »Das Archiv Will Grohmann« en bloc (darunter die zwei wichtigsten Graphikeditionen der 20er Jahre: alle Bauhaus-Mappen und »Die Schaffenden«) für die Staatsgalerie erworben hatte; was sie uns an Werken von Klee, Kandinsky (Abb. 18, S. 222), Miró und Kirchner hinterließ, wiegt den Kaufpreis des Archivs auf. Zuletzt, 1981, überraschte uns die Witwe des Malers Julius Bissier (geboren 1893 in Freiburg i. B., verstorben 1965 in Ascona) mit der Stiftung von 18 seiner Tuschen und Miniaturen als Dank für eine Ausstellung in der Staatsgalerie 1963.

Fünf ungewöhnliche Stiftungen sollen noch dankbar genannt sein: Der in Stuttgart aufgewachsene Daniel Henry Kahnweiler schickte uns 1964 in zwei Rollen acht graphische Blätter des von ihm frühzeitig erkannten Genies Pablo Picasso; Marktwert heute: mindestens eine halbe Million DM (darunter die zwei Hauptwerke der Linolschnitte: das Halbfigurenbild nach Cranach und das Stilleben unter der Lampe, siehe Katalog Picasso, Stuttgart 1981, Nr. 308, 327). – Ohne je unsere Dienste in Anspruch genommen zu haben, vermachte uns der Stuttgarter Major a. D. Kurt v. Marval ca. 80 Blatt englischer und französischer Graphik des 18. und 19. Jahrhunderts, darunter kostbare Farbstiche; Herr Kurt Reichardt hinterließ uns 1982 DM 70 000,– mit der Auflage, dafür Radierungen von Seymour Haden und James Whistler zu erwerben. Der langjährige Stuttgarter Akademieprofessor Karl Rössing schenkte uns nicht nur einen Großteil seines graphischen Werkes, sondern errichtete bei Lebzeiten die »Erika-und-Karl-Rössing-Stiftung«, deren Erlös für Ankäufe von jungen Künstlern zur Verfügung steht. Der vielseitige Stuttgarter Künstler Anton Stankowski hat die im Entstehen begriffene Abteilung alter Fotografien gefördert und will das auch weiterhin mit seiner »Stiftung« tun. – Mit der Stifterfreudigkeit in der Schweiz und den USA kann sich aber das auch wohlhabende Stuttgart nicht messen; die Zuwendungen an den »Galerieverein« kommen überwiegend der Gemäldegalerie zugute. Um so mehr ist es zu danken, daß eine Stiftergruppe, die Erbengemeinschaft von Dr. A. Klein, darüber hinaus immer wieder die Graphische Sammlung bedenkt, u. a. mit einer »Anthropometrie« von Yves Klein und einer bildmäßigen Gouache von Martial Raysse sowie illustrierten Büchern von Picasso und Max Ernst. –

Über die Tätigkeit des Stuttgarter Galerievereins berichtet der Direktor der Staatsgalerie in dieser Publikation (Seite 29–38), darum seien von den Stiftungen an die Gra-

Archive. Most recently, in 1981, the widow of the painter Julius Bissier (born 1893 in Freiburg in the Black Forest, died in Ascona 1965), surprised us with a donation of 18 of his ink drawings and miniatures. This donation was an expression of gratitude for the Staatsgalerie exhibition of 1963.

We ought to gratefully mention five other exceptional donations. In 1964 Daniel Henry Kahnweiler, who grew up in Stuttgart, sent us two rolls containing eight sheets of Pablo Picasso's graphic art. Kahnweiler had recognized Picasso's genius quite early. Today, the market value of these prints is at least half a million Deutschmarks. They include two main linocuts, the half-length figure after Cranach and the still life "Unter der Lampe" (Under a lamp) (see Picasso Catalogue, Stuttgart 1981, n. 308, 327). Without ever having rendered Major Kurt von Marval (Retd) of Stuttgart any of our services, he bequeathed to us some 80 sheets of English and French graphics of the 18th and 19th centuries, among them some valuable coloured engravings; Herr Kurt Reichardt left us DM 70,000.– in 1982 with the provision to use it to purchase etchings by Seymour Haden and James Whistler. Karl Rössing, professor for many years at the Stuttgart Academy, not only donated a large part of his graphic œuvre but established the during his lifetime the "Erika and Karl Rössing Foundation". It proceeds go towards making purchases of younger artists' work. The versatile Stuttgart artist, Anton Stankowski, has supported the department of early photography now being installed and will continue to do so with his "Foundation". But even prosperous Stuttgart can not vie with the enthusiasm for donating gifts found in Switzerland and the States; monetary gifts to the Galerieverein/Galerie Association are primarily intended for the Picture Gallery. Our debt is therefore all the greater to a group of donors, the heirs of Dr. A. Klein, for remembering the Collection of Graphic Art many times with their donations of such works like Yves Klein's "Anthropometrie" and a gouache painting by Martial Raysse, as well as illustrated books by Picasso and Max Ernst.

The Director of the Staatsgalerie expounded in detail on the activities of the Stuttgart Galerieverein in this publication (p. 29–38). For this reason, it may suffice to mention only the most precious of its donations to the Department of Graphic Art. They are: Albrecht Dürer's drawing of the martyrdom of the Saint Catherine (pl. 3, p. 234), and one of the three engravings known as the Master Engravings, the "Melancholia"; 200 Chodowiecky drawings[25]; four large studies by Renoir, the water-colour "Erinnerung an Orte" (Memory of Places) (1887) by Hans Thoma, Rouault's 58 etchings of the "Miserere" (1922–1927), a large water-colour by Miró (1942) and recently, Willi Baumeister's Gilgamesh cycle (pl. 40, p. 350), the key work of his asylum period in Urach from 1943 to 1945[26].

The ground for all these donations was facilitated by state funding; thanks to the continuity of this funding it was possible to aim for and realize a concept of collecting. The

20
Max Beckmann (1884—1950),
Bildnis von Margarete Wichert, der Tochter des
Direktors der Städelschule in Frankfurt a. M.,
Bleistiftzeichnung, entstanden 1930, gewidmet
1938.

20
Max Beckmann (1884—1950), Portrait of
Margarete Wichert, the daughter of the Director
of the Städelschule in Frankfurt-on-Main;
pencil drawing, 1930, dedicated in 1938.

phische Sammlung hier nur die kostbarsten genannt: von Albrecht Dürer die Zeichnung der Marter der hl. Katharina (Tafel 3, S. 234) und einer der drei sogenannten Meisterstiche, »Die Melancholie«, von Chodowiecki 200 Zeichnungen[25], von Renoir vier große Studienblätter, von Hans Thoma das bildmäßige Aquarell »Erinnerung an Orte« (1887), von Rouault die 58 Radierungen des »Miserere« (1922—1927), von Miró ein großes Aquarell (1942) und in jüngster Zeit die seit drei Jahrzehnten von uns umworbene Gilgamesch-Folge Willi Baumeisters (Tafel 40, S. 350), das zeichnerische Hauptwerk seines Uracher Asyls von 1943 bis 1945.[26]

Den Boden für all diese Stiftungen haben die staatlichen Mittel bereitet; dank ihrer Kontinuität konnte ein Sammlungskonzept anvisiert und realisiert werden. Die Absicht, in der Kunst des 20. Jahrhunderts die führende Position auszubauen (die im Bereich der alten Kunst nicht einzuholen war), dürfte erreicht worden sein. Dazu darf bei allem Respekt vor der Leistung Erwin Petermanns gesagt werden, daß er seinen Nachfolgern auf dem Gebiet des Konstruktivimus[27] und des Surrealismus alles zu tun übrig ließ (Abb. 17, 19, 21, S. 222 und 227), ebenfalls auf dem Gebiet der amerikanischen und englischen Graphik.[28] Die »Spitzenwerke« der internationalen Graphik verdanken wir unserem relativ geringen, absolut gesehen aber doch hohen Anteil an den staatlichen »Sondermitteln«; daß wir über eine breite Basis der zeitgenössischen deutschen Graphik verfügen, ist das Verdienst unseres Kultusministeriums, des heutigen Ministeriums für Wissenschaft und Kunst, und auch des Regierungspräsidiums, deren in Deutschland außerge-

intention, that of consolidating the leading position in 20th century art, has probably been attained (our former position in the areas of older art cannot be regained). We may qualify that — with respect to Erwin Petermann's achievement — by adding, that he left much for his successors to do in the areas of Constructivism[27] and Surrealism (ill. 17, 19, 21, p. 222 and 227) not to mention American and British graphic arts[28]. We owe our "key works" of international graphic to our relatively limited, but considered on an absolute scale, large share of the State's "special funds". That we have today a broad base of contemporary German prints and drawings is the merit of our Ministry of Culture, today's Ministry of Science and Art, and also of the District President's Office, whose support for artists in Germany has been unfailing. This has also been very advantageous because the District Office donates some of its purchases which enables us to spend more of our budgetary funds on older and foreign artwork.

A collection of prints and drawings that does not exhibit foregoes its existence in the public's mind. Unlike a gallery of painting, which is always evident, a collection of prints and drawings must justify itself through exhibitions of its own stock. It is a necessity that detracts from continuous scientific work, but it contributes to the profile of the Staatsgalerie as a whole. Since 1963 catalogues of exemplary design attest to this constant exhibition effort. The exhibition programme should not be at risk now that events are taking place in the new Staatsgalerie extension; the catalogues have documented all main areas of the collection, except the numerous German 15th to 18th

wöhnliche Künstlerförderung uns durch teilweise Überlassung ihrer Ankäufe sehr zugute kommt. Dadurch können die laufenden Etatmittel für ältere und ausländische Kunst eingesetzt werden.

Eine graphische Sammlung, die nicht ausstellt, existiert nicht im Bewußtsein des Publikums; anders als die immer präsente Gemäldegalerie muß sie ihre Ansprüche durch Ausstellungen — möglichst der eigenen Bestände — legitimieren. Dieser Zwang ist einer kontinuierlichen wissenschaftlichen Tätigkeit abhold, trägt aber zum Image der Staatsgalerie als Ganzes bei. Von jener permanenten Ausstellungstätigkeit, die angesichts der geplanten Veranstaltungen im Erweiterungsbau der Staatsgalerie nicht zum Erliegen kommen sollte, zeugen die seit 1963 vorbildlich gestalteten Kataloge, sie dokumentieren die Schwerpunkte unserer Sammlung; nur ein Gebiet ist davon noch ausgenommen: die zahlreichen deutschen Zeichnungen des 15. bis 18. Jahrhunderts[29] und auch die niederländischen, darunter drei von Rembrandt (Tafel 8, S. 256), von dem wir 300 Radierungen besitzen. Weitere Schwerpunkte bilden das zeichnerische Werk von Käthe Kollwitz (Tafel 24, S. 300), auf dessen Eigenständigkeit erstmals unser Katalog zu ihrem 100. Geburtstag im Jahre 1967 hinwies[30] sowie das graphische Werk Ernst Ludwig Kirchners, das umfangreichste des Expressionismus; sich frühzeitig die Kirchner-Sammlung des Schweizer Ehepaares Dr. Gervais (Tafel 27, S. 308) gesichert zu haben, gehört zu den Geniestreichen Erwin Petermanns.[31] Damit wurde die Basis für die sogenannte »Klassische Moderne« geschaffen, auf die wir heute nur noch ab und zu Glanzlichter setzen können. Im übrigen aber muß man den Mut haben, nach vorn zu sammeln.

Angesichts der Flut von Graphik-Editionen in den 60er Jahren entschlossen wir uns, bei der zeitgenössischen Kunst die Zeichnung gegenüber der Druckgraphik zu bevorzugen.[32] Die Entwicklung hat uns darin recht gegeben: Zeichnungen werden von Künstlern aller Art als autonomes Medium eingesetzt, weltweit gesammelt und ausgestellt (gleichzeitig mit unserem Erweiterungsbau wird das Museum of Modern Art in New York den seinen eröffnen und darin einen großen Trakt allein für die ständige Präsentation von Zeichnungen).

Erstmals ist hier versucht worden, eine Geschichte der Stuttgarter Graphischen Sammlung zu schreiben; die Triebfeder dazu — außer dem festlichen Anlaß des Erweiterungsbaues — war, ihre durch den Verlust aller Archivalien bedingte scheinbare »Geschichtslosigkeit« aufzuheben; zu Unrecht ist oft der Eindruck entstanden, sie sei dank der im Jahre 1958 geschaffenen »Sondermittel« ein Parvenü; diesen verdankt sie gewiß in der Kunst des 20. Jahrhunderts viele ihrer »Spitzenwerke«, aber nicht auf dem Gebiet der alten Graphik, da hat sie eine königliche Herkunft. — Gunther Thiem

drawings[29] and the Netherlands, including three Rembrandts (pl. 8, p. 257). There are 300 of his etchings in our collection; other focal points include, the drawings of Käthe Kollwitz (pl. 24, p. 300), whose artistic originality was first pointed out in our catalogue of 1967 published for her 100th birthday[30], and Ernst Ludwig Kirchner's graphic work, the most comprehensive of the Expressionists. It was one of Petermann's strokes of genius to have made a timely bid for the collection of Kirchners formerly in the possession of Dr. and Mme Gervais in Switzerland (pl. 27, p. 308)[31]. This collection forms the basis for our so-called "Classical Moderns", to which we can only occasionally add new highlights. Apart from this, one has to have the courage to collect in a forward direction.

Considering the tide of print editions in the 1960's, we resolved to focus on contemporary drawings rather than printed graphic[32]. Developments have since then warranted that decision. Drawings are an autonomous medium for all types of artists and they are collected and exhibited the world over. Coinciding with the opening of our new building extension, New York's Museum of Art has opened its own extension and dedicated a large section of it exclusively to the permanent presentation of drawings.

This is the first attempt to write a history of the Collection of Prints and Drawings at Stuttgart. Apart from celebrating the opening of our new wing, the motivating impulse behind this venture was to correct the illusion engendered by the loss of all the archives; namely that the Collection has no history at all. This is often coupled with the unjustified assumption that the Collection is a pervenu owing its existence to the establishment of the State's "special funds" in 1958. We certainly thank this fund for many of our "star-exhibitions" of 20th century art, but not for the graphic arts of preceeding centuries — in these the Collection has a royal lineage. — Gunther Thiem

21
Joseph Beuys, (1921—1986), Kreuz, Bleistift zum Teil durchgerieben auf dünnem vergilbtem Seidenpapier, signiert und datiert 1950.

21
Joseph Beuys (1921—1986), Cross, pencil, partly in frottage technique, on thin yellowed tissue paper, signed and dated 1950.

ZEICHNUNGEN
AQUARELLE
PASTELLE UND
COLLAGEN

———

DRAWINGS
WATER COLOURS
PASTEL DRAWINGS
AND COLLAGES

Schwäbischer Meister

1

Der Jesse-Baum

*Entstanden Ende des 15. Jahrhunderts
Federzeichnung in Bister, allseits
beschnitten,
28 × 32,3 cm
Beschriftet unten:
Nr. 3 – Martin Schön,
Maistre d'albert Durer.
Inv. Nr. 5*

Swabian Master

1

The Tree of Jesse

*End of the 15th century
Pen drawing in bistre, cut on all sides,
28 × 32.3 cm.
Inscription below:
Nr. 3 – Martin Schön,
Maistre d'albert Durer.
Inv. No. 5*

Wem die christliche Ikonographie nicht vertraut ist, dem wird diese »serielle« Komposition gestikulierender männlicher Halbfiguren in den Ranken eines Stammes seltsam vorkommen; zugrunde liegt die herkömmliche Form eines Stammbaums, der hier die Genealogie Christi verbildlicht; nach den Geschlechtsregistern der Evangelisten Matthäus und Lukas geht sie auf (den am Boden lagernden) Jesse zurück, dem die Könige von Juda und die Propheten im Traum erscheinen; daher die Bezeichnung Jesse-Baum oder auch Wurzel Jesse. Seit dem 11. Jahrhundert werden die Vorfahren Christi in Handschriften, Glas-, Decken- und Wandgemälden und Altären so dargestellt. Damit wird die königliche Herkunft der Muttergottes und ihres Sohnes nachgewiesen, die man sich auf unserer Zeichnung als Bekrönung in der Mitte des oben abgeschnittenen Blattes vorzustellen hat (nur der gezackte Rand der sie tragenden Blüte ist noch zu sehen).

Auf der vorliegenden Zeichnung – vermutlich ein Gemäldeentwurf – sind die für die Namen der Vorfahren Christi vorgesehenen Schriftbänder leer geblieben, daher lassen sich die Halbfiguren nicht ohne weiteres personifizieren; aber die wichtigste ist an ihrem Attribut, der Harfe, sofort zu erkennen: links oberhalb von Jesse der jugendliche David, König von Israel, der mit seinem Saitenspiel die Schwermut Sauls besänftigte.

27 Halbfiguren in fünf Reihen über- und nebeneinander darzustellen, das ist eine Aufgabe, bei der Monotonie unausbleiblich scheint. Aber hier erfreuen den Betrachter lebhafte Bewegungsmotive, deklamatorische Gesten und bizarre Einfälle der Hüte, Kronen und geflochtenen Bärte, vor allem aber besticht die hohe Qualität, die Prägnanz der wie ziselierten Strichführung. Dennoch sind Herkunft und Meister unserer Zeichnung nicht genau auszumachen. Der Vorbesitzer dachte an den oberrheinischen Maler und Stecher Martin Schongauer († 1491), dessen Namen er in französischer Schreibweise auf das Blatt setzte. Damit ist der deutsche Südwesten als Kunstlandschaft und die Zeitlage richtig angesprochen, wie ein um 1490 entstandener Kupferstich mit dem Jesse-Baum von Israhel van Meckenem, einem zeitweiligen Mitarbeiter des am Bodensee tätigen Meisters E. S., im Vergleich mit unserer Zeichnung belegt (siehe Abb. unten); diese unter-

To those unfamiliar with Christian iconography, this "serial" composition of gesticulating male half-length figures among the branches curling from a tree-trunk, will appear strange. The customary principle is that of a family tree, used here to visualise the genealogy of Christ. According to the Evangelists Matthew and Luke, Christ's ancestry can be traced back to Jesse (shown here lying on the ground). The kings of Juda and the prophets appear to him in a dream. Thus the term "tree of Jesse" or "root of Jesse". Since the 11th century Christ's ancestors have been depicted in this manner in manuscripts, painting on glass, walls and ceilings, as well as on altars. This is the substantiation for the royal lineage of the Virgin and her Son, both of whom are to be imagined in our drawing as the crowning element, top centre (the cut edge shows only the toothed lower petals of the blossom that would have carried them). In these drawings – presumable the design for a painting – the banderoles intended for the names of Christ's ancestors have been left blank, so we cannot readily identify the figures individually. However, the most important figure is immediately recognizable by his attribute, the harp. This figure on the left above Jesse is the youthful David, King of Isreal, whose playing soothed Saul's melancholy.

To depict five rows of 27 half-length figures next to and above each others, is a task in which monotony seems inevitable. Here, however, the beholder is entertained with lively cameos of motion, declamatory gestures and fanciful elaboration of the hats, crowns and plaited beards. Particularly enchanting is the high quality of the line, terse as if incised. Yet, the provenance and artist of our drawing cannot be determined with any precision. The previous owner thought it might have been the Upper-Rhenish painter and engraver, Martin Schongauer, whose name he wrote in French script on the sheet. This is a correct interpretation of the artistic milieu as southwestern Germany, as well as the timeperiod. A comparison with a Tree of Jesse copper engraving of about 1490 by Israhel van Meckenem, who worked with the E. S. Master at Lake Constance, illustrates this convincingly (see ill. below). The drawing differs from the ornamental engraving in its more impulsive poses and gestures, a quite Swabian joy in narrative which will does not refrain from

scheidet sich von dem ornamentalen Stich durch die impulsivere Mimik und Gestik, durch eine das Groteske nicht meidende Erzählfreude, die im Schwäbischen zu Hause ist. Mangels, der in so früher Zeit eminent raren deutschen Zeichnungen sei auf die acht artverwandten Brustbilder von Propheten unseres Pfullendorfer Marienaltars hingewiesen, der einem »selbständigen Mitarbeiter Zeitbloms in Ulm, um 1500« zugeschrieben wird (Katalog von 1957, S. 198, Abb. 9).

depicting the grotesque. For lack of German drawings (exceedingly rare from this very early period) compare eight related half-length prophet figures in our Pfullendorf Lady Altar. This is attributed to an "independent collaborator of Zeitblom's in Ulm, about 1500" (cat. 1957, p. 198, ill. 9).

Lucas Cranach

Geboren 1472 in Kronach (Oberfranken), gestorben 1553 in Weimar, 1501–1504 in Wien, seit 1505 als Hofmaler des sächsischen Kurfürsten Johann Friedrich u. a. in Wittenberg, Torgau und auf der Veste Coburg tätig; 1550–1552 in Augsburg bei seinem dort von Kaiser Karl V. nach der Schlacht bei Mühlberg gefangen gehaltenen Landesherrn.

2

Schreitendes Paar

Entstanden zwischen 1505 und 1509
Feder in Braun, grau laviert,
18,5 × 13,2 cm
Links unten die spätere Bezeichnung
»L Cranach«.
Aus dem ältesten Bestand der Sammlung,
da bereits in dem 1810 verfaßten, 1943
vernichteten »Catalogue des dessins de S. M.
le Roi« erwähnt (laut Rosenberg).
Inv. Nr. 4

Lucas Cranach

Born in Kronach (Upper Franconia) in 1472, died in Weimar in 1553. In Vienna, 1501–04; court painter to Johann Friedrich, Elector of Saxony, and others in Wittenberg, Torgau and the Residence at Veste Coburg. In Augsburg, 1550–52 worked for his ruler, who was being held captive by the Emperor Charles V after the Battle of Mühlberg.

2

Walking Couple

Between 1505 and 1509
Pen and brown ink, grey wash
18.5 × 13.2 cm
Below left later inscription "L. Cranach".
From the Collection's oldest stock as listed
according to Rosenberg, in the "Catalogue
des dessins de S. M le Roi of 1810
(destroyed 1943).
Inv. No. 4

So kräftig schreitet der von seinem Fräulein beglückte Ritter aus, daß ihm sein Federbarett vom Kopf in den Nacken gerutscht ist, während das ihre die hohe Stirn rahmt; als Gegengewicht zum heftig vorgestreckten Bein wirft der Mann frohgemut den Arm hoch, dabei schlägt sein Schwert fast waagerecht aus. Das will mehr besagen als »Vornehmer Mann mit Dame spazierend«, wie es jüngst im Basler Katalog heißt, das ist Ausdruck eines neuen, selbstherrlichen Lebensgefühls, wie es so unmittelbar unter all den großen Künstlern seiner Epoche wohl nur der Realismus Cranachs zu fassen vermag, besonders in seiner Frühzeit, als er in Österreich zum Begründer des expressiven »Donaustils« wurde.
Die Leibhaftigkeit der Bewegung, die mehr von dem Ritter als von dem artigen Fräulein ausgeht, läßt an Tänzer denken, vor allem an einen Holzschnitt mit vier Paaren vom jungen Dürer in der 1493 erschienenen Schedelschen Weltchronik (siehe Hollstein VII, S. 243; Hinweis von Dieter Koepplin) oder an den großen Stich eines Balles am Münchner Hof vom Meister M Z aus dem Jahre 1500 (siehe Katalog: Meisterwerke alter Druckgraphik aus der Staatsgalerie Stuttgart 1982, Nr. und Abb. 21). Cranach, der Martin Luther nahestand, hat dem Stuttgarter Paar etwas von der reformatorischen Lebensbejahung seiner Zeit verliehen: statt »Herbst des Mittelalters« (wie Johan Huizinga 1919 seine kulturgeschichtliche Abhandlung nannte) »Aufgang der Neuzeit« (wie eine erhellende Nürnberger Ausstellung von 1952 hieß).
Cranachs Wirkung ist von seinen Gemälden ausgegangen, weniger von seiner Graphik und seinen Zeichnungen, deren es kaum einhundert gibt. — Im 2. Band seines Basler Kataloges hat Dieter Koepplin herausgearbeitet, warum Cranach bei Künstlern des 20. Jahrhunderts, wie Ernst Ludwig Kirchner und Picasso, mehr Faszination als Albrecht Dürer ausgelöst hat: Es ist die frappante, mit einem Schuß Naivität verbundene Präsenz, die auch unser schreitendes Paar auszeichnet.

The knight favoured by his damsel struts out with such vigour that his feathered hat slids from his head to the nape of his neck while the lady's hat still frames her high forehead. Counterbalancing his left leg's forward thrust, the man throws his arm joyfully and his sword swings out almost horizontally. This says more than just a "Gentleman Walking with Lady", the caption in the recent Basel catalogue titling the drawing; it is the expression of a new, autocratic outlook on life as only the realism of a Cranach, of all the great artists of his era, was able to grasp. This is decidedly true of his early period when he founded the expressive "Danuabe Style" in Austria.
The vitality emanating more from knight's movements than from the demure young lady is reminiscent of dancers and reminds us in particular of a woodcut by the young Dürer in Schedels' Weltchronik (1493) (cf. Hollstein VII, p. 243; information from Dieter Koepplin). Or on the large engraving dated 1500 of a Munich court ball by the M Z Master (cf. catalogue "Meisterwerke alter Druckgraphik aus der Staatsgalerie Stuttgart", 1982, No. & ill. 21). Cranach, who was a friend of Luther's, has invested the Stuttgart couple with something of the contemporary Reformational affirmation of life. Not so much the "Autumn of the Middle Ages" (as Johan Huizinga titled his treatise on cultural history in 1919), but the "dawn of the modern era" (the title of an illuminating exhibition in Nuremberg of 1952).
Cranach's influence derives from his paintings. His prints and drawings (number less than 100) are less influential. In the second volume of his catalogue for Basel, Dieter Koepplin has elaborated on reasons why artists of the 20th century, such as E. L. Kirchner or Picasso, have been far more fascinated by Cranach than by Dürer: it is the striking presence, combined with a touch of naivity, that also distinguishes our couple out walking.

Literatur: Jakob Rosenberg, Die Zeichnungen Lucas Cranach d. Ä., Berlin 1960, Nr. 19, Tafel 19. — Dieter Koepplin, Tilman Falk, Katalog der Cranach-Ausstellung, Basel 1974, Bd. I, Nr. 22.

Bibliography: Jakob Rosenberg, Die Zeichnungen Lucas Cranach d. Ä. (Berlin, 1960) No. 19, pl. 19; Dieter Koepplin, Tilman Falk, Cat. for Cranach exh. (Basel, 1974), vol. I, No. 22.

Albrecht Dürer

Geboren 1471 in Nürnberg, gestorben daselbst 1528. Sohn eines Goldschmiedes. Lehrzeit als Malerknabe bei Michael Wohlgemut 1486–1490, dann Wanderschaft an den Oberrhein, nach Colmar und Basel. 1495 die erste Italienreise, Herbst 1505 bis Anfang 1507 die zweite mit Aufenthalt in Venedig, 1520/21 in den Niederlanden.

3

Die Marter der heiligen Katharina

Entstanden 1510
Federzeichnung in Braun (Bister), auf Büttenpapier aufgezogen, das rechte Viertel des Blattes durch Restaurierung gemindert, 22,5 × 33,3 cm
Entwurf eines nicht ausgeführten oder nicht erhaltenen Wandgemäldes, wie aus dem als Halbkreis links skizzierten Rundfenster und der bildmäßigen Komposition zu schließen ist.
In der Mitte unten die echte Signatur mit dem Monogramm AD und darüber die Jahreszahl 1510.
Erworben im November 1953 vom Stuttgarter Galerieverein aus der Fürstlich Liechtensteinschen Kunstsammlung in Vaduz auf der 18. Auktion von R. N. Ketterer, Stuttgart.
Inv. Nr. GVL 31

Albrecht Dürer

Born 1471 in Nuremberg. Died there in 1528. The son of a goldsmith, he was apprenticed to Michael Wohlgemut as "painter's lad" from 1486–90; as a journeyman he travelled to the Upper Rhine, Colmar and Basel. First journey to Italy in 1495; the second from autumn 1505 to early 1507 in Venice. Travel to the Netherlands, 1520–21.

3

The Martyrdom of St. Catherine

Dated 1510
Pen drawing in brown (bistre) mounted on handmade paper; the right-hand quarter of the sheet has been badly restored.
22.5 × 33.3 cm
Design for a mural not executed or preserved. Discernable from the semicircle sketched in for a roundel on the left and from the pictorial finish of the composition. At the centre, below, the genuine signature with the monogram AD, surmounted by the date 1510.
Acquired November 1953, from the Stuttgart Galerieverein, out of the Collection of the Prince of Liechtenstein at Vaduz, at the 18th auction at R. N. Ketterer, Stuttgart.
Inv. No. GVL 31

Nach der Präsenz von Cranachs schreitendem Paar muß der Betrachter hier bei Dürers zarter Zeichnung innehalten; sie gibt keine Momentaufnahme, sondern die Schilderung eines Ereignisses: eine Heiligenlegende mit einem Wunder. Beide Zeichnungen sind annähernd gleichzeitig von fast gleichaltrigen Künstlern entstanden, dabei grundverschieden; das liegt weniger im Motiv, hier religiös, dort weltlich, und im Zweck, hier Auftrag, dort Ungebundenheit, als vielmehr in der total anderen Mentalität Dürers und Cranachs und ihrer Entwicklung. — Cranach hat seinen ganz persönlichen Stil früh gefunden und ihn bis ins hohe Alter mit zunehmender Perfektion fortgeführt. Dürer hat sich, wie alle Genies, gewandelt. Mehr als Worte beweist das die Gegenüberstellung unserer Zeichnung von 1510 mit dem Holzschnitt desselben Themas aus Dürers Sturm- und Drangzeit (siehe Abbildung), als er die expressive »Apokalypse« schuf, 1498; dazwischen liegt die zweite lange Italienreise mit seiner Hinwendung zur klassischen Form. — Dieser adäquat ist die Beschreibung Meders, der das Blatt um die letzte Jahrhundertwende entdeckt und publiziert hat:
»Die Darstellung selbst ist, so flüchtig sie auch hingeschrieben erscheint, voll inneren Lebens, trefflicher, reicher Erzählung und ausgezeichneter Gruppierung. Das Naturwunder, die Zertrümmerung und Verzehrung des Folterrades durch ein himmlisches Feuer, ist hier nicht in untergeordneter Weise dargestellt, sondern beherrscht die Hälfte der Fläche, so daß der Flammenschein sich fast über den ganzen Himmel verbreitet. Man merkt in allem und jedem das decorative Element, welches die Composition durchbricht. Den Mittelpunkt der Zeichnung bildet die Heilige selbst, die als Profilfigur mit gefalteten Händen, ähnlich wie auf dem Flügel des Heller-Altares, nach links kniet, um mit dem Ausdruck frommer Ergebung den Todesstreich zu erwarten, zu welchem sich ein rechts hinter ihr stehender langbeiniger Geselle eben anschickt. Während er das Schwert aus der Scheide ziehen will, hält er einen Moment still und beobachtet mit zusammengekniffenen Augen die aufflammenden Trümmer des Rades und den wie aus geöffnetem Himmel niederprasselnden Feuerregen.
Die Wirkung dieses Wunders wird durch die fünf im Vordergrunde und zwei im Mittelgrund vor Schreck zusammengestürzten Marterknechte charakterisiert. Hinter dem Henker bäumt sich das Pferd des Königs hoch auf, so daß dieser ängstlich nach seiner Krone faßt, und ein Hündchen in der rechten Ecke ergreift eilends die Flucht. Das nach beiden Seiten aufsteigende, zum Teile bewachsene Terrain der Landschaft gestattet nur einen schmalen Ausblick in die Ferne, in welcher eine kleine Bergstadt mit einem davor liegenden Hafen sichtbar wird. . .«
Das Neue in Dürers Kompositionen seit seiner zweiten Italienreise ist eine Überschaubarkeit, bei der das Einzelne zugunsten des Ganzen zurücktritt. Diese folgenreiche »Wandlung um 1510« steht im Zentrum einer von Theodor Hetzer 1939 veröffentlichten Betrachtung mit dem Titel »Dürers

After the assertiveness of Cranach's walking couple, Dürer's sensitive drawing must make the beholder pause. This is not a record of the moment but the depiction of an event; the legend of a saint and a miracle. The two drawings have been done by artists of almost the same age, at roughly the same time — but they are entirely different. This difference has little to do with the motives — the one religious, the other secular, or with that of intent — the one is a commission, the other independent. Decisive is the utterly different mentality and development of the artists. Cranach found his markedly personal style early on and continued it with increasing perfection into his old age. Dürer, like all geniuses, changed. The juxtaposition of our drawing of 1510 with the woodcut on the same subject from the "Sturm und Drang" period in 1498 (see plate opposite) when he created his expressive Apocalypse, will prove the point better than words. Between these two works lay the second, long sojourn in Italy, with its attention to classical form. This is given rightful acknowledgement in Meder's description. Joseph Meder discovered and first published the drawing at the turn of the century:
"As hastily noted as it may appear, the representation itself is full of inner life, choice narrative and excellent grouping. The prodigy of the instrument of torture, the wheel, being shattered and consumed by a heavenly fire, is represented here in no subordinate manner; rather it dominates half the picture surface, so that the glow from the flames spreads over almost the whole sky. In all and in every detail, one notes the decorative element that penetrates the composition. The focus of the drawing consists of the Saint herself, a kneeling figure in profile, facing to the left, hands folded, like on the wing of the Heller Altar, awaiting with an expression of pious submission the death blow which a long-legged fellow standing behind her to the right is just preparing to deliver. Intending to draw the sword from its sheath, he pauses for a moment and, squinting, observes the flames bursting from the shattered wheel and the rain of fire bursting from the shattered wheel and the rain of fire hailing down as if from a sky rent open."
The effect of this miracle is characterised by the tormentors, five in the foreground and two in the middle, all struck down with fear. Behind the executioner, the king's horse rears up and the king fearfully seizes his crown and a little dog in the right-hand corner hastily takes flight. The landscape, a terrain rising steeply on both sides and partially overgrown with vegetation, allows only glimpse into the distance where a little mountain town with a harbour can be seen . . .
The innovation in Dürer's compositions after his second journey to Italy is seen in the clarity of composition; details recede in favour of the whole. This "change of c. 1510" was to have lasting consequences and is the central issue in an essay published by Theodor Hetzer in 1939, with the title, "Dürers Bildhoheit" ("The Majesty of Dürer's Pictures"). It is a study still worth

Dürer, »Die Marter der heiligen Katharina«,
Holzschnitt 1498.

Dürer, The Martyrdom of St. Catherine,
woodcut, 1498.

Bildhoheit«; lesenswert noch immer und erstaunlich, wenn man bedenkt, wie andere damals, als das »Nordische« gepriesen wurde, Dürers Rezeption der italienischen Kunst abqualifizierten.

reading and astonishing considering how others at that time, when "the Nordic" was put on a pedestal, were busy playing down Dürer's enthusiasm for Italian art.

Literatur: Joseph Meder, Eine neue Dürer-Zeichnung, in: Wiener Jahrbuch, Bd. 23, 1902, S. 68/69, Tafel VI. – Friedrich Winkler, Die Zeichnungen Albrecht Dürers, Band II, Berlin 1937, Nr. und Abb. 469. – Erwin Panofsky, Albrecht Dürer, Princeton 1948, Vol. II, Nr. 857.

Bibliography: Joseph Meder, "Eine neue Dürer-Zeichnung", Wiener Jahrbuch, Vol. 23 (1902), pp. 68–69, ill. VI; Friedrich Winkler, Die Zeichnungen Albrecht Dürers, Vol. II (Berlin, 1937), ill. 469; Erwin Panofsky, Albrecht Dürer, Vol. II (Princeton, 1948), No. 857.

3
Dürer, »Die Marter der heiligen Katharina«,
Zeichnung 1510.
3
Dürer, The Martyrdom of St. Catherine,
drawing, 1510.

Johann Heinrich Schönfeld

Geboren 1609 in Biberach a. d. Riß, gestorben 1684 in Augsburg. Entstammt einer Goldschmiede-Familie, lernte als Maler in Memmingen (1626) und Stuttgart (1627 bis 1629), 1633–1651 in Rom und 12 Jahre in Neapel, seit 1651 in Augsburg ansässig; viel für den habsburgischen Adel und den österreichischen Klerus tätig.

4

Saul spricht mit Samuels Geist bei der Hexe von Endor

Entstanden um 1670
Federzeichnung in Blaugrau, laviert, einen angefangenen Stich vollendend; gestochen sind der rechte Rand des Blattes, der kniende Saul und sein Schatten, in der linken unteren Ecke die Unterseite der Grabplatte, die Stirnseite der Gruft und das Gewand des daraus steigenden Samuel, 42,7 × 31,5 cm
Unbezeichnet, aufgezogen.
Links unten alte Nr. 12.
Gehört mit 21 weiteren Zeichnungen des Künstlers zum alten Bestand der Sammlung; vermutlich aus dem Nachlaß seines Schülers Gabriel Ehinger (1652–1736).
Inv. Nr. 517

Surreales gibt es nicht erst in der modernen Kunst, sondern schon seit Baldung Griens und Jacques de Gheyns Hexenszenen (s. Tafel 7, S. 252). Hier erscheint die Hexe als Wahrsagerin in einer nächtlichen Geisterbeschwörung, die auch ohne Kenntnis ihres Inhaltes fasziniert — und doch sollte man ihn in der Sprache der Bibel nachlesen, dann steigert sich die Sprache des Bildes. Im 28. Kapitel des 2. Buches Samuelis steht, wie der vor den Heeren der Philister verzagende König von Israel, Saul, eine Zauberin, die er des Landes verwiesen hatte, heimlich aufsucht, damit sie den Geist des verstorbenen Richters Samuel beschwöre, um von ihm Sieg oder Niederlage zu erfahren. — Halbnackt zieht die Hexe, während sie mit einer Hand die schattenwerfende Fackel hält, mit der Rute in der anderen Hand den magischen Doppelkreis, der mit einem Schädel als Zeichen der Vergänglichkeit und symbolträchtigem Getier wie Schlange, Kröte und Eule besetzt ist (die letztere verkündet nicht nur Klugheit, sondern lichtscheu auch Unheil). Die gegen den spukhaften Himmel offene Gruft umschließt eine von Sarkophagen bekrönte Mauer, ihnen entsteigen Gerippe, während Sauls Begleiter im Hintergrund gebannt der Dinge harren.

Auf den geistreichen Neapolitaner Salvator Rosa, einen Zeitgenossen Schönfelds, den er in Neapel so gut wie in Rom getroffen haben kann, hat die Forschung als seinen wichtigsten Anreger hingewiesen und speziell auf ein Gemälde des gleichen Themas von 1668 (jetzt im Louvre), das aber ganz anders komponiert ist. In dieser Zeichnung ist aber etwas unverwechselbar Neues entstanden, das das Spirituelle von Schönfelds besten Schöpfungen aufweist. Der eigentümlich verfeinerte Figurenstil hat weder in der deutschen noch in der italienischen Barockkunst seinesgleichen; er ist eine ganz persönliche Manier des Künstlers, der Linkshänder gewesen sein soll und auf einem Auge erblindet war. Schon 1927 hat der bahnbrechende Barock-Forscher Hermann Voss ihn als »den nächst Elsheimer und Liss feinsinnigsten Malerpoeten, dessen sich die deutsche Kunst des 17. Jahrhunderts rühmen darf« hervorgehoben (in: »Das Schwäbische Museum«, 1927, S. 57 ff.). Interessant ist die zweifache Technik unseres Blattes: Zuerst Kupferstich, dann Zeichnung; der Stich zeigt aber nicht Schönfelds zierlichen Stil, sondern einen handwerklichen. Wie die heutigen Künstler ihre Werke fotografieren lassen, so ließen die früheren die ihren stechen. Für Schönfeld tat das sein Schüler Ehinger. Der hier vorliegende Probeabzug einer unvollendeten Platte bezeugt, daß er begonnen hatte, das (inzwischen verschollene) Gemälde Schönfelds zu kopieren, aber wohl nicht zur Zufriedenheit des Meisters, so daß dieser korrigierend und vollendend mit Feder und Pinsel eingriff. Darauf nahm Ehinger eine neue Platte und radierte eine unserer Zeichnung entsprechende Darstellung, die er bezeichnete: J H Schönfeld Inventor / Gabriel Ehinger sculpsit (Kat. Ulm 1967, Abb. 241).

Johann Heinrich Schönfeld

Born in Biberach a. d. Riss in 1609, died in
Augsburg in 1684. From a family of gold-
smiths, apprenticed as a painter in Memmingen (1626) and Stuttgart (1627–29);
from (1633–51) in Rome and 12 years in
Naples. Resident of Augsburg from 1651. A
great deal of work for the Habsburg nobility
and the Austrian clergy.

4

Saul speaks with Samuel's Ghost at the Witch of Endor's

About 1670
Drawing in grey-blue ink and wash,
complete a begun engraving; the right-
hand edge of the picture, Saul (kneeling)
and his shadow, the underside of the
tombstone in the bottom left-hand corner,
the facing side of the tomb and Samuel's
garments (he is rising from the grave) are
engraved. 42.7 × 31.5 cm
Below left former designation No. 12
Unsigned, mounted.
One of 22 drawings by Schönfeld wich
belong to the Collection's old stock,
presumably from the estate of the artist's
pupil, Gabriel Ehinger (1652–1735).
Inv. No. 517

Surrealistic motives are not alone the prerogative of modern art; they are as old as
the witches' scenes in Baldung Grien and
Jacques de Gheyn works (cf. pl. 7, p. 252).
Here the witch appears as a soothsayer in a
nocturnal evocation of spirits. Even without
knowledge of the narrative content, the
scene is fascinating; though to read it in the
language of the Bible, is to appreciate the
language in the picture even more intensely. In I Samuel 28 we read how Saul, the
king of Isreal, despairs after seeing the size
of the Philistine armies against him. He has
banished all witches but now visits one in
secret, asking her to call up the spirit of the
judge Samuel, to hear from him the victory
or defeat to come. The half-naked soothsayer holds in one hand a torch that casts
deep shadows and in the other the rod,
with which she draws the magic double
circle full of portent symbols; the skull as
sign of mortality, a serpant, a toad and an
owl, which, in avoiding the light, embodies
not only wisdom but also disaster. The vault
opens to an eerie sky, surrounded by a wall
crowned with sarcophagi, from which skel-
etons rise. Saul's servants look on spellbound from the background.

Research has shown that Schönfeld's contemporary, the brilliant Neapolitan, Salvator Rosa, to be his most important inspiration. This inspiration is evident in a painting (1668) of the same subject (now in the
Louvre), although it is composed quite dif-
ferently. The two artists may very well have
met, either in Rome or Naples; but this
drawing evinces that something undeniably
new has come about, and it has the spiritual
quality of Schönfeld's best works. The cu-
riously refined figure style has no parallels
in either German or Italian Baroque art. It
is altogether a very personal style of the artist who is said to have been left-handed and
blind in one eye. Schönfeld was praised by
the pioneering scholar of the Baroque, Herman Voss, as long ago as 1927. He was considered "next to Elsheimer and Liss to be
the most subtle painter-poet that German
art of the 17th century can extol as its own"
(in: "Das Schwäbische Museum, 1927",
p. 57 ff.).

An interesting feature of this work is the
use of two different techniques. First copper
engraving, then drawing. The engraving
does not show Schönfeld's delicate approach, but rather that of the craftsman. At
that time artists had their works engraved,
today artists have their works photogra-
phed. In Schönfeld's case this was done by
his pupil Ehinger. Here we are looking at a
trial print from an unfinished plate. This
shows that he probably began to copy
Schönfeld's (since lost) painting but not to
the master's satisfaction; Schönfeld then
corrected and completed the picture with
pen and brush. Ehinger took a fresh plate to
engrave the scene as designed on our sheet.
He inscribed his copy: "J H Schönfeld In-
ventor/Gabriel Ehinger sculpsit" (cat., Ulm,
1967, ill. 241).

Literatur: Katalog der Ausstellung »Der barocke Himmel«, Staatsgalerie Stuttgart 1964, Nr. 9. – Herbert Pée, Katalog der Ausstellung, Johann Heinrich Schönfeld, Museum Ulm 1967, Nr. 168, Abb. 163. – Bruno Bushart, J. H. Schönfeld, Studien zur Biographie, in: Jahrbuch der Staatlichen Kunstsammlungen in Baden-Württemberg, 6. Band, 1969, S. 127 ff. – Rolf Biedermann, Die Zeichnungen des J. H. Schönfeld, ebenda, 8. Band, 1971, S. 164 ff., Abb. 48.

Bibliography: Cat. Der barocke Himmel, Staatsgalerie Stuttgart (1964), No. 9; Herbert Pee, cat. Johann Heinrich Schönfeld, Museum Ulm (1967), No. 168, ill. 163; Bruno Bushart, "J. H. S., Studien zur Biographie" in Jahrbuch der Staatlichen Kunstsammlungen in Baden-Württemberg VI (1969), 127 ff.; Rolf Biedermann, "Die Zeichnungen des J. H. S.", ibid., VIII (1971), 164 ff., ill. 48.

12.

Joseph Anton Feuchtmayr

Geboren 1696 in Linz (Oberösterreich), gestorben 1770 in Mimmenhausen bei Salem am Bodensee. Entstammt einer Wessobrunner Bildhauer- und Stukkatorenfamilie, lernte bei seinem Vater Franz Joseph Feuchtmayr und dem aus Como gebürtigen Diego Francesco Carlone; ab 1718 in Mimmenhausen eine umfangreiche Werkstatt begründend, schuf er im Bodenseegebiet Altarwerke (nicht zu verwechseln mit dem vorwiegend in Bayern tätigen Johann Michael Feichtmayr, 1709–1772).

5

Entwurf für den Hochaltar der Wallfahrtskirche Birnau

Entstanden 1748
Federzeichnung in Braun, grau laviert auf zwei Boden handgeschöpften Büttens, 84,5 × 44 cm
Rechts unten eigenhändig bezeichnet: Inv: von Jo: Faichtm. 1748; ferner am linken Rand Maßangaben: 1-2-3-4-5 Schuh – 25 gallery Höhe – 40 sch; unter dem Rahmenprofil Mitte rechts steht: »Rahm des / altar blatts fuer / dem Beylaster [Pilaster] / welches man im Riss nit / kan sehen. wohl aber / im werkh wen man auf der / Seiten steth.«; an dem Treppenprofil darüber: »gallery Höhe So durch die Kirchen geth – Stieg – ober der Rahm die gallery«; darüber beim Schnitt durch Altarkuppel und bekrönenden Obelisken: »profil oben der Cupl. – Spiegl – Spiegl.« –
Gehört zu einer Gruppe von neun zum Teil farbig ausgeführten Altarentwürfen Feuchtmayrs und seines engsten Mitarbeiters Johann Georg Dirr: alle 1931 inventarisiert.
Inv. Nr. C 31/6

Die ebenso beherrschend wie anmutig in Rebgärten über dem Bodensee liegende Birnau ist ein Kleinod des deutschen Rokoko; als schwäbische Schöpfung ebenbürtig den bayerischen. – Joseph Anton Feuchtmayr vollendete auf der Höhe seines Schaffens und seiner Epoche, ehe Klassizismus und Aufklärung rauschende Farben und verzückte Gebärden verachteten, die Ausstattung der Salemer Priorats- und Wallfahrtskirche Birnau – ein vollkommenes Gesamtkunstwerk, erbaut von Peter Thumb aus Bregenz, ausgemalt von Gottfried Bernhard Götz aus Augsburg.
Feuchtmayrs großformatiger Entwurf vereinigt simultan den architektonischen Aufbau, den plastischen Schmuck und das dekorative Beiwerk eines prunkvollen Altars mit den nötigen Angaben über die räumliche Anordnung in einem Kirchenchor; dazu genügte dem Auftraggeber und dem ausführenden Handwerker, daß jeweils nur eine Hälfte vom Ganzen fixiert ist. Die Zeichnung hatte also über ihren ästhetischen Reiz hinaus – der auch im scheinbar Unvollendeten liegt – eine praktische Funktion; sie unterscheidet sich von den farbigen Werkzeichnungen des Feuchtmayr-Schülers F. A. Dirr durch ihre graphische Qualität. Ein konsequentes System von Schraffuren in wechselnden Richtungen, das sich zuweilen punktförmig auflöst, bewirkt eine Vibration des Ganzen, die den malerischen Gesamteindruck des bewegten Formzusammenhangs anzudeuten vermag, während die zurückhaltende Lavierung für den plastischen Gehalt und die räumliche Tiefe sorgt.
Der Besucher Birnaus trifft heute den Hochaltar nicht mehr so an, wie er auf unserem Riß entworfen wurde: klassizistischer Gesinnung entsprechend wurde der Altar mit dem spätgotischen Gnadenbild, thronartig, horizontal gegliedert – gottlob ließ man Säulen und Baldachin-Kuppel stehen, aber das Altarbild, ein Gemälde J. C. Storers mit der Himmelfahrt Mariä, ersetzte man 1790 durch ein Engelsreigen-Relief und beraubte damit Feuchtmayrs brillante Figuren ihres farbigen Kontrastes.

Joseph Anton Feuchtmayr

Born in 1696 in Linz (Upper Austria). Died in 1770 in Mimmenhausen near Salem (Lake Constance). Came from a family of sculptors and stucco workers at Wessobrunn. Learned the trade from his father, Franz Joseph Feuchtmayr, and Diego Francesco Carlone, born in Como. Established a large work-shop at Mimmenhausen as of 1718 and produced altars for the Lake Constance region. (Not to be confused with his contemporary and namesake, Johann Michael Feichtmayr, 1709–72, who was active mainly in Bavaria).

5

Design for the High Altar of the Pilgrimage Church in Birnau

Dated 1748
Pen drawing in brown, with grey wash;
on two sheets of handmade paper
84.5 × 44 cm
Signed in his hand, below right "Inv: von Jo: Faichtm. 1748; dimensions are given with a scale along left edge of paper, 1-2-3-4-5 Schuh (ft.), with details on gallery height and glazing for the cupola of the altar.
One of a group of nine designs for the altar partly coloured, by Feuchtmayr and his closest collaborator Johann Georg Dirr: all catalogued in 1931.
Inv. No. C 31/6

Commanding as it is charming, the church at Birnau, set in the vineyard above Lake Constance, is a gem of the German Rococo. A Swabian creation that is equal to its Bavarian counterparts. At the height of his œuvre and his era, before Neo-Classicism did away with intoxicating colors and ecstatic gesture, Joseph Anton Feuchtmayr completed the decoration of the pilgrim and priory church of Birnau at Salem. It is a perfect Gesamtkunstwerk, built by Peter Thumb of Bregenz and painted by Gottfried Bernhard Götz of Augsburg.

Feuchtmayr's large-scale design simultaneously comprises the architectural construction, sculptural decoration and embellishments of a magnificent altar spatially integrated into the chancel. In order to execute this design, the commissioner and the craftsman needed to see only half of a given illustrated feature — so there is a practical reason behind the apparent incompleteness of the drawing. This incompleteness also contributes to the drawing's charm and its graphic qualities distinguish it from the coloured architectural drawings of Feuchtmayr's pupil, F. A. Dirr. A consistently applied system of hatching in different directions, occasionally dissolving into dots, sets the image into a state of vibration. This quite skillfully lends to the overall picturesque dynamism of forms, while the reticent wash adds sculptural sense and spatial depth.

Today's visitor to Birnau will not encounter the same high altar shown in this drawing. Falling in line with the classicising trend of the time, the altar with the Late Gothic Virgin figure was divided horizontally, like a throne. The columns and canopy have been left standing — thank goodness — but the altar painting by J. C. Storer of the Assumption of the Virgin, was replaced in 1790 with a relief of dancing angels, thus robbing Feuchtmayr's brilliant figures of a colourful contrast.

Literatur: H. Sauer, Zeichnungen der Mimmenhauser Bildner, Straßburg–Leipzig 1936. S. 22, 69, Kat. Nr. Stuttgart II A 2. – W. Boeck, Joseph Anton Feuchtmayr, Tübingen 1948, S. 142, Abb. 195. – Katalog der Ausstellung »Der barocke Himmel«, Staatsgalerie Stuttgart, 1964, Nr. 97, Abb. 24 (Ausschnitt), dort weitere zwei Altarentwürfe behandelt und ein neu bestimmtes Figurenblatt des Künstlers (Nr. 64, 80, 128). – Katalog der Ausstellung »Barock in Baden-Württemberg«, Schloß Bruchsal, 1981, S. 200, B. 43 (Eva Zimmermann).

Bibliography: H. Sauer, Zeichnungen der Mimmenhauser Bildner (Strasbourg-Leipzig, 1936), pp. 22, 69, cat. No. Stuttgart IIA2; W. Boeck, Joseph Anton Feuchtmayr (Tübingen, 1948), p. 142, ill. 195; cat. Der barocke Himmel (Staatsgalerie Stuttgart, 1964), No. 97, ill. 24 (detail), as well as descriptions of two other altar designs and a sheet of figures newly established as this artist's (No. 64, 80, 128); cat. Barock in Baden-Württemberg (Schloß Bruchsal, 1981), p. 200, ill. 43 (Eva Zimmermann).

245

Matthäus Günther

Geboren 1705 in Unterpeissenberg (Oberbayern), gestorben 1788 in Haid bei Wessobrunn. Lehrzeit in München bei Cosmas Damian Asam, beeinflußt von Johann Evangelist Holzer. Seit 1731 Meister in Augsburg, von 1762–1784 Direktor der dortigen »Reichsstädtischen Kunstakademie«. Arbeitet als Freskant zusammen mit Wessobrunner Stukkatoren in süddeutschen Kirchen.

6a
Flucht des Äneas aus Troja

6b
Äneas' Meerfahrt und Landung in Italien

Entstanden 1757
Entwürfe für das dreiteilige Deckenfresko Günthers über der südlichen Galerie des Neuen Schlosses in Stuttgart; 1944 zerstört, 1963 nach fotografischen Vorlagen erneuert. Feder in Braun und Bleistift, grau laviert, weiß gehöht auf rötlich-braun laviertem Papier. Wasserzeichen: Straßburger Lilie mit Monogramm WR (ähnlich Churchill 408). Das erste Blatt (6a) 33,2 × 31 cm (Bild 26,5 × 24 cm; oben beschnitten); das zweite, aus zwei Teilen zusammengesetzte Blatt (6b) 30,7 × 95,3 cm (Bild 24,4 × 87 cm; seitlich beschnitten, besonders rechts, wo man sich ein Tondo wie auf dem ersten Blatt vorzustellen hat). Herkunft: Architekt Anton Schmid, Wien.
Inv. Nr. C 52/433, C 52/432 a und b

Die Äneas-Fresken des Stuttgarter Neuen Schlosses, signiert: »M. Gündter Fecit. 1757«, sind der größte profane Auftrag für Günther gewesen; in Stuttgart aber nicht der einzige. Der an Cosmas Damian Asam geschulte bayerische Künstler war seit 1753 mehrfach für Herzog Carl Eugen von Württemberg tätig: bei der Ausmalung des Musiksaals und des Porzellankabinetts im Stuttgarter Schloß und des Stuttgarter Opernhauses (bereits 1762 zerstört) sowie des neuen Corps de Logis im Schloß Ludwigsburg, 1759, mit 16 Supraporten.
Angesichts der Zerstörung von Günthers Fresken in Stuttgart kommt den vorliegenden Entwürfen für sein Hauptwerk erhöhte Bedeutung zu, sowohl künstlerische wie dokumentarische. Dargestellt ist die von Vergil, dem größten römischen Epiker überlieferte Sage der Flucht des Äneas aus dem von den Griechen eroberten Troja über Karthago nach Italien; weniger eine Kriegsgeschichte als die Glorifizierung von Tugenden, die sich absolutistische Herrscher — wie Carl Eugen — gern andichten ließen: Mut — Beharrlichkeit — Frömmigkeit.

Auf dem ersten Blatt (6a) unten trägt Äneas seinen Vater auf den Schultern aus dem brennenden Troja, links seine Frau Kreusa, die Statuen der Stadtgötter tragend, rechts sein Sohn Ascanius; im Tondi darüber die Göttin Juno; dem Äneas feindlich gibt sie den Windgöttern (links) Weisung, seine Schiffe (rechts) zu zerstören.
Auf dem zweiten Blatt (6b) ist wie eine dreimal ansteigende Welle zu sehen: Äneas' Meerfahrt, Neptun, der Meeresgott mit dem Dreizack auf dem Muschelwagen, und die Landung Äneas' in Italien, dazu sein Dankopfer und der Empfang durch den Fürsten der Arkader, Evander. Darüber die Götter des Olymp: Juno, über der die Göttin der Gerechtigkeit, Justitia, schwebt, Venus mit dem Taubenwagen und Amor sowie (für den Betrachter auf dem Kopf stehend) Dido, die Königin von Karthago, die sich auf dem Scheiterhaufen verbrennen läßt, weil Äneas, ihr Geliebter, sie auf Geheiß der Götter verließ. — Im unvollständigen rechten Tondo empfängt Äneas von seiner Mutter Venus die von Vulkan geschmiedete Rüstung; es fehlt darunter die Darstellung des Zweikampfs mit dem italienischen Fürsten Turnus.
Obwohl die Entwürfe nicht skizzenhaft, sondern detailliert auf zart getöntem Papier mit spritzigen Weißhöhungen ausgeführt sind — so daß sie als Modelle zur Vorlage beim Auftraggeber geeignet waren — bewahren sie in ihrer Erzählfreude eine Frische und Großzügigkeit, wie sie den ausgeführten Fresken kaum eigen gewesen sein dürfte. Nur selten erreicht das fertige Werk des Künstlers die Intensität der ersten Idee. Daher kommt unsere hohe Wertschätzung der Barock-Bozzetti. — Johannes Zahlten hat die ikonographischen Vorbilder Günthers in den ein Jahrhundert früheren Äneas-Fresken des Pietro da Cortona von 1651/54 im römischen Palazzo Pamphili, bzw. in deren Nachstichen ausfindig gemacht. Das beweist die künstlerische Kontinuität und spricht nicht gegen die eigene Qualität, die Grazie des süddeutschen Rokoko; sie hatte sich gegen das Genie Tiepolos zu behaupten, der die Fresken der Würzburger Residenz schuf, als Günther 1752 das dortige Käppele ausmalte.

Matthäus Günther

Born in Unterpeissenberg (Upper Bavaria) in 1705, died 1788 in Haid near Wessobrunn. A pupil of Cosmas Damian Asam in Munich. Influenced by Johann Evengelist Holzer. Master in Augsburg from 1731, Director of the "Reichsstädtischen Kunstakademie" 1762–84. Worked as a fresco painter, together with stucco craftsmen from Wessobrunn, in southern German churches.

6 a

Flight of Aeneas from Troy

6 b

Aeneas' Passage and Landing in Italy

Dated 1757
Designs for Günther's three-part ceiling fresco over the south gallery of the Neues Schloß in Stuttgart. Destroyed 1944, restored after photographs in 1963.
Pen and brown ink, with pencil; grey wash with white highlights on red and brown washed paper. Watermark: Strasbourg lily with monogram WR (similiar to Churchill 408). The first sheet (6a), 33.2 × 31 cm picture area: 26.5 × 24 cm, cut above); the second (6b), 30.7 × 95.3 cm, consists of two sheets (picture: 24.4 × 87 cm; cut at the sides, especially on the right, where a tondo, like on the first sheet, is to be imagined).
Provenance: Anton Schmid, architect, Vienna
Inv. No. C 52/433, C 52/432 a & b

The Aeneas Frescoes in the Neues Schloß in Stuttgart, signed "M. Günther Fecit. 1757", were Günther's largest secular commission but not his only one in Stuttgart. The Bavarian artist, who trained under Cosmas Damian Asam, worked on many commissions for Duke Carl Eugen of Württemberg: the painting of the Music Room and the Porcelain Cabinet in Stuttgart's Schloß, the Stuttgart Opera (destroyed as early as 1762) and the new corps de logis built 1759 at Schloß Ludwigsburg with 16 supraporten.

In light of the destruction of Günther's frescoes in Stuttgart, the existing designs for his main project gain in both artistic and documentory value. They depict the legend as told by Virgil, the greatest Roman epic poet, of Aeneas's flight from Troy which has been taken by the Greeks, over Carthage to Italy. It is less a story of war than a glorification of certain virtues that absolutist rulers — like Carl Eugen — sought to be commended for, such as courage, perseverance and piety.

In the first drawing (sheet 6a), Aeneas, below, carries his father out of the flaming Troy on his shoulders; to the left, his wife, Creusa, carrying the statues of the city's gods; to the right, his son Ascanius; in the tondo above, the goddess, Juno. An enemy of Aeneas, she instructs the gods of the wind to destroy his ships.

The second drawing (6b) depicts, like a triple-crested wave, Aeneas' passage from Troy; Neptune, the god of the sea, with his trident riding in his sea-shell chariot; and Aeneas' landing in Italy, together with his offering of thanks and the reception by the Prince of the Arcadians, Evander. Above them the Olympian gods; Justitia, the goddess of justice hovers over Juno, Venus with the chariot of doves and Cupid. The Queen of Carthage, Dido, (from the viewer's standpoint) upside-down, who has herself burnt at the stake because her lover Aeneas, at the gods' command, abandoned her. In the incomplete tondo on the right, Aeneas receives, from his mother Venus, the armour that Vulcan has made for him. The scene where Aeneas and the Italian prince, Turnus, met in single combat, is missing.

Although these designs are not roughly sketched, but executed in fine detail on delicately toned paper with sparkling white highlights (good enough to be presented as a model to the commissioner), they retain a freshness and amplitude in the joy of narrative that could not have been imparted to the completed frescoes. Only rarely does an artist's finished work attain the intensity of the original idea. That is why we so value these Baroque bozzetti. Johannes Zahlten has discovered Günther's iconographic models in the Aeneas frescoes of Pietro da Cortona of a century before (1651–54) at the Palazzo Pamphili in Rome. This is proof of the underlying artistic continuity and does not detract from the later works' quality or the grace of the southern German Rococo. It had to assert itself in face of Tiepolo's genius. Tiepolo was working on the frescoesat the residential palace of Würzburg at the same time (1752) that Günther was there painting the chapel.

Literatur: B. Bushart /H. Geissler, Katalog der
Ausstellung »Der barocke Himmel«,
Handzeichnungen deutscher und ausländischer
Künstler in Deutschland, Staatsgalerie Stuttgart
1964. – H. A. Klaiber, Der Württembergische
Oberbaudirektor Philipp de la Guêpière,
Stuttgart 1959, S. 62, 75, Abb. 22, 23. – Katalog
der Ausstellung »Deutsche Zeichnungen 1400
bis 1900«, München 1956, S. 54, Nr. 133
(Inv. Nr. C 52/432 a und b). – Johannes Zahlten,
Das zerstörte Aeneas-Fresko Matthäus
Günthers im Stuttgarter Neuen Schloß, in:
Pantheon, Jhg. XXXVII, 1979, S. 150–163.

Bibliography: B. Bushart/H. Geissler, cat. Der
Barocke Himmel, drawings by German and
foreign artists in Germany, Staatsgalerie
Stuttgart (1964); H. A. Klaiber, Der
Württembergische Oberbaudirektor Philipp de
la Guêpière, (Stuttgart, 1959), pp. 62, 75, ills. 22,
23: cat. Deutsche Zeichnungen 1400–1900
(Munich, 1956), p. 54, No. 133 (inv. No. C 52/
432 a & b); Johannes Zahlten, "Das zerstörte
Aeneas-Fresko Matthäus Günthers im
Stuttgarter Neuen Schloß" in Pantheon, XXXVII
(1979), pp. 150–163.

6a
M. Günther, »Flucht des Äneas aus Troja«, 1757.

6a
M. Günther, Flight of Aeneas from Troy, 1757.

6b
M. Günther, »Äneas' Meerfahrt und Landung in
Italien«, 1757.

6b
M. Günther, Aeneas' Passage and Landing in
Italy, 1757.

Jacques de Gheyn

Kupferstecher und Maler, geboren 1565 in Antwerpen, gestorben 1629 in Den Haag. Seit 1585 Schüler des brillanten Stechers Hendrik Goltzius in Haarlem, seit 1591 in Amsterdam, 1594 Aufnahme in die Gilde von Den Haag. Arbeitet zunächst nach Vorlagen von Goltzius, Bloemaert und van Mander, später nach eigenen Erfindungen. Wendet sich nach 1600 der Malerei zu. Sein druckgraphisches Œuvre umfaßt 430 Blätter.

7

Die Hexenküche

Entstanden um 1600
Feder und Pinsel in Braun (Bister), grau laviert, auf Hadernpapier aufgezogen, in der Mitte durchgehende Horizontal- und Vertikalfalten, Fehlstellen unten in der Mitte und an den Ecken, 45 × 68,2 cm
Signiert unten links der Mitte in Ligatur: IDGheyn inv.
Herkunft: aus dem Nachlaß des Malers Joseph Anton von Gegenbaur (1800–1876). Inv.Nr. 1095

Jacques de Gheyn

Engraver and painter. Born 1565 in Antwerp. Died 1629 in The Hague. From 1585 pupil of the brilliant engraver, Hendrik Goltzius in Haarlem. In Amsterdam from 1591, accepted into the Guild at The Hague in 1594. Worked at first after originals by Goltzius, Bloemaert and van Mander, then developed own subjects. After 1600 turned to painting. His printed œuvre comprises 430 works.

7

The Witches' Kitchen

Circa 1600
Pen and brush in brown (bistre), with grey wash. Mounted on rag paper; horizontal and vertical bisection folds; damaged below centre and in left corner.
45 × 68.2 cm
signed bottom, left of centre, in ligatures: IDGheyn inv.
Source: from the estate of the painter Joseph Anton von Gegenbaur (1800–76). Inv.No. 1095

Zwischen Realismus und Phantastik, zwischen Naturbeobachtung und Wahnvorstellungen brodelt es in dieser Hexenküche; ihren Zauber im einzelnen zu entschlüsseln, ist nicht leicht, auch nicht das Zentralmotiv über den drei köchelnden Hexen (die vordere, ein feister Rückenakt, deutet auf Goyas »Koloß« voraus): jener auf Stufen getürmte, feuerspeiend explodierende Sarkophag, den Wolfgang Schöne als Altar ansieht, »was (wie in anderen Darstellungen des Hexensabbats beispielsweise verfallene, verwüstete Kirchen) auf den heillos widerchristlichen Charakter dieses Hexentreibens wiese«. Am Boden wimmelt abscheuliches Getier, im Himmel Ausgeburten der Hölle. Nur zweimal vermag man Menschen in alptraumhaften Situationen zu entdecken: in der linken unteren Ecke den aufgereckten Kopf eines Toten und rechts von den drei Hexen Gesäß und Bein eines Körpers, der in eine Erdspalte eingeklemmt ist. Darüber öffnet sich der Blick in eine »Weltlandschaft« mit Meeresbucht, Stadt und Bergen. Ganz rechts besteigt ein bekränzter Amor einen Drachen und erlegt mit Pfeilen ein Reptil und (in der Ecke) einen dicken Frosch, der, getroffen, Münzen unter sich wegrollen läßt. Ist das als Überwindung des damals grassierenden Hexenwahns durch Eros zu deuten oder vielmehr als dessen Mittäterschaft?

Für die Ikonographie bietet sich hier ein weites Feld, das von Hans Baldung Griens spätmittelalterlichen Hexenholzschnitten und der Dämonie des Hieronymus Bosch bis hin zu Johann Heinrich Füsslis »Nachtmahren« und Goyas »Hexensabbat« in den »Caprichos« reicht. Für den Leser von Goethes »Faust I.« ist die Walpurgisnacht mit dem Tanz der Hexen auf dem Blocksberg eine vertraute Vorstellung (dazu und über Goethes unterdrückte Fragmente zum Hexensabbat vergleiche das Walpurgisnacht-Kapitel in Albrecht Schöne: Götterzeichen, Liebeszauber, Satanskult. Neue Einblicke in alte Goethetexte. 2. Auflage München 1982).

Die reich instrumentierte Komposition bestätigt Oberhubers Urteil von de Gheyn als »Genialem Zeichner«, einem der geistreichsten seiner Zeit«. Die Datierung unserer Zeichnung »um 1600« wird gefestigt durch eine mit dem Jahr 1600 datierte Vorzeichnung der Eidechse rechts vorn im Bilde (Städel-Museum, Frankfurt). In den Umkreis von de Gheyns hervorragendem Blatt gehören in unserer Sammlung eine Gruppe farbiger Landschaftsskizzen von Roelant Savery, eine Goltzius-Zeichnung und der Anonymus des sogenannten Kurpfälzischen Skizzenbuches. Zeitlich etwas früher liegt das im einführenden Text des Bandes erwähnte niederländische Skizzenbuch des sogenannten Anonymus Fabriczy (Abb. 9, S. 211); am Anfang einer neuen Geistesrichtung steht dann die im folgenden behandelte Zeichnung Rembrandts.

Literatur: Bisher unveröffentlicht, auch nicht erwähnt in Konrad Oberhubers Albertina-Katalog »Zwischen Renaissance und Barock«, Wien 1968, der unter Nr. 330 den nach unserer Zeichnung ausgeführten Kupferstich würdigt und abbildet. Vorgesehen für die Monographie des jetzt verstorbenen J. Q. van Regteren-Altena.

In this witches kitchen, the brew bubbles between observations of nature and hallucinations, the realistic and the fantastic. To decipher the sorcery in detail is not an easy task. Not even the main motive above the three cooking witches is easily deciphered (the foremost of the witches, a corpulent backview nude, anticipates Goya's Colossus): namely the exploding, fire-spewing sarcophagus on top of towering steps, that Wolfgang Schöne views as altar, "which indicates (like in other depictions of the Witches' Sabbath; dilapidated, devastated churches) the utterly antichristian nature of these witches sorcery". The ground teems with horrible beasts; the sky with creatures from hell. Humans beings appear only twice and this in night-marish situations — in the left bottom corner the stretched head of a dead man, and to the right of the three witches, the buttocks and legs of a figure wedged into a cleft in the ground. Above the scene, the view opens to a "wordly landscape" with a bay, a city and mountains. At the far right, a Cupid wearing a wreath mounts a dragon and kills a reptile and (in the corner) a fat frog with his arrows. The frog writhes with pain while coins roll out from under him. Is this to be interpreted as Eros overcoming the obsession with witches prevalent at the time or rather his complicity?

In iconographic terms, the subject is vast and begins with Hans Baldung Grien's late medieval woodcuts of witches, the demonic images of Hieronymus Bosch, and extends to Johann Heinrich Füssli's "Nightmares" and Goya's "Witches' Sabbath" in the "Caprichos". The vision of Walpurgis night with dance of the witches on Blocksberg will be familiar to readers of Goethe's Faust I. On this and on Goethe's suppressed fragments for the Witches' Sabbath, cf. the chapter on Walpurgis night in Albrecht Schöne's Götterzeichen, Liebeszauber, Satanskult. Neue Einblicke in alte Goethetexte, 2nd edn. (Munich, 1982).

The richly orchestrated composition confirms Oberhuber's assessment of de Gheyn as "an inspired draftsman, one of the most ingenious of his time". The dating of our drawing as "c. 1600" is substantiated by a preliminary drawing of the lizard on the right foreground dated 1600 (Städel-Museum, Frankfurt). Other works in the collection which can be grouped with de Gheyn's superb drawing are: a cycle of coloured landscape sketches by Roelant Savery, a Goltzius drawing and the anonymous author of the so-called Kurpfälzisches Skizzenbuch. A somewhat earlier example is the Dutch sketchbook of the Anonymous Fabriczy (ill. 9, p. 211), mentioned in the introduction to this volume, while the Rembrandt drawing which follows marks the beginning of a new outlook.

Bibliography: Nothing published to date; the work is not mentioned in Konrad Oberhuber's Albertina catalogue, Zwischen Renaissance und Barock (Vienna, 1968), which praises and illustrates a copper engraving copied after our drawing (No. 330). Was to be included in the monography by the late J. Q. van Regteren-Altena.

7
De Gheyn, »Die Hexenküche«, Zeichnung um
1600.

7
De Gheyn, The Witches' Kitchen, drawing
c. 1600.

7
De Gheyn, »Die Hexenküche«, um 1600,
Ausschnitt der Zeichnung.

7
De Gheyn, The Witches' Kitchen, c. 1600, detail
of drawing on preceding page.

Rembrandt Harmensz van Rijn

Geboren 1609 in Leiden (Holland) als Sohn eines Müllers, dort besuchte er die Lateinschule und war an der Universität immatrikuliert; zuerst lernte er bei dem Historienmaler van Swanenburgh, dann bei Pieter Lastman in Amsterdam, wo er sich 1631 niederließ; 1634 heiratete er die Patriziertochter Saskia van Uylenburgh. Mit ihrem frühen Tod 1642 setzte die entscheidende Wende seines Lebens und seiner Kunst ein; er starb vereinsamt 1669.

8

Rebekkas Abschied von ihrem Elternhaus

Entstanden um 1637
Rohrfeder mit Bister, Lavierung und feinen Weißhöhungen,
auf Karton aufgezogen, 18,5 × 30,6 cm
Auf der Unterkante eigenhändig bezeichnet:
»dit behoorde vervoucht te weesen met veel gebueren die deese hoge bruijt sien vertreken« (zu deutsch: Dies sollte die Figuren vieler Nachbarn enthalten, die dem Abschied der hohen Braut beiwohnen),
darüber von fremder Hand: Rembrandt.
Rückseitig: Signaturstempel M. G. Kade (Lugt 1561a).
Herkunft (laut Benesch): Bis 1921 Lord Northwick (= E. G. Spencer-Churchill), bis 1926 De Robiano, Brüssel. — Max Kade, New York. — 1963 von ihm mit dem größten Teil seiner graphischen Sammlung als deren einzige Zeichnung geschenkt.
Inv. Nr. GL 936

Rembrandt stand der religiösen Reformbewegung des Jansenismus nahe; er las die Bibel und hat mit Vorliebe aus ihr seine Stoffe gewählt: hier die im 24. Kapitel des 1. Buches Mose überlieferte Geschichte, wie Abraham seinen ältesten Knecht mit einer Karawane nach Mesopotamien sendet, um seinem Sohn Isaak eine Braut aus seinem Vaterland zu freien; er trifft sie an einem Brunnen, wo »der Leute Töchter Wasser schöpfen«, beschenkt sie, nachdem seine Kamele getränkt wurden, und geleitet sie nach Hause; sie willigt in die Werbung ein und nimmt hier nun als »hohe Braut«, wie Rembrandt sagt, »Abschied von vielen Nachbarn«.
Wer die Hauptperson, Rebecca, in der Mitte der ungewöhnlich breit angelegten Komposition zu finden glaubt, sieht sich getäuscht; dort breitet sich eine kostbar verzierte Satteldecke über einem knienden Kamel aus und hält ein Diener in Erwartung Rebeccas einen Sonnenschirm, der die triptychonartige Szenerie diagonal verspannt; auf der Altane steht, das Geschehen mehr überschauend als lenkend, der Hausherr. Von links führen ins Bild hinein eine markante Repoussoirfigur und die bereits aufgesessene

Karawane. Der eigentliche Abschied spielt sich im rechten Bilddrittel ab; in einer Gruppe verneigt sich dort Rebecca mit Kranz und Schleier vor einer älteren Frau.
Die Dezentralisierung der Hauptperson ist ein gewagter Kunstgriff; doch bleibt der Zusammenhang mit dem Bildganzen gewahrt durch Rembrandts Licht, das auf ihr ruht. Es bedeutet auch: Mit dem Abschied aus dem Schatten des Elternhauses tritt Rebecca ins Licht der biblischen Geschichte. — Die malerisch lavierte, zart weiß gehöhte Zeichnung, zu der kein Gemälde bekannt ist, strahlt eine erwartungsvolle Feierlichkeit aus, die alle historischen Details überhöht. Der Reichtum ihrer Kompositionsform und die Lust am orientalischen Dekor weisen zusammen mit der Strichbildung auf ihre Entstehung in Rembrandts reifer Frühzeit, als er das Leben an Saskias Seite festlich empfand.

Rembrandt Harmensz van Rijn

Born in Leyden, Holland, the son of a miller in 1609. Attended latin school and was enrolled at the university; initially pupil of the history painter van Swanenburgh, then with Pieter Lastman in Amsterdam, where he settled in 1631. Married Saskia van Uylenburgh, a patrician's daughter in 1634. Her early death in 1642 marked the decisive turn in his life and art; he died desolate in 1669.

8

Rebecca Departs from her Parents' House

Circa 1637
Reed pen with bistre, wash and fine highlights mounted on cardboard,
18.5 × 30.6 cm
In his own hand along the bottom edge,
"dit behoorde vervoucht te weesen met veel gebueren die deese hoge bruijt sien vetreken"
(this should contain the figures of many neighbours who witness the departure of the noble bride), over this in another hand,
"Rembrandt".
On the reverse, the signature stamp of M. G. Knade (Lugt 1561a).
Provenance (according to Benesch): until 1921, Lord Northwick (= E. G. Spencer-Churchill), until 1926 De Robiano, Brussels; Max Kade, New York. Donated in 1963 along with the larger part of his entire graphic arts collection. This was only drawing donated.
Inv. No. GL 936

Rembrandt was sympathetic to the Jansenistic religious reform movement; he read the Bible and preferred to use biblical subject matter. Here, he focuses on the story (Genesis 24) how Abraham sends his oldest servant to Mesopotamia with a caravan to find a bride from his place of birth for his son Isaac. The servant encounters her at a well, where "the daughters of the men of the city come out to draw water". He gives her presents after she has watered his camels, and accompanies her home. She consents to the proposal; the "noble (high) bride" as Rembrandt calls her, is depicted "taking leave of the many neighbours."
The picture will deceive those expecting to see the main figure, Rebecca, in the center of the surprisingly wide pictorial composition. That place in the center of the composition is taken up by a richly decorated saddle blanket spread over a kneeling camel and a servant holding a parasol in anticipation of Rebecca, the rider; the sunshade is braced diagonally across the triptych-like composition of the scene. Surveying rather than directing the event, the master of the house stands on the balcony. From the left, a striking repoussoir figure leads our eye into the picture; behind him, the caravan is mounted and ready to go. The actual leave-taking takes place in the right third of the picture. Rebecca, wearing a wreath and veil, bows before an older woman.
The shift of the main figure from the centre is a daring gesture. Yet her significance within the whole is maintained through Rembrandt's light, which surrounds her. This can also be interpreted as Rebecca's forsaking the shade of her parental home to depart into the light of biblical history. The drawing with its painterly washes and delicate white highlights, radiates an expectant air of ceremony that transcends all historical details. The wealth of its compositional form and the sheer delight in oriental decor carried out in the particular line of Rembrandt's mature early period indicate a time when he found life at Saskia's side a celebration.

Literatur: Otto Benesch, The Drawings of Rembrandt, 1954, Vol. I, Nr. 147, Fig. 159. – Katalog der Ausstellung: Sammlung Max Kade, Staatsgalerie Stuttgart 1963, Nr. 116, Tafel 91 mit ergänzender Literatur. – Zuletzt als eigenhändig bestätigt von: Werner Sumowski, Drawings of the Rembrandt-School, Bd. 3, 1980, S. 1734, bei Nr. 806**. Dort wird die ausführliche Inschrift Rembrandts (siehe oben) als Hinweis für einen seiner Schüler erklärt.

Bibliography: Otto Benesch, The Drawings of Rembrandt (1954), I, No. 147, Fig. 159; cat. Sammlung Max Kade (Staatsgalerie Stuttgart, 1963), No. 116, plate 91, with additional literature; the latest confirmation of Rembrandt's hand comes from Werner Sumowski, Drawings of the Rembrandt School, vol. III (1980), p. 1734, for No. 806**. He postulates that Rembrandt's detailed inscription (see above) is an indication for one of his students.

Paolo Veronese

Geboren 1528 in Verona, gestorben 1588 in Venedig. Sein eigentlicher Name ist Caliari; er war Schüler des Antonio Badile in Verona und seit spätestens 1554 in Venedig tätig, 1560 Romreise. Vom Manierismus eines Tintoretto unberührt, stellt Veronese die Kontinuität der venezianischen Malerei her zwischen Renaissance und Barock, zwischen Tizian und Tiepolo.

9

Doppelseitiges Skizzenblatt

Entstanden gegen 1573
Feder in Braun, braun laviert und Rötel,
weiß gehöht auf bläulichem Papier,
29,6 × 27,4 cm
Bezeichnet auf der Rückseite unten:
Di Paulo Caliari Veronese. Daneben der
Sammlerstempel F. K. Z. F.
Herkunft: Sammlung Carl Faber
(1839–1903) Stuttgart; erworben auf
der 60. Versteigerung von H. G. Gutekunst,
Stuttgart, 10./12. 11. 1904, Nr. 59 als
Veronese.
Sammlung Schloß Fachsenfeld (in
Verwahrung der Staatsgalerie Stuttgart).
Inv. Nr. III/1256

Die Kreativität eines Künstlers spricht aus seinen Skizzenblättern, aus ihrer Reichhaltigkeit und ihrer Verve. Zwei Beispiele dafür werden in diesem Band vorgestellt, eines von dem Bolognesen Agostino Carracci (siehe Tafel 10, S. 264), und das vorliegende von dem zum Venezianer gewordenen Veronese. Das auf beiden Seiten mit kleinfigurigen Skizzen dicht gefüllte Blatt ist in seiner malerisch fluktuierenden, von Licht und Farbe gesättigten Erscheinungsweise ein typisches Beispiel der Zeichenkunst Venedigs. Wie eine Springflut scheinen die Bildideen im freien Spiel der Linien zu entstehen. Werner R. Deusch hat drei Gemälde Veroneses nachgewiesen, die hier ihre erste Formulierung gefunden haben: Im Querformat das über drei (!) Meter lange Bild der Rosenkranzmadonna, das von der Rosenkranz-Bruderschaft für San Pietro in Murano in Auftrag gegeben und von Mitarbeitern Veroneses laut Inschrift im Dezember 1573 vollendet wurde (jetzt Murano, Museo Vetrario; siehe Pignatti, op. cit. Nr. 216). Die zentrale Figur der Entwurfszeichnung ist auch die am stärksten durchgearbeitete: der heilige Dominikus; er steht zwischen der thronend-schwebenden Muttergottes, dem Papst einerseits, dem Dogen andererseits, ihrem Gefolge und Mitgliedern der Bruderschaft, an die er Rosen als Symbol des Rosenkranzes verteilt. — Was Veronese mit der links oben hingeworfenen Skizze einer Reiterin im Sinne hatte, vermag die Rückseite des Blattes zu erklären.
Die Aussaat der Ideenskizzen auf der Rückseite hat ein Zentrum und eine vertikale Achse. Die zentrale Gruppe ist auch die technisch reichste: Rötel und Deckweiß über brauner Feder stellen eine auf einem lagernden Tier sitzende, von ihren Gespielinnen umringte Frau dar; es ist der »primo pensiero« des Gemäldes »Raub der Europa«, die — laut den Metamorphosen des Ovid — eine von Jupiter in Gestalt eines Stieres nach Kreta entführte phönizische Königstochter war; sie ist die »Reiterin« auf der Vorderseite des Blattes. Das Gemälde dazu hängt im Dogenpalast, seine umstrittene Entstehungszeit erhält aufgrund dieses Blattes den Anhaltspunkt 1573, das Vollendungsdatum des Rosenkranzbildes; denn die Gleichzeitigkeit des schöpferischen Aktes der »primi pensieri« auf der Vorder- und Rückseite des Blattes steht außer Zweifel. — Zum »Raub der Europa« gehören auch die fliegenden Putten über der Gruppe und unten rechts eine sich graziös wendende Gespielin.
Die vertikale Achse verläuft am linken Bildrand. Der Reiter unten steht in loser Verbindung zu einer Hintergrundsfigur im »Raub der Europa«. — Darüber fanden in drängender Fülle noch zwei Skizzen eines Bildgedankens Platz: eine sogenannte Engelpietà, eine Dreiergruppe von zwei Engeln, die den toten Christus zwischen sich halten; ein Bildtypus, der in Oberitalien während des späten 15. Jahrhunderts von Mantegna, Bellini und Antonello da Messina ausgebildet und in der Zeit der Gegenreformation — das ist die Zeit unseres Blattes (1573) — wieder aktuell wurde. Von all den nur in Veroneses Spätzeit entstandenen Fassungen der Pietà steht den beiden Skizzen ein Berliner Gemälde relativ nahe, es ist aber eine Werkstattarbeit ohne Zusammenhalt der Gruppe (Berlin-West, Katalog der Gemäldegalerie 1975, Nr. 295 mit Abbildung). — So klein Veroneses Skizzen sind, haben sie doch etwas von der inneren Größe der späten Pietà-Skulpturen Michelangelos in Rom und Florenz (er hinterließ sie bei seinem Tod 1564 unvollendet).

Paolo Veronese

Born 1528 in Verona. Died 1588 in Venice. His real name was Caliari. He was a pupil of Antonio Badile at Verona and active in Venice by 1554 at the latest. Journey to Rome in 1560. Unaffected by the Mannerism of a Tintoretto, Veronese represents a link in the continuum of Venetian painting between the Renaissance and the Baroque; between Titian and Tiepolo.

9

Double-sided sheet of sketches

About 1573
Pen and brown ink, brown wash and sanguine heightened with white, on bluish paper, 29.6 × 27.4 cm
Inscribed on reverse, below, Di Paulo Caliari Veronese. Adjacent, the collector's stamp: F. K. Z. F.
Provenance: Collection Carl Faber (1839–1903), Stuttgart; acquired at 60th H. G. Gutekunst auction, Stuttgart, 10th/12th Nov. 1904. No. 59 als Veronese. Schloß Fachsenfeld Collection (in custody of Staatsgalerie Stuttgart).
Inv. No. III/1256

An artist's sketches can envince his creative powers with its visual wealth and verve. This volume contains two such instances, one by the Bolognese, Agostino Carracci (see pl. 10, p. 264), the other by Veronese, who became a Venetian. This sheet is a typical example of Venetian draughtsmanship in its painterly, fluctuating surface, saturated in light and colour, with both sides filled with sketched groups of little figures. The pictorial ideas emerge from the free play of lines like a spring tide. These sketches contain the prototypes for three paintings by Veronese identified by Werner R. Deusch. The horizontal-format work corresponds to the painting (more than three metres long) of the Madonna of the Rosery, commissioned by the Brotherhood of the Rosary for S. Pietro in Murano and, according to the inscription, completed by Veronese's assistents in December 1573 (now at Murano, Museo Vetrario; see Pignatti op. cit. 1976, No. 216). The central figure of St. Dominic in the draft sketch is also the most detailed. He stands between the Madonna, floating enthroned above, and, to either side of the Pope and of the Doge, their retinue and members of the Brotherhood, to whom he distributes roses as a sign of the rosary. What Veronese intended with the summary sketch of a female rider at the top left, becomes clear on the reverse of the sheet. The cluster of ideas sketched on the other side of the draft has a centre and a vertical axis. The central group is also the richest in technique. Sanguine and opaque white over pen drawing in brown ink are used to show a woman seated on a resting animal, surrounded by her playmates. This is the primo pensiero for the painting of the Rape of Europa. According to the Metamorphoses she is a royal Phoenician princess who Jupiter, in the form of a bull, abducts to Crete. This is the "rider" on the front of our sheet. The date of the painting, which is at the Doge's Palace, is still much debated, but our drawing places it with some certainty around 1573, the year the Madonna of the Rosary commission was completed. The primi pensieri on both sides of this sheet was created without a doubt at the same time. The flying putti above the Europa group and the graceful, turning figure of a companion in the bottom right-hand corner also form part of the painting at the Doge's Palace.

The vertical axis runs down the left-hand edge of the sheet. The rider, below, is loosely related to a background figure in the Rape of Europa. Above it, another pictorial conception has been elaborated in two sketches which pushes the space upwards — the so-called "Angel Pietà", i.e. the dead Christ supported by two angels. It is a type developed in Northern Italy during the late 15th century by Mantegna, Bellini and Antonello da Messina, and revived in the era of the Counter-Reformation. Our sheet falls into this period (1573). Of all Veronese's versions of the Pietà, a genre treated exclusively in his late period, the one in Berlin bears at least some relation to these two sketches; but it is a workshop piece lacking in the cohesive content of the group in the sketches (West Berlin, catalogue of the Gemäldegalerie (1975), No. 295, with ills.) — Small as Veronese's sketches are, they possess something of the inner grandeur of Michelangelo's late Pietà in Rome and Florence that he left unfinished at his death in 1564.

Literatur: Kat. Schloß Fachsenfeld 1967, Nr. 76.
– Werner R. Deusch, Ein unbekanntes
Skizzenblatt von Veronese, in: Pantheon XXVI,
4, 1968, S. 295 ff. – Terisio Pignatti, Veronese,
L'opera completa, Venezia 1976, Fig. 526 (unter
Nr. A 214 das »Rosenkranz«-Gemälde, unter
Nr. 216 »Raub der Europa«). – Kat. Schloß
Fachsenfeld 1978, Nr. 70, S. 150 (H. Geissler).

Bibliography: Schloß Fachsenfeld, cat. (1967),
No. 76; Werner R. Deusch, "Ein unbekanntes
Skizzenblatt von Veronese", Pantheon XXXVI,
4 (1968), 295 ff.; Terisio Pignatti, Veronese,
L'opera completa (Venice, 1976), Fig. 526 (also
No. A 214, the Rosary painting, No. 216, The
Rape of Europa); Schloß Fachsenfeld catalogue
(1978), No. 70, P. 150 (H. Geissler).

263

Agostino Carracci

Kupferstecher und Maler, geboren 1557 in Bologna als älterer Bruder des Annibale Carracci und Vetter des Lodovico; Agostinos Begabung liegt im graphischen Bereich (der Washingtoner Katalog von 1979 umfaßt 213 Stiche). 1597–1599 war er in Rom tätig, seitdem bis zum Tode 1602 in Parma.

10

Beweinung Christi

Entstanden um 1595
Verso: Studie zum heiligen Franziskus vom Engel getröstet und zum trauernden Johannes der Vorderseite (beide links unten), zu einem Putto und zwei Masken (oben links), außerdem Kalligraphie und Notizen.
Feder in Braun, braun laviert, linke obere Ecke ergänzt, teilweise mit Chiffon-Seide doubliert, 22 × 33 cm
Herkunft anhand der Sammlerstempel: Richard Cosway (Lugt 628). – Sir Thomas Lawrence (Lugt 2445). – Lord Francis Egerton, 1st Earl of Ellesmere (Lugt 2710 b). – Sotheby's London 1972. – Marianne Feilchenfeldt, Zürich.
Inv. Nr. C 77/2671

Agostino Carracci

Engraver and painter, born in Bologna in 1557, the older brother of Annibale Carracci and cousin of Lodovico. Agostino's strength lies in the graphic arts (the Washington catalogue of 1979 includes 215 engravings). Active in Rome, 1597–1599, thereafter in Parma until his death in 1602.

10

The Lamentation of Christ

About 1595
Verso: study for a St. Francis consoled by the Angel and the St. John mourning on front sheet (both below, left), for a putto and two masks (above left); calligraphy and notes. Pen and brown ink, brown wash; top left corner repaired, partially lined with silk chiffon. 22 × 33 cm
Provenance, according to collectors' stamps:
Richard Cosway (Lugt, 628); Sir Thomas Lawrence (Lugt 2445);
Lord Francis Egerton, 1st Earl of Ellesmere (Lugt 2710 b); Sotheby's, London, 1972; Marianne Feilchenfeldt, Zürich.
Inv. No. C 77/2671

Der Entschluß, aus der berühmten Ellesmere-Collection zwei kostbare Carracci-Zeichnungen zu erwerben (die andere, eine Landschaft von Annibale Carracci, siehe Abb. 10, S. 212), wurde im Hinblick auf die von uns seit 1966 wissenschaftlich betreute und seit 1976 in der Staatsgalerie deponierte Sammlung Schloß Fachsenfeld gefaßt. Denn in dieser, die fast 1000 bolognesische Zeichnungen des späten 16. bis frühen 19. Jahrhunderts umfaßt, sind die Carracci nicht mehr ihrer Bedeutung gemäß vertreten, und viele der alten Zuschreibungen an sie sind nicht mehr aufrechtzuerhalten, weil ihr Name als Inbegriff der Schule von Bologna bald ein Sammelname wurde und der Wunsch schon immer der Vater des Gedankens war.

Agostino Carracci führt uns die Beweinung des vom Kreuz genommenen Christus in einer ungewöhnlichen Doppelgruppe vor Augen, zusammengehalten durch die Blickrichtungen und malerische Lavierung wirkt sie monumental und beseelt zugleich. Die Bewegung ihrer Figuren zueinander entspricht ihrer inneren Bewegtheit; der starke Wechsel von Licht und Schatten suggeriert das Aufwühlende des Schmerzes. Die Komposition steht unverkennbar in der klassischen Tradition von Raffael (siehe dessen Beweinungsszene in einer Zeichnung des Oxforder Ashmolean-Museums) und Correggios Gemälde »Compianto su Cristo morto« in der Pinakothek zu Parma; neu an ihr ist eine Steigerung des Ausdrucks durch geballte Form, gewittrige Transparenz und leidenschaftliche Gebärde: das barocke Pathos.

Auf der Rückseite hat der Künstler seiner Feder freien Lauf gelassen zu einem faszinierenden Ensemble von »primi pensieri«, spontanen Einfällen und kalligraphischen Schwüngen. Das Bedeutendste ist die Skizze der Tröstung des heiligen Franziskus von Assisi, einer Vision, in der ihm ein Geige spielender Engel erscheint. Diese Skizze einschließlich der angedeuteten Landschaft steht in so engem Zusammenhang mit einem 1595 datierten Stich Agostinos nach einem Gemälde des Sienesen Francesco Vanni (Bartsch 67; abgebildet im zitierten Katalog von Washington), daß damit auch das Datum unserer Zeichnung fixiert ist. Links vom heiligen Franziskus hat Agostino die Figur des trauernden Johannes skizziert, der den Eckpfeiler der großen Komposition der Vorderseite bildet.

The decision to purchase two valuable Carracci drawings from the famous Ellesmere Collection (the second, a landscape by Annibale, see ill. 10, p. 212) is connected with our tending of the Schloß Fachsenfeld Collection which we have been researching since 1966 (in 1976 it was placed in our custody at the Staatsgalerie). Although this collection comprises almost a thousand Bolognese drawings from the late 16th to the early 19th century, the Carracci are not represented proportionally to their significance, since many of the former attributions can no longer be substantiated. Their name so epitomized the School of Bologna that it soon came to function as a collective term; and the wish was always father to the thought.

Here, Agostino shows depicts the Lamentation as Christ is being taken from the Cross in an unusual double group. The figures are united by common lines of vision and painterly washes; they are rendered at once monumental and full of life. The movement of the figures toward each other corresponds to their inner, moved state; the strong contrasts between light and shade connote their painful tumult. Without a doubt the composition continues in the classical tradition of Raphael (cf. his Lamentation scene in a drawing at the Ashmolean Museum, Oxford) and Correggio's painting, the "Compianto su Cristo morto" at the Galleria nazionale, Parma. Innovative is the intensified quality of expression achieved through the dense piling of forms, a stormy transparency and impassioned gesture – the ardour of the Baroque.

On the reverse, the artist has let his pen run free to compose a fascinating array of "primi pensieri", spontaneous ideas and calligraphic swirls. The most significant is a sketch of the Consolation of St. Francis of Assisi, where in a vision an angel, playing a violin, appears to him. This sketch, including its landscape setting, is so close to Agostino's engraving after a painting by the Sienese, Francesco Vanni (Bartsch 67; ill. in the Carracci catalogue, cited below) that it must share the engraving date of 1595. To the left of St. Francis, Agostino has sketched the grieving figure of St. John, the cornerstone of the large composition on the other side of the sheet.

Literatur: Christel Thiem, Italienische Zeichnungen 1500–1800, Katalog Graphische Sammlung Staatsgalerie Stuttgart 1977, Nr. 225 (mit aller früheren, bis 1836 reichenden Literatur). – Jahrbuch der Staatlichen Kunstsammlungen in Baden-Württemberg, Bd. XV, 1978, S. 199. – Diane DeGrazia Bohlin, Prints and related Drawings by the Carracci Family, Katalog Washington 1979, Nr. und Abb. 204b. – Christel Thiem, Disegni di Artisti Bolognesi dal Seicento all'Ottocento, Katalog Bologna 1983, Nr. 3.

Bibliography: Christel Thiem, Italienische Zeichnungen 1500–1800, catalogue of the Collection of Graphic Art, Staatsgalerie (1977), No. 225. With complete earlier Bibliography from 1836 on; Jahrbuch der Staatlichen Kunstsammlung in Baden-Württemberg XV (1978), 199; Diane Degrazia Bohlin, Prints and Related Drawings by the Carracci Family, catalogue (Washington, 1979), No. & ill. 204b; Christel Thiem, Disegni di Artisti Bolognesi dal Seicento all'Ottocento, catalogue (Bologna, 1983), No. 3.

Guercino

Geboren 1591 in Cento, gestorben 1666 in Bologna. Sein eigentlicher Name ist Giovanni Francesco Barbieri, genannt: Il Guercino, zu deutsch: Der Schieler; er ist einer der Hauptmeister der im Barock tonangebenden Maler von Bologna. Geschult an den Carracci, besonders an Lodovico, und den Venezianern, besonders an Tizian.

11

Studie zum Gewand der Madonna im Gemälde »Maria mit Kind und heiliger Anna« zu Senigallia

Entstanden 1642
Rötel, weiß gehöht auf blauem Papier,
32,8 × 26 cm
Unbezeichnet; rechts unten der
Sammlerstempel: F. K. Z. F. —
Auf der Rückseite des blauen Kartons die
Notiz: Sg. F. G. i. B. / Aus Libro I; das
bedeutet: Sammlung Francesco Giusti in
Bologna / Aus Band I (dieser inzwischen
aufgelöste Band trug die Aufschrift:
Libro I, Studi e Frammenti).
Herkunft: Werkstatt des Guercino, dann
dessen Neffe Cesare Gennari (1637—1688),
dann dessen Enkel Carlo Gennari
(1712—1790). — Francesco Giusti, Bologna
(1752—1828). — 1899 Franz Freiherr
Koenig-Fachsenfeld.
Sammlung Schloß Fachsenfeld (in
Verwahrung der Staatsgalerie Stuttgart).
Inv. Nr. III/67

Es ist ein Glücksfall für die Kunst und die Forschung gewesen, daß zufällig im 300. Todesjahr von Guercino, der zu den Hauptmeistern der Malerei des Barock — nicht nur in Bologna — zählt, eine große Gruppe seiner Zeichnungen auf einem Landschloß der Ostalb in Württemberg wiederentdeckt wurde; unter 935 Blättern bolognesischer Künstler fanden sich 116 mit der alten Zuschreibung an Guercino, vor allem Gewandstudien — eine Spezies, die in der bedeutendsten Guercino-Sammlung auf Windsor Castle fehlt, so daß man sie verloren glaubte. In drei mit Katalogen verbundenen Ausstellungen 1967, 1978 und 1982 haben die Wissenschaftler unserer Graphischen Sammlung sich bemüht, die Schätze dieser seit 1976 in ihrer Obhut befindlichen Privatsammlung von insgesamt 2700 auch deutschen, niederländischen und französischen Blättern zu heben. Der Block der bolognesischen Arbeiten rief sehr bald den besten Kenner Guercinos, Professor Denis Mahon auf den Plan; er und Christel Thiem haben sich der Detektivarbeit unterzogen, die Gewandstudien als Vorarbeiten für Gemälde zu identifizieren (im ersten Katalog von 1967 hieß es von dieser noch: »Verwendung in einem Gemälde nicht nachzuweisen«). — So beglückend der Fund der ca. 50 Gewandstudien ist, wird man für eine Sammlung seine Einseitigkeit bedauern, denn es fehlen ganz die freien Federzeichnungen seiner Landschaften und Capricci. Diese Einseitigkeit erklärt sich aus der Herkunft der Zeichnungen (siehe oben) und ihrer Gruppierung nach Motiven. Die einen gelangten schon 1763 von einem Nachfahren Guercinos über den Bibliothekar des englischen Königs Georgs III., Richard Dalton, nach Schloß Windsor, die anderen im Jahre 1899 mit der Sammlung des bolognesischen Altarmalers Francesco Giusti (1752—1828) an Franz Freiherrn von Koenig-Fachsenfeld. So wie man früher auf Auktionen alte Zeichnungen in Lots (Bündeln) versteigerte, sind sie auch in Giustis erhaltenen Inventaren registriert »Libro I di Studi e Frammenti come Guercino. Mani, piedi ed altri studi« — jetzt bildet eine jede eine Kostbarkeit!

Daß für den heutigen Betrachter eine Gewandstudie den Rang eines autonomen Kunstwerkes haben kann, hängt sowohl mit der Aktualität der Handzeichnung überhaupt als auch mit der Anerkennung des »Non finito«, des Unvollendeten als einer absoluten künstlerischen Aussage zusammen. Bei Guercino liegt im Konzept des Details eine solche Vollendung, daß man die fehlenden Partien der Figur nicht vermißt; durch die Geschlossenheit der Form und delikate Tonwerte entsteht ästhetisch ein Ganzes von absoluter Schönheit. Mit diesem Typ der formvollendeten Gewandstudie knüpft Guercino an die Meister der Hochrenaissance an und erreicht allen großen Künstlern des Barock voraus eine »kompositionell geschlossene Prägung« (Degenhart).

Guercino

Born 1591 in Cento. Died 1666 in Bologna. Il Guercino, nickname of Giovanni Francesco Barbieri, means "squint-eyed". He was one of the foremost figures among the painters of Bologna who were important during the Baroque period. Trained in the mode of the Carracci and in particular Lodovico, also influenced by the Venetians, especially Titian.

11

Study for the Madonna's robes in the painting of the Virgin with Child and St. Anne at Senigallia

Dated 1642
Ruddle with white highlights on blue paper, 32.8 × 26 cm
Unsigned; at bottom right, the collector's stamp, F. K. Z. F. — A note on the reverse, "Sg. F.G.i.B./ Aus Libro I", i.e., Collection of Francesco Giusti in Bologna / From Vol. I. This book, since dispersed, bore the inscriptio, Libro I, Studie Frammenti.
Provenance: Guercino's workshop; then his nephew, Cesare Gennari (1637–88), his grandson, Carlo Gennari (1712–90), Francesco Giusti, Bologna (1752–1828); and (1899) Franz Freiherr Koenig-Fachsenfeld.
Schloß Fachsenfeld Collection (in custody of the Staatsgalerie Stuttgart).
Inv. No. III/67

It is a happy coincidence for art and research that in the 300th anniversary of Guercino's death, numerous drawings of this notable painter of the Baroque — not just of Bologna — were discovered at a country seat in the Ostalb region of Württemberg. Among the 935 works by Bolognese artists, 116 were attributed to Guercino. Most of these studies are of drapery — a genre of Guercino's that was thought to be lost and not represented at all in the reputable Guercino collection at Windsor Castle. In three exhibitions with catalogues (1967, 1978 and 1982), our researchers at the Department of Graphic Art worked to evaluate the treasures in this private collection which has been in our custody since 1976. It also contains works by German, Netherlandish and French artists — 2700 sheets in all. This block of Bolognese works soon drew the best connoisseur of Guercino, Professor Denis Mohan, to the scene. He and Christel Thiem completed some dectective work that led them to identify the drapery studies as preliminary work for paintings (in the first catalogue of 1967 it was stated that their use in paintings "could not be verified"). As fortunate as this find of some 50 drapery studies is, it is also regrettable that the collection is so one-sided. There are no examples of the free pen and ink technique of his landscapes and Capricci. This is partially due to the origin of the drawings (see above) and the fact that they were complied according to subject. Some were brought to Windsor in 1763 by the English King George III's librarian, Richard Dolton, who got the sheets from a descendant of Guercino's. Others were added to Franz Freiherr von Koenig-Fachsenfeld's collection in 1899 as part of the Bolognese altarpiece painter, Francesco Giusti's collection. In Giusti's preserved inventories the old drawings are recorded in the way they would have been auctioned off — in lots (in bundles), "Libro I di Studi e Frammenti come Guercino. Mani, piedi ed altri studi". Today, each single sheet is a rare treasure! Here we lend a "working drawing" of drapery the consideration and importance that otherwise might have been reserved for autonomous works of art. This arises from both a modern repect for freehand drawing in general and the discovery of the "non finito" the incomplete, as a self-sufficient artistic statement. In Guercino, the study of detail is so conceptually complete that one does not miss the other parts of the figure. The coherence of form and delicate tonal values combine into an aesthetic whole of absolute beauty. With this type of formal perfection in a drapery study, Guercino resumes the qualities of the masters of the High Renaissance and, anticipating all the great artists of the Baroque, attains a "self-contained style of composition" (Degenhart).

Literatur: Kat. Fachsenfeld 1967, Nr. und
Abb. 40. – Denis Mahon, Il Guercino, Catalogo
critico dei disegni, Bologna 1968, Nr. und Abb.
148. – Christel Thiem, Unpublished Chalk
Drawings by Guercino in the Collection of
Schloß Fachsenfeld, in: Master Drawings,
Vol. XVII, No. 4, 1979, p. 401 ff. (mit weiteren
Zeichnungen zu dem Gemälde in Senigallia). –
Christel Thiem, Disegni di Artisti Bolognesi dal
Seicento all'Ottocento, Katalog Bologna 1983,
Nr. 34.

Bibliography: Fachsenfeld cat. 1967, No. &
ill. 40; Denis Mahon, Il Guercino, Catalogo
critico dei disegni (Bologna, 1968),
No. & ill. 148; Christel Thiem, "Unpublished
Chalk Drawings by Guercino in the Collection
of Schloß Fachsenfeld", in Master
Drawings XVIII, 4 (1979), 401 ff. (with our other
drawings for the painting at Senigallis);
Christel Thiem, Disegni di Artisti Bolognesi dal
Seicento all'Ottocento, cat. (Bologna, 1983),
No. 34.

Giovanni Benedetto Castiglione

Geboren in Genua um 1610. In der Frühzeit unter dem Einfluß van Dycks, der von 1621–1627 in Genua tätig war. Nach der Auseinandersetzung mit Rembrandts Radierungen geriet er in Rom, wo er seit 1634 als Mitglied der Accademia di San Luca nachweisbar ist, in den Kreis von Poussin und Claude Lorrain. 1651 verließ er Rom, um Hofmaler in Mantua zu werden, wo er 1663 zuletzt nachweisbar ist.

12

Campagna-Landschaft

Entstanden um 1650
Feder in Braun, laviert, 27,2 × 41 cm
Bez. links oben in Feder: G. B., rechts unten: 23
Herkunft: Durch Vernichtung der alten Inventare nicht mehr nachweisbar; 1922 als »Guercino« mit mindestens 18 anderen italienischen Zeichnungen in die Sammlung gekommen, vielleicht als Stiftung.
Inv. Nr. C 1922/68

Giovanni Benedetto Castiglione

Born about 1610 in Genoa. Influenced early on by van Dyck, who worked in Genoa from 1621 to 1627. Rembrandt's etchings were an important stimulus. In Rome he is documented as a member of the Accademia di San Luca from 1634, where he joined Poussin's and Lorrain's circle. In 1651 he left Rome to become court painter in Mantua. This is his last known whereabouts in 1663.

12

Landscape in the Campagna

About 1650
Pen and brown ink wash, 27.2 × 41 cm
Inscribed with pen top left, G. B.; below right, 23
Provenance: Information lost with the destruction of the old inventories; filed in the Collection, possibly as a donation, as "Guercino", along with at least 18 other Italian drawings.
Inv. No. C 1922/68

Die ebenso locker wie sicher gezeichnete »pastorale« Landschaft als eine Arbeit des einfallsreichen Genuesen Castiglione erkannt zu haben, ist ein Ergebnis der jüngsten Forschung. Nachdem Christel Thiem die Zuschreibung an den Bolognesen Guercino aufgrund von Stilkritik berichtigt hatte, stellte Ann Percy nach einem Hinweis von Felice Stampfle die Herkunft unseres Blattes aus einem Album Castigliones fest, wie die Maße und die Paginierung mit der Zahl 23 bestätigen. Die Zeichnungen des ehemaligen Albums — darunter auch Capricci, Allegorien und Satyrszenen — haben anders als die eines Skizzenbuches einen höheren Grad von Vollendung und tragen zum Teil das Monogramm der Taufnamen des Künstlers — wie hier links oben: G. B.
In die konzentrierte Auswahl dieses Bandes wurde die vorliegende Zeichnung nicht allein wegen ihrer lichterfüllten Schönheit aufgenommen, sondern auch als Repräsentantin unseres ansehnlichen Bestandes von 176 genuesischen Zeichnungen, die fast alle 1872 durch den »Vorstand des' königlichen Kupferstichkabinetts«, Karl August Kräutle, aus der Sammlung des Marchese Durazzo erworben wurden. Darunter eine Pinselzeichnung Castigliones, die zusammen mit denen in der Sammlung Schloß Fachsenfeld (siehe Katalog 1967 und 1978) ein beachtliches Ensemble bilden; dabei nicht zu vergessen seine schimmernden Radierungen (siehe Katalog »Meisterwerke alter Druckgraphik aus der Staatsgalerie Stuttgart«, 1982, Nr. 152, 153).
Castigliones Campagna-Landschaft — also die Landschaft vor den Toren Roms mit der Cestius-Pyramide im Zentrum des Mittelgrundes — verkörpert den Typus der »idealen« Landschaft; ihr erster Meister war Annibale Carracci (1560–1609), aus dessen Spätzeit wir die romantisch anmutende Skizze eines Sonnenuntergangs am Meer besitzen (siehe Abb. 10, S. 212). Castigliones Landschaft aber ist eher klassisch zu nennen, sowohl ihrer Topographie als auch ihrer Komposition nach. Vor Castiglione haben sich zwei Nordländer in ähnlicher Weise von der römischen Landschaft inspirieren lassen: Paul Bril (gestorben 1626 in Rom) und Adam Elsheimer (ebenfalls in Rom, 1610 begraben); ihre Erfindung ist das im Vordergrund dominierende Repoussoir der dunkel lavierten Baumgruppe, von der unser Blick in die Tiefe des Bildes geführt wird, wie auch die winzigen Figuren, die sich in der Landschaft ergehen. — Unter den Zeitgenossen Castigliones sind es wieder Nordländer wie Breenbergh (1600 bis 1657) und Rembrandt, die seinem Naturverständnis näherstehen als die Franzosen Poussin und Lorrain. — Erst im 19. Jahrhundert kam es zu einer erneuten künstlerischen Begegnung mit der südlichen Landschaft, vor allem durch die Deutschen in Rom (siehe in diesem Bande Blechens »Tempelruine« und Feuerbachs »Villa d'Este«, Tafel 21 und 23).

It is only very recently that research established this "pastoral" landscape, drawn in a manner as free as it is assured, as belonging to the imaginative Genoese, Castiglione. Christel Thiem corrected the former attribution to Guercino on a stylistic basis. Anne Percy was then able to ascertain the origin of our sheets as part of an album of Castiglione's. This followed a suggestion from Felice Stample. The inference is verified by the dimensions and pagination ("23") of the drawing. The drawings of the former album, including capricci, allegories and scenes with stayrs, achieve a greater degree of finish than those one might find in a sketch book. Some, like the landscape illustrated here, bear the monogram of the artist's Christian names — G. B. — seen here at the top left.
The beauty of this light-irradiated drawing was not the only reason that it was chosen for the limited selection of works illustrated in this volume; it also represents our fine stock of 176 Genoese drawings that were almost without exception, acquired in 1872 from the Marchese Durazzo's Collection by the "Vorstand des königlichen Kupferstichkabinetts", Karl August Kräutle. The acquisition included a brush drawing by Castiglione, which along with the works in the Schloß Fachsenfeld Collection (cats. 1967, 1978) form a substantial ensemble. Not to be forgotten however, his shimmering etchings (see cat., "Meisterwerke alter Druckgraphik aus der Staatsgalerie Stuttgart", 1982, No. 152, 153).
Castiglione's Campagna landscape — the vista before the gates of Rome, with the Cestius Pyramid at the centre of the middle ground — embodies the "ideal" landscape type. Its first master was Annibale Carracci (1560–1609), from whose late period we have a sketch of a sunset by the sea in romantic undertones (ill. 10, p. 212). Castiglione's landscape here is closer to the classical, both in topography and composition. Two Northerners were similarly inspired by the Roman landscape before Castiglione, Paul Bril, who died 1626 in Rome, and Adam Elsheimer, who also died in Rome in 1610. Their invention was the repoussoir of trees, dominating the foreground with their dark washes and leading the eye into the picture as well as the tiny figures moving through the landscape. Among Castiglione's contemporaries, it is once again northern artists such as Breenbergh (1600–1657) and Rembrandt who have more understanding for Castiglione's concept of nature than the French artists Poussin and Lorrain. Only in the 19th century is the artistic experience of this southern landscape taken up again, and then mainly by the Germans working in Rome (cf. Blechen's Tempelruine and Feuerbach's Villa d'Este, plates 21 and 23 in this volume).

Literatur: Christel Thiem, Neubestimmte
italienische Zeichnungen in der Graphischen
Sammlung der Staatsgalerie Stuttgart, in:
Jahrbuch der Staatlichen Kunstsammlungen in
Baden-Württemberg, VI, 1969, S. 189 ff. — Ann
Percy, A Castiglione Album, Master Drawings,
VI, 1968, p. 144 ff., Abb. 36. — Christel Thiem,
Italienische Zeichnungen 1500—1800,
Bestandskatalog Graphische Sammlung
Staatsgalerie Stuttgart, 1977, Nr. 67.

Bibliography: Christel Thiem, "Neubestimmte
italienische Zeichnungen in der Graphischen
Sammlung der Staatsgalerie Stuttgart" in
Jahrbuch der Staatlichen Kunstsammlung in
Baden-Württemberg VI (1969), 189 ff.; Anne
Percy, "A Castiglione Album", Master
Drawings VI (1968), 144 ff., ill. 36; Christel
Thiem, Italienische Zeichnungen 1550—1800,
Bestands Katalog Graphische Sammlung
Staatsgalerie Stuttgart (1977), No. 67.

Giambattista Tiepolo

Geboren 1696 als Sohn des Kaufmanns Domenico Tiepolo in Venedig. 1719 heiratet er die Schwester der Maler Antonio und Francesco Guardi. 1727 wird sein erster Sohn und wichtigster Mitarbeiter Domenico geboren, 1736 der zweite Sohn Lorenzo. Mit beiden trifft er im Dezember 1750 in Würzburg ein, um den Kaisersaal und dann das Treppenhaus der Residenz auszumalen. — Im November 1753 kehren sie nach Venedig zurück. 1762 werden sie nach Madrid berufen, wo Giambattista 1770 verstorben ist.

13

Hagar und Ismael vom Engel getröstet

Entstanden um 1732
Feder in Bister laviert über Bleistiftskizze,
41 × 28 cm
Unbezeichnet. Links der Mitte ergänzte
Fehlstelle. An den vier Ecken abgeschrägt.
Spätere Aufschrift in Blei rechts unten:
Gio. Batta Tiepolo. —
Rückseitig beschriftet: 3.f.C.M. No. 2826
(in Blei 622). — Es handelt sich um eine
Preisschätzung in österreichischer Währung,
wie sie in Venedig seit dem Frieden von
Campoformio, 1797, eingeführt worden
war; sie dürfte von dem 1804 verstorbenen
Sohn Domenico stammen und findet sich —
gleich wie die laufende vierstellige Nummer
— auf allen Tiepolo-Zeichnungen aus der
Sammlung Bossi-Beyerlen, der die unseren
entstammen:
»3.f.« bedeutet: 3 florin (zu je 60 Kreutzern),
»C.M.«: Conventions Münze.
Herkunft: Giovanni Domenico Bossi,
Münchner Hofmaler 1765—1853; dessen
Tochter Maria Theresa Karoline (geboren
1825 in Wien, seit 1853 in Stuttgart mit
Karl Christian Friedrich Beyerlen
verheiratet, gestorben 1881 in Stuttgart). —
1882 Auktion H.G. Gutekunst, Stuttgart,
dort vom »Vorstand des Kgl.
Kupferstichkabinetts«, Karl August Kräutle,
erworben.
Inv. Nr. 1423

Die Geschichte von der Flucht der Magd Hagar mit ihrem von Abraham gezeugten Sohn Ismael, den sie hier ermattet im Schoß hält, und der tröstenden Weisung eines Engels, wieder heimzukehren, wird im 16. Kapitel des 1. Buches Mose erzählt; ihr Klang wird von Tiepolo genau getroffen — die Atmosphäre der äußeren und der inneren Situation. Es gibt ein Gemälde von ihm zu diesem Thema, auch aus dem Beginn der 30er Jahre; es steht auf einer Staffelei in der Scuola di San Rocco zu Venedig (inmitten all der Riesenbilder Tintorettos), man bewundert die Brillanz des Kolorits, die Kostbarkeit des Stofflichen und die Beleuchtungseffekte, aber man ist nicht betroffen: die zusammengedrängte Komposition ist mehr eine Inszenierung als ein überirdisches Ereignis. Unserer Zeichnung bleibt es durch den aufstrebenden Diagonalzug, durch die sich treffenden Blicke und die Schwerelosigkeit der Lavierung vorbehalten, das Wunder der Erscheinung des Engels, einer Vorform der neutestamentlichen Verkündigung an Maria, glaubhaft zu machen.

Käme ein einziges Blatt von solcher Qualität heute auf den Markt, so würde es einen sechsstelligen Preis kosten; 1882, vor 100 Jahren also, erwarb Kräutle 20 dieser »Federskizzen in Sepia«, als sogenanntes Lot, auf einen Schlag (Nr. 1—20 im Stuttgarter Katalog von 1970). Zum Schluß hatte er 416 Goldmark für 168 Zeichnungen von Vater und Sohn Tiepolo zu zahlen. Dadurch erhielt Stuttgart nächst Leningrad, London, New York und Triest eine der großen Tiepolo-Sammlungen der Welt, zu der inzwischen auch vier Gemälde gehören (siehe Seite 106, Tafel 18).

Giambattista Tiepolo

Born in 1696, the son of a merchant, Domenico Tiepolo, in Venice. In 1719 he married the sister of the painters, Antonio and Francesco Guardi; their first son, Domenico, later his most important collaborator, was born in 1727. Their second son, Lorenzo, was born in 1736. In 1750 he arrived in Würzburg with his sons, to decorate the Kaisersaal and then the staircase of the Residenz. They returned to Venice in 1753. In 1762, they were called to Madrid; Giambattista died there in 1770.

13

Hagar and Ishmael comforted by the Angel

About 1732
Pen and bistre washed over pencil sketch, 41 × 28 cm. Unsigned. Left of centre, a repaired hole. The four corners trimmed off obliquely. Later inscription in lead, below right,
Gio. Batta Tiepolo; inscribed on reverse, 3.f.C.M. No. 2826 (in lead, 622). The figures reflect an estimate in Austrian currency, as introduced in Venice upon the Treaty of Campoformio in 1797.
It may be from the hand of Tiepolo's son, Domenico, who died in 1804, and is to be found along with the continuous four-figured numbering, on all Tiepolo drawings from the Bossi-Beyerlen Collection — the source of our own.
"3.f." stands for three florins (at 60 Kreutzer each),
"C. M." for Conventions Münze (conventional coin).
Provenance: Giovanni Domenico Bossi, Court Painter at Munich, 1765–1853; his daughter, Maria Theresa Karoline (b. in Vienna in 1825; in Stuttgart from 1853, married to Karl Christian Friedrich Beyerlen; d. in Stuttgart, 1881); 1882, auction at H. G. Gutekunst's, Stuttgart, where purchased by Karl August Kräutle, "Chairman of the Royal Copper Engraving Collection".
Inv. No. 1423

The story of the flight of Abraham's maidservant, Hagar, with Ishmael, her son by him, the exhausted child she is here depicted holding on her lap, and of the angel who reassures her that God has seen their plight, "opening her eyes" to a nearby well, is told in Genesis 21, 17. Tiepolo captures exactly the tone of the narrative, the atmosphere of the inner as well as the outward situation. On an easel in the Scuola di San Rocco at Venice is a painting of his on the same subject (amidst all those enormous Tintoretto paintings), also completed in the early 1730s. There one wonders at the brilliant palette, the precious material and lighting effects — but one is not in awe, the compressed composition being more a stage-set than an supernatural event. This our drawing is, by virtue of the upward-soaring diagonal, the glances of the angel and Hagar meeting, the weightlessness of the washes of colour; qualities which quite suspend disbelief in the miracle of the angel's appearing, as if in an Old Testament precursor to the Annunciation of the New.

A single sheet of this quality on the market today would fetch six-figure prices; a century ago, in 1882, Kräutle acquired twenty of these "sketches in pen and sepia" in what auctioneers would call one "lot" — literally (nos. 1–20 in the Stuttgart catalogue of 1970). The transaction ended with Kräutle's paying 416 gold marks for 168 drawings by Tiepolo father and son. It blessed Stuttgart with one of the great collections of their work (the others are in Leningrad, London, New York and Trieste), to which four paintings have since been added (cf. p. 106, plate 18).

Literatur: Tiepolo, Zeichnungen von
Giambattista, Domenico und Lorenzo Tiepolo
aus der Graphischen Sammlung der
Staatsgalerie Stuttgart, aus württembergischem
Privatbesitz und dem Martin-von-Wagner-
Museum der Universität Würzburg, bearbeitet
von George Knox und Christel Thiem, Katalog
der Staatsgalerie Stuttgart 1970 (1971 erschien
eine Auflage in Englisch), Nr. 7 (Abbildung als
Frontispiz) mit Angabe der früheren Œuvre-
Verzeichnisse: Molmenti 1909, p. 241, Nr. 1. —
Sack 1910, Nr. 220, repr. 266. — Hadeln 1927,
repr. 108.

Bibliography: Tiepolo, Zeichnungen von
Giambattista, Domenico und Lorenzo Tiepolo
aus der Graphischen Sammlung der
Staatsgalerie Stuttgart, aus württembergischem
Privatbesitz und dem Martin von Wagner
Museum der Universität Würzburg, eds
George Knox and Christel Thiem, catalogue
Staatsgalerie Stuttgart (1970; English edn,
1971), No. 7 (ill. as frontispiece) with
details of earlier catalogues raisonnés, i. e.,
Molmenti (1909), p. 241, No. 1; Sack (1910),
No. 220, repr. 266; Hadeln (1927),
repr. 108.

Giambattista Tiepolo

(Venedig 1696—Madrid 1770)

Biographie siehe Nummer 13

14

Kniender Mohr mit Sonnenschirm

Entstanden 1752/53
Rötel und weiße Kreide auf blauem Papier,
37,5 × 26,5 cm
Unbezeichnet.
Rückseitig beschriftet:
No. 3094 1 f. C. M.
(siehe dazu bei der vorigen Nummer).
Herkunft wie die vorhergehende
Tiepolo-Zeichnung.
Inv. Nr. 1470

Giambattista Tiepolo

(Venice, 1696—Madrid, 1770)

Biography: see No. 13

14

Kneeling Moor with Parasol

Dated 1752/53
Ruddle and white chalk on blue paper,
37.5 × 26.5 cm
Unsigned.
Inscribed on reverse, No. 3094 1f.C.M.
(cf. No. 13 above). Provenance as No. 13.
Inv. No. 1470

Im Treppenhaus der Würzburger Residenz malte Giambattista Tiepolo mit seinen beiden Söhnen innerhalb von 15 Monaten das große Fresko der vier Erdteile; darin wird Afrika von einer Negerfürstin verkörpert, vor der ein Mohr kniet, dessen Entwurf wir hier vor uns haben. Als »Nebenfigur« erscheint er in Rückenansicht mit verlorenem Profil, einen Köcher mit Pfeilen auf dem Rücken, in der Rechten hält er den Sonnenschirm für seine Gebieterin, mit der Linken streckt er ihr ein Weihrauchgefäß entgegen, während sie frontal auf einem Kamel vor einem Zelt thront. Da wir weitere 30 Rötelzeichnungen zu diesem größten und — man darf wohl sagen gelungensten — Deckenfresko Tiepolos besitzen, läßt sich feststellen, daß er dem reich gewandeten Mohren keine geringere zeichnerische Brillanz verliehen hat als der entblößten Stammesfürstin. Die Weißhöhungen blitzen nur so auf dem satten Rötel über dem lichtblauen Blattgrund. —

Das Zusammentreffen des genialsten Freskanten Italiens im Jahre 1750 mit dem bedeutendsten Baumeister Deutschlands, Balthasar Neumann in Würzburg, gehört zu den Sternstunden in der Geschichte der bildenden Künste; die Erwerbung der insgesamt 168, teilweise auch rückseitig bearbeiteten Blätter von Vater und Sohn Tiepolo im Jahre 1882 durch Karl August Kräutle gehört zu den Sternstunden des »königlichen Kupferstichkabinetts« in Stuttgart. Und daß die Würzburger Residenz 1944 im Bombenhagel zwar getroffen wurde, aber nicht zugrunde ging, ist ein Glück nicht nur für sie selbst als unersetzliches Gesamtkunstwerk, sondern auf immer für unsere Vorstellung von der Kultur des Abendlands in ihrem letzten europäischen Zenit.

It took Giambattista and his two sons no more than fifteen months to paint the large fresco of the four continents that decorates the staircase of the Residenz at Würzburg. In it, Africa is epitomised by a Negro princess, before whom a Moor kneels. This is the sketch for him. As a "secondary figure", we see him from behind in profil perdu, strung across his back a quiver of arrows, in his right hand the parasol for his sovereign while in his left he extends to her a censer; in the painting she sits enthroned upon a camel, in front view, before a tent. From our thirty further ruddle drawings for this largest, and, it will be readily affirmed, most successful of Tiepolo's ceiling frescoes, it is evident that he devoted no lesser brilliance of draughtsmanship to the splendidly clad Moor than to the naked tribal princess. White highlights flash scintillating across the full-bodied red chalk on the light-blue ground of the paper.

The meeting of the most inspired frescopainter in Italy and the most significant German architect, Balthasar Neumann, in Würzburg in 1750 was one of the most propitious events in the history of art; of like significance for the "Royal Copper Engraving Collection" in Stuttgart, was Karl August Kräutle's acquisition of sheets of drawings by Tiepolo, father and son, some of them worked on both sides, 168 sheets in all, in 1882. Finally, the fact that, though hit in bombing raids in 1944, the Residenz at Würzburg was not destroyed, was a stroke of luck not only for the building itself as an irreplaceable Gesamtkunstwerk, but also one of eternal value for our conception of Occidental culture in its last European zenith.

Literatur: Tiepolo-Katalog Stuttgart 1970 (siehe vorige Nummer), Nr. 85, Farbtafel S. 91; Molmenti 1909, p. 239, 1. Album, folio 4; Sack 1910, Nr. 300. — Hadeln 1927, repr. 145. — George Knox, Giambattista and Domenico Tiepolo, A study and Catalogue Raisonné of the Chalk Drawings, Clarendon Press Oxford 1980, Vol. I, M. 358, Pl. 146.

Bibliography: Tiepolo cat. Stuttgart (1970; see No. 13 above), No. 85, colour plate p. 91; Molmenti (1909), p. 239, 1st Album, folio 4; Sack (1910), No. 300; Hadeln (1927), repr. 145; George Knox, Giambattista and Domenico Tiepolo, A study and Catalogue Raisonné of the Chalk Drawings (Clarendon Press, Oxford, 1980), vol. I, M. 358, Pl. 146.

Honoré Daumier

Geboren 1808 in Marseille, als Junge Laufbursche bei einem Gerichtsvollzieher, nimmt Zeichen- und Malunterricht, lebt aber von seinen Lithographien, wird wegen politischer Karikaturen in Le Charivari 1832 zu einem halben Jahr Gefängnis verurteilt. 1856–1860 Bekanntschaft mit den Malern Corot und Millet. Seit 1873 Nachlassen der Sehkraft, 1879 in Valmondois gestorben.

15

Ein Advokat und seine Klientin

Entstanden um 1860
Schwarze Kreide, Aquarell und Deckfarbe auf hellgrau getöntem Bütten, aufgezogen, 21,9 × 17,8 cm
Bezeichnet oben links: H. Daumier
Herkunft laut Maison: Slg. Royer, Paris. – Decaux(?). – Eissler. – Ferner: Prochazka, New York. – Schweizer Kunsthandel.
Inv. Nr. C 64/1285

Honoré Daumier

Born in Marseilles, 1808. A bailiff's assistant while still a boy, took lessons in drawing and painting; earnt his living from his lithographs, goaled for six months in 1832 for his political caricatures in Le Charivari. Friendship with the painters, Corot and Millet, 1856–60. His eyesight deteriorated from 1873; died at Valmondois in 1879.

15

An Advocate and his Client

About 1860
Black chalk, water-colour and body colour on light-grey tinted handmade paper, mounted, 21.9 × 17.8 cm
Signed above left, H. Daumier
Provenance according to Maison: Coll. Royer, Paris; Decaux(?); Eissler; also Prochazka, New York; Swiss art market.
Inv. No. C 64/1285

Daumier ist in diesen Band ausgewählter Zeichnungen und Aquarelle nicht als Karikaturist aufgenommen worden, sondern als Künstler von Rang. Das eine schließt das andere nicht aus, trifft aber nur selten zusammen. Erst Daumier hob durch sein hohes Niveau de facto die Grenze zwischen Karikatur und Kunst auf. Die Karikaturen, denen er seine Popularität verdankt – über 4000 Blatt, davon sind 1250 Lithographien aus der Sammlung Loncle in Stuttgart vorhanden – waren sein Brotverdienst, aber schon früh in den 1830er Jahren setzt sein plastisches Werk mit den entlarvenden Büsten der Pariser Parlamentarier ein, und es drängte ihn immer, ein Maler zu sein, was ihm nur zwischen 1856 und 1860 vergönnt war. Aus diesem Zeitraum stammt unser Blatt, das sich durch intensive malerische Behandlung mit lasierenden und deckenden Farben über der Kreideskizze auszeichnet. Stahlblau ist der dominierende Farbton, undurchdringlich in der Robe des feisten Advokaten, transparent in der changierenden Mantille der puppenhaften Frau – sie scheint dem maliziösen Ungeheuer ausgeliefert zu sein, zugleich lockt sie ihn mit der roten Blume im Haar, dem Point de Vue des Bildes. Der dritte im Bunde, ein Kollege des Anwalts, rechts im Profil hämisch lachend, scheint sich sein Teil über diese Affäre zu denken; eine im Motiv verwandte Lithographie von 1864 trägt den Titel: »Une affaire d'adultère« (eine Ehebruchsgeschichte; Delteil No. 3333). – Aber es bedarf keiner Erklärung; so amüsant die zumeist von Daumiers Verleger Philipon zu den Karikaturen erfundenen »Bon mots« sein mögen, lenken sie doch von der Zeitlosigkeit der tiefer eindringenden bildnerischen Sprache ab. Daumier hat das selbst so empfunden und im Freundeskreis geäußert: »Wenn meine Zeichnung Euch nichts sagt, so heißt das, daß sie schlecht ist; die Legende wird sie deshalb nicht besser machen. Wenn sie gut ist, versteht Ihr sie von selbst – wozu dann also die Legende?«

Daumier's place in this volume of selected drawings and water-colours is not that of the caricaturist, but of an artist of eminence. One does not exclude the other, but the two qualities rarely coincide. It took the standard of a Daumier to raise by its very nature the borders between caricature and art. The caricatures to which he still owes his popularity – more than four thousand, of which 1250 lithographs from the Loncle Collection are at Stuttgart – were his bread and butter; but by the early 1830s he had already begun his sculptural œuvre with the revealing busts of Parisian government ministers. He always yearned to be a painter, a desire he was to fulfil only between 1856 and 1860. Our water-colour comes from this period. It is conspicuous for its intense, painterly handling in glazes and opaque body colour over the chalk sketch. Steely blue is the dominant colour, impenetrable in the obese advocate's gown, transparent in the iridescent tones of the doll-like woman's mantilla. She seems to be at the mercy of the malicious monster she simultaneously tempts with the red flower in her hair which is the viewpoint of the picture. The third party in the scene, a colleague of the lawyer's, occupies the right margin of the picture in profile and, with a knowing sneer, seems to have his own thoughts on the affair. A lithograph of 1864 on a related subject bears the title, "Une affaire d'adultère" ("A Tale of Adultery"; Delteil No. 3333). – Not that an explanation is necessary; amusing though the bon mots might be which Daumier's publisher, Philipon, mostly supplied for his caricatures, they detract from the timelessness of the more penetrating visual language. Daumier himself thought and said as much to his friends: "If my drawing conveys nothing to you, it must be bad; no caption will make it better. If the drawing is good, you'll be able to understand it anyway – so what is the point of a caption then?"

Literatur: Eduard Fuchs, Der Maler Daumier, München 1927, S. 54, Abb. 196a. – K.E. Maison, Honoré Daumier, Catalogue raisonné, Vol. II, 1968, Nr. 615, Pl. 232. – Katalog der Ausstellung: Von Ingres bis Picasso, Französische Zeichnungen des 19. und 20. Jahrhunderts aus der Graphischen Sammlung der Staatsgalerie Stuttgart, 1969, Nr. 28, Farbtafel. – Ulrike Gauß, Bestandskatalog der Zeichnungen und Aquarelle des 19. Jahrhunderts in der Graphischen Sammlung der Staatsgalerie Stuttgart, 1976, Nr. und Abbildung 167 mit weiterer Bibliographie. – Honoré Daumier, Kunst und Karikatur, Ausstellungskatalog Bremen, 1980, Nr. und Abb. 8.

Bibliography: Eduard Fuchs, Der Maler Daumier (Munich, 1927), p. 54, ill. 196a; K.E. Maison, Honoré Daumier, Catalogue raisonné, vol. II (1968), No. 615, Pl. 232; exh. cat., Von Ingres bis Picasso, Französische Zeichnungen des 19. und 20. Jahrhunderts aus der Graphischen Sammlung der Staatsgalerie Stuttgart (1969), No. 28, colour plate; Ulrike Gauss, Bestandskatalog der Zeichnungen und Aquarelle des 19. Jahrhunderts in der Graphischen Sammlung der Staatsgalerie Stuttgart (1976), No. and ill. 167 with further bibliography; Honoré Daumier, Kunst und Karikatur, exh. cat. (Bremen, 1980), No. and ill. 8.

Odilon Redon

Geboren 1840 in Bordeaux, durch Rodolphe Bresdin 1864 in die graphischen Techniken eingeführt, am stärksten beeindruckt durch die mythische Bildwelt Moreaus (1826–1898), befreundet mit den Dichtern des Symbolismus Huysmans und Mallarmé, später mit den »Nabis«, den Malern Denis, Bonnard, Vuillard, deren Wortführer er nach Gauguins Emigration 1891 wurde. Um 1900 endet sein graphisches Schaffen. 1916 in Paris verstorben.

16

La naissance de la pensée

Die Geburt des Gedankens

Entstanden um 1885
Kohle, Kreide, Rötel auf naturfarbenem
Papier mit rötlichen Fasern, fixiert und
gebräunt, 52,5 × 37,7 cm
Bezeichnet unten rechts zweimal in
Ligatur: odR
Herkunft: Galerie Georges Bernier, Paris. –
Privatsammlung Paris. – Paul Rosenberg,
New York. – Schweizer Kunsthandel.
Inv. Nr. C 79/2928

Odilon Redon

Born in Bordeaux in 1840, introduced to printmaking techniques by Rodolphe Bresdin in 1864; the strongest influence on him was the mythical iconography of Moreau (1826–98); a friend of the Symbolist poets, Huysmans and Mallarmé, and later of the "Nabis" – the painters Denis, Bonnard and Vuillard, whose spokesman he became upon Gauguin's emigration in 1891. His graphic output came to a standstill in 1900. Died in Paris in 1916.

16

La naissance de la pensée

The Birth of Thought

About 1885
Charcoal, chalk, ruddle, on natural paper
with reddish fibre, fixed and darkened.
52.5 × 37.7 cm
Signed twice in ligature, below right, odR
Provenance: Galerie Georges Bernier,
Paris; private collection, Paris; Paul
Rosenberg, New York; Swiss art dealers.
Inv. No. C 79/2928

Redon stand gegen den Impressionismus, dessen Generation er angehörte. »Le Noir est la couleur la plus essentielle . . . Il est agent de l'esprit«, schrieb er, der seine Kohlezeichnungen und schwarzen Lithographien »Mes Noirs« nannte; sie bilden den Schwerpunkt seines Schaffens bis 1890; der Tiefe ihrer Aussage ist man sich erst in jüngerer Zeit sub specie der »Traumdeutungen« Sigmund Freuds und des Surrealismus bewußt geworden. Obwohl Redon in der Spätzeit farbig arbeitete, erklärte er noch 1913: »Das Schwarz läßt sich nicht prostituieren . . . Die graphischen Sammlungen im Louvre enthalten eine Menge weitaus größerer reinerer Kunst als die Gemäldesammlungen.« Seine frühen Freunde waren weniger Maler als vielmehr Naturwissenschaftler und Dichter; er illustrierte Flaubert und E. A. Poe, studierte Rembrandt und Goya und traute der Musik irrationale Kräfte zu.

Redons Devise »Man sollte jede Schöpfung mit einem Geheimnis umkleiden«, weist auf die Grenzen des Verständnisses dieser im Bereich des Visionären angesiedelten Invention: Aus einer samtschwarzen Muschelform mit einer Aureole tritt ein introvertiertes Gesicht; man könnte an einen Mönch mit Kutte denken; aber es ist eine Erscheinung ohne Körper und Glieder, aus ihrer Mitte leuchtet wie ein Gestirn ein Strahlenkranz.

Das Traumhafte ist Redons Element, spätestens seit seinem Zyklus »Dans le rêve« (1879); aber was bedeutet das alles? – Die Strahlensonne auf der Brust zu tragen, ist unter den Heiligen Bernhard von Clairvaux und dem Bernhard von Siena vorbehalten; die Muschel ist seit der Antike Symbol der Schöpfung; und die Versunkenheit der schwerelosen Gestalt läßt an Verkörperungen buddhistischer Transzendenz denken. Man kann die einzelnen Motive auch sonst in Redons Werk nachweisen (eine Buddha-Lithographie schuf er 1895), hier aber hat er durchaus eine Synthese gestaltet, die dem hohen Anspruch seines Bildtitels »La Naissance de la Pensée« gerecht wird. – Und sollte er als Franzose nicht den Titel des Lebenswerkes von Pascal im Sinne gehabt haben: »Pensées«?! – Darüber hinaus liegt in Redons Verkörperung des Schöpfungsgedankens eine spezifisch symbolistische Note: die Melancholie. Sie resultiert aus dem Bewußtsein der Unvollkommenheit eines jeden Werkes gegenüber seiner ersten Idee; ihre Reinheit und Identität mit dem Schöpfer geht während des Schaffensprozesses verloren. So trägt die Geburt schon den Tod in sich.

Mit diesen Hinweisen ist Redons Schöpfung gewiß noch nicht ausgelotet. In kunstgeschichtlicher Hinsicht dürfen zwei gleichzeitige Meister des »Blanc et Noir« nicht ignoriert werden: Degas (1834–1917), der besonders in seinen Monotypien das Schwarz dämonisierte, und Seurat (1859 bis 1891), der von analytischen Denkprozessen ausgehend schon in den frühen 80er Jahren luzide Kohlezeichnungen schuf, die allein aus der Form und Wahl der Tonstufen ihre Faszination beziehen.

Redon was against Impressionism, though he belonged to that generation. "Le Noir est la couleur la plus essentielle . . . Il est agent de l'esprit", wrote the artist who called his charcoal drawings and lithographs "Mes Noirs". These are at the centre of his work until 1890; awareness of their depth of content has come only relatively recently come about in the wake of Freud's "Interpretation of Dreams" and of Surrealism. Though Redon turned to colour late in life, he still claimed in 1913, "Black will not be prostituted . . . the collections of prints and drawings at the Louvre contain a good deal of art by far greater and purer than the collections of paintings." His early friends were not so much painters as scientists and poets; he illustrated Flaubert and E. A. Poe and studied Rembrandt and Goya; to music he attributed irrational powers.

Redon's guiding principle, "Every creation ought to be clothed in a secret", implies the limits of rational comprehension of this invention whose place is within the realm of the visionary. – Out of a velvet-black shell-shape with an aureole, emerges an introverted face; a monk with a cowl comes to mind – but it is an apparition lacking body and limbs, a nimbus glowing star-like from its centre.

The dream-bound is Redon's element, beginning at the latest with his cycle, "Dans le rêve", of 1879; but what does all this signify? To bear the radiant sun upon his chest is the prerogative, among the saints, of Bernard of Clairvaux and Bernard of Siena; since Antiquity the cockle-shell has been a symbol of creation; while the pensive look of the weightless figure calls up Buddhist transcendence materialised. It is possible to locate individual aspects of this picture in Redon's other works (there is a Buddha lithograph of 1895), but here he has fused them into a synthesis which matches the high claim of his title, "La naissance de la pensée". The Frenchman Redon must have known the title of Pascal's life's work Pensées! All this apart, there is in Redon's incarnation of the notion of creation, a particularly Symbolist tone, that of melancholy. It arises from the awareness of the imperfection of any and every work in comparison to the original idea, whose purity and identity with its creator is lost in the process of creation. Thus birth already bears death within it.

These associations certainly cannot completely define Redon's creation. From an art-historical viewpoint, two contemporary masters of the "blanc et noir" should not be ignored – Degas (1834–1917), whose monotypes especially mystify the quality of black, and Seurat (1859–91), who, setting out from analytical thinking, had already created in the early 1880s lucid charcoal drawings whose fascination springs solely from their form and the choice of tonal gradations.

Literatur: Ausstellungskataloge: Les maîtres du dessin 1820—1920, Galerie Bernard Lorenceau, Paris 1968, Kat. Nr. 46 — Dessins et aquarelles du XIXe siècle, Galerie L'Œil, Paris 1970, Kat. Nr. 57 mit Abbildung.

Bibliography: Exhibition catalogues: Les maîtres du dessin 1820—1920, Galerie Bernard Lorenceau (Paris, 1968), cat. no. 46; Dessins et aquarelles du XIXe siècle, Galerie L'Œil (Paris, 1970), cat. no. 57, with ill.

Paul Cézanne

Geboren 1839 in Aix-en-Provence, wo er 1860/61 die Zeichenakademie besuchte; nach vergeblichem Versuch seiner Aufnahme in die Pariser Ecole des Beaux Arts lernte er im »Atelier Suisse«; 1874 und 1877 Teilnahme an der Impressionisten-Ausstellung, stößt jedoch auf Ablehnung und zieht sich 1879 nach Aix zurück, wo er — nach ersten Erfolgen in den 90er Jahren — 1906 verstorben ist.

17

Bords d'une Rivière

Flußufer

Entstanden um 1880
Aquarell über Bleistift auf vergilbtem
Bütten, Wasserzeichen MICHALLET,
ringsum bräunliche Lichtränder,
32,2 × 49,2 cm
Herkunft: Sammlung Ambroise Vollard,
Paris und M. Bromford, London. —
Privatbesitz Paris. — Schweizer
Kunsthandel.
Inv. Nr. C 74/2377

Paul Cézanne

Born in Aix-en-Provence in 1839, attended the Academy of Drawing, 1860/61. After attempting unsuccessfully to gain acceptance at the École des Beaux Arts in Paris, he studied at the "Atelier Suisse". Took part in the Impressionist Exhibitions of 1874 and 1877, but met with rejection; withdrew to Aix, 1879, where, after success in the 1890s, he died, in 1906.

17

Bords d'une Rivière

Riverbank

About 1880
Water-colour over pencil on yellowed
handmade paper with rough edges,
watermarked MICHALLET, edges
browned by exposure to light;
32.2 × 49.2 cm
Provenance: Collection Ambroise Vollard,
Paris, and M. Bromford, London; private
ownership, Paris; Swiss art market.
Inv. No. C 74/2377

Cézanne verlebte von 1879 bis 1882 die Herbstmonate auf dem Landsitz seines Freundes, des Schriftstellers Emile Zola: Médan heißt dieser 40 Kilometer von Paris gelegene Ort am Ufer der Seine. »Um in ganzer Breite das Seine-Ufer in den Blick zu bekommen, hatte er sich als Standort die teilweise zum Zolaschen Besitz gehörende Insel Platais gewählt.« Aufgrund von Götz Adrianis Tübinger Katalog (S. 61) können wir den Zeit- und Blickpunkt dieses Aquarells erstmalig so fixieren. Seine scheinbare Unfertigkeit ist Absicht, seine farbige Zartheit auch, aber sie dürfte sich im Lauf der Zeit noch verstärkt haben. Es gibt reichere Aquarelle Cézannes, aber — im Blick auf die Kunst unseres Jahrhunderts — kaum progressivere. Seine bildnerische Askese wird den sensiblen Betrachter stimulieren, wie schon Lionello Venturi in seinem Œuvrekatalog von 1936: »Puissance extraordinaire de suggestion, due à la rareté des touches, et à la complexité de l'effet obtenu des moyens matériels limités.«

Die Horizontale des Flußufers bringt Stille ins Bild; es gibt nur einen vertikalen Schnittpunkt, den mit der Baumgruppe und ihrem Spiegelbild. Damit das Bild durch diese Doppelung nicht rechtslastig wird, steht links der Mitte eine kleinere Baumgruppe und sind die Bildachsen durch die abgetreppten Umrisse von Giebelhäusern diagonal verzahnt. Der fast geraden Uferlinie unten antwortet die sanft geschwungene eines Höhenzuges oben. Alles bleibt in der Bildfläche. Dabei haben auch die leeren Flächen Funktion und Bedeutung. Sie vermitteln den Eindruck von Raum und Licht, sie steigern das meditative Element spiegelnden Wassers. Man kann die bewußte Leere auch existentiell interpretieren, wie Ursula Perucchi im genannten Katalog (S. 9): »Ähnlich wie bei den Ostasiaten weist bei ihm das Fragmentarische auf einen größeren Zusammenhang hin, letztlich auf das nicht mehr darstellbare Ganze.« Solches trifft in erhöhtem Maße auf unser späteres Cézanne-Aquarell zu: den »Pistazienbaum im Hof des Château Noir«.

Cézanne spent the autumn months of every year from 1879 to 1882 at the country estate of his friend, the writer, Emile Zola. Médan lies forty kilometres from Paris, on the banks of the Seine. "To gain a view of the Seine's bank in panoramic width, he had chosen as his standpoint the isle of Platais, part of which belonged to Zola's grounds." It is thanks to Götz Adriani's catalogue for Tübingen (p. 61) that we are able for the first time to establish both time and location of this water-colour so specifically. Its apparent unfinished state, like its delicacy of colour, is intentional; time may have further enhanced that effect. There are richer water-colours by Cézanne, but, looking forward to the art of our own century, hardly any as progressive. His pictorial asceticism will provoke the sensitive viewer today as did Lionello Venturi in his catalogue raisonné of 1936: "Puissance extraordinaire de suggestion, due à la rareté des touches, et à la complexité de l'effet obtenu des moyens matériels limités."

The horizontal of the riverbank introduces a calm into the picture; there is but one vertical to intersect it, in the clump of trees and their reflection. Then, preventing the composition from tipping down to the right, a smaller group of trees stands to the left of centre, while the gradated contours of the gabled houses interlock the axes of the picture diagonally. The almost straight shoreline below finds an echo in the gentle undulation of the line of hills above. Everything remains on the picture plane, in which the "blank" areas are as functional and significant as the others. They convey the impression of space and light, heightening the meditative element of the reflecting water surface. The conscious use of space can also be interpreted philosophically, as Ursula Perucchi has done (G. Adriani 1982, p. 9): "Rather as in Oriental art, the fragmentary in his own indicates a greater context and ultimately the whole, which eschews depiction." This applies even more to our late Cézanne water-colour, the "Pistachio in the Courtyard of Château Noir".

Literatur: Lionello Venturi, Cézanne, son art — son œuvre, Paris 1936, Nr. 1074, Abb. in Bd. 2, Tafel 312. — Jahrbuch der Staatlichen Kunstsammlungen in Baden-Württemberg, Bd. 12, 1975, S. 360, Abb. 15. — Ulrike Gauß, Die Zeichnungen und Aquarelle des 19. Jahrhunderts in der Graphischen Sammlung der Staatsgalerie Stuttgart, 1976, S. 22, Abb. Nr. 1635. — Götz Adriani, Paul Cézanne, Aquarelle, Katalog Tübingen und Zürich 1982, Nr. und Abb. 19.

Bibliography: Lionello Venturi, Cézanne, son art — son œuvre (Paris, 1936), No. 1074, ill. in vol. 2, pl. 312; Jahrbuch der Staatlichen Kunstsammlungen in Baden-Württemberg XII (1975) 360, ill. 15; Ulrike Gauss, Die Zeichnungen und Aquarelle des 19. Jahrhunderts in der Graphischen Sammlung der Staatsgalerie Stuttgart (1976), p. 22, ill. No. 1635; Gotz Adriani, Paul Cézanne, Aquarelle, cat. (Tübingen & Zürich, 1982), No. and ill. 19.

283

Vincent Willem van Gogh

Geboren 1853 als ältester Sohn eines calvinistischen Pastors in Groot-Zundert (Holland). 1869–1876 im Kunsthandel tätig; unstetes Leben u. a. als Laienprediger im Bergwerksgebiet Borinage. 1880 Entschluß, Künstler zu werden. Mit dem Besuch in Paris 1886 bei seinem lebenslang hilfreichen Bruder Theo konstituiert sich sein Stil, der seine Höhe 1888 in Arles erreicht. 1890 nimmt er sich in Auvers-sur-Oise das Leben.

18

»Le Pont de Langlois«

Entstanden Frühjahr 1888
Rohr- und Kielfeder in Braun über
Bleistiftskizze auf gebräuntem Papier,
ringsum bräunliche Lichtränder.
Wasserzeichen: P. L. BAS, 30,7 × 47,7 cm
Herkunft: Frau J. van Gogh-Bonger,
Amsterdam. — Dr. Hugo Cassirer, Berlin. —
1933–1939 Leihgabe im Gemeente
Museum, Den Haag (Kat. 1935, S. 77). —
Familie Cassirer, Johannesburg. — Baronin
Rothschild, New York. — J. K. Thannhauser
Art Gallery, New York. — Arthur
Goldschmidt, Paris. — Schweizer
Kunsthandel.
Inv. Nr. C 67/1491

Wenn man von einem ausländischen Künstler sagen kann, daß er bei uns »volkstümlich« wurde, so nur von Vincent van Gogh; für die Generation der Expressionisten war er eine Vaterfigur, die Jugend liebte ihn — den missionarischen Menschen, den verkannten Künstler. Seine Hauptwerke sind millionenfach reproduziert worden und manch ein Betrachter wird in unserer Zeichnung (auf der folgenden Doppeltafel) die Zugbrücke von Arles wiedererkennen, die van Gogh mehrfach dargestellt hat; sie ist aber nicht vom Ufer her gesehen, wie auf dem Kölner Gemälde (siehe Abbildung gegenüber), sondern von einer Biegung der Straße her, die auf sie zuführt. Man weiß, daß sie nach dem Namen des Brückenwärters »Le Pont de Langlois« hieß, ehe sie im letzten Weltkrieg zerstört wurde; mehrere solcher Brücken überqueren den schiffbaren Kanal, sie sind das Werk eines holländischen Ingenieurs aus der Zeit von 1820 bis 1830 und waren Vincent wohl besonders sympathisch, weil sie ihn an seine Heimat erinnerten; jedenfalls hat er kein Motiv so häufig behandelt wie dieses, aber nie wieder so wie hier.

Das eigentliche Thema der Stuttgarter Zeichnung ist nicht die Brücke, sondern die in verkürzter Perspektive ansteigende Straße; leergefegt unter gleißendem Licht öffnet sie sich in voller Breite dem Betrachter, nur die Schatten von zwei schütteren Bäumchen links züngeln über ihre Fläche; Bordsteine, runde und eckige, die an Grabsteine erinnern, fassen sie ein. Etwas von Aufbruch, vielleicht auch von Sehnsucht — verkörpert in dem ausschreitenden Paar, das mit der Brücke und den Häusern die dominierende Horizontalachse der Komposition bildet, ergreift uns. Van Goghs Briefe aus Arles an seinen Bruder Theo erlauben, von einem durch die südliche Landschaft überwältigten Lebensgefühl zu sprechen; in dem flammenden Zypressenpaar gewinnt es durch die impulsiven Hiebe der Rohrfeder eine für die Erregung des Künstlers spezifische Gestalt.

Noch im Frühjahr 1886 — also zwei Jahre vor unserer Zeichnung — hat die Akademie von Antwerpen van Gogh, der sich dort als Schüler beworben hatte, erklärt, daß er nicht zeichnen könne. Aber so wie er zeichnete ja auch sonst keiner — auch keiner der anderen »Bahnbrecher«: weder Seurat, den er studierte, noch Gauguin, mit dem er zwei Monate im Herbst des Jahres 1888 eine Arbeitsgemeinschaft in Arles versucht hatte, noch Cézanne, der auch in der Provence zurückgezogen lebte; sie alle waren systematischer und ästhetischer als der Holländer, der immer wieder sich aussetzend mit Mühe zur eigenen Form gelangte. Hier hat er sie gefunden, sowohl in dem frappierenden Bildausschnitt als auch im spannungsgeladenen Duktus der Feder. Ein souveränerer Strich ist kaum denkbar, nicht kreisend, das Blatt randvoll füllend wie sonst in den letzten Jahren, sondern kantig bauend, den freien Blattgrund sprechen lassend — wie beim späten Rembrandt.

Vincent Willem van Gogh

Born in 1853, the eldest son of a Calvinist pastor in Groot-Zundert (Holland). 1869 till 76, worked for art dealers; then an unsettled life which included that of a lay preacher in the Dutch mining district of Borinage. In 1880 he resolved to become an artist. His style asserted itself with his visit to his lifelong support, his brother Theo, in Paris in 1886; it reached its highpoint in 1888 at Arles. He took his own life at Auvers-sur-Oise in 1890.

18

"Le Pont de Langlois"

Spring, 1888
Rush and quill pens in brown ink over pencil sketch on brown-toned paper, all edges browned by exposure to light. Watermark P. L. BAS. 30.7 × 47.7 cm Provenance: Mrs. J. van Gogh-Bonger, Amsterdam; Dr. Hugo Cassirer, Berlin; 1933–39, on loan to the Gemeente Museum, The Hague (cat., 1935, p. 77); the Cassirer family, Johannesburg; Baroness de Rothschild, New York; J. K. Thannhauser Art Gallery, New York; Arthur Goldschmidt, Paris; Swiss art market. Inv. No. C 67/1491

If it can be said of any foreign artist that he became part of our own "folklore", then surely and only of van Gogh. For the Expressionists' generation he was a father-figure, the young loved him, the missionary, the unappreciated artist. His main works have been reproduced in millions and many a beholder of the drawing overleaf below will recognise the drawbridge at Arles, which van Gogh drew and painted several times. Here it is not seen from the bank as in the painting at Cologne (see facing page), but from a bend in the road leading to it. We know that it was called "Le Pont de Langlois" after the one-time attendant at the bridge — until it was destroyed in the last War. A number of bridges like it span the navigable canal, all being the work of a Dutch engineer, c. 1820–30 and thus likely to have appealed to Vincent as reminders of his home. He certainly treated this more often than any other subject; but never again as in our drawing.

The actual subject of the Stuttgart drawing is not so much the bridge as the foreshortened view of the rising road. Swept bare under the glowing heat it opens out to the viewer in full breadth, only the shadows of two thin trees tongue across the surface. Kerbstones, round and angular, reminiscent of gravestones, border it. A sense of departure touches us, of presence gone, possibly of longing too, materialised in the couple stepping out onto the bridge with which they and the houses form the dominant horizontal axis of the composition. Van Gogh's

letters from Arles to his brother, Theo, justify our speaking of a sense of life overwhelmed by the southern landscape; in the twin flames of the cypresses, the impulsive strokes of the rush-pen, this has found a form specific to the agitated state of the artist.

It was only two years before the date of this drawing, in the spring of 1886, that the Academy at Antwerp explained to van Gogh upon his applying to study there, that he could not draw. But then no-one drew as he did, the other innovators included — not Seurat, whom he studied, nor Gauguin, with whom he spent two months in an attempt at a working community at Arles in autumn 1888, nor Cézanne, who lived likewise in seclusion in the Provenance. They were all more systematic and aesthetic than the Dutchman, whose way to his own language was always fraught with effort, a continual exposure. That language is articulate here, both in the striking view and the tension-charged pen line. A hand more in command is hardly conceivable — not circling, filling the paper with line to the very edge as in the years leading up to this work, but building up in an angular mode, letting the untouched material support speak: like the later Rembrandt.

Literatur: Julius Meier-Graefe, Vincent van Gogh, München 1922, Bd. II, Tafel 55; ds. Van Gogh als Zeichner, München 1928, Tafel 24. – J.-B. de la Faille, V. van Gogh, Catalogue raisonné, Paris 1928, Bd. III, Nr. 1470; ds. Neuauflage 1970, F 1470, Abb. S. 512. – Von Ingres bis Piacsso, Kat. Staatsgalerie Stuttgart 1969, Nr. 52, Doppeltafel S. 22/23. – Sylvia Rathke-Köhl, van Gogh, Zeichnungen und Aquarelle, Katalog, Frankfurter Kunstverein, 1968, Nr. und Abb. 45. – Ulrike Gauß, Katalog der Zeichnungen und Aquarelle des 19. Jahrhunderts in der Graphischen Sammlung der Staatsgalerie Stuttgart, 1976, Nr. und Abb. 422 mit ausführlicher Bibliographie.

Bibliography: Julius Meier-Graefe, Vincent van Gogh (Munich, 1922), vol. II, pl. 55, & Van Gogh als Zeichner (Munich, 1928), pl. 24; J.-B. de la Faille, V. van Gogh, catalogue raisonné (Paris, 1928) III, No. 1470, new edn (1970), F 1470, ill. p. 512; Von Ingres bis Picasso, cat., Staatsgalerie Stuttgart (1969), No. 52, double pl. p. 22/23; Sylvia Rathke-Köhl, van Gogh, Zeichnungen und Aquarelle, cat., Frankfurter Kunstverein (1968), No. & ill. 45; Ulrike Gauss, Katalog der Zeichnungen und Aquarelle des 19. Jahrhunderts in der Graphischen Sammlung der Staatsgalerie Stuttgart (1976), No. and ill. 422 with detailed bibliography.

Vincent van Gogh, Gemälde der »Zugbrücke
von Arles«, 1888, Wallraf-Richartz-Museum,
Köln.

Vincent van Gogh, painting of the Drawbridge
at Arles, 1888, Wallraf-Richartz-Museum,
Cologne.

18
Vincent van Gogh, »Le Pont de Langlois«,
Zeichnung Frühjahr 1888.

18
Vincent van Gogh, Le Pont de Langlois,
drawing, spring 1888.

Joseph Anton Koch

Geboren 1768 im Tiroler Lechtal als Sohn eines Bauern und einer Rheinländerin, wuchs als Hirtenjunge auf, kam über die Schule in Dillingen 1785 an die Hohe Carlsschule in Stuttgart, lernte bei Harper und Hetsch, entzog sich dem militärischen Regime 1791 durch die Flucht nach Straßburg und anschließend 1792–1794 in die Schweiz. Seit 1795 bis zu seinem Tode 1839 lebte er in Rom, wo er Senior und Mittelpunkt der deutschen Künstlerkolonie war.

19

»Spital auf der Grimsel«

Das Hospiz am Grimselpaß

Entstanden 1805
Feder in Schwarzgrau, aquarelliert, auf geripptem Bütten, aufgezogen, Randlinie in Bleistift, 37 × 52 cm
Bez. rechts unten: Spital auf der Grimsel, links: 5.
Herkunft: Im Bestand vor 1906.
Inv. Nr. 4170

Joseph Anton Koch

Born in 1768 in the Lech Valley in Tyrol, where his father farmed; his mother was from the Rhineland. Boyhood as a shepherd; from school at Dillingen, entered the Hohe Carlsschule in Stuttgart (1785), studying under Harper and Hetsch. Fled the military regime, travelling first to Strasbourg, then (1792–94) to Switzerland. From 1795 to his death in 1839, he lived in Rome, where he was the senior and central figure of the German artists' colony.

19

"Spital auf der Grimsel"

The Hospice on the Grimsel Pass

Dated 1805
Pen and dark grey ink, water-colour, on laid handmade, rough-edged paper, mounted; pencilled margin; 37 × 52 cm
Inscribed below right, Spital auf der Grimsel; left, 5.
Provenance: In our collection before 1906.
Inv. No. 4710

Diese transparente Zeichnung des Hochgebirges mit spiegelndem See übertrifft unsere Vorstellung von der Landschaft in der Kunst um 1800: Sie hat nicht die Gefälligkeit des von Goethe geschätzten Klassizisten Philipp Hackert (gestorben 1811), nicht die Poesie der Romantiker und nicht das Visionäre William Turners, der 1802 seine erste Reise in die Schweizer Alpen unternahm. Kochs Darstellung ist kühl, gläsern, nicht nur im Atmosphärischen, sondern auch im Graphischen; eher distanziert als fasziniert.

Wir wissen von einer ersten Fassung in Aquarell auf einem Skizzenbuchblatt vor der Natur 1793/94 entstanden (Wien, Akademie der bildenden Künste) und von einer quadrierten Federzeichnung (Basel, Kunstmuseum), die gewiß zur Vorbereitung der beiden Gemäldefassungen von 1813 in Leipzig (1931 im Glaspalast zu München verbrannt) und in Karlsruhe gedient hat. In einem Brief J. A. Kochs an den Freiherrn von Uexküll vom 9. 2. 1805 (Lutterotti: op. cit. S. 205) schreibt er, er habe »einige Naturgegenden auf den ersten Strich fertig gemalt in drei oder vier Tagen«, darunter auch »Das Spital auf der Grimsel im Kanton Bern, umgeben mit Felsen und Gletschern; öde Partie, weder Laub noch Gras, nichts als bemooste Trümmer und einen See von stigischer Schwärze, im Hintergrund finstre Wolken, welche Schnee verkündigen; die Maultiertreiber und Säumer von Italien nach Deutschland im Vordergrunde« (sie finden sich sehr klein am linken Blattrand, vorangeeilt ist der Hund).

Die Übereinstimmung dieser Briefstelle mit unserem Blatt sowohl in der Ortsangabe wie in der Darstellung, dazu die Akkuratesse des Striches und die vorzügliche Erhaltung machen es wahrscheinlich, daß wir die genannte Fassung von 1805 vor uns haben; auch die Numerierung und bildmäßige Einfassungslinie lassen auf eine Reinschrift der Naturstudie von 1793/94 schließen. Nichtsdestoweniger fasziniert sie durch das – wie Hölderlin zu jener Zeit dichtete: »heilig nüchterne«. In dem Karlsruher Gemälde ist das Ausgesetztsein des Menschen in der Einsamkeit der Berge durch Staffagefiguren verharmlost. – Aus unserem großen Bestand von Zeichnungen Kochs – darunter Karikaturen auf das Regime der Stuttgarter Carlsschule (siehe Abb. 3, S. 202), Fragmente des illustrierten Bodensee-Tagebuchs, »historische und dichterische Landschaften« im Stile Poussins sowie Dante-Illustrationen – ragt das »Spital auf der Grimsel« durch eine Absolutheit des Naturerlebnisses hervor, die Koch wie keinen anderen seiner Zeit zur Gestaltung »heroischer« Landschaft befähigte; er stand dabei in der großen, von den Carracci begründeten Tradition des »Ideale classico« (siehe Abb. 10, S. 212).

This transparent drawing of the alpine landscape with the mirror of the lake exceeds our notions of landscape in art around 1800: It has neither the easy appeal of the classicist Philipp Hackert (d. 1811), whom Goethe venerated, nor the lyrical qualities of the Romantics, nor the visionary qualities of William Turner, who undertook his first journey to the Swiss Alps in 1802. Koch's image is cool, glassy, in his graphic technique as much as in atmosphere – detached rather than fascinated.

We know of a first version in water-colour, on a sheet from a sketchbook, done from nature in 1793/94 (Vienna, Akademie der bildenden Künste) and of a squared pen drawing (Basel, Kunstmuseum), which must certainly have served as a preparation for the two painted versions of 1813 in Leipzig (destroyed by fire at the Glaspalast in Munich, 1931) and Karlsruhe. In a letter to Baron von Uexküll, dated 9th February 1805 (Lutterotti, 1940, p. 205), Koch writes that he has "finished painting several wild landscapes in one session, over three or four days", including "The Hospital on the Grimsel in the Canton of Berne, surrounded by rocks and glaciers; a bleak part, neither leaves nor grass, nothing but moss-grown debris and a lake of Stygian blackness, in the background dark clouds, foretelling snow; the mule-drivers and sumpters from Italy to Germany in the foreground" (minute figures entering from the left-hand edge, far behind their dog in the foreground).

The co-incidence between the description in the letter and our drawing, both in name and appearance of place, along with the precision of line and wonderful state of preservation, make it probable that the work before us is that of 1805. The numbering and framing margin along the bottom edge also support the identification of a "fine" version of the study from the life of 1793/94. Nonetheless, it fascinates in its quality of what a contemporary poem of Hölderlin's calls "sacred sobriety". In the painting at Karlsruhe the utter vulnerability of man in the desolation of the mountains forfeits its drama by the addition of staffage figures; in our extensive collection of Koch drawings, which includes caricatures of the Carlsschule at Stuttgart (see ill. 3, p. 202 above), fragments from the illustrated Lake Constance Diary, "historic and poetic landscapes" in the manner of Poussin, and illustrations of Dante, the "Spital auf der Grimsel" is preeminent for its absolute experience of nature – that which endowed Koch beyond all his contemporaries with the power to create "heroic" landscapes. It places him in the grand tradition established by the Carracci, of the "Ideale classico" (cf. ill. 10, p. 212).

Literatur: Otto R. v. Lutterotti, Joseph Anton Koch, Werkverzeichnis Berlin 1940, Z. 621. – Ausstellungskatalog Nationalgalerie Berlin 1939, Nr. 84. – Ulrike Gauß, Die Zeichnungen und Aquarelle des 19. Jahrhunderts in der Graphischen Sammlung der Staatsgalerie Stuttgart, 1976, Nr. und Abb. 765.

Bibliography: Otto R. von Lutterotti, Joseph Anton Koch, œuvre catalogue (Berlin, 1940), ill. 621; exh. cat., Nationalgalerie Berlin (1939), No. 84; Ulrike Gauss, die Zeichnungen und Aquarelle des 19. Jahrhunderts in der Graphischen Sammlung der Staatsgalerie Stuttgart (1976), No. & ill. 765.

Spital auf dem Grimsel

Carl Philipp Fohr

Geboren 1795 in Heidelberg, dort erster Zeichenunterricht bei Friedrich Rottmann. 1811—1813 in Darmstadt gefördert durch die Erbprinzessin Wilhelmine Louise, für die er die Skizzenbücher der Neckargegend und des Schwarzwalds schuf. Juli 1815 bis Mai 1816 an der Münchner Akademie, dann wieder in Heidelberg im Kreise der Burschenschaftler; am 18. Oktober 1816 Abreise nach Rom, wo er im Juni 1818 im Tiber ertrank.

20

Bildnis Heinrich Karl Hofmann

Entstanden zwischen Mai und Oktober 1816
Feder in Braungrau über Bleistift auf hell bräunlichem Papier, an drei Kanten mit Goldschnitt, 25,4 × 21,1 cm
Auf der Rückseite mit dem Stempel der Sammlung Dr. Heinrich Stinnes und dessen Erwerbungsnotiz »Ludwigs-Galerie / 27. XII. 930« sowie die Aufschrift: »Wird von H Schilbach / für Jurist Hofmann aus / Darmstadt gehalten.«
Herkunft: Dr. Edmund Schilling, Frankfurt a. M. — Ludwigsgalerie München (seit 1927). — Dr. H. Stinnes (seit 1930). — Kunsthandel Stuttgart.
Inv. Nr. C 51/343

Carl Philipp Fohr

Born in Heidelberg, 1795; first lessons in drawing there under Friedrich Rottmann. Patronised in Darmstadt, 1811—13, by the Crown Princess Wilhelmine Louise, for whom he completed sketchbooks of the River Neckar landscapes and the Black Forest. July 1815—May 1816, at the Munich Academy; then in Heidelberg again, in student league circles. Left for Rome, 18th October 1816; drowned in the Tiber in June, 1818.

20

Portrait of Heinrich Karl Hofmann

Between May and October, 1816
Pen and grey-brown ink over pencil on light-brown tinted paper, gilt-edged on three sides, 25.4 × 21.1 cm
On the reverse, the collector's stamp of Dr. Heinrich Stinnes and his acquisition note, "Ludwigs-Galerie / 27. XII.930" and the inscription, "Held by H Schilbach / as [the portrait of] the lawyer Hofmann from / Darmstadt."
Provenance: Dr. Edmund Schilling, Frankfurt-on-Main; Ludwigsgalerie, Munich (from 1927); Dr. H. Stinnes (from 1930); Stuttgart art dealers.
Inv. No. C. 51/343

Bis zu den Silberstiftzeichnungen des älteren Holbein müßte man zurückgehen — also bis zur Schwelle vom Mittelalter zur Neuzeit — um eine solche Präzision der Details bei unverminderter Totalität der psychologischen Erfassung wiederzufinden. Am genauesten ist das Dreiviertelprofil des Gesichtes gezeichnet; die uns zugewandte Seite ist mit Kreuzschraffuren exakt durchmodelliert, sie verlaufen bis zur Augenbraue und dem Nasenrücken, während die abgewandte Seite und die Stirn blank im Licht liegen. Aus dieser hellsten Partie stechen die schwarzen Augen hervor. Das offene strähnige Haar erhöht den Eindruck verdeckter Leidenschaft, wie auch die blitzende Binnenzeichnung des hochgeknöpften Wamses mit dem steilen »Schillerkragen«. Zartheit und Schärfe des Strichs sind gleichermaßen zwingend. In der Balance von Größe der Form und Genauigkeit, von Distanzierung und Wahrheit erweist sich die Genialität des 20jährigen Künstlers.

Das Freundschaftsbild — um ein solches handelt es sich hier im Gegensatz zum konventionellen Auftragsbild — ist eine Schöpfung der Romantik (Klaus Lankheit hat ihm 1952 eine umfassende Publikation gewidmet). Zumeist hält es Bildnisse und Bildnisgruppen befreundeter Künstler fest; hier ist das Bildnis zugleich ein politisches Bekenntnis zu einem gleichaltrigen Juristen und Journalisten namens Heinrich Karl Hofmann, der als Mitarbeiter von Görres am »Rheinischer Merkur« begonnen hatte und »ein süddeutscher Vorkämpfer des deutschen Einheitsgedankens« war, wie der Untertitel seiner Biographie von Herman Haupt in den »Quellen und Darstellungen zur Geschichte der Burschenschaft und der deutschen Einheitsbewegung« (Heidelberg 1912) lautet. Diese nach ihrer Verbindung »Teutonen« genannten jungen Menschen hatten ihre patriotische Gesinnung zumeist noch in den Freiheitskriegen bewiesen und bekundeten sie durch das Tragen altdeutscher Tracht mit langem Haar; eine Reihe von ihnen hat Fohr in einem aufgelösten Album, das sich weitgehend rekonstruieren ließ, porträtiert; aus ihm stammt auch unser Blatt, an dessen Kanten der Goldschnitt noch sichtbar ist.

One would have to look back to the silverpoint drawings of the elder Holbein, in other words, to the threshold from the medieval to the modern era, to find a match for this precision of detail, yet unstinted totality of psychological observation. The three-quarter profile drawing of the face is the most precisely detailed, the side nearest us being fully and accurately modelled in cross-hatching which runs up to the eyebrow and the bridge of the nose, while averted side and the forehead are white in the light. Black eyes pierce from this lightest part of the face. The loose hair, in strands, intensifies the impression of concealed passion — as does the interior drawing of the jacket, buttoned up to the open "Schiller collar". Delicacy and incisiveness of line are equally cogent. The balance between grand scale of form and precision, detachment and truth, evince the genius of the twenty-year-old artist.

This is not a conventional, commissioned drawing, but a "friendship picture" ("Freundschaftsbild"), a genre created by the Romantics (to which Klaus Lankheit devoted a comprehensive study in 1952). Most of these were single or group portraits of artist friends. In this case the likeness is also a political declaration of faith in a lawyer and journalist of Fohr's age named Heinrich Karl Hofmann, who had begun as a collaborator of Görres' at the "Rheinischer Merkur", becoming "a South-German pioneer of the concept of German unity", as the subtitle of Herman Haupt's biography of him in his "Sources and Accounts relating to the History of the Students' Societies and the Movement for German Unity" has it ("Quellen und Darstellungen zur Geschichte der Burschenschaft und der deutschen Einheitsbewegung" Heidelberg, 1912). Most of these young men, whose pledge lent them the name of "Teutons", had for the most part proved their patriotic convictions in the Wars of Liberation and attested to them by wearing old German costume and long hair. Fohr portrayed a number of them in an album, since dispersed, but which it has been possible to reconstruct to a large extent. The present drawing, comes from this source as well, its gilt edging is still visible.

Literatur: L. Grote, Das Antlitz eines Jugendbundes, Berlin o. J. (1943, Kunstbrief, Gebr. Mann Verlag), S. 18/19. — J. E. v. Borries, Zeichnungen des 19. und 20. Jahrhunderts in der Graphischen Sammlung der Staatsgalerie Stuttgart, 1960, Nr. 43, Abb. 4. — J. Chr. Jensen, Carl Philipp Fohr in Heidelberg und im Neckartal, Karlsruhe 1968, Nr. 41, Abb. 40. — Ulrike Gauß, Die Zeichnungen und Aquarelle des 19. Jahrhunderts in der Graphischen Sammlung der Staatsgalerie Stuttgart, 1976, Nr. und Abb. 261 (mit weiterer Bibliographie).

Bibliography: L. Grote, Das Antlitz eines Jugendbundes, Berlin, without date) (1943), Kunstbrief, Gebr. Mann Verlag, pp. 18, 19; J. E. von Borries, Zeichnungen des 19. und 20. Jahrhunderts in der Graphischen Sammlung der Staatsgalerie Stuttgart (1960), No. 43, ill. 4; J. C. Jensen, Carl Philipp Fohr in Heidelberg und im Neckartal (Karlsruhe, 1968), No. 41, ill. 40; Ulrike Gauss, Die Zeichnungen und Aquarelle des 19. Jahrhunderts in der Graphischen Sammlung der Staatsgalerie Stuttgart (1976), No. and ill. 261 (with extended bibliography).

Carl Blechen

Geboren 1798 in Cottbus, zunächst Bankkaufmann, ab 1822 Schüler der Berliner Akademie, 1824–1827 Bühnenmaler am Königstädtischen Theater in Berlin, Oktober 1828 bis Ende 1829 als stärkstes künstlerisches Erlebnis Reise nach Italien, seit 1831 Professor für Landschaftsmalerei, seit 1836 zunehmend gemütskrank, gestorben 1840 in Berlin.

21

Italienische Landschaft mit antikem Tempel

Entstanden 1829
Aquarell über Bleistiftspuren, in der Mitte
Horizontalfalte, angeschnittenes
Wasserzeichen: JV(?), 20,1 × 34,7 cm
Herkunft: Nachlaß Blechens (Stempel Lugt
263 b). – Sammlung H. F. W. Brose, Berlin
(Stempel Lugt 307 c), versteigert 1928. –
Sammlung Julius Freund, dann Frau
Dr. G. Freund, Buenos Aires. – Galerie
Fischer, Luzern. – Sammlung v. Kreibig,
München.
Inv. Nr. C 70/1780

Carl Blechen

Born in Cottbus in 1798. Began as a bank clerk; student at the Academy in Berlin from 1822; 1824–27, scene painter at the Königstädtisches Theater in Berlin. His most telling artistic experience was his journey to Italy. Professor for landscape painting from 1831. Increasingly mentally disturbed from 1836 on, died in Berlin in 1840.

21

Italian Landscape with Antique Temple

Dated 1829
Water-colour over traces of pencil,
horizontal fold through the centre, cut
watermark: JV(?), 20.1 × 34.7 cm
Provenance: Blechen's estate (stamp: Lugt
263 b); collection H. F. W. Brose, Berlin
(stamp: Lugt 307 c), auctioned 1928;
collection Julius Freund, then Frau Dr.
G. Freund, Buenos Aires; Galerie Fischer,
Lucerne; von Kreibig Collection, Munich.
Inv. No. C 70/1780

Hier wird ein Bildganzes allein aus transparenten Farbflecken und -flächen im Zusammenklang mit dem ausgesparten Weiß des Blattes geschaffen. Das hatte es damals in Deutschland noch nicht gegeben; die Romantiker, also Blechens Zeitgenossen, aquarellierten innerhalb eines Liniennetzes, sie legten ihre Zeichnungen z.T. farbig an, sie »lavierten«, aber sie erlaubten der Farbe nicht, zu fließen, wie hier, wo sie aufgehellt oder verdichtet die Formen frei erschafft. Das strahlende Licht löst alle festen Konturen auf; so erscheinen nicht nur Busch und Baum schwerelos, sondern ebenso die Ruine eines darin eingebetteten Tempels vor einem zum Meer abfallenden, lichten Höhenzug. Den Gesetzen der Schwerkraft spottend, hält alles luftig zusammen: die farbstarke Mittelzone des Aquarells schwebt zwischen dem nur hauchzart angedeuteten Vordergrund, der durch eine geschwungene Schattenbahn ausponderiert ist, und dem offenen Himmel. Ein so freies Spiel der Kräfte, das weder den Pinsel des Malers noch die Phantasie des Betrachters begrenzt, erlaubt nur das Aquarell.

Das Revolutionäre von Blechens Sicht ist innerhalb dieses Bandes im Rückblick auf J. A. Kochs lavierte Federzeichnung des Grimselpasses (siehe Tafel 19, S. 290) und im Hinblick auf Cézannes Aquarell eines spiegelnden Flußufers (siehe Tafel 17, S. 282) zu erkennen: der künstlerische Zusammenhang mit der fünfzig Jahre späteren Arbeit Cézannes ist enger als mit der 25 Jahre früheren von J. A. Koch. – Man hat mit Recht darauf hingewiesen, daß Blechens italienische Aquarelle (nahezu eintausend innerhalb eines Jahres als der quantitative und qualitative Höhepunkt seines Schaffens) den Impressionismus vorwegnehmen, aber daß ihre Struktur und ihr Freiraum die Rhythmisierung und Imaginationskraft eines Cézanne erreichen, ist noch nicht beachtet worden, wohl weil Blechens Œuvre zu sehr im geteilten Berlin verborgen war; es ist noch nie international herausgekommen. Das liegt auch am frühen Tod des Künstlers und der langen Verkennung des Ertrages seines italienischen Jahres als bloßen »Studienmaterials«.

Max Liebermann hat dessen Wert begriffen, als er 1932 schrieb: »Die Studien . . . geben das Höchste, was ein Maler zu geben hat, sie geben das wieder, was Blechen gesehen hat: das Einfachste und das Schwerste« (zitiert nach dem Katalog der Blechen-Ausstellung in Berlin-Ost, 1973).

Here a pictorial whole is created solely from translucent areas and dabs of colour orchestrated with the unpainted white of the paper. In Germany this was an unprecedented phenomenon. The Romantics, Blechen's contemporaries, used water-colour within a line network and would occasionally apply colour to their drawings; they "washed" them over – but they did not let the paint flow like in this picture, creating forms freely in the play of denser or lighter washes. The radiant light dissolves all hard contours. Thus not only bushes and trees, but also the ruins of a temple nestling amidst them, seem weightless before the backdrop of an airy height sloping down to the sea. Making a mockery of the laws of gravity, all coheres in an airiness; the concentration of local colour about the middle zone of the picture hovers between the foreground, barely hinted at in the slightest tone, and held in equilibrium by a sweeping band of shade, and the open sky. A play of forces so free, encumbering neither the painter's brush nor the beholder's imagination, is possible only in water-colour.

The revolutionary quality of Blechen's prospect becomes obvious, in comparison with J. A. Koch's colour-washed pen drawing of the Grimsel Pass (pl. 19, p. 290) and, looking ahead, with Cézanne's water-colour of a riverbank and its reflection (pl. 17, p. 282). The artistic link with Cézanne's work, fifty years on, is stronger than that with J. A. Koch's of twenty-five years before. The claim has justifiably been made that Blechen's Italian water-colours (almost a thousand within a single year, the quantitative and qualitative summit of his œuvre) anticipate Impressionism; but that their structure and use of free space attain the mastery of rhythm and imaginative power of a Cézanne. This has yet to be acknowledged, probably because Blechen's work is too inaccessible in divided Berlin: it has never been shown at an international level. This is also a result of his early death and the inability to see in the work of his year in Italy anything more than "study material".

Max Liebermann understood its value when he wrote, in 1932, "The studies . . . render the utmost a painter can give, they render that which Blechen saw: the simplest and the most difficult thing." (Quoted in the Blechen exhibition catalogue, East Berlin, 1973.)

Literatur: Paul Ortwin Rave, Karl Blechen – Leben, Würdigungen, Werk, Berlin 1940, Nr. 1240. – Katalog der Ausstellung: Das Aquarell, München 1972/73, Nr. 160, Abb. S. 167. – Ulrike Gauß, Die Zeichnungen und Aquarelle des 19. Jahrhunderts in der Graphischen Sammlung der Staatsgalerie Stuttgart, 1976, Nr. und Abb. 22, mit weiterer Bibliographie.

Bibliography: Paul Ortwin Rave, Karl Blechen – Leben, Würdigungen, Werk (Berlin, 1940), No. 1240; Das Aquarell, exh. cat. (Munich, 1972/73), No. 160, ill. p. 167; Ulrike Gauss, Die Zeichnungen und Aquarelle des 19. Jahrhunderts in der Graphischen Sammlung der Staatsgalerie Stuttgart (1976), No. and ill. 22, with further bibliography.

Moritz von Schwind

Geboren 1804 in Wien, seit 1823 Studium an der dortigen Akademie bei Schnorr von Carolsfeld, befreundet u. a mit den Brüdern Olivier, Franz Schubert, Lenau, Grillparzer; seit 1828 in München als Schüler von Cornelius; zahlreiche Freskenaufträge, u. a. für die Kunsthalle in Karlsruhe (1840–1842). 1835 Italienreise. Seit 1847 bis zu seinem Tode 1871 in München. In den letzten Jahren befreundet mit Mörike.

22

Die Sängerin Karoline Hetzenecker

im Kostüm der Valentine in Meyerbeers Oper »Die Hugenotten«

Entstanden um 1848
Bleistift, mit Deckweiß gehöht auf
olivgrünem Karton, Goldstaub auf dem
Armreif, 41,6 × 30,9 cm
Im Bestand vor 1906 wie auch zwei weitere
Kostümbildnisse der Sängerin; weitere drei
gingen während des 2. Weltkrieges verloren.
Inv. Nr. 5195.

Moritz von Schwind

Born in Vienna in 1804; 1823, began studies at the academy there, under Schnorr von Carolsfeld; friends included the Olivier brothers, Franz Schubert, Lenau and Grillparzer. In Munich from 1828 as a pupil of Cornelius. Many fresco commissions, such as that for the Kunsthalle (gallery) at Karlsruhe (1840–42). Journey to Italy in 1835. In Munich from 1847 to his death in 1871. In his last years a friend of Mörike's.

22

The singer, Karoline Hetzenecker

Costumed as Valentine in Meyerbeer's opera, Les Huguenots

Dated 1848
Pencil with opaque white highlights on
olive green card, golddust on the bangle,
41.6 × 30.9 cm
Part of the Gallery's collection before 1906,
along with two other costume portraits of
the singer; another three were lost in the
Second World War.
Inv. No. 5195

Von dem Schleier geht der Zauber dieser Zeichnung aus; ohne ihn wäre es gewiß noch eine der anmutigsten unter den zahlreichen, von Sammlern schon immer begehrten »Kostümbildnissen« der Münchner Hofopernsängerin Karoline Hetzenecker. Der Schleier gehört zur Romantik wie der Heiligenschein zur Religion; er ist ihr sichtbares Symbol. Schiller schrieb 1795 ein »philosophisches Gedicht« mit dem Titel »Das verschleierte Bild zu Sais« — ein Stoff, mit dem sich auch Novalis befaßte.
Schwind verbindet in unserer Zeichnung das Schwere mit dem Leichten durch den Fluß der Bewegung. Ohne die Plastizität des Faltenrocks würde sich die Transparenz des wehenden Schleiers verringern; unter ihm strecken sich die Hände wie die eines Dirigenten aus, der Pianissimo gebietet. Und tatsächlich ist es in Meyerbeers Oper, dessen Textbuch der erfolgreichste Bühnenschriftsteller seiner Zeit, Eugéne Scribe, verfaßte, die verschleierte Valentine, die versucht, die verfeindeten Katholiken und Hugenotten zu besänftigen. Diese dramatische Spannung hat Schwind in der Balance der Figur verkörpert, die wie eine Fee auf der Spitze ihres Fußes zu schweben scheint. Schwinds Ehrgeiz waren unter dem Einfluß seines Lehrers Cornelius die Fresken. Viele Jahre seines Lebens hat er in München, Hohenschwangau, Karlsruhe, Frankfurt und der neuerbauten Wiener Oper damit vergeudet, die Schöpfungen seiner Phantasie auf monumentale Formate vergrößert selbst auf die Wand zu malen; ohne im eigentlichen Sinne Maler zu sein, von der Farbe auszugehen. — Seine Popularität verdankt er den Bildergeschichten in den »Fliegenden Blättern« und den »Münchner Bilderbogen« des Verlages Braun und Schneider; sie sind etwa gleichzeitig mit unserem Blatt entstanden. »Freie« Kunst hier und »angewandte« dort sind für einen Künstler von Rang nicht unverträglich. —
Schwinds bleibende Größe liegt in seinen Zeichnungen, dort offenbart sich seine Empfindsamkeit überzeugend; noch intimer als die großzügigen Zeichnungen in Feder wirken die in Bleistift wie die vorliegende, die unter 30 Arbeiten unserer Sammlung ausgewählt wurde; sie entstand, nachdem er »lange genug unter dem Glück fürstlicher Aufträge geschmachtet« hatte (so in einem Brief an Bonaventura Genelli vom 23. April 1846).

It is from the veil that the spell of this drawing emanates; without it it would still be one of the most charming of the numerous, always eagerly collected "costume portraits" of Karoline Hetzenecker, a singer at the Hofoper at Munich. The veil is as much a part of Romanticism as the halo of religion; it is its visible symbol. In 1795, Schiller wrote a "philosophical poem" with the title, "Das verschleierte Bild zu Sais" (The veiled Image at Sais) — a subject also treated by Novalis. In our drawing, Schwind combines weight with lightness through the flow of movement. Without the tangible volume of the pleated skirt the transparency of the wafting veil would be reduced: under it the singer's hands are extended like a conductor's in eliciting a pianissimo. This is altogether apt: in Meyerbeer's opera with the libretto by the most successful dramatist of his time, Eugène Scribe, the Valentine is the character who, veiled, attempts to calm the opposing Catholics and Huguenots. Schwind has embodied this dramatic tension in the figure's equilibrium as she seems to hover like a fairy on the tips of her toes.
Under the influence of his teacher, Cornelius, Schwind's ambition was devoted to his frescoes. He squandered many years of his life painting monumentally enlarged versions of the products of his own imagination onto walls — without being a painter in the real sense of starting from colour — in Munich, Hohenschwangau, Karlsruhe, Frankfurt and at the newly constructed Vienna Opera House. He owes his popularity to the illustrated stories in the "Fliegende Blätter" and the "Münchner Bilderbogen" of the Munich publisher, Braun und Schneider. These appeared at about the same time as our drawing. For an artist of stature "fine" art of the one and "applied" art of the other are not incompatible.
Schwind's permanent greatness lies in his drawings, where his sensibility is revealed in cogent form. More intimate still than the generous pen drawings are those in pencil such as the present one, selected from 30 in our collection. It was completed after he had "languished long enough under the fortune of royal commissions" (in a letter to Bonaventura Genelli, dated 23rd April, 1846).

Literatur: Otto Weigmann, Moritz v. Schwind, des Meisters Werke, Stuttgart 1906, Abb. S. 260. – Peter Halm, Katalog der Schwind-Ausstellung, Karlsruhe 1937, Nr. 78. – Ulrike Gauß, Die Zeichnungen und Aquarelle des 19. Jahrhunderts in der Graphischen Sammlung der Staatsgalerie Stuttgart, 1976, Nr. und Abb. 1436.

Bibliography: Otto Weigmann, Moritz von Schwind, des Meisters Werke (Stuttgart, 1906), ill. p. 260; Peter Halm, Schwind exh. cat. (Karlsruhe, 1937), No. 78; Ulrike Gauss, Die Zeichnungen und Aquarelle des 19. Jahrhunderts in der Graphischen Sammlung der Staatsgalerie Stuttgart (1976), No. and ill. 1436.

Anselm Feuerbach

Geboren 1829 in Speyer. 1845–1848 Schüler von Schadow und Schirmer in Düsseldorf, dann bis 1850 in München, anschließend in Antwerpen und Paris, wo er 1853/54 bei Couture lernte. 1855 Aufbruch nach Italien in Begleitung des Dichters Victor v. Scheffel, traf über Venedig und Florenz 1856 in Rom ein, wo er bis 1873 lebte. Bis 1876 Professur in Wien. Seit 1877 meist in Venedig, wo er 1880 einem Herzschlag erlag.

23

Allee im Park der Villa d'Este in Tivoli

Entstanden Juli 1857
Schwarze Kreide und Deckfarben auf
braunem Papier, 45,1 × 31,2 cm
Bez. links unten: AF (verbunden); auf der
Rückseite: 464. Park-Allee.
Herkunft: Nachlaß des Künstlers 1880. –
Großherzog von Oldenburg.
Inv. Nr. C 20/5

Anselm Feuerbach

Born in Speyer, 1829. A pupil of Schadow and Schirmer in Düsseldorf, 1845–48; then in Munich until 1850, followed by Antwerp and Paris, where he studied under Couture, 1853/54. In 1855 he accompanied the poet, Victor von Scheffel, to Italy, arriving in Rome in 1856, via Venice and Florence. Lived in Rome until 1875; professor at Vienna until 1876, returning in 1877 to Italy (Venice), where he largely remained until his death of heart failure in 1880.

23

Avenue in the Park of the Villa d'Este at Tivoli

July, 1857
Black chalk and body colour on brown
paper, 45.1 × 31.2 cm
Signed, below left, AF (ligature);
on the reverse, 464. Park-Allee.
Provenance: the artist's estate, 1880;
Grand Duke of Oldenburg.
Inv. No. C 20/5

Wem der Name des Malers Anselm Feuerbach, der mit Böcklin und Hans von Marees zu den letzten Deutsch-Römern gehört, etwas bedeutet, der wird in der strengen Auswahl dieses Buches eine seiner repräsentativen Modellstudien zur »Iphigenie« oder zur »Medea« erwarten, die er selbst für »exquisit« erachtete. Obwohl wir solche besitzen, haben wir uns aber für eine seiner drei frühen römischen Landschaften entschieden. Die vorliegende, farbig auf braungetöntem Papier entworfene »Allee im Park der Villa d'Este« wurde gegenüber den herberen Campagna-Landschaften bevorzugt als die für Feuerbachs künstlerische Herkunft und Absicht bedeutendere. Damit wird der weniger bekannte, frühe Feuerbach vorgestellt.

Ohne Vordergrundsmotiv wächst aus der verschatteten Mitte des Blattes eine Baumgruppe auf; zart begrünt steht sie links frei vor den Blautönen des Himmels; rechts verschmilzt sie mit dem Braunton des Papiergrundes. Die Sonnenflecken auf dem Weg, die den Blick zu einer Nischenfigur in der Tiefe des Parkes führen, und das durchbrochene Laubwerk darüber nehmen den Impressionismus voraus. Durch die Spontaneität des Vortrags und das Verwischen der Kreide erscheint alles offen, erwartungsvoll wie vor einem Auftritt. Nichtsdestoweniger spürt man ein klares Gefühl für die Bildmäßigkeit des Gesehenen, wie auch in den Campagna-Landschaften; wir wissen, daß sie alle vor der Natur entstanden sind, auf Ausflügen mit dem Freund und Biographen Allgeyer und dem Bildhauer Reinhold Begas.

Für eine malerische Zeichenweise von solcher Raffinesse gibt es – wie der Rückblick auf J. A. Koch, Blechen und Schwind zeigt – bis zur Mitte des 19. Jahrhunderts in Deutschland kein Vorbild. Dank der Forschungen von Marianne Küffner wissen wir, daß Feuerbach bei Thomas Couture in Paris so zu zeichnen lernte – und es ist erhellend, daß dieser wenig später (1855/56) der Lehrer Edouard Manets geworden ist. »Die von Couture übernommene freie Kreidetechnik hat der Künstler von der Pariser Zeit an für alle größeren Entwürfe und Modellstudien beibehalten ... er hat sie noch weiter ins Malerische gesteigert ... Ihren vollendetsten Ausdruck hat sie in den Landschaftsstudien der Jahre 1857 und 1858 gefunden. Diese Blätter gehören zu den bedeutendsten Leistungen der europäischen Landschaftszeichnung des 19. Jahrhunderts. Sie führen die heroische Landschaft der vorausgegangenen Generation ... zu einer bis dahin unerreichten Naturwahrheit, ohne den Sinn für die klassische Form der italienischen Landschaft aufzugeben« (im zitierten Karlsruher Katalog S. 116/117).

Literatur: Julius Allgeyer, Anselm Feuerbach, 2. Auflage, Berlin und Stuttgart 1904, Bd. 1, S. 366, Bd. 2, Nr. 330. – Marianne Küffner, Katalog der Ausstellung: Feuerbach als Zeichner, Heidelberg und Speyer 1969, Nr. 30, Abb. Taf. XIII. – Ulrike Gauß, Die Zeichnungen und Aquarelle des 19. Jahrhunderts in der Graphischen Sammlung der Staatsgalerie Stuttgart, 1976, Nr. und Abb. 254. – Katalog der Ausstellung: Anselm Feuerbach, Karlsruhe 1976, Nr. Z. 16, Abb. S. 285.

Those to whom Anselm Feuerbach's is a familiar name as belonging to one of the last Deutsch-Römer along with Böcklin and Hans von Marees, will expect us to have chosen in the selection for this book one of his exemplary model studies for "Iphigenia" or his "Medea" — especially since he himself esteemed them as "exquisite". Although we have some of these in our collection, we have opted for one of his three early Roman landscapes. The "Avenue in the Park of the Villa d'Este" opposite, sketched out in colour on brown-tinted paper, was chosen rather than the starker Campagna landscapes; it is more significant than these for Feuerbach's artistic origins and intentions, and shows him at a lesser known, earlier stage.

Without any foreground motif, a group of trees grows out of the shady centre area of the sheet: given delicate patches of green, the trees on the left stand free against the blues of the sky; on the right they merge with the brown of the paper. The patches of sunlight on the path, leading the eye to a statue in a niche in the depths of the park, and the interspersal of foliage and sky above, anticipate Impressionism. Spontaneity of technique and the smudging of the chalk lend everything an open look, expectant as if before a stage performance. Yet there is also quite clearly a feeling for the pictorial quality of what has been seen, just as there is in the Campagna landscapes. We know that all of them were done "from life", during excursions with Feuerbach's friend and biographer, Allgeyer, and the sculptor, Reinhold Begas.

Painterly drawing of such sophistication has no precedent in Germany — as comparison with J. A. Koch, Blechen and Schwind, above, shows — until the middle of the 19th century. It is now known, thanks to the research of Marianne Küffner, that Feuerbach acquired this approach to drawing while studying under Thomas Couture in Paris; and it is illuminating that Couture became Edouard Manet's teacher only a little later (1855/56). "From his period in Paris onward, the artist retained the free chalk technique he had taken on from Couture, applying it in all the larger designs and figure studies ... pushing it further still into the painterly ... It found its most perfect expression in the landscape studies of 1857 and 1858. These are amongst the most significant achievements in European landscape drawing of the 19th century. They take the heroic landscape of the preceding generation ... to a truth to nature hitherto unattained, without relinquishing the sense for the classical form of the Italian landscape." (In the Karlsruhe catalogue cited below, pp. 116/7.)

Bibliography: Julius Allgeyer, Anselm Feuerbach, 2nd edn (Berlin and Stuttgart, 1904), vol. 1, p. 366, vol. 2, No. 330; Marianne Küffner, exh. cat., Feuerbach als Zeichner (Heidelberg and Speyer, 1969), No. 30, ill. pl. XIII; Ulrike Gauss, Die Zeichnungen und Aquarelle des 19. Jahrhunderts in der Graphischen Sammlung der Staatsgalerie Stuttgart (1976), No. and ill. 254; exh. cat., Anselm Feuerbach (Karlsruhe, 1976), No. Z. 16, ill. p. 285.

Käthe Kollwitz
(geborene Schmidt)

Geboren 1867 in Königsberg (Ostpreußen), studierte 1885/86 in Berlin bei dem Graphiker Stauffer-Bern, 1889/90 in München bei dem Maler Herterich. 1891 Heirat mit dem Armenarzt Dr. Kollwitz; 1904 in Paris, wo sie Rodin und Steinlen besuchte. Seit 1928 Meisteratelier für Graphik an der Berliner Akademie, 1933 entlassen, seit 1936 Ausstellungsverbot. 1945 in Moritzburg bei Dresden gestorben.

24

Schlafendes Kind und Kinderkopf

Entstanden 1903
Kohle, vielfach gewischt, links schwarze Tusche und grünes Pastell, die Gesichter weiß gehöht, über der Stirn des linken gelbe Wischer, auf braungrauem Zeichenkarton mit gerissenen Rändern, 51 × 63 cm
Bez. rechts unten: Kollwitz
Herkunft: Sammlung Hudtwalcker, Hamburg. — Kornfeld und Klipstein, Bern, 96. Auktion 1959, Nr. 352, Tafel 19.
Inv. Nr. C 60/931

Käthe Kollwitz (née Schmidt)

Born in Königsberg, East Prussia, in 1867; studied in Berlin under the painter and engraver, Stauffer-Bern, in 1885/86, and in Munich under the painter, Herterich (1889/90). Married Dr. Kollwitz, a public assistance doctor, in 1891. In Paris in 1904, visited Rodin and Steinlen. Led a "master studio" for printing and drawing at the Berlin Academy from 1928, dismissed in 1933, banned from exhibiting her work from 1936 on. Died in Moritzburg, near Dresden, 1945.

24

Sleeping child and child's head

Dated 1903
Charcoal, rubbed in many places, on left, black Indian ink and green pastel; faces with white highlights, yellow smudges over forehead of figure on left; on grey-brown cartridge with torn edges, 51 × 63 cm
Signed below right, Kollwitz
Provenance: Hudtwalcker Collection, Hamburg; Kornfeld und Klipstein, Berne, 96th auction, 1959, No. 352, plate 19.
Inv. No. C 60/931

Schlafende Kinder pflegen auch für Künstler ein Bild reinen Friedens zu sein; in dieser durch Lichtführung, Farbakzente und Verdopplung des Motivs aufregenden Zeichnung ist das nicht ganz so. Ein Lichtschein, der tiefen Schatten wirft, hebt den Halbakt des Kindes aus dem Dunkel heraus; dadurch rückt seine Kreatürlichkeit bedrängend nahe. Um so mehr empfinden wir unsere Ferne von seiner mehr geträumten als bewußten, ahnungsvollen Welt. Wie ein Reflex von ihr ist das überschattete Grün, auf dem Kopf und Schultern des Kindes wie schwebend lagern. Die Künstlerin hat den Kopf allein auf demselben Blatt wiederholt — in vergrößerter Form dem vollen Licht ausgesetzt und etwas nach vorn gedreht. Solch eine erneute Befragung des Motivs auf Studienblättern ist nichts Ungewöhnliches, führt aber selten wie hier zu einer Steigerung des Ausdrucks. — Vor aller Kinder- und Traumpsychologie wurde hier eine in Worten kaum faßbare Ebene unserer Existenz erkannt und ans Licht gehoben. Das hat zu jener Zeit kein deutscher Künstler vermocht; in Europa nur Edvard Munch (geb. 1863), von dem die Staatsgalerie das schicksalsbeladene Gemälde der »Vier Mädchen in Aasgaardstrand« von 1902 besitzt.

Der Anlaß, ein schlafendes bzw. totes Kind darzustellen, war der graphische Zyklus »Bauernkrieg«, an dem die Künstlerin seit 1902 arbeitete. Dort war ein Blatt mit dem Begräbnis des gefallenen Sohnes vorgesehen, daraus wurde dann die »Schlachtfeld« betitelte Radierung von 1907, auf der die Mutter des Nachts gebeugt mit einer Lampe den toten Sohn sucht. Eine unmittelbare Vorstufe unseres Blattes in der Sammlung Walter Bareiss (siehe deren Ausstellungskatalog, Staatsgalerie Stuttgart, 1965, S. 19; Nagel-Timm Nr. 253) ist 1903 datiert; ein großes Jahr, wie unter den 50 Zeichnungen der Künstlerin in Stuttgart außerdem die Entwürfe zur Lithographie »Pietà« und zur monumentalen Radierung »Frau mit totem Kind« erweisen. — Als Modell diente der elfjährige Sohn Hans.

Ohne sich einer Gruppe anzuschließen, hat Käthe Kollwitz die Fesseln der von Allegorie und Historie belasteten Kunst des 19. Jahrhunderts abgeworfen, um im Sprung über den herrschenden Jugendstil und Impressionismus (der gleichaltrige Max Slevogt malt zur selben Zeit den »Weißen d'Andrade« in Stuttgart!) wieder das Elementare der menschlichen Existenz zu vergegenwärtigen. Mit diesem Anliegen, das sie dank angeborenen Wirklichkeitssinnes und technischer Meisterschaft bewältigte, steht sie in Deutschland zu Beginn unseres Jahrhunderts allein.

For artists, too, sleeping children tend to be an image of pure peace. In this drawing, dramatic by virtue of its lighting, accentuating use of colour and the double motif, this is not quite the case. A beam of light, casting deep shadows picks the semi-nude figure of the child out from the dark; this brings its physical humanity alarmingly close. We find ourselves all the more sensitised to the distance that separates us from the child's more dreamed-of than conscious, more apprehended world. Like a reflection of it the overshadowed green appears upon which head and shoulders seem to float as much as lie. The artist has repeated the head alone on the same sheet, enlarged and exposed to full light, and turned a little forward. Second inquiries into the subject are common enough in studies, but only rarely do they intensify the expressive quality, as in this drawing. Predating any psychology of the child or of dreams, we see here an awareness and highlighting of a stratum of our existence that we can hardly find words for. It is a feat with which Kollwitz stands alone amongst German artists of the time, and in Europe her one match was Edvard Munch (b. 1863), whose portentaden painting of the "Four Girls in Aasgaardstrand" of 1902 is in the Staatsgalerie's Collection.

The motive for depicting a sleeping or dead child was the graphic series, "Peasant War", on which the artist had been working since 1902. One image she intended was the burial of the fallen son; this materialised as the etching entitled "Schlachtfeld" ("Battlefield") of 1907, showing a mother searching for her dead son at night, bent over a lantern. An immediate predecessor of our work, in the Bareiss Collection (see the Bareiss catalogue, Staatsgalerie Stuttgart, 1965, p. 19, and Nagel-Timm, No. 253), is dated 1903 — a high-point for Kollwitz, as (amongst the fifty drawings in Stuttgart) her sketches for the lithograph Pietà and for the monumental etching "Frau mit totem Kind" ("Woman with dead Child") like the present drawing, substantiate. Her model was her eleven-year-old son, Hans.

Without joining a group, Käthe Kollwitz shook off the ties of 19th century art with its ballast of allegory and history, and, bypassing the then dominant Art Nouveau current and Impressionism (at the same time Max Slevogt, her equal in age, was painting the "White d'Andrade" in Stuttgart!), rediscovered the essence of human existence. With this concern, which a native sense for reality coupled with technical mastery enabled her to work out, she is a figure alone in the Germany of the early twentieth century.

Literatur: J. E. v. Borries, Zeichnungen des 19. und 20. Jahrhunderts in der Graphischen Sammlung der Staatsgalerie Stuttgart, 1960, Nr. 87, Abb. 34. — G. Thiem, Die Zeichnerin Käthe Kollwitz, Ausstellungskatalog Staatsgalerie Stuttgart 1967, Nr. 23, Abb. S. 39. — Nagel-Timm, Käthe Kollwitz, Die Handzeichnungen, Berlin 1972, Nr. und Abb. 256.

Bibliography: J. E. von Borries, Zeichnungen des 19. und 20. Jahrhunderts in der Graphischen Sammlung der Staatsgalerie Stuttgart (1960), No. 87, pl. 34; G. Thiem, die Zeichnerin Käthe Kollwitz (exh. cat., Staatsgalerie Stuttgart, 1967), No. 23, ill. p. 39; Nagel-Timm, Käthe Kollwitz, Die Handzeichnungen (Berlin, 1972), No. and ill. 256.

Karl Schmidt-Rottluff

Geboren 1884 in Rottluff bei Chemnitz, Besuch des Gymnasiums, Freundschaft mit Erich Heckel, studierte mit ihm und E.L. Kirchner in Dresden Architektur und begründete mit ihnen 1905 die Künstlergemeinschaft »Brücke«. 1911 Übersiedlung nach Berlin, dem er bis zu seinem Tode 1976 die Treue hielt. In den Sommermonaten lebte er in Fischerdörfern der Nord- und Ostsee. Als Gegner des Nationalsozialismus aus der Preußischen Akademie der Künste 1933 ausgeschlossen und 1941 mit Malverbot belegt.

25

Sitzender Frauenakt

Entstanden 1911
Schwarze, gelbe, blaue und rote Kreide,
42,5 × 32 cm
Bez. oben rechts: S-Rottluff 1911, unten
links: Frau Dehmel zu eigen
Herkunft: Nachlaß des Dichters Richard
Dehmel (1863–1920). – Auktion 101,
Dr. Hauswedell Hamburg, 1960, Nr. 612. –
Galerie Nierendorf Berlin.
Inv. Nr. C 65/1412

Ein 26jähriger, der nie eine Akademie besuchte, hat 1911 aus dem »Geist der Revolte« diesen lapidaren Akt gezeichnet und der Frau des Dichters Richard Dehmel in Hamburg geschenkt. Gemessen an dem, was heute, 70 Jahre danach, die »Neuen Wilden« uns anbieten, hat diese Zeichnung klassisches Maß in expressiver Gestalt; ihre Monumentalität beruht auf ihrer strengen Achsialität und Frontalität. Die in der Schwere des gesenkten Kopfes und des hochgezogenen Knies angestaute plastische Kraft wird durch die diagonal aufgestützten Arme in die Bildfläche gebunden. Der Ausdruck liegt in der Kraft der Linie; jede für sich genommen ist energiegeladen, könnte abstrahiert vom Akt bestehen (wie es zur gleichen Zeit Kandinsky unternahm). – »Klassisch« ist auch der Dreiklang der primären Farben Gelb, Blau, Rot, in körniger Transparenz aufgehellt als Gegenstimmen zur archaischen Strenge des Ganzen. – Die beiden Beschriftungen des Blattes, die Widmung unten links und die Signatur oben rechts sind Bestandteile der Komposition und ihrer vollendeten »mise en page«.
Das Jahr 1911 bringt den Höhepunkt des von Kirchner, Heckel und Schmidt-Rottluff ausgebildeten »Brücke«-Stils und zugleich die Individuation eines jeden; ein Jahr darauf zerfiel die Gemeinschaft. Es gibt ein Gegenstück zu diesem sitzenden Akt, einen lagernden, ebenfalls von 1911, den Schmidt-Rottluff »Herrn Dehmel« widmete; in ihm verbindet sich die Strenge des Künstlers mit der Eleganz Kirchners. Hier aber nicht, da ist Schmidt-Rottluff ganz unverkennbar er selbst. Seine Kunst, die manchmal barbarisch anmutet, ist so recht aus dem Geiste des revolutionären Richard Dehmel, der großen Einfluß auf die Jugend seiner Generation ausübte; man muß nur einmal sein Essay über »Kunst und Persönlichkeit« mit dem Untertitel »Perspektiven ins Unpersönliche« nachlesen (Gesammelte Werke, Berlin 1920, 3. Band, S. 117), z.B. auf S. 122: »Es hat schon manchen Sittenprediger, auch manchen Schöngeist kopfscheu gemacht, daß oft gerade Kunstwerke, die am stärksten auf Umfassung der Lebensgewalten, auf Beherrschung der Naturkräfte ausgehn, obenhin fast den Eindruck machen, als handle sich's um Verherrlichung brutaler persönlicher Instinkte. Das wäre freilich das Gegenteil von einer Kunst der Naturbeherrschung. Aber man wird nicht leugnen können: wo geherrscht werden soll, muß etwas da sein, das der Beherrschung wert und bedürftig ist. Der lenkende Geist ohne starke Triebe wäre ein Reiter ohne Pferd; wie hinwider selbst das edelste Vollblut nichtsnutzig wird und niederträchtig, wenn nicht ein ebenbürtiger Herr es mit Geschick zu bändigen weiß.« – Ist das nicht wie eine Übersetzung der gebändigten Leidenschaft in Schmidt-Rottluffs Akt?

Karl Schmidt-Rottluff

Born in Rottluff near Chemnitz in 1884 where he attended secondary school. Friendship with Erich Heckel, studied architecture with him and E. L. Kirchner in Dresden, the three of them went on to found "Die Brücke" group in 1905. Settled in Berlin in 1911 and stayed loyal to that city until his death in 1976. Spent the summer months in fishing villages on the North Sea and Baltic coasts. An opponent of National Socialism, was expelled from the Prussian Academy of Arts in 1933 and prohibited from painting in 1941.

25

Seated female nude

Dated 1911
Black, yellow, blue and red chalk,
42.5 × 32 cm
Signed above right, S-Rottluff 1911,
dedicated below left, Frau Dehmel zu eigen
Provenance: Estate of the poet, Richard
Dehmel (1863–1920); Auction 101,
Dr. Hauswedell, Hamburg, 1960, No. 612;
Galerie Nierendorf, Berlin.
Inv. No. C 65/1412

In 1911, a twenty-six-year-old who never attended a school of art drew this terse nude out of a "spirit of revolt" and presented it to the wife of the poet, Richard Dehmel, in Hamburg. Compared to what the "New Fauves" give us today, seventy years later, this drawing has classical scale in expressive form. Its monumentality resides in its strictly axial and frontal perspective. The corporeal force latent in the weight of the inclined head and the raised knee is reintegrated into the picture plane by the diagonals of the model's arms by which she props herself up. The expression lies in the power of line, each being charged with energy in its own right — each could subsist alone, abstracted from the depiction of the nude (as Kandinsky was doing at that very time). "Classical", too, is the triad of the primary colours, yellow, blue and red, lightened into a grainy transparency by the texture of the paper, a counterpoint to the archaic terseness of the whole. The two inscriptions on the sheet, the dedication below left and the signature above right, are constituent parts of the composition and its perfect "mise en page".

1911 was the year in which the "Brücke" style evolved by Kirchner, Heckel and Schmidt-Rottluff reached a high-point, simultaneously with the individuation of each: a year later, the group broke up. There is a counterpiece to this seated nude, a reclining figure, also done in 1911, which Schmidt-Rottluff dedicated to "Herrn Dehmel". This combines his stringency with the elegance of Kirchner; not so in the drawing opposite, there Schmidt-Rottluff is utterly, unmistakably himself. His art, with its occasional barbaric feel, is quite in the spirit of the revolutionary Richard Dehmel, who exercised great influence upon young people of his generation. One has only to read his essay on "Art and Personality", subtitled, "Perspectives into the Impersonal" ("Kunst und Persönlichkeit", "Perspektiven ins Unpersönliche", in his collected works "Gesammelte Werke", Berlin, 1920, vol. 3, p. 117), thus on p. 122, "Many a moraliser, many a bel esprit besides, has been made to shy by the fact that the very works of art most given to harnessing the powers of life, to mastering nature's forces, superficially seem almost to suggest the glorification of brutal personal instincts. Admittedly, that would be the opposite of an art of control over nature. But one will not be able to deny it, where there is to be mastery, there has to be something there worthy and needy of being mastered. The directing spirit without strong urges would be a rider without a horse; as, by the same token, even the noblest thoroughbred becomes worthless and low if it does not meet its match in a master who has the skill and understanding to tame it." — Does this not read like a translation of the mastered passion in Schmidt-Rottluff's nude?

Literatur: G. Thiem, Schmidt-Rottluff,
Aquarelle und Zeichnungen, München 1963,
S. 16, Abb. S. 78. — Katalog der Ausstellung:
Schmidt-Rottluff, Hannover, Essen, Frankfurt,
Berlin 1963/64, Nr. 29, Abb. S. 60. — G. Thiem,
»Herrn Dehmel zu eigen — S. Rottluff Hamburg
1911«, in Festschrift für Dr. h. c. Eduard
Trautscholdt, Hamburg 1965, S. 195, Abb. 115. —
Katalog der Ausstellung Schmidt-Rottluff
Aquarelle, Farbstift- und Tuschblätter,
Staatsgalerie Stuttgart 1969, Nr. 10, Farbtafel.

Bibliography: G. Thiem, Schmidt-Rottluff,
Aquarelle und Zeichnungen (Munich, 1963),
p. 16, ill. p. 78; exh. cat., Schmidt-Rottluff
(Hanover, Essen, Frankfurt, Berlin, 1963/64),
No. 29, ill. p. 60; G. Thiem, "Herrn Dehmel zu
eigen — S. Rottluff Hamburg 1911", in
Festschrift für Dr. h. c. Eduard Trautscholdt
(Hamburg, 1965), p. 195, ill. 115; exh. cat.
Schmidt-Rottluff, Aquarelle, Farbstift- und
Tuschblätter (Staatsgalerie Stuttgart, 1969),
No. 10, colour plate.

Frau Dehmel zueigen

Erich Heckel

Geboren 1883 in Döbeln (Sachsen), besuchte in Chemnitz das Gymnasium und befreundete sich mit Karl Schmidt-Rottluff; studierte mit ihm und E.L. Kirchner in Dresden Architektur; als Autodidakten gründeten sie 1905 die Künstlergruppe »Brücke«. 1911 siedelte er nach Berlin über und lebte im Sommer an der Ostsee; im 3. Reich als Expressionist geächtet und 1944 ausgebombt, zog er nach Hemmenhofen am Bodensee, wo er 1970 verstarb.

26

Die Schaukel

Entstanden 1912
Schwarze Kreide, Deckfarben und etwas Ölfarbe (in den Haarpartien) auf grauweißem Papier, 46,6 × 38 cm
Bez. rechts unten: Heckel 12. Die Schaukel.
Herkunft: aus dem Nachlaß des Künstlers geschenkt von Frau Siddi Heckel.
Inv. Nr. C 73/2322

Erich Heckel

Born at Döbeln (Saxony) in 1883, attended secondary school at Chemnitz and became a friend of Karl Schmidt-Rottluff; studied architecture at Dresden, with him and E.L. Kirchner. All of them self-taught, they founded the artists' group "Die Brücke" in 1905. Heckel moved to Berlin in 1911, spending summers on the Baltic coast. Spurned as an Expressionist in the Third Reich and bombed out in 1944, he moved to Hemmenhofen (Switzerland) by Lake Constance, where he died in 1970.

26

The Swing

Dated 1912
Black chalk, body colour, some oil paint (for the hair), on pale grey paper,
46.6 × 38 cm
Signed below right, Heckel 12.
Die Schaukel.
Provenance: from the artist's estate, donated by Frau Siddi Heckel.
Inv. No. C 73/2322

Mit den gestreckten Füßen wippend, sitzen zwei Mädchen auf dem Rundholz einer Schaukel, das größere faßt um das kleinere Mädchen und hält sich am vorderen Seil der Schaukel fest, die dadurch eine leichte Drehung erfährt. Die Figuren zeichnen sich in spitzen Zügen vor dem ockergelben Vorhang ab, dessen exotische Ornamentik wir aus anderen Interieurs von Heckel und Kirchner kennen, sie geht auf die Kenntnis der indischen Ajanta-Fresken zurück. Auch die kindhaften Modelle kommen dem Kenner der frühen »Brücke«-Kunst vertraut vor, Marcella und Fränzi glaubt man zu erkennen. Jedoch würde das der Datierung Heckels widersprechen: 1912 — denn er verließ schon im Herbst 1911 Dresden, wo die zwei Mädchen zurückblieben. — Es ist dem Scharfblick Karlheinz Gablers zu verdanken, im Vergleich mit dem 1913 datierten Aquarell »Innenraum« (Brücke-Museum Berlin, Katalog 1967, Nr. 72, Tafel 28) erkannt zu haben, daß wir hier »den ersten Zustand des Ateliers Mommsenstraße 60 in Berlin—Steglitz mit Blick auf die Küchentüre« vor uns haben. »Bei den Dargestellten handelt es sich um Heckels Nachbarn.« — Heckels Neffe, Hans Geißler, hält die grazile vordere Figur für die jugendliche Tänzerin Siddi, die der Künstler 1915 heiratete.
Die von Siddi Heckel gestiftete Zeichnung ist exemplarisch für den »Brücke«-Stil, für die kurze Zeit enger Zusammenarbeit des Künstlers mit Kirchner und Schmidt-Rottluff, die mit der Übersiedlung aller nach Berlin und der offiziellen Auflösung der »Brücke« im Jahre 1913 endete. — Das für Heckel spezifische dieses Interieurs ist seine Intimität, seine Stille, die sich auch im beruhigten Farbton kundtut; dem Sujet der Schaukel entspricht der pendelnde Rhythmus der Linien, die nur an den Längsseiten raumbegrenzend gerade verlaufen. Die zwei halbwüchsigen Mädchen sind keß, aber keineswegs frivol, nicht einmal auf den Beschauer bezogen (wie auf Fragonards berühmtem Bild der hochfliegenden Schaukel mit Voyeur). — Das Expressive mit dem Anmutigen versteht sich in der deutschen Kunst fast immer von selbst, aber Charme höchst selten.

Waggling their outstretched feet, two girls sit upon the round bar of a swing, the larger's arm around the smaller, her hand clasping the nearer rope, which gives the swing a slight twist. The figures stand out in sharp contours against the yellow-ochre curtain whose exotic ornamentation is familiar from other interiors in the works of Heckel and Kirchner; this can be traced to their knowledge of the Ajanta Frescoes in India. The childlike models, too, will be familiar to connoisseurs of the early works of the "Brücke", as — it would seem — Marcella and Fränzi. But this identification does not tally with Heckel's dating of 1912, since he had already left Dresden and the two girls of the earlier work behind him in autumn of the preceding year. We owe it to the keen-sightedness of Karlheinz Gabler to have identified, by comparison with the water-colour "Interior", dated 1913 (Innenraum; in the 1967 catalogue of the Brücke-Museum, Berlin, No. 72, plate 28), that this is "the first state of the studio at Mommsenstrasse 60 in Steglitz, Berlin, facing the kitchen door". "The figures are Heckel's neighbours." Heckel's nephew, Hans Geissler, judges the delicate nearer figure to be that of the youthful dancer, Siddi, whom the artist married in 1915.
It was she who donated the drawing, one typical of the "Brücke" style, of that short period of the artist's collaboration with Kirchner and Schmidt-Rottluff that ended with all of them moving to Berlin and the official break up of the "Brücke" in 1913. What is specific to Heckel in this interior is its intimacy, its stillness, of which the calm colours also speak. The theme of the swing is resumed in the oscillating rhythm of the lines, which straighten out only near the lateral edges of the paper, framing the depicted space. The two adolescent girls are cheeky, but far from frivolous even in relation to the viewer (unlike Fragonard's famous painting of the soaring swing and a voyeur below). To unite the expressive with the charming is Heckel's particular gift. Expression can almost be taken for granted in German art — charm is exceedingly rare.

Literatur: G. Thiem, Katalog der Ausstellung: Erich Heckel, Farbholzschnitte, Zeichnungen, Aquarelle, Stuttgart 1973/74, Nr. 52, Farbtafel S. 39.

Bibliography: G. Thiem, Erich Heckel, Farbholzschnitte, Zeichnungen, Aquarelle, exh. cat. (Stuttgart, 1973/74), No. 52, p. 39.

Ernst Ludwig Kirchner

Geboren 1880 in Aschaffenburg, 1901 in Dresden Studium der Architektur, 1905 gründete er mit Heckel und Schmidt-Rottluff die Künstlergruppe »Brücke«, 1911 zog er mit ihnen nach Berlin, 1914 zum Militär eingezogen, erlitt er 1915 einen Nervenzusammenbruch. 1917 Übersiedlung nach Davos, wo er sich 1938 in seinem Haus auf dem Wildboden das Leben nahm.

27

Rote Kokotte

Entstanden 1914
Farbkreiden und Tempera weiß gehöht, die schwarzen Partien im oberen rechten Blattviertel aufgerauht, 41 × 30,2 cm
Bez. rechts unten: »E L Kirchner 14« sowie am rechten Rand 12 cm unterhalb der Oberkante, etwas überdeckt: E L Kirchner; auf der Rückseite: KFZ6 (das ist die Inventarnummer des Vorbesitzers und heißt: Katalog Farb-Zeichnungen Nr. 6).
Herkunft: Sammlung des Schweizer Ehepaares Dr. Gervais, die zum größten Teil nach Stuttgart kam
Inv. Nr. C 57/745

Ernst Ludwig Kirchner

Born at Aschaffenburg in 1880. Studied architecture at Dresden, 1901; in 1905, established the "Brücke" group with Heckel and Schmidt-Rottluff, moving with them to Berlin in 1911. Called up for military service in 1914, he suffered a nervous breakdown the following year. Moved to Davos in 1917, where, at his house at the Wildboden, he committed suicide in 1938.

27

Red Cocotte

Dated 1914
Coloured chalk and tempera with white highlighting, areas of black in upper left quarter of paper roughened, 41 × 30.2 cm
Signed below right, "E L Kirchner 14", and at right edge, 12 cm below top edge, partly obscured, "E L Kirchner"; on reverse, KFZ6 (the previous owner's inventory number with the initials for Katalog Farb-Zeichnungen, catalogue / coloured drawings).
Provenance: Collection of M. & Mme Gervais, Switzerland, most of which came to Stuttgart.
Inv. No. C 57/745

Keilförmig stoßen die Straßen auf uns zu; auf ihrem fächerförmig weiß gehöhten Blauviolett gleitet eine gesichtslose Prozession in Schwarz dem sich spreizenden roten Ziel zu, das Blickpunkt und Schnittpunkt der Bildachsen zugleich ist. Die Kokotte flackert in Rottönen, die vom fahlen Grün ihres Stehkragens, dem blassen Rosé ihres animalischen Kopfes und dem bleichen Federbusch ihres monströsen Radhutes zersetzt werden. Die Farben sind so dekadent wie das Milieu. − Den manieristischen Tiefenzug der Szene hält nur die Halbfigur vorn links auf; sie ist nicht unbeteiligt, aber nicht verstrickt; im scharfen, vom hohen Hut pronocierten Profil spielt sie die Doppelrolle des Beobachters und des Vermittlers; kompositionell hat sie die Funktion einer sogenannten Repoussoirfigur gegen die stürzenden Bildelemente; bedeutungsmäßig ist eine Selbstidentifikation Kirchners, der gern das Treiben anderer beäugte, nicht auszuschließen.

Die Berliner Straßenbilder von 1913 und 1914 gelten heute als der frühe Höhepunkt in Kirchners Werk (siehe unser Gemälde »Berlin Friedrichstraße«, S.141, Tafel 35). Gegenüber allen anderen Fassungen zeichnet sich die vorliegende durch Konzentration im Bildbau aus. Der Berliner Kirchner-Katalog von 1979/80, der diese Bildgruppe umfassend vorstellt, würdigt im Zusammenhang mit der Ideenskizze (Abb. 183) und dem durch Übermalung entstellten Gemälde (Abb. 184) unser »berühmtes Pastell« (auf S. 192); es fasziniert über die erotische Brisanz hinaus durch die vollkommene Identität von Farbe, Form und Aussage. Kirchner hat sich von früh an über das aktuelle Kunstgeschehen orientiert und das Spezifische seiner Arbeit unter Pseudonymen wie »L. de Marsalle« − zuerst 1920 in der Zeitschrift »Genius« anhand seiner Zeichnungen − selbst interpretiert; er wird auch, wie Erhard Göpel vermutete (E.L. Kirchner, Farbige Graphik, München 1959, S. 42), auf die Straßenbilder des Futurismus mit ihren »fast mechanischen Bewegungsabläufen« in den Ausstellungen von Herwarth Waldens »Sturm« gestoßen sein. Gewiß hat Kirchner − darin Picasso nicht unähnlich − alles ihm Dienliche aufgegriffen, aber die Thematik des Straßenlebens war ihm a priori auf den Leib geschrieben, die Hektik Berlins war nur ihr Katalysator; was er von dem Phänomen Großstadt, von der Anonymität und Triebhaftigkeit ihrer Menschen in seiner nervigen Pinselschrift aufzeigt, bleibt seine alleinige Leistung.

Like a wedge the roads come at us. Upon their ultramarine-violet, overlaid with white in a loose fan pattern, a faceless procession in black glides towards its strutting goal which is both the focal point and the point of intersection of the picture's axes. The cocotte flickers and flares in tones of red which are undermined by the pallid green of her stand-up collar, the pale pink of her sensual head and the wan plume on her monstrous broad-rimmed hat. The colours are as decadent as the milieu. The mannerist, plummetting depth of perspective is arrested only by the half-length figure in the left foreground, who is not neutral, but not directly part of the drama; in his acute profile accentuated by the tall hat he plays the double part of the onlooker and mediator. In compositional terms he performs the function of a repoussoir figure, offsetting the tumbling components of the picture. As for interpretation, it would not be amiss to consider Kirchner's identification with a figure that, as he liked to do, observes the activities of others.

The pictures of Berlin street life of 1913 and 1914 are esteemed today as the early summit of Kirchner's œuvre (see our painting, Berlin Friedrichstraße, p. 142, pl. 35). In comparison with all the other versions, the one opposite is unique in its compositional concentration. This group of pictures is presented exhaustively in the Berlin Kirchner catalogue of 1979/80, where, in the context of the draft sketch of the idea (ill. 183) and the painting in which overpainting has quite altered the image (ill. 184), regard is given to our "famous pastel" (on p. 192). Its magnetism springs from both the explosively erotic subject and, more, the complete identity of colour, form and message. Kirchner informed himself early on as to current artistic developments and interpreted the specific quality of his own work under pseudonyms such as "L. de Marsalle", beginning in 1920 in the journal Genius, where he focussed on his drawings; it is also probable, as Erhard Göpel supposed (E.L. Kirchner, Farbige Graphik, Munich 1959, p. 42), that he encountered the Futurists' street pictures with their "almost mechanical sequences of motion" in the exhibitions of Herwarth Walden's Sturm. Certainly Kirchner − not unlike Picasso in this aspect − took up everything that would serve his purpose; but the subject of street life was written upon his soul at the outset, the fever of Berlin being only its catalyst. What he reveals in his vigorous painter's script of the phenomenon of the metropolis, of the anonymity and impulsiveness of its inhabitants, is his achievement alone.

Literatur: Erwin Petermann, Katalog der Kirchner-Ausstellung im Künstlerhaus Sonnenhalde, Stuttgart 1948, Nr. 33, Farbtafel. − H. Geissler, Zeichen und Farbe, Katalog der Ausstellung: Aquarelle und Pastelle seit 1900 in der Staatsgalerie Stuttgart, 1972, Nr. 70, Abb. S. 21. − Ketterer und v. Manteuffel, E.L. Kirchner, Zeichnungen und Pastelle, Stuttgart 1979, Nr. 52, Farbtafel. − G. Thiem im Katalog der Ausstellung: E.L. Kirchner in der Graphischen Sammlung der Staatsgalerie Stuttgart, 1980, Nr. 33, Farbtafel (mit weiterer Bibliographie).

Bibliography: Erwin Petermann, cat. of the Kirchner Exhibition at the Künstlerhaus Sonnenhalde, Stuttgart (1948), No. 33, colour plate; H. Geissler, Zeichen und Farbe, cat. of the exhibition, Aquarelle und Pastelle seit 1900 in der Staatsgalerie Stuttgart (1972), No. 70, ill. p. 21; Ketterer & von Manteuffel, E.L. Kirchner, Zeichnungen und Pastelle (Stuttgart, 1979), No. 52, colour plate; G. Thiem in the cat. for the exhibition, E.L. Kirchner in der Graphischen Sammlung der Staatsgalerie Stuttgart (1980), No. 33, colour plate (with further bibliography).

Egon Schiele

Geboren 1890 in Tulln a. d. Donau, 1906 bis 1909 Besuch der Wiener Akademie, 1907 die entscheidende Begegnung mit Gustav Klimt (1862–1918). 1909 Mitbegründer der »Neukunstgruppe«, 1915–1917 Kriegsdienst. Gestorben in Wien 1918 an der Spanischen Grippe, drei Tage nach seiner Frau, im gleichen Jahr wie Klimt.

28

Selbstbildnis im Hemd (Kniestück)

Entstanden 1914
Farbstifte und Deckfarbe über Bleiskizze auf Japanpapier, 48,5 × 32 cm
Bez. links unten innerhalb eines Quadrates: EGON SCHIELE 1914
Herkunft: Architekt Anton Schmid, München—Wien.
Inv. Nr. C 63/1063

Egon Schiele

Born in 1890 at Tulln on the Danube, attended the Academy at Vienna 1906–09; in 1907, his decisive meeting with Gustav Klimt (1862–1918). Co-founder of the "Neukunstgruppe" in 1909, called up for active service in 1915–17. Died in Vienna in the Spanish Influenza epidemic of 1918 — three days after his wife and in the same year as Klimt.

28

Self-Portrait in Shirt (Knee-Piece)

Dated 1914
Coloured pencil and opaque paint over pencil sketch on Japan paper, 48.5 × 32 cm
Signed below left, within a square, EGON SCHIELE 1914
Provenance: Anton Schmid, architect, Munich & Vienna.
Inv. No. C 63/1063

Das Selbstbildnis war schon immer, das heißt seit dem frühen Dürer, Selbstbefragung, psychologische Selbsterfahrung; van Gogh stellte sich erstmals in Selbstverstümmelung dar (1889 mit Kopfverband, nachdem er sich das Ohr abgeschnitten hatte); danach E. L. Kirchner 1915 als Soldat mit abgehackter Hand (Oberlin College, Ohio; Gordon Nr. 435); von dort ist es nur noch ein Schritt zur Selbstzerstörung (Arnulf Rainer) und dem weitgehenden Verlust des Bildnisses in der modernen Kunst.

Die Expressionisten waren allesamt Bekenner, Ekstatiker, Propheten des Untergangs der alten Welt schon vor dem Ersten Weltkrieg. Schiele, obwohl der Jüngste unter ihnen, trägt am frühesten das Kainszeichen tödlicher Bedrohung, schon auf unserem »Der Prophet« genannten Gemälde, einem Doppelbildnis von 1911, das ein Totentanz des 20jährigen ist (siehe S.152, Tafel 40). — Und gebärdet er sich hier auf dem Selbstbildnis vom Jahre des Kriegsausbruchs 1914 nicht auch als Tänzer? Die gespreizte Schrittstellung und die Exaltation der Pantomime sprechen dafür. Der Kopf ist wie bei einem plötzlichen Staccato zurückgeworfen, diesem Ruck des Entsetzens folgen die Skeletthände; die deckende Farbe des Hemdes durchbrechend, legen sich ihre gespreizten Finger um den tiefroten Mund. Blutige Flecken wie Stigmata tragen die Handrücken und das Gesicht; ein rotes Band zieht sich bis zum Ohr unter dem Haarkranz.

Im leidenschaftlichen Drang zur Offenbarung, zur Preisgabe, die keine Tabus kennt, die das Obszöne — wie hier im »Kniestück« — einkalkuliert, verkörpert Schieles Selbstbildnis Hellsichtigkeit und Angst, Abwehr und Aggression. — »Der Künstler selbst ist, im wahrsten Sinne des Wortes, der Brennpunkt, in dem das Zeitgeschehen sein Symbol besitzt« (Werner Hofmann im Katalog der Ausstellung: »Experiment Weltuntergang, Wien um 1900«, Hamburg 1981, S. 150).

Always, since the early Dürer, that is, the self-portrait has been a questioning of the self, a psychological experiencing of the self. Van Gogh was the first to show himself in self-mutilation (in 1889, with his head bandaged after he had cut off his ear); then, in 1915, we see E. L. Kirchner as a soldier with one hand cut off (Oberlin College, Ohio, Gordon No. 435); thence it is but a step to self-destruction (Arnulf Rainer) and the extensive loss of portraiture in modern art.

The Expressionists were all of them confessors, ecstatics, prophets of the downfall of the old world even before the Great War. Schiele, though the youngest of them, is the first to bear mark of Cain of mortal danger, as early as 1911 in our painting entitled "The Prophet", a Dance of Death of the twenty-year-old (cf. p.152, pl. 40). Is his pose in this self-portrait of 1914, the year in which the War broke out, not again that of a dancer? His legs spread as if in a step, the highly-strung gesture, would seem to confirm this. The head is thrown back as if at a sudden staccato, a jerk of horror; it is followed by the skeletal hands. Breaking through the opaque colour of the shirt, their splayed fingers are laid about the deep-red mouth. Stains red as blood like stigmata mark the backs of his hands and his face; a red band is drawn up to the ear and under the hair-line.

In its passionate urge for revelation, for disclosure that knows no taboos and which takes the obscene into account, as this "Knee-Piece" does, Schiele's self-portrait epitomises vision and dread, defence and aggression. — "The artist himself is, in the true sense of the word, the burning focus in which current events possess their symbol" (Werner Hofmann, in the catalogue for the exhibition, "Experiment Weltuntergang, Wien um 1900", Hamburg, 1981, p. 150).

Literatur: W. Hofmann, Katalog der Ausstellung Egon Schiele (2. Internationale der Zeichnung), Darmstadt 1967, Nr. 61, Abbildung. — H. Geissler, Zeichen und Farbe, Katalog der Ausstellung: Aquarelle und Pastelle seit 1900 in der Staatsgalerie Stuttgart, 1972, Nr. 124, Farbtafel S. 27.

Bibliography: W. Hofmann, exh. cat. Egon Schiele (2nd Internationale of Drawing, Darmstadt, 1967), No. 61, ill.; H. Geissler, Zeichen und Farbe, exh. cat. for the exhibition, Aquarelle und Pastelle seit 1900 in der Staatsgalerie Stuttgart (1972), No. 124, colour plate p. 27.

Fernand Léger

Geboren 1881 in Argentan (Normandie), 1897–1902 Lehre als Architekt, besuchte seit 1900 in Paris die Ecole des Arts Decoratifs, 1908 Kontakt mit Delaunay, 1914–1916 Soldat, gründete 1920 mit Le Corbusier die Zeitschrift »L'Esprit Nouveau«, 1928 erste Reise nach Amerika, wo er sich 1940–1945 aufhielt, gestorben 1954 in Gif-sur-Yvette.

29

Les Fumées sur les toits

Rauch über den Dächern

Entstanden 1912
Rohrfeder und Pinsel in Schwarz über
Bleistift auf braunem Papier, auf Pappe
aufgezogen, 61,4 × 43,4 cm
Bez. rechts unten: F Léger; auf der Pappe:
Les fumées sur les Toits / Dessin pour une
Composition /No 2.
Herkunft: Laut Klebezettel auf der
Rückseite 1913 in Herwarth Waldens
»Erstem deutschen Herbstsalon« in Berlin
ausgestellt (mit weiteren 14 Arbeiten). –
Sammlung Ida Bienert, Dresden. –
Kunsthandel London.
Inv. Nr. C 68/1675

Fernand Léger

Born at Argentan, Normandy, in 1881. Trained as an architect 1897–1902, attended the École des Arts Décoratifs in Paris from 1900. Met Delaunay in 1908; soldier 1914 till 16; in 1920, founded the journal L'Esprit Nouveau, with Le Corbusier. First journey to America, 1928; lived there 1940–45. Died at Gif-sur-Yvette in 1954.

29

Les Fumées sur les toits

Smoke above the roofs

Dated 1912
Rush pen and brush in black over pencil
on brown paper, mounted on card,
61.4 × 43.4 cm
Signed below with, F Léger; on the card:
Les fumées sur les Toits / Dessin pour une
Composition / No 2.
Provenance: according to label on reverse,
shown in 1913 at Herwarth Walden's
"First German Autumn Salon" in Berlin
(with fourteen other works);
Collection Ida Bienert, Dresden;
London art dealers.
Inv. No. C 68/1675

Der Titel »Rauch – Rauchwolken über den Dächern« hört sich wie der eines impressionistischen Bildes an; man könnte dabei an das lichterfüllte Basler Gemälde Vincent van Goghs von 1886 mit dem Blick über die Häuser des Montmartre denken. Hier aber geht es um eine neuartige Aktivierung des Betrachters, der aus fragmentarischen Formen das Bild in seiner Vorstellung zu ergänzen hat. Das ist die Methode des analytischen Kubismus. Der Bildraum entsteht aus der Verzahnung geometrischer Elemente. Eckige Gebäudeteile mit spitzen und flachen Dächern sind von Kreissegmenten durchsetzt, die sich durchdringen und teilweise wie Polster ausbuchten: das sind Légers »Rauchwolken« in einem letzten Stadium formaler Autonomie, wie aus der Entwicklung dieses »Städtebildes« von der ersten Fassung in einem Karlsruher Gemälde bis zu der vorliegenden, am stärksten abstrahierten und damit freiesten Form ersichtlich ist. Die für die avantgardistische Kunst des 20. Jahrhunderts gültige Devise Légers: »Der realistische Wert eines Werkes ist von jeder imitativen Qualität vollkommen unabhängig« (erstmals 1913 bei einem Vortrag in Berlin so formuliert), ließ auch realiter nicht definierbare, zugunsten des Bildorganismus erfundene Formen entstehen. Das sind hier vor allem die keilförmigen schwarzen Flächen oben, rechts und unten: Sie bilden zu den zentrifugalen, um eine offene Mitte schwingenden Kräften der labilen Komposition die Gegengewichte.

Der Ausgangspunkt der Konzeption ist wie stets bei Léger ein Seherlebnis – in seiner Abwandlung wird es immer mehr Vorwand als Vorwurf des Bildes – wie hier in hohem Maße. Letztlich ist es noch immer der Blick aus seinem 1911 bezogenen Atelier in der Rue de l'Ancienne Comédie über das Quartier Latin bis hin zu Notre Dame, deren einer Turm unter dem oberen Keil durch das Relikt der abschließenden Balustrade zu identifizieren ist. Aber geworden ist daraus ein Bild ganz eigener rhythmischer Prägung, gewiß nicht ohne Kenntnis der Eiffelturmbilder Delaunays und des Futurismus; etwas sehr anderes als die zentrierte Bildordnung des gleichzeitigen synthetischen Kubismus von Braque und Picasso. In Légers Bildwelt hat erstmalig die Dynamik der Großstadt und der Technik Eingang gefunden und sich bis zuletzt behauptet. Hier ist alles noch in einer frühen, offenen Form voller Elan; sie steht an der Wende zur Geschlossenheit der »Contrastes de formes«, die zum Inbegriff von Légers Schaffen wurden (exemplarisch dafür unser Gemälde »Eléments géométriques« von 1913).

From the title, "Smoke" or "Clouds of smoke over the rooftops", we might be looking at an Impressionist picture, or be reminded of Vincent van Gogh's luminescent painting of 1886 (now at Basle) with the view over the houses of Montmartre. Not so; this is a new kind of stimulation for the beholder to complete the picture in his mind from the fragmentary forms before him. It is the method of Analytical Cubism. Pictorial space is created out of the enmeshing of geometric elements. Angular parts of buildings with pointed and flat roofs are interspersed with segments of circles which in turn cut across each other and occasionally bulge as if upholstered: these are Léger's "clouds of smoke" in a final stage of autonomy, as the development of this "townscape" from the first version in a painting at Karlsruhe to the present, most drastically abstracted and thus freest form shows. Léger's premise that "the realistic value of a work of art is completely independent of any imitative quality" first formulated at a lecture in Berlin in 1913, was to be valid for the avant-garde art of this century; it allowed for the emergence of forms not definable by recourse to known reality, but invented to suit the pictorial organism. Here this applies especially to the wedge-shaped areas towards the top, right and bottom of the picture. They form counterweights to the centrifugal forces of a composition rotating, unstable, about an open centre.

As always with Léger, the starting-point of his concept is a visual experience which, as it evolves, becomes increasingly the pretext rather than the plan for a picture. This drawing is an extreme instance of the process. Ultimately, it is still the view from his studio in the Rue de l'Ancienne Comédie, which he took in 1911, across the Quartier Latin all the way to Notre Dame, the one tower still identifiable under the upper wedge, by its vestige of balustrading. But what this has become is a picture with its own rhythmic metre, certainly not in ignorance of the pictures of the Eiffel Tower by Delaunay and the Futurists, definitely distinct from the centralised pictorial order of the contemporary movement of Synthetic Cubism of Braque and Picasso. In Léger's iconography the dynamics of the metropolis and of technology first found expression, and asserted themselves to the last. Here all that is still in an early, open form full of élan – at the turning point to the compactness of the "Contrastes de formes" that were to epitomise Léger's work (as exemplified by our painting, "Eléments géometriques" of 1913).

Literatur: Will Grohmann, Die Sammlung Ida Bienert Dresden, Potsdam 1933, Abb. 12. – U. Gauss, Katalog der Ausstellung: Von Ingres bis Picasso, Französische Zeichnungen des 19. und 20. Jahrhunderts aus dem Besitz der Graphischen Sammlung der Staatsgalerie Stuttgart, 1969, Nr. 70, Abb. S. 37. – A. Franzke, Fernand Léger, Fumées sur les toits, in: Jahrbuch der Staatlichen Kunstsammlungen in Baden-Württemberg, Band 15, 1978, S. 87, Abb. 13. – M. Moeller, Katalog der Ausstellung: Léger zum 100. Geburtstag, Staatsgalerie Stuttgart 1981/82, Nr. 4 (fälschlich datiert: 1913).

Bibliography: Will Grohmann, Die Sammlung Ida Bienert, Dresden (Potsdam, 1933), ill. 12. – U. Gauss, exh. cat. Von Ingres bis Picasso, Französische Zeichnungen des 19. und 20. Jahrhunderts aus dem Besitz der Graphischen Sammlung der Staatsgalerie Stuttgart (1969), No. 70, ill. p. 37; A. Franzke, "Fernand Léger, Fumées sur les toits" in Jahrbuch der Staatlichen Kunstsammlungen in Baden-Württemberg XV (1978), p. 87, ill. 13; M. Moeller, cat. for the exhibition, Léger zum 100. Geburtstag (Staatsgalerie Stuttgart, 1981/82), No. 4 (mistakenly dated 1913).

Piet Mondrian

Geboren 1872 in Amersfoort (Holland), 1892 Diplom als Zeichenlehrer, seitdem Studium an der Rijksacademie Amsterdam, kommt in Berührung mit der Theosophie, 1911–1914 in Paris, 1916 Begegnung mit Bart van der Leck und Theo van Doesburg, Gründung der De Stijl-Gruppe. 1919–1938 erneut in Paris, 1938–1940 in London, seitdem in New York bis zu seinem Tode 1944.

30

Das Meer

Entstanden 1914
Kohle, teils gewischt, auf grauem Papier,
auf Karton aufgezogen, Fehlstellen am
linken Rand und unten, Blindstempel
rechts oben: Hand mit Beil im Kreis,
50,2 × 63 cm
Bez. unten rechts der Mitte: PM '14
Herkunft: H. L. C. Jaffé, Amsterdam. —
Brook Street Gallery, London. — Jorge
Coumandari, Santiago. — Galerie Tarica,
Paris.
Inv. Nr. C 75/2509

Aus einem rechteckigen Boden grauen Papiers wurde ein Queroval als Bildfeld ausgegrenzt. Mondrian will sich damit von seinen bisherigen, naturgebundenen Darstellungen absetzen und einen vom Abbild unabhängigen, geistigen Bereich prästabilieren. Das Oval, von der Theosophie als kosmisches Ei, als Urform angesehen, soll hier die Autonomie des Bildes garantieren. Das Erlebnis der Unermeßlichkeit des sich zwischen Himmel und Erde wiegenden Meeres wird von Mondrian in eine Zeichensprache übersetzt, die bei aller Einfachheit reich an Nuancen ist und wegweisend für die Kunst unseres Jahrhunderts wurde. — Die dominierenden langen Horizontalstriche, die hin und wieder von kurzen Vertikalen gekreuzt werden, bezeichnen den Wellenschlag. Wechselnde Dichte und leichte Verwerfung der fein gewischten Strichlagen suggerieren das Schwanken des Meeresspiegels, der sich in den aufgelichteten Randzonen mit der Atmosphäre zu verbinden scheint. Zwei ausnahmsweise gewölbte Linien in der Mitte oben sind — wie alles bei Mondrian — sowohl als Kompositionselemente wie als Metaphern zu verstehen: als weitgespannte Bogen wirken sie stabilisierend und zentrierend, als Brücken — mit angedeuteten Eckpfeilern am unteren Bogen — überbrücken sie nicht allein Wasser und Erde, sondern alles Getrennte.
Als diese Zeichnung im Sommer 1914 entstand, war der Krieg ausgebrochen. Expressionisten wie E. L. Kirchner reflektierten die Hochspannung als Morbidität in den Berliner Straßenbildern (siehe Tafel 27, S. 308) oder wie der Österreicher Schiele als Schock im Selbstbildnis (siehe Tafel 28, S. 310); die Kunst des introvertierten Holländers Mondrian blieb davon unberührt, obwohl er unmittelbar betroffen wurde: Er lebte in Paris, besuchte im Juli seinen todkranken Vater in Holland, konnte aber nicht mehr zurückkehren — und wurde so im Jahre 1916 zum Mitbegründer der De Stijl-Gruppe. — Seine expressive Phase schicksalsschwerer Bäume und einsamer Dünen hatte er hinter sich und strebte zu einer absoluten Kunst universaler Harmonie. An dieser vom Kubismus bestärkten Wende, bei der sich das Seherlebnis zusehends in Bildgeometrie verwandelt, entstand die vorliegende Zeichnung »Das Meer«.
Es wird Betrachter geben, die keinen solchen Titel brauchen, denen die reine Ästhetik einer gegenstandsfreien Komposition genügt. Andere aber werden hier den Anfang vom Ende der Kunst sehen. Dabei wollte Mondrian mit seiner Kunst die Welt verbessern! — Vielleicht ist der Gedanke nicht abwegig, daß nur ein am nördlichen Meer Aufgewachsener und ein holländischer Calvinist die Abstraktion so konsequent vorantreiben konnte wie er. — Als Mondrian um 1920 den Prozeß der Abstraktion vom Naturvorbild durch die Reduktion allein auf Senkrechte und Waagerechte sowie auf die Primärfarben Blau, Rot, Gelb abgeschlossen hatte, hörte er auf zu zeichnen; als Mittel der Auseinandersetzung mit der sichtbaren Realität war das überflüssig geworden. Zum ersten »neoplastizistischen« Gemälde von 1921 bediente er sich ein letztes Mal eines — in unserer Sammlung befindlichen — Kartons (Katalog Stuttgart 1981, op. cit. Nr. und Abbildung 105).

Piet Mondrian

Born at Amersfoort (Holland) in 1872. After obtaining a diploma as teacher of drawing, studied at the Rijksacademie in Amsterdam; contact with Theosophy; in Paris, 1911—14. Meit Bart van der Leck and Theo van Doesburg in 1916, founded the group De Stijl. 1919—38, in Paris again, 1938—40 in London, then New York, where he died in 1944.

30

The Sea

Dated 1914
Charcoal, partly smudged, on grey paper mounted on card; portions missing at corner bottom left and below; stamp in relief, top right, a hand with axe in circle, 50.2 × 63 cm
Signed below, right of centre, PM '14
Provenance: H.C.L. Jaffé, Amsterdam; Brook Street Gallery, London; Jorge Coumandari, Santiago; Galerie Tarica, Paris.
Inv. No. C 75/2509

On a rectangular sheet of grey paper, a horizontal oval has been marked out as the picture area. It is Mondrian's relinquishing of his previous, naturalistic images in favour of pre-stabilising a spiritual sphere independent of illustration. The oval, regarded by Theosophists as a cosmic egg, a primeval form, is here intended to vouchsafe the autonomy of the picture. The experience of the immeasurable vastness of the sea undulating between heaven and earth has been translated by Mondrian into a sign language rich in nuance for all its simplicity and which became a pioneering act for the art of our century. The dominant long horizontal lines, here and there crossed by short verticals, signify the lapping of the waves. Variations in density and slight play in the horizontality of the horizontals, the regularity of the strata of finely blurred lines, suggest the swaying of the surface of the sea. At the lightened periphery it seems to unite with the atmosphere. Two lines that break the rule and describe arcs across the top of the picture's vertical axis can be taken — like every element in Mondrian — both as compositional factors and metaphors. As wide arcs they have a stabilising and centring effect; as bridges, with the suggestion of anchoring turrets framing the lower line, they span not only water and earth, but all that is separate.

When this drawing came about, in the summer of 1914, war had broken out. Expressionists such as E. L. Kirchner were reflecting the high tension as morbidity in Berlin street scenes (see plate 27, p. 308) or, like the Austrian, Schiele, as shock in self-portraits (see plate 28, p. 310); it left the art of Mondrian, the introvert, untouched, although he was directly affected. He was living in Paris, visited his mortally ill father in Holland in July, but could not return to France — and thus, in 1916, found himself co-founding the De Stijl group. He had his expressive phase of fateful trees and solitary dunes behind him, and was striving for an absolute art of universal harmony. It is from this fulcrum that, encouraged by Cubism and in the transformation of visual experience into pictorial geometry, our drawing, "The Sea", emerged.

There will be beholders who have no need of such titles, the pure aesthetic of a non-representational composition sufficing entirely. Others will see here the beginning of the end for art. As for Mondrian — for him his art was a means for reforming the world! It is perhaps not too far-fetched to think that only one who grew up by the northern sea and a Dutch Calvinist could push abstraction forward so rigorously as he. In about 1920, when he had completed the process of abstraction from nature as a model by reduction to verticals and horizontals alone, and to the primary colours, blue, red and yellow, he stopped drawing. As a means of coming to terms with visible reality, it had ceased to be relevant. For his first "Neo-Plasticist" painting of 1921, he was to avail himself for the last time of a preparatory drawing (in our Collection; see the Stuttgart catalogue cited below, 1981, No. and ill. 105).

Literatur: Jahrbuch der Staatlichen Kunstsammlungen in Baden-Württemberg, Band 13, 1976, S. 229 mit Abb. (dort auch die gleichzeitig erworbene Zeichnung einer Polderlandschaft Mondrians von 1906/08 abgebildet, Inv. Nr. C 75/2508). – U. Gauss, Katalog der Ausstellung: Mondrian – Zeichnungen und Aquarelle, Staatsgalerie Stuttgart, Den Haag, Baltimore 1981, Nr. 95 (die genannte Polderlandschaft: Nr. 26). – Siegmar Holsten, Kosmische Bilder in der Kunst des 20. Jahrhunderts, Katalog der Ausstellung in der Kunsthalle Baden-Baden 1983/84, Nr. 116, Abb. 63.

Bibliography: Jahrbuch der Staatlichen Kunstsammlungen in Baden-Württemberg XIII (1976), p. 229 with ill. (also of his drawing, acquired at the same time, of a polder landscape, 1906/08, Inv. No. C 75/2508); U. Gauss, exh. cat. Mondrian – Zeichnungen und Aquarelle, (Drawings, Water Colours, New York Paintings), Staatsgalerie Stuttgart, The Hague, Baltimore (1981), No. 95; the polder landscape is No. 26; Siegmar Holsten, Kosmische Bilder in der Kunst des 20. Jahrhunderts, exh. cat. Kunsthalle Baden-Baden (1983/84), No. 116, ill. 63.

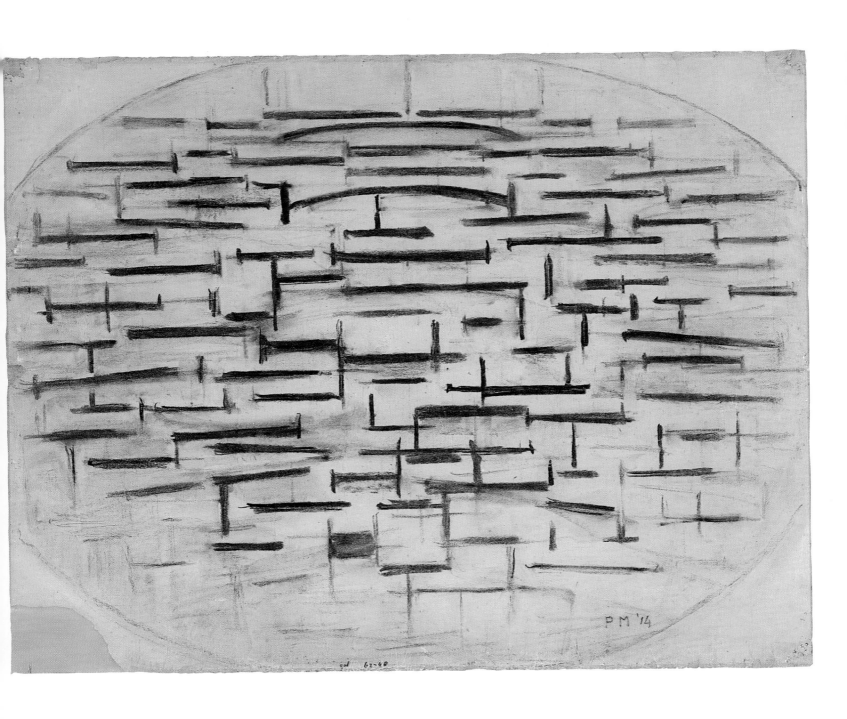

Francis Picabia

Geboren 1879 in Paris. Maler und Schriftsteller von sprunghafter Entwicklung. 1910 erste Begegnung mit Duchamp; mit ihm und Man Ray traf er 1915 in New York zusammen und gründete eine DADA-Gruppe, weitere folgten 1917 in Zürich mit Tzara und Arp und 1920 in Paris. 1921 Bruch mit den Dadaisten, seit 1924 Kontakt mit den Surrealisten. Zog sich an die Riviera zurück und verstarb 1953 in Paris.

31

Gabrielle Buffet

Entstanden 1915
Tuschpinsel und Aquarell in Rosé und
Hellgrün über Bleistift auf kaschiertem
Whatman-Karton, 58,5 × 46,8 cm
Bez. links oben: GABRIELLE BUFFET,
rechts unten: ELLE CORRIGE LES
MOEURS EN RIANT: LE FIDELE/
Picabia.
Herkunft: Marcel Duchamp. — Brook Street
Gallery, London. — Cordier-Ekstrom, New
York. — Sammlung Arthur A. Cohen, New
York. — Galerie Tarica, Paris.
Inv.Nr. C 79/2984

»Kunst ist ein pharmazeutisches
Produkt für Narren«
Picabia in »Manifeste Dada«, 1920

chen. — Wäre Picabias Einfall nur ein Einzelfall, müßte man ihn nicht hervorheben, aber er ist exemplarisch für das Bedeutendste, was er dank seiner antikünstlerischen Haltung erfunden hat: die Mécaniques.
Die Mécaniques sind ironische Metaphern für menschliches Verhalten, sie wollen die vielgepriesene Menschenwürde und die akademische Kunst provozieren, mit den Traditionen brechen, nachdem ihre Brüchigkeit im Ersten Weltkrieg offenbar wurde. Außerdem kann man die Maschinenbilder, meist sind es Räderwerke, die Picabia von 1915 bis 1921 ersann, als Hohn und Abwehr des uns vergewaltigenden Maschinenzeitalters interpretieren. Auf jeden Fall sind es Vorboten der DADA-Rebellion; die vorliegende Invention, bei der das Aggressive in Picabia dank der Hommage an seine Frau weniger in Erscheinung tritt, gehört zu den frühesten; sie war im Januar 1916 bereits in New York ausgestellt. —
Den Anfang mit ingenieurhaften, konzeptuellen Zeichnungen machte Duchamp, von dem der Funke auf Picabia 1915 in der Freiheit New Yorks übersprang. Zu Duchamps Hauptwerk, dem »Großen Glas«, auch die »Junggesellenmaschine« genannt, besitzen wir die 1914 datierte große Zeichnung der »Siebe« (siehe Abb. 17 und den Essay von Gudrun Inboden, in: »Studien zur Kunst«, Gunther Thiem zum 60. Geburtstag, Edition Cantz, Stuttgart 1977). — Die Folgen der »Mécaniques« sind sichtbar bei Max Ernst (siehe Tafel 34, S. 330) und bis heute u. a. bei Tinguely, Klapheck, Panamarenko.

Paradoxie und Ironie sind die Waffen Picabias, der dank seines väterlichen Vermögens ein unabhängiges Leben führen konnte und elegante Autos zu einer Zeit, wo sie noch Seltenheitswert besaßen, liebte. Dieses seiner Frau Gabrielle Buffet gewidmete Blatt aus dem Besitz von Marcel Duchamp stellt die aufgeklappten Windschutzscheiben eines offenen »Oldtimers« dar; man kann sie verstellen, so wie eine Frau ihr Gesicht zu verstellen weiß. Und eine Frau kann — so besagt es die Inschrift des »getreuen Picabia« — mit einem Lächeln Sitten und Gebräuche abändern. Im Kriegsjahr 1915 hatte das für den als Soldaten ausgebildeten Picabia eine sehr aktuelle Bedeutung: ohne den »Schutzschild« der aus einflußreicher Familie stammenden Gabrielle Buffet wäre er aufgrund seiner Emigration nach den Vereinigten Staaten als Deserteur eingestuft worden. — Der Mechanismus der abgewinkelten Scheiben, in deren Luftzug das Spruchband in Schwingung gerät, wird vor diesem biographischen Hintergrund zu einer Art Bildnis von Picabias Frau; dadurch gewinnt er nicht nur menschliche, sondern sogar charmante Züge: Die Beweglichkeit der beiden in Rosé und Grün spiegelnden Scheiben kann man als den Augenaufschlag oder das Mienenspiel einer Frau ansehen; auch mit ihren Launen, je nachdem, woher der Wind weht, verglei-

Francis Picabia

Born in Paris in 1879. A painter and writer whose career was fast and erratic. 1910, first encounter with Duchamp. Met him and Man Ray in New York in 1915, and founded a DADA group. Others followed, in Zurich with Tristan Tzara and Arp in 1917, and in Paris in 1920. Broke with the Dadaists in 1921, in touch with the Surrealists from 1924. Withdrew to the Riviera. Died in Paris in 1953.

31

Gabrielle Buffet

Dated 1915
Ink-drawing brush and water-colour in
pink and light green over pencil on lined
Whatman card, 58.5 × 46.8 cm
Inscribed above left, GABRIELLE
BUFFET, below to right, ELLE CORRIGE
LES MOEURS EN RIANT / LE
FIDÈLE / Picabia.
Provenance: Marcel Duchamp; Brook
Street Gallery, London; Cordier-Ekstrom,
New York; Collection Arthur A. Cohen,
New York; Galerie Tarica, Paris.
Inv. No. C 79/2984

"Art is a pharmaceutical
product for fools"
Picabia in "Manifeste Dada", 1920

Paradox and irony are the weapons of Picabia, whose father's wealth allowed him to lead an independent life and indulge his passion for elegant cars at a time when they were still a rarity. This work, which was dedicated to his wife, Gabrielle Buffet, and once belonged to Marcel Duchamp, shows the opened windscreen sections of a roofless "old-timer". The panes can be adjusted, just as a woman knows how to regulate her face; and a woman, so the "faithful Picabia's" inscription would have us know, can alter custom and morals with a smile. In the war-year of 1915 and for the trained soldier Picabia, this assertion was full of significance. Without the "screen" of Gabrielle Buffet, who came from an influential family, his emigration to the United States would have marked him as a deserter. Against this autobiographical background, the mechanies of the tilted panes, with the banderole of script waving in the resultant breeze becomes a kind of portrait of Picabia's wife. Thus it acquires not just anthropomorphic traits, but charm. — The mobility of the two panes, reflecting in pink and green respectively, could be viewed as a woman's eyes glancing up, or her changing expressions — along with her mood, too, according to how the wind blows. If Picabia's idea were unique, it would not need highlighting; but it is typical of the most important invention his anti-art stance led him to contrive — the "Mécaniques".

The Mécaniques are ironic metaphors for human behaviour, intended to provoke that much-praised human dignity and academic art, to break with traditions whose brittleness became manifest in the Great War. This apart, the machine pictures (mostly of wheel mechanisms) which Picabia conceived from 1915 to 1921 can be interpreted as contempt for and rejection of the machine age by which mankind is violated. Whatever else they may signify, they are heralds of the DADA rebellion. The invention before us, in which Picabia's aggressive element is mitigated by the homage to his wife, is one of the earliest; by January 1916 it was already on exhibition in New York.

The pioneer in quasi-engineering, conceptual drawings had been Duchamp, from whom Picabia picked up the spark in 1915, in the freedom of New York. In our possession is the large drawing of the "Sieves", dated 1914, which Duchamp executed for his major work, the Great Glass, or, as it is also known, the "Bachelor Machine" (cf. ill. 17 and Gudrun Inboden's essay in "Studien zur Kunst, Gunther Thiem zum 60. Geburtstag", Edition Cantz, Stuttgart, 1977). The further consequences of the Mécaniques are visible in Max Ernst (see plate 34, p. 330) and to the present day in the work of Tinguely, Klapheck and Panamarenko, to name just a few.

Literatur: Katalog der Picabia-Ausstellung, Modern Gallery, New York, Januar 1916, Nr. 10. — Katalog der Duchamp-Auktion, Hôtel Drouot, Paris 1926, Nr. 18. — Katalog der Picabia-Ausstellung, S. R. Guggenheim Foundation, New York 1970, Nr. 43, Abb. S. 89. — Katalog der Picabia-Ausstellung Paris 1976, Nr. 55, Abb. S. 76. — W. A. Camfield, Francis Picabia, Princeton 1979, S. 83, Abb. 111. — Katalog der Picabia-Ausstellung, Düsseldorf und Zürich, 1983/84, Nr. 22, Abb. S. 45.

Bibliography: Picabia Exhibition Catalogue, Modern Gallery, New York, January 1916, No. 10; cat. of the Duchamp Auction, Hôtel Drouot, Paris, 1926, No. 18; cat. of the Picabia Exhibition, S. R. Guggenheim Foundation, N.Y., 1970, No. 43, ill. p. 89; cat. of Picabia Exh., Paris, 1976, No. 55, ill. p. 76; W. A. Camfield, Francis Picabia (Princeton, N. J., 1979), p. 83, ill. 111; Picabia Exh. cat., Düsseldorf & Zurich, 1983/84, No. 22, ill. p. 45.

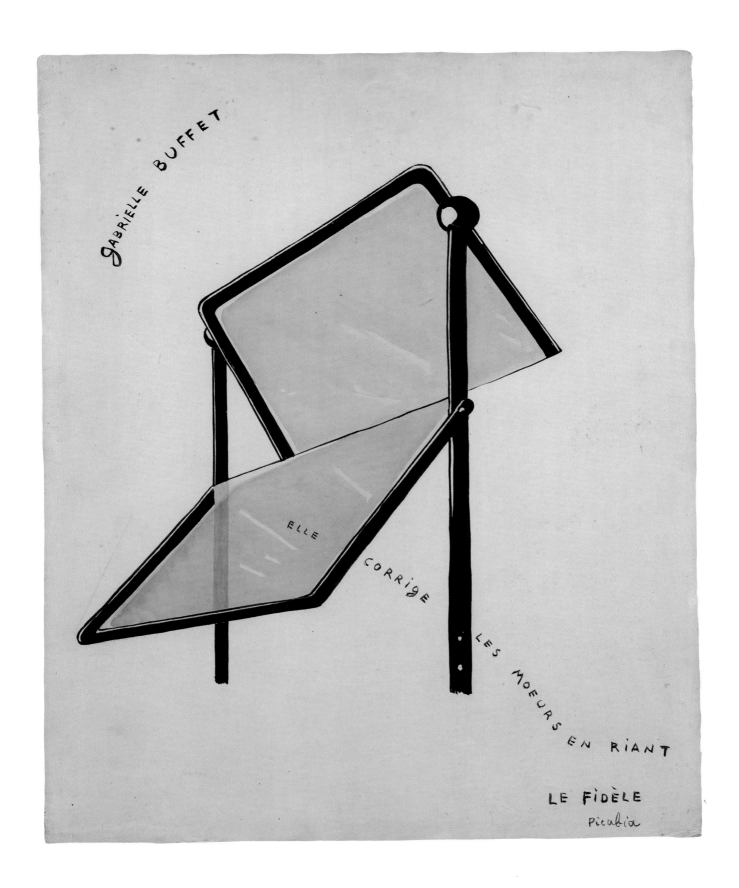

GABRIELLE BUFFET

ELLE

CORRIGE

LES MOEURS EN RIANT

LE FIDÈLE

Picabia

Paul Klee

Geboren 1879 in Münchenbuchsee bei Bern. 1898–1901 Studium bei Knirr und Stuck in München, wohin er 1906 übersiedelte, Freundschaft mit den Künstlern des »Blauen Reiters«, 1914 Reise nach Tunis, 1916–1918 Soldat auf dem Flugplatz Gersthofen, seit 1920 am »Bauhaus«, seit 1931 an der Düsseldorfer Akademie, 1933 entlassen, ging im Dezember nach Bern zurück, wo er 1940 starb.

32

Warnung der Schiffe

Entstanden 1917
Tuschfeder und Aquarell auf Fabriano-Papier, 18,8 × 14,2 cm, montiert auf rosagefärbtes Untersatzpapier 24,1 × 15,6/16,3 cm
Bez. links unten: 1917.108. Warnung der Schiffe; links oben, kaum sichtbar: Klee Herkunft: Ausstellung in Herwarth Waldens Berliner »Sturm«, Dezember 1917 (eines der vier verkauften von insgesamt 30 Blättern). – Rechtsanwalt Frings, Stuttgart. – Galerie Valentien, Stuttgart. – Dort 1934 von Hugo Borst, Stuttgart, für RM 155,– erworben. Inv. Nr. C 68/1608

Am 10. Juli 1917 notierte Klee: »Ein Aquarell in der Art der Miniaturen entstand, eine gute Erweiterung der Serie«; zu dieser gehört auch »Warnung der Schiffe«. – Miniaturartig ist die Dichte und Schwerelosigkeit der Komposition; sie gewinnt an Reiz, wenn man sie dreht und dabei entdeckt, daß Segelschiffe nicht nur den unteren, sondern auch den oberen Rand durchziehen; schwarz sind sie und werden allseits bedroht; besonders unten rechts, wo sich über dem Boot mit dem winzigen Männchen ein riesiges Rohr aufrichtet, desgleichen links ein Rohr aus einem Kopf mit Papierhelm. Die Assoziation Kanone oder Fernrohr führt – so banal es angesichts von Klees lyrischer Gestimmtheit erscheinen mag – zu der Frage, ob der Titel unseres Aquarells wie auch der seines Gegenstückes »Unstern der Schiffe« nicht mit der folgenschweren Erklärung des totalen U-Bootkrieges seitens der Deutschen am 1. Februar 1917 zu tun hat. Dem Soldaten Klee kann das nicht entgangen sein, der am 9. September 1917 niederschrieb: »Ein leidenschaftlicher Zug nach Verklärung ist doch mit Produkt des äußeren Erlebens.« Es ist die lichte Farbigkeit harmonischer Blau-Gelb-Töne auf rosa Grund und die Imagination des Kosmischen, die in uns Vorstellungen von Spiel, Märchen und »Verklärung« hervorrufen, wo doch im Grunde alles unheilverkündend ist. Im Zentrum richtet sich ein Fischvogel auf, dessen Bedrohlichkeit zwei Ausrufungszeichen und ein schwarzer Stern hervorheben; Sonne und Mond sind verdunkelt, spitz gezeichnete Wesen tauchen wie Schlingpflanzen aus dem Grunde auf, und von allen Seiten stoßen schwarze Dreieckssegel vor. – Was im ersten Augenblick spielerisch erscheint, erweist sich als »Warnung«, als »memento mori«.

Paul Klees Reaktion auf den Ersten Weltkrieg war: »Ich habe diesen Krieg in mir längst gehabt. Daher geht er mich innerlich nichts an« (Tagebuch 1914/952); er konnte ihn aber doch nur verdrängen. In seinem Etappendasein auf einem Flugplatz hat er sich durch Ignoranz und Ironie vom Kriegsgeschehen distanziert, es aber künstlerisch reflektiert, zunehmend in poetischem Gewande. Wie aus Klees Tagebüchern hervorgeht, hat er sich gegen Ende des Jahres 1917 – auch aus merkantilen Gesichtspunkten – entschlossen, sowohl die Titel seiner Blätter zu poetisieren, da die Leute nichts mehr vom Krieg wissen wollten, als auch den strengen kristallinischen Stil zu reduzieren, den noch die zwei Lithographien unserer Sammlung »Der Tod für die Idee« (1914/15) und »Zerstörung und Hoffnung« (1916) zeigen.

Paul Klee

Born in 1879, at Münchenbuchsee near Berne. Studied with Knirr and Stuck at Munich, 1898—1901, and settled there in 1906. Friendship with "Blaue Reiter" artists; 1914, travels to Tunis, 1916—18 soldier at Gersthofen aerodrome. At the "Bauhaus" from 1920, appointed to the Accademy at Düsseldorf in 1931; dismissed in 1933, returned to Berne in September of that year and died there in 1940.

32

Ships' Warning

Dated 1917
Drawing-pen and water-colour on Fabriano paper, 18.8 × 14.2 cm, mounted on pink-stained mounting paper, 24.1 × 15.6/16.3 cm
Inscribed bottom left, 1917.108.
Warnung der Schiffe; top left, barely discernible, Klee
Provenance: exhibited in Herwarth Walden's Berlin Sturm, December, 1917 (one of the four works sold out of a total of thirty); Frings, Stuttgart; Galerie Valentien, Stuttgart; acquired there by Hugo Borst, Stuttgart, in 1934, for 155 Reichsmark.
Inv. No. C 68/1608

On July 10th, 1917, Klee noted, "A watercolour done in the manner of miniatures, a good extension to the series." "The series" includes "Warnung der Schiffe": both density and weightlessness of the composition are "miniaturesque". Its charm is enhanced when one turns the composition and finds sailing-boats cruising not only along the bottom edge, but also, the top. They are black, and under threat from all sides; particularly below on the right, where, over the boat with the tiny mannikin, an enormous tube rises. Another juts out from a head wearing a paper helmet on the left. The association of a cannon or a telescope elicits the question, banal though it may seem in contrast to Klee's lyrical tenor, as to whether the title of our water-colour painting is not connected with the fateful declaration of an all-out U-boat war by the Germans on 1st February, 1917. It cannot have escaped the soldier, Klee, who wrote on 9th September, 1917: "A passionate bent for transfiguration is, after all, also the product of outward experience."

It is the bright colourfulness of harmonising blue-and-yellow tones upon the pink base, and the visualisation of the cosmic, that evoke in us images of play, fairy-tale and "transfiguration" in the midst of what is essentially a single message of disaster. At the centre a fish-bird rears, it maleficence underscored by two exclamation marks and a black star. Sun and moon are darkened, creatures sharply contoured, emerge like climbing, creeping plants from the picture ground, and from all sides black triangular sails advance. What at first glance appears playful turns out to be a "warning", a "memento mori".

Paul Klee's reaction to the First World War was, "I have long had this war within me. Therefore it is no concern of mine, inwardly" (Diary, 1914/952); but he could do no more than repress it. In the relative safety of his life at an airfield behind the lines, ignorance and irony helped him to remain detached from the events of the War, but he reflected it through his art and this increasingly in lyrical garb. As his diaries reveal, Klee resolved towards the end of 1917, also for mercantile reasons, to cast the titles for his work in a more poetic register since people wanted to hear no more of the War, and to reduce the stringent, crystalline style still evident, for example, in two lithographs in our collection — "Death for the Idea" (1914/15) and "Destruction and Hope" (1916).

Literatur: Die Sammlung Hugo Borst in Stuttgart, Stuttgart 1970, Farbtafel XV. – H. Geissler, Zeichen und Farbe, Katalog der Ausstellung: Aquarelle und Pastelle in der Staatsgalerie Stuttgart, 1972, Nr. 75, Farbtafel S. 45. – Katalog der Ausstellung: Paris–Berlin 1900–1933, Paris 1978/79, Farbtafel S. 244 der deutschen Ausgabe. – M. Droste, Klee und Kandinsky, Katalog der Ausstellung der Staatsgalerie Stuttgart 1979, Nr. 20, Farbtafel. – Katalog der Ausstellung: Paul Klee – Das Frühwerk, München 1979/80, Nr. 326, Abbildung. – O.K.Werkmeister, Versuche über Paul Klee, Frankfurt 1981, S. 57.

Bibliography: Die Sammlung Hugo Borst in Stuttgart (Stuttgart, 1970), colour plate XV; H. Geissler, Zeichen und Farbe, cat. of the exh., Aquarelle und Pastelle in der Staatsgalerie Stuttgart (1972), No. 75, colour plate, p. 45; exh. cat. Paris–Berlin 1900–1933 (Paris, 1978/79), colour plate 244 in German edn; M. Droste, Klee und Kandinsky, exh. cat. at Staatsgalerie Stuttgart (1979), No. 20, colour plate; exh. cat. Paul Klee – Das Frühwerk (Munich, 1979/80), No. 326, ill.; O. K. Werkmeister, Versuche über Paul Klee (Frankfurt, 1981), p. 57.

1917. 108. Warnung der Schiffe

George Grosz

Geboren 1893 in Berlin. 1909 Studium in Dresden und ab 1912 in Berlin bei Emil Orlik, 1914 Infanterist, Anfang 1916 wegen Krankheit entlassen, 1917/18 Heeresdienst, Nervenheilanstalt, Militärgericht, Mitbegründer der Berliner DADA-Gruppe; 1932 Reise und 1933 Übersiedlung nach New York, Lehrer an der Art Students League, 1951 erstmals wieder in Deutschland, 1959 in Berlin gestorben.

33

Niederkunft

Entstanden 1917
Tuschfeder und Aquarell auf gegilbtem
Zeichenkarton, 50,8 × 35 cm
Bez. rechts unten: GROSZ / August 17 /
Im. . .; darunter: dem Theodor Däubler zur
Erinnerung in Herzlichkeit / 25. März 1918
/ Babelsbergerstr.
Herkunft: Der Dichter und Kunstkritiker
Theodor Däubler (1876–1934) und dessen
Freund Will Frieg (1885–1968), über den
Werner Helwig in seinem Buch: Capri,
Magische Insel, Frankfurt 1979, berichtet.
Inv. Nr. C 66/1447

big vom Blattgrund abgesetzten Dreiecksform hervorgerufen; die dreht sich wie ein Karussell um ihre Spitze, in der eine Zirkustänzerin mit Zylinder die Arme hebt. Durch die andrängenden, mit spitzer Feder demaskierten »Typen« und das Changieren morbider Farben steigert sich das Bewegungsmoment. — Von zentrifugalen Kräften erfaßt ist auch unser großes, kurz nach diesem Aquarell entstandenes Gemälde »Widmung an Oskar Panizza« (siehe S. 156, Tafel 42), das man fälschlich, aber seinem Gehalt nach richtig, ein »Begräbnis« genannt hat.

Ein 24jähriger, der Berlin kaum verlassen hatte und wider Willen in die Uniform gesteckt wurde, erweist sich hier künstlerisch absolut auf der Höhe seiner Zeit, ideologisch war er wie kein anderer gegen sie. Nur wenn beides zusammentrifft — wie auch bei Daumier — hat die Gesellschaftskritik in der Kunst eine Chance, den Tag zu überleben. — Es ist staunenswert, wie Grosz seine geschmeidige frühe Zeichenweise durch Elemente des Kubismus und Futurismus auf eigene Faust während des Krieges in ein messerscharfes Instrument verwandelt hat. Unsentimental und entlarvend wie sein ätzender Strich sind auch seine Titel: »Ach knallige Welt, du seliges Abnormitätenkabinett« — »Professor Freud gewidmet« — »Der Mensch ist gut«.

1917 geriet die alte Welt mit der Russischen Revolution aus den Fugen. Was die Bilder der Expressionisten prophezeiten (siehe Tafel 25, 27, 28) und poetisch verschlüsselt — auch Klees »Warnung der Schiffe« von 1917 (siehe vorige Tafel), seziert George Grosz in »Ecce homo« (»sehet, welch ein Mensch«), einem Band mit 84 gesellschaftskritischen Federzeichnungen und 16 Aquarellen, darunter das vorliegende; schon der religiöse Titel des Bandes ist eine Blasphemie. Der Zeichner und sein Verleger standen wegen Gotteslästerung und Beleidigung mehrfach vor Gericht. Vor dem Todesurteil wegen Meuterei rettete den Soldaten Grosz 1918 die Intervention des Grafen Kessler in Weimar, eines Freundes von Hugo v. Hofmannsthal, Henry van de Velde und Maillol. — Theodor Däubler, der hymnische Dichter des »Nordlichts« und hellsichtige Kunstinterpret eines »Neuen Standpunkts« (1916) setzte als erster auf Grosz; zum Dank erhielt er dieses Aquarell.

Die Niederkunft vollzieht sich wie in einem Kaleidoskop, wo Gestalten facettenhaft schillernd kommen und gehen; ohne dieses futuristische Bewegungsmoment wäre die Thematik, die alle unsere Vorstellungen von Geburtsszenen in der Kunst brüskiert, schwer erträglich. Die Schlagkraft der Komposition liegt in der Schräge, mit der sie — wie der Fetzen einer Abreißcollage — aufs Blatt gesetzt ist. Stürzende Formen erwekken die Assoziation einer Sturzgeburt. Der Effekt der Simultaneität wird durch die Verschränkung aller Bildelemente in einer far-

George Grosz

Born in Berlin in 1893. Studied at Dresden in 1909, from 1912 at Berlin under Emil Orlik; 1914, infantryman, but discharged on ground of illness early in 1916; 1917/18, military service, psychiatric clinic, court martial, co-fo under of the Berlin DADA group; 1932, went to New York, settling there in 1933. Taught at Art Students League. Revisited Germany in 1951; died in Berlin in 1959.

33

In Childbirth

Dated 1917
Drawing-pen and water-colour on yellowed drawing card, 50.8 × 35 cm
Signed below right, GROSZ / August 17 / Im. . .; below this, dem Theodor Däubler zur Erinnerung in Herzlichkeit [to T. D., in sincere remembrance] / 25. März 1918 / Babelsbergerstr.
Provenance: the poet and art-critic, Theodor Däubler (1876–1934) and his friend, Will Frieg (1885–1968), on whom Werner Helwig writes in his book, Capri, Magische Insel (Frankfurt, 1979).
Inv. No. C 66/1477

With the year 1917 and the Russian Revolution, the old world fell apart. What the pictures of the Expressionists had been prophesying (cf. plates 25, 27, 28), as had Klee's "Ships' Warning" in its poetically coded way (see preceding plate) in 1917, George Grosz now dissected in "Ecce homo" (Behold the man), a volume containing eighty-four socially critical pen drawings and sixteen water-colours, the work opposite among them. The blasphemy begins with the religious title of the book; both draughtsman and publisher were called to court more than once to face that charge and that of insult. In 1918 Grosz the soldier had narrowly escaped execution for insubordination, when Count Kessler, a friend of Hugo von Hofmannsthal, Henry van de Velde and Maillol in Weimar, interceded on his behalf. Theodor Däubler, the hymnic poet of "Das Nordlicht" and far-sighted art-historical interpreter of a "Neuer Standpunkt", 1916 was the first to place his confidence in Grosz. This water-colour was given to him in gratitude.
The childbirth takes place as if in a kaleidoscope, figures coming and going as shimmering fragments. Grosz's subject plays merciless havoc with all our notions of the image of birth in art; were it not for this futuristic element of dynamism, the scene would be almost impossible to endure. The composition's impact lies in its oblique axis on the sheet, placed there as if it were a torn fragment in a décollage. Tumbling forms evoke the association of a precipitate delivery. The effect of simultaneity is created by the overlapping of all the elements of the picture in a rough triangle shape set off by its colours from the monochrome picture ground. This interior shape appears to revolve like a merry-go-ro and about its point, at which a circus dancer with a top hat raises her arms. The dynamism is intensified further by the "customers" drawing insistently near — characterised and unmasked with an incisive pen — and the scintillation of morbid colours. Such centrifugal energy also informs our large painting, "Widmung an Oskar Panizza" ("Dedicated to Oskar Panizza") (see page 156, pl. 42), which was completed shortly after this water-colour and which has been mistakingly called a "funeral" — an error, but not in relation to its "message".
A twenty-four-year-old, having hardly left Berlin behind him and put into uniform against his will, here shows himself artistically as absolutely in tune with his time as he was ideologically against it more than anyone. Only when the two coincide, as they do in Daumier, to name another instance, does social criticism in art have a chance of survival beyond its time. It is astounding how, during the War, Grosz's own initiative led him to transform his smooth early drawing technique through Cubist and Futurist elements into the acutest surgical instrument. If his mordant line is unsentimental and exposing, so are his titles: "O gaudy World, you blessed Freak-show; Dedicated to Professor Freud"; "Man is Good".

Literatur: George Grosz, Ecce Homo, Berlin 1923, Farbtafel VI. — Katalog der Ausstellung: George Grosz — John Heartfield, Kunstverein Stuttgart 1969, Nr. 7, Abb. S. 52. — H. Geissler, Zeichen und Farbe, Katalog der Ausstellung: Aquarelle und Pastelle seit 1900 in der Staatsgalerie Stuttgart, 1972, Nr. 49, Farbtafel S. 29.

Bibliography: George Grosz, Ecce Homo (Berlin, 1923), colour pl. VI; exh. cat. George Grosz — John Heartfield, Kunstverein Stuttgart (1969), No. 7, ill. p. 52; H. Geissler, Zeichen und Farbe, cat. for exh., Aquarelle und Pastelle seit 1900 in der Staatsgalerie Stuttgart (1972), No. 49, colour pl. p. 29.

Max Ernst

Geboren 1891 in Brühl bei Köln, 1909 bis 1914 Studium der Philosophie in Bonn, 1914–1918 Soldat, 1919 Gründung der Kölner DADA-Gruppe mit Hans Arp. Seit 1922 in Paris, 1924 Mitbegründer der surrealistischen Bewegung. 1941–1953 in den USA, 1954 wieder in Paris, wo er 1976 verstarb.

34

Frau Wirtin an der Lahn

Entstanden 1920
Bleistift und Tuschfeder über Gouache auf bedrucktem Papier (Häkelmusterblatt),
auf braunes Tonpapier aufgezogen,
24,3 × 31 cm auf 26 × 34 cm
Bez. rechts unten: Max Ernst; am unteren Rand: frau wirtin an der lahn, schutzengelin der deutschen, dein ist die industrie anatomie paläontologie schenk uns kleine frohlocken. — Auf der Rückseite handschriftlicher Zettel: Jury der Jungen / Gruppe 1924 / Max Ernst / Adr. Ey Düsseldorf Hindenburgwall 11 / Frau Wirtin an der Lahn / Preis 350 Mark / Vers.: 350 Mark.
Herkunft: Johanna Ey, Düsseldorf. —
20. Auktion, Stuttgarter Kunstkabinett, 24.–26. II. 1954, II. Teil, Nr. 1063. —
Erich Schurr, Stuttgart.
Inv. Nr. C 80/3022

Wer sich mit »Dadamax« einläßt, gerät leicht auf Glatteis; es ist sehr viel über ihn geschrieben worden, aber zu fassen kriegt man ihn schwer. So ist die vorliegende Arbeit, eine der raffiniertesten seiner drei Kölner DADA-Jahre, zwar mehrfach veröffentlicht, aber wirklich untersucht hat sie keiner. De facto ist sie keine Collage, sondern erweckt nur den Anschein eines »Klebebildes«. Genaues Hinsehen und Abtasten ergeben, daß ein durchlaufendes Vorlageblatt für Häkelarbeiten zugrunde liegt, dessen Muster (die zwei radförmigen links und die beiden teppichartigen in der Mitte) sich durch Übermalen und Überzeichnen der anliegenden Flächen reliefartig, wie Fotocollagen, herausheben: Verwirrspiel von »Dadamax« — »jenseits der Malerei«, wie seine Devise gegen die konventionelle Kunstästhetik lautete.

Das Ganze dieser Schein-Collage ist mehr als die Summe ihrer merkwürdigen Teile; isoliert sind sie trivial bis anstößig, als Ganzes vielschichtig in ein Bezugssystem gebracht, aber poetisch. Das ist die erklärte Absicht des Künstlers, der als Quintessenz seiner Definition der Collage von dem »Funken Poesie« spricht, »welcher bei der Annäherung dieser Realitäten überspringt.« Ähnliches könnte Paul Klee gesagt haben, dem die Metamorphose der Dinge etwas Vertrautes war. Max Ernst kannte den 12

Jahre älteren Künstler, wie aus einem Besuch bei ihm in München 1919 hervorgeht, wo er für eine Klee-Ausstellung in Köln 33 Arbeiten erhielt.

Das skurrile Räderwerk auf unserem Blatt (sein Bezugswort in der Aufschrift unten ist: »die industrie«) läßt auf Kenntnis der absurden »Mécaniques« von Picabia schließen (siehe sein »Bildnis« der Gabrielle Buffet von 1915 auf Tafel 31, S. 318), der seit 1917 auf der Züricher DADA-Szene mitwirkte und mit Marcel Duchamp befreundet war. Dessen Hauptwerk, die »Junggesellenmaschine« von 1914, kommt einem in den Sinn (siehe unsere Zeichnung dazu, Abbildung 17, S. 223), sobald man auf der vorliegenden Gouache entdeckt hat, daß von dem Rand oben in der Mitte ein Phallus herabhängt, der sich im Getriebe der Häkelvorlagen reibt. Jetzt gibt es auch keinen Zweifel mehr, worauf die Anrufung der »Frau Wirtin an der Lahn« abzielt: Die Studentenlieder und die Knittelverse über sie — dem ehemaligen »Landser« Max Ernst wohl vertraut — sind erotisch mehr als gepfeffert. Mutter Ey, Max Ernsts Düsseldorfer »Wirtin« und Erstbesitzerin dieser »Maschinerie«, muß nicht zimperlich gewesen sein. — Wer weiß, was sie unter »anatomie« und »paläontologie«, die in der fiktiven Widmung nach der »industrie« zitiert werden, verstanden hat; man kann die Anatomie als Hinweis auf den sezierenden Denk- und Werkprozeß Max Ernsts verstehen, der wie die Paläontologie Verschüttetes und damit Unbewußtes zutage fördert, aber man muß es nicht zu »ernst« nehmen. — Max Ernst ist auch in der verbalen Deutung ein Verweigerer par excellence. Die Ironie, die aus seinen edlen Gesichtszügen blitzte, steckt bei den frühen Arbeiten wie dieser hier nicht allein im Bild-Schock, sondern geradeso im Wortspiel.

Max Ernst

Born in Brühl, near Cologne, in 1891. Studied philosophy at Bonn, 1914—18 soldier, 1919 founded the Cologne DADA group with Hans Arp. In Paris from 1922; cofounder of Surrealist movement, 1924. In United States from 1941—53, returned to Paris in 1954; died there in 1976.

34

My Lady Host by the Lahn

Dated 1920
Pencil and drawing pen over gouache on printed paper (crochet pattern), mounted on brown coloured paper, 24.3 × 31 cm on 26 × 34 cm
Inscribed below right, Max Ernst; along bottom edge: frau wirtin an der lahn, schutzengelin der deutschen, dein ist die industrie anatomie paläontologie schenk uns kleine frohlocken (lady host by the lahn, guardian angel of the germans, thine is the industry anatomy palaeontology grant us little jubilations); a handwritten label on the reverse, Jury der Jungen/ Gruppe 1924/ Max Ernst/ Adr. Ey Düsseldorf Hindenburgwall 11/Frau Wirtin an der Lahn/ Preis 350 Mark/ Vers. ("Ins."): 350 Mark.
Provenance: Johanna Ey, Düsseldorf; 20th Auction at Stuttgart Kunstkabinett, 24th—26th II. 1954, Section II, No. 1063; Erich Schurr, Stuttgart.
Inv. No. C 80/3022

Becoming involved with "Dadamax" can easily mean landing on black ice. A great deal has been written about him, but he is nonetheless not easy to pin down. The work opposite, one of the most ingenious to come out of Ernst's three years of DADA activity in Cologne, has been published a number of times, but no-one has really examined it. In fact it is not even a collage, although its appearance suggests just that. Closer inspection and touch reveal that the base is a continuous, intact pattern sheet for crochet work, the patterns themselves (the pair on the left, like wheels, and the carpet-like pair in the centre) project in relief against the painted and drawn-over surrounding areas, like a photo collage: a teasing puzzle of "Dadamax's", "beyond painting", this according to his motto contrary to conventional art aesthetic.

The totality of this bogus collage is more than the sum of its strange parts; in isolation, they range from trivial to offensive, as a whole, they are brought together in a manifold relational context, and this poetically. This is the declared intent of an artist whose essential definition of collage lies in the "spark of poetry that flashes over when approaching these realities". Paul Klee, with his familiarity with the metamorphosis of things, could have said very much the same. Max Ernst knew Klee (Klee was twelve years his senior) and he visited him in 1919 in Munich to collect 33 works for a Klee exhibition in Cologne.

The whimsical system of wheels in the work before us (with the corresponding word below, "die industrie", suggests that he had seen Picabia's absurd "Mécaniques" (cf. his "protrait" of Gabrielle Buffet of 1915, pl. 31, p. 319 above). Picabia, a friend of Marcel Duchamp's, collaborated since 1917 in the Zurich DADA scene.

Duchamp's major work, the "Bachelor Machine" of 1914 (cf. the drawing for it in our possession, ill. 17, p. 223) comes to mind as soon as one discovers, suspended from the middle of the upper green margin on our gouache, a phallus, rubbed by the wheels and gears of the crochet pattern. Now there can be no doubts as to what the invocation of the "hostess by the Lahn" intends; the doggerel and the student songs about her, which Max Ernst, the former private, must have known very well, are more than spiced with eroticism. Johanna ("Mutter") Ey, Max Ernst's "hostess" in Düsseldorf (her inn was a regular artists' rendezvous) and the first owner of this "machinery", cannot have been squeamish. Who knows how she interpreted out of "anatomy" and "palaeontology" cited after "industry" in the fictitious dedication. Anatomy could be seen as an allusion to the incisiveness of Ernst's thought processes and work, bringing to the light of day as a palaeontologist might, that which has been obscured with sedimental ballast and thus rendered subconscious — but we should not take it all too much in "e(a)rn(e)st". In verbal interpretation, too, Max Ernst is a refuser par excellence. The irony that flashed from his aristocratic physiognomy is matched in his early works such as this one, both in the shock of the image, and, patently, in his play on words.

Literatur: Katalog der Ausstellung: Neuere
Kunst aus württembergischem Privatbesitz I.,
Staatsgalerie Stuttgart 1973, Nr. 29 Abb. S. 32
(B. Rau). — Werner Spies, Max Ernst — Collagen,
Köln 1974, Farbtafel 20. — Spies-Metken, Max
Ernst, Werke 1906—25, Köln 1975, Nr. 405,
Abb. S. 206 (mit Bibliographie). — Jahrbuch
der Staatlichen Kunstsammlungen in Baden-
Württemberg, XVIII. Band, 1981, S. 174/175 mit
Abbildung.

Bibliography: cat. for the exhibition, Neuere
Kunst aus württembergischem Privatbesitz I
(Staatsgalerie Stuttgart, 1973), No. 29, ill. p. 32
(B. Rau); Werner Spies, Max Ernst — Collagen
(Cologne, 1974), col. pl. 20; Spies-Metken,
Max Ernst, Werke 1906—25 (Cologne, 1975),
No. 405, ill. p. 206 (with bibliography);
Jahrbuch der Staatlichen Kunstsammlungen in
Baden-Württemberg XVIII (1981), 174/75
with ill.

frau wirtin an der lahn, schutzengel der deutschen. dein ist die industrie anatomie paläontologie schenk uns kleine frohlocken

max ernst

Lovis Corinth

Geboren 1858 in Tapiau (Ostpreußen), nach der Ausbildung an der Königsberger und Münchner Akademie (1880–1884) ging er über Antwerpen nach Paris bis 1887. Seit 1900 in Berlin. Mitglied und Präsident der Sezession. Seit 1918 alljährlich in Urfeld am Walchensee. Gestorben auf einer Reise in Zandvoort (Holland) 1925.

35

Walchensee im Winter

Entstanden 6. Januar 1924
Aquarell und Deckweiß auf gegilbtem Aquarellkarton mit unregelmäßigen gebräunten Rändern, 43 × 48,8 cm
Bez. unten links der Mitte in Feder:
5 — verändert in: 6. Januar 1924 /
Lovis Corinth
Herkunft: Erich Cohn, New York. —
Dr. Walter Feilchenfeldt, Zürich
Inv. Nr. C 72/2220

Lovis Corinth

Born in Tapiau, East Prussia, in 1858. After training at the Academies at Königsberg and Munich (the latter 1880–84) he moved via Antwerp, to Paris, where he stayed until 1887. In Berlin from 1900. Member and president of the Sezession. From 1918, annual visits to Urfeld by the Walchensee. Died on a visit to Zandvoort (Holland) in 1925.

35

Walchensee in Winter

6th January, 1924
Water-colour and opaque white on yellowed water-colour card with irregular browned edges, 43 × 48.8 cm
Inscribed below left of centre, in pen: 5 [altered to:] 6. Januar 1924 / Lovis Corinth
Provenance: Erich Cohn, New York;
Dr. Walter Feilchenfeldt, Zurich.
Inv. No. C 72/2220

Vom Dreigestirn der deutschen Impressionisten hat sich nur Lovis Corinth in der Avantgarde der stürmischen 20er Jahre unseres Jahrhunderts behauptet. Anders als der zehn Jahre ältere Max Liebermann und der zehn Jahre jüngere Max Slevogt, die ihn beide überlebten, hat der 60jährige einen dynamischen Spätstil entfaltet, der zur Zeit der nationalsozialistischen Kunstdiktatur als »entartet« galt und heute — besonders in den Walchensee-Bildern — als Krönung seines Lebenswerkes gilt. Dies um so mehr, als Corinth eine Autonomie der Pinselschrift und eine Absolutheit der Farbe erreichte, die heute wie ein Vorgriff auf den Tachismus der 50er Jahre anmutet.

Das vorliegende ist ein untypisches Walchenseebild, man würde es kaum als solches erkennen, wenn der Titel nicht darauf hinwiese; es verschließt sich im ersten Augenblick, ist nicht beglückend (wie unser Walchensee-Gemälde von 1923), sondern bestürzend im Verglühen des Tages und des Lebens. — Obwohl gewiß vor der Natur bei einem winterlichen Sonnenuntergang entstanden, hat das künstlerische Resultat dieser Impression mit Landschaftsmalerei wenig zu tun, aber mit den Grenzerfahrungen unserer Existenz sehr viel; mit ihnen war der sonst vital erscheinende Corinth seit der Erschütterung durch einen Schlaganfall im 53. Lebensjahr vertraut, er hat sie weit vor den psychischen Improvisationen eines Wols oder Michaux bildnerisch bewältigt (» . . . jede Arbeit endet mit Depressionen, dieses Leben noch weiter führen zu müssen«, schrieb er).

Obwohl das Großartige an diesem Aquarell »die Abwesenheit jedes Gegenstandes« ist, wie Erwin Petermann schlagend formulierte, seien aus der Kenntnis anderer Walchenseebilder, gleichsam als Sehhilfen, einige topographische Hinweise angefügt. Den Standpunkt des Malers hat man sich auf der »Kanzel« oberhalb des Wohnhauses in Urfeld zu denken, dessen verschneites Dach sich am linken Bildrand hinter Busch und Baum abzeichnet, rechts davon strebt eine schneebedeckte Lärche auf, dahinter breitet sich schwarzblau der See, über dem die Sonne wie blutend untergeht. — Hier hat Corinth, was ihm als letztes Ziel vorschwebte, verwirklicht: »Die wahre Kunst ist Unwirklichkeit üben. Das Höchste!« — niedergeschrieben im Jahre der Entstehung dieses visionären Aquarells, 1924.

Of the triumvirate of German Impressionists, only Lovis Corinth asserted himself in the avant-garde of the tumultuous twenties of this century. Unlike Max Liebermann, who was ten years older, or Max Slevogt, ten years his junior (both of whom survived him) Corinth developed at sixty a dynamic late style which was labelled "degenerate" under the Nazis' dictatorship of the arts. Today, however, this style, especially in the Walchensee landscapes, is prized as the summit of his life's work. This is even more the case in retrospect, Corinth having attained a hand so autonomous and colour so absolute that he seems all but to anticipate the "tachisme" of the 1950s.

Ours is not a typical Walchensee picture; it would hardly be recognisable as such without the help of the title; and, rather than instilling joy (as our Walchensee painting of 1923 does), the first impression is one of withdrawal and then of our dismay, of fading daylight and life. Though certainly executed from nature during a winter sunset, the artistic result of this impression has precious little in common with landscape painting — and a great deal with the border experiences of our existence. To Corinth, whose general impression was one of great vitality, they were nothing new since his crippling stroke at the age of fifty-three. Long before the psychic improvisations of a Wols or a Michaux, he overcame excruciation through his creativity (". . . every piece of work ends with depression at having to continue this life", he wrote).

Although the masterly achievement in this water-colour is "the absence of any object", as Erwin Petermann has observed so cogently, some topographical notes based on Corinth's other Walchensee paintings may aid our vision here. The painter's standpoint must have been on the "Kanzel" (a high promontory, the "pulpit" above his house at Urfeld, its snow-covered roof seen toward the far left through shrubs and trees; to its right a snowy larch rises, behind lies the blue-black expanse of the lake and over that, as if bleeding, the sun sets. Here, Corinth has realised what he projected as his culminating aim — "The real art is to practise unreality. The ultimate!" This he noted in the year in which our visionary water-colour painting came about, 1924.

Literatur: Katalog der Lovis Corinth-Ausstellung, Wolfsburg 1958, Nr. 277. — H. Geissler, Zeichen und Farbe, Katalog der Ausstellung: Aquarelle und Pastelle seit 1900 in der Staatsgalerie Stuttgart, 1972, Nr. 23, Abb. 59.

Bibliography: cat. of Lovis Corinth Exhibition, Wolfsburg (1958), No. 277; H. Geissler, Zeichen und Farbe, cat. for the exhibition, Aquarelle und Pastelle seit 1900 in der Staatsgalerie Stuttgart (1972), No. 23, ill. 59.

Oskar Schlemmer

Geboren 1888 in Stuttgart, 1906—1914 an der Stuttgarter Akademie bei v. Keller, Landenberger und Hölzel, Freundschaft mit Baumeister, Meyer-Amden und Itten. 1914—1918 Kriegsdienst, 1921—1925 am »Bauhaus« in Weimar und bis 1928 in Dessau, 1929—1932 an der Akademie Breslau, nach deren Schließung Notzeiten. Gestorben 1943 in Baden-Baden.

36

Vier Figuren in Raumperspektive

Entstanden 1924/25
Aquarell, mit Kreide gehöht, über Bleistift auf weißem Seidenpapier (oben Rest einer Zähnung), zweifach montiert auf Untersatzblatt und starkem Papier, 27/27,3 × 21,9 cm
Nicht signiert
Herkunft: 1951 von Tut Schlemmer aus dem Nachlaß erworben.
Inv. Nr. C 51/354

Der Titel des in Komposition und Aussage ungewöhnlichen Blattes: »Vier Figuren in Raumperspektive« besagt, worum es Schlemmer nach seiner ersten Schaffensperiode »systematischer Entpersönlichung« ging: um die Figur im Raum. Das war damals eine Kampfansage. Denn das figürliche Element und damit der Mensch drohte durch die Abstraktion der russischen und holländischen Avantgarde verlorenzugehen, und der Raum war durch die Expressionisten der Tiefe enthoben in die Bildfläche verlegt worden. Dieses Aquarell macht klar, daß Schlemmer Figur und Raum unabhängig von der Tradition neu begreift.
Durch vertikale Dreiteilung in einen schachtartigen Korridor links, eine dunkle Wand rechts und eine Zelle in der Mitte entsteht eine gestaffelte Raumfolge aus der Tiefe bis in die Ebene des Betrachters. Die progressiv aufgestellten Figuren sind in der Raumkulisse abgekapselt, aber der Betrachter kann sie alle mit einem Blick von der Nähe bis in die imaginäre Ferne erfassen. Nur auf einer Bühne kann man so verfahren. Schlemmer war bekanntlich auch Bühnenbildner und Tänzer. Die kleinste, links aus der Tiefe hervortretende Figur hat die stärkste Ausstrahlung, ein weiß gehöhter Lichthof umgibt sie, und ihr Gesicht bildet den Fluchtpunkt der Raumperspektive. Das feierliche Schwarz der Kleidung und der wie beim Überbringen eines Geschenkes angehobene Arm betonen ihre Bedeutung. Im Spannungsverhältnis dazu steht der hermetische Profilkopf vorn rechts; kompositionell hat er die Funktion eines Repoussoirs — inhaltlich die eines Gegenspielers. Während jene eintretende kleine Figur er-

wartungsvoll dünkt, ist diese an Schlemmers Masken erinnernde abweisend. Zwischen jenen beiden männlichen Figuren steht in einer Zelle eingeschlossen ein Paar, nach den langen Gewändern und den Frisuren zu schließen, sind es zwei Frauen. Wirft diese Konstellation nicht die Frage auf: Was wird hier gespielt? Für das Verständnis von Schlemmers Bildwelt mag das sonst sekundär erscheinen, hier aber, bei einem »Blattbild«, dem er prinzipiell »individuelle Freiheit/Formfreiheit« zugesteht, verbirgt sich in der verklammerten Konfiguration eine dramatische Situation. Die Frage danach dürfte nicht müßig sein, zumal schon andere Bildideen aus dieser Zeit — wie »Anklage«, »Tischgesellschaft« oder »Gegeneinander« existentiell gedeutet wurden.
Im flüssigen Aquarell hat Schlemmer die Gefahr der Starrheit, die in seinem neuen Ausgangspunkt von De Chiricos »Pittura metafisica« lag, am leichtesten überwunden und gelangt er über komplizierte vielfigurige »Raumperspektiven« wie diese zur Klarheit und Monumentalität seiner drei Jahre später begonnenen Folkwang-Bilder.

Oskar Schlemmer

Born in Stuttgart, 1888. 1906—14, at the Stuttgart Academy, under von Keller, Landenberger and Hölzel; frequented Baumeister, Meyer-Amden and Itten. War service, 1914—18. At the "Bauhaus" in Weimar 1921—25, then in Dessau, until 1928; Academy at Breslau (Wroclaw), 1929—32, followed by hardship and official suppression. Died in Baden-Baden in 1943.

36

Four Figures in Spatial Perspective

Dated 1924/25
Water-colour with chalk highlights, over pencil on white tissue paper (remains of serration visible above), mounted twice on support paper and stiff paper,
27/27.3 × 21.9 cm
Unsigned
Provenance: acquired from Tut Schlemmer, from the estate, in 1951.
Inv. No. C 51/354

The title of this water-colour, an unusual work both in composition and content, "Four Figures in Spatial Perspective", expresses Schlemmer's concern following his first period of work, his "systematic depersonalisation". At the centre now was the figure in space. Then, it amounted to a challenge; for the figurative element and with it the human, looked as if it was about to be lost, displaced by the abstraction of the Russian and Dutch avant-garde; while space had been raised by the Expressionists out of depth onto the picture surface. This picture shows clearly that Schlemmer was focussing on both the figure and space again, but in a new way, independent of tradition.
The vertical division of the picture into three sections — a shaft-like passage to the left, a dark wall on the right and in between, a cell or cubicle, creates a staggered sequence of spaces from a depth up to the viewer's own plane. The progressively placed figures are contained, separate within the stage set for them, but the viewer can take them all in at one glance, from the nearest down to the imaginary distance. It is only on a stage, in fact, that this effect can be realised in pratice: and, of course, Schlemmer was both a set-designer and dancer. The strongest presence is that of the smallest figure, advancing from the furthest background on the left, surrounded by a halo of (back-)light from beyond the corridor, heightened in white. The figure's face coincides with the perspectival vanishing point. The stately black of his clothing and the one arm raised as if proffering a gift enhance the figure's significance. In spatially and emotively tense opposition to it is the hermetic profile head in the foreground on the right: compositionally, acting in the role of a repoussoir, in "meaning", that of a stage antagonist. While the former, emerging little figure suggests anticipation, the nearer, reminiscent of Schlemmer's masks, wards off. Between these two male figures, enclosed in a cell, is a duo whose long robes and hairstyles suggest the figures of two women. Does this constellation not elicit the question, what is the drama we are witness to? Normally it would seem a question of only secondary relevance for the understanding of Schlemmer's imagery; but here, in the case of a "Blattbild" ("sheet" or "paper" picture), a category of his coining to which he allotted "individual freedom / freedom of form" as a matter of principle, the configuration locked inward conceals a dramatic situation. The question may not be so inappropriate given that other pictorial ideas from this period, such as "Anklage" ("Indictment"), "Tischgesellschaft" ("Dinner Party"), "Gegeneinander" ("Conflict") have been interpreted on an existential basis.
In this fluid water-colour, Schlemmer has succeeded in overcoming the danger of rigidity inherent in his assumption of De Chirico's "Pittura metafisica" as a new starting-point; complex "patial perspectives" densely peopled, like the work opposite, would to lead him to the clarity and monumentality of the Folkwang pictures that he began three years later.

Literatur: Hans Hildebrandt, Oskar Schlemmer (mit Œuvreverzeichnis der Gemälde und Aquarelle), München 1952, Nr. 538. — Karin v. Maur, Katalog der Ausstellung zu Schlemmers 80. Geburtstag, Staatsgalerie Stuttgart 1968, Nr. 95, Farbtafel S. 75. — H. Geissler, Zeichen und Farbe, Katalog der Ausstellung: Aquarelle und Pastelle in der Staatsgalerie Stuttgart 1972, Nr. 127. — Karin v. Maur, Oskar Schlemmer, Band II, Œuvrekatalog, München 1979, Nr. A 199 (mit Bibliographie); Farbtafel Nr. 20 in Band I Monographie.

Bibliography: Hans Hildebrandt, Oskar Schlemmer (with cat. raisonné of paintings and water-colours; Munich, 1952); No. 538; Karin von Maur, cat. of exhibition on eightieth anniversary of Schlemmer's birth, Staatsgalerie Stuttgart (1968), No. 95, colour pl. p. 75; H. Geissler, Zeichen und Farbe, cat. of exh., Aquarelle und Pastelle in der Staatsgalerie Stuttgart (1972), No. 127; Karin von Maur, Oskar Schlemmer (Munich, 1979), vol. 2, cat. raisonné, No. A 199 (with bibliography); col. pl. No. 20 in vol. 1, monograph.

Laszlo Moholy-Nagy

Maler, Graphiker, Fotograf und Typograf. Geboren 1895 in Bàcsborod (Ungarn). 1914—1917 Soldat. Schloß sich der Gruppe MA in Budapest an und wanderte 1919 über Wien nach Berlin aus. 1923—1928 am »Bauhaus« als Leiter des Vorkurses und der Metallwerkstatt. Bis 1934 wieder in Berlin, dann in Amsterdam und London; seit 1937 in Chicago als Leiter des »New Bauhaus« und der »School of Design«, dort 1946 verstorben.

37

Transparente Konstruktion

Entstanden 1923/25
Tusche und Aquarell über Vorzeichnung auf weißem Bütten, collagiert auf bräunlichen Karton, der schwarzgrau überspritzt ist, 37,4 × 49,8 cm
Bez. auf dem weißen Papier rechts unten: Moholy-Nagy; auf der Rückseite des Kartons in Blei: Moholy-Nagy 23/25; in Blockschrift der Stempel des Künstlers und in Tusche: P 15.
Herkunft: Galerie Dr. Klihm, München. — Dr. Ernst Hauswedell, Hamburg, Katalog der 187. Auktion, 1972, Nr. 1621.
Inv. Nr. C 72/2285

Laszlo Moholy-Nagy

Painter, graphic artist, photographer and typographer. Born in Bàcsborod, Hungary, in 1895. 1914—17, military service. Joined the MA Group in Budapest; emigrated to Berlin via Vienna in 1919. Headed the preparatory course and the metal workshop at the "Bauhaus", 1923—28. In Berlin again until 1934, then in Amsterdam and London. To Chicago in 1937, where he was the head of the "New Bauhaus" and "School of Design"; died in Chicago in 1946.

37

Transparent Construction

Dated 1923/25
Ink and water-colour over preliminary drawing on white deckle-edged handmade paper, stuck to brown card sprayed thinly with dark grey, 37.4 × 49.8 cm
Signed at lower right edge of white inset, Moholy-Nagy on reverse of card, in pencil: Moholy-Nagy 23/25; in block printing, the artist's stamp, and in Indian ink, P 15.
Provenance: Galerie Dr. Klihm, Munich; Dr. Ernst Hauswedell, Hamburg, catalogue of 187th Auction, 1972, No. 1621.
Inv. No. C 72/2285

Das Licht unabhängig von einem Gegenstand, rein darzustellen als Lichtbahn, -bündel, -raum, das ist Moholys Beitrag zum Konstruktivismus und über ihn hinaus weiterwirkend bis heute. Als er 1920 aus Ungarn in Berlin eintraf und den Suprematismus der Russen Malewitsch und El Lissitzky kennenlernte und im Jahre 1921 mit der holländischen De Stijl-Gruppe einen »Aufruf zur elementaren Kunst« unterzeichnete, hatte er nicht das Gefühl zu spät, sondern in eine Welt progressiver Ideen hineingeboren zu sein. Die Technik in die Kunst zu integrieren, wurde sein Hauptanliegen und machte ihn zum richtungweisenden Kopf im »Bauhaus« seit 1923. Assistiert von seiner Frau, der Fotografin Lucia Schultz, »entwickelte« er (im doppelten Sinn des Wortes) neue Arten von Licht-Bildern: Fotogramme und Fotocollagen, die die bisherige Statik der Motive in Bewegung setzten. Das führte zwangsläufig zur Kinetik, das heißt zu Abläufen von Licht-Phänomenen. Seit 1922 konstruierte Moholy dazu eine Maschine: den Licht-Raum-Modulator (das Original heute im Busch-Reisinger-Museum, Cambridge, Mass., zwei Repliken in Eindhoven und im Bauhaus-Archiv, Berlin). Was sich da mit elektrisch angetriebenen Reflektoren und Metallschablonen an Lichteffekten abspielt, geschieht auf dem vorliegenden Blatt in konzentrierter Momentaufnahme; die Beschränkung, aber auch Sensibilisierung der Mittel und die harmonische Farbtrias der diagonalen Lichtbahnen erwecken eine kosmische Vorstellung von Raum und Zeit.
»Von der Pigmentmalerei bis zu der in den Raum geworfenen Lichtgestaltung« heißt der Titel eines Aufsatzes von Moholy aus dem Jahre 1925 (im Katalog des Vereins der Leipziger Jahresausstellungen); treffender als mit dieser Formulierung ist das auf unserem Blatt Sichtbare gar nicht zu definieren; es entzieht sich, auch in seinem visionären Charakter, einer detaillierten Beschreibung. — Seine Datierung 1923/25 läßt auf eine Entstehung in zwei Arbeitsprozessen schließen, was der technische Befund bestätigt. Zuerst muß das weiße Blatt mit den diagonalen Strahlen und den zwei raumperspektivischen Flächen in Schwarz und Rot entstanden sein. Moholy signierte es, hielt es also für fertig; später aber hinterlegte er es mit einem dunkleren Karton, um die Räumlichkeit zu steigern. Alsdann tat er den entscheidenden Schritt, der die Komposition aus der Nachfolge von Mondrians Gestaltungsprinzipien heraushebt. Er bediente sich dazu eines neuartigen Instrumentes: der Spritzpistole, deren Pigmentzerstäubung einen atmosphärischen Reiz hervorruft. Ausgespart aber mit Hilfe abdeckender Streifen blieb ein rechtwinkliges helles Gitternetz, das die beiden Blätter immateriell durchdringt. Balance und Transparenz schaffen einen imaginären Lichtraum.

To have depicted light independently of an object, in its pure state as a beam, bundled rays or space, this was Moholy's contribution to Constructivism, and one whose influence was to outlast it and continue to the present day. When he arrived in Berlin from Hungary in 1920 and encountered the Suprematism of the Russians, Malevich and El Lissitsky, and, in 1921, signed an "Appeal for elementary art" with the Dutch De Stijl group, he did not feel that he had been born too late, but rather that he had been born into a world of progressive ideas. His chief concern became the integration of technology into art and it made him the determining head at the "Bauhaus" from 1923 on. Assisted by his wife, the photographer, Lucia Schultz, he "developed" (in both senses) new kinds of photo (light) graphs; photogrammes and photocollages which dynamised his hitherto static motifs. That could only lead to kinetics, that is, sequences of phenomena with light. In 1922, Moholy constructed the first of a series of machines, the Light-Space Modulator (the original now at the Busch-Reisinger Museum, Cambridge, Mass., and two replicas at Eindhoven and at the Bauhaus Archives, Berlin). What occurs with these electrically driven reflectors and metal templates is an orchestration of light effects. This is done in the work illustrated with a concentrated, instantaneous perspective. The restriction, but also sensitisation, of the means, and the harmonic triad of colour of the diagonal beams of light, engender a cosmic conception of time and space.
"From Pigment-painting to the Shaping of Light projected into Space" ("Von der Pigmentmalerei bis zu der in den Raum geworfenen Lichtgestaltung") is the title of an essay Moholy wrote in 1925 for the catalogue of the Leipzig Annual Exhibition Society.
There could be no better articulation of what is visible in our work; its visionary nature eschews detailed description. The date, 1923—25, shows that the work was created in two distinct phases. This is corroborated by the results of technical research. The earlier piece is the white sheet with the diagonal rays and two space creating panels in black and red. Moholy signed it and so must have considered it complete. Later he affixed it to a darker coloured sheet of cardboard in order to heighten the spatial quality. In doing so, he took the significant step that raised the composition out of the wake of Mondrian's principles of design. Moholy discovered a new kind of tool: the spraygun. Its fine dispersal of pigment casts an evocative atmospheric charm; applied over stencil strips however, we are left with a rectangular, light gridh that permeates both sheets in an ethereal way. Balance and transparency create an imaginary space of light.

Literatur: St. v. Wiese, Katalog der Ausstellung:
Der Konstruktivismus und seine Nachfolge,
Staatsgalerie Stuttgart 1974, Nr. 43, Farbtafel
S. 37. – G. Thiem im Katalog der Ausstellung:
Zeichnungen von Bildhauern des 20. Jahr-
hunderts, Staatsgalerie Stuttgart 1980, Nr. 84,
Abbildung. – Siegmar Holsten, Kosmische
Bilder in der Kunst des 20. Jahrhunderts,
Katalog der Ausstellung in der Kunsthalle
Baden-Baden 1983/84, Nr. 113, Abb. 91.

Bibliography: Stephan von Wiese, exh. cat.
Der Konstruktivismus und seine Nachfolge
(Staatsgalerie Stuttgart, 1974), No. 43, colour pl.
p. 37; G. Thiem in the exh. cat. of Zeichnungen
von Bildhauern des 20. Jahrhunderts
(Staatsgalerie Stuttgart, 1980), No. 84, ill.;
Siegmar Holsten, Kosmische Bilder in
der Kunst des 20. Jahrhunderts, cat. of the
exhibition at Kunsthalle Baden-Baden
(1983–84), No. 113, ill. 91.

Pablo Picasso

Geboren 1881 in Malaga. 1892–1898 an spanischen Kunstschulen, 1900 erstmalig in Paris, wohin er 1904 übersiedelte. 1906 Kontakt mit Braque und Kahnweiler. 1917 in Italien. Seit 1919 im Sommer an der Côte d'Azur. Seit 1930 auf Schloß Boisgeloup in der Normandie. Bleibt während des Zweiten Weltkrieges in Paris. Seit 1946 in Südfrankreich: Antibes, Vallauris (1947–1955), Cannes (1955–1958), Vauvernagues bei Aix (1958–1961), seit 1961 in Mougins, wo er 1973 verstarb.

38

Mädchenkopf frontal und im Profil

Entstanden 1926
Tuschfeder in Schwarz über schwarzer, tonig gewischter Kreide und weißer, z. T. mit Wasser vermalter Kreide über lichtem graubraunem Ingres-Bütten; kleinere Korrekturen in Deckfarben, 62 × 47 cm
Bez. in Feder rechts unten: Picasso 26.
Herkunft: Galerie Flechtheim, Berlin und Düsseldorf. – 1930 L. Beith v. Speyer, Berlin (laut Unterschrift der Abbildung im »Kunstblatt« von 1930). – Theodor Werner, Berlin; von ihm 1949 erworben.
Inv. Nr. C 49/147

Pablo Picasso

Born in Malaga, 1881. Attended art schools in Spain 1892–98, first visit to Paris in 1900, settled there in 1904. Became acquainted with Braque and Kahnweiler in 1906. 1917, Italy. From 1917, spent his summers on the Côte d'Azur. Moved to château at Boisgeloup, Normandy, in 1930. Remained in Paris during WW2, then, from 1946, in the Midi: Antibes, Vallauris (1947–55), Cannes (1955–58), Vauvernagues near Aix (1958 till 61) and from 1961 at Mougins, where he died in 1973.

38

Girl's Head, Front View and Profile

Dated 1926
Drawing-pen and black ink over black chalk blurred in tonal gradations and white chalk partly dispersed with water, on light grey-brown handmade deckle-edged Ingres paper; minor alterations in poster-colours, 62 × 47 cm
Signed in pen, below right, Picasso 26.
Provenance: Galerie Flechtheim, Berlin and Düsseldorf; 1930, L. Beith von Speyer, Berlin (thus a subscript to the illustration in Kunstblatt, 1930); Theodor Werner, Berlin; acquired from him in 1949.
Inv. No. C 49/147

»In Bildern wie Picassos »Kopf«... leben die Masselosigkeit, die Allseitigkeit des Raumes, die Relativität des Standpunkts in neuer Verbindung mit gegenständlichen und daran hängenden psychischen Vorstellungen fort.« Mit diesen Begriffen hat der Hannoveraner Museumsmann Dorner schon vor 50 Jahren die Bedeutung dieses überlebensgroßen Kopfes erkannt (siehe Literatur). Der Überraschungseffekt der simultanen Metamorphose, bei der unser Blick das eine Profil nicht ohne das andere fixieren kann und beide sogleich zu einem En face verschmelzen, überwindet die Statik des Bildes, die Picasso in seinen klassizistischen Arbeiten der frühen 20er Jahre wieder betont hatte, zugunsten einer »neuen Raumvorstellung«. Man könnte von einer figürlichen Kinetik sprechen – gegenüber der abstrakten bei den gleichzeitigen Konstruktivisten (siehe Moholy-Nagy, Tafel 37, S. 340). Entscheidend für das Gelingen eines solchen Formenspieles ist, daß trotz der wechselnden Ansichten die Komposition nicht in ihre Teile zerfällt; hier sind sie wie Intarsien vollkommen ineinandergewachsen durch das kurvo-lineare Formsystem, durch Tonstufen und einen von der Weißhöhung suggerierten Lichteinfall.

Picasso hat das Prinzip der Metamorphose bereits im Jahre 1924 in zahlreichen Tuschzeichnungen durchgespielt, die man kaum kennen würde, hätte der Verleger Ambroise Vollard sie nicht in Holz schneiden lassen und »En manière d'introduction« Picassos Illustrationen zu Balzacs »Le chef d'Œuvre inconnu« von 1931 vorangestellt (es ist wie viele andere der »großen Bücher« Picassos als Vorzugsausgabe in unserer Graphischen Sammlung vorhanden). – Das wichtigste Gemälde im Stil und Ton unserer Zeichnung ist ein lichtdurchflossenes Interieur, »Das Atelier der Putzmacherin« in Paris vom Januar 1926; es hat den Charakter einer Grisaille. – Das Prinzip der geteilten, aber korrespondierenden Formen, das in Henry Moores Plastik beherrschend wurde, hat Picasso in den flachen, teils geschnittenen, teils gefalteten Holz- und Blechfiguren der 50er und 60er Jahre wieder aufgegriffen.

Unter unseren 16 von 1904 bis 1968 datierenden Zeichnungen und Pastellen Picassos (siehe auch Abb. 15 und 16, S. 220/221) wurde diese von 1926 wegen ihrer Bildhaftigkeit und Innovationskraft gewählt; sie beinhaltet die formalen Errungenschaften seines kubistischen Frühwerkes und weist weit in das spätere Schaffen voraus.

"In pictures like Picasso's Head..., absence of mass, ubiquity of space, the relativity of one's standpoint, live on in a new association with objective conceptions and psychic ones dependent upon them."
In these terms, the Hanover museum curator Dorner had recognised the significance of this larger-than-head more than 50 years ago (cf. bibliography below). We are surprised by the simultaneous metamorphosis. Our gaze cannot register one profile, without taking in the other at the same time, both instantaneously merging into a single en face. Here was Picasso's answer to the static quality of the image that he returned to in the classicising works of the 1920's, displacing this now with a "new concept of space". It could be called a kind of figurative kineticism as opposed to the abstract version of contemporary Constructivists (see Moholy-Nagy, pl. 37, p. 340). Decisive for the success of such a formal game is the cohesiveness of the composition despite alternating viewpoints. Here the parts are completely, interlocked and interwoven, like inlay work, by virtue of the curvilinear system of form. Graduations of shade and the suggestion of light is arrived at by means of white highlighting.

Two years previously, Picasso had experimented with the metamorphic principle in numerous ink drawings. These drawings would be scarcely known, had the publisher Ambroise Vollard not had them carved in wood and used Picasso's illustrations in 1931 "en manière d'introduction" to Balzac's "Un chef d'Œvre inconnu" (it is, like many other of Picasso's "great books", a special edition that can be seen in our Collection of Graphic Art).
The most important painting in the style and tone of our drawing is an interior flooded with light, "The Milliner's Workshop" (now in Paris) of January, 1926. It has the characteristics of a grisaille. The principle of divided but corresponding forms, a trait which became dominant in Henry Moore's sculpture, was something Picasso resumed in the flat, partly carved, partly folded wood and sheet metal figures of the 1950s and 60s.

Among our collections sixteen Picasso drawings and pastels dated between 1904 and 1968 (see also ills 15 and 16, p. 220/221 above), this one of 1926 was chosen for its vividness and innovative power. It incorporates the formal attainments of his early, Cubist œuvre and points far ahead to his later work.

Literatur: »Das Kunstblatt«, XIV., 1930, S. 129 (ganzseitiges Frontispiz). – A. Dorner, Die neue Raumvorstellung in der bildenden Kunst, in: Museum der Gegenwart, II., 1931/32, S. 35, Abb. 37. – Zervos, Picasso VII, 1926–32, Paris 1955, Nr. 7, Taf. 4. – Katalog der Ausstellung: Zeichnungen von Bildhauern des 20. Jahrhunderts, Staatsgalerie Stuttgart 1980, Nr. 68. – Ebenda: G. Thiem, Katalog der Ausstellung Pablo Picasso, 1981, Nr. 22, Farbtafel.

Bibliography: Das Kunstblatt XIV (1930), 129 (whole-page frontispiece); A. Dorner, "Die neue Raumvorstellung in der bildenden Kunst" in Museum der Gegenwart II (1931/32), 35, ill. 37; Zervos, Picasso VII; 1926–32 (Paris, 1955), No. 7, pl. 4; exh. cat. for Zeichnungen von Bildhauern des 20. Jahrhunderts (Staatsgalerie Stuttgart, 1980), No. 68; G. Thiem, exh. cat. for Pablo Picasso, also at Stuttgart, 1981, No. 22, colour pl.

Henry Moore

Geboren 1898 in Castleford (Yorkshire).
1917 Kriegsdienst. 1919—1921 an der Kunstschule in Leeds, dann am Royal College of
Art in London, seit 1924 Lehrauftrag daselbst. Begegnete 1931/32 in Paris Giacometti und Arp. 1932—1939 Lehrer an der
Kunstschule in Chelsea. Seit 1940 in Much
Hadham (Hertfordshire) ansässig. 1940 bis
1942 »Official War Artist«. Nach 1945 zahlreiche Reisen, auch nach Deutschland.

39

Zwei Schlafende

»Shelter-Drawing«

Entstanden 1941
Feder in Schwarz über farbigen Fettkreiden,
aquarelliert auf gelblichem Papier, auf
Karton aufgezogen, 38 × 55,6 cm
Bez. rechts unten: Moore 41
Herkunft: Marlborough Fine Art, London
Inv. Nr. GL. 464

Der Bildhauer Henry Moore gehört zu den
großen Zeichnern unseres Jahrhunderts;
darin Rodin im 19. Jahrhundert vergleichbar; er umkreist sein Werk von früh an skiz-
zierend als ein »Mittel zur Erweckung von
Einfällen«... »ich suche den Grundgedan-
ken — und eine Methode, um Ideen zu sor-
tieren und weiterzuentwickeln«. In Stuttgart haben wir fünf solcher Blätter von ihm
aus den Jahren 1927—1951; außerdem noch
zwei bildmäßige farbige Zeichnungen, die
mit seinen Skulpturen nicht unmittelbar zusammenhängen, sondern Beobachtungen
als »Official War Artist« von 1940—1942 ent-
sprungen sind, als er wegen der »Schlacht
um England« keine Bildwerke schaffen
konnte; eine davon ist die vorliegende.
Das Motiv zweier Schlafender, einer Frau in
halbwacher Haltung links, und eines wie
hingestreckten Mannes rechts, könnte
harmlos erscheinen, spürte man nicht sofort an den aggressiven Farben und der vehement sich über das Paar hinwälzenden
Decke, daß es nicht in Frieden ruht, sondern von Schlaf überwältigt ist. Die aufbre-
chenden Farbschichten und das gitterartige
Liniennetz signalisieren Schwere und Un-
entrinnbarkeit von Alpträumen. Bei diesen
»Liegenden« (Moores Generalthema seit
den 30er Jahren) geht es weniger um
die Bewältigung formaler Probleme als um
die Erfassung einer extremen Situation;
und zwar um Menschen, die aus Angst
vor nächtlichen Bombenangriffen in die
U-Bahn-Schächte Londons, die »Shelters«,
geflohen sind und sich dort eng gedrängt
lagern. Dieses Betroffensein von bedrohten
Menschen fixierte Moore in einem Skizzenbuch von 1940/42, das ihm zu großen bildhaften Blättern wie diesem diente. Daß er
die beklemmenden Eindrücke jener »Unter-

welt« ins Allgemeingültige unserer Existenz
zu erheben vermochte, verdankt er der
Entwicklung seines bisherigen Schaffens:
Moore war darauf vorbereitet, »ein Visio-
när des Wirklichen zu werden, als er an
das Shelter-Thema heranging«, resümierte
R. Melville in einer Untersuchung über dessen Vorformen, die man im Stuttgarter Katalog von 1967 nachlesen kann.
Dort steht auch Erwin Petermanns Interpretation der Shelter-Drawings aus der
Sicht eines selbst in jener Zeit schwer be-
troffenen Zeitgenossen; ihre Aktualität ist
heute größer denn je: »In den Shelterblät-
tern findet sich aus der Zeit heraus Über-
zeitliches, von dem man eher fürchtet, daß
es kommende Generationen noch mehr be-
treffen kann als uns, die Zeitgenossen. Es
sind die Menschen im Untergrund. Sie können gelesen werden als Lebende oder als
Tote, als Schlafende oder Gestorbene, als
Reihen von Lebenden oder Leichenhaufen,
wie sie sich in den Kammern der Konzen-
trationslager fanden. Nirgends ist Pathos
oder Protest... Besonders eindrucksvoll
sind die Schläfer, häufig wiederkehrend.
»Zwei Menschen unter einer Decke« und
immer wieder ergreifend der einzelne
Mensch ohne Kontakt. Menschen liegen
wie verschnürte Pakete, andere erscheinen
mit Auferstehungsgebärden wie in mittelalterlichen Bildern (siehe nebenstehende Abbildung): es sind die in Katakomben Lebenden und die darin Mumifizierten, Men-
schenbehauptung und zugleich Ende des
Menschlichen.«

Henry Moore

Born in Castleford, Yorks, 1898. Active service, 1917. Trained at Leeds 1919—21, then at the Royal College of Art in London, where he obtained a teaching post in 1924. In 1931/32, met Giacometti and Arp in Paris. 1932—39, teacher at Chelsea School of Art. Lived at Much Hadham (Herts.) from 1940. "Official War Artist", 1940—42. Undertook many journeys abroad after 1945, also to Germany.

39

Two Sleeping Figures

"Shelter Drawing"

Dated 1941
Pen and black ink on coloured grease-crayon, water-colour, on buff paper, mounted on cardboard, 38 × 55.6 cm
Signed below right, Moore 41
Provenance: Marlborough Fine Art, London
Inv. No. GL 464

The sculptor, Henry Moore, was also one of the great draughtsmen of our century, comparable in this to Rodin in the nineteenth. From an early stage he would approach his work through of sketches as a "means of awakening ideas"; "I look for the basic notion — and a method to sort ideas out and develop them further." In Stuttgart we have five such drawings, dating from 1927 to 1951. In addition two coloured drawings that were conceived in their own right, not connected directly with his sculpture, but induced by observations made during his period as "Official War Artist" in 1940—42, when, with the Battle of Britain waging overhead, he was unable to work sculptures. Our double-page plate is one of this pair.
The subject of two sleeping figures, a woman whose position suggests she is half-awake on the left and a man lying stretched out on the right, would seem innocent enough if we did not at once begin to feel, through the aggressive colouring and the tumultuous billows of the blanket over the couple, that theirs is no tranquil rest but an overwhelming by sleep. The fragmented layers of colour and the network of lines like a wire mesh indicate weight and the inescapability of nightmares. In these "lying figures" (Moore's major theme from the 1930s on), his concern is less the mastering of formal problems than recording of an extreme situation — people in fear of the nightly bombing-raids have fled into the "shelters" improvised in London's underground system, to rest there cheek-by-jowl. The effect of people under threat is what Moore recorded in a sketchbook of 1940/42, which then led him to large, vivid pictures such as this. He owed his ability to transform those oppressive impressions of the "underworld" into a general statement with validity for our existence to the way he had been developing until then: Moore was well-prepared to become "a visionary of reality, by the time he took on the shelter theme", as R. Melville summarises in an examination of his precursors (included in the Stuttgart catalogue of 1967).
In the same catalogue, Erwin Petermann interprets the Shelter Drawings from the point of view of a contemporary who was himself deeply involved. Today his conclusions are more relevant than ever: "In the Shelter sheets datable events give rise to the timeless, so that one fears that events might effect coming generations harder than us, the contemporaries. Here are people underground. They can be read as living or dead, sleeping or lifeless, rows of living people or heaped corpses like they were found in the chambers of the concentration camps. Nowhere is there pathos or protest... particularly impressive are the sleepers, frequently recurring as "Two People under a Blanket", and again and again, the touching image of the solitary human being without contact. People lie like strung parcels, others appear in gestures of resurrection as in medieval pictures (see illustration opposite): they are those who live in catacombs and those mummified in them, assertion of humanity and simultaneously the end of the human kind.

Henry Moore,
Drei stehende Figuren in »Shelter«,
Feder und Fettkreiden,
aquarelliert,
1941/42.

Henry Moore,
Three standing Figures in Shelter,
pen and grease-crayon,
water-colour,
1941/42.

Literatur: J. E. v. Borries, Zeichnungen des
19. und 20. Jahrhunderts in der Graphischen
Sammlung der Staatsgalerie Stuttgart, 1960,
Nr. 121, Abb. 76. – E. Petermann / K. v. Maur,
Katalog der Ausstellung: Die Shelter-
zeichnungen des Henry Moore, Staatsgalerie
Stuttgart 1967, Nr. 103 mit doppelseitiger
Farbtafel. – Nicht bei H. Read, Henry Moore I,
Sculpture and Drawings, 4. Auflage
(»completely revised«), London 1957.

Bibliography: J. E. von Borries, Zeichnungen
des 19. und 20. Jahrhunderts in der
Graphischen Sammlung der Staatsgalerie
Stuttgart (1960), No. 121, ill. 76; E. Petermann,
K. von Maur, exh. cat.: Die Shelterzeichnungen
des Henry Moore (Staatsgalerie Stuttgart, 1967),
No. 103, with double-page colour plate; not in
H. Read, Henry Moore I, Sculpture and
Drawings, 4th edn ("completely revised"),
London, 1957.

39
Henry Moore, »Zwei Schlafende«, Feder und
Fettkreiden, aquarelliert, 1941.

39
Henry Moore, Two Sleeping Figures, pen and
grease-crayon, water-colour washes, 1941.

Willi Baumeister

Geboren 1889 in Stuttgart. 1910 Aufnahme in die »Komponierklasse« von Adolf Hölzel, Freundschaft mit Oskar Schlemmer und Meyer-Amden. 1914—1918 Kriegsdienst. 1928 Berufung an die Städelsche Kunstschule in Frankfurt a. M., 1933 Entlassung. 1943 wegen der Bombenzerstörungen im Stuttgarter Haus Übersiedlung nach Urach. Seit 1946 Professur an der Akademie in Stuttgart, wo er 1955 verstarb.

40

Blatt 8 des Gilgamesch-Zyklus

Entstanden 1943
Kohle gewischt, die hellen Ränder radiert,
über Frottage in schwarzer Fettkreide auf
altrosa Papier, 24 × 31,5 cm
Nicht signiert, auf der Rückseite der
Stempel: atelier willi baumeister. Auf dem
Untersatzkarton ein Zettel mit dem
betreffenden Gilgamesch-Text: Am dritten
Tag kamen sie an und fanden sich ein auf
dem Feld der Bestimmung . . .»Da ist er,*
Weib! Löse das Tuch deines Busens.
Begierde errege in ihm, lock ihn ins
Fangwerk des Weibes. Fremd wird ihm
werden sein Vieh, das mit ihm wuchs auf
dem Felde.«
Herkunft: Nachlaß des Künstlers;
erworben 1980
Inv. Nr. GVL 214,8 (Leihgabe des
Stuttgarter Galerievereins)

Auf den ersten Blick scheint es eine abstrakte Komposition zu sein; die Wucht ihrer Zeichensprache erinnert an Keilschrift. Bei längerem Hinsehen schließt sich ein Komplex gerundeter Formen zusammen — archetypischer Zeichen des Weiblichen mit einem winzigen Kopf und riesigen Brüsten über den mächtigen Schenkeln, sie lassen sich als Fragmente zu einer Figur ergänzen. Diese Rundungen werden von eckigen Elementen umklammert und durchdrungen; ihre Vereinigung ist evident. An der Aggressivität der zugespitzten männlichen Teile läßt ihre aufgerichtete Diagonale keinen Zweifel und an der Bereitschaft der weiblichen — ihre allseitige Offenheit. — Das Ganze mutet wie ein Relief aus Bruchstücken an, die trotz ihrer Schwerkraft vor dem durchgeriebenen Bildgrund zu schweben scheinen. Das entrückt die Szene jeder übermäßigen Deutlichkeit ins zeitlos Mythische. Das Gestalthafte in Baumeisters Abstraktionen ist so eindringlich, daß es auch ohne Titel oder Text — hier der des Gilgamesch-Epos — lesbar bleibt. Das erhebt seine 64 davon inspirierten Zeichnungen über den Charakter der Illustration in das Überzeitliche einer Text-Illumination.
»Da ist er, Weib!« — heißt es in jenem ältesten Epos der Menschheit aus Mesopota-

mien: »Er«, das ist Enkidu, der Mann aus der Steppe, der mit den Tieren lebt und den es zu domestizieren gilt — mit Hilfe eines Weibes, einer Dienerin der babylonischen Liebesgöttin Ischtar. Für ihn löst sie das Tuch ihres Busens und enthüllt sie den Hügel der Freude, wie es weiter heißt, aber die Tiere, die Gazellen, meiden ihn fortan; sie werden in unserer Zeichnung rechts oben durch die heraldische Formulierung eines gehörnten Wildes vergegenwärtigt (eine jedem Kenner primitiver Kulturen oder Höhlenzeichnungen vertraute Bildsprache). — Im Epos tritt dann Enkidu dem Herren von Uruk, Gilgamesch, gegenüber, dieser besiegt ihn, tötet ihn aber nicht, sondern sagt zu ihm: »Du bist mein Freund. Nun streite an meiner Seite.«
Der Gilgamesch-Zyklus ist ein Höhepunkt des Schaffens von Willi Baumeister, er entstand 1943 in der Abgeschiedenheit der Provinzstadt Urach als Frucht des inneren Widerstands gegen »diese scheußlichste aller Zeiten«; sie zwang den lebensfrohen Künstler zur Konzentration und Meditation, aber auch mangels Malmaterial den Pinsel mit dem Zeichenstift zu vertauschen. — Sein Interesse an archaischer Kunst datiert etwa seit seiner Entlassung aus dem Frankfurter Lehramt im März 1933. Damals wurde die sumerische Kunst durch Ausgrabung ihrer wichtigsten Stätten — darunter Uruk, wo das Gilgamesch-Epos spielt — weithin bekannt. Baumeister hatte Zeit, die bebilderten Berichte und den als Inselbüchlein erschienenen Text des Epos zu studieren. Dessen Wortgewalt und tragischer Ausgang — mit der vergeblichen Suche des Helden nach dem ewigen Leben — hat ihn in seiner »fast zum Erlöschen gebrachten letzten Virulenz« erregt; so stark, daß er dem Gilgamesch-Zyklus die biblischen Folgen »Saul«, »Esther«, »Salome« folgen ließ — und daß noch das malerische Spätwerk von den »Urzeitgestalten« (1946) bis zu den Aru-Bildern seines Todesjahres davon überstrahlt wird.

Willi Baumeister

Born in Stuttgart in 1889. Accepted into the "Composition" class of Adolf Hölzel in 1910, friendship with Oskar Schlemmer and Meyer-Amden. 1915–18, war service. Appointed to the Städelsche Kunstschule, Frankfurt-on-Main, in 1928, but dismissed in 1933. In 1943, when his house was bombed, moved from Stuttgart to Urach. Professor at Stuttgart Academy from 1946; died in Stuttgart in 1955.

40

Sheet 8 of the Gilgamesh Cycle

Dated 1943
Wiped-over charcoal, light edges etched, over frottage in black grease-crayon on dark-salmon coloured paper, 24 × 31.5 cm
Not signed, but stamp on reverse, atelier willi baumeister. On base card a label with the pertinent Gilgamesh quotation: On the third day they arrived and convened in the Field of Destiny . . . "There he is, woman! Loose the cloth of your bosom. Arouse desire in him, tempt him into the woman's snare.
His cattle will become alien to him, that grew with him in the field."
Provenance: the artist's estate; acquired in 1980.
Inv. No. GVL 214,8 (on loan from the Stuttgarter Galerieverein)

At first glance this appears to be an abstract composition. The bulk boldness of its sign language recalls cuneiform script. A longer look reveals a coherent system of rounded shapes, giving an archetypal token of the female, with a minuscule head and colossal breasts over mighty thighs — they coalesce as fragments into a figure. These rounded forms are enclosed and permeated by angular elements, their union is evident. The rising diagonal leaves no doubt as to the aggressive nature of the tapering male aspects, or to the all-round willingness on the part of the female. The whole has the atmosphere of a relief composed of fragments which, despite their mass, appear to float in front of the frottage picture-ground. This shifts the scene from any overstatement into the timelessness of myth. The figurative element in Baumeister's abstractions is so forceful that it would be tangible even without title or text (in this case, taken from the "Gilgamesh" epic). It raises the sixty-four drawings the legend inspired Baumeister to do, beyond the character of illustration into the timelessness of text illumination.

"There he is, woman!" says that oldest known epic of mankind from Mesopotamia. "He" is Enkidu, the man from the steppes who lives with the animals and who is now to be domesticated with the aid of a woman, a servant of the Babylonian goddess of love, Ishtar. For him she loosens the cloth of her bosom and reveals the hill of joy, as the legend reads on, but the animals, the gazelles, avoid it from that moment on; they are betokened in our drawing to the top right, in the heraldic formulation of horned game in a pictogramme familiar to anyone conversent with primitive cultures or cave drawings. What follows in the epic is that Enkidu faces the Lord of Uruk, Gilgamesh, who conquers him. He does not kill him, however, but says to him, "You are my friend. Now fight at my side."

The Gilgamesh Cycle is a climax in Willi Baumeister's œuvre. It was completed in 1943 in the isolation of the provincial town of Urach as the fruit of his inner resistance against "this most monstrous of all times" which enforced upon this vital, spirited artist a period of concentration and meditation — and, for lack of painting materials, the necessity of exchanging the brush for the pencil. His interest in archaic art dated from about the time he was dismissed from his teaching post at Frankfurt, in March 1933. It was about that time that Sumerian art became widely known through excavations at its most important sites, Uruk among them, the scene of the Gilgamesh legend. Now, Baumeister had time enough to study the illustrated reports and the text of the epic, which Insel-Verlag published in their series of little paperbacks. The power of words and tragic dénouement of the hero's vain search for eternal life excited the artist in their "last virulence taken almost to the point of obliteration", so much so that he followed his Gilgamesh Cycle with the Bible sequences dedicated to Saul, "Esther" and "Salome" — to the extent, that this power overshadows even his late painting from the Urzeitgestalten (Figures of Prehistory) (1946) to the "Aru" paintings done in his last year of life.

Literatur: Lise Lotte Möller, Katalog der
Ausstellung: Gilgamesch, Museum für Kunst
und Gewerbe, Hamburg, 1964, Nr. 100. —
H. Geissler, Katalog der Ausstellung: Willi
Baumeister, Die 5 Zeichnungs-Folgen aus seiner
Uracher Zeit 1943—45, Staatsgalerie Stuttgart,
1965, S. 7, Nr. 8. — G. Adriani, Katalog der
Ausstellung, Willi Baumeister, Zeichnungen und
Gouachen, Kunsthalle Tübingen 1975, Nr. 138,
Tafel S. 16/17. — Werner Haftmann, Willi
Baumeister, Gilgamesch, Köln 1976, Tafel 8.

Bibliography: Lise Lotte Möller, cat. for the
exhibition, Gilgamesch (Museum für Kunst und
Gewerbe, Hamburg, 1964), No. 100; H. Geissler,
exh. cat., Willi Baumeister, Die 5 Zeichnungs-
Folgen aus seiner Uracher Zeit 1943—45
(Staatsgalerie Stuttgart, 1965), p. 7, No. 8;
G. Adriani, exh. cat. Willi Baumeister,
Zeichnungen und Gouachen (Kunsthalle
Tübingen, 1975), No. 138, pl. pp. 16/17; Werner
Haftmann, Willi Baumeister, Gilgamesch
(Cologne, 1976), pl. 8.

ANMERKUNGEN

NOTES

1 H.Th. Musper, Einige Handzeichnungen in der Stuttgarter Graphischen Sammlung, in: Schwäbische Heimat, 4. Jg. Stuttgart 1953, S. 100.

2 Glaubrecht Friedrich, in: 400 Jahre Dresdner Kunstsammlungen, Absatz C: Graphik, Zeichnungen, 1960, S. 34.

3 Hans Ebert, Zur Vor- und Frühgeschichte des Berliner Kupferstichkabinetts zwischen 1640 und 1840, in: Staatliche Museen zu Berlin (DDR), Forschungen und Berichte, Bd. 20/21, 1980, S. 343–383; mit vielen Informationen zu der weit älteren Dresdner graphischen Sammlung.

4 Peter Halm, Hundert Meisterzeichnungen aus der Staatlichen Graphischen Sammlung München, München 1958, S. 6–16: Zur Entstehungsgeschichte der Sammlung. – Zuletzt Dieter Kuhrmann im Katalog: »Zeichnungen aus der Sammlung des Kurfürsten Carl Theodor«, München 1983/84.

5 Seine Bücher gelangten 1720 in die Bibliothek der Stadt Heilbronn, sein Ex Libris von 1643 ist abgebildet im Ausstellungskatalog des Stadtarchivs von 1981: Kostbarkeiten in Schrift und Druck aus Heilbronn, bearbeitet von H. Hummel, Nr. 231. – Wolfskeels Monogramm trägt auch der Kupferstich des Bellini-Schülers Girolamo Mocetto: »Die Taufe Christi« (entstanden nach 1507). Siehe Katalog »Meisterwerke alter Druckgraphik aus der Staatsgalerie Stuttgart«, 1983/84, Nr. 36 mit Abb.

6 Rolf Biedermann, die Zeichnungen des Johann Heinrich Schönfeld, in: Jahrbuch der Staatlichen Kunstsammlungen in Baden-Württemberg, VIII, 1971, S. 119ff., Anm. 8.

7 Pierre Rosenberg, Dandré-Bardon as a Draughtsman, A group of Drawings at Stuttgart, in: Master Drawings, 1974, XII, 2, p. 137–151, sowie Pierre Rosenberg und Heinrich Geissler, Un nouveau groupe de dessins de Jean Restout (1692–1768) au Musée de Stuttgart, in: Jahrbuch der Staatlichen Kunstsammlungen in Baden-Württemberg, XVII, 1980, S. 133–154.

8 Il libro di schizzi d'un pittore olandese nel museo di Stuttgart, in: Archivio Storico dell'Arte, 1893, 6. Jhg., p. 106–126. – Der 1839 in Ungarn geborene Autor war zuerst Eisenbahningenieur in württembergischen Diensten, seit 1879 publizierte er auch in deutschen Zeitschriften besonders über toskanische Künstler; sein Hauptwerk ist eine Brunelleschi-Monographie von 1892 (Neuauflage Florenz 1979). Er war in Stuttgart mit einer Sofia Ziegler verheiratet und starb 1910. Nekrolog und Bibliographie in Rivista d'Arte, Bd. 7, 1910, S. 157–166; ungarisches Schrifttum siehe bei: Max Arnim, Internationale Personalbibliographie 1800–1943, 2. verb. und verm. Aufl., Bd. I: A–K, Stuttgart 1952, S. 352 (alle Hinweise von Dr. H.-J. Eberhardt, München).

9 H.Th. Musper, Der Anonymus Fabriczy, in: Jahrbuch der preußischen Kunstsammlungen, 57. Band 1936, S. 238–246. – Über eine Gleichsetzung mit dem aus Brüssel gebürtigen Adrian de Weerdt (gestorben um 1590 in Köln), siehe: K.G. Boon, Netherlandish Drawings of the 15. and 16. centuries in the Rijksmuseum Amsterdam, 1978, Nr. 483–485. – Zuletzt Heinrich Geissler im Katalog: Zeichnung in Deutschland – Deutsche Zeichner 1540–1640, Staatsgalerie Stuttgart, Band II, 1980, S. 80.

1 H.T. Musper, "Einige Handzeichnungen in der Stuttgarter Graphischen Sammlung", Schwäbische Heimat 4 (Stuttgart, 1953), p. 100.

2 Glaubrecht Friedrich, in 400 Jahre Dresdner Kunstsammlungen, Section C: "Graphik, Zeichnungen" (1960), p. 34.

3 Hans Ebert, "Zur Vor- und Frühgeschichte des Berliner Kupferstichkabinetts zwischen 1640 und 1840" in Staatliche Museen zu Berlin (DDR), Forschungen und Berichte, vol. 20/21 (1980), pp. 343–383. Much information on the far older collection of prints and drawings at Dresden.

4 Peter Halm, Hundert Meisterzeichnungen aus der Staatlichen Graphischen Sammlung München (Munich, 1958), pp. 6–16. On the origins of the Collection, most recently, Dieter Kuhrmann in the catalogue, Zeichnungen aus der Sammlung des Kurfürsten Carl Theodor (Munich, 1983/84).

5 His books entered the Library of the City of Heilbronn in 1720; his ex-libris of 1643 is illustrated in the City Archive exhibition catalogue of 1981, Kostbarkeiten in Schrift und Druck aus Heilbronn, ed. H. Hummel, No. 231. Wolfskeel's monogram also appears on the copper engraving The Baptism of Christ, executed after 1507 by Girolamo Mocetto, a pupil of Bellini's. See catalogue Meisterwerke alter Druckgraphik aus der Staatsgalerie Stuttgart of 1983/84, No. 36, and ill.

6 Rolf Biedermann, "Die Zeichnungen des Johann Heinrich Schönfeld", Jahrbuch der Staatlichen Kunstsammlungen in Baden-Württemberg, VIII (1971), pp. 119 ff, note 8.

7 Pierre Rosenberg, "Dandré-Bardon as a Draughtsman, A Group of Drawings at Stuttgart", Master Drawings XII, 2 (1974), 137 bis 51; also Pierre Rosenberg & Heinrich Geissler, "Un nouveau groupe de dessins de Jean Restout (1692–1768) au Musée de Stuttgart", Jahrbuch (. . .) XVII (1980), pp. 133–54.

8 "Il libro di schizzi d'un pittore olandese nel museo di Stuttgart", Archivio Storico dell'Arte 6 (1893), 106–26. The author, born in Hungary in 1839, began as a railway engineer for the state of Württemberg. From 1879 he also published in German journals, notably on Tuscan artists; his main work is a monograph on Brunelleschi (1892; new edn Florence, 1979). He was married to a Sofia Ziegler in Stuttgart and died in 1910. Obituary and bibliography in Rivista d'Arte 7 (1910), 157–66. For his writings in Hungarian, see Max Arnim, Internationale Personalbibliographie 1800–1943, 2nd revised edn, I: A–K (Stuttgart, 1952), p. 352 (all references from Dr. H.-J. Eberhard, Munich).

9 H.T. Musper, "Der Anonymus Fabriczy", Jahrbuch der Preussischen Kunstsammlungen 57 (1936), pp. 238–46. On an identification with Adrian de Weerdt, who was born in Brussels (d. c. 1590, Cologne), see K.G. Boon, Netherlandish Drawings of the 15. and 16. centuries in the Rijksmuseum Amsterdam (1978), Nos 483–5, and most recently, Heinrich Geissler in the catalogue, Zeichnung in Deutschland – Deutsche Zeichner 1540–1640, Staatsgalerie Stuttgart, vol. II (1980), p. 80

10 Otto Fischer, "Oberdeutsche Federzeichnungen aus den Jahren 1457 und 1483" in Gesellschaft für zeichnende Künste (5th

10   Otto Fischer, Oberdeutsche Federzeichnungen aus den Jahren 1457 und 1483, in: Gesellschaft für zeichnende Künste, 5. Druck, München 1923, S. 5/6. (O.C. Hecht Verlag; Druck Bruckmann; bei uns unter den Mappen mit Reproduktionsgraphik aufbewahrt.) Laut Fischer wurde der Sammelband »zwischen 1893 und 1909« (also nach Fabriczys Publikation) aufgelöst und die Blätter aufgelegt.

11   Siehe den Katalog der Graphischen Sammlung Albertina von 1976: Giacomo Conte Durazzo, 1717–1794, Diplomat aus Genua, Hoftheaterdirektor und Cavagliere di Musica in Wien, Gesandter Österreichs in Venedig, Initiator der Kunstsammlung Herzog Alberts von Sachsen-Teschen.

12   Bereits 1852 hatte König Wilhelm I. († 1864) mit der Gemäldesammlung Barbini-Breganze Giambattista Tiepolos faszinierenden Ölbozzetto für das Deckenfresko des Würzburger Kaisersaales erworben (siehe Band I Farbtafel 13).

13   Beim Umzug im Jahre 1930 wurden die künstlerisch geringeren württembergischen Ansichten und Bildnisse — einige tausend Stück — unserer Landesbibliothek übergeben, die erstrangigen behielt man im Kupferstichkabinett; jedoch kamen viele Dubletten von der Landesbibliothek später wieder in unseren Bestand zurück.

14   Es mag den Außenstehenden wundern, daß wiederauftauchende Blätter — und das trifft auch auf die Gemälde zu — nach 1945 nur selten zurückgekauft wurden. Man hatte in Stuttgart besonders auf dem Gebiet des Expressionismus den Nachholbedarf anderweitig gedeckt und im Abstand von rund zwei Jahrzehnten einen Qualitätsmaßstab entwickelt, dem die ehemaligen Erwerbungen oft nicht mehr standhielten; die besten der beschlagnahmten Stücke hatte sich das Ausland, vor allem die Museen in Basel und New York, gesichert.

15   Während bei den Illustrierten Büchern schon ein ansehnlicher Bestand vom späten 15. bis 19. Jahrhundert vorhanden war, der inzwischen karteimäßig nach Autoren, Künstlern und Schlagworten erfaßt ist, wurden Plakate erst nach 1946 gesammelt, das heißt die künstlerisch wertvollen, die wir zugesandt bekamen, wurden alphabetisch nach Herkunftsorten aufbewahrt. Erst durch die Übernahme der alle Gebiete umfassenden, bis ins späte 19. Jahrhundert zurückreichenden Sammlung von 12 000 Plakaten des Stuttgarter Landesgewerbeamts im Jahr 1973 erhielten wir eine den weiteren Ausbau lohnende Basis.

16   Näheres über Max Kade siehe in »Neue Deutsche Biographie«, Bd. 10, 1974, Spalte 719/720.

17   Mit Hilfe der Max-Kade-Foundation in zwei Bänden veröffentlicht: »Kaiser Maximilians I. Weisskunig«, herausgegeben von H.Th. Musper in Verbindung mit Rudolf Buchner, Heinz-Otto Burger und Erwin Petermann, Stuttgart 1956. — Siehe auch den Ausstellungs-Katalog »Hans Burgkmair zum 500. Geburtstag, Das Graphische Werk«, umfaßt von R. Biedermann, T. Falk und H. Geissler, Stuttgart und Augsburg 1973.

18   Katalog »Sammlung Max Kade«, Ausstellung Graphische Sammlngen Stuttgart und München 1963/64. — Der Katalog

impression, Munich, 1923) p. 5/6 (O.C. Hecht Verlag; printed by Bruckmann; we have it amongst our folders of reproduction graphics). Fischer asserts that the portfolio was taken apart "between 1893 and 1909" (i.e. after Fabriczy's publication) and the drawings mounted separately.

11   Cf. the catalogue of the Graphische Sammlung Albertina of 1976, Giacomo Conte Durazzo, 1717–1794, Diplomate from Genua, Manager of the Hoftheater and Cavagliere di Musica in Vienna, Austrian Envoy in Venice; Initiator of the Art Collection of Duke Albert of Saxony-Teschen.

12   As early as 1852, King Wilhelm I (d. 1864) had acquired the Barbini-Breganze collection of paintings and with it Giambattista Tiepolo's fascinating oil sketch for the ceiling fresco in the Imperial Hall at Würzburg (see vol. 1, colour plate 13).

13   With the move in 1930, the Württemberg landscapes and portraits of lesser artistic value, several thousand of them, were passed to our Land (Regional) Library, the best remaining in the Department of Prints and Drawings; but many duplicates later returned from the Landesbibliothek into our stock.

14   To an onlooker it may seem strange that after 1945, lost items have only rarely been repurchased on appearing again — and this applies to paintings as well as graphics. In Stuttgart the need to make good, especially in Expressionists, was felt to lie in other works, and in the course of some two decades a set of standards had been developed which the former acquisitions frequently no longer matched, while the best of the requisitioned works had been secured abroad, particularly by the museums in Basel and New York.

15   While the Illustrated Books already made up a sizeable stock in examples from the late 15th to the 19th century (since documented under the headings of author, artist and subject), posters have only been collected since 1946, the artistically valuable ones were sent being stored alphabetically according to place of origin. But it was only from 1973, when we had transferred to us the collection of the Land Department of Trade in Stuttgart, consisting of 12 000 posters, that we had the foundations to justify further expansion.

16   For more on Max Kade, cf. Neue Deutsche Biographie, X (1974), col. 719/720.

17   Published in two parts, with the aid of the Max Kade Foundation. — Kaiser Maximilians I. Weisskunig, ed. H.T. Musper with Rudolf Buchner, Heinz-Otto Burger and Erwin Petermann, (Stuttgart, 1956); see also the exhibition catalogue, Hans Burgkmair zum 500. Geburtstag, Das Graphische Werk, compiled by R. Biedermann, T. Falk & H. Geissler (Stuttgart and Augsburg, 1973).

18   Catalogue, Sammlung Max Kade; exhibited by the Departments of Prints and Drawings at Stuttgart and Munich, 1963/64. The catalogue, Meisterwerke alter Druckgraphik aus der Staatsgalerie Stuttgart — Zum 100. Geburtstag des Stifters Max Kade (Stuttgart, 1982/83) also illustrates outstanding prints from Kade's own collection.

19   Unbekannte Handzeichnungen alter Meister ("Unknown drawings by Old Masters"), exhibited in Stuttgart, Basel, Ellwangen, 1967;

»Meisterwerke alter Druckgraphik aus der Staatsgalerie Stuttgart – Zum 100. Geburtstag des Stifters Max Kade«, Stuttgart 1982/83 – enthält außerdem hervorragende Blätter aus eigenem Besitz.

19   »Unbekannte Handzeichnungen alter Meister«, ausgestellt in Stuttgart, Basel, Ellwangen, 1967; »Sammlung Schloß Fachsenfeld, Zeichnungen aus fünf Jahrhunderten«, verfaßt von U. Gauß, H. Geissler, V. Schauz und Ch. Thiem, Stuttgart, 1978; »Bolognesische Zeichnungen 1600–1830 mit Leihgaben aus Windsor Castle und der Fondazione Cini Venedig«, verfaßt von Ch. Thiem, Stuttgart, 1982; zuletzt der Katalog: »Disegni di Artisti Bolognesi dal Seicento all'Ottocento«, a cura di Christel Thiem, Bologna, Edizioni ALFA, 1983/84.

19a   Seine Werke in der Staatsgalerie Stuttgart und ihrer graphischen Sammlung erfaßt der Katalog von U. Gauß und Ch. v. Holst: »Gottlieb Schick – Ein Maler des Klassizismus«, Stuttgart 1976.

20   Zeichnungen des 19. und 20. Jahrhunderts, Neuerwerbungen seit 1945, verfaßt von J. E. v. Borries, Stuttgart 1960; Von Ingres bis Picasso (130), Französische Zeichnungen des 19. und 20. Jahrhunderts, verfaßt von U. Gauß, Stuttgart 1969; von derselben der eingangs genannte Gesamtkatalog der Zeichnungen des 19. Jahrhunderts, 1976.

21   1965 erschien als Jahresgabe der Höheren Fachschule für das Graphische Gewerbe, Stuttgart, ein bebilderter Gesamtkatalog unter dem Titel »Französische Maler illustrieren Bücher«, verfaßt von Ch. und G. Thiem.

22   Siehe unseren von Karin v. Maur verfaßten Bestandskatalog »Oskar Schlemmer. Ausstellung zum 80. Geburtstag. Zeichnungen – Aquarelle – Pastelle und Folkwang-Entwürfe«, Stuttgart 1968.

23   Siehe unseren Katalog »Erich Heckel, Farbholzschnitte – Zeichnungen und Aquarelle. Ausstellung zum 90. Geburtstag«, Stuttgart 1973/74.

24   Siehe das von K. v. Maur und G. Thiem verfaßte Heft »Stiftung Adolf Fleischmann«, Stuttgart 1976.

25   Davon sind 36 der schönsten erfaßt von Kurt Löcher in dem Katalog: »Daniel Chodowiecki und Johann Karl Schultz, zwei Danziger Künstler«, Stuttgart 1965.

26   Willi Baumeister »Gilgamesch«. Mit einer Einführung von Werner Haftmann. Köln 1976 (mit Faksimiles der 64 Zeichnungen und Frottagen).

27   »Der Konstruktivismus und seine Nachfolge in Beispielen aus dem Bestand der Staatsgalerie Stuttgart und ihrer Graphischen Sammlung«, 1974, bearbeitet von Stephan v. Wiese und Bernd Rau.

28   »Amerikanische und englische Graphik der Gegenwart aus der Graphischen Sammlung der Staatsgalerie Stuttgart«, 1973, bearbeitet von Ulrich Arnold.

Sammlung Schloss Fachsenfeld, Zeichnungen aus fünf Jahrhunderten, ed. U. Gauss, H. Geissler, V. Schauz & C. Thiem (Stuttgart, 1978); Bolognesische Zeichnungen 1600–1830 mit Leihgaben aus Windsor Castle und der Fondazione Cini Venedig, ed. C. Thiem (Stuttgart, 1982); finally, the catalogue, Disegni di Artisti Bolognesi dal Seicento all'Ottocento, a cura di Christel Thiem, Bologna, Edizioni ALFA, 1983/84.

19a   His works in the Staatsgalerie Stuttgart and its Collection of Graphic Art are documented in the catalogue by U. Gauss and C. v. Holst, Gottlieb Schick – Ein Maler des Klassizismus (Stuttgart, 1976).

20   Zeichnungen des 19. und 20. Jahrhunderts, Neuerwerbungen seit 1945, ed. J. E. v. Borries (Stuttgart, 1960); Von Ingres bis Picasso (130) Französische Zeichnungen des 19. und 20. Jahrhunderts, ed. U. Gauss (Stuttgart, 1969; also by U. Gauss, the comprehensive catalogue of nineteenth-century drawings mentioned in the introduction (1976).

21   The Presentation Annual of the Höhere Fachschule für das Graphische Gewerbe at Stuttgart in 1965 was an illustrated comprehensive catalogue entitled Französische Maler illustrierter Bücher, compiled by C. & G. Thiem.

22   Cf. our stock catalogue, Oskar Schlemmer. Ausstellung zum 80. Geburtstag. Zeichnungen – Aquarelle – Pastelle und Folkwang-Entwürfe, by Karin v. Maur (Stuttgart, 1968).

23   Cf. our catalogue, Erich Heckel, Farbholzschnitte – Zeichnungen und Aquarelle. Ausstellung zum 90. Geburtstag (Stuttgart, 1973/74).

24   See the brochure, Stiftung Adolf Fleischmann (Stuttgart, 1976), compiled by K. v. Maur and G. Thiem.

25   36 of the finest of these have been documented in Kurt Löchner's catalogue, Daniel Chodowiecki und Johann Karl Schulz, zwei Danziger Künstler (Stuttgart, 1965).

26   Willi Baumeister, Gilgamesch. With an introduction by Werner Haftmann (Cologne, 1976): includes facsimiles of the 64 drawings and frottages.

27   Der Konstruktivismus und seine Nachfolge in Beispielen aus dem Bestand der Staatsgalerie Stuttgart und ihrer Graphischen Sammlung (1974) edited by Stephan von Wiese and Bernd Rau.

28   "Amerikanische und englische Graphik der Gegenwart aus der Graphischen Sammlung der Staatsgalerie Stuttgart" (1973), ed. Ulrich Arnold.

29   Part of the stock has been illustrated in Der barocke Himmel, Handzeichnungen deutscher und ausländischer Künstler in Deutschland (Stuttgart, 1964), eds. Bruno Bushart, Heinrich Geissler and Eckhard v. Knorre.

29   Ein Teil des Bestandes veröffentlicht in:
»Der barocke Himmel, Handzeichnungen
deutscher und ausländischer Künstler in
Deutschland«, Stuttgart 1964, bearbeitet von
Bruno Bushart, Heinrich Geissler und Eckhard
v. Knorre.

30   »Die Zeichnerin Käthe Kollwitz, Katalog
zum 100. Geburtstag der Künstlerin«, Stuttgart
1967, verfaßt von Gunther Thiem.

31   »Ernst Ludwig Kirchner in der
Graphischen Sammlung der Staatsgalerie
Stuttgart«, 1980, verfaßt von Karin Becker
und Gunther Thiem.

32   »Die Handzeichnung der Gegenwart«,
Katalog Stuttgart 1970, bearbeitet von Marina
Schneede-Sczesny. — »Zeichnungen von
Bildhauern des 20. Jahrhunderts«, Stuttgart
1980, bearbeitet von K. Becker, U. Gauss,
Ch. und G. Thiem. — »Handzeichnungen der
Gegenwart II, Erwerbungen seit 1970«, Stuttgart
1982, bearbeitet von U. Gauss, H. Geissler,
M. Moeller und G. Thiem.

30   Die Zeichnerin Käthe Kollwitz,
Katalog zum 100. Geburtstag der Künstlerin
(Stuttgart, 1967), compiled by Gunther Thiem.

31   Karin Becker & Gunther Thiem,
Ernst Ludwig Kirchner in der Graphischen
Sammlung der Staatsgalerie Stuttgart
(1980).

32   Die Handzeichnung der Gegenwart
(Stuttgart, 1970), ed. Marina Schneede-Sczesny;
Zeichnungen von Bildhauern des 20. Jahr-
hunderts (Stuttgart, 1980), ed. K. Becker,
U. Gauss, C. & G. Thiem; Handzeichnungen der
Gegenwart II, Erwerbungen seit 1970 (Stuttgart,
1982), ed. U. Gauss, H. Geissler, M. Moeller &
G. Thiem.